TRADITIONS & ENCOUNTERS

To access the *Traditions & Encounters* online resource package please visit
www.mhhe.com/bentleybrief and use the following code: **G8JR-Y9P7-TTEH-9487-THW4**

TRADITIONS & ENCOUNTERS

A Brief Global History
Volume II: From 1500 to the Present

Jerry H. Bentley
University of Hawai'i

Herbert F. Ziegler
University of Hawai'i

Heather E. Streets
Washington State University

Boston   Burr Ridge, IL   Dubuque, IA   Madison, WI   New York
San Francisco   St. Louis   Bangkok   Bogotá   Caracas   Kuala Lumpur
Lisbon   London   Madrid   Mexico City   Milan   Montreal   New Delhi
Santiago   Seoul   Singapore   Sydney   Taipei   Toronto

Higher Education

Published by McGraw-Hill, an imprint of The McGraw-Hill Companies, Inc., 1221 Avenue of the Americas, New York, NY 10020. Copyright © 2008. All rights reserved. No part of this publication may be reproduced or distributed in any form or by any means, or stored in a database or retrieval system, without the prior written consent of The McGraw-Hill Companies, Inc., including, but not limited to, in any network or other electronic storage or transmission, or broadcast for distance learning.

This book is printed on acid-free paper.

1 2 3 4 5 6 7 8 9 0 DOW/DOW 0 9 8 7 6

ISBN: 978-0-07-320703-2
MHID: 0-07-320703-9

Editor in Chief: *Emily Barrosse*
Publisher: *Lisa Moore*
Sponsoring Editor: *Jon-David Hague*
Marketing Manager: *Jennifer Reed*
Director of Development: *Lisa Pinto*
Developmental Editor: *Angela Kao*
Editorial Coordinator: *Nicole Caddigan*
Project Manager: *Christina Gimlin*
Manuscript Editor: *Carole Crouse*
Art Director: *Jeanne Schreiber*
Design Manager: *Kim Menning*
Text Designer: *Linda Robertson*
Art Editor: *Katherine McNab*
Manager, Photo Research: *Brian J. Pecko*
Supplements Producer: *Louis Swaim*
Production Supervisor: *Richard DeVitto*
Composition: *10/12 Galliard by Thompson Type*
Printing: *45 # Publisher's Matte, R. R. Donnelley & Sons*

Cover credits: Royal Standard of Ur, © Erich Lessing/Art Resource, NY; Han emperor with Confucian scholars, © Bibliotheque Nationale, Paris, France/The Bridgeman Art Library; faithful before the Kaaba in Mecca, © Topkapi Palace Museum, Istanbul, Turkey, Bildarchiv Steffens/The Bridgeman Art Library; merchants and customers in a town market, © Scala/Art Resource, NY; Doña Marina, Hernán Cortés, and Tlaxcala, © The Granger Collection, New York; young woman at work in a mechanized mill, © Bettmann/Corbis; Himid, Lubaina (b. 1954), *Between the two my heart is balanced*, 1991, © Tate Gallery, London/Art Resource, NY. Used by permission of Lubaina Himid.

Credits: The credits section for this book begins on page C-1 and is considered an extension of the copyright page.

Library of Congress Cataloging-in-Publication Data

Bentley, Jerry H., 1949–
  Traditions and encounters : a brief global history / by Jerry H. Bentley, Herbert F. Ziegler, and Heather E. Streets.
    p. cm.
  Brief ed. of: Traditions and encounters / Jerry H. Bentley, Herbert F. Ziegler. 3rd ed.
  Includes index.
  ISBN-13: 978-0-07-353453-4 (alk. paper)
  ISBN-10: 0-07-353453-6 (alk. paper)
    1. World history. 2. Intercultural communication--History. I. Ziegler, Herbert F., 1949– II. Streets, Heather E. III. Title. IV. Title: Traditions and encounters.

D20.B42 2006
909—dc22   2006046708

The Internet addresses listed in the text were accurate at the time of publication. The inclusion of a Web site does not indicate an endorsement by the authors or McGraw-Hill, and McGraw-Hill does not guarantee the accuracy of the information presented at these sites.

www.mhhe.com

Brief Table of Contents

Table of Contents

Preface xv

PART V

THE ORIGINS OF GLOBAL INTERDEPENDENCE, 1500–1800 354

PART VI

AN AGE OF REVOLUTION, INDUSTRY, AND EMPIRE, 1750–1914 434

PART VII

CONTEMPORARY GLOBAL REALIGNMENTS 560

35 The End of Empire and the Emergence of a World without Borders 657

Primary Sources from the Past

Preface

How is it possible to make sense of the entire human past?

The study of world history is an exhilarating project that offers unparalleled opportunities to understand oneself and one's society in relation to the larger world. Given the range of human diversity, however, world history also presents a daunting challenge. Human communities have adopted widely varying forms of political, social, and economic organization, and they have elaborated even more diverse cultural, religious, and philosophical legacies.

We wrote *Traditions & Encounters* to offer a global perspective on the past—a vision of history that is meaningful and appropriate for the interdependent world we live in today. During an era when peoples from all parts of the earth meet, interact, and do business with one another, a global perspective has become an essential tool for informed and responsible citizenship. Because global interactions profoundly influence the fortunes of peoples in all lands, it is impossible to understand the contemporary world by approaching it exclusively from the viewpoint of western Europe, the United States, Japan, or any other individual society, or the historical experience of any one society.

We wrote *Traditions & Encounters: A Brief Global History* to offer an option to instructors who want to provide a global perspective to their students with a briefer text, allowing more flexibility in the way they present the exciting stories of world history to their students.

Of course, a brief text must offer more than just brevity. It must also provide a sound organizational structure, strong themes that provide a systematic framework for interpreting history, an engaging narrative, strong visual appeal, and solid pedagogy. *Traditions & Encounters: A Brief Global History* offers all of these elements.

ORGANIZATIONAL STRUCTURE

We discuss the world's development through time by organizing it into *seven eras of global history.* These eras, treated successively in the seven parts of this book, represent coherent epochs that form the larger architecture of world history as we see it. The eras owe their coherence in large part to the networks of transportation, communication, and exchange that have linked peoples of different societies at different times in the past. This structure allows us to make cross-cultural comparisons that help frame world history for students to put events in a perspective that renders them more understandable.

UNIFYING THEMES

The themes of traditions and encounters that give this book its title bring focus to the human experience. Together they account for much of the historical development of human societies.

The theme of *tradition* draws attention to the dynamics of individual societies. From their earliest days on earth, human groups have generated distinctive political, social, economic, and cultural traditions that have guided affairs in their own societies. Some of these traditions arose and disappeared relatively quickly, while others influenced human affairs over the centuries and millennia, sometimes down to the present day.

The world's peoples have interacted with one another since the earliest days of history. The theme of *encounters* directs attention to the elements that have linked individual societies to their neighbors and others in the larger world. Whether in the form of mass migrations, the spread of infectious diseases, imperial expansion, long-distance trade, or the multitude of other ways in which peoples interact, these encounters have profoundly influenced the experiences of individual societies and the development of the world as a whole.

Like the structure, the strong themes illuminate the events of history for students, enhancing their understanding of and appreciation for world history in a way they can use and apply to their point of view as world events unfold throughout their lives.

ENGAGING NARRATIVE

The structure and themes provide a strong foundation on which the story of global history can be told in an engrossing way. Each chapter-opening narrative tells the story of a man or woman caught in the currents of movement and exchange. Whether it be Xuanzang, a Chinese monk who illegally travels to India to study Buddhism and bring it back to his native land, or Doña Marina, a slave girl of noble descent in Central Mexico who serves as translator and aid to the Spanish conquistador, Hernán Cortés, as he conquers her native land, each story serves as portal to engage students and to foster their enthusiasm for the study of the world's past.

STRONG VISUAL APPEAL

Throughout the book, *images* are seamlessly integrated into the narrative to enhance and support the stories of history that unfold through the themes of traditions and encounters. Students interested in the story of Xuanzang can see a scroll depicting his return to China with caravan of oxen carrying 657 books, relics, and images.

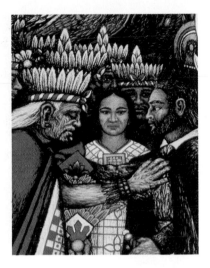

And in Chapter Twenty-two a depiction of the controversial figure, Doña Marina, shows her standing centrally between Hernán Cortés and a Tlaxcala ruler as they enter into an alliance against the Aztecs. All of the images in the book were carefully researched and chosen to support and enlighten the stories of the past.

Each *map* in the book provides a clear pedagogical purpose to enrich student's understanding of the relationship between geography and history. Interactive maps are also available on the book's website, and they are called out throughout the text with this icon.

SOLID PEDAGOGY

This text contains a carefully selected range of tools to enhance student comprehension and enthusiasm.

Part openers explain the rationale behind a major era of human history, and all part openers combine to provide a cohesive summary of the seven-era scheme, the larger interpretive framework of the book.

CHAPTER 16

States and Societies of Sub-Saharan Africa

Chapter-opening vignettes draw the reader into the larger story and allow students to remember that world history is really about people.

Sources from the Past, a primary source excerpt, are in every chapter. These excerpts were selected to illustrate fundamental ideas raised in the text and to provide individual voices from the human past.

SOURCES FROM THE PAST

First Impressions of Spanish Forces

As the Spanish army made its way to Tenochtitlan, Motecuzoma dispatched a series of emissaries to communicate with Cortés and learn his intentions. The reports that came back were not reassuring. They brought disturbing news about Spanish weapons, armor, horses, and dogs that were much larger and more aggressive than the small, barkless animals that were native to Mexico.

And when [Motecuzoma] had heard what the messengers reported, he was terrified, he was astounded. . . .

Especially did it cause him to faint away when he heard how the gun, at [the Spaniards'] command, discharged [the shot]; how it resounded as if it thundered when it went off. It indeed bereft one of strength; it shut off one's ears. And when it discharged, something like a round pebble came forth from within. Fire went showering forth; sparks went blazing forth. And its smoke smelled very foul; it had a fetid odor which verily wounded the head. And when [the shot] struck a mountain, it was as if it were destroyed, dissolved. And a tree was pulverized; it was as if it vanished; it was as if someone blew it away.

All iron was their war array. In iron they clothed themselves. With iron they covered their heads. Iron were their swords. Iron were their crossbows. Iron were their shields. Iron were their lances.

And those which bore them upon their backs, their deer [that is, horses], were as tall as roof terraces.

And their bodies were everywhere covered; only their faces appeared. They were very white; they had chalky faces; they had yellow hair, though the hair of some was black. Long were their beards; they also were yellow. They were yellow-headed. [The black men's hair] was kinky, it was curly.

And their food was like fasting food—very large, white, not heavy like [tortillas]; like maize stalks, good-tasting as if of maize stalk flour; a little sweet, a little honeyed. It was honeyed to eat; it was sweet to eat.

And their dogs were very large. They had ears folded over; great dragging jowls. They had fiery eyes—blazing eyes; they had yellow eyes—fiery yellow eyes. They had thin flanks—flanks with ribs showing. They had gaunt stomachs. They were very tall. They were nervous; they went about panting, with tongues hanging out. They were spotted like ocelots; they were varicolored.

And when Motecuzoma heard all this, he was much terrified. It was as if he fainted away. His heart saddened; his heart failed him.

*   *In light of the reports that he received, what were Motecuzoma's options for dealing with the Spanish threat?*

SOURCE: Bernardino de Sahagún. *Florentine Codex: General History of the Things of New Spain,* 13 vols. Trans. by Arthur J. O. Anderson and Charles E. Dibble. Salt Lake City: University of Utah Press, 1950–82, 13:19–20. (Translation slightly modified.)

Running Pronunciation Guide at the bottom of each page helps readers with unfamiliar words and names. An audio version is also available online.

formed sacrifices similar to those conducted by the *brahmins* in India. Like the Aryans, the ancient Persians glorified strength and martial virtues, and the cults of both peoples sought principally to bring about a comfortable material existence for their practitioners.

During the classical era Persian religion underwent considerable change, as moral and religious thinkers **Zarathustra** sought to adapt their messages to the circumstances of a complex, cosmopolitan society. One result was Zoroastrianism, which emerged from the teachings of Zarathustra. Though Zarathustra was undoubtedly a historical person, little certain information survives about his life and career. It is not even clear when he lived, though most scholars date his life to the late seventh and early sixth centuries

Avesta. Nevertheless, many of Zarathustra's own compositions survive because of the diligence by which *magi* preserved them through oral transmission. Known as the *Gathas*, Zarathustra's works were hymns that he composed in honor of the various deities that he recognized. Apart from the *Gathas*, ancient Zoroastrian literature included a wide variety of hymns, liturgical works, and treatises on moral and theological themes. Though some of these works survive, the arrival of Islam in the seventh century C.E. and the subsequent decline of Zoroastrianism resulted in the loss of most of the Avesta and later Zoroastrian works.

Zarathustra and his followers were not strict monotheists. They recognized Ahura Mazda as a supreme

Zoroastrianism (zohr-oh-ASS-tree-ahn-iz'm)

Zarathustra (zar-uh-THOO-struh)
Gathas (GATH-uhs)

Liu Bang called the new dynasty the Han, in honor of his native land. The Han dynasty turned out to be one of the longest and most influential in all of Chinese history. It lasted for more than four hundred years, from 206 B.C.E. to 220 C.E., although for a brief period (9–23 C.E.) a usurper temporarily displaced Han rule. Thus historians conventionally divide the dynasty into the Former Han (206 B.C.E.–9 C.E.) and the Later Han (25–220 C.E.).

The Han dynasty consolidated the tradition of centralized imperial rule that the Qin dynasty had pioneered. During the Former Han, emperors ruled from Chang'an, a cosmopolitan city near modern Xi'an that became the cultural capital of China. During the Later Han, the emperors moved their capital east to Luoyang, also a cosmopolitan city and second in importance only to Chang'an throughout Chinese history.

During the early days of the Han dynasty, Liu Bang attempted to follow a middle path between the decen-**Early Han Policies** tralized political alliances of the Zhou dynasty and the tightly centralized state of the Qin to save the advantages and avoid the excesses of both. On the one hand, he allotted large landholdings to members of the imperial family, in the expectation that they would provide a reliable network

Domestically, Han Wudi worked strenuously to increase the authority and prestige of the central government. He built an enormous bu-**Han Centralization** reaucracy to administer his empire, and he relied on Legalist principles of government. He also continued the Qin policy of building roads and canals to facilitate trade and communication between China's regions. To finance the vast machinery of his government, he levied taxes on agriculture, trade, and craft industries, and he established imperial monopolies on the production of essential goods such as iron and salt. In building such an enormous governmental structure, Han Wudi faced a serious problem of recruitment. He needed thousands of reliable, intelligent, educated individuals to run his bureaucracy, but there was no institutionalized educational system in China that could provide a continuous supply of such people.

Han Wudi addressed that problem in 124 B.C.E. by establishing an imperial university that prepared young men for government service. Personally, **The Confucian Educational System** the Martial Emperor cared little for learning. In that respect he resembled all the other early Han emperors: Liu Bang once emptied his bladder in the distinctive cap worn by Confucian scholars in order to demonstrate his con-

The Marginal Key Terms highlight events and concepts as they appear within the narrative.

A *Chronology* at the end of each chapter lists the key dates and events of the chapter to provide an easy overview.

CHRONOLOGY	
1ST TO 6TH CENTURY	Kingdom of Funan
606–648	Reign of Harsha
670–1025	Kingdom of Srivijaya
711	Conquest of Sind by Umayyad forces
850–1267	Chola kingdom
889–1431	Kingdom of Angkor
1001–1027	Raids on India by Mahmud of Ghazni
11TH TO 12TH CENTURY	Life of Ramanuja
12TH CENTURY	Beginning of the bhakti movement
1206–1526	Sultanate of Delhi
1336–1565	Kingdom of Vijayanagar

Summaries: Each chapter ends with a clearly written, paragraph-long summary to remind students of the highlights they have just read.

SUMMARY

After gaining independence from European colonial powers, the states of the western hemisphere worked to build stable and prosperous societies. The independent American states faced difficult challenges as they sought to construct viable societies on the Enlightenment principles of freedom, equality, and constitutional government. The United States and Canada built large federal societies in North America, whereas a series of smaller states governed affairs in Latin America. Throughout the hemisphere descendants of European settlers subdued indigenous American peoples and built societies dominated by Euro-American peoples. They established agricultural economies, exploited natural resources, and in some lands launched processes of industrialization. They accepted streams of European and Asian migrants, who contributed to American cultural diversity. All American lands experienced tensions arising from social, economic, cultural, and ethnic differences, which led occasionally to violent civil conflict and often to smoldering resentments and grievances. The making of independent American societies was not a smooth process, but it reflected the increasing interdependence of all the world's peoples.

And, finally, *For Further Reading* provides an annotated list of references that students can use for research assignments or their own study.

FOR FURTHER READING

Colin G. Calloway. *First Peoples: A Documentary Survey of American Indian History.* Boston, 1999. A fine text on native American history, written by a knowledgeable scholar in the field.

Fernando Henrique Cardoso and Enzo Faletto. *Dependency and Development in Latin America.* Berkeley, 1979. A sophisticated treatment of economic development in Latin America.

William Cronon. *Nature's Metropolis: Chicago and the Great West.* New York, 1991. A valuable study exploring the role of Chicago in the economic development of the American west.

Tulio Halperín Donghi. *The Contemporary History of Latin America.* Trans. by J. C. Chasteen. Durham, 1993. An influential general history of Latin America from a Latin American point of view.

Ellen C. DuBois. *Feminism and Suffrage: The Emergence of an Independent Women's Movement in America, 1848–1869.* Ithaca, 1984. Traces the rise and character of the U.S. women's movement in the nineteenth century.

Patricia Nelson Limerick. *The Legacy of Conquest: The Unbroken Past of the American West.* New York, 1987. A provocative work exploring the influences of race, class, and gender in the conquest of the American west.

Leon F. Litwack. *Been in the Storm So Long: The Aftermath of Slavery.* New York, 1979. The best study of the promises and perils of life for freed slaves after the U.S. Civil War.

J. R. Miller. *Skyscrapers Hide the Heavens: A History of Indian-White Relations in Canada.* Toronto, 1989. An important study of Canadian policies toward indigenous peoples.

Walter Nugent. *Crossings: The Great Transatlantic Migrations, 1870–1914.* Bloomington, 1992. Provides an overview and analysis of the mass migrations to North America in the nineteenth and twentieth centuries.

Ronald Takaki. *A Different Mirror: A History of Multicultural America.* Boston, 1993. A spirited account of the contributions made by peoples of European, African, Asian, and Native American ancestry to the modern American society.

Throughout the three editions of *Traditions & Encounters: A Global Perspective on the Past,* upon which this text is based, we have benefited from the feedback of instructors and students. Our approach to world history and the manner in which it resonates in the text has been honed by classroom experiences that many others have so generously shared with us. We hope the dialogue continues with the publication of *Traditions & Encounters: A Brief Global History* and that our approach can continue to evolve. World history is a passion for all three of us, and we hope that our texts help to instill in students today a lifelong appreciation for the field as well.

Jerry H. Bentley
Herbert F. Ziegler
Heather E. Streets

Acknowledgments

Many individuals have contributed to this book, and the authors take pleasure in recording deep thanks for all the comments, criticism, advice, and suggestions that helped to improve the work. Special thanks to the editorial and production teams at McGraw-Hill: Lyn Uhl, Jon-David Hague, Angela Kao, Lisa Pinto, Christina Gimlin, Kim Menning, and Brian Pecko who provided crucial support by helping the authors work through difficult issues and solve the innumerable problems of content, style, and organization that arise in any project to produce a history of the world. Finally, we would like to express our appreciation for the advice of the following individuals who read and commented on the original manuscript and previous editions of this text.

Heather J. Abdelnur
Blackburn College

Wayne Ackerson
Salisbury University

William H. Alexander
Norfolk State University

Michael Balyo
Chemeketa Community College

Diane Barefoot
*Caldwell Community College,
Watauga Campus*

Gene Barnett
Calhoun Community College

John Boswell
San Antonio College

W. H. Bragg
Georgia College and State University

Robert Brown
UNC Pembroke

Gayle Brunelle
California State University, Fullerton

Marybeth Carlson
University of Dayton

Kay J. Carr
Southern Illinois University

Jon Davidann
Hawaii Pacific University

Mitch Driebe
Andrew College

Shannon Duffy
Loyola University of New Orleans

Shawn Dry
Oakland Community College

Robert J. Flynn
Portland Community College

Deanna D. Forsman
North Hennepin Community College

Kristine Frederickson
Brigham Young University

James Fuller
University of Indianapolis

Jessie Ruth Gaston
California State University, Sacramento

George W. Gawrych
Baylor University

Deborah Gerish
Emporia State University

Gary G. Gibbs
Roanoke College

Candace Gregory
California State University, Sacramento

Jillian Hartley
Arkansas Northeastern College

Gregory Havrilcsak
The University of Michigan, Flint

John K. Hayden
Southwest Oklahoma State University

Thomas J. Hegarty
University of Tampa

Michael Hickey
Bloomsburg University

Tamara Hunt
University of Southern Indiana

Wallace Hutcheon
Northern Virginia Community College

Karen Irizarry
Southwestern College

Christopher Johnson
Palomar College

Roger L. Jungmeyer
Lincoln University of Missouri

Carole A. Keller
San Antonio College

Charles Keller
Southern Arkansas University

Mee-Ae Kim
Albertson College of Idaho

Mark Konnerty
University of Calgary

Alan D. Lane
Barton College

Marcus Larsen
University of Wisconsin–Eau Claire

Laurence W. Marvin
*Evans School of Humanities,
Berry College*

Ken Millen-Penn
Fairmont State University

April Najjaj
Greensboro College

Kenneth Osgood
Florida Atlantic University

Patrick Peebles
University of Missouri, Kansas City

Phyllis E. Pobst
Arkansas State University

Ronald E. Powaski
Cleveland State University

Dave Pretty
Winthrop University

Tracie Provost
Middle Georgia College

Paul C. Rosier
Villanova University

Margaret Sankey
Minnesota State Moorhead

Daniel Sarefield
Ohio State University

Thomas Saylor
Concordia University, St. Paul

Stuart Schaar
Brooklyn College

Timothy Schroer
University of West Georgia

Francis M. Stackenwalt
East Central University

Gordon C. Thomasson
Broome Community College

John Tucker
East Carolina University

Sara Tucker
Washburn University

Wendy Turner
August State University

David Ulbrich
Ball State University

Rick Whisonant
York Technical College

Pingchao Zhu
University of Idaho

About the Authors

Jerry H. Bentley is professor of history at the University of Hawai'i and editor of the *Journal of World History*. He has written extensively on the cultural history of early modern Europe and on cross-cultural interactions in world history. His research on the religious, moral, and political writings of the Renaissance led to the publication of *Humanists and Holy Writ: New Testament Scholarship in the Renaissance* (1983) and *Politics and Culture in Renaissance Naples* (1987). His more recent research has concentrated on global history and particularly on processes of cross-cultural interaction. His book *Old World Encounters: Cross-Cultural Contacts and Exchanges in Pre-Modern Times* (1993) studies processes of cultural exchange and religious conversion before modern times, and his pamphlet *Shapes of World History in Twentieth-Century Scholarship* (1996) discusses the historiography of world history. His current interests include processes of cross-cultural interaction and cultural exchange in modern times.

Herbert F. Ziegler is an associate professor of history at the University of Hawai'i. He has taught world history since 1980 and currently serves as director of the world history program at the University of Hawai'i. He also serves as book review editor of the *Journal of World History*. His interest in twentieth-century European social and political history led to the publication of *Nazi Germany's New Aristocracy* (1990). He is at present working on a study that explores from a global point of view the demographic trends of the past ten thousand years, along with their concomitant technological, economic, and social developments. His other current research project focuses on the application of complexity theory to a comparative study of societies and their internal dynamics.

Heather Streets is an associate professor of history at Washington State University, where she teaches world history at the graduate and undergraduate levels. She has been teaching at WSU since 1998 and is the director of the WSU history department's world history Ph.D. program. Streets is also co-editor of *World History Connected: the ejournal of Learning and Teaching*. Recent publications include *Martial Races: The Military, Race, and Masculinity in British Imperial Culture, 1857–1914* (2004). She is currently researching 19th and 20th century imperialism as a global phenomenon rather than as a strictly national issue. Her next book will explore the connections between French Indochina, the Dutch East Indies, and British India as a way of demonstrating that the various national empires learned from, imitated, and stayed in contact with one another.

Connections in History, Connections in Class:
Resources for Students and Instructors

Texts these days abound in print and media resources for students and instructors, and we begin to wonder what instructor or student has time to sort through all of the resources available and make use of them in class or for studying. As we developed the text, we worked to discover exactly what tools instructors and students need to be successful in the course, and how to make these resources as easy to use as possible.

As a result of extensive research, we have streamlined the traditional laundry list of ancillary items available with texts these days onto a single rich Web site to support teaching and learning with *Traditions & Encounters: A Brief Global History*.

THE ONLINE LEARNING CENTER FOR STUDENTS

We have created tools for students that reinforce the text's chapters and encourage their interest in world history. The Online Learning Center, or OLC, serves two purposes: 1) Help students prepare for exams, and 2) Help students conduct research for papers and presentations. The OLC is a complete, straightforward media resource that provides a multitude of practice quizzes as well as readings and images for outside research.

To simplify matters for instructors, we provide a map of every feature on the OLC in a downloadable Faculty Guide, so that instructors can see exactly what kind of study tools the student is using and coordinate those tools with their own class assignments. (See below for more information.)

Primary Source Investigator (PSI) on the Online Learning Center

Beginning historians must learn to use primary and secondary sources to formulate and defend their arguments. Available online for the first time, McGraw-Hill's *Primary Source Investigator* (*PSI*) is designed to support and enrich the text discussion in *Traditions & Encounters: A Brief Global History.*

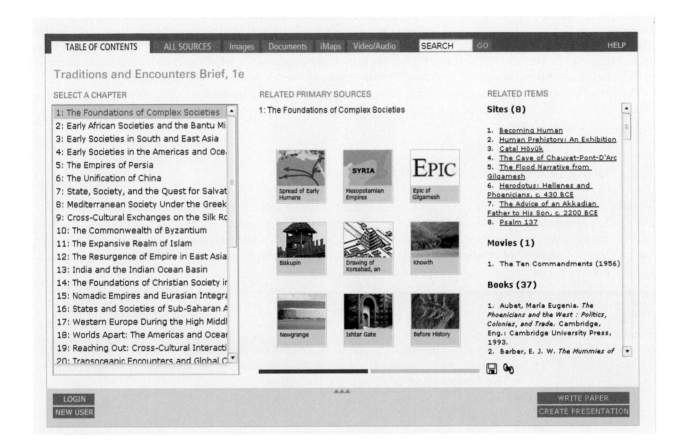

Access to Sources:

A selection of the resources available through PSI are integrated into the text itself. Throughout the text, marginal icons show that an additional source is available for free on the OLC.

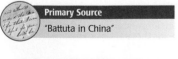

- **Primary Source Documents**: Documents include contemporary accounts of events that appeared in books, newspapers, or private letters of an era as well as government documents.

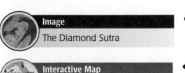

- **Images:** These include photographs of artifacts and buildings as well as contemporary paintings, engravings, and drawings.

- **Interactive Maps:** These maps actively illustrate historical changes over time.

Additional secondary sources materials such as videos are available on PSI but not integrated into the text. Informative and of high quality, the videos engage student interest in topics such as Islamic scientific advances or Mesoamerican civilizations.

Create a Presentation:

Using the sources available through *PSI*, students and teachers can choose sources to build a custom presentation. Teachers can use this tool for presentations during lectures and students for in-class presentation assignments.

Write a Paper:

This useful tool guides students through the process of creating and supporting a thesis around the *PSI* sources they are exploring.

Study Tools on the Online Learning Center

We understand that research is only part of a world history course. This portion of the OLC provides students with study tools to aid in exam preparation.

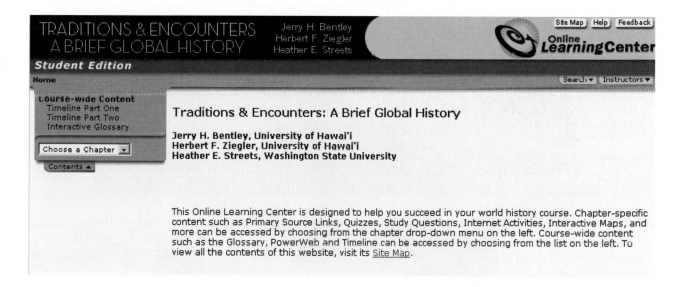

- **Blank Maps:** All of the maps from the book are available for download without any labels, keys, or captions. Students can print these out to quiz themselves on geography.

- **Interactive Glossary:** A textbook for world history naturally spans many different countries and languages. This interactive glossary is formatted in a flashcard template with over 600 terms, definitions, and an audio pronunciation guide.

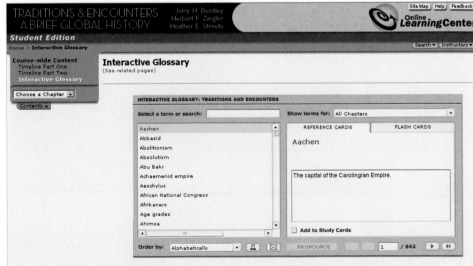

- **Practice Quizzes:** Each chapter contains a variety of quizzes with questions in a variety of formats: multiple choice, true/false, short answer, and essay.

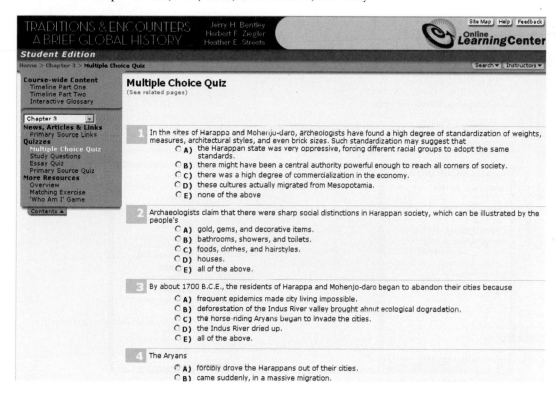

- **Review Summaries:** A chapter outline and overview help to reinforce the big picture of each chapter.

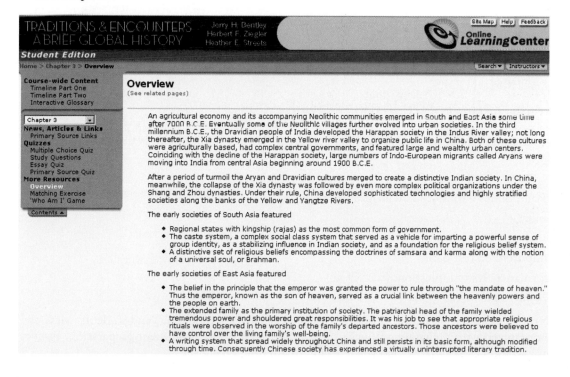

- **Interactive Maps with Quizzes:** Created directly from the maps in the book, the online interactive maps in each chapter are accompanied by critical thinking questions.

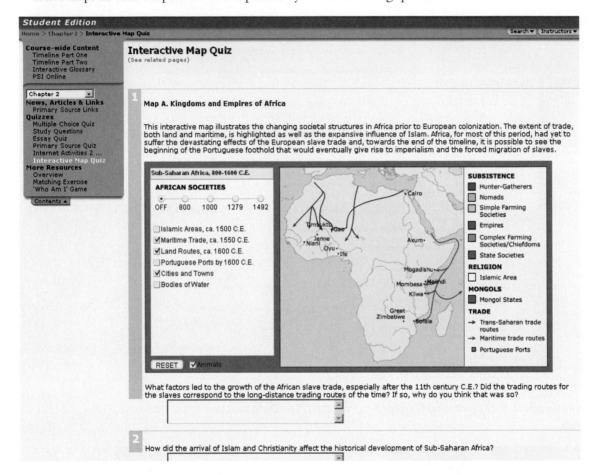

EFFORTLESS TEACHING TOOLS:
THE ONLINE *FACULTY GUIDE* WITH INSTRUCTOR'S RESOURCE

This instructor's tool contains the best of the premier resources that are traditionally available for the larger version of this text:

- Image bank
- Premier PowerPoint Slides with over 100 images and maps
- Instructor's Manual
- Test Bank
- EZ TEST (a computerized test bank)
- Classroom Performance System questions (see below)
- New *Faculty Guide* to resources

The *Faculty Guide* provides easy reference to all learning assets available to both teachers and students. McGraw-Hill resources are organized within chapter outlines to streamline lecture and assignment preparation. Faculty will see the options and sources at a glance, and where to find them on the Web site.

ADDITIONAL TOOLS FOR THE INSTRUCTOR

We identified two other resources that are in high demand for classroom use, and so they are included in the resource package for instructors as well:

- The same maps and illustrations that are available in the Faculty Guide as PowerPoint slides may also be ordered as *overhead transparencies.*

- A *classroom response system* using electronic "clickers" is available. McGraw-Hill's Classroom Performance System (CPS) by eInstruction allows instructors to gauge immediately what students are learning during lectures. Instructors can ask questions, take polls, host classroom demonstrations, and get instant feedback. In addition, CPS makes it easy to take attendance, give and grade pop quizzes, or give formal paper-based class tests with multiple versions of the test using CPS for immediate grading.

Instructors can contact their McGraw-Hill sales representative for all of the above resources. You can find your sales representative at www.mhhe.com/rep.

We hope that these tightly integrated resources make the teaching and learning of world history more manageable than ever before.

J. H. B.
H. F. Z.
H. E. S.

B y 1500 C.E. peoples throughout the world had built well-organized societies with distinctive cultural traditions. Powerful agricultural societies dominated most of Asia, the Mediterranean basin, Europe, much of sub-Saharan Africa, Mexico, and the central Andean region. By 1500 peoples of the world had also established intricate transportation networks that supported travel, communication, and exchange. Although pioneered by merchants in the interests of trade, religion, food crops, animal stocks, and disease pathogens also traveled these routes.

Yet the commercial, cultural, and biological exchanges of premodern times prefigured much more intense cross-cultural interactions after 1500. Beginning in the fifteenth century, European mariners established trade routes linking the lands of the Indian, Atlantic, and Pacific Ocean basins. These routes in turn fostered direct contact between the peoples of the eastern hemisphere, the western hemisphere, and Oceania.

The establishment of links between all the world's regions and peoples gave rise to the early modern era of world history, approximately 1500 to 1800 C.E. The early modern era differed from the period from 1000 to 1500, when there were only sporadic contacts between peoples of the eastern hemisphere, the western hemisphere, and Oceania. It also differed from the modern era, from 1800 to the present, when national states, heavy industry, powerful weapons, and efficient technologies of transportation and communication enabled peoples of European ancestry to achieve political and economic dominance in the world.

During the early modern era, several global processes touched peoples in all parts of the world and influenced the development of their societies. One involved biological exchange: plants, animals, diseases, and human communities crossed the world's oceans and established themselves in new lands, where they dramatically affected both

the natural environment and established
societies. Another involved commercial exchange:
merchants took advantage of newly established sea lanes to
inaugurate a genuinely global economy. Yet another process involved the diffusion of
technologies and cultural traditions: printing and gunpowder spread throughout the
world, and Christianity and Islam attracted increasing numbers of converts.

These global processes had different effects for different peoples. In the Americas
and Oceania, diseases introduced from the eastern hemisphere ravaged indigenous
populations and sometimes led to the collapse of whole societies. In contrast, Europeans

THE ORIGINS OF GLOBAL INTERDEPENDENCE, 1500–1800

claimed vast stretches of land in the Americas, where they founded colonies and
cultivated crops for sale on the open market. In sub-Saharan Africa, millions of enslaved
individuals underwent a forced migration to the western hemisphere, where they
suffered both physical and psychological abuse. Meanwhile, east Asian and Islamic
peoples prospered from increased trade but restricted the introduction of foreign ideas
and technologies into their societies.

Although European peoples benefited from global processes of the period 1500
to 1800, by no means did they dominate world affairs in early modern times. Indeed,
most of the western hemisphere and Africa lay beyond their control until the nineteenth
century. Nevertheless, European peoples played a more prominent role in world affairs
than any of their ancestors, and their efforts helped foster the development of an
increasingly interdependent world.

CHAPTER 20

Transoceanic Encounters and Global Connections

On 8 July 1497 the Portuguese mariner Vasco da Gama led a small fleet of four armed merchant vessels with 170 crewmen out of the harbor at Lisbon. His destination was India, which he planned to reach by sailing around the continent of Africa and through the Indian Ocean. He carried letters of introduction from the king of Portugal as well as cargoes of gold, wool textiles, and other goods that he hoped to exchange for pepper and spices in India.

Before there would be an opportunity to trade, however, da Gama and his crew had a prolonged voyage through two oceans. They sailed south from Portugal to the Cape Verde Islands off the west coast of Africa, where they took on fresh provisions. On 3 August they headed southeast into the Atlantic Ocean to take advantage of the prevailing winds. For the next ninety-five days, the fleet saw no land. By October, da Gama had found westerly winds in the southern Atlantic, rounded the Cape of Good Hope, and entered the Indian Ocean. The fleet slowly worked its way up the east coast of Africa as far as Malindi, where da Gama secured the services of an Indian Muslim pilot to guide his ships across the Arabian Sea. On 20 May 1498—more than ten months after its departure from Lisbon—the fleet anchored at Calicut in southern India.

In India the Portuguese fleet found a wealthy, cosmopolitan society. The markets of Calicut offered not only pepper, ginger, cinnamon, and spices but also rubies, emeralds, gold jewelry, and

OPPOSITE PAGE: *A Chinese lacquer screen from the 17th century depicts Portuguese ships and sailors.*

fine cotton textiles. Alas, apart from gold and some striped cloth, the goods that da Gama had brought attracted little interest among merchants at Calicut. Nevertheless, da Gama managed to exchange gold for a cargo of pepper and cinnamon that turned a handsome profit when the fleet returned to Portugal in August 1499. Da Gama's expedition also opened the door to direct maritime trade between European and Asian peoples and helped to establish permanent links between the world's various regions.

Cross-cultural interactions have been a persistent feature of historical development. Even in ancient times mass migration, campaigns of imperial expansion, and long-distance trade deeply influenced societies throughout the world. Yet after 1500 C.E. cross-cultural interactions took place on a much larger geographic scale than ever before, and encounters were often more disruptive than in earlier centuries. Equipped with advanced technologies and a powerful military arsenal, western European peoples began to cross the world's oceans in large numbers during the early modern era. At the same time, Russian adventurers built an enormous Eurasian empire and ventured tentatively into the Pacific Ocean.

Europeans were not the only peoples who actively explored the larger world during the early modern era. In the early fifteenth century, the Ming emperors of China sponsored a series of seven enormous maritime expeditions that visited all parts of the Indian Ocean basin. In the sixteenth century Ottoman mariners also ventured into the Indian Ocean. Following the Ottoman conquest of Egypt in 1517, both merchant and military vessels established an Ottoman presence throughout the Indian Ocean basin.

Although other peoples also made their way into the larger world, only Europeans linked the lands and peoples of the eastern hemisphere, the western hemisphere, and Oceania. Because of that, European peoples benefited from unparalleled opportunities to increase their power, wealth, and influence. As a result, after 1500 European peoples became much more prominent in the larger world than before.

The expansion of European influence resulted in the establishment of global networks of transportation, communication, and exchange. Indeed, a worldwide diffusion of plants, animals, diseases, and human communities followed European ventures across the oceans, and intricate trade networks eventually gave birth to a global economy.

THE EUROPEAN RECONNAISSANCE OF THE WORLD'S OCEANS

Between 1400 and 1800, European mariners launched a remarkable series of exploratory voyages that took them to nearly all the earth's waters. Those voyages were very expensive affairs. Yet private investors and government authorities had strong motives to underwrite the expeditions and outfit them with the latest nautical technology. The voyages of exploration paid large dividends: they enabled European mariners to

Image
Mediterranean map—17th century

chart the world's ocean basins and develop an accurate understanding of world geography. On the basis of that knowledge, European merchants and mariners established global networks of communication, transportation, and exchange—and profited handsomely from their efforts.

Motives for Exploration

A complex combination of motives prompted Europeans to explore the world's oceans. Most important of those motives were the search for basic resources and lands suitable for the cultivation of cash crops, the desire to establish new trade routes to Asian markets, and the aspiration to expand the influence of Christianity.

Mariners from the relatively poor kingdom of Portugal were most prominent in the search for fresh resources and lands. Beginning in the thirteenth century, Portuguese seamen ventured away from the coasts and into the open Atlantic Ocean to supplement their own meager resources. By the early fourteenth century, they had discovered the uninhabited Azores and Madeiras Islands and called frequently at the Canary Islands, inhabited by the indigenous Guanche people. These Atlantic islands proved ideal for the cultivation of sugar, a product that enjoyed a strong European demand. In the fifteenth century, Italian investors—who had organized sugar plantations in the Mediterranean since the twelfth century—helped Portuguese mariners establish plantations in the Atlantic islands. Continuing Portuguese voyages also led to the establishment of plantations on the Cape Verde Islands, São Tomé, Principe, and Fernando Po.

Portuguese Exploration

The Lure of Trade Even more alluring than the exploitation of fresh lands and resources was the goal of establishing maritime trade routes to the markets of Asia. During the era of the Mongol empires, European merchants often traveled overland as far as China to trade for Asian goods. When the Mongol empires collapsed and bubonic plague spread across Eurasia in the fourteenth century, however, travel on the silk roads became much more dangerous. As a result, Europeans relied on Muslim mariners to bring Asian goods through the Indian Ocean and the Red Sea to Cairo, where Italian merchants purchased them for distribution in western Europe. But prices at Cairo were high, and Europeans sought ever-larger quantities of Asian goods, particularly spices.

By the fourteenth century the wealthy classes of Europe regarded Indian pepper and Chinese ginger as expensive necessities, and they especially prized cloves and nutmeg from the spice islands of Maluku. Merchants and monarchs alike realized that by gaining direct access to Asian markets and eliminating Muslim intermediaries, they could increase the quantities of spices and other Asian goods available in Europe while making enormous profits.

African trade also beckoned to Europeans and called them to the sea. Since the twelfth century, Europeans had purchased west African gold, ivory, and slaves brought to north African ports by Muslim merchants. West African gold was especially important to Europeans because it was their principal form of payment for Asian luxury goods. As in the case of Asian trade, Europeans realized that they could profit from eliminating Muslim middlemen and establishing maritime routes that offered direct access to African markets.

Missionary Efforts Alongside material incentives, the goal of expanding the boundaries of Christianity drove Europeans into the larger world. Like Buddhism and Islam, Christianity is a missionary religion that directs believers to spread the faith. Sometimes such efforts were attempted through peaceful persuasion. At other times the expansion of Christianity could be quite violent. Beginning in the eleventh century, for example, western Europeans launched a series of crusades against Muslims in Palestine, the Mediterranean islands, and Iberia. In Iberia, in fact, the Muslim kingdom of Granada fell to Spanish Christian forces just weeks before Christopher Columbus set sail on his famous first voyage to the western hemisphere in 1492. Whether through persuasion or violence, overseas voyages offered fresh opportunities for western Europeans to spread their faith.

In practice, the various motives for exploration combined and reinforced one another. When the Portuguese mariner Vasco da Gama reached the Indian port of Calicut in 1498, local authorities asked him what he wanted there. His reply: "Christians

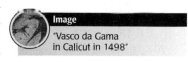

Image
"Vasco da Gama in Calicut in 1498"

A detail from the Catalan Atlas, a magnificent illustrated representation of the known world produced about 1375, depicts a camel caravan traveling from China to Europe across the silk roads.

and spices." The goal of spreading Christianity thus became a powerful justification and reinforcement for the more material motives for the voyages of exploration.

The Technology of Exploration

Without advanced nautical technology and navigational skills, even the strongest motives would not have enabled European mariners to reconnoiter the world's oceans. They also needed sturdy ships, good navigational equipment, and knowledge of sailing techniques. These they devised by combining Chinese and Arabic technologies with their own inherited nautical technologies from the Mediterranean and northern Europe.

Ships and Sails From their experiences in the rough coastal waters of the Atlantic, European sailors learned to construct ships strong enough to brave most adverse conditions. Beginning about the twelfth century, they increased the maneuverability of their craft by building a rudder onto the stern. (The sternpost rudder was a Chinese invention that had diffused across the Indian Ocean.) They outfitted their vessels with two types of sails: square sails (which enabled them to take full advantage of a wind blowing from behind) and triangular lateen sails (which could catch winds from the side as well as from behind). With a combination of square and lateen sails, European ships were able to use whatever winds arose. Their ability to tack—to advance against the wind by sailing across it—was crucial for the exploration of regions with uncooperative winds.

Navigational Instruments The most important navigational equipment on board these vessels were magnetic compasses (which determined heading) and astrolabes (which determined latitude). The compass was a Chinese invention that had diffused throughout the Indian Ocean basin in the eleventh century and had reached European mariners by the mid–twelfth century. The astrolabe was a simplified version of an instrument used by Greek and Persian astronomers to measure the angle of the sun or the pole star above the horizon. In the late fifteenth century, however, Portuguese mariners encountered Arab sailors in the Indian Ocean using simpler and more serviceable instruments for determining latitude, which the Portuguese then used as models for the construction of cross-staffs and back-staffs.

Image
18th-century magnetic compass

By using cross-staffs to measure the angle of the sun or the pole star above the horizon, mariners could determine latitude.

Knowledge of Winds and Currents European mariners' ability to determine direction and latitude enabled them to assemble a vast body of data about the earth's geography and to find their way around the world's oceans with tolerable accuracy and efficiency. Equipped with advanced technological hardware, European mariners ventured into the oceans and gradually compiled a body of practical knowledge about winds and currents. Indeed, as they became familiar with the wind systems of the world's oceans, European mariners developed the ability to travel reliably to coastlines throughout the world.

Voyages of Exploration: From the Mediterranean to the Atlantic

Although European exploratory voyaging began as early as the thirteenth century, the pace quickened decisively after 1415. In that year, Prince Henry of Portugal (1394–1460), often called Prince Henry the Navigator, conquered the Moroccan port of Ceuta and sponsored *Prince Henry of Portugal* a series of voyages down the west African coast. Portuguese merchants soon established fortified trading posts at São Jorge da Mina (in modern Ghana) and other strategic locations. There they exchanged European horses and goods for gold and slaves. Portuguese explorations continued after Henry's death, and in 1488 Bartolomeu Dias rounded the Cape of Good Hope and entered the Indian Ocean. He did not proceed farther because of storms and a restless crew, but the route to India, China, and the spice-bearing islands of southeast Asia lay open. The sea route to the Indian Ocean offered European merchants the opportunity to buy silk, spices, and pepper at the source, rather than through Muslim intermediaries, and to take part in the flourishing trade of Asia.

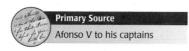

Primary Source

Afonso V to his captains

As we have already seen, in 1497 Vasco da Gama sought to do just that, departing Lisbon with a fleet of four armed merchant ships bound for India. His experience was not altogether pleasant. His fleet went more than three months without seeing land, and his cargoes excited

Vasco da Gama

Map 20.1 Voyages of European exploration in the Atlantic Ocean between 1486 and 1498. Observe the difference between Bartolomeu Dias's journey and Vasco da Gama's journey around the Cape of Good Hope. Why did da Gama go so far out into the Atlantic before rounding the Cape?

little interest in Indian markets. Moreover, less than half of his crew made it safely back to Portugal. Yet his cargo of pepper and cinnamon was hugely profitable, and Portuguese merchants began immediately to organize further expeditions. By 1500 they had built a trading post at Calicut, and Portuguese mariners soon called at ports throughout the Indian Ocean basin. By the late sixteenth century, English and Dutch mariners followed suit.

While Portuguese navigators plied the sea route to India, the Genoese mariner Cristoforo Colombo, *Christopher Columbus* known in English as Christopher Columbus (1451–1506), proposed sailing to the markets of Asia by a western route. On the basis of wide reading in the existing geographical literature, Columbus believed that earth was a relatively small sphere with a circumference of about 17,000 nautical miles. (In fact, the earth's circumference is almost 25,000 nautical miles.) By Columbus's calculations, Japan should have been less than 2,500 nautical miles west of the Canary Islands. (The actual distance is more than 10,000 nautical miles.) This geography suggested that sailing west from Europe to Asian markets would be profitable, and Columbus sought royal sponsorship for a voyage to prove his ideas.

Eventually Fernando and Isabel of Spain agreed to underwrite Columbus's expedition, and in August 1492 his fleet of three ships departed southern Spain. He sailed south to the Canaries, picked up supplies, and then turned west with the trade winds. On the morning of 12 October 1492, he made landfall at an island in the Bahamas that the native Taino inhabitants called Guanahaní and that Columbus rechristened San Salvador (also known as Watling Island). Thinking that he had arrived in the spice islands known familiarly as the Indies, Columbus called the Tainos "Indians." He sailed around the Caribbean for almost three months in search of gold, and at the large island of Cuba he sent a delegation to seek the court of the emperor of China. When Columbus returned to Spain, he reported to his royal sponsors that he had reached islands just off the coast of Asia.

Columbus never reached the riches of Asia, and he obtained very little gold in the Caribbean. Yet news of his voyage spread rapidly throughout Europe, and hundreds of Spanish, English, *Hemispheric Links* French, and Dutch mariners soon followed in his wake. Initially, many of them continued to seek the passage to Asian waters that Columbus himself had pursued. Over a longer term, however, it became clear that the American

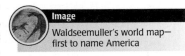

Image
Waldseemuller's world map— first to name America

can continents and the Caribbean islands themselves held abundant opportunities for entrepreneurs. Thus

A map prepared about 1512 by the Polish cartographer Jan Stobnicza shows eloquently that it took a long time for geographers to realize the extent of the Americas and the Pacific Ocean. Here "Cipangu" (Japan) lies just west of Mexico, with the Asian mainland nearby.

Christopher Columbus's First Impressions of American Peoples

Christopher Columbus kept journals of his experiences during his voyages to the western hemisphere. The journal of his first voyage survives mostly in summary, but it clearly communicates Columbus's first impressions of the peoples he met in the Caribbean islands. The following excerpts show that Columbus, like other European mariners, had both Christianity and commerce in mind when exploring distant lands.

■ ■ ■

Thursday, 11 October [1492]. . . .
I . . . in order that they would be friendly to us—because I recognized that they were people who would be better freed [from error] and converted to our Holy Faith by love than by force—to some of them I gave red caps, and glass beads which they put on their chests, and many other things of small value, in which they took so much pleasure and became so much our friends that it was a marvel. Later they came swimming to the ships' launches where we were and brought us parrots and cotton thread in balls and javelins and many other things, and they traded them to us for other things which we gave them, such as small glass beads and bells. In sum, they took everything and gave of what they had willingly.

But it seemed to me that they were a people very poor in everything. All of them go as naked as their mothers bore them; and the women also, although I did not see more than one quite young girl. And all those that I saw were young people, for none did I see of more than 30 years of age. They are very well formed, with handsome bodies and good faces. Their hair [is] coarse—almost like the tail of a horse—and short. They wear their hair down over their eyebrows except for a little in the back which they wear long and never cut. . . .

They do not carry arms nor are they acquainted with them, because I showed them swords and they took them by the edge and through ignorance cut themselves. They have no iron. Their javelins are shafts without iron and some of them have at the end a fish tooth and others of other things. All of them alike are of good-sized stature and carry themselves well. I saw some who had marks of wounds on their bodies and I made signs to them asking what they were; and they showed me how people from other islands nearby came there and tried to take them, and how they defended themselves and I believed and believe that they come here from *tierra firme* [the continent] to take them captive. They should be good and intelligent servants, for I see that they say very quickly everything that is said to them; and I believe that they would become Christians very easily, for it seemed to me that they had no religion. . . .

Monday, 12 November. . . .
They are very gentle and do not know what evil is; nor do they kill others, nor steal; and they are without weapons and so timid that a hundred of them flee from one of our men even if our men are teasing them. And they are credulous and aware that there is a God in heaven and convinced that we come from the heavens; and they say very quickly any prayer that we tell them to say, and they make the sign of the cross. So that Your Highnesses ought to resolve to make them Christians: for I believe that if you begin, in a short time you will end up having converted to our Holy Faith a multitude of peoples and acquiring large dominions and great riches and all of their peoples for Spain. Because without doubt there is in these lands a very great quantity of gold; for not without out cause do these Indians that I bring with me say that there are in these islands places where they dig gold and wear it on their chests, on their ears, and on their arms, and on their legs; and they are very thick bracelets. And also there are stones, and there are precious pearls and infinite spicery. . . . And also here there is probably a great quantity of cotton; and I think that it would sell very well here without taking it to Spain but to the big cities belonging to the Grand [Mongol] Khan.

- *On the basis of Columbus's account, what inferences can you draw about his plans for American lands and peoples?*

SOURCE: Christopher Columbus. *The* Diario *of Christopher Columbus's First Voyage to America*. Trans. by Oliver Dunn and James E. Kelley Jr. Norman: University of Oklahoma Press, 1989, pp. 65–69, 143–45.

Map 20.2 Voyages of European exploration in the Pacific Ocean between 1519 and 1780. Note the vast expanses of blue water mariners had to cross in these voyages. What technologies made such extensive voyages possible?

Columbus's voyages to the western hemisphere had unintended but momentous consequences, since they established links between the eastern and western hemispheres and paved the way for the conquest, settlement, and exploitation of the Americas by European peoples.

Voyages of Exploration: From the Atlantic to the Pacific

While some Europeans sought opportunities in the Americas, others continued to seek a western route to Asian markets. However, in the early sixteenth century no one suspected the vast size of the Pacific Ocean, which covers one-third of the earth's surface.

The reconnaissance of the Pacific Ocean basin began with the Portuguese navigator Fernão de Magalhães (1480–1521), better known as Ferdinand Magellan. While sailing in the service of Portugal, Magellan had visited ports throughout the Indian Ocean basin and had traveled east as far as the spice islands of Maluku. He believed that the spice islands and Asian markets lay fairly close to the western coast of the Americas, and he decided to pursue Christopher Columbus's goal of establishing a western route to Asian waters. Because

Ferdinand Magellan

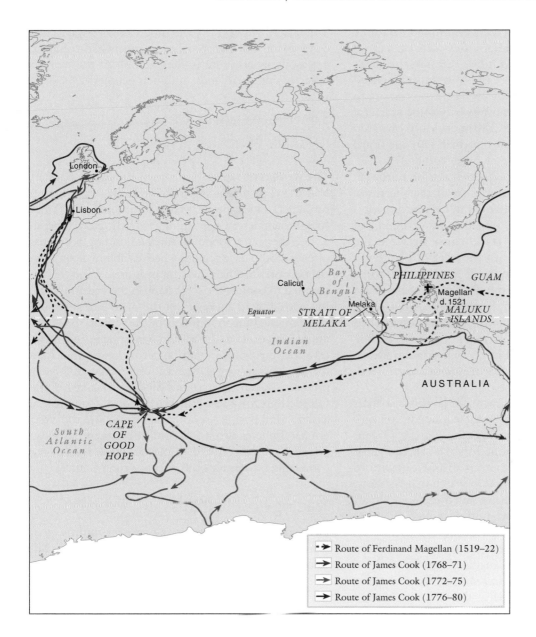

Route of Ferdinand Magellan (1519–22)
Route of James Cook (1768–71)
Route of James Cook (1772–75)
Route of James Cook (1776–80)

Portuguese mariners had already reached Asian markets through the Indian Ocean, they had little interest in Magellan's proposed western route. Thus, on his Pacific expedition and circumnavigation of the world (1519–1522), Magellan sailed in the service of Spain.

Magellan's voyage was an exercise in endurance. He began by probing the eastern coast of South *The Circumnavigation* America in search of a strait leading to the Pacific. Eventually he found and sailed through the treacherous Strait of Magellan near the southern tip of South America. His fleet then sailed almost four months before taking on fresh provisions at Guam.

During that period crewmen survived on worm-ridden biscuits, ship's rats, leather they had softened in the ocean, and water gone foul. Lacking fresh fruits and vegetables in their diet, many of the crew fell victim to the dreaded disease of scurvy, which caused painful rotting of the gums, loss of teeth, abscesses, hemorrhaging, and in most cases death. Scurvy killed twenty-nine members of Magellan's crew during the Pacific crossing.

Conditions improved after the fleet called at Guam, but its ordeal had not come to an end. From Guam, Magellan proceeded to the Philippine Islands, where he and 40 of his crew were killed in a local political dispute. The survivors continued on to the spice islands of Maluku, where they took on a cargo of cloves. They then sailed home through the familiar waters of the Indian Ocean—and thus completed the first circumnavigation of the world—returning to Spain after a voyage of almost exactly three years. Of Magellan's five ships and 280 men, only one ship with 18 of the original crew returned. (An additional 17 crewmen returned later by other routes.)

The Pacific Ocean is so vast that it took European explorers almost three centuries to chart its features. *Exploration of the Pacific* Spanish merchants built on information gleaned from Magellan's expedition and established a trade route between the Philippines and Mexico, but they did not continue to explore the ocean basin itself. English navigators, however, ventured into the Pacific in search of a northwest passage from Europe to Asia. While searching for a passage, English mariners established many of the details of Pacific geography. In the sixteenth century, for example, Sir Francis Drake scouted the west coast of North America as far north as Vancouver Island.

Russian expansion was mostly a land-based affair in early modern times, but by the eighteenth century Russians also were exploring the Pacific Ocean. Russian officials commissioned the Danish navigator Vitus Bering to undertake two maritime expeditions (1725–1730 and 1733–1742) in search of a northeast passage to Asian ports. Bering sailed through the icy Arctic Ocean and the Bering Strait, which separates Siberia from Alaska.

Other Russian explorers made their way from Alaska down the western Canadian coast to northern California. By 1800 Russian mariners were scouting the Pacific Ocean as far south as the Hawaiian Islands. Indeed, they built a small fort on the island of Kaua`i and engaged in trade there for a few years in the early nineteenth century.

Alongside Magellan, however, the most important of the Pacific explorers was Captain James Cook *Captain James Cook* (1728–1779), who led three expeditions to the Pacific and died in a scuffle with the indigenous people of Hawai`i. Cook charted eastern Australia and New Zealand, and he added New Caledonia, Vanuatu, and Hawai`i to European maps of the Pacific. He probed the frigid waters of the Arctic Ocean and spent months at a time in the tropical islands of Tahiti,

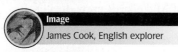
Image
James Cook, English explorer

Tonga, and Hawai`i. By the time Cook's voyages had come to an end, European geographers had compiled a reasonably accurate understanding of the world's ocean basins, their lands, and their peoples.

TRADE AND CONFLICT IN EARLY MODERN ASIA

The voyages of exploration taught European mariners how to sail to almost any coastline in the world and return safely. Once they arrived at their destinations, they sought commercial opportunities. In the eastern hemisphere they built a series of fortified trading posts that offered footholds in regions where established commercial networks had held sway for centuries. They even attempted to control the spice trade in the Indian Ocean, but with limited success. For the most part, they did not have the human numbers or the military power to impose their rule in the eastern hemisphere. In a parallel effort involving expansion across land rather than the sea, Russian explorers and adventurers established a presence in central Asia and Siberia, thus laying the foundations for a vast Eurasian empire. Commercial and political rivalries in both the eastern and the western hemispheres also led to conflict between European peoples, which resulted in numerous wars between competing powers for both territory and resources.

Trading-Post Empires

Portuguese mariners built the earliest trading-post empire. Their goal was not to conquer territories but to control trade routes by forcing merchant vessels to call at fortified trading sites and pay duties there. Vasco da Gama obtained *Portuguese Trading Posts* permission from local authorities to establish a trading post at Calicut when he arrived there in 1498. By the mid–sixteenth century, Portuguese merchants had built more than fifty trading posts between west Africa and east Asia.

Equipped with heavy artillery, Portuguese vessels were able to overpower most other craft that they encountered, and they sometimes trained their cannon effectively onshore. The *Afonso d'Alboquerque* architect of their aggressive policy was Afonso d'Alboquerque, commander of Portuguese forces in the Indian Ocean during the early sixteenth century. Alboquerque's fleets seized Hormuz in 1508, Goa in 1510, and Melaka in 1511. From these strategic sites, Alboquerque sought to control Indian

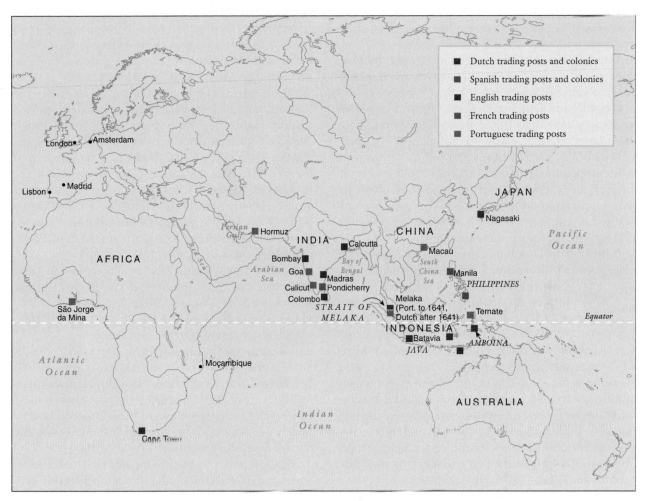

Map 20.3 European trading posts in Africa and Asia about 1700. Note how many more trading posts there were in Asia than in Africa. What accounts for the difference?

Ocean trade by forcing all merchant ships to purchase safe-conduct passes and present them at Portuguese trading posts. Ships without passes were subject to confiscation, along with their cargoes. Alboquerque's forces punished violators of his policy by executing them or cutting off their hands. Alboquerque was confident of Portuguese naval superiority and its ability to control trade in the Indian Ocean.

In reality, however, Portuguese forces did not have enough vessels to enforce their commander's orders. Arab, Indian, and Malay merchants continued to play prominent roles in Indian Ocean commerce, usually without taking the precaution of securing a safe-conduct pass. Indeed, Arab vessels continued to deliver shipments of pepper and spices through the Red Sea, which Portuguese forces never managed to control, to Cairo and Mediterranean trade routes.

By the late sixteenth century, Portuguese hegemony in the Indian Ocean was growing weak. Portugal was a small country with a small population—about one million in 1500—and was unable to sustain its large seaborne trading empire. In addition, by the late sixteenth century, investors in other lands began to organize their own expeditions to Asian markets. Most prominent of those who followed the Portuguese into the Indian Ocean were English and Dutch mariners.

Like their predecessors, English and Dutch merchants built trading posts on Asian coasts and sought to channel trade through them, but they did not attempt to control shipping on the high seas. They also occasionally seized Portuguese sites, although Portuguese authorities held many of their trading posts into the twentieth century. Meanwhile,

English and Dutch Trading Posts

English and Dutch entrepreneurs established parallel networks. English merchants concentrated on India and built trading posts at Bombay, Madras, and Calcutta, while the Dutch operated more broadly from Cape Town, Colombo, and Batavia (modern Jakarta on the island of Java).

English and Dutch merchants enjoyed two main advantages over their Portuguese predecessors. They sailed faster, cheaper, and more powerful ships, which offered both an economic and a military edge over their competitors. Furthermore, they conducted trade through an exceptionally efficient form of commercial organization—the joint-stock company—which enabled investors to realize handsome profits while limiting the risk to their investments.

The Trading Companies English and Dutch merchants formed two especially powerful joint-stock companies: the English East India Company, founded in 1600, and its Dutch counterpart, the United East India Company, known from its initials as the VOC (Vereenigde Oost-Indische Compagnie), established in 1602. Private merchants advanced funds to launch these companies, outfit them with ships and crews, and provide them with commodities and money to trade. Although they enjoyed government support, the companies were privately owned enterprises. Unhampered by political oversight, company agents concentrated strictly on profitable trade. Their charters granted them the right to buy, sell, build trading posts, and even make war.

The English and Dutch companies experienced immediate financial success. In 1601, for example, five English ships set sail from London with cargoes mostly of gold and silver coins valued at thirty thousand pounds sterling. When they returned in 1603, the spices that they carried were worth more than one million pounds sterling. Because of their advanced nautical technology, powerful military arsenal, efficient organization, and relentless pursuit of profit, the English East India Company and the VOC contributed to the early formation of a global network of trade.

European Conquests in Southeast Asia

Following voyages of exploration to the western hemisphere, Europeans conquered indigenous peoples, built territorial empires, and established colonies settled by European migrants. In the eastern hemisphere, however, they were mostly unable to force their will on large Asian populations and powerful centralized states. With the decline of the Portuguese effort to control shipping in the Indian Ocean, Europeans mostly traded peacefully in Asian waters alongside Arab, Indian, Malay, and Chinese merchants.

Yet in two island regions of southeast Asia—the Philippines and Indonesia—Europeans conquered existing authorities and imposed their rule. Though densely populated, neither the Philippines nor Indonesia had a powerful state when Europeans arrived there in the sixteenth century. Nor did imperial authorities in China or India lay claim to the island regions. Heavily armed ships enabled Europeans to bring overwhelming force to bear and to establish imperial regimes that favored the interests of European merchants.

Conquest of the Philippines Spanish forces approached the Philippines in 1565 under the command of Miguel López de Legazpi, who named the islands after King Philip II of Spain. Because the Philippines had no central government, there was no organized resistance to the intrusion. By 1575 Spanish forces controlled the coastal regions of the central and northern islands, and during the seventeenth century they extended their authority to most parts of the archipelago except the southern island of Mindanao, where a large Muslim community stoutly resisted Spanish expansion.

Manila Spanish policy in the Philippines revolved around trade and Christianity. Manila soon emerged as a bustling, multicultural port city—an entrepôt for trade, particularly in silk—and it quickly became the hub of Spanish commercial activity in Asia. Chinese merchants were especially prominent in Manila. They occupied a specially designated commercial district of the city and supplied silk goods that Spanish traders shipped to Mexico in the so-called Manila galleons. Their commercial success brought suspicion on the Chinese community, however, and resentful Spanish and Filipino residents massacred Chinese merchants in several eruptions of violence over the next few hundred years. Meanwhile, the Spanish also sought to Christianize the Philippines. Spanish rulers and missionaries pressured prominent Filipinos to convert to Christianity in hopes of persuading others to follow their example. They opened schools to teach the fundamentals of Christian doctrine, along with basic literacy, in densely populated regions throughout the islands. Although Spanish missionaries initially faced resistance, over the long term Filipinos turned increasingly to Christianity, and by the nineteenth century the Philippines had become one of the most fervent Roman Catholic lands in the world.

Conquest of Java   Dutch mariners who imposed their rule on the islands of Indonesia did not worry about seeking converts to Christianity but concentrated instead on the trade in spices, particularly cloves, nutmeg, and mace. The architect of Dutch policy was Jan Pieterszoon Coen, who in 1619 founded Batavia on the island of Java to serve as an entrepôt for the VOC. Coen's plan was to establish a VOC monopoly over spice production and trade, thus enabling Dutch merchants to reap enormous profits in European markets. Coen brought his naval power to bear on the small Indonesian islands and forced them to deliver spices only to VOC merchants. By the late seventeenth century, the VOC controlled all the ports of Java as well as most of the important spice-bearing islands throughout the Indonesian archipelago.

Dutch numbers were too few for them to rule directly over their whole southeast Asian empire. They made alliances with local authorities to maintain order in most regions, reserving for direct Dutch rule only Batavia and the most important spice-bearing islands. The Dutch did not embark on campaigns of conquest for purposes of adding to their holdings, but they uprooted spice-bearing plants on islands they did not control and mercilessly attacked peoples who sold their spices to merchants not associated with the VOC. Monopoly profits from the spice trade not only enriched the VOC but also made the Netherlands the most prosperous land in Europe throughout most of the seventeenth century.

Foundations of the Russian Empire in Asia

While western European peoples were building maritime empires, Russians were laying the foundations for a vast land empire that embraced most of northern Eurasia. This round of expansion began in the mid–sixteenth century, as Russian forces took over several Mongol khanates in central Asia. Those acquisitions resulted in Russian control over the Volga River and offered opportunities for trade with the Ottoman empire, Iran, and even India through the Caspian Sea. In the eighteenth century, Russian forces extended their presence in the Caspian Sea region by absorbing much of the Caucasus, a vibrant multiethnic region embracing the modern-day states of Georgia, Armenia, and Azerbaijan.

Far more extensive were Russian acquisitions in northeastern Eurasia. The frozen tundras and dense forests of Siberia posed formidable challenges, *Siberia* but explorers and merchants made their way into the region in a quest for fur. In the late sixteenth century, Russian explorers pushed into the interior regions of Siberia by way of the region's great rivers. By 1639 they had made their way across the Eurasian landmass and reached the Pacific Ocean.

Siberia was home to about twenty-six major ethnic groups that lived by hunting, trapping, fishing, or herding reindeer. These indigenous peoples varied widely in language and *Native Peoples of Siberia* religion, and they responded in different ways to the arrival of Russian adventurers who sought to exact tribute from them by coercing them to supply animal pelts on a regular basis. Some groups readily accepted iron tools, woven cloth, flour, tea, and liquor for the skins of fur-bearing animals such as otter, lynx, and especially sable. Others resented the ever-increasing demands for tribute and resisted Russian encroachment on their lands. For example, the Yakut people of the Lena and Aldan river

Harvesting mace on the island of Lontor in the Banda Islands.

valleys in central Siberia mounted a revolt against Russian oppression in 1642. The Russian response was brutal: over a period of forty years, Russian forces forced many Yakut out of their settlements and reduced their population by an estimated 70 percent. Quite apart from military violence, the peoples of Siberia reeled from epidemic diseases that reduced many populations by more than half.

Despite the region's harsh climate, Russian migrants—some of whom were social misfits or con-

The Russian Occupation of Siberia

victed criminals—gradually filtered into Siberia and thoroughly altered its demographic complexion. Small agricultural settlements grew up near many trading posts, particularly in the fertile Amur River valley. Over time, Siberian trading posts developed into Russian towns with Russian-speaking populations attending Russian Orthodox churches. By 1763 some 420,000 Russians lived in Siberia, nearly double the number of indigenous inhabitants. In the nineteenth century, large numbers of additional migrants moved east to mine Siberian gold, silver, copper, and iron, and the

Russian state was well on the way toward consolidating its control over the region.

European Commercial Rivalries

Exploration and imperial expansion led to conflicts not only between Europeans and Asians but also among Europeans themselves. Mariners competed vigorously for trade in Asia and the Americas, and their efforts to establish markets—and sometimes monopolies—led frequently to clashes with their counterparts from different lands.

Indeed, throughout the seventeenth and early eighteenth centuries, commercial and political rivalries led to running wars between ships flying different flags. Dutch vessels were most numerous in the Indian Ocean, and they enabled the VOC to dominate the spice trade. Dutch forces expelled most Portuguese merchants from southeast Asia and prevented English mariners from establishing secure footholds there. By the early eighteenth century, trade in Indian cotton and tea from

Competition and Conflict

Map 20.4 Russian expansion between 1462 and 1795. Observe how vast the empire became after it added the territory of Siberia. How did Russians exert their control over such a huge and unforgiving territory?

Ceylon had begun to overshadow the spice trade, and English and French merchants working from trading posts in India became the dominant carriers in the Indian Ocean. Fierce competition again generated violence: in 1746 French forces seized the English trading post at Madras, one of the three principal centers of British operations in India.

Commercial competition led to conflict also in the Caribbean and the Americas. English pirates and privateers preyed on Spanish shipping from Mexico, often seizing vessels carrying cargoes of silver. English and French forces constantly skirmished and fought over sugar islands in the Caribbean while also contesting territorial claims in North America. In addition, almost all conflicts between European states in the eighteenth century spilled over into the Caribbean and the Americas.

GLOBAL EXCHANGES

European explorers and those who followed them established links between all lands and peoples of the world. Interaction between peoples in turn resulted in an unprecedented volume of exchange across the boundary lines of societies and cultural regions. Some of that exchange involved biological species: plants, food crops, animals, human populations, and disease pathogens all spread to regions they had not previously visited. These biological exchanges had differing and dramatic effects on human populations, destroying some of them through epidemic diseases while enlarging others through increased food supplies and richer diets. Commercial exchange also flourished in the wake of the voyages of exploration as European merchants traveled to ports throughout the world in search of trade. Indeed, by the mid–eighteenth century they had established globe-girdling networks of trade and communication.

The Columbian Exchange

Processes of biological exchange were prominent features of world history well before modern times. The early expansion of Islam, for example, had facilitated *Biological Exchanges* the diffusion of plants and food crops throughout much of the eastern hemisphere during the period from about 700 to 1100 C.E., some of which helped spark demographic and economic growth in the lands where they took root. Yet the "Columbian exchange"—the global diffusion

of plants, food crops, animals, human populations, and disease pathogens that took place after voyages of exploration by Christopher Columbus and other European mariners—had consequences much more profound than earlier rounds of biological exchange. Unlike earlier processes, the Columbian exchange involved lands with radically different flora, fauna, and diseases. For thousands of years the various species of the eastern hemisphere, the western hemisphere, and Oceania had evolved along separate lines. By creating links between these biological zones, the European voyages of exploration set off a round of biological exchange that permanently altered the world's human geography and natural environment.

Beginning in the early sixteenth century, infectious and contagious diseases brought sharp demographic losses to indigenous peoples of the Americas and the Pacific islands. The worst scourge was smallpox, but measles, diphtheria, whooping cough, and influenza also took heavy tolls. Before the voyages of exploration, none of the peoples of the western hemisphere or Oceania possessed inherited or acquired immunities to those pathogens. In the eastern hemisphere, these diseases were endemic: they claimed a certain number of victims from the ranks of infants and small children, but survivors gained immunity to the diseases through exposure at an early age. In some areas of Europe, for example, smallpox was responsible for 10 to 15 percent of deaths, but most victims were age ten or younger. Although its individual effects were tragic, smallpox did not pose a threat to European society as a whole because it did not carry away economically and socially productive adults.

When infectious and contagious diseases traveled to previously unexposed populations, however, they touched off ferocious epidemics that sometimes destroyed entire societies. Beginning in 1519, epidemic smallpox ravaged the Aztec empire in combination with other diseases, and within a century the indigenous population of Mexico had declined by as much as 90 percent, from about 17 million to 1.3 million. By that time Spanish conquerors had imposed their rule on Mexico, and the political, social, and cultural traditions of the indigenous peoples had either disappeared or fallen under Spanish domination.

Epidemic Diseases and Population Decline

Imported diseases took their worst tolls in densely populated areas such as the Aztec and Inca empires, but they did not spare other regions. Smallpox and other diseases were so easily transmissible that they

Smallpox victims in the Aztec empire. The disease killed most of those it infected and left disfiguring scars on survivors.

raced to remote areas of North and South America and sparked epidemics well before the first European explorers arrived in those regions. By the 1530s smallpox may have spread as far from Mexico as the Great Lakes in the north and the pampas of Argentina in the south.

When introduced to the Pacific islands, infectious and contagious diseases struck vulnerable populations with the same horrifying effects as in the Americas. All told, disease epidemics sparked by the Columbian exchange probably caused the worst demographic calamity in all of world history. Between 1500 and 1800, upward of one hundred million people may have died of diseases imported into the Americas and Pacific islands.

Over a longer term, however, the Columbian exchange increased rather than diminished human population because of the global spread of *Food Crops and Animals* food crops and animals that it sponsored. For example, wheat, vines, horses, cattle, pigs, sheep, goats, and chickens went from Europe to the Americas, where they sharply increased supplies of food and animal energy. Food crops native to the Americas also played prominent roles in the Columbian exchange. American crops that took root in Africa, Asia, and Europe include maize, potatoes, beans, tomatoes, peppers, peanuts, manioc, papayas, guavas, avocados, tobacco, pineapples, and cacao, to name only a few. Residents of the eastern hemisphere only gradually developed a taste for American crops, but by the eighteenth century maize and potatoes had contributed to a sharply increased number of calories in Eurasian diets. In tropical regions, peanuts and manioc flourished in soils that otherwise would not produce large yields or support large populations.

The Columbian exchange of plants and animals fueled a surge in world population. In 1500, as Eurasian peoples were recovering from epidemic bubonic plague, world population stood at about 425 million. By 1600 it had increased more than 25 percent, to 545 million. By 1750 human population stood at 720 million, and by 1800 it had surged to 900 million, having grown by almost 50 percent during the previous century. Much of the rise was due to the increased nutritional value of diets enriched by the global exchange of food crops and animals. *Population Growth*

Alongside disease pathogens and plant and animal species, the Columbian exchange involved the spread of human populations through transoceanic migration, whether voluntary or forced. *Migration* During the period from 1500 to 1800, the largest contingent of migrants consisted of enslaved Africans transported involuntarily to the Americas. A smaller migration involved Europeans who traveled to the Americas and settled in lands depopulated by infectious and contagious diseases. During the nineteenth century, European peoples traveled in huge numbers to the western hemisphere and also to south Africa, Australia, and Pacific islands, and Asian peoples migrated to tropical and subtropical destinations throughout much of the world. In combination, those migrations have profoundly influenced modern world history.

The Origins of Global Trade

The trading-post empires established by Portuguese, Dutch, and English merchants linked Asian markets with European consumers and offered opportunities for European mariners to participate in the carrying trade within Asia. Indeed, by the late sixteenth century, European merchants carrying carpets, spices, silks, and silver were as prominent as Arabs in the trading world of the Indian Ocean basin.

Besides stimulating commerce in the eastern hemisphere, the voyages of European merchant mariners encouraged the emergence of a genuinely global trading system. As Europeans established colonies in the Caribbean and *Transoceanic Trade* the Americas, for example, trade networks extended to all corners of the Atlantic Ocean basin. European manufactured goods traveled west across the Atlantic in exchange for silver from Mexican and Peruvian mines and agricultural products such as sugar and tobacco, both of which were in high demand among European con-

Illustrations in an early-seventeenth-century book depict pineapple, potatoes, and cassava—all plants native to the Americas and unknown to Europeans before the sixteenth century.

sumers. Trade in human beings also figured in Atlantic commerce. European manufactured goods went south to west Africa, where merchants exchanged them for African slaves, who then went to the tropical and subtropical regions of the western hemisphere to work on plantations.

The experience of the Manila galleons illustrates the early workings of the global economy in the Pacific Ocean basin. For 250 years, from 1565 to 1815, Spanish galleons—sleek, fast, heavily armed ships capable of carrying large cargoes—regularly plied the waters of the Pacific Ocean between Manila in the Philippines and Acapulco on the west coast of Mexico. From Manila they took Asian luxury goods to Mexico and exchanged them for silver. Most of the precious metal made its way to China, where a thriving domestic economy demanded increasing quantities of silver. Meanwhile, some of the Asian luxury goods from Manila remained in Mexico or went to Peru, where they contributed to a comfortable way of life for Spanish ruling elites. Most, however, went overland across Mexico and then traveled by ship across the Atlantic to Spain and European markets.

The Manila Galleons

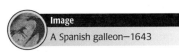

As silver lubricated growing volumes of global trade, pressures increased on several animal species that had the misfortune to become commodities on the world market. Fur-bearing animals came under particularly intense pressure, as hunters sought their pelts for sale to consumers in China, Europe, and North America. During the seventeenth century, an estimated two hundred to three hundred thousand sable pelts flowed annually from Siberia to the global market, and during the eighteenth century, more than sixteen million North American beaver pelts fed consumers' demands for fur hats and cloaks. Wanton hunting of fur-bearing animals soon drove many species into extinction or near extinction, permanently altering the environments they had formerly inhabited. Early modern hunters also harvested enormous numbers of deer, codfish, whales, walruses, and seals as merchants sought to supply animal products for global consumers.

Environmental Effects of Global Trade

In the seventeenth and eighteenth centuries, the volume of global trade expanded rapidly. During the seventeenth century, for example, Dutch merchants imported, among other commodities, wheat from south Africa, cowry shells from India, and sugar from Brazil. The wheat fed domestic consumers, who increasingly worked as merchants, bankers, or manufacturers rather than as cultivators. English, Dutch, and other merchants eagerly purchased the cowry shells—which served as currency in much of sub-Saharan Africa—and exchanged them for slaves destined for plantations in the western hemisphere. The sugar went on the market at Amsterdam and found its way to consumers throughout Europe. And that was just the beginning. By 1750 all parts of the world except Australia participated in global networks of commercial relations in which European merchant mariners played prominent roles.

SUMMARY

Global commercial and biological exchanges arose from the efforts of European mariners to explore the world's waters and establish sea lanes that would support long-distance trade. Their search for sea routes to Asia led them to the western hemisphere and the vast expanse of the Pacific Ocean. The geographic knowledge that they accumulated enabled them to link the world's regions into a finely articulated network of trade. But commercial exchange was not the only result of this global network. Food crops, animal stocks, disease pathogens, and human migrants also traveled the sea lanes and dramatically influenced societies throughout the world. Transplanted crops and animal species led to improved nutrition and increasing populations throughout the eastern hemisphere. Epidemics sparked by unfamiliar disease pathogens ravaged indigenous populations in the Americas and the Pacific islands. Mass migrations of human communities transformed the social and cultural landscape of the Americas and encouraged increased mingling of the world's peoples. The European voyages of exploration, transoceanic trade networks, and the Columbian exchange pushed the world's regions toward interdependence and global integration.

CHRONOLOGY

1394–1460	Life of Prince Henry the Navigator of Portugal
1488	Bartolomeu Dias's voyage around the Cape of Good Hope into the Indian Ocean
1492	Christopher Columbus's first voyage to the western hemisphere
1497–1499	Vasco da Gama's first voyage to India
1519–1522	Ferdinand Magellan's circumnavigation of the world
1565–1575	Spanish conquest of the Philippines
1768–1780	Captain James Cook's voyages in the Pacific Ocean

FOR FURTHER READING

K. N. Chaudhuri. *Trade and Civilisation in the Indian Ocean: An Economic History from the Rise of Islam to 1750.* Cambridge, 1985. A brilliant analysis that places the European presence in the Indian Ocean in its larger historical context.

Christopher Columbus. *The Diario of Christopher Columbus's First Voyage to America.* Trans. by Oliver Dunn and James E. Kelley Jr. Norman, Okla., 1989. A careful translation.

Alfred W. Crosby. *The Columbian Exchange: Biological and Cultural Consequences of 1492.* Westport, Conn., 1972. Focuses on early exchanges of plants, animals, and diseases between Europe and America.

Philip D. Curtin. *Cross-Cultural Trade in World History.* New York, 1984. Focuses on the roles of cross-cultural brokers in facilitating trade between different societies.

Andre Gunder Frank. *ReORIENT: Global Economy in the Asian Age.* Berkeley, 1998. Important and challenging analysis of global economic integration in the early modern world.

Antonio Pigafetta. *Magellan's Voyage: A Narrative Account of the First Circumnavigation.* 2 vols. Trans. by R. A. Skelton. New Haven, 1969. Valuable account by a crewman on Magellan's circumnavigation of the world.

Kenneth Pomeranz. *The Great Divergence: China, Europe, and the Making of the Modern World Economy.* Princeton, 2000. Path-breaking scholarly study that illuminates the economic history of the early modern world through comparison of economic development in Asian and European lands.

John F. Richards. *The Unending Frontier: An Environmental History of the Early Modern World.* Berkeley, 2003. Thoroughly explores the environmental effects of the global historical processes that shaped the early modern world.

Stuart B. Schwartz, ed. *Implicit Understandings: Observing, Reporting, and Reflecting on the Encounters between Europeans and Other Peoples in the Early Modern Era.* Cambridge, 1994. Fascinating collection of essays by specialists on cross-cultural perceptions in early modern times.

Yuri Slezkine. *Arctic Mirrors: Russia and the Small Peoples of the North.* Ithaca, N.Y., 1994. Thoughtful analysis of Russian relations with the hunting, fishing, and herding peoples of Siberia.

M · L

In silencio et spe erit   Fortitudo vestra

·5· 29

CHAPTER 21

The Transformation of Europe

In 1517 an obscure German monk posed a challenge to the Roman Catholic church. Martin Luther of Wittenberg denounced the church's sale of indulgences, a type of pardon that excused individuals from doing penance for their sins. Indulgences had been available since the eleventh century, but to raise funds for the reconstruction of St. Peter's basilica in Rome, church authorities began to market indulgences aggressively in the early sixteenth century. From their point of view, indulgences were splendid devices: they encouraged individuals to reflect piously on their behavior while also bringing large sums of money into the church's treasury.

To Martin Luther, however, indulgences were signs of greed, hypocrisy, and moral rot in the Roman Catholic church. Luther believed that no human being had the power to absolve individuals of their sins and grant them admission to heaven, so for him the sale of indulgences constituted a vast fraud. In October 1517, following academic custom, he offered to debate publicly with anyone who wished to dispute his views, and he denounced the sale of indulgences in a document called the *Ninety-five Theses*.

Luther did not nail his work to the church door in Wittenberg, although a popular legend credits him with that gesture, but news of the *Ninety-five Theses* spread instantly: within a few weeks, printed copies were available throughout Europe. Luther's challenge galvanized both strong support and severe criticism. Religious and political authorities seeking to maintain the established order were especially critical. Church officials judged Luther's views erroneous,

OPPOSITE PAGE: *Martin Luther at age forty-two, depicted as a conscientious and determined man by the German painter Lucas Cranach in 1525.*

and in 1520 Pope Leo X excommunicated him. In 1521 the Holy Roman emperor Charles V, a devout Roman Catholic, summoned Luther and demanded that he recant his views. Luther's response: "I cannot and will not recant anything, for it is neither safe nor right to act against one's conscience. Here I stand. I can do no other. God help me. Amen."

Martin Luther's challenge held enormous religious and political implications. Though expelled from the church, Luther still considered himself Christian, and he held religious services for a community of devoted followers. By the 1520s, religious dissent had spread through much of Germany and Switzerland. During the 1530s dissidents known as Protestants—because of their protest against the established order—organized movements also in France, England, the Low Countries, Italy, and Spain. By mid-century Luther's act of individual rebellion had mushroomed into the Protestant Reformation, which shattered the religious unity of western Christendom.

For all its unsettling effects, the Protestant Reformation was only one of several powerful movements that transformed European society during the early modern era. Another was the consolidation of strong centralized states, which took shape partly because of the Reformation. Between the sixteenth and eighteenth centuries, monarchs in western Europe took advantage of religious quarrels to tighten control over their societies. By the mid–eighteenth century, some rulers had concentrated so much power in their own hands that historians refer to them as absolute monarchs.

Alongside religious conflict and the building of powerful states, capitalism and early modern science profoundly influenced western European society in early modern times. Early capitalism encouraged European merchants and manufacturers to reorganize their businesses in search of maximum efficiency. Early modern science challenged traditional ways of understanding the world and the universe and prompted European intellectuals to seek an entirely rational understanding of human society as well as the natural world.

Thus between 1500 and 1800, western Europe underwent a thorough transformation. Although the changes were unsettling and often disruptive, they also strengthened European society. Indeed, by 1800 several European states had become especially powerful, wealthy, and dynamic. They stood poised to play major roles in world affairs during the nineteenth and twentieth centuries.

THE FRAGMENTATION OF WESTERN CHRISTENDOM

Although the peoples of western Europe spoke different languages and observed different customs, the church of Rome provided them with a common religious and cultural heritage. During the sixteenth and seventeenth centuries, however, revolts against the Roman Catholic church shattered the religious unity of western Europe. Followers of Martin Luther and other Protestant reformers established a series of churches independent of Rome, and Roman Catholic leaders strengthened their own church against the challengers. Throughout early modern times, religious controversies fueled social tensions.

The Protestant Reformation

Martin Luther (1483–1546) quickly attracted enthusiastic support from others who resented the policies of the Roman church. Luther was a talented writer, and he published scores of works condemning the Roman church. His cause benefited enormously from the printing press, which had first appeared in Europe in the mid–fifteenth century. A sizable literate public inhabited European cities and towns, and readers eagerly consumed printed works on religious as well as secular themes. Printed editions of Luther's writings appeared throughout Europe and sparked spirited debates on theological issues. His supporters and his critics took their own works to the printers, and religious controversies kept the presses busy churning out pamphlets and treatises for a century and more.

Martin Luther

Image
Martin Luther posting *Ninety-five Theses*

Luther attacked the Roman church for a wide range of abuses and called for thorough reform of Christendom. He advocated the closure of monasteries, translation of the Bible from Latin into vernacular languages, and an end to priestly authority, including the authority of the pope himself. Most important, Luther believed that salvation could never be earned through good works or through the prayers of others. Instead, he argued, humans could be saved only through faith in the promises of God as revealed in the Bible. This idea of "justification by faith alone" became the core of Protestant belief. When opponents

vernacular (ver-NA-kyoo-lar)

pointed out that Luther's reform program ran counter to church policy, he rejected the authority of the church hierarchy and proclaimed that the Bible was the only source of Christian religious authority.

Luther's works drew an enthusiastic popular response, and in Germany they fueled a movement to reform the church along the lines of Luther's teachings. Lay Christians flocked to hear Luther preach in Wittenberg, and several princes of the Holy Roman Empire warmed to Luther's views—partly because of personal conviction but partly also because religious controversy offered opportunities for them to build their own power bases. During the 1520s and 1530s, many of the most important German cities—Strasbourg, Nuremberg, and Augsburg, among others—passed laws requiring all religious services to follow Protestant doctrine and procedures. By the mid-sixteenth century about half the German population had adopted Lutheran Christianity, and reformers had launched Protestant movements and established alternative churches in other lands as well. By the late 1520s the prosperous cities of Switzerland—Zurich, Basel, and Geneva—had fledgling Protestant churches. The heavily urbanized Low Countries also responded enthusiastically to Protestant appeals. Protestants appeared even in Italy and Spain, although authorities in those lands handily suppressed their challenge to the Roman church.

Reform outside Germany

Meanwhile, an even more influential reformation was taking shape in France and French-speaking Switzerland. The initiator was a French lawyer, John Calvin (1509–1564), who in the 1530s converted to Protestant Christianity. Because the French monarchy sought to suppress Protestants, Calvin moved to French-speaking Geneva in Switzerland, where he organized a tight-knit Protestant community. Calvin also composed an influential treatise, *Institutes of the Christian Religion* (first published in 1536), that presented Protestant teachings as a coherent and organized package. Although Calvin believed in the basic elements of Luther's Protestant teachings, his ideas differed from those of Luther in important ways. Most fundamentally, Calvin emphasized the awesome power of God more than Luther did. Indeed, he believed not only that humans could never earn salvation but also that God had in fact already determined which individuals would be saved from damnation before they were even born. These individuals, known as "the elect," were predestined to salvation regardless of their deeds on earth. This doc-

John Calvin

trine of "predestination," as it became known, grew increasingly important to the Calvinist church in the generations after Calvin's death.

Calvin's Geneva was based on a strict code of morality and discipline. Calvinists were supposed to dress simply, to study the Bible regularly, and to refrain from activities such as playing cards and dancing. It was, in effect, a model Protestant community. Geneva also became an important missionary center from which Calvinist doctrine spread to other parts of Europe. Calvinist missionaries were most active in France, where they attracted strong interest in the cities, but they ventured also to Germany, the Low Countries, England, Hungary, and—most successfully—the Netherlands and Scotland.

In England a reformation took place for political as well as religious reasons. Lutherans and other Protestants worked to build a following in England from the 1520s on, but they faced stout government resistance until King Henry VIII (reigned 1509–1547) came into conflict with the pope. Henry wanted to divorce his wife, who had not borne a male heir, but the pope refused to allow him to do so. Henry's response was to sever relations with the Roman church and make himself supreme head of the Anglican church—an English pope, as it were. While Henry reigned, the theology of the English church changed little, but his successors replaced Roman Catholic with Protestant doctrines and rituals. By 1560 England had permanently left the Roman Catholic community. Indeed, by the late sixteenth century, Lutherans, Calvinists, and Anglicans in Europe had built communities large enough that a return to religious unity in western Christendom was inconceivable.

The English Reformation

The Catholic Reformation

In response to the Protestant Reformation, Roman Catholic authorities undertook a wide-ranging reform effort of their own. Their purpose was to clarify differences between Roman and Protestant churches, to persuade Protestants to return to the Roman church, and to deepen the sense of spirituality and religious commitment in their own community. Taken together, their efforts constituted the Catholic Reformation.

Two institutions were especially important for defining the Catholic Reformation and advancing its goals—the Council of Trent and the Society of Jesus. The Council of Trent was an assembly of high church officials who met intermittently between 1545 and

Under inspiration of the Catholic Reformation, many devout individuals sought mystic union with God. One of the most famous of the mystics was St. Teresa of Avila (in Spain), who founded a strict order of nuns and often experienced religious visions. A famous sculpture by the Italian artist Gianlorenzo Bernini depicts St. Teresa in an ecstatic trance accompanied by an angel.

that ended his military career. While recuperating he read spiritual works and popular accounts of saints' lives, and he resolved to put his energy into religious work. In 1540, together with a small band of disciples, he founded the Society of Jesus.

Ignatius required that members of the society, known as Jesuits, complete a rigorous and advanced education in theology, philosophy, languages, history, literature, and science. As a result of that preparation, the Jesuits made extraordinarily effective missionaries. They also acquired a reputation for discipline and determination, and often served as counselors to kings and other rulers. They also were the most prominent of the early Christian missionaries outside Europe: in the wake of the European reconnaissance of the world's oceans, Jesuits attracted converts in India, China, Japan, the Philippines, and the Americas, thus making Christianity a genuinely global religion. *The Society of Jesus*

Witch-Hunts and Religious Wars

Europeans took religion seriously in the sixteenth century, and religious divisions helped to fuel social and political conflict. Apart from wars, the most destructive violence that afflicted early modern Europe was the hunt for witches, which was especially prominent in regions, such as the Rhineland, where tensions between Protestants and Roman Catholics ran high.

Like many other peoples, Europeans had long believed that certain individuals possessed unusual or supernatural powers. During the late fifteenth century, theologians developed a theory that some of these people were witches who derived their powers—such as the ability to fly through the night on brooms or pitchforks—from the devil. Theorists believed that witches regularly flew off to distant places to attend the "witches' sabbath," a gathering that featured devil worship and the concoction of secret potions and culminated in sexual relations with the devil himself. Indeed, witchcraft became a convenient explanation for any unpleasant turn of events—failure of a crop, an unexpected death, or inability to conceive a child.

In the sixteenth and seventeenth centuries, fears that individuals were making alliances with the devil sparked a widespread hunt for witches. About 110,000 individuals underwent trial as suspected witches, and about 60,000 of them died either by hanging or by burning at the stake. Most of the victims—perhaps 95 percent—were poor, *Witch-Hunting*

1563 to address matters of doctrine and reform. During the meetings, the council defined the elements of Roman Catholic theology in detail. The council also took steps to reform the church by demanding that church authorities observe strict standards of morality and requiring them to establish schools and seminaries to prepare priests properly for their roles. *The Council of Trent*

While the Council of Trent dealt with doctrine and reform, the Society of Jesus sought to extend the boundaries of the reformed Roman church. The society's founder was St. Ignatius Loyola (1491–1556), a Basque nobleman and soldier who in 1521 suffered a leg wound *St. Ignatius of Loyola* old, single, or widowed women who lived on the margins of their societies and thus were easy targets for accusers. Although the fear of witches had largely diminished by 1700, the intermittent pursuit of witches for the better part of two centuries revealed clearly the stresses and strains—both secular and religious—that afflicted European society during early modern times.

Religious Wars

Religious tensions also led to outright war between Protestant and Roman Catholic communities. Religious wars wracked France for thirty-six years (1562–1598), for example, and they also complicated relations between Protestant and Roman Catholic states. In 1588 King Philip II of Spain (reigned 1556–1598) attempted to force England to return to the Roman Catholic church by sending the Spanish Armada—a huge flotilla consisting of 130 ships and 30,000 men—to dethrone the Protestant Queen Elizabeth. The effort collapsed, however, when English forces disrupted the Spanish fleet by sending blazing, unmanned ships into its midst. Then a ferocious gale scattered Spanish vessels throughout the North Sea.

Religious convictions also aggravated relations between the Netherlands and Spain by fueling the revolt of the Dutch provinces from their overlord, the king of Spain. In 1567 resistance escalated into a full-scale rebellion. By 1610 the seven northern provinces (the modern Netherlands) had won their independence and formed a republic known as the United Provinces, leaving ten southern provinces (modern Belgium) under Spanish and later Austrian rule until the late eighteenth century.

The Thirty Years' War

The religious wars culminated in a great continental conflict known as the Thirty Years' War (1618–1648). The war opened after the Holy Roman emperor attempted to force his Bohemian subjects to return to the Roman Catholic church, and the main battleground was the emperor's territory in Germany. By the time the war ended, however, Spanish, French, Dutch, German, Swedish, Danish, Polish, Bohemian, and Russian forces had taken part in the conflict. The war itself was the most destructive European conflict before the twentieth century. Quite apart from violence and brutalities committed by undisciplined soldiers, the war damaged economies and societies throughout Europe and led to the deaths of about one-third of the German population. And though religious differences were not the only issues of the war, they complicated other issues and made them more difficult to resolve.

THE CONSOLIDATION OF SOVEREIGN STATES

Although fundamentally a religious movement, the Reformation had strong political implications, and centralizing monarchs readily made use of religious issues in their efforts to strengthen their states and enhance their authority. Indeed, after the devastation of the Thirty Years' War, rulers of these states devised a diplomatic system that sought to maintain order among the many independent and competitive European states.

The Attempted Revival of Empire

After the dissolution of the Carolingian empire in the ninth century C.E., there was no effective imperial government in western Europe. The so-called Holy Roman Empire emerged in the tenth century, but its authority extended only to Germany and northern Italy, and even there its power was contested. During the early sixteenth century, it seemed that Emperor Charles V (reigned 1519–1556) might establish the Holy Roman Empire as the preeminent political authority in Europe, but by midcentury it was clear that there would be no revival of empire. Thus, unlike China, India, and the Ottoman empire, early modern Europe developed as a region of independent states.

Charles V

After 1438 the Habsburg family, with extensive dynastic holdings in Austria, dominated the Holy Roman Empire. Through marriage alliances, the Habsburgs accumulated rights and titles to lands throughout Europe and beyond. Indeed, when Charles V became emperor in 1519, his empire stretched from Vienna in Austria to Cuzco in Peru. In spite of his far-flung holdings, Charles did not extend his authority throughout Europe. Part of the reason was that throughout his reign Charles had to devote much of his attention and energy to the Lutheran movement and to putting down imperial princes who took advantage of religious controversy to assert their independence. Foreign difficulties also played a role, because Charles's neighbors to the west and east—in France and the Ottoman empire, respectively—actively opposed the creation of a powerful Holy Roman Empire.

To ensure that Charles's territories remained in disarray, for example, the Roman Catholic French kings aided German Lutherans in their rebellion against the Holy Roman Empire. The French kings even allied with the Muslim Ottoman Turks against the emperor.

Map 21.1 European states and territories in the sixteenth century. Note the extent of Habsburg territories, and the wide boundaries of the Holy Roman Empire. With such powerful territories, what prevented the Habsburgs from imposing imperial rule on most of Europe?

For their part, the Ottoman sultans did not want a powerful Christian empire to threaten their holdings in eastern Europe and the Mediterranean basin. With the encouragement of the French king, Turkish forces conquered Hungary in 1526, and three years later they even laid siege briefly to Vienna. Moreover, during the early sixteenth century Ottoman forces im-

posed their rule beyond Egypt and embraced almost all of north Africa.

Thus domestic and foreign problems prevented Charles V from establishing his vast empire as the supreme political authority in Europe. In 1556, disappointed especially in his inability to suppress the Lutherans in his territories, the emperor abdicated his throne and retired to a monastery in Spain. His empire did not survive. Charles bestowed his holdings in Spain, Italy, the Low Countries, and the Americas on his son, King Philip II of Spain, and his brother Ferdinand inherited the Habsburg family lands in Austria and the imperial throne.

The New Monarchs

In the absence of effective imperial power, public affairs fell to the various regional states that had emerged during the middle ages. In this period, however, the most powerful European states were the kingdoms of England, France, and Spain. During the late fifteenth and sixteenth centuries, rulers of these lands, known as the "new monarchs," marshaled their resources, curbed the nobility, and built strong centralized regimes.

The new monarchs included Henry VIII of England, Louis XI and Francis I of France, and Fernando and Isabel of Spain. All the new monarchs sought to enhance their treasuries by developing new sources of finance. The French kings levied direct taxes on sales, households, and the salt trade. A new sales tax dramatically boosted Spanish royal income in the sixteenth century, and English kings increased *Finance* revenues by raising fines and fees for royal services. Moreover, after Henry VIII severed ties between the English and Roman churches, he confiscated all church properties in England, which dramatically increased the size and wealth of the state.

With their increased income the new monarchs enlarged their administrative staffs, which enabled them to collect taxes and implement royal policies more reliably than before. In-*State Power* creased wealth also allowed the new monarchs to raise powerful armies when the need arose. That, in turn, resulted in increased control over the nobility, who could no longer compete with the power and wealth of the state.

The debates and disputes launched by the Protestant Reformation also helped monarchs increase their power. Whereas monarchs in Protestant lands—including England, much of Germany, Denmark, and

When the Spanish Inquisition detected traces of Protestant heresy, the punishment could be swift and brutal. In this engraving of about 1560, a large crowd observes the execution of heretics (top right) by burning at the stake.

Sweden—expropriated church wealth to expand their powers, others relied on religious justifications to advance state ends. The Spanish Inquisition was the most distinctive institution of that kind. Fernando and Isabel founded the Spanish Inquisition in 1478, and they obtained papal license to operate the institution as a royal agency. Its original task was to ferret out those who secretly practiced Judaism or Islam, but Charles V charged it with responsibility also for detecting Protestant heresy in Spain.

The Spanish Inquisition

Inquisitors had broad powers to investigate suspected cases of heresy. Popular legends have created an erroneous impression of the Spanish Inquisition as an institution running amok, framing innocent victims and routinely subjecting them to torture. In fact, inquisitors usually observed rules of evidence, and they released many suspects after investigation. Yet when they detected heresy, inquisitors could be ruthless. They sentenced hundreds of victims to hang from the gallows or burn at the stake and imprisoned many others for extended periods of time. Fear of the inquisition deterred nobles from adopting Protestant views out of political ambition, and inquisitors also used their influence to silence those who threatened the Spanish monarchy. From 1559 to 1576, for example, inquisitors imprisoned the archbishop of Toledo—the highest Roman Catholic church official in all of Spain—because of his political independence.

Constitutional States

During the seventeenth and eighteenth centuries, as they sought to restore order after the Thirty Years' War, European states developed along two lines. Rulers in England and the Netherlands shared authority with representative institutions and created constitutional states, whereas monarchs in France, Spain, Austria, Prussia, and Russia concentrated power in their own hands and created a form of state known as absolute monarchy.

During the seventeenth century the island kingdom of England and the maritime Dutch republic evolved governments that recognized rights pertaining to individuals and representative institutions. Their constitutional states took different forms: in England a constitutional monarchy emerged, whereas the Netherlands produced a republic based on representative government. In neither land did constitutional government come easily into being: in England it followed a civil war (1642–1649), and in the Nether-

Constitutional States

In this contemporary painting, the executioner holds up the just-severed head of King Charles I of England. The prospect of a royal execution overcomes one woman, who faints (at bottom).

lands it emerged after a long struggle for independence in the late sixteenth century. In both lands, however, constitutional government strengthened the state and provided a political framework that enabled merchants to flourish as never before in European experience.

Constitutional government came to England after political and religious disputes led to the English civil war. Politically, disputes arose *The English Civil War* between king and the parliament over the king's ability to institute new taxes without parliamentary approval, while religious tensions between the Anglican king and a vocal group of zealous, reform-minded Calvinists in Parliament created a deep rift between the two branches of government. By 1641 King Charles I and Parliament were at loggerheads. Both sides raised armies. In the conflicts

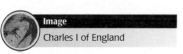
Charles I of England

that followed, Parliamentary forces captured Charles and in 1649 executed him for tyranny. Yet English problems of government continued through a dictatorial Puritan regime as well as the restoration of the monarchy in 1660, until in 1688 Parliament deposed King James II and invited his daughter Mary and her Dutch husband, William of Orange, to assume the throne. The resulting arrangement provided that kings would rule in cooperation with Parliament, thus guaranteeing that nobles, merchants, and other constituencies would enjoy representation in government affairs.

As in England, a combination of political and religious tensions led to conflict from which constitutional government emerged in the Netherlands. In the mid–sixteenth century, *The Dutch Republic* authority over the Low Countries, including modern-day Belgium as well as the Netherlands, rested with King Philip II of Spain. In 1566 Philip, a devout Roman Catholic, moved to suppress an increasingly popular Calvinist movement in the Netherlands—a measure that provoked large-scale rebellion against Spanish rule. In 1581 a group of Dutch provinces proclaimed themselves the independent United Provinces. Representative assemblies organized local affairs in each of the provinces, and on that foundation political leaders built a Dutch republic. Although Spain did not officially recognize the independence of the United Provinces until 1648, the Dutch republic was effectively organizing affairs in the northern Low Countries by the early seventeenth century.

In both England and the Dutch republic, merchants were especially prominent in political affairs, and state policy in both lands favored maritime trade and the building of commercial empires overseas. The constitutional states allowed entrepreneurs to pursue their economic interests with minimal interference from public authorities, and during the late seventeenth and eighteenth centuries both states experienced extraordinary prosperity as a result of those policies. Indeed, in many ways the English and Dutch states represented an alliance between merchants and rulers that worked to the benefit of both. Merchants supported the state with the wealth that they generated through trade—especially overseas trade—and rulers followed policies that looked after the interests of their merchants.

Absolute Monarchies

Whereas constitutional states devised ways to share power and authority, absolute monarchies stood on a theoretical foundation known as the divine right of kings. This theory held that kings derived their authority from God and served as "God's lieutenants upon earth." There was no role in divine-right theory for common subjects or even nobles in public affairs: the king made law and determined policy. In fact, absolute monarchs always relied on support from nobles and other social groups, but the claims of divine-right theory clearly reflected efforts at royal centralization.

The most conspicuous absolutist state was the French monarchy. The architect of French absolutism was a prominent church official, Cardinal Richelieu, who served as chief minister to King Louis XIII from 1624 to 1642. Richelieu worked systematically to undermine the power of the nobility and enhance the authority of the king. He destroyed nobles' castles and ruthlessly crushed aristocratic conspiracies. As a counterweight to the nobility, Richelieu built a large bureaucracy staffed by commoners loyal to the king. He also appointed officials to supervise the implementation of royal policy in the provinces.

The ruler who best epitomized royal absolutism was King Louis XIV (reigned 1643–1715). In fact, Louis XIV once reportedly declared that he was himself the state: "*l'état c'est moi.*" Known as *le roi soleil*—"the sun king"—Louis surrounded *The Sun King* himself with splendor befitting one who ruled by divine right. During the 1670s he built a magnificent residence at Versailles, and in the 1680s he moved his court there. Louis's palace at Versailles was the largest building in Europe, with 230 acres of formal gardens and 1,400 fountains. All prominent nobles established residences at Versailles for their families

King Louis XIV and his entourage approach the main gate of Versailles (bottom right). Though only partially constructed at the time of this painting (1668), Versailles was already a spacious and luxurious retreat for Louis and his court.

and entourages. Louis strongly encouraged them to live at court, where he and his staff could keep an eye on them, and ambitious nobles gravitated there anyway in hopes of winning influence with the king. While nobles living at Versailles mastered the intricacies of court ritual and attended banquets, concerts, operas, balls, and theatrical performances, Louis and his ministers ran the state, maintained a huge army, waged war, and promoted economic development. In effect, Louis provided the nobility with luxurious accommodations and endless entertainment in exchange for absolute rule.

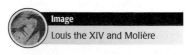

Image
Louis the XIV and Molière

Louis XIV was not the only absolute monarch of early modern Europe: Spanish, Austrian, and Prussian rulers embraced similar policies. Yet the potential of absolutism to increase state power was particularly conspicuous in the case of Russia, where tsars of the Romanov dynasty (1613–1917) tightly centralized government functions. Most important of the Romanov tsars was Peter I (reigned 1682–1725), widely known as Peter the Great, who inaugurated a thoroughgoing process of state transformation. Peter had a burning desire to transform Russia, a huge but underpopulated land, into a great military power like those that had recently emerged in western Europe. In 1697–1698 he led a large party of Russian observers on a tour of Germany, the Netherlands, and England to learn about western European administrative methods and military technology. His traveling companions often behaved crudely by western European standards: they consumed beer, wine, and brandy in quantities that astonished their hosts, and King William III sent Peter a bill for damages done by his entourage at the country house where they lodged in England.

Absolutism in Russia under Peter I

Versailles (vehr-SEYE)

Upon return to Moscow, Peter set Russia spinning. He reformed the army by providing his forces with extensive training and equipping them with modern weapons. He ordered aristocrats to study mathematics and geometry so that they could calculate how to aim cannons accurately, and he began the construction of a navy. He also overhauled the government bureaucracy to facilitate tax collection and improve administrative efficiency. He even commanded his aristocratic subjects to wear western European fashions and ordered men to shave their traditional beards. These measures provoked spirited protest among those who resented the influence of western European ways. Yet Peter was so insistent on the observance of his policies that he reportedly went into the streets and personally hacked the beards off recalcitrants' faces. Perhaps the best symbol of his policies was St. Petersburg, a newly built seaport that Peter opened in 1703 to serve as a magnificent capital city and a haven for Russia's fledgling navy.

The most able of Peter's successors was Catherine II (reigned 1762–1796), also known as Catherine the Great. Like Peter, Catherine sought to *Catherine II and the Limits of Reform* make Russia a great power. She worked to improve governmental efficiency, and she promoted economic development in Russia's towns. For a while, she even worked to improve the conditions of Russia's oppressed peasantry by restricting the punishments—such as torture, beating, and mutilation—that noble landowners could inflict on the serfs who worked their lands.

However, Catherine's interest in social reform cooled rapidly when it seemed to inspire challenges to her rule. She faced a particularly unsettling trial in 1773 and 1774, when a disgruntled former soldier named Yemelian Pugachev mounted a rebellion in the steppe lands north of the Caspian Sea. Pugachev raised a motley army of adventurers, exiles, peasants, and serfs who killed thousands of noble landowners and government officials before imperial forces crushed the uprising. Government authorities took the captured Pugachev to Moscow in chains, beheaded him, quartered his body, and displayed his parts throughout the city as a warning against rebellion. Thereafter, Catherine's first concern was the preservation of autocratic rule rather than the transformation of Russia according to western European models.

Thus, in Russia as in other European lands, absolutist policies resulted in tight centralization and considerable strengthening of the state. The enhanced power that flowed from absolutism became dramatically clear in the period 1772 to 1797, when Austria, Prussia, and Catherine II's Russia picked the weak kingdom of Poland apart. In a series of three "partitions," the predatory absolutist states seized Polish territory and absorbed it into their own realms, ultimately wiping Poland entirely off the map. The lesson of the partitions was clear: any European state that hoped to survive needed to construct an effective government that could respond promptly to challenges and opportunities.

The European States System

Whether they relied on absolutist or constitutional principles, European governments of early modern times built states much more powerful than those of their medieval predecessors. This round of state development led to difficulties within Europe, since conflicting interests fueled interstate competition and war. In the absence of an imperial authority capable of imposing and maintaining order in Europe, sovereign states had to find ways to resolve conflicts by themselves.

The Thirty Years' War demonstrated the chaos and devastation that conflict could bring. In an effort to avoid tearing their society apart, European states ended the Thirty Years' War with the *The Peace of Westphalia* Peace of Westphalia (1648), which laid the foundations for a system of independent, competing states. By the treaty's terms, the European states regarded one another as sovereign and equal. They also mutually recognized their rights to organize their own domestic and religious affairs

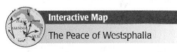

Interactive Map
The Peace of Westphalia

and agreed that political and diplomatic affairs were to be conducted by states acting in their own interests. European religious unity had disappeared, and the era of the sovereign state had arrived.

The Peace of Westphalia did not bring an end to war. Indeed, war was almost constant in early modern Europe. Most conflicts were minor affairs, but some grew to sizable proportions. Most notable among them were the wars of Louis XIV and the Seven Years' War. Between 1668 and 1713, the sun king sought to expand his borders east into Germany and to absorb Spain and the Spanish Netherlands into his kingdom. That prospect prompted England, the United Provinces, and Austria to mount a coalition against Louis. Later the Seven Years' War (1756–1763) pitted France, Austria, and Russia against Britain and Prussia, and it merged with conflicts between France and Britain in India and North America to become a global war for imperial supremacy.

Map 21.2 European states and territories after the Peace of Westphalia in 1648. Compare this map with Map 21.1. How have the boundaries of the Holy Roman Empire changed, and why?

The Balance of Power

These shifting alliances illustrate the principal foundation of European diplomacy in early modern times—the balance of power. No ruler wanted to see another state dominate all the others. Thus, when any particular state began to wax strong, others formed coalitions against it. By playing balance-of-power politics, states-men prevented the building of empires and ensured that Europe would be a land of independent, sovereign, competing states.

Frequent wars and balance-of-power diplomacy drained the resources of individual states but strength-ened European society as a whole. European states competed vigorously and sought to develop the most expert military leadership and the most effective weapons for their arsenals. States organized military *Military Development* academies where officers received advanced education in strategy and tactics. Demand for powerful weapons stimulated the development of a sophisticated armaments industry. Gun foundries manufactured cannons of increasing size, range, power, and accuracy as well as small arms that allowed infantry to unleash withering volleys against their enemies.

In China, India, and Islamic lands, imperial states had little incentive to encourage similar technological innovation in the armaments industry. These states possessed the forces and weapons they needed to maintain order within their boundaries, and they rarely encountered foreign threats backed up with superior armaments. In Europe, however, failure to keep up with the latest improvements in arms technology could lead to defeat on the battlefield and decline in state power. Thus Europeans continuously sought to improve their military arsenals, and as a result, by the eighteenth century European armaments outperformed all others.

EARLY CAPITALIST SOCIETY

While the Protestant Reformation and the emergence of sovereign states brought religious and political change, a rapidly expanding population and economy encouraged the development of capitalism, which in turn led to a restructuring of European economy and society. Technologies of communication and transportation enabled businessmen to profit from distant markets, and merchants and manufacturers increasingly organized their affairs with the market rather than local communities in mind. Although capitalism generated considerable wealth, its effects were uneven and sometimes unsettling. Even in western Europe, where development and prosperity were most noticeable, early capitalism sometimes required painful adjustments to new conditions.

Population Growth and Urbanization

The foundation of European economic expansion in early modern times was a rapidly growing population, which reflected improved nutrition and decreasing mortality. The Columbian exchange enriched European diets by introducing new food crops to European fields and tables. Most notable of the introductions was the potato, which provided a welcome and inexpensive source of carbohydrates for peasants and laborers all over Europe. Other American *American Food Crops* crops, such as tomatoes and peppers, added vitamins and tangy flavor to European diets.

Since better-nourished populations are less susceptible to illness, new food crops also improved the overall resistance of Europeans to old diseases such as smallpox, dysentery, influenza, and typhus. Bubonic plague, a devastating epidemic killer during the fourteenth and fifteenth centuries, also

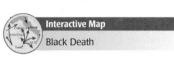
Interactive Map
Black Death

receded from European society. Although plague made periodic appearances throughout the early modern era, epidemics were rare and isolated events after the mid–seventeenth century.

Although European birthrates did not rise dramatically in early modern times, decreasing mortality resulted in rapid population growth. In 1500 the population of Europe, including Russia, was about 81 million. By *Population Growth and Urbanization* 1700 the population had risen to 120 million, and in the next century it reached 180 million. Such rapid population growth drove a process of equally rapid urbanization. In the mid–sixteenth century, for example, the population of Paris was about 130,000, and London had about 60,000 inhabitants. A century later the populations of both cities had risen to half a million. Other European cities also experienced rapid growth, including Madrid, Amsterdam, Berlin, Copenhagen, Dublin, Stockholm, and Vienna, to name only a few.

Early Capitalism and Protoindustrialization

Population growth and rapid urbanization helped spur a round of remarkable economic development. That economic growth coincided with the emergence of capitalism—an economic system in which private parties make their goods and services available on a free market and seek *The Nature of Capitalism* to take advantage of market conditions to profit from their activities. Private parties own the land, machinery, tools, equipment, buildings, workshops, and raw materials needed for production. Private parties also hire workers and decide for themselves what to produce: economic decisions are the prerogative of capitalist businessmen, not governments or social superiors. The center of a capitalist system is the market in which businessmen compete with one another, and the forces of supply and demand determine the prices received for goods and services. The goal is to realize handsome profits from these activities.

Supply and Demand

The desire to accumulate wealth and realize profits was by no means new. Indeed, for several thousand years before the early modern era, merchants in China, southeast Asia, India, southwest Asia, the Mediterranean basin, and sub-Saharan Africa had pursued commercial ventures in hopes of realizing profits. During early modern times, however, European merchants and entrepreneurs transformed their society in a way that none of their predecessors had done. The capitalist economic order developed as businessmen learned to take advantage of market conditions in distant places via efficient networks of transportation and communication. For example, Dutch merchants might purchase cheap grain from Poland, store it in Amsterdam until they learned about a famine in the Mediterranean, and then transport it and sell it in southern France or Spain at an enormous profit.

Private parties organized an array of institutions and services to support early capitalism. Banks, for example, appeared in all the major commercial cities of Europe: they held funds on account for safekeeping and granted loans to merchants or entrepreneurs launching new business ventures. Insurance companies mitigated financial losses from risky undertakings such as transoceanic voyages, and stock exchanges provided markets where investors could buy and sell shares in joint-stock companies and trade in other commodities as well.

Joint-Stock Companies

Joint-stock companies were especially important institutions in early capitalist society. Large trading companies such as the English East India Company and its Dutch counterpart, the Vereenigde Oost-Indische Compagnie (VOC), spread the risks attached to expensive business enterprises and also took advantage of extensive communications and transportation networks. The trading companies organized commercial ventures on a larger scale than ever before in world history. They were the principal foundations of the global economy that emerged in early modern times, and they were the direct ancestors of contemporary multinational corporations.

Capitalism did not develop in a political vacuum. On the contrary, it emerged with the active support of government authorities who saw a capitalist order as the one best suited to their individual and collective interests. Merchants were especially influential in the affairs of the English and Dutch states, so it is not surprising that these lands adopted policies that were most favorable to capitalist enterprises throughout the early modern era. The English and Dutch states recognized individuals' rights to possess private property and protected their financial interests. They also authorized joint-stock companies to explore and colonize distant lands in search of commercial opportunities. Indeed, imperial expansion and colonial rule were crucial for the development of capitalism, since they enabled European merchants to gain access to the natural resources and commodities that they distributed so effectively through their transportation networks.

Politics and Empire

Quite apart from its influence on trade and the distribution of goods, capitalism also encouraged European entrepreneurs to organize new ways to manufacture goods. For centuries, craft guilds had monopolized the production of goods such as textiles and metalwares in European towns and cities. Guilds fixed prices and wages, and they regulated standards of quality. They sought not to realize profits so much as to protect markets and preserve their members' places in society. As a result, they actively discouraged competition.

Capitalist entrepreneurs seeking profits found the guilds inflexible, so they sidestepped them and moved production into the countryside. There, they organized a "putting-out system" by which they delivered unfinished materials such as raw wool to rural households. Men and women in the countryside would spin and weave the wool into cloth and then cut and assemble the cloth into garments. The entrepreneur picked up the finished goods, paid the workers, and sold the items on the market for a handsome profit. The putting-out system represented an early effort to organize efficient industrial production and remained a prominent feature of European society until the nineteenth century. In fact, some historians refer to the seventeenth and eighteenth centuries as an age of "protoindustrialization."

The Putting-Out System

Social Change in Early Modern Europe

Capitalist economic development brought unsettling change to European lands. In western Europe, the putting-out system introduced considerable sums of

An anonymous engraving depicts activity in a Dutch shipyard, where workers build a massive, oceangoing sailing ship. In the seventeenth century, Dutch ships were inexpensive to operate, yet they accommodated abundant cargoes.

money into the countryside, which tended to undermine long-established patterns of rural life even as it brought material benefits such as improved food, clothing, and furnishings to rural households. Increased wealth meant that individuals suddenly acquired incomes that enabled them to become financially independent of their families and neighbors, and many feared that these individuals—especially young adults and women—might abandon their kin and way of life altogether as a result.

In eastern Europe, the putting-out system did not become a prominent feature of production, but early capitalism prompted deep social change there as well. Eastern Europe had very few cities in early modern times, so in agrarian states such as Poland, Bohemia, and Russia, most people had no alternative to working in the countryside. Landlords took advantage of this situation by forcing peasants to work under extremely harsh conditions.

Serfdom in Russia   Russia in particular was a vast but sparsely populated empire with little trade or manufacturing. Out of a concern to retain the allegiance of the powerful nobles who owned most of Russia's land, the Romanov tsars restricted the freedoms of most Russian peasants and tied them to the land as serfs. The institution of serfdom had emerged in the early middle ages as a labor system that required peasants to provide labor services for landowners and prevented them from marrying or moving away without their landlords' permission. Although serfdom came to an end in western Europe after the fifteenth century, in eastern Europe landowners and rulers tightened restrictions on peasants during the sixteenth century. In Russia, for example, landlords commonly sold serfs to one another as if they were private property. In effect, the Romanovs won the support of the Russian nobles by ensuring them that laborers would be available to work their estates, which otherwise would have been worthless. Under these conditions, landlords operated estates with inexpensive labor and derived enormous incomes from the sale of agricultural products on the market.

These arrangements played crucial roles in the emergence of capitalism. In the larger economy of early modern Europe, eastern European lands produced agricultural products and raw materials based on semifree labor, which were then exported to western Europe to sustain its large and growing free wage labor force. Already by the early sixteenth century, consumers in the Netherlands depended for their survival on grains imported from Poland and Russia through the Baltic Sea. Thus it was possible for capitalism to flourish in western Europe only because the peasants and semifree serfs of eastern Europe provided inexpensive foods and raw materials that fueled economic development. From its earliest days, capitalist economic organization had implications for peoples and lands far removed from the centers of capitalism itself.

Capitalism also posed moral challenges. Medieval theologians had regarded profit making as morally *Profits and Ethics* dangerous, since profiteers looked to their own advantage rather than the welfare of the larger community. But capitalism found advocates who sought to explain its principles and portray it as a socially beneficial form of economic organization. Most important of the early apostles of capitalism was the Scottish philosopher Adam Smith (1723–1790), who held that society would prosper when individuals pursued their own economic interests.

Nevertheless, prosperity was unattainable for all or even most early modern Europeans, which meant that the transition to capitalist economic practices was a long and painful process that generated deep social strains throughout Europe. Those strains often manifested themselves in violence: bandits plagued the countryside of early modern Europe, and muggers turned whole sections of large cities into danger zones. Some historians believe that witch-hunting activities reflected social tensions generated by early capitalism and that accusations of witchcraft represented hostility toward women who were becoming economically independent of their husbands and families.

In some ways capitalism favored the nuclear family as the principal unit of society. Although for centuries European couples had set up *The Nuclear Family* independent households, early capitalism offered further opportunities for independent families to increase their wealth by producing goods for sale on the market. As nuclear families became more important economically, they also became more socially and emotionally independent. Love between a man and a woman became a more important consideration in the making of marriages than the interests of the larger extended families, and affection between parents and their children became a more important ingredient of family life. Capitalism did not necessarily cause these changes in family life, but it may have encouraged developments that helped to define the nature and the role of the family in modern European society.

SCIENCE AND ENLIGHTENMENT

While experiencing religious, political, economic, and social change, western Europe also underwent intellectual and cultural transformation. Astronomers and physicists rejected classical Greek and Roman authorities, whose theories had dominated scientific thought during the middle ages, and based their understanding of the natural world on direct observation and mathematical reasoning. During the seventeenth and eighteenth centuries, they elaborated a new vision of the earth and the larger universe in a process known as the scientific revolution. Some European intellectuals then sought to use scientific methods and reason to overhaul moral, social, and political thought. In the process, they weakened the influence of churches in western Europe and encouraged the development of secular values.

The Reconception of the Universe

Until the seventeenth century, European astronomers based their understanding of the universe on the work of the Greek scholar Claudius Ptolemy of Alexandria. In the middle of the second century C.E., Ptolemy produced a work known *The Ptolemaic Universe* as the *Almagest,* which envisioned a motionless earth surrounded by a series of nine hollow, concentric spheres that revolved around it. Each of the first seven spheres had one of the observable heavenly bodies embedded in its shell. The eighth sphere held the stars, and an empty ninth sphere surrounded the whole cosmos and provided the spin that kept all the others moving. Beyond the spheres Christian astronomers located heaven, the realm of God.

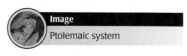
Image
Ptolemaic system

Following Ptolemy, astronomers believed that the heavens consisted of a pure substance that did not experience change or corruption and was not subject to the physical laws that governed the world below the moon. They also held that heavenly bodies followed perfect circular paths in making their revolutions around the earth.

This cosmology, however, did not mesh readily with the erratic movements of the planets, which sometimes slowed down, stopped, or even turned back on

Ptolemaic (TAWL-oh-may-ihk)

SOURCES FROM THE PAST

Adam Smith on the Capitalist Market

Adam Smith devoted special thought to the nature of early capitalist society and the principles that made it work. In 1776 he published a lengthy book titled An Inquiry into the Nature and Causes of the Wealth of Nations, *a vastly influential work that championed free, unregulated markets and capitalist enterprise as the principal ingredients of prosperity. Smith's optimism about capitalism sprang from his conviction that society as a whole benefits when individuals pursue their own economic interests and trade on a free market.*

■ ■ ■

Every individual is continually exerting himself to find out the most advantageous employment for whatever capital he can command. It is his own advantage, indeed, and not that of the society, which he has in view. . . .

As every individual, therefore, endeavours as much as he can both to employ his capital in the support of domestic industry, and so to direct that industry that its produce may be of the greatest value, every individual necessarily labours to render the annual revenue of the society as great as he can. He generally, indeed, neither intends to promote the public interest, nor knows how much he is promoting it. By preferring the support of domestic to that of foreign industry, he intends only his own security; and by directing that industry in such a manner as its produce may be of the greatest value, he intends only his own gain, and he is in this, as in many other cases, led by an invisible hand to promote an end which was no part of his intention. Nor is it always the worse for the society that it was no part of it. By pursuing his own interest he frequently promotes that of the society more effectually than when he really intends to promote it. I have never known much good done by those who affected to trade for the public good. It is an affectation, indeed, not very common among merchants, and very few words need be employed in dissuading them from it.

What is the species of domestic industry which his capital can employ, and of which the produce is likely to be of the greatest value, every individual, it is evident, can, in his local situation, judge much better than any statesman or lawgiver can do for him. The statesman, who should attempt to direct private people in what manner they ought to employ their capitals, would not only load himself with a most unnecessary attention, but assume an authority which could safely be trusted, not only to no single person, but to no council or senate whatever, and which would nowhere be so dangerous as in the hands of a man who had folly and presumption enough to fancy himself fit to exercise it.

To give the monopoly of the home market to the produce of domestic industry, in any particular art or manufacture, is in some measure to direct private people in what manner they ought to employ their capitals, and must, in almost all cases, be either a useless or a hurtful regulation. If the produce of domestic can be brought there as cheap as that of foreign industry, the regulation is evidently useless. If it cannot, it must generally be hurtful. It is the maxim of every prudent master of a family, never to attempt to make at home what it will cost him more to make than to buy. The tailor does not attempt to make his own shoes, but buys them of the shoemaker. The shoemaker does not attempt to make his own clothes, but employs a tailor. The farmer attempts to make neither the one nor the other, but employs those different artificers. All of them find it for their interest to employ their whole industry in a way in which they have some advantage over their neighbours, and to purchase with a part of its produce, or, what is the same thing, with the price of a part of it, whatever else they have occasion for.

- *To what extent do you think Adam Smith's analysis reflected the experiences of his own times, and to what extent did they represent universally valid observations?*

SOURCE: Adam Smith. *An Inquiry into the Nature and Causes of the Wealth of Nations.* Edinburgh, 1863, pp. 198–200.

A woodcut illustration depicts the Ptolemaic universe with the earth at the center surrounded by spheres holding the planets and the stars.

The Scientific Revolution

In time, though, Copernicus's theory inspired some astronomers to examine the heavens in fresh ways, using precise observational data and mathematical reasoning. Gradually, they abandoned the Ptolemaic in favor of the Copernican model of the universe. Some also began to apply their analytical methods to mechanics—the branch of science that deals with moving bodies—and by the mid–seventeenth century accurate observation and mathematical reasoning dominated both mechanics and astronomy. Indeed, reliance on observation and mathematics transformed the study of the natural world and brought about the scientific revolution.

The works of two mathematicians—Johannes Kepler of Germany and Galileo Galilei of Italy—rang the death knell for the Ptolemaic universe. *Galileo Galilei* Kepler (1571–1630) demonstrated that planetary orbits are elliptical, not circular as in Ptolemaic theory. Galileo (1564–1642) showed that the heavens were not the perfect, unblemished realm that Ptolemaic astronomers assumed. Using the recently invented telescope, Galileo was able to observe spots on the sun and mountains on the moon. He also caught sight of distant stars previously undetectable to the naked eye, which implied that the universe was much larger than anyone had previously suspected.

The new approach to science culminated in the work of the English mathematician Isaac Newton (1642–1727), who depended on accu- *Isaac Newton* rate observation and mathematical reasoning to construct a powerful synthesis of astronomy and mechanics. Newton outlined his views on the natural world in an epoch-making volume of 1687 titled *Mathematical Principles of Natural Philosophy.* Newton's work united the heavens and the earth in a vast, cosmic system. He argued that a law of universal gravitation regulates the motions of bodies throughout the universe, and he offered precise mathematical explanations of the laws that govern movements of bodies on the earth. His laws also allowed him to explain a vast range of seemingly unrelated phenomena, such as the ebb and flow of the tides and the eccentric orbits of planets and comets. Until the twentieth century, Newton's universe served as the unquestioned framework for the physical sciences.

Inspired by the dramatic discoveries of astronomers and physicists, other scientists began to construct fresh approaches to understanding the natural world. During the seventeenth and eighteenth

their courses. Astronomers went to great lengths to explain planetary behavior as the result of perfect circular *Planetary Movement* movements. The result was an awkward series of adjustments known as epicycles—small, circular revolutions that planets made around a point in their spheres, even while the spheres themselves revolved around the earth.

In 1543, however, the Polish astronomer Nicolaus Copernicus published *On the Revolutions of the Heav-* *The Copernican* *enly Spheres,* which broke with Ptole- *Universe* maic theory. Copernicus argued that the sun rather than the earth stood at the center of the universe and that the planets, including the earth, revolved around the sun. Although this new theory harmonized much better with observational data, it did not receive a warm welcome. Copernicus's ideas not only challenged prevailing scientific theories but also threatened cherished religious beliefs, which held that the earth and humanity were unique creations of God.

centuries, anatomy, physiology, microbiology, chemistry, and botany underwent a thorough overhaul, as scientists tested their theories against direct observation of natural phenomena and explained them in rigorous mathematical terms.

The Enlightenment

Newton's vision of the universe was so powerful and persuasive that its influence extended well beyond science. His work suggested that rational analysis of human behavior and institutions could lead to fresh insights about the human as well as the natural world. From Scotland to Sicily and from Philadelphia to Moscow, European and Euro-American thinkers launched an ambitious project to discover natural laws that governed human society in the same way that Newton's laws regulated the universe. They went about this project in different ways. Some, such as John Locke (1632–1704), sought the natural laws of politics. Others, such as Adam Smith, sought to comprehend the laws of economics. Like the early modern scientists, however, they all abandoned Aristotelian philosophy and Christian religion as sources of authority in their quest to subject the human world to purely rational analysis. The result of their work was a movement known as the Enlightenment.

The center of Enlightenment thought was France, where prominent intellectuals known collectively as *philosophes* ("philosophers") advanced the cause of reason. The philosophes addressed their works more to the educated public than to scholars: instead of formal philosophical treatises, they mostly composed histories, novels, dramas, satires, and pamphlets on religious, moral, and political issues.

More than any other philosophe, François-Marie Arouet (1694–1778) epitomized the spirit of the Enlightenment. Writing under the pen name *Voltaire*, he championed individual freedom and attacked any institution sponsoring intolerant or oppressive policies. Targets of his often caustic wit included the French monarchy and the Roman Catholic church. When the king of France sought to save money by reducing the number of horses kept in royal stables, for example, Voltaire suggested that it would be more effective to get rid of the asses who rode the horses. Voltaire also waged a long literary campaign against the Roman Catholic church, which he held responsible for fanaticism, intolerance, and incalculable human suffering. Indeed, Voltaire himself—like many other philosophes—was a deist and denied the supernatural teachings of Christianity. Instead, deists held that

Primary Source
Voltaire on nobility

Voltaire (vohl-TAIR)
deism (DEE-iz'm)

Socially prominent women deeply influenced the development of Enlightenment thought by organizing and maintaining salons—gatherings where philosophes, scientists, and intellectuals discussed the leading ideas of the day. Though produced in 1814, this painting depicts the Parisian salon of Mme. Geoffrin (center left), a leading patron of the French philosophes, about 1775. In the background is a bust of Voltaire, who lived in Switzerland at the time.

although a powerful god had created the universe, once created, the universe operated by itself according to rational and natural laws.

The Theory of Progress   Most philosophes were optimistic about the future of the world and humanity. In fact, they believed that rational understanding of human and natural affairs would bring about a new era of progress and individual freedom and would lead to the construction of a prosperous, just, and equitable society. Although those fond wishes did not come to pass, the Enlightenment did indeed help to bring about a thorough cultural transformation of European society. For one thing, it weakened the influence of organized religion by encouraging the replacement of Christian values with a new set of secular values based on reason. Furthermore, the Enlightenment encouraged political and cultural leaders to subject society to rational analysis and intervene actively in its affairs in the interests of promoting progress and prosperity. In many ways the Enlightenment legacy continues to influence European and Euro-American societies.

SUMMARY

During the early modern era, European society experienced a series of profound and sometimes unsettling changes. The Protestant Reformation ended the religious unity of western Christendom and led to more than a century of religious conflict. Centralizing monarchs strengthened their realms and built a society of sovereign, autonomous, and intensely competitive states. Capitalist entrepreneurs reorganized the production and distribution of manufactured goods, and although their methods led to increased wealth, their quest for efficiency and profits clashed with traditional values. Modern science based on direct observation and mathematical explanations emerged as a powerful tool for the investigation of the natural world. Some people used scientific methods to investigate the human world and created a new moral thought based strictly on science and reason. At just the time that European merchants, colonists, and adventurers were seeking opportunities in the larger world, European society was becoming more powerful, more experimental, and more competitive than ever before.

CHRONOLOGY

1473–1543	Life of Nicolaus Copernicus
1478	Foundation of the Spanish Inquisition
1483–1546	Life of Martin Luther
1517	Publication of the *Ninety-five Theses*
1540	Foundation of the Society of Jesus
1545–1563	Council of Trent
1564–1642	Life of Galileo Galilei
1571–1630	Life of Johannes Kepler
1618–1648	Thirty Years' War
1632–1704	Life of John Locke
1642–1727	Life of Isaac Newton
1648	Peace of Westphalia
1694–1778	Life of Voltaire
1723–1790	Life of Adam Smith

FOR FURTHER READING

Fernand Braudel. *Civilization and Capitalism, 15th to 18th Century.* 3 vols. Trans. by S. Reynolds. New York, 1981–84. A rich analysis of early capitalist society by one of the greatest historians of the twentieth century.

Paul Dukes. *The Making of Russian Absolutism, 1613–1801.* 2nd ed. London, 1990. A succinct study of two disparate centuries, the seventeenth and eighteenth, and two influential tsars, Peter and Catherine.

Robert S. Duplessis. *Transitions to Capitalism in Early Modern Europe.* Cambridge, 1997. A valuable synthesis of recent research on early capitalism and protoindustrialization.

Margaret Jacob. *The Cultural Meaning of the Scientific Revolution.* New York, 1989. Explores the larger cultural and social implications of early modern science.

E. L. Jones. *The European Miracle: Environments, Economies, and Geopolitics in the History of Europe and Asia.* 2nd ed. Cambridge, 1987. Examines European politics and economic growth in comparative perspective.

Thomas S. Kuhn. *The Structure of Scientific Revolutions.* 3rd ed. Chicago, 1997. An influential theoretical work that views scientific thought in larger social and cultural context.

William H. McNeill. *The Pursuit of Power: Technology, Armed Force, and Society since A.D. 1000.* Chicago, 1982. Insightful analysis exploring the influence of sovereign states and early capitalism on military technology and organization.

Eugene F. Rice Jr. and Anthony Grafton. *The Foundations of Early Modern Europe, 1460–1559.* 2nd ed. New York, 1994. Excellent introduction to political, social, economic, and cultural developments.

Simon Schama. *The Embarrassment of Riches: An Interpretation of Dutch Culture in the Seventeenth Century.* New York, 1987. A marvelous popular study of the wealthy Dutch republic at its height.

Keith Thomas. *Religion and the Decline of Magic.* New York, 1971. A riveting analysis of popular culture in early modern times, especially strong on the explanation of magic and witchcraft.

CHAPTER 22

New Worlds: The Americas and Oceania

A remarkable young woman played a pivotal role in the Spanish conquest of Mexico. Originally called Malintzin, she is better known by her Spanish name, Doña Marina. Born about 1500 to a noble family in central Mexico, Doña Marina's mother tongue was Nahuatl, the principal language of the Aztec empire. When she was a girl, Doña Marina's family sent her to the Mexican coast as a slave. Her new family later passed her on to their neighbors on the Yucatan peninsula, where she also became fluent in the Maya language.

When Hernán Cortés arrived on the Mexican coast in 1519, only one of his soldiers could speak the Maya language spoken by coastal peoples. But he had no way to communicate with the Nahuatl-speaking peoples of central Mexico until a Maya chieftain presented him with twelve young women, including Doña Marina, as a token of alliance. Doña Marina's linguistic talents enabled Cortés to communicate through an improbable chain of languages—from Spanish to Maya to Nahuatl and then back again— while making his way to the Aztec capital of Tenochtitlan. (Doña Marina soon learned Spanish and thus eliminated the Maya link in the linguistic chain.)

Doña Marina provided Cortés with intelligence and diplomatic as well as linguistic services. On several occasions she learned of plans by native peoples to overwhelm and destroy the tiny Spanish army, and she alerted Cortés to the danger in time for him to forestall an attack. She also helped Cortés negotiate with emissaries from the major cities of central Mexico. Indeed, in the absence of Doña

OPPOSITE PAGE: *Doña Marina is depicted between a Tlaxcalan chief and Hernando Cortés.*

Marina's services, it is difficult to see how Cortés's small band could have survived to see the Aztec capital.

Apart from facilitating the Spanish conquest of the Aztec empire, Doña Marina also played a role in the formation of a new society in Mexico. In 1522 she gave birth to a son fathered by Cortés, and in 1526 she bore a daughter to a Spanish captain whom she had married. Her offspring thus symbolize the early emergence of a mestizo population in Mexico. Doña Marina died soon after the birth of her daughter, probably in 1527, but during her short life she contributed to the thorough transformation of Mexican society.

Until 1492 the peoples of the eastern and western hemispheres had few dealings with one another. Sporadic encounters between Europeans and North Americans did occur, and it is likely that an occasional Asian or Austronesian mariner reached the Pacific coast of the Americas before 1492. Yet travel between the eastern hemisphere, the western hemisphere, and Oceania was too irregular and infrequent to generate sustained interaction until the fifteenth century.

After 1492, however, the voyages of European mariners led to permanent and continuous contact between the peoples of all these areas. The resulting encounters brought profound and often violent change to both American and Pacific lands. European peoples possessed powerful weapons, horses, and ships that provided them with technological advantages over the peoples they encountered in the Americas and the Pacific islands. Moreover, most Europeans also enjoyed complete or partial immunity to diseases that caused devastating epidemics when introduced to the western hemisphere and Oceania. Because of their technological advantages and the depopulation that followed from epidemic diseases, European peoples were able to establish a presence throughout the Americas and much of the Pacific Ocean basin.

COLLIDING WORLDS

When European peoples first sought to establish their presence in the Americas, they brought technologies unavailable to the peoples they encountered in the western hemisphere. More important than technology, however, were the divisions between indigenous peoples that Europeans were able to exploit and the effects of epidemic diseases that devastated native societies. Soon after their arrival in the western hemisphere, Spanish conquerors toppled the Aztec and

Inca empires and imposed their own rule in Mexico and Peru. In later decades Portuguese planters built sugar plantations on the Brazilian coastline. French, English, and Dutch migrants displaced indigenous peoples in North America and established settler colonies under the rule of European peoples.

The Spanish Caribbean

The first site of interaction between European and American peoples was the Caribbean. When Spanish mariners arrived there, the Tainos (also known as Arawaks) were the most prominent people in the region. The Tainos cultivated manioc and *Tainos* other crops, and they lived in small villages under the authority of chiefs who allocated land to families and supervised community affairs.

Christopher Columbus and his immediate followers made the island of Hispaniola (which embraces modern Haiti and the Dominican Republic) the base of Spanish opera- *Spanish Arrival* tions in the Caribbean. Columbus's original plan was to build forts and trading posts where merchants could trade with local peoples for products desired by European consumers. However, it soon became clear that the Caribbean region offered no silks or spices for the European market. If Spanish settlers wanted to maintain their presence in the Caribbean, they would need to find some way to make a living.

The settlers first attempted to support their society by mining gold. Spanish settlers were few in number and were not inclined to perform heavy labor, so they recruited the labor they needed from the ranks of the Tainos. This was done through an institution known as the *encomienda,* which gave Spanish settlers (*encomenderos*) the right to compel Tainos to work in their mines or fields. In return for 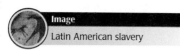 labor, *encomenderos* were supposed to look after their workers' welfare and encourage their conversion to Christianity.

Conscription of Taino labor was a brutal business. *Encomenderos* worked their charges hard and punished them severely. Tainos occasionally organized rebellions, but their bows, arrows, and slings had little effect against Spanish steel. By about 1515, social disruption and physical abuse caused Taino popula-

---

Taino (tah-EE-noh)
encomienda (ehn-koh-MYEN-dah)

One of the earliest European depictions of native Americans was this engraving of 1505. The caption informed readers that American peoples lived in communal society, where men took several wives but none had private possessions, and that they routinely smoked and consumed the bodies of slain enemies.

tions to decline on the large Caribbean islands—Hispaniola, Jamaica, Puerto Rico, and Cuba—favored by Spanish settlers.

After 1518 serious demographic decline set in when smallpox reached the Caribbean and touched off devastating epidemics. To replace laborers

Smallpox

lost to disease, *encomenderos* resorted to kidnapping and enslaving Tainos and other peoples. That tactic, however, only exposed additional victims to disease. As a result of epidemic disease, the native population of the Caribbean plummeted from about four million in 1492 to a few thousand in the 1540s. Entire native societies passed out of existence. By the middle of the sixteenth century, a few surviving words—*canoe, hammock, hurricane, barbecue, maize,* and *tobacco*—were all that was left of Taino society.

After the mid–sixteenth century, when it was clear that gold supplies in the region were thin, the Carib-

bean became a sleepy backwater of the Spanish empire. In the 1640s, French, English, and Dutch settlers began to take the place of the Spanish and flocked to the Caribbean with the intention of establishing plantations. Indeed, they found that the Caribbean offered ideal conditions for the cultivation of cash crops, particularly sugar and tobacco. Meanwhile, because indigenous populations were extinct, planters imported several million slaves to provide labor. By 1700 Caribbean society consisted of a small class of European administrators and large numbers of African slaves.

From Mining to Plantation Agriculture

The Conquest of Mexico and Peru

Spanish interest shifted quickly from the Caribbean to the American mainland in the quest for resources.

During the early sixteenth century, Spanish *conquistadores* ("conquerors") pressed west into Mexico and south into Panama and Peru. Between 1519 and 1521 Hernán Cortés and a small band of men brought down the Aztec empire in Mexico, and between 1532 and 1533 Francisco Pizarro and his followers toppled the Inca empire in Peru. Those conquests laid the foundations for colonial regimes that would transform the Americas.

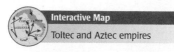

In Mexico and Peru, Spanish explorers found societies quite different from those of the Caribbean islands. Both Mexico and Peru had been sites of agricultural societies, cities, and large states for more than a millennium. In the early fifteenth century, both lands fell under the sway of powerful imperial states: the Mexica people and their allies founded the Aztec empire, which expanded to embrace most of Mesoamerica, and the Incas imposed their rule on a vast realm extending from modern Ecuador in the north to modern Chile in the south. (See chapter 18.)

The conquest of Mexico began in 1519 when Cortés led about 450 soldiers from Veracruz on the Gulf coast to the island city of Tenochtitlan, the stunningly beautiful Aztec capital situated in Lake Texcoco. They seized the emperor Motecuzoma II, who died in 1520 during a skirmish between Spanish forces and residents of Tenochtitlan. Aztec forces soon drove the conquistadores from the capital, but Cortés built a small fleet of ships, placed Tenochtitlan under siege, and in 1521 starved the city into surrender.

Hernán Cortés

Spanish weapons and horses offered Cortés and his soldiers some advantage over the forces they met and help to account for the Spanish conquest of the Aztec empire. Yet weaponry alone clearly was not enough to overcome such a large, densely populated society. Indeed, Cortés's expedition also benefited from divisions among the indigenous peoples of Mexico and made important alliances with peoples who resented Aztec domination. Native allies reinforced the small Spanish army with thousands of veteran warriors and provided Spanish forces with logistical support and secure bases in friendly territory.

Epidemic disease also aided Spanish efforts. During the siege of Tenochtitlan, smallpox raged through the city, killing inhabitants by the tens of thousands. It then spread beyond the capital and raced through Mexico, carrying

Epidemic Disease

off so many people that Aztec society was unable to function. Only in the context of this enormous depopulation is it possible to understand the Spanish conquest of Mexico.

Francisco Pizarro experienced similar results when he led a Spanish expedition from Central America to Peru. Pizarro set out in 1530 with 180 soldiers, later joined by reinforcements to make a force of about 600. The conquistadores arrived in Peru just after a bitter dispute within the Inca ruling house, and it was easy for them to exploit differences between the factions. By 1533 they had taken the Inca capital at Cuzco. Under pretext of holding a conference, they called the Inca ruling elites together, seized them, and killed most of them. They spared the Inca ruler Atahualpa until he had delivered a large quantity of gold to Pizarro. Then they strangled him and decapitated his body. Pizarro and his conquistadores proceeded to loot gold and silver from Cuzco's temples and public buildings, and even to loot jewelry and ornaments from the embalmed bodies of deceased Inca rulers.

Francisco Pizarro

In this illustration from Felipe Guaman Poma de Ayala's letter of complaint to the Spanish king, conquistadores decapitate Atahualpa after executing him by strangulation in 1533.

conquistadores (kon-kees-tah-DOH-rayz)

SOURCES FROM THE PAST

First Impressions of Spanish Forces

As the Spanish army made its way to Tenochtitlan, Motecuzoma dispatched a series of emissaries to communicate with Cortés and learn his intentions. The reports that came back were not reassuring. They brought disturbing news about Spanish weapons, armor, horses, and dogs that were much larger and more aggressive than the small, barkless animals that were native to Mexico.

And when [Motecuzoma] had heard what the messengers reported, he was terrified, he was astounded. . . .

Especially did it cause him to faint away when he heard how the gun, at [the Spaniards'] command, discharged [the shot]; how it resounded as if it thundered when it went off. It indeed bereft one of strength; it shut off one's ears. And when it discharged, something like a round pebble came forth from within. Fire went showering forth; sparks went blazing forth. And its smoke smelled very foul; it had a fetid odor which verily wounded the head. And when [the shot] struck a mountain, it was as if it were destroyed, dissolved. And a tree was pulverized; it was as if it vanished; it was as if someone blew it away.

All iron was their war array. In iron they clothed themselves. With iron they covered their heads. Iron were their swords. Iron were their crossbows. Iron were their shields. Iron were their lances.

And those which bore them upon their backs, their deer [that is, horses], were as tall as roof terraces.

And their bodies were everywhere covered; only their faces appeared. They were very white; they had chalky faces; they had yellow hair, though the hair of some was black. Long were their beards; they also were yellow. They were yellow-headed. [The black men's hair] was kinky, it was curly.

And their food was like fasting food—very large, white, not heavy like [tortillas]; like maize stalks, good-tasting as if of maize stalk flour; a little sweet, a little honeyed. It was honeyed to eat; it was sweet to eat.

And their dogs were very large. They had ears folded over; great dragging jowls. They had fiery eyes—blazing eyes; they had yellow eyes—fiery yellow eyes. They had thin flanks—flanks with ribs showing. They had gaunt stomachs. They were very tall. They were nervous; they went about panting, with tongues hanging out. They were spotted like ocelots; they were varicolored.

And when Motecuzoma heard all this, he was much terrified. It was as if he fainted away. His heart saddened; his heart failed him.

- *In light of the reports that he received, what were Motecuzoma's options for dealing with the Spanish threat?*

SOURCE: Bernardino de Sahagún. *Florentine Codex: General History of the Things of New Spain,* 13 vols. Trans. by Arthur J. O. Anderson and Charles E. Dibble. Salt Lake City: University of Utah Press, 1950–82, 13:19–20. (Translation slightly modified.)

As Cortés's expedition had done to the Aztecs in Mexico, Pizarro's tiny force toppled the Inca empire by exploiting divisions among native peoples. Many Inca subjects despised their overlords and thus either allied with or did not resist Pizarro's forces. In addition, smallpox had spread to the Inca empire in the 1520s, long before Pizarro's arrival, and had already taken a heavy toll among Andean populations. As a result, by 1540 Spanish forces had established themselves securely as lords of the land.

Iberian Empires in the Americas

The conquests of Mexico and Peru were the results not of Spanish royal policy but, rather, of individual efforts by freelance adventurers. Gradually, however, the Spanish monarchy extended its control over the growing American empire, and by about 1570 it had established formal rule under the Spanish crown. Spanish administrators established two main centers of

Spanish Colonial Administration

authority in the Americas—Mexico (which they called New Spain) and Peru (known as New Castile)—each governed by a viceroy who was responsible to the king of Spain. In Mexico they built a new capital, Mexico City, on top of Tenochtitlan. In Peru they moved the seat of government from the high-altitude Inca capital of Cuzco to the Peruvian coast and in 1535 founded the new capital of Lima.

The viceroys were the king's representatives in the Americas, and they wielded considerable power. The kings of Spain attempted to hold them in check by subjecting them to the review of courts known as *audiencias* staffed by university-educated lawyers. The *audiencias* heard appeals against the viceroys' decisions and policies and had the right to address their concerns directly to the Spanish king. Furthermore, the *audiencias* conducted reviews of viceroys' performance at the end of their terms, and negative reviews could lead to severe punishment.

In many ways, Spanish administration in the Americas was a ragged affair. Transportation and communication difficulties limited the ability of viceroys to supervise their own extensive territories. The jurisdiction of the viceroyalty of New Spain, for example, reached from Mexico City as far as St. Augustine in Florida (founded in 1565). Distance also prevented Spanish monarchs from exercising much influence on American affairs. It often took two years for the central government in Spain to respond to a query from Mexico or Peru, and when viceroys received clear orders that they did not like, it was easy to procrastinate.

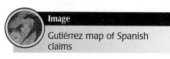

While the Spanish built a territorial empire in Mexico and Peru, Portuguese forces established an imperial presence in Brazil. The Portuguese presence came about by an odd twist of diplomatic convention. In 1494 Spain and Portugal signed the Treaty of Tordesillas, which divided the world along an imaginary north-south line 370 leagues west of the Azores and Cape Verde Islands. According to this agreement, Spain could claim any non-Christian lands west of that line, and Portugal gained the same rights for lands east of the line. Thus Portugal gained territory along the northeastern part of the South American continent, a region known as Brazil from the many brazilwood trees that grew along the coast, and the remainder of the western hemisphere fell under Spanish control. Brazil did not attract significant Portuguese interest, however, until entrepreneurs began establishing sugar plantations on

Portuguese Brazil

the coast after the mid–sixteenth century. Once it was clear the plantations would be profitable, Portuguese interest—and settlement—surged.

Both the Spanish and the Portuguese rapidly established cities throughout their territories. Like their compatriots in Europe, colonists preferred to live in cities even when they derived their income from the agricultural production of their landed estates, and they made every attempt to model their new cities along European lines. Away from urban areas, however, indigenous ways of life largely persisted. In places such as the Amazon basin and Paraguay, for example, where there were no mineral deposits to attract European migrants, European visitors learned to adapt to indigenous societies and customs: they ate bread made of manioc flour, made use of native hammocks and canoes, and communicated in the Guaraní and Tupí languages. Indeed, indigenous languages flourish even today throughout much of Latin America: among the more prominent are Nahuatl in Mexico, Quiché in Mexico and Guatemala, Guaraní in Paraguay, and Quechua in the Andean highlands of Peru, Ecuador, and Bolivia.

Colonial American Society

Spanish and Portuguese peoples always saw the western hemisphere more as a land to exploit and administer than as a place to settle and colonize. Nevertheless, upward of five hundred thousand Spaniards and one hundred thousand Portuguese settled permanently in the Americas between 1500 and 1800. Their presence contributed to the making of a new world—a world characterized by intense interaction between the peoples of Europe, Africa, and the Americas—in the western hemisphere.

Settler Colonies in North America

Throughout the sixteenth century, Spanish explorers sought opportunities north of Mexico and the Caribbean. They established towns, forts, and missions from modern Florida as far north as Virginia, and they scouted shorelines off Maine and Newfoundland. On the west coast they established a fort on Vancouver Island in modern Canada. By midcentury, however, French, English, and Dutch mariners were dislodging Spanish colonists north of Florida. Originally, they came in a fruitless search for a northwest passage to Asia. Instead, they found immense quantities of codfish, which they exploited from the banks off Labrador, Newfoundland, Nova Scotia, and New England.

More important, in the early seventeenth century they began to plant permanent colonies on the North

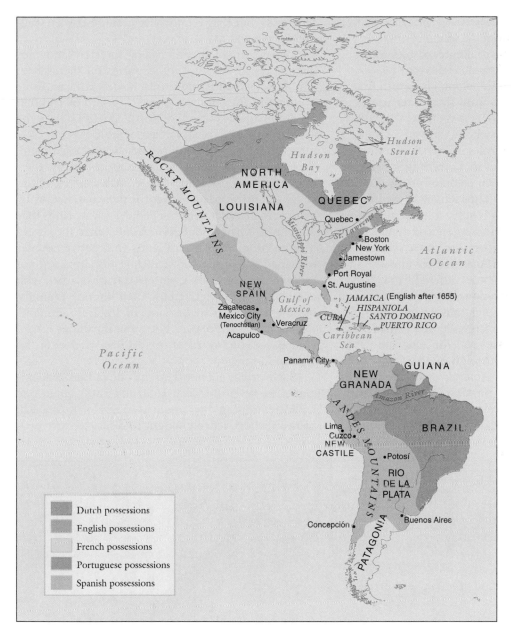

Map 22.1 European empires and colonies in the Americas about 1700. Locate the major cities and settlements of each imperial power. What factors decided where settlements would be placed, and why are there so few settlements in the interior of either North or South America?

American mainland. French settlers established colonies at Port Royal (Nova Scotia) in 1604 and Quebec in 1608, and English migrants founded Jamestown in 1607 and the Massachusetts Bay Colony in 1630. Dutch entrepreneurs built a settlement at New Amsterdam in 1623, but in 1664 an English fleet seized and rechristened it New York and absorbed it into English colonial holdings. During the seventeenth and eighteenth centuries, French migrants settled in eastern Canada, and French explorers and traders scouted the St. Lawrence, Ohio, and Mississippi rivers, building forts

Foundation of Colonies

all the way to the Gulf of Mexico. Meanwhile, English settlers established colonies along the east coast of the present-day United States of America.

Life in those early settlements was extremely difficult. Most of the settlers hoped to sustain their communities not through farming but by producing valuable commodities such as fur, pitch, tar, or lumber, if not silver and gold. They relied heavily on provisions sent from Europe, and when supply ships did not arrive as expected, they sometimes avoided starvation only because indigenous peoples provided them with food. In Jamestown, food shortages and disease became so severe that only sixty of the colony's five hundred inhabitants survived the winter of 1609–1610. Some settlers went so far as to disinter corpses and consume the flesh of their departed neighbors.

Colonial Government

The French and English colonies in North America differed in several ways from Iberian territories to the south. Whereas Iberian explorations had royal backing, private investors played larger roles in French and English colonial efforts. Because of that, individuals retained much more control over their colonies' affairs than did their Iberian counterparts. Thus settlers in the English colonies—though ultimately subject to royal authority—maintained their own assemblies and influenced the choice of royal governors: there were no viceroys or *audiencias* in the North American colonies.

Relations with Indigenous Peoples

French and English colonies differed from Iberian territories also in their relationships with indigenous peoples. French and English migrants did not find large, densely settled, centralized states like the Aztec and Inca empires. Although many of the native societies in eastern North America practiced agriculture, most also relied on hunting and consequently moved their villages frequently in pursuit of game. They did not claim ownership of precisely bounded territories, but they regularly migrated between well-defined regions.

When European settlers saw forested lands not bearing crops, they staked out farms for themselves. The availability of fertile farmland soon attracted large numbers of European migrants. Upward of 150,000 English migrants moved to North America during the seventeenth century alone, and sizable French, German, Dutch, and Irish contingents soon joined them.

European migrants took pains to justify their claims to American lands. Some, such as the English, sought to provide legal cover for their settlements by negotiating treaties with the peoples whose lands they colonized. Other migrants claimed that they were making productive use of lands that native peoples only used as hunting parks. Such justifications did not convince native peoples, who frequently clashed with colonists over the right to use their hunting grounds, whether treaties existed or not. In 1622, for example, native peoples angry over European intrusions massacred almost one-third of the English settlers in the Chesapeake region.

Such attacks did not stem the tide of European migrants, however. Between 1600 and 1800, about one million European migrants arrived in North America, many of whom actively sought to displace native peo-

A painting of the English settlement at Jamestown in the early seventeenth century illustrates the precarious relations between European settlers and indigenous peoples. Note the heavy palisades and numerous cannons deployed within the fort, as well as the imposing figure of the native chief Powhatan depicted outside the settlement's walls.

ples from their lands. Violent conflict, indeed, took a heavy toll on native populations. Yet as in the Iberian territories, epidemic disease also dramatically reduced the indigenous population of North America in early modern times. In 1492 the native population of the territory now embraced by the United States was greater than five million, perhaps as high as ten million. By the mid–sixteenth century, however, smallpox and other diseases spread north from Mexico and ravaged native societies in the plains and eastern woodlands of North America. By 1800 only six hundred thousand indigenous peoples remained, as against almost five million settlers of European ancestry and about one million slaves of African ancestry. Although the settler colonies of North America differed markedly from the Iberian territorial empires, they too contributed greatly to the transformation of the western hemisphere.

COLONIAL SOCIETY IN THE AMERICAS

The European migrants who flooded into the western hemisphere interacted both with the native inhabitants and with African peoples whom they imported as enslaved laborers. Throughout the Americas, relations between individuals of American, European, and African ancestry soon led to the emergence of mestizo populations. Yet European peoples and their Euro-American offspring increasingly dominated political and economic affairs in the Americas. They mined precious metals, cultivated cash crops such as sugar and tobacco, and trapped fur-bearing animals to supply capitalist markets that met the voracious demands of European and Asian consumers. Over time they also established their Christian religion as the dominant faith of the western hemisphere.

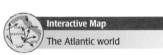

The Formation of Multicultural Societies

Many parts of the Americas remained outside European control until the nineteenth century. Only rarely did Europeans venture into the interior regions of the American continents in the sixteenth century, and those who did often found themselves at the mercy of the native inhabitants. But even though their influence reached the American interior only gradually, European migrants radically transformed the social order in the regions where they established colonies.

In Spanish and Portuguese territories, society quickly became both multicultural and ethnically mixed, largely because of migration patterns. Indeed, more than 85 percent of Spanish migrants were men, and the percentage of men was even higher for the Portuguese. Because there were so few European women, Spanish and Portuguese migrants entered into relationships with native women, which soon gave rise to an increasingly mestizo society.

Mestizo Societies

This pattern was especially pronounced in the Portuguese colony of Brazil, where there were very few European women. There, Portuguese men entered into relationships with both native and African slave women. Brazil soon had large populations not only of mestizos but also of mulattoes, born of Portuguese and African parents; *zambos,* born of indigenous and African parents; and other combinations arising from these groups themselves. Indeed, marriages between members of different racial and ethnic communities became very common in colonial Brazil.

In both the Spanish and the Portuguese colonies, migrants born in Europe known as *peninsulares* (people from the Iberian peninsula) stood at the top of the social hierarchy, followed by *criollos,* or creoles, individuals born in the Americas of Iberian parents. As the numbers of mestizos grew, they also became essential contributors to their societies, especially in Mexico and Brazil. Meanwhile, mulattoes, zambos, and other individuals of mixed parentage became prominent groups in Brazilian society, although they were usually subordinate to peninsulares, creoles, and even mestizos. In all the Iberian colonies, imported slaves and native peoples stood at the bottom of the social hierarchy.

The Social Hierarchy

The social structure of the French and English colonies in North America differed markedly from that of the Iberian colonies. Women were more numerous, especially among the English migrants, and settlers mostly married within their own groups. Although French fur traders often associated with native women and

North American Societies

mestizo (mehs-TEE-soh)

zambos (SAHM-bohs)
peninsulares (pehn-IHN-soo-LAH-rayz)
criollos (KRYO-yohs)

generated *métis* (the French equivalent of mestizos) in regions around trading posts, such arrangements were less common in French colonial cities such as Port Royal and Quebec.

Mingling between peoples of different ancestry was least common in the English colonies of North America. Colonists regarded the native peoples they encountered as lazy heathens who did not exert themselves to cultivate the land. Later they also scorned African slaves as inferior beings. Those attitudes fueled a virulent racism, and English settlers worked to maintain sharp boundaries between themselves and peoples of American and African ancestry.

Yet English settlers readily borrowed useful cultural elements from other communities. From native communities, for example, they learned about American plants and animals, and they adapted moccasins and deerskin clothes. From their slaves they borrowed African food crops and techniques for the cultivation of rice. Yet, unlike their Iberian neighbors, English settlers strongly discouraged relationships between individuals of different ancestry and mostly refused to accept offspring of mixed parentage.

---

métis (may-TEE)

Mining and Agriculture in the Spanish Empire

From the Spanish perspective, the greatest attractions of the Americas were precious metals. Once the conquistadores had thoroughly looted the treasures of the Aztec and Inca empires, their followers opened mines to extract the mineral wealth of the Americas in a more systematic fashion.

Silver was the most abundant American treasure, and much of Spain's American enterprise focused on its extraction. Silver production con-*Silver Mining* centrated on two areas: the thinly populated Mexican north, particularly the region around Zacatecas, and the high central Andes, particularly the stunningly rich mines of Potosí. Both sites employed large numbers of indigenous laborers. Many laborers went to Zacatecas voluntarily to escape the pressures of conquest and disease. Over time they became professional miners, spoke Spanish, and lost touch with the communities of their birth.

Meanwhile, Spanish prospectors discovered a large vein of silver near Potosí in 1545 and began large-scale mining there in the 1580s. By 1600 Potosí had a booming population of 150,000. Such rapid growth

Mining operations at Potosí gave rise to a large settlement that housed miners and others who supplied food, made charcoal, fashioned tools, and supported the enterprise. In this illustration from the mid-1580s, llamas laden with silver ore descend the mountain (background) while laborers work in the foreground to crush the ore and extract pure silver from it.

created an explosive demand for labor. As in the Mexican mines, Spanish administrators relied mostly on voluntary labor, but they also adapted the Inca practice of requisitioning draft labor, known as the *mita* system, to recruit workers for particularly difficult and dangerous chores. Under the *mita* system, each native village was required to send one-seventh of its male population to work for four months in the mines at Potosí. Draft laborers received very little payment for their work, and conditions were extremely harsh. Death rates of draft laborers were high, and many native men sought to evade *mita* obligations by fleeing to cities or hiding in distant villages.

The Global Significance of Silver   The mining industries of Mexico and Peru powered the Spanish economy in the Americas and even stimulated the world economy of early modern times. Indeed, the Spanish government's share—one-fifth of all silver production, called the *quinto*—represented the principal revenue the crown derived from its American possessions. Most American silver made its way across the Atlantic to Spain, where it financed Spain's army and bureaucracy and lubricated markets throughout Europe. From Europe, merchants used it to trade for silk, spices, and porcelain in the markets of Asia. Silver also traveled from Acapulco on the west coast of Mexico across the Pacific in the Manila galleons, and from Manila it also made its way to Asian markets. No matter which direction it went, American silver powerfully stimulated global trade.

The Hacienda   Apart from mining, the principal occupations in Spanish America were farming, stock raising, and craft production. By the seventeenth century the most prominent site of agricultural and craft production in Spanish America was the estate, or hacienda, which produced goods for sale to local markets in nearby mining districts, towns, and cities. Bordering the large estates were smaller properties owned by Spanish migrants or creoles as well as sizable tracts of land held by indigenous peoples who practiced subsistence agriculture.

Labor Systems   The major source of labor for the haciendas was the indigenous population. As in the Caribbean, Spanish conquerors first organized native workforces under the *encomienda* system. Yet from the 1520s to the 1540s, this system led to rampant abuse, as Spanish landowners overworked their laborers and skimped on their maintenance. After midcentury, *encomenderos* in agriculturally productive regions increasingly required their subject populations to provide tribute but not labor. That didn't solve the problem of labor, however, so Spanish landowners resorted to a system of debt peonage to recruit workers for their haciendas. Under this system, landowners advanced loans to native peoples so that they could buy seeds, tools, and supplies for their own farms. The debtors then repaid the loans with labor, but wages were so low that they were never able to pay off their debts. Thus, landowners helped create a cycle of debt that ensured them a dependent labor force to work their estates.

Resistance to Spanish Rule   The Spanish regimes in the Americas met considerable resistance from indigenous peoples. Resistance took various forms: armed rebellion, halfhearted work, and retreat into the mountains and forests. On some occasions, indigenous peoples turned to Spanish law in search of aid against oppressive colonists. In 1615, for example, Felipe Guaman Poma de Ayala, a native of Peru, fired off a 1,200-page letter to King Philip III of Spain asking for protection for native peoples against rapacious colonists. He wrote passionately of men ruined by overtaxation and women driven to prostitution, of Spanish colonists who grabbed the lands of native peoples and Spanish priests who seduced the wives of native men. Guaman Poma warned the king that if Philip wanted anything to remain of his Andean empire, he should intervene and protect the indigenous peoples of the land. Unfortunately for Guaman Poma, the king never saw the letter. Instead, it ended up in Denmark, where it remained unknown in a library until 1908.

Sugar and Slavery in Portuguese Brazil

Whereas the Spanish American empire concentrated on the extraction of silver, the Portuguese empire in Brazil depended on the production and export of sugar. The different economic and social foundations of the Spanish and Portuguese empires led to different patterns of labor recruitment. The Spanish forced native peoples to provide labor; the Portuguese relied instead on imported African slaves. Because of that, Africans and their descendants became the majority of the population in Brazil.

Colonial Brazilian life revolved around the sugar mill, or *engenho,* which came to represent a complex of

---

quinto (KEEN-toh)
hacienda (ah-SYEN-dah)

land, labor, buildings, animals, capital, and technical skills related to the production of sugar. Unlike other

The Engenho

crops, sugarcane required extensive processing to yield molasses or refined sugar. Thus *engenhos* needed both heavy labor for the planting and harvesting of cane and specialized skills for the intricacies of processing.

Like their Spanish counterparts, Portuguese colonists first tried to enlist local populations as laborers.

The Search for Labor

Unlike the inhabitants of Mexico and Peru, however, the peoples of Brazil were not sedentary cultivators. They resisted efforts to commandeer their labor and evaded the Portuguese simply by retreating to interior lands. In addition, in Brazil as elsewhere in the Americas, epidemic diseases devastated indigenous populations. After smallpox and measles ravaged the Brazilian coast in the 1560s, Portuguese settlers had a hard time even finding potential laborers, let alone forcing them to work.

Faced with those difficulties, the colonists turned to another labor source: African slaves. Portuguese

Slavery

plantation managers imported slaves as early as the 1530s, but they began to rely on African labor on a large scale only in the 1580s. The toll on slave communities was extremely heavy: arduous working conditions, mistreatment, poor nutrition, and inadequate housing combined to produce high rates of disease and mortality. Indeed, *engenhos* typically lost 5 to 10 percent of their slaves annually, so there was a constant demand for more slaves.

Owners had little economic incentive to improve conditions for slaves or to encourage them to reproduce naturally. If a slave lived five to six years, the investment of the average owner doubled and permitted him to purchase a new and healthy slave without taking a monetary loss. Children required financial outlays for at least twelve years, which from the perspective of the owner represented a financial loss. To them the balance sheet of sugar production was about profit, not about slaves' lives. All told, the business of producing Brazilian sugar was so brutal that every ton of the sweet substance cost one human life.

Fur Traders and Settlers in North America

European mariners first frequented North American shores in search of fish. Over time, though, trade in furs became far more lucrative. After explorers found a convenient entrance to rich fur-producing regions through the Hudson Strait and Hudson Bay, they began to con-

nect large parts of the North American interior by a chain of forts and trading posts. Indigenous peoples trapped animals for Europeans and exchanged the pelts for manufactured goods. The hides went mostly to Europe, where there was strong demand for beaver skin hats and fur clothing.

The Fur Trade

Primary Source
Champlain's explorations

The fur trade generated tremendous conflict between native groups. As overhunting caused American beaver populations to plummet, native trappers constantly had to push farther inland in search of hides. This frequently led native peoples to invade others' territories, which in turn often led to war. The fur trade also took place in the context of competition between European states. This competitive atmosphere contributed to further conflict, as indigenous peoples became embroiled in their patrons' rivalries.

Effects of the Fur Trade

European settler-cultivators posed an even more serious challenge to native ways of life than the fur traders, since they displaced indigenous peoples from the land and turned hunting grounds into plantations. And, as colonists' numbers increased, they sought to integrate their American holdings into the larger economy of the

Settler Society

Primary Source
Conditions in the Virginia colony

Atlantic Ocean basin by producing cash crops—such as tobacco, rice, and indigo—that they could market in Europe.

Cash-crop plantations created high demand for cheap labor. Unlike their counterparts in the Spanish territories, indigenous peoples in North America could not be induced to labor in the colonists' fields. Instead, planters turned to indentured servants from Europe for their labor needs. Under this system, people who had little future in Europe—the chronically unemployed, orphans, criminals—received free passage across the Atlantic in exchange for providing four to seven years of labor. Although thousands of indentured servants came to the American colonies with high hopes for making a new start, the system was far from ideal—many died of disease or overwork before completing their terms of labor, and others found only marginal employment.

Indentured Labor

English settlers in North America also found uses for African slaves. In 1619 a group of about twenty Africans reached Virginia, where they worked along-

European moralists often denounced tobacco as a noxious weed, and they associated its use with vices such as drunkenness, gambling, and prostitution. Nevertheless, its popularity surged in Europe, and later in Africa and Asia as well, after its introduction from the Americas.

side European laborers as indentured servants. After about 1680, however, planters increasingly replaced *Slavery in North America* indentured servants with African slaves. By 1750 some 120,000 black slaves tilled Chesapeake tobacco, and 180,000 others cultivated Carolina rice.

Slave labor was not prominent in the northern colonies, mostly because the land and the climate were not suitable for the cultivation of labor-intensive cash crops. Nevertheless, the economies of these colonies also profited handsomely from slavery. Many New England merchants traded in slaves destined for the West Indies: by the mid–eighteenth century, half the merchant fleet of Newport carried human cargo. The economies of New York and Philadelphia also benefited from the building and outfitting of slave vessels, and the seaports of New England became profitable centers for the distillation of rum. The chief ingredient of that rum was slave-produced sugar from the West Indies, and merchants traded much of the distilled spirits for slaves on the African coast. Thus, although the southern plantation societies became most directly identified with slavery, all the North American colonies participated in and profited from the slave trade.

Christianity and Native Religions in the Americas

Like Buddhists and Muslims in earlier centuries, European explorers, conquerors, merchants, and settlers took their religious traditions with them when they traveled overseas. The desire to spread Christianity was a prominent motive behind European ventures overseas, and missionaries soon made their way to the Americas.

From the beginning of Spanish colonization in Mexico and Peru, Franciscan, Dominican, and Jesuit missionaries campaigned to Christianize indigenous peoples. Over time, and despite considerable initial resistance, Christianity did win adherents in Spanish America. In the wake of conquest and epidemic disease, many native leaders in Mexico concluded that their gods had abandoned them and looked to the missionaries for spiritual guidance. When native peoples adopted Christianity, however, they blended their own interests and traditions with the faith taught by Spanish missionaries. When they learned about Roman Catholic saints, for example, they revered saints with qualities like those of their inherited gods or those whose feast days coincided with traditional celebrations. *Spanish Missionaries*

In Mexico, Christianity became especially popular after the mid–seventeenth century, as an increasingly mestizo society took the Virgin of Guadalupe almost as a national symbol. According to legends, the Virgin Mary appeared before a peasant near Mexico City in 1531. The site of the apparition soon became a popular local shrine visited mostly by Spanish settlers. By the 1640s the shrine attracted pilgrims from all parts of Mexico, and the Virgin of Guadalupe gained a reputation for working miracles on behalf of individuals who visited her shrine. The popularity of the Virgin of Guadalupe helped to ensure that Roman Catholic Christianity would dominate cultural and religious matters in Mexico. *The Virgin of Guadalupe*

French and English missionaries did not attract nearly as many converts to Christianity in North America as their Spanish counterparts did in Mexico and Peru, partly because French and English colonists

An eighteenth-century engraving depicts work on a plantation: African slaves prepare flour and bread from manioc (left) while others hang tobacco leaves to dry in a shed (right). A male turkey—a fowl native to the Americas—ignores the bustle and displays his feathers (right foreground).

did not rule over sedentary cultivators: it was much more difficult to conduct missions among peoples who frequently moved about the countryside than among those who lived permanently in villages, towns, or cities. Even so, French missionaries did work actively among native communities in the St. Lawrence, Mississippi, and Ohio river valleys and experienced modest success for their efforts. English colonists, in contrast, displayed little interest in converting indigenous peoples to Christianity, nor did they welcome native converts into their agricultural and commercial society. Yet even without native conversion to Christianity, the growing settlements of French and especially English colonists guaranteed that European religious traditions would figure prominently in North American society.

French and English Missions

EUROPEANS IN THE PACIFIC

Though geographically distant from the Americas, Australia and the Pacific islands underwent experiences similar to those that transformed the western hemisphere in early modern times. Like their American counterparts, the peoples of Oceania had no inherited or acquired immunities to diseases that were common to peoples throughout the eastern hemisphere, and their numbers plunged when epidemic disease struck their populations. For the most part, however, Australia and the Pacific islands experienced epidemic disease and the arrival of European mi-

grants later than did the Americas. European mariners thoroughly explored the Pacific basin between the sixteenth and eighteenth centuries, but only in Guam and the Mariana Islands did they establish permanent settlements before the late eighteenth century. Nevertheless, their scouting of the region laid a foundation for much more intense interactions between European, Euro-American, Asian, and Oceanic peoples during the nineteenth and twentieth centuries.

Australia and the Larger World

At least from the second century C.E., European geographers had speculated about *terra australis incognita*—"unknown southern land"—that they thought must exist in the world's southern hemisphere to balance the huge landmasses north of the equator. Although Portuguese mariners most likely charted much of the western and northern coasts of Australia as early as the 1520s, Dutch sailors based in the Indonesian islands made the first recorded European sighting of the southern continent in 1606. The Dutch VOC authorized exploratory voyages, but mariners found little to encourage further efforts. In 1623, after surveying the landscape of western Australia, the Dutch mariner Jan Carstenzs described the land as "the most arid and barren region that could be found anywhere on earth."

Dutch Exploration

Nevertheless, Dutch mariners continued to visit Australia. By the mid–seventeenth century they had scouted the continent's northern, western, and southern coasts and had fleeting encounters with indigenous populations. Yet because those peoples were nomadic foragers rather than sedentary cultivators, Europeans mostly considered them wretched savages. In the absence of tempting opportunities to trade, European mariners made no effort to establish permanent settlements in Australia.

Only after James Cook charted the eastern coast in 1770 did European peoples become seriously inter-

British Colonists ested in Australia. Cook dropped anchor for a week at Botany Bay (near modern Sydney) and reported that the region was suitable for settlement. In 1788 a British fleet arrived at Sydney carrying about one thousand passengers, eight hundred of them convicts, who established the first European settlement in Australia as a penal colony. For half a century Europeans in Australia numbered only a few thousand, most of them convicts. In fact, free settlers did not outnumber convicted criminal migrants

until the 1830s. Thus, despite early fleeting encounters between European and aboriginal Australian peoples, it was only in the nineteenth and twentieth centuries that a continuing stream of European migrants and settlers linked Australia more directly to the larger world.

The Pacific Islands and the Larger World

The entry of European mariners into the Pacific Ocean basin did not bring immediate change to most of the Pacific islands. In these islands, as in Australia, European merchants and settlers did not arrive in large numbers until the late eighteenth century. However, in Guam and the Mariana Islands, dramatic change was already under way by the sixteenth century.

Ferdinand Magellan and his crew became the first Europeans to cross the Pacific Ocean, in 1521. Before reaching the Philippines, they encountered only one inhabited island group—the Marianas, dominated by

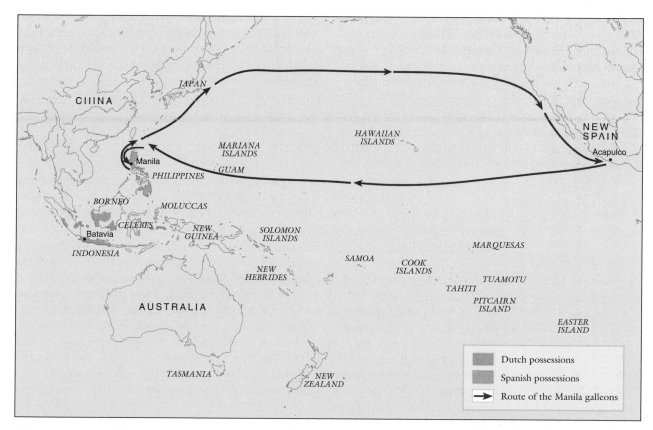

Map 22.2 The Manila galleon route and the lands of Oceania between 1500 and 1800. Note the route taken by the Manila galleons in relation to the majority of the Pacific islands. Why weren't Spanish mariners more interested in exploring the rest of the Pacific as they made their way to the Philippines?

Guam. In 1565 Spanish mariners inaugurated the Manila galleon trade between Manila and Acapulco.

Spanish Voyages in the Pacific

Because their primary goal was to link New Spain to Asian markets, they rarely went out of their way to explore the Pacific Ocean or to search for other islands. Although a few Spanish vessels visited some of the other Pacific islands in the sixteenth century, Spanish mariners found little to interest them and did not establish regular communications with island peoples.

The only Pacific islands that attracted substantial Spanish interest in the sixteenth century were Guam

Guam

and the Marianas. Manila galleons called regularly at Guam, which lay directly on the route from Acapulco to Manila. For more than a century, they took on fresh provisions and engaged in mostly peaceful trade with the indigenous Chamorro people. Then, in the 1670s and 1680s, Spanish authorities decided to bring the Mariana Islands under the control of the viceroy of New Spain in Mexico. They dispatched military forces to the islands to impose Spanish rule and subject the Chamorro to the spiritual authority of the Roman Catholic church. The Chamorro stoutly opposed those efforts, but a smallpox epidemic in 1688 severely reduced their numbers and crippled their resistance. By 1695 the Chamorro population had declined from about fifty thousand at midcentury to five thousand, mostly because of smallpox.

By the end of the seventeenth century, Spanish forces had established garrisons throughout the Mariana Islands and relocated surviving Chamorro into communities supervised by Spanish authorities.

By the late eighteenth century, growing European and Euro-American interest in the Pacific Ocean basin led to sharply increased interactions between islanders and mariners. English and French mariners explored the Pacific basin

Visitors and Trade

in search of commercial opportunities and the elusive northwest passage from Europe to Asia. They frequently visited Tahiti after 1767, and they soon began to trade with the islanders: European mariners received provisions and engaged in sexual relations with Tahitian women in exchange for nails, knives, iron tools, and textiles.

After 1778 the published writings of Captain James Cook, who happened across the Hawaiian Islands in that year, galvanized even greater interest in the Pacific. European whalers, missionaries, and planters came

Captain Cook and Hawai`i

in large numbers in search of opportunities. As a result, by the early nineteenth century, European and Euro-American peoples had become prominent figures in all the major Pacific island groups. In the next two centuries, interactions between islanders, visitors, and migrants brought rapid and often unsettling change to Pacific island societies.

SUMMARY

The Americas underwent thorough transformation in early modern times. Smallpox and other diseases sparked ferocious epidemics that devastated indigenous populations and undermined their societies. In the wake of severe depopulation, European peoples toppled imperial states, established mining and agricultural enterprises, imported enslaved African laborers, and founded colonies throughout much of the western hemisphere. Some indigenous peoples disappeared entirely as distinct groups. Others maintained their communities, identities, and cultural traditions but fell increasingly under the influence of European migrants and their Euro-American offspring. In Oceania only Guam and the Mariana Islands felt the full effects of epidemic disease and migration in the early modern era. By the late eighteenth century, however, European and Euro-American peoples with advanced technologies had thoroughly explored the Pacific Ocean basin, and epidemic diseases traveled with them to Australia and the Pacific islands. As a result, during the nineteenth and twentieth centuries, Oceania underwent a social transformation similar to the one experienced earlier by the Americas.

CHRONOLOGY

1492	First voyage of Christopher Columbus to the western hemisphere
1494	Treaty of Tordesillas
1518	Smallpox epidemic in the Caribbean
1519–1521	Spanish conquest of Mexico
1532–1540	Spanish conquest of Peru
1545	Spanish discovery of silver near Potosí
1604	Foundation of Port Royal (Nova Scotia)
1607	Foundation of Jamestown
1608	Foundation of Quebec
1623	Foundation of New Amsterdam
1630	Foundation of the Massachusetts Bay Colony
1688	Smallpox epidemic on Guam
1754–1763	French and Indian war in North America
1763	Transfer of French Canadian possessions to British rule
1768–1779	Captain James Cook's exploration of the Pacific Ocean
1788	Establishment of the first European colony in Australia

FOR FURTHER READING

Colin G. Callaway. *New Worlds for All: Indians, Europeans, and the Remaking of Early America*. Baltimore, 1997. Scholarly synthesis examining interactions and cultural exchanges between European and indigenous American peoples.

William Cronon. *Changes in the Land: Indians, Colonists, and the Ecology of New England*. New York, 1983. Brilliant study concentrating on the different ways English colonists and native peoples in colonial New England used the environment.

Philip D. Curtin. *The Rise and Fall of the Plantation Complex: Essays in Atlantic History*. 2nd ed. Cambridge, 1998. Examines plantation societies and slavery as institutions linking lands throughout the Atlantic Ocean basin.

K. R. Howe. *Where the Waves Fall: A New South Sea Island History from First Settlement to Colonial Rule*. Honolulu, 1984. A thoughtful survey of Pacific island history emphasizing interactions between islanders and visitors.

John E. Kicza. *Resilient Cultures: America's Native Peoples Confront European Colonization, 1500–1800*. Upper Saddle River, N.J., 2002. A comprehensive comparative study assessing the impact of colonization on indigenous American peoples as well as native influences on American colonial history.

Karen Ordahl Kupperman. *Indians and English: Facing Off in Early America*. Ithaca, N.Y., 2000. Fascinating reconstruction of the early encounters between English and indigenous American peoples, drawing on sources from all parties to the encounters.

Miguel León-Portilla. *The Broken Spears: The Aztec Account of the Conquest of Mexico*. Rev. ed. Boston, 1992. Offers translations of indigenous accounts of the Spanish conquest of the Aztec empire.

James Lockhart and Stuart B. Schwartz. *Early Latin America: A History of Colonial Spanish America and Brazil*. New York, 1982. The best survey of colonial Latin American history.

Gary B. Nash. *Red, White, and Black: The Peoples of Early America*. 3rd ed. Englewood Cliffs, N.J., 1992. Outstanding survey of early American history focusing on the interactions between peoples of European, African, and American ancestry.

Steve J. Stern. *Peru's Indian Peoples and the Challenge of Spanish Conquest*. 2nd ed. Madison, 1993. Scholarly analysis concentrating on the social history of indigenous peoples following the Spanish conquest of Peru.

Fig.2.
A
B
C

CHAPTER 23

Africa and the Atlantic World

B etween 1760 and 1792, a west African man known as Thomas Peters crossed the Atlantic Ocean four times. In 1760 slave raiders captured Peters, whose original African name is unknown, marched him to the coast, and sold him to French slave merchants. He traveled in a slave ship to the French colony of Louisiana, where he probably worked on a sugar plantation. But Peters was not a docile servant. He attempted to escape at least three times, and his master punished him by beating him and branding him with a hot iron. During the 1760s his French master sold Peters to an English planter, and about 1770 a Scottish landowner in North Carolina bought him.

During the 1770s, as English colonists in North America prepared to rebel against the British government, slaves of African an-

cestry considered their own prospects and looked for ways to obtain personal freedom. Peters was among them. When war broke out, he made his way with his wife and daughter to British lines and joined the Black Pioneers, a company of escaped slaves who fought to maintain British rule in the colonies. When the colonists won the war, Peters escaped to Nova Scotia with his family and many other former slaves.

Blacks were legally free in Nova Scotia, but the white ruling elites forced them to till marginal lands and live in segregated villages. In hopes of improving their lot, some two hundred black families sent Peters to London in 1790, where he promoted the establishment of a colony for former slaves in Sierra Leone. His efforts succeeded, and the next year he returned to Nova Scotia to seek

OPPOSITE PAGE: *An 18th-century engraving shows the slave trade in Africa, and the slaving ships that were used.*

recruits for the colony. In 1792 he led 1,196 blacks aboard a convoy of fifteen ships and began his fourth crossing of the Atlantic Ocean. The colonists arrived safely at Freetown, and Peters served as a leader of the black community there. Although he lived less than four months after arriving in Sierra Leone, his life and experiences personified the links connecting the lands of the Atlantic Ocean basin.

For the most part, the peoples of sub-Saharan Africa continued to follow established patterns of life in early modern times. They built states and organized societies based on kinship groups, and in west Africa and coastal east Africa they continued to trade regularly with Muslim merchants from north Africa and southwest Asia.

Yet the establishment of global trade networks brought deep change to sub-Saharan Africa. Commercial opportunities drew Europeans to the coasts of west Africa, and maritime trade soon turned west African attention to the Atlantic. Maritime commerce also helped promote the emergence of prosperous port cities and the establishment of powerful coastal kingdoms that traded through the ocean rather than the desert. In central Africa and south Africa, European merchants brought the first substantial opportunities for long-distance trade, since Muslim merchants had not ventured to those regions in large numbers.

Trade through the Atlantic profoundly affected African society because it involved human beings. Slavery had been a part of African societies for centuries, and Africans had long supplied slaves to Muslim merchants involved in trans-Saharan trade networks. The Atlantic slave trade, however, was vastly larger than the African and Islamic slave trades, and it had more serious consequences for African society. Between the fifteenth and the nineteenth centuries, it not only siphoned millions of people from their own societies but also provoked turmoil in much of sub-Saharan Africa.

The vast majority of Africans sold into the Atlantic slave trade went to the Caribbean or the Americas. Most worked on plantations cultivating cash crops for export, although some worked as domestic servants, miners, or laborers. Together they made up the largest migration in history before the nineteenth century and gave rise to an African diaspora in the western hemisphere. Under the restrictive conditions of slavery, they could not reconstitute African societies, but they preserved some African traditions and blended them with European and American traditions to create hybrid African-American societies.

AFRICAN POLITICS AND SOCIETY IN EARLY MODERN TIMES

At the start of the early modern era, African peoples lived under a variety of political organizations, including clans governed by kinship groups, regional kingdoms, city-states, and large imperial states that drew their power from the trans-Saharan trade. Under the influence of maritime trade, however, African patterns of state development changed. In west Africa, regional kingdoms replaced imperial states as peoples organized their societies to take advantage of Atlantic as well as trans-Saharan commerce. In east Africa, Swahili city-states fell under the domination of Portuguese merchant-mariners seeking commercial opportunities in the Indian Ocean basin. The extension of trade networks also led to the formation of regional kingdoms in central Africa and south Africa. As the volume of long-distance trade grew, both Islam and Christianity became more prominent in sub-Saharan African societies.

The States of West Africa and East Africa

Between the eighth and the sixteenth centuries, powerful kingdoms and imperial states ruled the savannas of west Africa. The earliest was the kingdom of Ghana, which originated as early as the fourth or fifth century and established its dominance in the region in the eighth century. By controlling and taxing the trans-Saharan trade in gold, the kings of Ghana gained the resources they needed to field a large army and influence affairs in much of west Africa. In the thirteenth century the Mali empire replaced Ghana as the preeminent power in west Africa and continued the Ghana policy of controlling trans-Saharan trade.

In the fifteenth century the expansive state of Songhay emerged to take Mali's place as the dominant power of the western grasslands. Based in the trading city of Gao, Songhay rulers built a flourishing city-state as early as the eighth century. In the early fifteenth century, they rejected Mali authority, and in 1464 the Songhay ruler Sunni Ali (reigned 1464–1493) conquered his neighbors and consolidated the Songhay empire (1464–1591). He brought the important trading cities of Timbuktu and Jenne under his control and used their wealth to dominate the central Niger valley.

The Songhay Empire

Timbuktu, the commercial and cultural center of the Mali and Songhay empires, as sketched by a French traveler in 1828. Though long in decline, the city's mosques, mud-brick dwellings, and crowds of people bespeak a prosperous community.

Sunni Ali built an elaborate administrative and military apparatus to oversee affairs in his realm. He

Songhay Administration

instituted a hierarchy of command that turned his army into an effective military force. He also created an imperial navy to patrol the Niger River, which was an extremely important commercial highway. Songhay military might enabled Sunni Ali's successors to extend their authority north into the Sahara, east toward Lake Chad, and west toward the upper reaches of the Niger River.

The Songhay emperors presided over a prosperous land. The capital city of Gao had about seventy-five thousand residents, many of whom participated in the lucrative trans-Saharan trade that brought salt, textiles, and metal goods south in exchange for gold and slaves. The emperors were all Muslims: they supported mosques, built schools to teach the Quran, and maintained an Islamic university at Timbuktu. Like the rulers of Ghana and Mali, the Songhay emperors valued Islam as a cultural foundation for cooperation with Muslim merchants and Islamic states in north Africa.

The Songhay empire dominated west Africa for most of the sixteenth century, but it was the last of the great imperial states of the grasslands. In 1591 a musket-bearing Moroccan army trekked across the Sahara and opened fire on the previously invincible Songhay military machine.

Fall of Songhay

Songhay forces withered under the attack, and subject peoples took the opportunity to revolt against Songhay domination.

As the Songhay empire crumbled, a series of small, regional kingdoms and city-states emerged in west Africa. On the coasts Diula, Mande, and other trading peoples established a series of states that entered into commercial relations with European merchant-mariners who called at west African ports after the fifteenth century. The increasing prominence of Atlantic trade in west African society worked against the interests of imperial states such as Mali and Songhay, which had relied on control of trans-Saharan trade to finance their empires.

While regional states displaced the Songhay empire in west Africa, the Swahili city-states of east Africa fell on hard times. In 1505 a huge Portuguese naval expedition subdued all the Swahili cities from Sofala to

Swahili (swah-HEE-lee)

Map 23.1 Major sub-Saharan African states between 1500 and 1650. Locate the three largest states of Songhay, Kongo, and Kanem-Bornu. What was it about their respective locations that favored the development of such large polities?

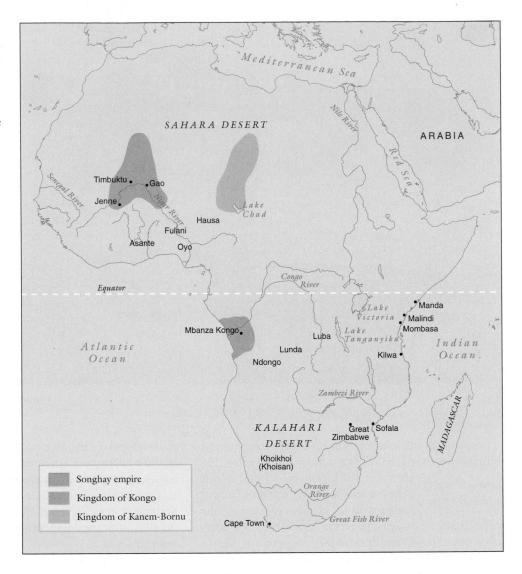

Mombasa. Portuguese forces built administrative centers at Mozambique and Malindi and constructed *Swahili Decline* forts throughout the region in hopes of controlling trade in east Africa. They did not succeed in that effort, but they disrupted trade patterns enough to send the Swahili cities into a decline from which they never fully recovered.

The Kingdoms of Central Africa and South Africa

As trade networks multiplied and linked all regions of sub-Saharan Africa, an increasing volume of commerce encouraged state building in central and south Africa. In central Africa the principal states were the kingdoms

of Kongo, Ndongo, Luba, and Lunda in the Congo River basin. Best known of them was the kingdom of Kongo, which emerged in the fourteenth century. Its rulers built a centralized state *The Kingdom of Kongo* with officials overseeing military, judicial, and financial affairs, and by the late fifteenth century Kongo embraced much of the modern-day Republic of the Congo and Angola.

In 1483 a small Portuguese fleet initiated commercial relations with the kingdom of Kongo. Within a few years, Portuguese merchants had established a close political and diplomatic relationship with the kings of Kongo. They supplied the kings with advi-

---

Ndongo (n'DAWN-goh)

sors, provided a military garrison to support the kings and protect Portuguese interests, and brought artisans and priests to Kongo.

The kings of Kongo converted to Christianity as a way to establish closer commercial and diplomatic relations with the Portuguese. The kings appreciated the

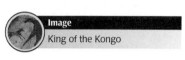
Image
King of the Kongo

fact that Christianity offered a strong endorsement of their monarchical rule and found similarities between Roman Catholic saints and the spirits recognized in Kongolese religion. King Nzinga Mbemba of Kongo, also known as King Afonso I (reigned 1506–1542), became a devout Roman Catholic and sought to convert all his subjects to Christianity. Portuguese priests in Kongo reported that he attended religious services daily and studied the Bible so zealously that he sometimes neglected to eat.

Relations with Portugal brought wealth and foreign recognition to Kongo but also led eventually to the destruction of the kingdom. In ex-

Slave Raiding in Kongo

change for their goods and services, Portuguese merchants sought high-value merchandise such as copper, ivory, and, most of all, slaves. They sometimes embarked on slaving expeditions themselves, but more often they made alliances with local authorities in interior regions and provided them with weapons in exchange for slaves. Such tactics undermined the authority of the kings, who appealed repeatedly for the Portuguese to cease or at least to limit their trade in slaves.

Over time, relations between Kongo and Portugal deteriorated, particularly after Portuguese agents began to pursue opportunities south of Kongo. In 1665 Portuguese colonists to the south even went to war with Kongo. Portuguese forces quickly defeated the Kongolese army and decapitated the king. Soon thereafter, Portuguese merchants began to withdraw from Kongo in search of more profitable business in the kingdom of Ndongo to the south. By the eighteenth century the kingdom of Kongo had largely disintegrated.

Meanwhile, Portuguese explorers were developing a brisk slave trade to the south in the kingdom of

The Kingdom of Ndongo

Ndongo, which the Portuguese referred to as Angola from the title of the king, *ngola*. During the sixteenth century, Ndongo had grown from a small chiefdom subject to the kings of Kongo to a powerful regional kingdom, largely on the basis of the wealth it was able to attract by trading directly with Portuguese merchants rather

than through Kongolese intermediaries. After 1611 the Portuguese steadily increased their influence inland by allying with neighboring peoples who delivered increasing numbers of war captives to feed the growing slave trade. Over the next several decades, Portuguese forces campaigned in Ndongo in an effort to establish a colony that would support large-scale trading in slaves.

The conquest of Angola did not come easily. For forty years Queen Nzinga (reigned 1623–1663) led spirited resistance against Portuguese forces. Nzinga came from a long line of

Queen Nzinga

warrior kings. She dressed as a male warrior when leading troops in battle and insisted that her subjects refer to her as king rather than queen. She mobilized central African peoples against her Portuguese adversaries, and she allied with Dutch mariners who also traded on the African coast. Her aim was to drive the Portuguese from her land, then expel the Dutch, and finally create a central African empire embracing the entire lower Congo basin.

Although she was an effective military leader, Nzinga was unable to oust Portuguese forces from Ndongo. When Nzinga died, Portuguese forces faced less capable resistance, and they both extended

The Portuguese Colony of Angola

and tightened their control over Angola, the first European colony in sub-Saharan Africa.

In south Africa, as in central Africa, regional kingdoms dominated political affairs. Kingdoms had begun to emerge as early as the eleventh century, largely under the influence of trade. Merchants from the Swahili city-states of coastal east Africa sought gold, ivory, and

Regional Kingdoms in South Africa

slaves from the interior regions of south Africa. By controlling local commerce, chieftains increased their wealth, enhanced their power, and extended their authority. By 1300 rulers of one such kingdom had built a massive, stone-fortified city known as Great Zimbabwe, near the city of Nyanda in modern Zimbabwe, and they dominated the gold-

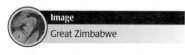
Image
Great Zimbabwe

bearing plain between the Zambesi and Limpopo rivers until the late fifteenth century.

After the fifteenth century a series of smaller kingdoms displaced the rulers of Great Zimbabwe, and Portuguese and Dutch mariners began to play a role in south African affairs. They became especially active

---

Zimbabwe (zihm-BAHB-way)

King Afonso I Protests Slave Trading in the Kingdom of Kongo

King Afonso I of Kongo wrote some twenty-four official letters to his fellow monarchs, the kings of Portugal. The letters touch on many themes—relations between Portugal and Kongo, Afonso's devotion to Christianity, and the slave trade. The following excerpts come from two letters of 1526, when Portuguese slave trading was causing serious disruption in Kongo, prompting Afonso to request help in controlling the activities of Portuguese merchants.

■ ■ ■

And we cannot reckon how great the damage [caused by Portuguese merchants] is, since the mentioned merchants are taking every day our natives, sons of the land and the sons of our noblemen and vassals and our relatives, because the thieves and men of bad conscience grab them wishing to have the things and wares of this Kingdom which they are ambitious of; they grab them and get them to be sold; and so great, Sir, is the corruption and licentiousness that our country is being completely depopulated, and Your Highness should not agree with this nor accept it as in your service. And to avoid it we need from [your] Kingdoms no more than some priests and a few people to teach in schools, and no other goods except wine and flour for the holy sacrament. That is why we beg of Your Highness to help and assist us in this matter, commanding your factors that they should not send here either merchants or wares, because it is *our will that in these Kingdoms there should not be any trade of slaves nor outlet for them.* Concerning what is referred [to] above, again we beg of Your Highness to agree with it, since otherwise we cannot remedy such an obvious damage. . . .

Moreover, Sir, in our Kingdoms there is another great inconvenience which is of little service to God, and this is that many of our people, keenly desirous as they are of the wares and things of your Kingdoms, which are brought here by your people, and in order to satisfy their voracious appetite, seize many of our people, freed and exempt men, and very often it happens that they kidnap even noblemen and the sons of noblemen, and our relatives, and take them to be sold to the white men who are in our Kingdoms. . . .

And as soon as they are taken by the white men they are immediately ironed and branded with fire, and when they are carried to be embarked, if they are caught by our guards' men the whites allege that they have bought them but they cannot say from whom, so that it is our duty to do justice and to restore to the freemen their freedom, but it cannot be done if your subjects feel offended, as they claim to be.

And to avoid such a great evil we passed a law so that any white man living in our Kingdoms and wanting to purchase goods [i.e., slaves] in any way should first inform three of our noblemen and officials of our court whom we rely upon in this matter, . . . who should investigate if the mentioned goods are captives or free men, and if cleared by them there will be no further doubt nor embargo for them to be taken and embarked. But if the white men do not comply with it they will lose the aforementioned goods. And if we do them this favor and concession it is for the part Your Highness has in it, since we know that it is in your service too that these goods are taken from our Kingdom, otherwise we should not consent to this.

• *On the basis of these letters, does it appear that King Afonso opposed all slave trading or only certain kinds of slave trading?*

SOURCE: Basil Davidson. *The African Past.* Boston: Little, Brown, 1964, pp. 191–93.

Queen Nzinga of Ndongo speaks with the Portuguese governor of Angola at his headquarters. The diplomat refused to provide Nzinga with a chair, so she seated herself on the back of a servant while her "concubines" looked on at the right.

after Dutch mariners built a trading post at Cape Town in 1652. With the aid of firearms, they claimed *European Arrival in South Africa* lands for themselves and commandeered the labor of indigenous Khoikhoi peoples. By 1700 large numbers of Dutch colonists had begun to arrive in south Africa, and by midcentury they had established settlements in the region. Their conquests laid the foundation for a series of prosperous Dutch and British colonies in sub-Saharan Africa.

Islam and Christianity in Early Modern Africa

Indigenous religions remained influential throughout sub-Saharan Africa in early modern times. Although many African peoples recognized a supreme, remote creator god, they devoted most of their attention to powerful spirits who were thought to intervene directly in human affairs. Some of those spirits were associated with geographic features such as mountains, waters, or forests, and others were believed to be the spirits of ancestors who roamed the world.

Although most Africans continued to observe their inherited religions, both Islam and Christianity attracted increasing interest in sub-Saharan Africa.

Islam was most popular in the commercial centers of west Africa and the Swahili city-states of east Africa. In the sixteenth century the trading city of Timbuktu had a prominent Islamic university and 180 schools that *Islam in Sub-Saharan Africa* taught the Quran. Students flocked to Timbuktu by the thousands from all parts of west Africa.

Most African Muslims blended Islam with indigenous beliefs and customs. The result was a syncretic brand of Islam that not only made a place for African beliefs but also permitted men and women to associate with one another on much more familiar terms than was common in north Africa and Arabia. This syncretic Islam frequently struck many devout Muslims as impure and offensive. Muslim merchants and travelers from north Africa and Arabia often commented on their shock at seeing women in tropical Africa who went out in public with bare breasts and socialized freely with men outside their own families.

Some Muslims in sub-Saharan Africa also shared these concerns about the purity of Islam. Most important of them were the Fulani of the west African savannas, who observed a strict form of Islam like that

---

Fulani (foo-LAH-nee)

practiced in north Africa and Arabia. Beginning about 1680 and continuing through the nineteenth century, the Fulani led a series of military campaigns to establish Islamic states and impose their own brand of Islam in west Africa. They founded powerful states in what is now Guinea, Senegal, Mali, and northern Nigeria, and they promoted the spread of Islam beyond the cities to the countryside by establishing Islamic schools in remote towns and villages. Their campaigns did not stamp out African religions, but they strengthened Islam in sub-Saharan Africa and laid a foundation for new rounds of Islamic state-building and conversion efforts in the nineteenth and twentieth centuries.

The Fulani and Islam

Like Islam, Christianity blended with traditional beliefs and customs when it spread in sub-Saharan Africa and sometimes formed syncretic cults. A particularly influential syncretic cult was the Antonian movement in Kongo, which flourished in the early eighteenth century. The Antonian movement began in 1704 when an aristocratic woman named Doña Beatriz proclaimed that St. Anthony of Padua had possessed her and chosen her to communicate his messages. St. Anthony was a thirteenth-century Franciscan missionary and popular preacher, and he became the patron saint of Portugal. Doña Beatriz gained a reputation for working miracles and curing diseases, and she used her prominence to promote an African form of Christianity. She taught that Jesus Christ had been a black African man, that Kongo was the true holy land of Christianity, and that heaven was for Africans. She urged Kongolese to ignore European missionaries and heed her disciples instead, and she sought to harness the widespread popular interest in her teachings and use it to end the wars plaguing Kongo.

Christianity in Sub-Saharan Africa

Doña Beatriz's movement was a serious challenge to Christian missionaries in Kongo. In 1706 they persuaded King Pedro IV of Kongo to arrest the charismatic prophetess on suspicion of heresy. Upon examining her, the missionaries determined that Doña Beatriz knowingly taught false doctrine. On their recommendation the royal government sentenced her to death and burned her at the stake. Yet the Antonian movement did not disappear: in 1708 an army of almost twenty thousand Antonians challenged King Pedro, whom they considered an unworthy ruler. Their efforts illustrate clearly the tendency of Kongolese Christians to fashion a faith that reflected their own needs and concerns as well as the interests of European missionaries.

Social Change in Early Modern Africa

Despite increased state-building activity and political turmoil, African society followed long-established patterns during the early modern era. Kinship groups, for example, continued to serve as the basis of social organization and sometimes political organization as well. Within agricultural villages throughout sub-Saharan Africa, clans under the leadership of prominent individuals organized the affairs of their kinship groups and disciplined those who violated community standards. Even in lands ruled by formal states, clan leaders usually implemented state policy at the village level.

Yet interaction with European peoples brought change to African society in early modern times. Trade brought access to European textiles and metal goods, which became popular as complements to native African wares. Trade also brought new food crops to sub-Saharan Africa. In the mid–sixteenth century, American crops such as manioc, maize, and peanuts arrived in Africa aboard Portuguese ships. These crops supplemented bananas, yams, rice, and millet, the principal staple foods of sub-Saharan Africa. The most important American crop was manioc because of its high yield and be-

American Food Crops in Sub-Saharan Africa

cause it thrived in tropical soils not well suited to cultivation of the other crops.

By the eighteenth century, bread made from manioc flour had become a staple food in much of west Africa and central Africa, where it helped to underwrite steady population growth. In 1500 C.E. the population of sub-Saharan Africa was about thirty-four million. By 1600 it had increased to forty-four million, and it continued climbing to sixty million in 1800. This strong demographic expansion is all the more remarkable because it took place precisely when millions of Africans underwent an involuntary, forced migration to destinations in the Caribbean and the Americas.

Population Growth

THE ATLANTIC SLAVE TRADE

Of all the processes that linked Africa to the larger Atlantic world in early modern times, the most momentous was the Atlantic slave trade. From the fifteenth to the nineteenth century, European peoples looked to

Africa as a source of labor for large plantations that they established in the western hemisphere. In exchange for slaves, African peoples received European manufactured products—most notably firearms. Only in the nineteenth century did the Atlantic slave trade and, in most places, slavery itself come to an end.

Foundations of the Slave Trade

Until the nineteenth century many settled peoples of the world utilized slave labor in some form. Slavery was common throughout Africa after the Bantu migrations spread agriculture to all parts of the continent. As in other societies, most slaves in Africa were war captives, although criminals and individuals expelled from their clans also fell into slavery. Once enslaved, an individual had no personal or civil rights. Owners could punish slaves at will and sell them as chattel. African slaves usually worked as cultivators in societies far from their homes, although some worked as administrators, soldiers, or even highly placed advisors. The Songhay emperors, for example, often employed slaves as administrators and soldiers, since the rulers distrusted free nobles, whom they considered excessively ambitious and undependable.

Slavery in Africa

Law and society made African slavery different from bondage in Europe, Asia, and other lands. African law did not recognize private property but, rather, vested ownership of land in communities. Thus wealth and power in Africa came not from the possession of land but from control over the human labor that made land productive. Slaves were thus an important means of measuring wealth. Those who controlled large numbers of individuals were able to harvest more crops and accumulate more wealth than others. Africans routinely purchased slaves to enlarge their families, and they often assimilated slaves into their kinship groups so that within a generation a slave might obtain both freedom and an honorable position in a new family or clan.

After the eighth century, Muslim merchants from north Africa, Arabia, and Persia sought African slaves for sale and distribution to destinations in the Mediterranean basin, southwest Asia, India, and even southeast Asia and China. When traditional sources proved insufficient to satisfy the demand for slaves, merchants created new supplies by raiding villages and capturing innocent individuals. Merchants then transported the freshly recruited slaves across the Sahara desert or boarded them on ships at the Swahili port cities of east Africa.

The Islamic Slave Trade

Between the eighth and the twentieth centuries, as many as ten million Africans may have left their homeland to feed the Islamic slave trade.

By the time Europeans ventured to sub-Saharan Africa in the fifteenth and sixteenth centuries, traffic in slaves was a well-established feature of African society, and a system for capturing, selling, and distributing slaves had functioned effectively for more than five hundred years. After 1450 European peoples tapped existing networks and dramatically expanded commerce in African slaves even as they shifted its focus to the Atlantic Ocean basin. This Atlantic slave trade profoundly influenced the development of societies throughout the Atlantic Ocean basin.

Human Cargoes

The Atlantic slave trade began small, but it grew steadily and eventually reached enormous proportions. The earliest European slave traders were Portuguese explorers who, in 1441, seized twelve African men and took them to Portugal as slaves. Portuguese mariners encountered stiff resistance when they attempted to capture slaves, as African warriors fired thousands of poison-tipped arrows at gangs of would-be slave raiders. Soon, however, the mariners learned that they could purchase slaves rather than capture them. By 1460 they were delivering five hundred slaves per year to Portugal and Spain, where they usually worked as miners, porters, or domestic servants.

Image
Slave-trading post on the African coast

Slave traders also delivered their human cargoes to Portuguese island colonies in the Atlantic. There was no supply of labor to work plantations in the Azores, the Madeiras, the Cape Verde Islands, and São Tomé, all of which were uninhabited when explorers discovered them in the fifteenth century. Sugar planters on the island of São Tomé in particular called for slaves in increasing quantities. By the 1520s some two thousand slaves per year went to São Tomé. By the 1530s Portuguese entrepreneurs had extended the use of slave labor to Brazil, which eventually became the wealthiest of the sugar-producing lands of the western hemisphere.

The Early Slave Trade

Spanish explorers and conquerors also sought laborers to work lands in the Caribbean and the Americas. As imported diseases ravaged indigenous populations, the conquerors found themselves with few laborers to work the land. Gradually Spanish settlers began to rely on imported African slaves as laborers. In 1518 the first shipment of slaves went directly from west Africa to the Caribbean, where they worked on recently established sugar plantations. By the early seventeenth century, English colonists had introduced slaves also to the North American mainland.

The demand for labor in the western hemisphere stimulated a profitable commerce known as the trian-

Triangular Trade

gular trade, since European ships often undertook voyages of three legs. On the first leg they carried horses and European manufactured goods—especially firearms—which they exchanged in Africa for slaves. The second leg took Africans to Caribbean and American destinations.

Upon arrival merchants sold their human cargoes to plantation owners for two to three times what they had cost in Africa. In sugar-producing regions they often bartered slaves for sugar or molasses. Then they filled their vessels' hulls with American products before embarking on their voyage back to Europe.

At every stage of the process, the slave trade was a brutal and inhumane business. The original capture of slaves in Africa was almost always a violent affair. As European demand for slaves grew, some African chieftains organized raiding parties to seize individuals from neighboring societies. Others launched wars for the purpose of capturing victims for the slave trade. They often snatched individuals right out of their homes, fields, or villages: millions of lives changed instantly, as slave raiders grabbed their quarries and then immediately spirited them away in captivity. Bewilderment and anger was the lot not only of the captives but also of their family members, who would never again see their kin.

Following capture, enslaved individuals underwent a forced march to the coast, where they lived in hold-

The Middle Passage

ing pens until a ship arrived to transport them to the western hemisphere. Then they embarked on the dreadful "middle passage," the trans-Atlantic journey aboard filthy and crowded slave ships. Enslaved passengers traveled belowdecks in hideously cramped quarters. Conditions were so bad that many slaves attempted to starve themselves to death or mounted revolts. Ship crews often treated the unwilling passengers with cruelty and con-

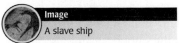
Image
A slave ship

tempt. Crew members used tools to pry open the mouths of those who refused to eat and pitched sick individuals into the ocean rather than have them waste limited supplies of food.

A bronze plaque from Benin offers an early African view of Europeans: it depicts a Portuguese soldier armed with a musket and accompanied by a dog.

Barring difficulties, the journey to Caribbean and American destinations took four to six weeks, during which heat, cold, and disease levied a heavy toll on the human cargo. During the early days of the slave trade, mortality could exceed 50 percent. As the volume of the trade grew, slavers provided better nourishment and facilities for their cargoes, and mortality eventually declined to about 5 percent per voyage. Over the course of the Atlantic slave trade, however, approximately one-quarter of individuals enslaved in Africa did not survive the middle passage.

The Impact of the Slave Trade in Africa

Before 1600 the Atlantic slave trade operated on a modest scale: on average about two thousand slaves left Africa annually during the late fifteenth and six-

Volume of the Slave Trade
teenth centuries. During the seventeenth century, slave exports rose dramatically to twenty thousand per year. The high point of the slave trade came in the eighteenth century, when the number of slaves exported to the Americas averaged fifty-five thousand per year. During the 1780s slave arrivals averaged eighty-eight thousand per year, and in some individual years they exceeded one hundred thousand. From beginning to end the Atlantic slave trade brought about twelve mil-

lion Africans to the western hemisphere. An additional four million or more died before arriving.

The impact of the slave trade varied over time and from one African society to another. Some societies largely escaped the slave trade because their lands were distant from the major slave ports on the west African coast. Those societies that raided, took captives, and sold slaves to Europeans profited handsomely from the trade, as did the port cities and the states that coordinated trade with European merchants. Asante, Dahomey, and Oyo peoples, for example, took advantage of the slave trade to obtain firearms from European merchants and build powerful states in west Africa.

On the whole, however, Africa suffered serious losses from the slave trade. The Atlantic slave trade

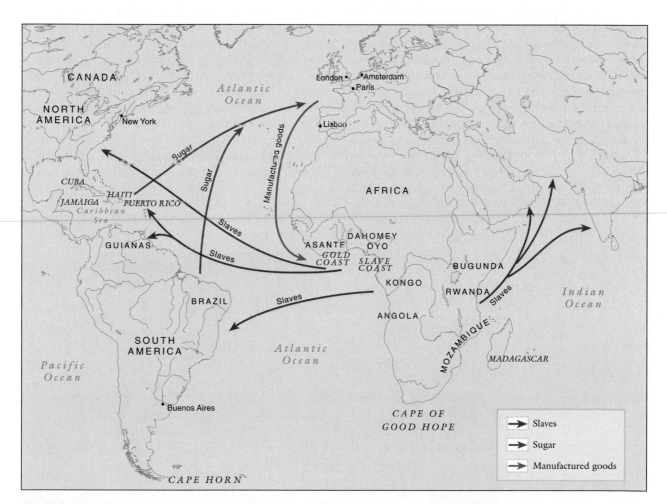

Map 23.2 Origins and destinations of slaves, sugar, and manufactured goods in the Atlantic slave trade between 1500 and 1800.
Note the "triangular" pattern of the Atlantic trade routes between Europe, Africa, and the Americas. Why were most slaves in the Atlantic system taken from west/central Africa, and where were they taken?

alone deprived African societies of about sixteen million individuals, in addition to several million others

Social Effects of the Slave Trade

consumed by the continuing Islamic slave trade during the early modern era. Although total African population rose during the early modern era, partly because American food crops enriched diets, several individual societies experienced severe losses because of the slave trade. West African societies between Senegal and Angola were especially vulnerable to slave raiding because of their proximity to the most active slave ports.

While diverting labor from Africa to other lands, the slave trade also distorted African sex ratios, since approximately two-thirds of all exported slaves were males. Slavers preferred young men between fourteen and thirty-five years of age, since they had the best potential to provide heavy labor over an extended period of time. This preference for male slaves had social implications for lands that provided slaves. By the late eighteenth century, for example, women made up more than two-thirds of the adult population of Angola. This sexual imbalance encouraged Angolans to practice polygamy and forced women to take on duties that in earlier times had been the responsibility of men.

Apart from its demographic and social effects, the slave trade brought turmoil to African societies. Vio-

Political Effects of the Slave Trade

lence escalated especially after the late seventeenth century, when African peoples increasingly exchanged slaves for European firearms. When the kingdom of Dahomey obtained effective firearms, for example, its armies were able to capture slaves from unarmed neighboring societies and exchange them for more weapons. During the eighteenth century, Dahomey expanded rapidly and absorbed neighboring societies by increasing its arsenal of firearms and maintaining a constant flow of slaves to the coast. By no means did all African states take such advantage of the slave trade, but Dahomey's experience illustrates the potential of the slave trade to alter the patterns of African politics and society.

THE AFRICAN DIASPORA

Some slaves worked as urban laborers or domestic servants, and in Mexico and Peru many worked also as miners. The vast majority, however, provided agricultural labor on plantations in the Caribbean or the Americas. There they cultivated cash crops that made their way into commercial arteries linking lands throughout the Atlantic Ocean basin. Although deprived of their freedom, slaves often resisted their bondage, and they built hybrid cultural traditions compounded of African, European, and American elements. Most European and American states ended the slave trade and abolished slavery during the nineteenth century. By that time the African diaspora—the dispersal of African peoples and their descendants—had left a permanent mark throughout the western hemisphere.

Armed escorts march a group of freshly captured Africans to the coast for sale in slave markets.

Plantation Societies

Most African slaves went to plantations in the tropical and subtropical regions of the western hemisphere. Spanish colonists established the first of these plantations in 1516 on the island of Hispaniola (which embraces modern Haiti and the Dominican Republic) and soon extended them to Mexico as well. Beginning in the 1530s Portuguese entrepreneurs organized plantations in Brazil, and by the early seventeenth century English, Dutch, and French plantations had also appeared in the Caribbean and the Americas.

Cash Crops Many of these plantations produced sugar, which was one of the most lucrative cash crops of early modern times. But plantations produced other crops as well, including tobacco, rice, and indigo. By the eighteenth century many plantations concentrated on the cultivation of cotton, and coffee had begun to emerge as a plantation specialty.

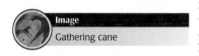

Regardless of the crops they produced, Caribbean and American plantations had certain elements in common. All of them specialized in the production and export of commercial crops. They all also relied almost exclusively on slave labor. Plantations also featured a sharp, racial division of labor: small numbers of European or Euro-American supervisors governed plantation affairs, and large numbers of African or African-American slaves performed most of the community's physical labor.

Regional Differences In spite of their structural similarities, plantation societies differed considerably from one region to another. In the Caribbean and South America, slave populations usually were unable to sustain their numbers by natural means. This was due partly to the impact of tropical diseases such as malaria and yellow fever, and partly to the brutal working conditions the slaves faced on the plantations. Moreover, since most slaves were male, slave communities did not reproduce quickly.

Thus, in the Caribbean and South America, plantation owners demanded a continuous supply of slaves to maintain their workforces. Of all the slaves delivered from Africa to the western hemisphere, about half went to Caribbean destinations, and a third more went to Brazil.

Only about 5 percent of enslaved Africans went to North American destinations. Diseases there were less threatening than in the Caribbean and Brazil. More-over, North American planters imported larger numbers of female slaves and encouraged their slaves to form families and bear children.

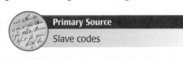

Their support for slave families was especially strong in the eighteenth century, when the prices of slaves direct from Africa rose dramatically.

Resistance to Slavery No matter where they lived, slaves did not meekly accept their status but, like Thomas Peters, resisted it in numerous ways. Some forms of resistance were mild but costly to slave owners: slaves often worked slowly for their masters but diligently in their own gardens, for example. Sometimes they sabotaged plantation equipment or work routines. More seriously, slaves resisted by running away. Runaways known as maroons gathered in remote regions and built their own self-governing communities. Many maroons had gained military experience in Africa, and they organized escaped slaves into effective military forces. Maroon communities flourished throughout slave-holding regions of the western hemisphere, and some of them survived for centuries. In present-day Suriname, for example, the Saramaka people maintain an elaborate oral tradition that traces their descent from eighteenth-century maroons.

Slave Revolts The most dramatic form of resistance to slavery was the slave revolt. Slaves far outnumbered others in most plantation societies, and thus slave revolts brought stark fear to plantation owners and supervisors. Yet slave revolts almost never brought slavery itself to an end, because the European and Euro-American ruling elites had access to military forces that extinguished most rebellions. Only in the French sugar colony of Saint-Domingue did a slave revolt abolish slavery as an institution (1793). Indeed, the slaves of Saint-Domingue declared independence from France, renamed the land Haiti, and established a self-governing republic (1804). The Haitian revolution terrified slave owners and inspired slaves throughout the western hemisphere, but no other slave rebellion matched its accomplishments.

Slavery and Economic Development The physical labor of African and African-American slaves made crucial contributions to the building of new societies in the Americas and also to the making of the early modern world as a whole. Slave labor cultivated many of the crops and extracted many of the minerals that made their way around the world in the global trade networks of the early modern era. Although slaves themselves did not enjoy the fruits of

Slaves were vulnerable to cruel treatment that often provoked them to run away from their plantations or even mount revolts. A French visitor to Brazil in the early nineteenth century depicted a Portuguese overseer administering a brutal whipping to a bound slave on a plantation near Rio de Janeiro.

their labors, without them it would have been impossible for prosperous new societies to emerge in the Americas during the early modern era.

The Making of African-American Cultural Traditions

Enslaved Africans did not enjoy the luxury of maintaining their inherited cultural traditions in the western hemisphere. When packed in slave ships for the middle passage, they found themselves in the company of Africans from societies other than their own. When sold to masters in the Caribbean and the Americas, they joined societies shaped by European and American traditions. In those new circumstances, then, slaves constructed distinctive African-American cultural traditions.

European languages were the dominant tongues in the slave societies of the western hemisphere, but slave communities frequently spoke a creole tongue that drew on several African and European languages. In the low country of South Carolina and Georgia, for example, slaves made up about three-quarters of the population in the eighteenth century and regularly communicated in the creole languages Gullah and Geechee, respectively.

African and Creole Languages

Like their languages, slaves' religions combined elements from different societies. Some slaves from Africa were Christians, and many others converted to Christianity after their arrival in the western hemisphere. Most Africans and African-Americans, however, practiced a syncretic faith that made considerable room for African interests and traditions. Because they developed mostly in plantation societies under conditions of slavery, these syncretic religions usually did not create an institutional structure or establish a hierarchy of priests and officials. Yet in several cases—most notably Vodou in Haiti, Santeria in Cuba, and Candomblé in Brazil—they became exceedingly popular.

African-American Religions

All the syncretic African-American religions drew inspiration from Christianity: they met in parish churches, sought personal salvation, and made use of Christian paraphernalia such as holy water, candles, and statues. Yet they also preserved African traditions. They associated African deities with Christian saints and relied heavily on African rituals such as drumming, dancing, and sacrificing animals. They also preserved beliefs in spirits and supernatural powers: magic, sorcery, witchcraft, and spirit possession all played prominent roles in African-American religions.

African-American Cultural Traditions

African traditions also made their effects felt throughout much of the western hemisphere. Slaves introduced African foods to Caribbean and American societies and helped give rise to distinctive hybrid cuisines. They combined African okra, for example, with European-style sautéed vegetables and American shellfish to produce magnificent gumbos, which found their way to Euro-American as well as African-American tables. Slaves introduced rice cultivation to tropical and subtropical regions. They also built houses, fashioned clay pots, and wove grass baskets in west African styles. In many ways the African diaspora influenced the ways all peoples lived in plantation societies.

The End of the Slave Trade and the Abolition of Slavery

Olaudah Equiano

Almost as old as the Atlantic slave trade itself were voices calling for its abolition. The American and French revolutions, with their calls for liberty and universal human rights, stimulated the abolitionist cause. Africans also took up the struggle to abolish commerce in human beings. Frequent slave revolts in the eighteenth and nineteenth centuries made the institution of slavery an expensive and dangerous business. Some freed slaves contributed to the abolitionist cause by writing books that exposed the brutality of institutional slavery. Most notable of them was the west African Olaudah Equiano (1745–1797), who in 1789 published an autobiography detailing his experiences as a slave and a free man. Captured at age ten in his native Benin (in modern Nigeria), Equiano worked as a slave in the West Indies, Virginia, and Pennsylvania. He accompanied one of his masters on several campaigns of the Seven Years' War before purchasing his freedom in 1766. The book became a best-seller, and Equiano traveled throughout the British isles giving speeches and denouncing slavery as an evil institution. He lobbied government officials and members of Parliament, and his efforts strengthened the antislavery movement in England.

The Economic Costs of Slavery

Quite apart from moral and political arguments, economic forces contributed to the end of slavery and the slave trade. Indeed, it gradually became clear that slave labor did not come cheap. The possibility of rebellion forced slave societies to maintain expensive military forces. Even in peaceful times slaves were often unwilling and unproductive workers. Further-

Olaudah Equiano as depicted in the first edition of his autobiography (1789).

more, in the late eighteenth century a rapid expansion of Caribbean sugar production led to declining prices. About the same time, African slave traders and European merchants sharply increased the prices they charged for fresh slaves.

As the profitability of slavery declined, Europeans began to shift their investments from sugarcane and slaves to newly emerging manufacturing industries. Investors soon found that wage labor in factories was cheaper than slave labor on plantations. As an additional benefit, free workers spent much of their income on manufactured goods. Meanwhile, European investors realized that leaving Africans in Africa, where they could secure raw materials and buy manufactured goods in exchange, was good business.

End of the Slave Trade

In 1803 Denmark abolished trade in slaves, and other lands followed suit: Great Britain in 1807, the United States in 1808, France in 1814, the Netherlands in 1817, and Spain in 1845. The end of the slave trade did not abolish the institution of slavery itself, however, and as long as plantation slavery continued, a clandestine trade shipped slaves across the Atlantic. British naval squadrons sought to prevent this trade by conducting search-and-seizure operations, and gradually the illegal slave trade ground to a halt. The last documented ship that carried slaves across the Atlantic arrived in Cuba in 1867.

The abolition of the institution of slavery itself was a long-drawn-out process: emancipation of all slaves came in 1833 in British colonies, 1848 in French colonies, 1865 in the United States, 1886 in Cuba, and 1888 in Brazil. Saudi Arabia and Angola abolished slavery in the 1960s. Officially, slavery no longer exists, but millions of people live in various forms of involuntary servitude even today. According to the Antislavery Society for the Protection of Human Rights, debt bondage, contract labor, sham adoptions, servile marriages, and other forms of servitude still oppress more than two hundred million people, mostly in Africa, south Asia, and Latin America. Meanwhile, the legacy of the Atlantic slave trade remains visible throughout much of the western hemisphere, where the African diaspora has given rise to distinctive African-American communities.

SUMMARY

During the early modern era, the peoples of sub-Saharan Africa built states and traded with Islamic societies as they had since the eighth century C.E. Yet African peoples also experienced dramatic changes as they participated in the formation of an integrated Atlantic Ocean basin. The principal agents of change were European merchant-mariners who sought commercial opportunities in sub-Saharan Africa. They brought European manufactured goods and introduced American food crops that fueled population growth throughout Africa. But they also encouraged vast expansion of existing slave-trading networks as they sought laborers for plantations in the western hemisphere. The Atlantic slave trade violently removed at least sixteen million individuals from their home societies and caused political turmoil and social disruption throughout much of sub-Saharan Africa. Enslaved Africans and their descendants were mostly unable to build states or organize societies in the western hemisphere. But they formed an African diaspora that maintained some African traditions and profoundly influenced the development of societies in all slave-holding regions of the Caribbean and the Americas. They also collaborated with others to bring about an end to the slave trade and the abolition of slavery itself.

eighteenth century, industrialization spread rapidly to western Europe and North America, and by the late nineteenth century to Russia and Japan as well.

Alongside increased material standards of living, industrialization brought political, military, and economic strength. In western Europe, the United States, and Japan, industrialization helped underwrite processes of imperialism and colonialism. Railroads, steamships, telegraphs, and lethal weapons enabled industrial powers to impose their rule in most of Asia and Africa in the nineteenth century, just as Euro-American settlers relied on industrial technologies to drive the indigenous peoples of North

AN AGE OF REVOLUTION, INDUSTRY, AND EMPIRE, 1750–1914

America and South America onto marginal lands.

Revolution, industrialization, and imperialism had effects that were felt around the world. Western European and North American peoples vastly strengthened their position in the world by exercising political or economic influence over other societies. They also inspired sustained resistance among colonized peoples, which eventually led to the organization of anticolonial movements. Indeed, revolution, industry, and empire fueled conflict throughout the world in the nineteenth century, and in combination they forced the world's peoples to deal with one another more systematically than ever before in history.

During the period from about 1750 to 1914, European peoples parlayed the profits they had gained from early modern trade, as well as their recent and advantageous domination of the Americas, into global hegemony. In stark contrast to the period from 1500 to 1800, by the late nineteenth century European powers controlled affairs in most of Asia and almost all of Africa, and their Euro-American cousins continued to dominate the Americas. Three historical developments—revolution, industrialization, and imperialism—help to explain how European and Euro-American peoples came to dominate so much of the world.

Revolution transformed societies in North America, France, Haiti, and South America during the late eighteenth and early nineteenth centuries. Although the results of each revolution were different, Enlightenment values of freedom, equality, and popular sovereignty played a large role in each. Revolutions also had a profound effect on the organization of societies in the Atlantic Ocean basin. First in Europe and later in the Americas as well, revolutions and the conflicts that followed from them encouraged the formation of national identities.

The idea of organizing states around national communities eventually influenced political development throughout the world. While organizing themselves into national states, western European and North American peoples also embarked on processes of industrialization. Although industrialization initially caused a great deal of discomfort and dislocation for workers, over time industrial societies became economically much stronger than agricultural societies, and industrial production brought about general improvement in material standards of living. After originating in Britain in the late

CHRONOLOGY

1441	Beginning of the Portuguese slave trade
1464–1493	Reign of Sunni Ali
1464–1591	Songhay Empire
1506–1542	Reign of King Afonso I of Kongo
1623–1663	Reign of Queen Nzinga of Ndongo
1706	Execution of Doña Beatriz
1745–1797	Life of Olaudah Equiano
1793–1804	Haitian revolution
1807	End of the British slave trade
1865	Abolition of slavery in the United States

FOR FURTHER READING

Michael L. Conniff and Thomas J. Davis. *Africans in the Americas: A History of the Black Diaspora.* New York, 1994. A comprehensive survey of African-European relations, the slave trade, and the African diaspora.

Philip D. Curtin. *The Rise and Fall of the Plantation Complex: Essays in Atlantic History.* 2nd ed. Cambridge, 1998. Examines plantation societies and slavery as institutions linking lands throughout the Atlantic Ocean basin.

———, ed. *Africa Remembered: Narratives by West Africans from the Era of the Slave Trade.* Madison, 1967. Translations of works in which ten enslaved Africans recounted their memories of early modern Africa.

Christopher Ehret. *The Civilizations of Africa: A History to 1800.* Charlottesville, Va., 2002. An important contribution that views Africa in the context of world history.

David Eltis. *The Rise of African Slavery in the Americas.* Cambridge, 1999. Emphasizes both the economic and the cultural foundations of Atlantic slavery.

Joseph E. Harris, ed. *Global Dimensions of the African Diaspora.* 2nd ed. Washington, 1993. A collection of scholarly essays on Africans in the Americas and the larger world.

Patrick Manning. *Slavery and African Life: Occidental, Oriental, and African Slave Trades.* Cambridge, 1990. Concentrates on the impact of the slave trade on Africa.

Sidney Mintz. *Sweetness and Power: The Place of Sugar in Modern History.* New York, 1985. Important study of sugar, slavery, politics, and society by a prominent anthropologist.

John Thornton. *Africa and Africans in the Making of the Atlantic World, 1400–1800.* 2nd ed. New York, 1997. A rich analysis of African peoples and their roles in the Atlantic Ocean basin.

Jan Vansina. *Paths in the Rainforest: Toward a History of Political Tradition in Equatorial Africa.* Madison, 1990. A thoughtful analysis that considers both native traditions and external influences on African history.

CHAPTER 24

Tradition and Change in East Asia

In January 1601 a mechanical clock chimed the hours for the first time in the city of Beijing. In the early 1580s, devices that Chinese called "self-ringing bells" had arrived at the port of Macau with Portuguese merchants. Reports of them soon spread to the emperor in Beijing. The Roman Catholic missionary Matteo Ricci conceived the idea of awing the emperor with mechanical clocks and then persuading him and his subjects to convert to Christianity. From his post at Macau, Ricci let imperial authorities know that he could supply the emperor with a chiming clock. When the emperor Wanli granted him permission to travel to Beijing and establish a mission, Ricci took with him a large mechanical clock intended for public display and a smaller clock for the emperor's personal use.

Chiming mechanical clocks enchanted Wanli and his court and soon became the rage in elite society throughout China. Wealthy Chinese merchants paid handsome sums for them, and Europeans often found that business went better if they presented clocks to the government officials they dealt with. By the eighteenth century the imperial court maintained a workshop to manufacture and repair mechanical clocks and watches. Although most Chinese could not afford to purchase mechanical clocks, commoners could admire the large, chiming clock Matteo Ricci installed outside his residence in Beijing.

Chiming clocks did not have the effect that Ricci desired. The emperor showed no interest in Christianity, and the missionaries attracted only small numbers of

Wanli (wahn-LEE)

OPPOSITE PAGE: *European-style buildings on the waterfront in eighteenth-century Guangzhou, where foreign merchants conducted their business.*

Chinese converts. Yet, by opening the doors of the imperial court to the missionaries, the self-ringing bells symbolized the increasing engagement between Asian and European peoples.

By linking all the world's regions and peoples, the European voyages of exploration inaugurated a new era in world history. Yet transoceanic connections influenced different societies in very different ways. In contrast to sub-Saharan Africa, where the Atlantic slave trade provoked turmoil, east Asian lands benefited greatly from long-distance trade, since it brought silver, which stimulated their economies. East Asian societies benefited also from American plant crops that made their way across the seas as part of the Columbian exchange.

Unlike societies in the Americas, where Europeans profoundly influenced historical development from the time of their arrival, east Asian societies largely controlled their own affairs until the nineteenth century. Because of its political and cultural preeminence, China remained the dominant power in east Asia. China was also a remarkably prosperous land. Indeed, with its huge population, enormous productive capacity, and strong demand for silver, China was a leading economic powerhouse driving world trade in early modern times. By the late eighteenth century, however, China was experiencing social and economic change that eventually caused instability.

During the seventeenth and eighteenth centuries, Japan also underwent major transformations. The Tokugawa shoguns unified the Japanese islands for the first time and laid a foundation for long-term economic growth. While tightly restricting contacts and relations with the larger world, Tokugawa Japan generated a distinctive set of social and cultural traditions. Those developments helped fashion a Japan that would play a decisive role in global affairs by the twentieth century.

THE QUEST FOR POLITICAL STABILITY

During the thirteenth and fourteenth centuries, China was ruled by the Yuan dynasty (1279–1368) of nomadic Mongol warriors. Mongol overlords ignored Chinese political and cultural traditions, and they displaced Chinese bureaucrats in favor of foreign administrators. When the Yuan dynasty came to an end, the

Tokugawa (TOH-koo-GAH-wah)
shogun (SHOH-gun)

Ming emperors who succeeded it sought to erase all signs of Mongol influence and restore traditional ways to China. Looking to the Tang and Song dynasties for inspiration, they built a powerful imperial state, revived the civil service staffed by Confucian scholars, and promoted Confucian thought. Rulers of the succeeding Qing dynasty were themselves Manchus of nomadic origin, but they too worked zealously to promote Chinese ways. Ming and Qing emperors alike were deeply conservative: their principal concern was to maintain stability in a large agrarian society, so they adopted policies that favored Chinese political and cultural traditions. The state they fashioned governed China for more than half a millennium.

The Ming Dynasty

When the Yuan dynasty collapsed, the Ming dynasty (1368–1644) restored native rule to China. Hongwu (reigned 1368–1398), founder of the Ming ("brilliant") dynasty, built a tightly centralized state. As emperor, Hongwu made extensive use of mandarins, imperial officials who oversaw implementation of government policies throughout China. He also placed great trust in eunuchs on the assumption that they could not generate families who might one day challenge imperial authority. The emperor Yongle (reigned 1403–1424) launched a series of naval expeditions that went as far as Malindi in east Africa. Yongle's successors discontinued the expeditions but maintained the centralized state that Hongwu had established.

Ming Government

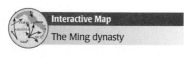

The Ming emperors were determined to prevent new invasions. In 1421 Yongle moved the capital from Nanjing in the south to Beijing to keep closer watch on the Mongols and other nomadic peoples in the north. The later Ming emperors sought to protect their realm by building new fortifications, including the Great Wall of China, along the northern border. The Great Wall had precedents dating back to the fourth century B.C.E., but its construction was a Ming-dynasty project. Workers by the hundreds of thousands labored throughout the late fifteenth and sixteenth centuries to build a stone and brick barrier

The Great Wall

Qing (chihng)

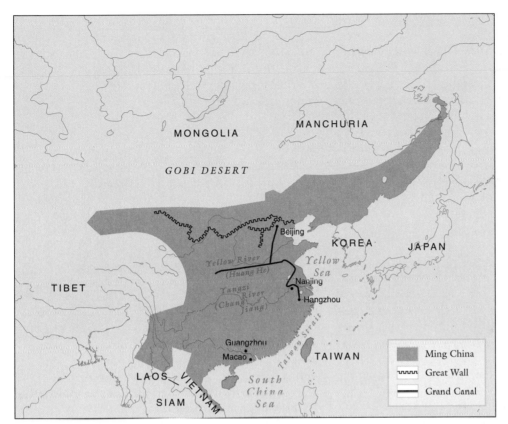

Map 24.1 Boundaries of Ming China from 1368 until 1644. Locate the old Ming capital at Nanjing and the new Ming capital at Beijing. Why would the Ming emperors have wanted to move so far north?

that ran some 2,500 kilometers (1,550 miles). The Great Wall was 10 to 15 meters (33 to 49 feet) high, and it featured watch towers, signal towers, and accommodations for troops deployed on the border.

The Ming emperors also set out to eradicate Mongol and other foreign influences and to create a stable society in the image of the Chinese past. Respect for Chinese traditions facilitated the restoration of institutions that the Mongols had ignored or suppressed. The government sponsored study of Chinese cultural traditions, especially Confucianism and the reestablishment of imperial academies and regional colleges. Most important, the Ming state restored the system of civil service examinations that Mongol rulers had neglected.

The vigor of early Ming rule did not survive beyond the mid–sixteenth century, when a series of problems weakened the dynasty. From the 1520s *Ming Decline* to the 1560s, pirates and smugglers operated almost at will along the east coast of China. Suppression of pirates took more than forty years, partly because of an increasingly inept imperial government.

The later Ming emperors lived extravagantly in the Forbidden City, a vast imperial enclave in Beijing, and received news about the outside world only from eunuch servants and administrators. The emperors sometimes ignored government affairs for decades on end, while powerful eunuchs won favor by providing for their amusement. As the eunuchs' influence increased, corruption and inefficiency spread throughout the government and weakened the Ming state.

When a series of famines struck China during the early seventeenth century, the government was unable to organize effective relief efforts. During the 1630s peasants organized revolts *Ming Collapse* throughout China. To complicate matters further, Manchu forces invaded from the north. In 1644 Chinese rebel forces captured the Ming capital at Beijing. Manchu invaders allied with an army loyal to the Ming, crushed the rebels, and recovered Beijing. The Manchus portrayed themselves as avengers who saved the capital from dangerous rebels, but they neglected to restore Ming rule. Instead, they moved their own capital to Beijing and displaced the Ming dynasty.

The emperor Yongle designed the Forbidden City as a vast, walled imperial retreat in central Beijing. Here a sculptured lion guards the Forbidden City's Gate of Supreme Harmony.

The Qing Dynasty

When the Ming dynasty fell, Manchus poured south into China from their homeland of Manchuria. The victors proclaimed a new dynasty, the Qing ("pure"), *The Manchus* which ruled China until the early twentieth century (1644–1911). The Manchus mostly were pastoral nomads whose remote ancestors had traded with China since the Qin dynasty. During the late sixteenth and early seventeenth centuries, an ambitious chieftain named Nurhaci (reigned 1616–1626) unified Manchu tribes into a centralized state and organized a powerful military force. During the 1620s and 1630s, the Manchu army captured Korea and Mongolia and launched small-scale invasions into China. After their seizure of Beijing in 1644, the Manchus moved to extend their authority throughout China. By the early 1680s they had consolidated the Qing dynasty's hold throughout the land.

The establishment of the Qing dynasty was due partly to Manchu military prowess and partly to Chinese support for the Manchus. During the 1630s and 1640s, many Chinese generals and Confucian scholar-bureaucrats deserted the Ming dynasty because of its corruption and inefficiency. The Manchu ruling elites were schooled in Chinese language and Confucian thought, and they often enjoyed more respect from the scholar-bureaucrats than the high administrators of the Ming dynasty itself.

The Manchus were careful to preserve their own ethnic and cultural identity. They outlawed intermarriage between Manchus and Chinese and forbade Chinese to travel to Manchuria or to learn the Manchurian language. Qing authorities also forced Chinese men to shave the front of their heads and grow a Manchu-style queue as a sign of submission to the dynasty.

The long reigns of two particularly effective emperors, Kangxi (1661–1722) and Qianlong (1736–1795), helped mute the tensions between Manchus and Chinese and allowed the Manchus to consolidate their hold on China. *Kangxi and His Reign* Kangxi was a Confucian scholar as well as an enlightened ruler. He studied the Confucian classics and sought to apply their teachings through his policies. Thus, for example, he organized flood-control and irrigation projects on the Confucian precept that rulers should look after the welfare of their subjects and promote agriculture. He also generously patronized Confucian schools and academies.

Kangxi was also a conqueror, and he oversaw the construction of a vast Qing empire. He conquered the island of Taiwan, where Ming loyalists had retreated after their expulsion from southern China, and absorbed it into his empire. Like his predecessors of the

Map 24.2 **Boundaries of the Qing empire from 1644 until 1911.** Compare this map with Map 24.1. Why would the Qing emperors have wanted to incorporate such extensive territories in Mongolia and Tibet into their empire?

Han and Tang dynasties, Kangxi sought to forestall problems with nomadic peoples by projecting Chinese influence into central Asia. His conquests in Mongolia and central Asia extended almost to the Caspian Sea, and he imposed a Chinese protectorate over Tibet. Kangxi's grandson Qianlong continued this expansion of Chinese influence by consolidating Kangxi's conquests in central Asia and by making Vietnam, Burma, and Nepal vassal states of the Qing dynasty.

Qianlong's reign marked the height of the Qing dynasty. Like Kangxi, Qianlong was a sophisticated *Qianlong and* and learned man. During his long, sta-*His Reign* ble, and prosperous reign, the imperial treasury bulged so much that on four occasions Qianlong canceled tax collections. Toward the end of his reign, however, Qianlong delegated many responsibilities to his favorite eunuchs. His successors continued that practice, and by the nineteenth century the Qing dynasty faced serious difficulties. Throughout the reign of Qianlong, however, China remained a wealthy and well-organized land.

The Son of Heaven and the Scholar-Bureaucrats

Although Qing rulers usually appointed Manchus to the highest political posts, they relied on the same governmental apparatus that the Ming emperors had established. Indeed, for more than five hundred years, the autocratic state created by the Ming emperor Hongwu governed China's fortunes.

If the emperor of China during the Ming and Qing dynasties was not quite a god, he certainly was more than a mere mortal. Chinese tradition held that he was the "Son of Heaven," the human *The Son* being designated by heavenly powers to *of Heaven* maintain order on the earth. He led a privileged life within the walls of the Forbidden City. Hundreds of concubines resided in his harem, and thousands of eunuchs looked after his desires. Everything about his person and the institution he represented conveyed a sense of awesome authority. The imperial wardrobe and personal effects bore designs forbidden to all others, for

Though painted in the nineteenth century, this portrait depicts Kangxi in his imperial regalia as he looked at about age fifty.

Preparations for the examinations began at an early age, either in local schools or with private tutors. By the time students were eleven or twelve years old, they had memorized several thousand characters that were necessary to deal with the Confucian curriculum, including the *Analects* of Confucius and other standard works. They followed those studies with instruction in calligraphy, poetry, and essay composition.

The examinations consisted of a battery of tests administered at the district, provincial, and metropolitan levels. Stiff official quotas restricted the number of successful candidates in each examination—only three hundred students could pass metropolitan examinations—and students frequently took the examinations several times before earning a degree.

Civil Service Examinations

The possibility of bureaucratic service—with prospects for rich social and financial rewards—ensured that competition for degrees was ferocious at all levels. Yet a degree did not ensure government service. During the Qing dynasty the empire's one million degree holders competed for twenty thousand official civil service positions, and only those who passed the metropolitan examinations could look forward to powerful positions in the imperial bureaucracy.

The Examination System and Chinese Society

Yet the examination system was a pivotal institution. By opening the door to honor, power, and rewards, the examinations encouraged serious pursuit of a formal education. Furthermore, since the system did not erect social barriers before its recruits, it provided an avenue for upward social mobility. Finally, in addition to selecting officials for government service, the education and examination system molded the personal values of those who managed day-to-day affairs in imperial China. By concentrating on Confucian classics and neo-Confucian commentaries, the examinations guaranteed that Confucianism would be at the heart of Chinese education and that Confucians would govern the state.

ECONOMIC AND SOCIAL CHANGES

By modeling their governmental structure on the centralized imperial states of earlier Chinese dynasties, the Ming and Qing emperors succeeded in their goal of restoring and maintaining traditional ways in China. They also sought to preserve the traditional hierarchical and patriarchal social order. Yet, while the emperors promoted conservative political and social policies,

instance, and the written characters of the emperor's name were taboo throughout the realm. Individuals who had the rare privilege of a personal audience with the emperor had to perform the kowtow—three kneelings and nine head knockings. Those who gave even minor offense faced having their bare buttocks flogged with bamboo canes.

Day-to-day governance of the empire fell to scholar-bureaucrats appointed by the emperor. With few exceptions these officials came from the class of well-educated and highly literate men known as the scholar-gentry. These men had earned academic degrees by passing rigorous civil service examinations, and they dominated China's political and social life.

The Scholar-Bureaucrats

China experienced economic and social changes, partly as a result of influences from abroad. Agricultural production increased dramatically and fueled rapid population growth, and global trade brought China enormous wealth. These developments deeply influenced Chinese society and partly undermined the stability that the Ming and Qing emperors sought to preserve.

The Patriarchal Family

Moralists portrayed the Chinese people as one large family, and they extended family values to the larger society. Filial piety, for example, implied not only duties of children toward their fathers but also loyalty of subjects toward the emperor. Like the imperial government, the Chinese family was hierarchical, patriarchal, and authoritarian. The father was head of the household, and he passed leadership of the family to his eldest son. The veneration of ancestors, which the state promoted as a matter of Confucian propriety, strengthened the authority of the patriarchs by honoring the male line of descent. Filial piety was the cornerstone of family values. Children had the duty to look after their parents' happiness and well-being, especially in their old age. Young children heard stories of sons who went so far as to cut off parts of their bodies to ensure that their parents had enough to eat!

Filial Piety

The social assumptions of the Chinese family extended into patrilineal descent groups such as the clan. Clans—whose members sometimes numbered in the thousands—assumed responsibilities such as the maintenance of local order, organization of local economies, and provision for welfare. Clan-supported education gave poor but promising relatives the opportunity to succeed in the civil service examinations. Finally, clans served as a means for the transmission of Confucian values from the gentry leaders to all social classes within the clan.

Within the family, Confucian principles subjected women to the authority of men. The subordination of females began at an early age. Chinese parents preferred boys over girls. Whereas a boy might have the opportunity to take the official examinations and become a government official, parents regarded a girl as a social and financial liability. Under those circumstances it was not surprising that girls were the primary victims of infanticide.

Gender Relations

During the Ming and Qing dynasties, patriarchal authority over females probably became tighter than ever before in China. Since ancient times, relatives had discouraged widows from remarriage, but social pressures increased during the Ming dynasty. Friends and relatives not only encouraged widows to honor the memory of their departed husbands but also heaped posthumous honors on those who committed suicide and followed their spouses to the grave.

Moreover, foot binding, a custom that probably originated in the Song dynasty, became exceptionally popular during the late Ming and Qing dynasties. Tightly constrained and deformed by strips of linen, bound feet could not grow naturally and so would not support the weight of an adult woman. Bound feet were small and dainty, and they sometimes inspired erotic arousal among men.

Foot Binding

The practice of foot binding became most widespread among the wealthy classes, since

Image
Chinese foot binding

it demonstrated an ability to support women who could not perform physical labor, but commoners sometimes bound the feet of especially pretty girls in hopes of arranging favorable marriages.

Marriage itself was a contractual affair whose principal purpose was to continue the male line of descent. A bride became a member of the husband's family, and her position there was one of unambiguous subservience. Women could not divorce their husbands, but men could put aside their wives in cases where there were no offspring or where the wife was guilty of adultery, theft, or disobedience.

Thus custom and law combined to strengthen patriarchal authority in Chinese families during the Ming and Qing dynasties. Yet, while family life continued to develop along traditional lines, the larger Chinese society underwent considerable change between the sixteenth and the eighteenth centuries.

Population Growth and Economic Development

China was a predominantly agricultural society, a fact that meshed agreeably with the Confucian view that land was the source of everything praiseworthy. Yet only a small fraction of China's land is suitable for planting: even today only about 11 percent is in cultivation. To feed the country's large population, China's farmers relied on intensive, garden-style agriculture that was highly productive. On its strong agrarian foundation, China supported a large population and built the most highly commercialized economy of the preindustrial world.

By intensively cultivating every available parcel of land, Chinese peasants increased their yields of tradi-

American Food Crops

tional food crops—especially rice, wheat, and millet—until the seventeenth century. As peasants approached the upper limits of agricultural productivity, Spanish merchants coming by way of the Philippines introduced American food crops to China. American maize, sweet potatoes, and peanuts permitted Chinese farmers to take advantage of soils that previously had gone uncultivated. The introduction of new crops increased the food supply and supported further population growth.

In spite of recurring epidemic diseases such as plague, China's population rose rapidly from 100 mil-

Population Growth

lion in 1500 to 160 million in 1600. By 1750 it had surged to 225 million. However, this rapid demographic growth set the stage for future economic and social problems, since agricultural production could not keep pace with population over a long term.

Although an increasing population placed pressure on Chinese resources, it offered opportunities for entrepreneurs. Indeed, entrepreneurs had access to a large labor force, which meant they were able to recruit workers readily at low cost. After the mid–sixteenth century the Chinese economy benefited also from the influx of Japanese and American silver, which stimulated trade and financed further commercial expansion.

Global trade brought tremendous prosperity to China, especially during the early Qing dynasty. Chinese workers produced vast quantities of silk, porcelain, lacquerware, and tea for consumers in the Indian Ocean basin, central Asia, and Europe. Chinese imports were relatively few, and thus the most important form of compensation for ex-

Foreign Trade

A Ming-era vase painting depicts a woman weaving silk as an attendant pours tea.

ports was silver bullion, which supported the silver-based Chinese economy and fueled manufacturing.

Economic growth and commercial expansion took place mostly in an atmosphere of tight government regulation. Although the Ming emperor Yongle had sponsored a series of maritime expeditions (1405–1433) in the Indian Ocean basin, his successors withdrew their support for such activities and even tried to prevent Chinese subjects from dealing with foreign peoples. In its effort to pacify southern China during the later seventeenth century, the Qing government tried to end maritime activity altogether. An imperial edict of 1656 forbade "even a plank from drifting to the sea," and in 1661 the emperor Kangxi ordered evacuation of the southern coastal regions. Those policies had only a limited effect, and when Qing forces pacified southern China in the 1680s, government authorities rescinded the strictest measures. Thereafter, however, Qing authorities closely supervised the activities of foreign merchants in China. Portuguese merchants were allowed to operate only at the port of Macau, and British agents had to deal exclusively with the official merchant guild in Guangzhou.

Government policies also discouraged the organization of large-scale commercial ventures by Chinese merchants. As a result, it was impossible to maintain shipyards that could construct large sailing ships capable of traveling long distances. Similarly, it was impossible to organize large trading firms like the English East India Company or the Dutch VOC.

Nevertheless, thousands of Chinese merchants worked either individually or in partnerships, plying *Trade and* the waters of the China seas to link *Migration to* China with global trade networks. Chi-*Southeast Asia* nese merchants were especially prominent in Manila, where they exchanged silk and porcelain for American silver that came across the Pacific Ocean from Mexico. They were also frequent visitors at the Dutch colonial capital of Batavia, where they supplied the VOC with silk and porcelain in exchange for silver and Indonesian spices. Entrepreneurial Chinese merchants ventured also to lands throughout southeast Asia in search of exotic tropical products for Chinese consumers. Indeed, the early modern era was an age when merchants established a prominent Chinese presence throughout southeast Asia.

China's economic expansion took place largely in the absence of technological innovation. During the Tang and Song dynasties, Chinese engineers had produced a veritable flood of inventions, and China was the world's leader in technology. Yet by early Ming times, technological innovation had slowed. Part of the explanation for the slowdown has to do with role of the government. Dur-*Government and Technology* ing the Tang and Song dynasties, the imperial government had encouraged technological innovation as a foundation of military and economic strength. In contrast, the Ming and Qing regimes favored political and social stability over technological innovation.

Image
Beijing Observatory

Alongside government policy, the abundance of skilled workers discouraged technological innovation. When employers wanted to increase production, they found that hiring additional workers was less costly than making investments in new technologies. In the short run this tactic kept most of China's population gainfully employed. Over the longer term, however, it meant that China lost technological ground to European peoples, who embarked on a round of stunning technological innovation beginning about the mid–eighteenth century.

Gentry, Commoners, Soldiers, and Mean People

Besides the emperor and his family, scholar-bureaucrats and gentry occupied the most exalted positions in Chinese society. Scholar-bureaucrats had much in common with the gentry: they came *Privileged Classes* largely from gentry ranks, and after leaving government service they usually rejoined gentry society. The scholar-bureaucrats and the gentry functioned as intermediaries between the imperial government and local society. By organizing water-control projects and public security measures, they played a crucial role in the management of local society.

Scholar-bureaucrats and gentry were easy to identify. They wore distinctive clothing—black gowns with blue borders adorned with various rank insignia—and commoners addressed them with honorific terms. They also received favorable legal treatment and enjoyed immunity from corporal punishment as well as exemption from labor service and taxes.

Most of the gentry owned land, which was their major source of income. Some were also silent business partners of merchants and entrepreneurs. Their principal source of income, however, was the government service to which their academic degrees gave them access. In contrast to landed elites elsewhere, who

SOURCES FROM THE PAST

Qianlong on Chinese Trade with England

Qing administrators tightly restricted foreign trade. Foreign merchants had to deal with government-approved agents outside the city walls of Guangzhou and had to depart as soon as they had completed their business. In 1793 a British diplomat representing King George III of England bestowed gifts on the emperor Qianlong and petitioned for the right to trade at ports other than Guangzhou. In a letter to King George, Qianlong outlined his views on Chinese trade with England. His letter also bespeaks clearly the importance of government policy for commerce and economic affairs in China.

■   ■   ■

You, O king, from afar have yearned after the blessings of our civilization, and in your eagerness to come into touch with our influence have sent an embassy across the sea bearing a memorandum. I have already taken note of your respectful spirit of submission, have treated your mission with extreme favor and loaded it with gifts, besides issuing a mandate to you, O king, and honoring you with the bestowal of valuable presents. . . .

Yesterday your ambassador petitioned my ministers to memorialize me regarding your trade with China, but his proposal is not consistent with our dynastic usage and cannot be entertained. Hitherto, all European nations, including your own country's barbarian merchants, have carried on their trade with our Celestial Empire at Guangzhou. Such has been the procedure for many years, although our Celestial Empire possesses all things in prolific abundance and lacks no product within its own borders. There was therefore no need to import the manufactures of outside barbarians in exchange for our own produce. But as the tea, silk, and porcelain which the Celestial Empire produces are absolute necessities to European nations and to yourselves, we have permitted, as a signal mark of favor, that trading agents should be established at Guangzhou, so that your wants might be supplied and your country thus participate in our beneficence. But your ambassador has now put forward new requests which completely fail to recog-

nize our throne's principle to "treat strangers from afar with indulgence," and to exercise a pacifying control over barbarian tribes the world over. . . . Your England is not the only nation trading at Guangzhou. If other nations, following your bad example, wrongfully importune my ear with further impossible requests, how will it be possible for me to treat them with easy indulgence? Nevertheless, I do not forget the lonely remoteness of your island, cut off from the world by intervening wastes of sea, nor do I overlook your excusable ignorance of the usages of our Celestial Empire. I have consequently commanded my ministers to enlighten your ambassador on the subject, and have ordered the departure of the mission. . . .

If, after the receipt of this explicit decree, you lightly give ear to the representations of your subordinates and allow your barbarian merchants to proceed to Zhejiang and Tianjin, with the object of landing and trading there, the ordinances of my Celestial Empire are strict in the extreme, and the local officials, both civil and military, are bound reverently to obey the law of the land. Should your vessels touch the shore, your merchants will assuredly never be permitted to land or to reside there, but will be subject to instant expulsion. In that event your barbarian merchants will have had a long journey for nothing. Do not say that you were not warned in due time! Tremblingly obey and show no negligence! A special mandate!

• *What considerations might have prompted the Chinese government to take such a restrictive approach to foreign trade?*

SOURCE: J. O. P. Bland. *Annals and Memoirs of the Court of Peking.* Boston: Houghton Mifflin, 1914, pp. 325–31. (Translation slightly modified.)

This engraving depicts a peasant couple in harness pulling a plow. Note that the man wears the braided queue that Manchus required their male Chinese subjects to wear.

often lived on rural estates, China's gentry resided largely in cities and towns, where they tended to political, social, and financial affairs.

Confucian tradition ranked three broad classes of commoners below the gentry: peasants, artisans or *Working Classes* workers, and merchants. By far the biggest class consisted of peasants· a designation that covered everyone from day laborers to petty landlords. Confucian principles regarded peasants as the most honorable of the three classes, since they performed honest labor and supplied the entire population with food.

The category of artisans and workers encompassed a wide spectrum of occupations. Despite their lower status, crafts workers, tailors, barbers, and physicians generally enjoyed higher income than peasants did. Artisans and workers were usually employees of the state or of gentry and merchant families, but they also pursued their occupations as self-employed persons.

Merchants, from street peddlers to individuals of enormous wealth and influence, ranked at the bottom *Merchants* of the Confucian social hierarchy. Because moralists looked upon them as unscrupulous social parasites, merchants enjoyed little legal protection. Yet Chinese merchants often garnered official support for their enterprises through bribery of government bureaucrats or through profit-sharing arrangements with gentry families. Indeed, the participation of gentry families in commercial ventures such as

warehousing, money lending, and pawnbroking blurred the distinction between gentry and merchants. In addition, merchants blurred the distinction further by preparing their sons for government examinations, which could result in appointment to civil service positions and promotion to gentry status.

Although China was still a basically agricultural land under the Ming and the Qing, the increasing prominence of artisans and merchants demonstrated that manufacturing and commerce had become much more economically important than in ancient times. As a result, those who could exploit opportunities had the potential to lead comfortable lives and even to climb into the ranks of the privileged gentry class. Yet Chinese merchants and artisans did not forge cooperative relationships with government authorities as their counterparts in England and the Netherlands did.

The principal concern of late Ming and Qing authorities was to preserve the stability of a large agrarian society, not to promote rapid economic development through trade. Thus Chinese authorities did not adopt policies designed to strengthen both merchants and the state by authorizing merchants to pursue their efforts aggressively in the larger world.

Beyond the Confucian social hierarchy were members of the military forces and the so-called mean people, such as slaves, indentured servants, *Lower Classes* entertainers, and prostitutes. Confucian moralists regarded armed forces as a wretched but necessary evil and attempted to avoid military dominance of society by placing civilian bureaucrats in the highest command positions, even at the expense of military effectiveness.

THE CONFUCIAN TRADITION AND NEW CULTURAL INFLUENCES

The Ming and Qing emperors looked to Chinese traditions for guidance in framing their cultural as well as their political and social policies. They provided generous support for Confucianism, and they ensured that formal education in China revolved around Confucian thought and values. Yet demographic and urban growth also encouraged the emergence of a vibrant popular culture in Chinese cities, and European missionaries acquainted the Chinese with Roman Catholic Christianity and European science and technology as well.

Neo-Confucianism and Pulp Fiction

Imperial sponsorship of Chinese cultural traditions meant primarily support for the Confucian tradition, especially as systematized by the Song dynasty scholar Zhu Xi, the most prominent architect of neo-Confucianism. Zhu Xi combined the moral, ethical, and political values of Confucius with the logical rigor and speculative power of Buddhist philosophy. He emphasized the values of self-discipline, filial piety, and obedience to established rulers, all of which appealed to Ming and Qing emperors seeking to maintain stability in their vast realm. To promote Confucian values, the Ming and Qing emperors supported educational programs at many levels throughout the land.

While the imperial courts promoted Confucianism, a lively popular culture took shape in the cities of China. *Popular Culture* Most urban residents did not have an advanced education and knew little about Confucius. Many were literate, however, and they found that popular novels met their needs for entertainment and diversion. Although Confucian scholars thought popular novels were crude, printing made it possible to produce them cheaply and in large numbers, and urban residents eagerly consumed them. Many of the novels had little literary merit, but their tales of conflict, horror, wonder, excitement, and sometimes unconcealed pornography appealed to readers.

Some popular novels, however, did offer thoughtful reflections on the world and human affairs. The historical novel *The Romance of the Three Kingdoms,* *Popular Novels* for example, explored the political intrigue that followed the collapse of the Han dynasty. *The Dream of the Red Chamber* told the story of cousins deeply in love who could not marry because of their families' wishes. Through the prism of a sentimental love story, the novel shed fascinating light on the dynamics of wealthy scholar-gentry families.

The Return of Christianity to China

Nestorian Christians had established churches and monasteries in China as early as the seventh century C.E., and Roman Catholic communities were prominent in Chinese commercial centers during the Yuan dynasty. After the outbreak of epidemic plague and the collapse of the Yuan dynasty in the fourteenth century, however, Christianity disappeared from China. When Roman Catholic missionaries returned in the sixteenth century, they had to start from scratch in their efforts to win converts.

Founder of the mission to China was the Italian Jesuit Matteo Ricci (1552–1610), who had the ambitious goal of converting China to Christianity, beginning with the Ming emperor Wanli. *Matteo Ricci* Ricci was a brilliant and learned man as well as a polished diplomat, and he became a popular figure at the Ming court. Upon arrival at Macau in 1582, Ricci immersed himself in the study of the Chinese language and the Confucian classics. By the time he first traveled to Beijing and visited the imperial court in 1601, Ricci was able to write learned Chinese and converse fluently with Confucian scholars.

Ricci's mastery of Chinese language and literature opened doors for the Jesuits, who then dazzled their hosts with European science, technology, and mechanical gadgetry such as glass prisms, harpsichords, and especially "self-ringing bells"—spring-driven mechanical clocks that chimed the hours.

The Jesuits sought to capture Chinese interest with European science and technology, but their ultimate goal was to win converts. Ricci, for example, tried to make Christianity seem familiar by arguing that the doctrines of Confucius and Jesus were very similar, if not identical. *Confucianism and Christianity* The Jesuits also held religious services in the Chinese language and allowed converts to continue the time-honored practice of venerating their ancestors.

In spite of their tolerance, flexibility, and genuine respect for their hosts, the Jesuits attracted few converts in China. By the mid–eighteenth century, Chinese Christians numbered about 200,000—a tiny proportion of the Chinese population of 225 million. Many Chinese hesitated to adopt Christianity partly because of its exclusivity: like Islam, Christianity claimed to be the only true religion, so conversion implied that the time-honored traditions of Confucianism, Daoism, and Buddhism were fallacious creeds—a proposition most Chinese were unwilling to accept.

Ultimately, the Roman Catholic mission in China came to an end because of squabbles between the Jesuits and members of the Franciscan and Dominican orders, who also sought converts in China. Jealous of the Jesuits' *End of the Jesuit Mission* presence at the imperial court, they complained to the pope about their rivals' tolerance of Chinese traditions. The pope sided with the critics and in the early eighteenth century issued several proclamations ordering missionaries in China to conduct services according to

Zhu Xi (ZHOO SHEE)
neo-Confucianism (NEE-oh kuhn-FYEW-shuhn-iz'm)

Buddhism (BOO-diz'm)

European standards. In response, the emperor Kangxi ordered an end to the preaching of Christianity in China. By the mid–eighteenth century, the mission had weakened so much that it had effectively come to an end.

The Roman Catholic mission to China did not attract large numbers of converts, but it nonetheless had important cultural effects. In letters, reports, and other writings distributed widely throughout Europe, the Jesuits described China as an orderly and rational society. The rational morality of Confucianism appealed to the Enlightenment philosophes, who sought alternatives to Christianity as the foundation for ethics and morality. Thus for the first time since Marco Polo, strong European interest in east Asian societies was stimulated.

THE UNIFICATION OF JAPAN

During the late sixteenth and early seventeenth centuries, the political unification of Japan ended an extended period of civil disorder. Like the Ming and Qing emperors in China, the Tokugawa shoguns

sought to lay a foundation for long-term political and social stability by promoting conservative values and tightly restricting foreign influence in Japan. As in China, however, demographic expansion and economic growth fostered social and cultural change in Japan, and merchants introduced Chinese and European influences into Japan.

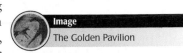
Image
The Golden Pavilion

The Tokugawa Shogunate

From the twelfth through the sixteenth century, a *shogun* ("military governor") ruled Japan through retainers who received political rights and large estates in exchange for military services. Theoretically, the shogun ruled as a temporary stand-in for the Japanese emperor. In fact, however, the emperor was nothing more than a figurehead. After the fourteenth century the conflicting ambitions of shoguns and retainers led to constant turmoil, and by the sixteenth century Japan was in a state of civil war. Japanese historians often refer to the sixteenth century as the era of *sengoku*, "the country at war."

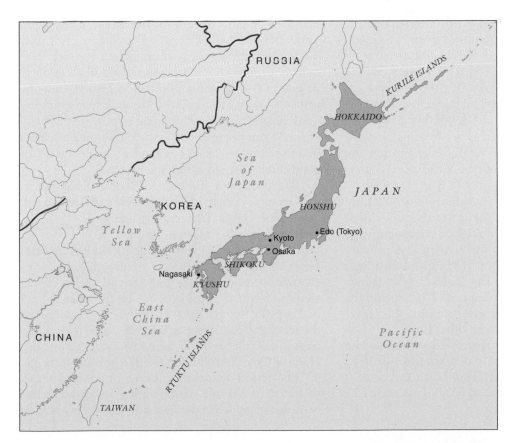

Map 24.3 Territories of Tokugawa Japan from 1600 to 1867. Consider Japan's position with regard to China, Korea, and Russia. Would it have been easy or difficult to enforce the ban on foreign trade during most of this period?

Toward the end of the sixteenth century, a series of military leaders brought about the unification of the land. In 1600 the last of those *Tokugawa Ieyasu* leaders, Tokugawa Ieyasu (reigned 1600–1616), established a military government known as the Tokugawa *bakufu* ("tent government," since it theoretically was only a temporary replacement for the emperor's rule). Ieyasu and his descendants ruled the bakufu as shoguns from 1600 until the end of the Tokugawa dynasty in 1867.

The principal aim of the Tokugawa shoguns was to prevent the return of civil war. Consequently, the shoguns needed to control the *daimyo* ("great names"), powerful territorial lords who ruled most of Japan from their vast, hereditary landholdings. Each maintained a government, an independent judiciary, and schools, and each circulated paper money. Moreover, after the mid–sixteenth century, many daimyo established relationships with European mariners, from whom they learned how to manufacture and use gunpowder weapons, which they turned against one another.

From the castle town of Edo (modern Tokyo), the shogun sought to extend his control over the daimyo *Control of the Daimyo* through the policy of "alternate attendance," which required daimyo to maintain their families at Edo and spend every other year at the Tokugawa court. This policy enabled the shoguns to keep an eye on the daimyo, and it encouraged daimyo to spend their money on comfortable lives in Edo rather than on military forces that could challenge the bakufu. The shoguns also discouraged the daimyo from visiting one another and even required daimyo to obtain permission to meet with the emperor.

In an effort to prevent European influences from destabilizing the land, the Tokugawa shoguns closely *Control of Foreign Relations* controlled relations between Japan and the outside world. A primary concern was that Europeans might threaten the bakufu by making alliances with daimyo and supplying them with weapons. Thus during the 1630s the shoguns issued a series of edicts sharply restricting Japanese relations with other lands.

The policy forbade Japanese to go abroad on pain of death and prohibited the construction of large ships. It expelled Europeans from Japan and prohib-

daimyo (DEYEM-yoh)

ited foreign merchants from trading in Japanese ports. The policy did, however, allow carefully controlled trade with Asian lands, and it also permitted small numbers of Chinese and Dutch merchants to trade under tight restrictions at the southern port city of Nagasaki. As a result, Japan was never completely isolated from the outside world.

Economic and Social Change

By ending civil conflict and maintaining political stability, the Tokugawa shoguns set the stage for economic growth in Japan. Ironically, peace and a booming economy encouraged social change that undermined the order that the bakufu sought to preserve. Economic growth had its roots in increased agricultural production, especially of rice, cotton, silk, and indigo. In many parts of Japan, villages moved away from subsistence farming in favor of production for the market.

Increased agricultural production brought about rapid demographic growth: during the seventeenth century the Japanese population rose by almost one-third, from twenty-two million *Population Growth* to twenty-nine million. Thereafter, however, many families practiced population control to maintain or raise their standard of living. Between 1700 and 1850 the Japanese population grew only moderately, from twenty-nine million to thirty-two million. Contraception, late marriage, and abortion all played roles in limiting population growth, but the principal method of control was infanticide, euphemistically referred to as "thinning out the rice shoots." Japanese families resorted to these measures primarily because Japan was land poor, which made it easy for populations to strain available resources.

The Tokugawa era was an age of social as well as demographic change in Japan. Because of Chinese cultural influence, the Japanese social hier- *Social Change* archy followed Confucian precepts in ranking the ruling elites—including the daimyo and samurai warriors—as the most privileged class of society, followed by peasants and artisans. As in China, merchants ranked at the bottom. Yet the extended period of peace ushered in by Tokugawa rule undermined the social position of the ruling elites, who found their traditional role as local administrators redundant. Many of the ruling elite also fell into financial difficulty in this period because of rising prices and lavish lifestyles. As a result, many became indebted to rice brokers and gradually declined into genteel poverty.

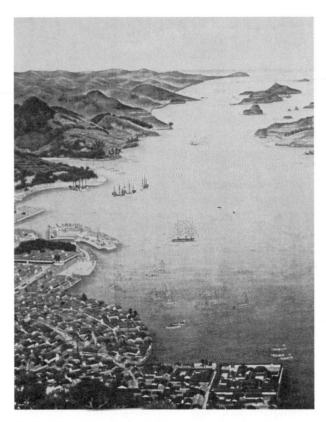

Dutch sailing ships and smaller Japanese vessels mingle in Nagasaki harbor. Dutch merchants conducted their business on the artificial island of Deshima, at left.

Meanwhile, as in China, merchants in Japan became increasingly wealthy and prominent. Japanese cities flourished throughout the Tokugawa era—the population of Edo approached one million by 1700—and merchants prospered in the vibrant urban environment. Rice dealers, pawnbrokers, and sake merchants soon controlled more wealth than the ruling elites.

Neo-Confucianism and Floating Worlds

Japan had gone to school in China, and the influence of China continued throughout the Tokugawa era. Formal education began with study of Chinese language and literature. As late as the nineteenth century, many Japanese scholars wrote their philosophical, legal, and religious works in Chinese. The common people embraced Buddhism, which had come to Japan from China, and Confucianism was the most influential philosophical system. Indeed, by the early

Neo-Confucianism in Japan

eighteenth century, neo-Confucianism had become the official ideology of the Tokugawa bakufu.

Yet even with Tokugawa sponsorship, neo-Confucianism did not dominate intellectual life in Japan. Some scholars sought to establish a sense of Japanese identity *Native Learning* that did not depend on cultural kinship with China. Particularly during the eighteenth century, scholars of "native learning" scorned neo-Confucianism and even Buddhism as alien cultural imports and emphasized instead the importance of folk traditions and the indigenous Shinto religion for Japanese identity. Many scholars of native learning viewed Japanese people as superior to all others and glorified the supposed purity of Japanese society before its adulteration by Chinese and other foreign influences.

Meanwhile, the emergence of a prosperous merchant class encouraged the development of a vibrant popular culture. During the seventeenth and eighteenth centuries, an exuberant middle-class culture flourished in cities such as Kyoto, Edo, and Osaka. In those and other cities, Japan's finest creative talents catered to middle-class appetites.

The centers of Tokugawa urban culture were the "floating worlds" *(ukiyo)*, entertainment and pleasure quarters where teahouses, theaters, brothels, and public baths *Floating Worlds* offered escape from the rigid rules of conduct that governed public behavior in Tokugawa society. In contrast to the solemn, serious proceedings of the imperial court and the bakufu, the popular culture of urban residents was secular, satirical, and even scatological. The main expressions of this lively culture were prose fiction and new forms of theater.

Ihara Saikaku (1642–1693), one of Japan's most prolific poets, helped create a new genre of prose literature, the "books of the floating world." Much of his fiction revolved around the theme of love. In *The Life of a Man Who Lived for Love,* for example, Ihara chronicled the experiences of a townsman who devoted his life to a quest for sexual pleasure. Ihara's treatment of love stressed the erotic rather than the aesthetic, and the brief, episodic stories that made up his work appealed to literate urban residents who were not inclined to pore over dense neo-Confucian treatises.

Beginning in the early seventeenth century, two new forms of drama became popular in Japanese cities. One was *kabuki* theater, which usually featured several

Shintoism (SHIHN-toh-iz'm)
kabuki (kah-BOO-kee)

A colored woodcut by Okumura Masanobu depicts the audience at a seventeenth-century kabuki theater. Enthusiastic actors often ran down wooden ramps and played their roles among the audience.

acts consisting of lively and sometimes bawdy skits where stylized acting combined with lyric singing, dancing, and spectacular staging. The other new dramatic form was *bunraku,* the puppet theater. In bunraku, chanters accompanied by music told a story acted out by puppets. Manipulated by a team of three, each puppet could execute the subtlest and most intricate movements, such as brushing a tear from the eye with the sleeve of a kimono. Both kabuki and bunraku attracted enthusiastic audiences in search of entertainment and diversion.

Christianity and Dutch Learning

Christian missionaries and European merchants also contributed their own distinctive threads to the cultural fabric of Tokugawa Japan. The Jesuit Francis

Christian Missions

Xavier opened the first Roman Catholic mission in 1549 and for a few decades experienced remarkable success. Several powerful daimyo adopted Christianity and ordered their subjects to do likewise. Many Japanese converts became enthusiastic Christians and worked to convert their compatriots to the new faith. By the 1580s about 150,000 Japanese had converted to Christianity, and by 1615 Japanese Christians numbered about 300,000.

Although Christians were only a tiny minority of the Japanese population, the popularity of Christianity generated a backlash among those seeking to preserve Japanese religious and cultural traditions. The Tokugawa shoguns restricted European access to Japan largely because of concerns that Christianity might serve as a cultural bridge for alliances between daimyo and European adventurers, which in turn could threaten the bakufu. Meanwhile, Buddhist and Confucian scholars resented the Christian conviction that their faith was the only true doctrine.

Between 1587 and 1639, shoguns promulgated several decrees ordering a halt to Christian missions and commanding Japanese Christians to renounce their faith. In 1612 the shoguns began rigorous enforcement

Anti-Christian Campaign

of these decrees. They tortured and executed European missionaries who refused to leave the islands as well as Japanese Christians who refused to abandon their faith. The campaign was so effective that even some European missionaries abandoned Christianity. Most notable was the Por-

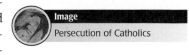
Image
Persecution of Catholics

tuguese Jesuit Christovão Ferreira, head of the Jesuit mission in Japan, who gave up Christianity under torture, adopted Buddhism, and interrogated many Europeans who fell into Japanese hands in the mid–seventeenth century. By the late seventeenth century, the anti-Christian campaign had claimed tens of thousands of lives, and Christianity survived only as a secret, underground religion.

Tokugawa policies ensured that Christianity would not soon reappear in Japan, but they did not entirely *Dutch Learning* prevent contacts between Europeans and Japanese. After 1639 Dutch merchants trading at Nagasaki became Japan's principal source of information about the world beyond east Asia. A small number of Japanese scholars learned Dutch to communicate with the foreigners. Their studies, which they called "Dutch learning," brought considerable knowledge of the outside world to Japan. After 1720 Tokugawa authorities lifted the ban on foreign books, and Dutch learning—especially European art and science—began to play a significant role in Japanese intellectual life. Indeed, by the mid-eighteenth century the Tokugawa shoguns themselves had become enthusiastic proponents of Dutch learning, and schools of European medicine and Dutch studies flourished in several Japanese cities.

SUMMARY

Both China and Japan controlled their own affairs throughout the early modern era and avoided the turmoil that afflicted societies in the Americas and much of sub-Saharan Africa. Rulers of the Ming dynasty built a powerful centralized state in China. They worked diligently to restore traditional ways by reviving Chinese political institutions and providing state sponsorship for neo-Confucianism. In the interest of stability, authorities also restricted foreign merchants' access to China and limited the activities of Christian missionaries. The succeeding Qing dynasty pursued similar policies. The Ming and Qing dynasties both brought political stability, but China experienced considerable social and economic change in early modern times. American food crops helped increase agricultural production, which fueled rapid population growth, and global trade stimulated the Chinese economy, which improved the position of merchants and artisans in society. The experience of the Tokugawa era in Japan was much like that of the Ming and Qing eras in China. The Tokugawa bakufu brought political order to the Japanese islands and closely controlled foreign relations, but a vibrant economy promoted social change that enhanced the status of merchants and artisans.

CHRONOLOGY

1368–1644	Ming dynasty (China)
1368–1398	Reign of Hongwu
1403–1424	Reign of Yongle
1552–1610	Life of Matteo Ricci
1572–1620	Reign of Emperor Wanli
1600–1867	Tokugawa shogunate (Japan)
1616–1626	Reign of Nurhaci
1642–1693	Life of Ihara Saikaku
1644–1911	Qing dynasty (China)
1661–1722	Reign of Kangxi
1736–1795	Reign of Qianlong
1793	British trade mission to China

FOR FURTHER READING

Timothy Brook. *The Confusions of Pleasure: Commerce and Culture in Ming China.* Berkeley, 1998. Fascinating social and cultural analysis of Ming China focusing on the role of commerce as an agent of social change.

Mark C. Elliott. *The Manchu Way: The Eight Banners and Ethnic Identity in Late Imperial China.* Stanford, 2001. Important scholarly study focusing on relations between Manchus and Chinese during the Qing dynasty.

Mark Elvin. *The Pattern of the Chinese Past: A Social and Economic Interpretation.* Stanford, 1973. A brilliant analysis of Chinese history concentrating on economic, social, and technological themes.

Ray Huang. *1587: A Year of No Significance.* New Haven, 1981. A very good history of the late Ming, with insights into daily life.

Susan Naquin and Evelyn S. Rawski. *Chinese Society in the Eighteenth Century.* New Haven, 1987. A lucid and well-organized discussion of Chinese social history.

Kenneth Pomeranz. *The Great Divergence: China, Europe, and the Making of the Modern World Economy.* Princeton, 2000. Path-breaking scholarly study that illuminates the economic history of the early modern world through comparison of economic development in Asian and European lands.

Jonathan D. Spence. *The Death of Woman Wang.* New York, 1978. Engaging reconstruction of life in rural China during the early Qing dynasty.

Conrad Totman. *Early Modern Japan.* Berkeley, 1993. An outstanding survey of Tokugawa ecological, political, social, economic, and cultural history.

H. Paul Varley. *Japanese Culture.* 4th ed. Honolulu, 2000. Places the cultural history of the Tokugawa era in its larger historical context.

Frederic Wakeman Jr. *The Great Enterprise: The Manchu Reconstruction of the Imperial Order in Seventeenth-Century China.* 2 vols. Berkeley, 1985. Important scholarly analysis of early Qing history.

CHAPTER 25
The Islamic Empires

In 1635 Shah Jahan, the emperor of Mughal India, took his seat on the Peacock Throne. Seven years in the making, the Peacock Throne is probably the most spectacular seat on which any mortal human being has rested. Shah Jahan ordered the throne encrusted with ten million rupees' worth of diamonds, rubies, emeralds, and pearls. Atop the throne itself stood a magnificent, golden-bodied peacock with a huge ruby and a fifty-carat, pear-shaped pearl on its breast and a brilliant tail fashioned of sapphires and gems.

Yet, for all its splendor, the Peacock Throne ranks a distant second among Shah Jahan's artistic projects: pride of place goes to the incomparable Taj Mahal. Built over a period of eighteen years as a tomb for Shah Jahan's beloved wife, Mumtaz Mahal, who died during childbirth in 1631, the Taj Mahal is a graceful and elegant monument both to the departed empress and to Shah Jahan's Islamic faith.

The emperor and his architects conceived the Taj Mahal as a vast allegory in stone symbolizing the day when Allah would cause the dead to rise and undergo judgment. Its gardens represented the gardens of paradise, and the four water channels running through them symbolized the four rivers of the heavenly kingdom. The domed marble tomb of Mumtaz Mahal represented the throne of Allah. The main gateway to the structure features the entire text of the chapter promising that on the day of judgment, Allah will punish the wicked and gather the faithful into his celestial paradise.

The Peacock Throne and the Taj Mahal testify to the wealth of

OPPOSITE PAGE: *The Taj Mahal, a sumptuous mosque and tomb built between 1632 and 1649 by Shah Jahan in memory of his wife, Mumtaz Mahal.*

the Mughal empire, and the tomb of Mumtaz Mahal bespeaks also the fundamentally Islamic character of the ruling dynasty. But the Mughal realm was not the only well-organized Islamic empire of early modern times. The Ottoman dynasty ruled a powerful empire that expanded from its base in Anatolia to embrace much of eastern Europe, Egypt, and north Africa. The Safavid dynasty challenged the Ottomans for dominance in southwest Asia and prospered from its role in trade networks linking China, India, Russia, southwest Asia, and the Mediterranean basin.

All three Islamic empires of early modern times had dynasties that originated with nomadic, Turkish-speaking peoples from the steppes of central Asia. All three dynasties retained political and cultural traditions that their ancestors had adopted on the steppes, but they also adapted readily to the city-based agricultural societies that they conquered. The Ottoman dynasty made especially effective use of gunpowder weapons, and the Safavids and the Mughals also incorporated gunpowder weapons into their arsenals. All three dynasties officially embraced Islam and drew cultural guidance from Islamic values.

During the sixteenth and early seventeenth centuries, the three Islamic empires presided over expansive and prosperous societies. About the mid–seventeenth century, however, they all began to weaken. Each empire waged long, costly wars that drained resources without bringing compensating benefits. The empires also faced domestic difficulties. Each of them was an ethnically and religiously diverse realm, and each experienced tensions when conservative Muslim leaders lobbied for strict observance of Islam while members of other communities sought greater freedom for themselves. Furthermore, the Islamic empires made little investment in economic and technological development. By the mid–eighteenth century the Safavid empire had collapsed, and the Ottoman and Mughal realms were rapidly falling under European influence.

FORMATION OF THE ISLAMIC EMPIRES

The Islamic empires began as small warrior principalities in frontier areas. As they grew, they devised elaborate administrative and military institutions. Under the guidance of talented and energetic rulers, each empire organized an effective governmental apparatus and presided over a prosperous society.

The Ottoman Empire

The Ottoman empire was an unusually successful frontier state. The term *Ottoman* derived from Osman Bey, founder of the dynasty that continued in unbroken succession from 1289 until the dissolution of the empire in 1923. Osman was chief *(bey)* of a band of seminomadic Turks who migrated to north-western Anatolia in the thirteenth century. Osman and his followers sought above all to become *ghazi*, Muslim religious warriors who fought on behalf of the faith.

Osman

Interactive Map
The Ottoman empire

The Ottomans' location on the borders of the Byzantine empire afforded them ample opportunity to wage holy war. Their first great success came in 1326 with the capture of the Ana-tolian city of Bursa, which became the capital of the Ottoman principality. About 1352 they established a foothold in Europe when they seized the fortress of Gallipoli. The city of Edirne (Adrianople) became a second Ottoman capital and served as a base for further expansion into the Balkans. As warriors settled in frontier districts and pushed their boundaries forward, they took spoils and gathered revenues that enriched both the *ghazi* and the central government.

Ottoman Expansion

Driving Ottoman expansion was a formidable military machine, which included light cavalry, volunteer infantry, and—as the state grew larger—heavy cavalry. After expanding into the Balkans, the Ottomans created an important force composed of slave troops. Through an institution known as the *devshirme*, the Ottomans required the Christian population of the Balkans to contribute young boys to become slaves of the sultan. The boys received special training, learned Turkish, and converted to Islam. According to individual ability, they entered either the Ottoman civilian administration or the military. Those who became soldiers were known as Janissaries, from the Turkish *yeni cheri* ("new troops"). The Janissaries quickly gained a reputation for esprit de corps, loyalty to the sultan, and readiness to employ new military technology. The Ottomans also outfitted their forces with gunpowder weapons and used them effectively in battles and sieges.

The capture of Constantinople in 1453 by Mehmed II (reigned 1451–1481)—known as Mehmed the Con-

---

ghazi (GAH-zee)
Byzantine (BIHZ-uhn-teen)

Map 25.1 Islamic empires from 1500 to 1800. Locate the Ottoman capital of Istanbul, the Safavid capital of Istahan, and the Mughal capital of Delhi. What strategic or commercial purposes did each of these capitals fulfill, and how would their locations have aided or hindered imperial administration?

queror—opened a new chapter in Ottoman expansion. With its superb location and illustrious heritage, Con-

Mehmed the Conqueror

stantinople became the new Ottoman capital, subsequently known as Istanbul. With the capture of the great city behind him, Mehmed presented himself not just as a warrior sultan but as a true emperor. He laid the foundations for a tightly centralized, absolute monarchy, and his army faced no serious rival. He completed the conquest of Serbia, moved into southern Greece and Albania, eliminated the last Byzantine outpost at Trebizond, captured Genoese ports in the Crimea, initiated a naval war with Venice in the Mediterranean, and reportedly hoped to march on Rome and capture the pope himself. Toward the end of his life, he launched an invasion of Italy and briefly occupied Otranto, but his successors abandoned plans for expansion in western Europe.

The Ottomans continued their expansion in the early sixteenth century by occupying Syria and Egypt. Ottoman imperialism climaxed in the reign of Süleyman the Magnificent (reigned 1520–1566). In 1534

Süleyman conquered Baghdad and added the Tigris and Euphrates valleys to the Ottoman domain. In Europe he kept the rival Habsburg empire on the defensive throughout his reign. He captured Belgrade in 1521, defeated

Süleyman the Magnificent

and killed the king of Hungary at the battle of Mohács in 1526, and in 1529 subjected the Habsburgs' prized city of Vienna to a brief but nonetheless terrifying siege.

Under Süleyman the Ottomans also became a major naval power. In addition to their own Aegean and Black Sea fleets, the Ottomans inherited the navy of the Mamluk rulers of Egypt. A Turkish corsair, Khayr al-Din Barbarossa Pasha, placed his pirate fleet under the Ottoman flag and became Süleyman's leading admiral. With such resources and leadership, Süleyman was able to challenge Christian vessels throughout the Mediterranean as well as Portuguese fleets in the Red Sea and the Indian Ocean.

Süleyman (SOO-lehy-mahn)

Sultan Süleyman (center, on horse) leads Ottoman forces as they march on Europe.

The Safavid Empire

In 1499 a twelve-year-old boy named Ismail left the swamps of Gilan near the Caspian Sea, where he had hidden from the enemies of his family for five years, to seek his revenge. Two years later he entered Tabriz at the head of an army and laid claim to the ancient Persian imperial title of shah. The young Shah Ismail (reigned 1501–1524) also proclaimed that the official religion of his realm would be Twelver Shiism, and he proceeded to impose it, by force when necessary, on the formerly Sunni population. Over the next decade he seized control of the Iranian plateau and

launched expeditions into the Caucasus, Anatolia, Mesopotamia, and central Asia.

Shah Ismail and his successors traced their ancestry back to Safi al-Din (1252–1334), leader of a Sufi religious order in northwestern Persia. The famous tomb and shrine of Safi al-Din at Ardabil became the home of Shah Ismail's family (named "Safavids" after the holy man himself), the headquarters of his religious movement, and the center of a determined, deliberate conspiracy to win political power for his descendants. The Safavids changed their religious preferences several times in the hope of gaining popular support before settling on a form of Shiism that appealed to the nomadic Turkish tribes who were moving into the area. *The Safavids*

Twelver Shiism held that there had been twelve infallible imams (or religious leaders) after Muhammad, beginning with the prophet's cousin and son-in-law Ali. The twelfth, or "hidden," imam had gone into hiding about 874 to escape persecution, but the Twelver Shiites believed he was still alive and would one day return to take power and spread the true religion. Ismail's father had instructed his Turkish followers to wear a distinctive red hat with twelve pleats in memory of the twelve Shiite imams, and they subsequently became known as the *qizilbash* ("red heads"). Safavid propaganda also suggested that Ismail was himself the hidden imam, or even an incarnation of Allah. Although most Muslims would have regarded those pretensions as utterly blasphemous, the *qizilbash* enthusiastically accepted them, since they resembled traditional Turkish conceptions of leadership that associated military leaders with divinity. The *qizilbash* believed that Ismail would make them invincible in battle, and they became fanatically loyal to the Safavid cause. *Twelver Shiism*

Shah Ismail's curious blend of Shiism and Turkish militancy created some powerful enemies. Foremost among them were the staunchly Sunni Ottomans, who detested the Shiite Safavids and feared the spread of Safavid propaganda among the nomadic Turks in their own territory. As a result, Ottomans launched a full-scale invasion of Safavid territory in the early sixteenth century.

At a battle on the plain of Chaldiran (1514), the Ottomans deployed heavy artillery and thousands of

Shiism (SHEE-izm)
Sunni (SOON-nee)
Safavid (SAH-fah-vihd)
qizilbash (gih-ZIHL-bahsh)

Battle of Chaldiran

Janissaries equipped with firearms behind a barrier of carts. Although the Safavids knew about gunpowder technology, they declined to use devices that they saw as unreliable and unmanly. Trusting in the protective charisma of Shah Ismail, the *qizilbash* cavalry fearlessly attacked the Ottoman line and suffered devastating casualties. Ismail had to slip away, and the Ottomans temporarily occupied his capital at Tabriz. The Ottomans badly damaged the Safavid state but lacked the resources to destroy it, and the two empires remained locked in intermittent conflict for the next two centuries.

Shah Abbas the Great

Later Safavid rulers prudently abandoned the extreme Safavid ideology that associated the emperor with Allah in favor of more conventional Twelver Shiism, from which they still derived legitimacy as descendants and representatives of the imams. In the late sixteenth century, Shah Abbas the Great (reigned 1588–1629) fully revitalized the Safavid empire. He moved the capital to the more central location of Isfahan, encouraged trade with other lands, and reformed the administrative and military institutions of the empire. With newly strengthened military forces, Shah Abbas led the Safavids to numerous victories. He attacked and defeated the nomadic Uzbeks in central Asia, expelled the Portuguese from Hormuz, and harassed the Ottomans mercilessly in a series of wars from 1603 to the end of his reign. His campaigns brought most of northwestern Iran, the Caucasus, and Mesopotamia under Safavid rule.

The Mughal Empire

Babur

In 1523 Zahir al-Din Muhammad, known as Babur ("the Tiger"), a Chagatai Turk who claimed descent from both Chinggis Khan and Tamerlane, appeared in northern India. Unlike the Ottomans or Safavids, who fought on behalf of Islam, Babur made little pretense to be anything more than a soldier of fortune in the manner of his illustrious ancestors. His father had been the prince of Farghana, and Babur's great ambition was to transform his inheritance into a glorious central Asian empire. Yet envious relatives and Uzbek enemies frustrated his ambitions.

Unable to accomplish his goals in central Asia, Babur turned his attention to India. With the aid of gunpowder weapons, including artillery and firearms, Babur took Delhi in 1526. Ironically, Babur cared little for the land he had conquered. Many in his entourage wanted to take their spoils of war and leave the hot and humid Indian climate, which ruined their finely crafted compound bows, but Babur elected to stay. By the time of his death in 1530, Babur had built a loosely knit empire that stretched from Kabul through the Punjab to the borders of Bengal. He founded a dynasty called the *Mughal* (a Persian term for "Mongol"), which expanded to embrace almost all the Indian subcontinent.

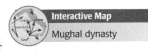

Shah Ismail and the *qizilbash.* This miniature painting from a Safavid manuscript depicts the shah and his *qizilbash* warriors wearing the distinctive red pleated cap that was their emblem of identity.

Mughal (MOO-guhl)

SOURCES FROM THE PAST

A Conqueror and His Conquests: Babur on India

Babur was a talented writer as well as a successful warrior. His memoirs make fascinating reading and provide a unique perspective on early Mughal India. His writings include his reflections on the territories he conquered in India, which he compared unfavorably to his central Asian homeland, and on his decision to stay in India and found an empire.

■ ■ ■

Most of the inhabitants of India are infidels, called Hindus, believing mainly in the transmigration of souls; all artisans, wage-earners and officials are Hindus. In our countries the desert dwellers get tribal names; here people settled in the cultivated villages also get tribal names. Again, every artisan follows the trade handed down to him from his forefathers.

India is a country of few charms. The people lack good looks and good manners. They have no social life or exchange of visits. They have no genius or intelligence, no polite learning, no generosity of magnanimity, no harmony or proportion in their arts and crafts, no lead-wire or carpenter's square. They lack good horses and good dogs; grapes, melons, and any good fruit; ice and cold water; good food or good bread in the markets. They have no baths and no advanced educational institutions. . . . There are no running streams in their gardens or residences, no waters at all except the large rivers and the swamps in the ravines and hollows. Their residences have no pleasant and salubrious breezes, and in their construction [there is] no form or symmetry. . . .

Among the charms that India does possess is that it is a large country, with large quantities of gold and silver. Its air in the rainy season is very fine. Sometimes it rains ten or fifteen or even twenty times a day, and in such torrents that rivers flow where no water was previously. While it rains, and throughout the rainy season, the air is remarkably fine, not to be surpassed for mildness and pleasantness. Its only fault is its great humidity, which spoils bows. . . .

It was the hot season when we came to Agra. All the inhabitants had run away in terror. We could find neither grain for ourselves nor corn for our horses. The villages, out of hostility and hatred for us, had taken to thieving and highway-robbery, and it was impossible to travel on the roads. We had not yet the opportunity to distribute the treasure and to assign men in strength to each district. Moreover, the year was a very hot one, pestilential simooms [sandstorms] were striking people down in heaps, and masses were beginning to die off.

For all these reasons, most of the best warriors were unwilling to stay in India; in fact, they determined to leave. . . .

When I discovered this unsteadiness among my people, I summoned all the leaders and took counsel. I said, "Without means and resources there is no empire and conquest, and without lands and followers there is no sovereignty and rule. By the effort of long years, through much tribulation and the crossing of distant lands, by flinging ourselves into battle and danger, we have through God's favor overcome so many enemies and conquered such vast lands. And now, what force compels us, what necessity has arisen, that we should, without cause, abandon a country taken at such risk of life? And if we returned to Kabul, we would again be left in poverty and weakness. Henceforth, let no well-wisher of mine speak of such things! But let not those turn back from going who cannot bear the hardship and have determined to leave." With such words I reasoned with them and made them, willy-nilly, quit their fears.

• *What does Babur's reaction to India suggest about his views of his own central Asian homeland?*

SOURCE: Babur. *The Babur-nama in English (Memoirs of Babur)*. Trans. by Annette Susannah Beveridge. London: Luzac, 1922. (Translation slightly modified.)

The real architect of the Mughal empire was Babur's grandson Akbar (reigned 1556–1605), a brilliant and charismatic ruler. During his reign, Akbar created a centralized administrative structure with ministries regulating the various provinces of the empire. His military campaigns consolidated Mughal power in Gujarat and Bengal. He destroyed the Hindu kingdom of Vijayanagar, thus laying the foundation for later Mughal expansion in southern India.

Akbar

In addition to being an able ruler, Akbar was a thoughtful, reflective man deeply interested in religion and philosophy. He pursued a policy of religious toleration that he hoped would reduce tensions between Hindu and Muslim communities in India. Although illiterate (probably due to dyslexia), he was extremely intelligent and had books read to him daily. Instead of imposing Islam on his subjects, he encouraged the elaboration of a syncretic religion called the "divine faith" that focused attention on the emperor as a ruler common to all the religious, ethnic, and social groups of India.

The Mughal empire reached its greatest extent under Aurangzeb (reigned 1659–1707). During his long reign, Aurangzeb waged a relentless campaign of expansion. By the early eighteenth century, Mughals ruled the entire subcontinent except for a small region at the southern tip. Although he greatly expanded Mughal boundaries, Aurangzeb presided over a troubled empire. Aurangzeb was a devout Muslim, and he broke with Akbar's policy of religious toleration. He demolished several famous

Aurangzeb

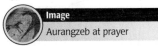
Image
Aurangzeb at prayer

Hindu temples and replaced them with mosques. He also imposed a tax on Hindus in an effort to encourage conversion to Islam. His promotion of Islam appealed strongly to Indian Muslims, but it provoked deep hostility among Hindus and enabled local leaders to organize movements to resist or even rebel against Mughal authority.

IMPERIAL ISLAMIC SOCIETY

Despite many differences, there were striking similarities in the development of Ottoman, Safavid, and Mughal societies. All relied on bureaucracies that drew inspiration from the steppe traditions of Turkish and Mongol peoples as well as from the heritage of Islam. They adopted similar economic policies and sought ways to maintain harmony in societies that embraced

This manuscript illustration from about 1590 depicts Akbar (at top, shaded by attendants) inspecting construction of a new imperial capital at Fatehpur Sikri.

many different religious and ethnic groups. Rulers of all the empires also sought to enhance the legitimacy of their regimes by providing for public welfare and associating themselves with literary and artistic talent.

The Dynastic State

The Ottoman, Safavid, and Mughal empires were all military creations, regarded by their rulers as personal possessions by right of conquest. The rulers exercised personal command of the armies, appointed and dismissed officials at will, and adopted whatever policies they wished. In theory, the emperors owned all land

and granted use of it in return for the payment of fixed taxes. The emperors and their families derived revenues from crown lands, and revenues from other lands supported military and administrative officials.

In the Ottoman, Safavid, and Mughal empires, the prestige and authority of the dynasty derived

The Emperors and Islam

from the personal piety and the military prowess of the ruler and his ancestors. Devotion to Islam encouraged rulers to extend their faith to new lands. Moreover, the *ghazi* ideal of spreading Islam by fighting infidels or heretics resonated with the traditions of Turkish and Mongolian peoples, who were accustomed both to warfare and to leadership by warriors.

The autocratic authority wielded by the rulers of the Islamic empires also reflected steppe traditions.

Steppe Traditions

The early emperors largely did as they pleased, irrespective of religious and social norms. The Ottoman sultans, for example, unilaterally issued numerous legal edicts, and Safavid and Mughal rulers unabashedly asserted their spiritual authority over their subjects. Yet steppe practices also brought problems to the Islamic empires, especially regarding succession issues. In the steppe empires the ruler's relatives often managed components of the states, and succession to the throne became a hot contest between competing members of the family. This was reflected in the Mughal empire, where conflicts among princes and rebellions of sons against fathers were recurrent features throughout its history. The Safavids also engaged in murderous struggles for the throne. Shah Abbas himself lived in fear that another member of the family would challenge him. He kept his sons confined to the palace and killed or blinded relatives he suspected, almost wiping out his family in the process.

Succession issues also became a problem for the Ottomans. After the fifteenth century, the sultans increasingly moved to protect their position by eliminating family rivals. Mehmed the Conqueror decreed that a ruler could legally kill off his brothers after taking the throne. His successors observed that tradition in Turko-Mongol style—by strangling victims with a silk bow string so as not to shed royal blood—until 1595, when the new sultan executed nineteen brothers, many of them infants, as well as fifteen expectant mothers. After that episode, sultans confined their sons in special quarters of the imperial harem and forbade them to go outside except to take the throne.

Even though Muslim theorists universally agreed that women should have no role in public affairs, women played important roles in managing the Islamic empires. Many Ottoman, Safavid, and Mughal emperors followed the example of Chinggis Khan, who revered his mother and his first wife. In the Islamic empires the ruler's

Women and Politics

mother and his chief wife or favorite concubine enjoyed special privileges and authority. Ottoman courtiers often complained loudly about the "rule of women," thus offering eloquent testimony to the power that women could wield. Süleyman the Magnificent, for example, became infatuated with Hürrem Sultana (also known as Roxelana), a concubine of Ukrainian origin. Süleyman elevated her to the status of a legal wife, consulted her on state policies, and deferred to her judgment even to the point of executing his eldest son when Hürrem wanted to secure the succession of her own child.

Women also played prominent political roles in the Safavid and Mughal empires. In Safavid Persia, Mahd-e Olya, the wife of one shah, was the de facto ruler. Her efforts to limit the power of the *qizilbash* so enraged them that they murdered her. The aunt of another shah scolded the ruler for neglecting his duties and used her own money to raise an army to put down a revolt. The Mughal emperor Jahangir was content to let his wife Nur Jahan run the government, and even the conscientious Muslim Aurangzeb listened to his daughter's political advice.

Agriculture and Trade

Productive agricultural economies were the foundations of all the Islamic empires. Each empire extracted surplus agricultural production and used it to finance armies and bureaucracies. Mostly the Islamic empires relied on crops of wheat and

Food Crops

rice that had flourished for centuries in the lands they ruled. The Columbian exchange brought American crops to all the Islamic empires but without the same dramatic effects as in Europe, east Asia, and Africa. European merchants did introduce maize, potatoes, tomatoes, and other crops to the Islamic empires, however, and although the new arrivals did not become staples, they enlivened regional cuisines with new tastes and textures.

Two products of the Columbian exchange that caught on extremely well in both the Ottoman and the Safavid empires were coffee and tobacco. Although native to Ethiopia and cultivated in southern Arabia, coffee did not become popular in Islamic lands until the sixteenth century. Like sugar, coffee had traveled to Europe and from there to the Americas, where plantations specialized in the production of both tropical crops for the world market. By the eighteenth century, American producers and European merchants supplied Muslim markets with coffee as well as sugar.

According to the Ottoman historian Ibrahim Pechevi, English merchants introduced tobacco about *Tobacco* 1600, claiming it was useful for medicinal purposes. Within a few decades it had spread throughout the Ottoman empire. The increasing popularity of coffee drinking and pipe smoking encouraged entrepreneurs to establish coffeehouses where customers could indulge their appetites for caffeine and nicotine at the same time. The popularity of coffeehouses provoked protest from moralists who worried that these popular attractions were dens of iniquity. Pechevi himself complained about the hideous odor of tobacco and the messy ashes, and religious leaders claimed that it was worse to frequent a coffeehouse than a tavern. Sultan Murad IV went so far as to outlaw coffee and tobacco and to execute those who continued to partake. That effort, however, was a losing battle. Both pastimes eventually won widespread acceptance, and the coffeehouse became a prominent social institution in the Islamic empires.

American food crops had less demographic effect in the Islamic empires than in other parts of the world. The population of India surged during early modern times, growing from 105 million in 1500 to 190 million in 1800. But population growth in India resulted more from intensive agriculture along traditional lines than from the influence of new crops. The *Population* Safavid population grew less rapidly, from 5 *Growth* million in 1500 to 8 million in 1800. Ottoman numbers grew from 9 million in 1500 to about 24 million about 1800, but those numbers reflect territorial additions more than fertility increases. Even in the Ottoman heartland of Anatolia, population did not expand nearly as dramatically as it did in other lands in early modern times. From 6 million in 1500, the population of Anatolia rose to just 9 million in 1800.

The Islamic empires ruled lands that had figured prominently in long-distance trade for centuries and participated actively in global trade networks in *Trade* early modern times. In the Ottoman empire, for example, the early capital at Bursa was also the terminus of a caravan route that brought raw silk from Persia to supply the Italian market. The Ottomans also granted special trading concessions to merchants from England and France to cement alliances against common enemies in Spain and central Europe, and the city of Aleppo became an emporium for foreign merchants engaged primarily in the spice trade.

Shah Abbas promoted Isfahan as a commercial center and extended trading privileges to foreign merchants to help create a favorable environment for trade. European merchants sought Safavid raw silk, carpets, and ceramics. The English East India Company, the

In this anonymous painting produced about 1670, Dutch and English ships lie at anchor in the harbor of the busy port of Surat in northwestern India.

French East India Company, and the Dutch VOC all traded actively with the Safavids. To curry favor, the English company even sent military advisors to help introduce gunpowder weapons to Safavid armed forces and provided a navy to help them retake Hormuz in the Persian Gulf from the Portuguese.

The Mughals did not pay as much attention to foreign trade as the Ottomans and the Safavids, partly because of the enormous size and productivity of the domestic Indian economy and partly because the Mughal rulers had little interest in maritime affairs. Nevertheless, the Mughal treasury derived significant income from foreign trade. The Mughals allowed the creation of trading stations and merchant colonies by Portuguese, English, French, and Dutch merchants. Meanwhile, Indian merchants formed trading companies of their own, venturing both overland as far as Russia and by sea to ports all over the Indian Ocean.

Religious Affairs in the Islamic Empires

All the Islamic empires had populations that were religiously and ethnically diverse, and imperial rulers had the daunting challenge of maintaining harmony among different religious communities. The Ottoman empire included large numbers of Christians and Jews in the Balkans, Armenia, Lebanon, and Egypt. The Safavid empire embraced sizable Zoroastrian and Jewish communities as well as many Christian subjects in the Caucasus. The Mughal empire was especially diverse. Most Mughal subjects were Hindus, but large numbers of Muslims lived alongside smaller communities of Jains, Zoroastrians, Christians, and devotees of syncretic faiths such as Sikhism.

Religious Diversity

In India, Akbar was especially tolerant of diverse religions and worked to find a religious synthesis that would serve as a cultural foundation for unity in his diverse empire. As part of that effort, he supported the early Sikhs, who combined elements of Hinduism and Islam in a new syncretic faith. He also attempted to elaborate his own "divine faith," which emphasized loyalty to the emperor while borrowing eclectically from different religious traditions. Akbar never explained his ideas systematically, but it is clear that they drew most heavily on Islam. The divine faith was strictly monotheistic, and it reflected the influence of Shiite and Sufi teachings.

Akbar's Divine Faith

But it also glorified the emperor: Akbar even referred to himself as the "lord of wisdom," who would guide his subjects to an understanding of god. The divine faith was tolerant of Hinduism, and it even drew inspiration from Zoroastrianism in its effort to bridge the gaps between Mughal India's many cultural and religious communities.

The Islamic empires relied on a long-established model to deal with subjects who were not Muslims. They did not require conquered peoples to convert to Islam but extended to them the status of a protected people (*dhimmi*). In return for their loyalty and payment of a special tax known as *jizya*, dhimmi communities retained their personal freedom, kept their property, practiced their religion, and handled their own legal affairs. In the Ottoman empire, for example, autonomous religious communities known as *millet* retained their own civil laws, traditions, and languages. *Millet* communities usually also assumed social and administrative functions in matters concerning birth, marriage, death, health, and education.

Status of Religious Minorities

The situation in the Mughal empire was different, since its large number of religious communities made a *millet* system impractical. Mughal rulers reserved the most powerful military and administrative positions for Muslims, but in the day-to-day management of affairs, Muslims and Hindus cooperated closely. Some Mughal emperors, such as Akbar, worked particularly hard to forge links between religious communities and to integrate Muslim and Hindu elites. Indeed, in an effort to build bridges between the different religious communities of his realm, he abolished the *jizya* and sponsored discussions and debates between Muslims, Hindus, Jains, Zoroastrians, and Christians.

Policies of religious tolerance were not popular with many Muslims, who worried that toleration might lead to their absorption into Hindu society. They therefore insisted that Mughal rulers create and maintain an Islamic state based on Islamic law. When Aurangzeb reached the Mughal throne in 1659, that policy gained strength. Aurangzeb reinstated the *jizya* and promoted Islam as the official faith of Mughal India. His policy satisfied zealous Muslims but at the cost of deep bitterness among his Hindu subjects. Tension between Hindu and Muslim communities in India persisted throughout the Mughal dynasty and beyond.

Promotion of Islam

Sikhs (SIHKS)

dhimmi (DIHM-mee)
jizya (JIHZ-yuh)

Cultural Patronage of the Islamic Emperors

As the empires matured, the Islamic rulers sought to enhance their prestige through public works projects and patronage of scholars. They competed to attract outstanding religious scholars, artists, and architects to their courts and lavished resources on public buildings.

Capital cities and royal palaces were the most visible expressions of imperial majesty. The Ottomans took *Istanbul* particular pride in Istanbul, which quickly revived after conquest and became a bustling, prosperous city of more than a million people. At its heart was the great Topkapi palace, which housed government offices and meeting places for imperial councils. At its core was the sultan's residence with its harem, gardens, pleasure pavilions, and a repository for the most sacred possessions of the empire, including the mantle of the prophet Muhammad. Sultan Süleyman the Magnificent was fortunate to be able to draw on the talents of the architectural genius Sinan Pasha (1489–1588) to create the vast religious complex called the Süleymaniye, which blended Islamic and Byzantine architectural elements. It combined tall, slender minarets with large domed buildings supported by half domes in the style of the Byzantine church Hagia Sofia (which the Ottomans converted into the mosque of Aya Sofya).

Shah Abbas made his capital, Isfahan, into one of the most precious jewels of urban architectural de-*Isfahan* velopment anywhere in the world. Abbas concentrated markets, the palace, and the royal mosque around a vast polo field and public square. Broad, shaded avenues and magnificent bridges linked the central city to its suburbs. Safavid architects made use of monumental entryways, vast arcades, spacious courtyards, and intricate, colorful decoration. Unlike the sprawling Ottoman and Mughal palaces, the Safavid palaces in Isfahan were relatively small and emphasized 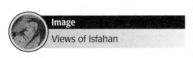 natural settings with gardens, pools, and large, open verandas. The point was not only to enable the shah to observe outside activities but also to emphasize his visibility and accessibility, qualities long esteemed in the Persian tradition of kingship.

In India, Mughal architects skillfully blended central Asian traditions with elements of Hindu architecture, and they built on a scale that left no doubt about their wealth and resources. They constructed

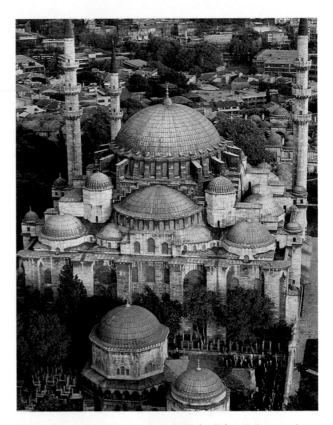

The massive Süleymaniye mosque built for Sultan Süleyman the Magnificent by the Ottoman architect Sinan Pasha in 1556.

scores of mosques, fortresses, and palaces and sometimes created entire cities.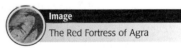

The best example was Fatehpur Sikri, a city planned and constructed by Akbar that served as his capital from 1569 to 1585. With its *Fatehpur Sikri* mint, records office, treasury, and audience hall, the new city demonstrated Akbar's strength and imperial ambitions. Fatehpur Sikri was also a private residence and retreat for the ruler, reproducing in stone a royal encampment with exquisite pleasure palaces where Akbar indulged his passions for music and conversation with scholars and poets. At yet another level, it was a dramatic display of Mughal piety and devotion, centered on the cathedral mosque and the mausoleum of Akbar's Sufi guru, Shaykh Salim Chisti. Despite their intensely Islamic character, many of the buildings consciously incorporated Indian elements, such as verandas supported by columns and decorations of stone elephants. Unfortunately, Akbar

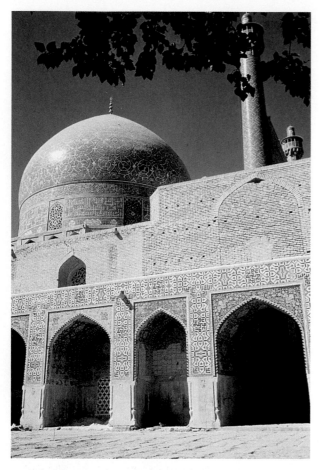

The Royal Mosque of Isfahan, centerpiece of the city as rebuilt by Shah Abbas at the end of the sixteenth century. With its combination of an open space flanked by markets, the palace, and religious structures, Isfahan stands as a unique example of urban planning in Islamic lands.

had selected a poor site for the city and soon abandoned it because of its bad water supply.

The most famous of the Mughal monuments—and one of the most prominent of all Islamic edifices—was

The Taj Mahal the Taj Mahal. Shah Jahan had twenty thousand workers toil for eighteen years to erect the exquisite white marble mosque and tomb. He originally planned to build a similar mausoleum out of black marble for himself, but his son Aurangzeb deposed him before he

could carry out the project. Shah Jahan spent his last years confined to a small cell with a tiny window, and only with the aid of a mirror was he able to catch the sight of his beloved wife's final resting place.

THE EMPIRES IN TRANSITION

The Islamic empires underwent dramatic change between the sixteenth and the eighteenth centuries. The Safavid empire disappeared entirely. In 1722 a band of Afghan tribesmen marched all the way to Isfahan, blockaded the city until its starving inhabitants resorted to cannibalism, forced the shah to abdicate, and executed thousands of Safavid officials as well as many members of the royal family. After the death of Aurangzeb in 1707, Mughal India experienced provincial rebellions and foreign invasions. By midcentury the subcontinent was falling under British imperial rule. By 1700 the Ottomans, too, were on the defensive: the sultans lost control over provinces such as Lebanon and Egypt, and throughout the eighteenth and nineteenth centuries European and Russian states placed political, military, and economic pressure on the shrinking Ottoman realm.

The Deterioration of Imperial Leadership

Strong and effective central authority was essential to the Islamic empires, and Muslim political theorists never tired of emphasizing the importance of rulers who were diligent, virtuous, and just. Weak, negligent, and corrupt rulers would allow the social order to break down. The Ottomans were fortunate in having a series of talented sultans for three centuries, and the Safavids and the Mughals produced their share of effective rulers as well.

Eventually, however, all three dynasties had rulers who were incompetent or irresponsible about tending to affairs of state. Moreover, all three *Dynastic Decline* dynasties faced difficulties because of suspicion and fighting among competing members of their ruling houses. In the Ottoman empire alone, notorious examples of problem rulers included Süleyman's successor, Selim the Sot (reigned 1566–1574) and Ibrahim the Crazy (reigned 1640–1648), who taxed and spent to such excess that government officials deposed and murdered him. Indeed, after the late seventeenth century, weak rule increasingly provoked mutinies in the army, provincial revolts, political corruption, and insecurity throughout the Ottoman realm.

Political troubles often arose from religious tensions. Conservative Muslim clerics had considerable influence in the Islamic empires because of their monopoly on education and their deep involvement in

Fatehpur Sikri, built by Akbar in the 1570s, commemorated the emperor's military conquests and housed the tomb of his religious guide. It included a palace, an audience hall where Akbar attended religious and philosophical debates, and a great mosque.

Religious Tensions

the everyday lives and legal affairs of ordinary subjects. The clerics mistrusted the emperors' interests in unconventional forms of Islam such as Sufism, complained bitterly when women or subjects who were not Muslims played influential political roles, and protested any exercise of royal authority that contradicted Islamic law.

In the Ottoman empire, disaffected religious students often joined the Janissaries in revolt. A particularly serious threat came from the Wahhabi movement in Arabia, which denounced the Ottomans as dangerous religious innovators who were unfit to rule. Conservative Muslims fiercely protested the construction of an astronomical observatory in Istanbul and forced the sultan to demolish it in 1580. In 1742 they also forced the closure of the Ottoman printing press, which they regarded as an impious technology.

Image
The observatory in Istanbul, 1580

In the Safavid empire, rulers fell under the domination of conservative Shiite clerics. Shiite leaders pressured the shahs to persecute Sunnis, non-Muslims, and even the Sufis who had helped establish the dynasty. Religious tensions also afflicted Mughal India. In the mid–eighteenth century, as Aurangzeb strug-gled to claim the Mughal throne, he drew on conservative Islamic ideas when he required non-Muslims to pay the poll tax and ordered the destruction of Hindu temples. Those measures inflamed tensions between the various Sunni, Shiite, and Sufi branches of Islam and also fueled animosity among Hindus and other Mughal subjects who were not Muslims.

Economic and Military Decline

In the sixteenth century, all the Islamic empires had strong domestic economies and played prominent roles in global trade networks. By the eighteenth century, however, domestic economies were under great stress, and foreign trade had declined dramatically or had fallen under the control of European powers. The Islamic empires were well on their way to becoming marginal lands that depended on goods produced elsewhere.

Economic Difficulties

The high cost of maintaining an expensive military and administrative apparatus helped to bring about economic decline in the Islamic empires. As long as the empires were expanding, they were able to finance their armies and bureaucracies with fresh resources extracted from newly conquered lands. When expansion slowed, ceased, or reversed, however, they faced the problem of supporting their institutions with limited resources.

Sufis (SOO-fees)

The long, costly, and unproductive wars fought by the Ottomans with the Habsburgs in central Europe, by the Safavids and Ottomans in Mesopotamia, and by Aurangzeb in southern India exhausted the treasuries of the Islamic empires without making fresh resources available to them.

As expansion slowed and the empires lost control over remote provinces, officials reacted to the loss of revenue by raising taxes, selling public offices, accepting bribes, or resorting to simple extortion. All those measures did long-term economic damage. To make matters worse, the governments viewed foreign trade as just another opportunity to bring in revenue. The Ottomans expanded the privileges enjoyed by foreign merchants, and the Mughals encouraged the establishment of Dutch and English trading outposts and welcomed the expansion of their business in India. In other words, imperial authorities were content to have foreign traders come to them. None made serious efforts to establish commercial stations abroad, although Indian merchants organized their own private trading companies.

Military Decline As they lost initiative to western European peoples in economic and commercial affairs, the Islamic empires also did not seek actively to improve their military technologies. During the sixteenth and early seventeenth centuries, the Islamic empires were able to purchase European weapons in large numbers and attract European expertise that kept their armies supplied with powerful gunpowder weapons. By about the mid–seventeenth century, however, European military technology was advancing so rapidly that the Islamic empires could not keep pace. None of the empires had a large armaments industry, so they had to rely on foreign suppliers. They still were able to purchase European weapons and expertise, but their arsenals became increasingly dated, since they depended on technologies that European peoples had already replaced. By the late eighteenth century, even the once-influential Ottoman navy was closing its shipbuilding operations and ordering new military vessels from foreign shipyards.

Cultural Conservatism

While experiencing economic and military decline, the Islamic empires also neglected cultural developments in the larger world. Europeans who visited the Islamic empires attempted to learn as much as possible about the language, religion, social customs, and history of the host countries. They published accounts of their travels that became extremely popular in their homelands, and they advocated serious study of Islamic lands.

Piri Reis Meanwhile, the Islamic empires expressed only limited interest in world affairs. In the sixteenth century, just as European mariners were scouting Atlantic waters, Ottoman mariners did reconnoiter the Indian Ocean basin from east Africa to Indonesia. Ottoman geographers also manifested great interest in European knowledge of geography, some of which had considerable military value. The Ottoman admiral and cartographer Piri Reis produced several large-scale maps and a major navigational text, the *Book of Seafaring*, which drew on reports and maps from European mariners and explorers. Some of Piri Reis's maps included the Atlantic coast of North America and the lands visited by Columbus, which the cartographer probably learned

Ottoman cartographer Piri Reis drew on European charts when preparing this map of the Atlantic Ocean basin in 1513. Caribbean and South American coastlines are visible at left, and Iberian and west African coastlines appear in the upper right corner.

about from Spanish sailors captured in naval conflicts with Ottoman forces.

On the whole, however, few Muslims traveled willingly to the infidel lands of "the Franks." Muslim *Cultural Conservatism* rulers and their Muslim subjects were confident that they had nothing to learn from Europeans. As a result, most Muslims remained largely oblivious to European cultural and technological developments. Not until 1703 was there an attempt to introduce European scientific instruments such as the telescope into astronomical observatories. Then conservative Muslim clerics soon forced the removal of the foreign implements, which they considered impious and unnecessary.

The early experience of the printing press in the Islamic empires illustrates especially well the resis- *The Printing Press* tance of conservative religious leaders to cultural imports from western Europe. Jewish refugees from Spain introduced the first printing presses to Anatolia in the late fifteenth century. Ottoman authorities allowed them to operate presses in Istanbul and other major cities as long as they did not print books in the Turkish or Arabic language. Not until 1729 did government authorities lift the ban on the printing of such books. During the next thirteen years, a Turkish press published seventeen books dealing mostly with history, geography, and language before conservative Muslims forced its closure in 1742. Only in 1784 did a new Turkish press open.

Printing also caught on slowly in Mughal India. Jesuit missionaries in Goa published books, including translations of the Bible into Indian and Arabic languages, as early as the 1550s. Yet Mughal rulers displayed little interest in the press, and printing did not become prominent in Indian society until the establishment of British colonial rule in Bengal in the eighteenth century.

To some extent, aesthetic considerations stood in the way of the printing press: particularly in the Ottoman and Safavid empires, scholars and general readers alike preferred elegant handwritten books to cheaply produced printed works. Yet resistance to printing also reflected the concerns of conservative religious leaders that readily available printed books would introduce all manner of new and dangerous ideas to the public.

Thus, like imperial China and Tokugawa Japan, the Islamic empires resisted the introduction of cultural influences from western European societies. Rulers of the Islamic empires readily accepted gunpowder weapons as enhancements to their military and political power, but they and their subjects drew little inspiration from European religion, science, or ideas. Moreover, under the influence of conservative religious leaders, Islamic authorities actively discouraged the circulation of ideas that might pose unsettling challenges to the social and cultural order. Like the Ming, Qing, and Tokugawa rulers, the Ottoman, Safavid, and Mughal emperors preferred political and social stability to the risks that foreign cultural innovations might bring.

SUMMARY

Like China and Japan, the Islamic empires largely retained control of their own affairs throughout the early modern era. Ruling elites of the Ottoman, Safavid, and Mughal empires came from nomadic Turkish stock, and they all drew on steppe traditions in organizing their governments. But the rulers also devised institutions that maintained order over a long term. During the sixteenth and seventeenth centuries, all the Islamic empires enjoyed productive economies that enabled merchants to participate actively in the global trade networks of early modern times. By the early eighteenth century, however, these same empires were experiencing economic difficulties that led to political and military decline. Like the Ming, Qing, and Tokugawa rulers in east Asia, the Islamic emperors mostly sought to limit foreign and especially European influences in their realms. The Islamic emperors ruled lands that were religiously and ethnically diverse, and most of them worried that such influences would threaten political and social stability. They allowed their subjects to practice faiths other than Islam, and a few emperors actively worked to defuse religious tensions in their realms.

For the most part, however, rulers of the Islamic empires followed the advice of conservative Muslim clerics, who promoted Islamic values and fought the introduction of foreign cultural imports that might undermine their authority. By the late eighteenth century, the Safavid empire had collapsed, and economic difficulties and cultural insularity had severely weakened the Ottoman and Mughal empires.

CHRONOLOGY

1289–1923	Ottoman dynasty
1451–1481	Reign of Mehmed the Conqueror
1453	Ottoman conquest of Constantinople
1501–1524	Reign of Shah Ismail
1501–1722	Safavid dynasty
1514	Battle of Chaldiran
1520–1566	Reign of Süleyman the Magnificent
1526–1858	Mughal dynasty
1556–1605	Reign of Akbar
1588–1629	Reign of Shah Abbas the Great
1659–1707	Reign of Aurangzeb

FOR FURTHER READING

Esin Atil. *The Age of Sultan Süleyman the Magnificent*. Washington, 1987. Richly illustrated volume that emphasizes Süleyman's role as a patron of the arts.

Palmira Brummett. *Ottoman Seapower and Levantine Diplomacy in the Age of Discovery*. Albany, 1994. A scholarly study of Ottoman military strategy and diplomacy in the Mediterranean during the sixteenth century.

Stephen Frederic Dale. *Indian Merchants and Eurasian Trade, 1600–1750*. Cambridge, 1994. Examines the workings of an Indian trading community that conducted business in Persia, central Asia, and Russia.

Halil Inalçik. *The Ottoman Empire: The Classical Age, 1300–1600*. New York, 1973. A reliable survey by the foremost historian of the early Ottoman empire.

Çemal Kafadar. *Between Two Worlds: The Construction of the Ottoman State*. Berkeley, 1995. Studies the origins and early development of the Ottoman empire.

Bernard Lewis. *The Muslim Discovery of Europe*. New York, 1982. An important study that charts Muslim interest in European affairs.

Leslie Pierce. *The Imperial Harem: Women and Sovereignty in the Ottoman Empire*. Oxford, 1993. Challenges many stereotypes about the role of women in the imperial Ottoman elite.

John F. Richards. *The Mughal Empire*. Cambridge, 1993. A concise and reliable overview of Mughal history, concentrating on political affairs.

Roger Savory. *Iran under the Safavids*. Cambridge, 1980. A rich and authoritative survey of Safavid history, especially interesting for its views on Safavid origins, culture, and commercial relations.

CHAPTER 26
Revolutions and National States in the Atlantic World

Marie Gouze was a French butcher's daughter who educated herself by reading books, moved to Paris, and married a junior army officer. Under the name Olympe de Gouges she won some fame as a journalist, actress, and playwright. Gouges was as flamboyant as she was talented, and her well-publicized love affairs scandalized Parisian society.

Gouges was also a revolutionary and a strong advocate of women's rights. She responded enthusiastically when the French revolution broke out in July 1789, and she applauded in August when revolutionary leaders proclaimed freedom and equality for all citizens in the *Declaration of the Rights of Man and the Citizen*. It soon became clear, however, that freedom and equality pertained only to male citizens. Revolutionary leaders welcomed women's contributions to the revolution but refused to grant them political and social rights.

Gouges demanded that women share equal rights in family property and campaigned for equal education. She even appealed to Queen Marie Antoinette to use her influence to advance women's rights. In 1791 Gouges published a *Declaration of the Rights of Woman and the Female Citizen*, which claimed the same rights for women that revolutionary leaders had granted to men in August 1789. She insisted on the rights of women to vote, speak their minds freely, participate in the making of law, and hold public office.

Gouges's declaration attracted a great deal of attention but little support. Revolutionary leaders dismissed her appeal, and in 1793 they executed her because of her affection for Marie Antoinette

OPPOSITE PAGE: *Liberty, personified as a woman, leads the French people in a famous painting by Eugène Delacroix.*

475

and her persistent crusade for women's rights. Yet Gouges's campaign illustrated the power of the Enlightenment ideals of freedom and equality. Revolutionary leaders stilled her voice, but once they had proclaimed freedom and equality as universal human rights, they were unable to suppress demands to extend them to new constituencies.

A series of violent revolutions brought dramatic political and social change to lands throughout much of the Atlantic Ocean basin in the late eighteenth and early nineteenth centuries. Revolution broke out first in the British colonies of North America, where colonists founded a new republic. A few years later, revolutionaries abolished the French monarchy and thoroughly reorganized French society. Revolutionary ideas soon spread, prompting Latin American peoples to seek independence from Spanish and Portuguese colonial rule. In Saint-Domingue, revolution led to the abolition of slavery as well as independence from French rule. By the 1830s, peoples had reorganized political and social structures throughout western Europe and the Americas.

The revolutions of the late eighteenth and early nineteenth centuries had two results of deep global significance. First, they helped to spread a cluster of Enlightenment ideas concerning freedom, equality, and popular sovereignty. Revolutionary leaders argued that political authority arose from the people rather than the rulers and often sought to establish republican forms of government in which the people selected delegates to represent their interests. In fact, early revolutionaries extended political rights only to a privileged group of white men, but they justified their actions in general terms that prompted disenfranchised groups to seek freedom, equality, and a political voice as well. Indeed, such ideas spread globally in the nineteenth and twentieth centuries as social reformers and revolutionaries struggled to make freedom and equality a reality for oppressed groups throughout the world.

Second, while promoting Enlightenment values, revolutions encouraged the consolidation of national states as the principal form of political organization. As peoples defended their states from enemies and sometimes mounted attacks on foreign lands, they developed a powerful sense of identity with their compatriots. During the nineteenth century, strong national identities led to movements to build national states, which in turn profoundly influenced the political experiences of European states. During the late nineteenth and twentieth centuries, efforts to harness nationalist sentiments and form states based on national identity became one of the most powerful and dynamic movements in world history.

POPULAR SOVEREIGNTY AND POLITICAL UPHEAVAL

Drawing on Enlightenment ideals, revolutionaries of the eighteenth and nineteenth centuries sought to fashion equitable societies by instituting governments that were responsive to the peoples they governed. In justifying their policies, revolutionaries argued for popular sovereignty—the notion that legitimate political authority resides not in kings but, rather, in the people who make up a society. In North America, colonists declared independence from British rule and instituted a new government founded on the principle of popular sovereignty. Soon thereafter, French revolutionaries abolished the monarchy and revamped the social order. Yet revolutionaries in France were unable to devise a stable alternative to the monarchy. In the early nineteenth century, Napoleon Bonaparte imposed military rule on France and helped spread revolutionary ideas to much of western Europe.

Enlightened and Revolutionary Ideas

Throughout history kings or emperors ruled almost all settled agricultural societies. In justifying their rule, they often identified themselves with deities or claimed divine sanction for their authority. In imperial China, for example, dynastic houses claimed to rule in accordance with the "mandate of heaven," and in early modern Europe centralizing monarchs often asserted a "divine right of kings" to rule as absolute monarchs.

During the seventeenth and eighteenth centuries, philosophes and other advocates of Enlightenment ideas (discussed in chapter 21) began to question such notions and argued that kings should be responsible to the people they governed. The English philosopher John Locke (1632–1704), for example, regarded government as a contract between rulers and ruled. In his *Second Treatise of Civil Government,* published in 1690, Locke held that individuals granted political rights to their rulers but retained personal rights to life, liberty, and property. Furthermore, according to Locke, rulers de-

Popular Sovereignty

rived their authority from the consent of those they governed. If rulers broke the contract, the people had the right to replace their rulers. In effect, Locke's political thought relocated sovereignty, removing it from rulers as divine agents and vesting it in the people of a society.

Individual Freedom   Enlightenment thinkers addressed issues of freedom and equality as well as sovereignty. Philosophes such as Voltaire (1694–1778) resented the persecution of religious minorities as well as royal censorship. Philosophes called for religious toleration and freedom to express their views openly. Thus, when censors prohibited the publication of their writings in France, they often published their books in Switzerland or the Netherlands and smuggled them across the border into France.

Political and Legal Equality   Many Enlightenment thinkers also called for equality. They argued that privileged aristocrats made no more contribution to the larger society than peasants, artisans, or workers and recommended the creation of a society in which all individuals would be equal before the law. The most prominent advocate of political equality was the French-Swiss thinker Jean-Jacques Rousseau (1712–1778). In his influential book *The Social Contract* (1762), Rousseau argued that members of a society were collectively the sovereign. In an ideal society all individuals would participate directly in the formulation of policy and the creation of laws.

Global Influence of Enlightenment Values   Most Enlightenment thinkers were of common birth but comfortable means. Though seeking to limit the prerogatives of ruling and aristocratic classes, they did not envision a society in which they would share political rights with women, children, peasants, laborers, or slaves. Nevertheless, Enlightenment thought constituted a serious challenge to long-established notions of political and social order. Although arguments for freedom, equality, and popular sovereignty originally served the interests of relatively privileged European and Euro-American men, many other groups made effective use of them in seeking the extension of political rights.

The American Revolution

In the mid–eighteenth century there was no sign that North America would become a center of revolution. Residents of the thirteen British colonies there regarded themselves as British subjects: they recognized British law, read English-language books, and benefited hand-somely from British rule. Trade brought prosperity to the colonies, and British military forces protected colonists' interests. From 1754 to 1763, for example, British forces waged an expensive conflict in North America known as the French and Indian War. That conflict merged with a larger contest for imperial supremacy, the Seven Years' War (1756–1763), in which British and French forces battled each other in Europe and India as well as North America. Victory in the Seven Years' War ensured that Britain would dominate global trade and that British North America would prosper.

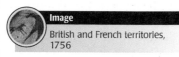

Tightened British Control of the Colonies   After the mid-1760s, however, North American colonists became increasingly disenchanted with British imperial rule. Faced with staggering financial difficulties arising from the Seven Years' War, the British parliament expected that the North American colonies would bear a fair share of the cost through new taxes. But new taxes proved extremely unpopular in North America. Colonists especially resented the imposition of taxes on molasses by the Sugar Act (1764), on publications and legal documents by the Stamp Act (1765), on a variety of imported items by the Townshend Act (1767), and on tea by the Tea Act (1773). Colonists also took offense at the Quartering Act (1765), which required them to provide housing and accommodations for British troops.

Colonists argued that they should pay such taxes only if the North American colonies were represented in the British parliament, arguing that there should be "no taxation without representation." They boycotted British products, physically attacked British officials, and mounted protests. They also organized the Continental Congress (1774), which coordinated the colonies' resistance to British policies. By 1775 tensions were so high that British troops and a colonial militia skirmished at the village of Lexington, near Boston. The war of American independence had begun.

The Declaration of Independence   On 4 July 1776 the Continental Congress adopted a document titled "The unanimous Declaration of the thirteen united States of America." This Declaration of Independence drew deep inspiration from Enlightenment political thought in its insistence "that all men are created equal, that they are endowed by their Creator with certain unalienable

Rights, that among these are Life, Liberty, and the pursuit of Happiness." It echoed John Locke's contractual theory of government in arguing that governments derive their power and authority from "the consent of the governed." When any government infringes upon individuals' rights, the document continued, "it is the Right of the People to alter or abolish it, and to institute new Government." The Declaration of Independence presented a long list of specific abuses charged to the British crown and concluded by proclaiming the colonies "Free and Independent States."

It was one thing to declare independence, but a different matter to make independence a reality. Britain enjoyed many advantages over the rebels: a strong government, the most powerful navy in the world, a com-

petent army, and a sizable population of loyalists in the colonies. But the colonies were far away, and British opponents were many. In addition, many European states were eager to see Britain lose its colonies: France, Spain, the Netherlands, and several German principalities all contributed militarily and economically to the American quest for independence. Moreover, George Washington (1732–1799) provided strong and imaginative military leadership for the colonial army while local militias employed guerrilla tactics effectively against British forces.

By 1780 all combatants were weary of the conflict. In October 1781 British forces surrendered to American and French forces commanded by George Washington at Yorktown, Virginia. In September 1783 diplomats concluded the Peace of Paris, by

Map 26.1 The thirteen colonies that rebelled against the British during the American Revolution. Note the location of both the major towns and cities in the colonies and the location of the major battles that occurred during the revolution. Why were both situated so close to the eastern coast?

In this painting by American artist John Trumbull, authors of the Declaration of Independence, including John Adams, Thomas Jefferson, and Benjamin Franklin, stand before a desk at the Continental Congress in Philadelphia.

which the British government formally recognized American independence.

The leaders of the fledgling republic organized a state that reflected Enlightenment principles. In 1787 a constitutional convention drafted the Constitution of the United States, which emphasized the rights of individuals. American leaders based the federal government on popular sovereignty, and they agreed to guarantee individual liberties such as freedom of speech, of the press, and of religion. Full political and social rights, however, were accorded only to men of property: landless men, women, slaves, and indigenous peoples were not included. Over the long term, however, disenfranchised groups claimed and struggled for political and legal rights and helped broaden the implications of the Enlightenment values of freedom and equality as well as popular sovereignty.

Building an Independent State

The French Revolution

French revolutionaries also drew inspiration from Enlightenment political thought, but the French revolution was a more radical affair than its American counterpart. American revolutionary leaders sought independence from British imperial rule, but they were content to retain British law and much of their British social and cultural heritage. In contrast, French revolutionary leaders repudiated existing society, often referred to as the *ancien régime* ("the old order"), and sought to replace it with new political, social, and cultural structures.

Serious financial, political, and social problems put France on the road to revolution. When Louis XVI (reigned 1774–1793) became king, he inherited an enormous debt from his predecessors, most of which had been incurred during France's many wars in the seventeenth and eighteenth centuries. To make matters worse, the French government had spent large sums of money helping the Americans in their war of independence. As a result, by the 1780s half of the French royal government's revenues went to pay off the national debt, and an additional quarter supported the French armed forces. Although France was a wealthy country in the eighteenth century, it did not have a national banking system to finance loans, and it did not have an efficient system of tax collection. Even if it had, the wealthiest French classes—including the nobility and the clergy—were exempt from most taxes, which meant that nearly

The Estates General

all direct taxes had to be levied on the already poor and overburdened French peasantry.

By 1787 King Louis XVI was desperate for money. When he turned to the French nobility and clergy for help, however, they refused. They did so in part to protect their financial status, but they also wanted to demonstrate to the king their ability to act independently. If the king wanted their help, they argued, he was going to have to allow the nobility a larger share of power. This issue of power was one that the king and the nobles had clashed over repeatedly in the past, and it was one over which the king was not willing to compromise. In the hope that Louis would be forced to institute reforms to their liking, then, the nobility demanded that Louis summon the Estates General, an assembly that represented the entire French population through three groups, known as estates. The first estate consisted of about one hundred thousand Roman Catholic clergy, and the second included some four hundred thousand nobles. The third estate embraced the rest of the population—about twenty-four million serfs, free peasants, and urban residents. It had as many delegates as the other two estates combined.

The National Assembly

In May 1789 King Louis called the Estates General into session at the royal palace of Versailles in hopes that it would authorize new taxes. But the mood of many of the representatives was grim. People of the third estate, in particular, were extremely dissatisfied with Louis. The middle classes resented the assumption of the best jobs and offices by the nobility and were also influenced by

Versailles

calls for political reforms that were making their way through France and the Atlantic world. The poorer classes, meanwhile, resented the burden of taxation they had to carry and were in any case feeling desperate because of economic hardship brought about by extremely bad harvests in 1788.

It quickly became clear to the members of the third estate that the members of the first and second estates wanted to maintain control by insisting that each estate cast only one vote. Members of the third estate insisted, in contrast, that the estates vote together by head. Disillusioned by weeks of arguing, on 17 June 1789 representatives of the third estate took the dramatic step of seceding from the Estates General and proclaiming themselves to be the National Assembly. Three days later, members of the new Assembly swore not to disband until they had provided France with a new constitution. The next month, on 14 July 1789,

a Parisian crowd stormed the Bastille, a royal jail and arsenal, in search of weapons to defend themselves from what they feared would be a royal crackdown on supporters of the Assembly. The military garrison protecting the Bastille surrendered to the crowd but only after killing many of the attackers. To vent their rage, members of the crowd hacked the

The Bastille

defenders to death. News of the event soon spread, sparking insurrections in cities throughout France. Those insurrections grew even more intense when rumors spread that armed bands organized by nobles were moving through the countryside to restore order. This "Great Fear" prompted the peasantry all over France to burn monasteries, public records offices, and the houses of nobles.

Fearing that the revolution would swing out of their control unless they acted quickly, the National Assembly undertook a broad program of political and social reform. The *Declaration of the Rights of Man and the Citizen,* which the National Assembly promulgated in August 1789, articulated the guiding principles of the program. Reflecting the influence of American revolutionary ideas, the *Declaration of the Rights of Man and the Citizen* proclaimed the equality of all men, declared that sovereignty resided in the people, and asserted individual rights.

Liberty, Equality, and Fraternity

Between 1789 and 1791 the National Assembly reconfigured French society. Taking the Enlightenment ideals of "liberty, equality, and fraternity" as its goals, the Assembly abolished the old social order. It seized church lands, abolished the first estate, defined clergy as civilians, and required clergy to take an oath of loyalty to the state. It also produced a constitution that left the king in place but deprived him of legislative authority. France became a constitutional monarchy in which men of property—about half the adult male population—had the right to vote in elections to choose legislators.

The Convention

The revolution soon took a radical turn. Many Parisians who were supposed to be represented by the third estate felt that the changes effected by the revolution were not radical enough and favored transforming France into a republic. The desire for a more radical approach was further encouraged by the efforts of the French nobility to ally with foreign powers—especially Austria and Prussia—to help restore the ancien régime. Faced with this threat to the survival of the revolution, the Assem-

SOURCES FROM THE PAST

Declaration of the Rights of Man and the Citizen

While developing their program of reform, members of the National Assembly consulted closely with Thomas Jefferson, the principal author of the American Declaration of Independence, who was the U.S. ambassador to France in 1789. Thus it is not surprising that the Declaration of the Rights of Man and the Citizen *reflects the influence of American revolutionary ideas.*

■ ■ ■

First Article. Men are born and remain free and equal in rights. Social distinctions may be based only on common utility.

Article 2. The goal of every political association is the preservation of the natural and inalienable rights of man. These rights are liberty, property, security, and resistance to oppression.

Article 3. The principle of all sovereignty resides essentially in the nation. No body and no individual can exercise authority that does not flow directly from the nation.

Article 4. Liberty consists in the freedom to do anything that does not harm another. The exercise of natural rights of each man thus has no limits except those that assure other members of society their enjoyment of the same rights. These limits may be determined only by law.

Article 6. Law is the expression of the general will. All citizens have the right to participate either personally or through their representatives in the making of law. The law must be the same for all, whether it protects or punishes. Being equal in the eyes of the law, all citizens are equally eligible for all public honors, offices, and occupations, according to their abilities, without any distinction other than that of their virtues and talents.

Article 7. No person shall be accused, arrested, or imprisoned except in the cases and according to the forms prescribed by law. Any one soliciting, transmit-

ting, executing, or causing to be executed, any arbitrary order, shall be punished. But any citizen summoned or arrested in virtue of the law shall submit without delay, as resistance constitutes an offense.

Article 9. As all persons are held innocent until they shall have been declared guilty, if arrest shall be deemed indispensable, all harshness not essential to the securing of the prisoner's person shall be severely repressed by law.

Article 11. The free communication of thoughts and opinions is one of the most precious rights of man: every citizen may thus speak, write, and publish freely, but will be responsible for abuse of this freedom in cases decided by the law.

Article 13. For the maintenance of public military force and for the expenses of administration, common taxation is necessary: it must be equally divided among all citizens according to their means.

Article 15. Society has the right to require from every public official an accounting of his administration.

Article 16. Any society in which guarantees of rights are not assured and separation of powers is not defined has no constitution at all.

Article 17. Property is an inviolable and sacred right. No one may be deprived of property except when public necessity, legally determined, clearly requires it, and on condition of just and prearranged compensation.

- *In what ways do the principles established in the Declaration reflect the political transformations taking place throughout the age of Atlantic revolutions?*

SOURCE: *Déclaration des droits de l'homme et du citoyen.* Translated by Jerry H. Bentley.

bly declared war against Austria and Prussia in April 1792. In the following year, revolutionary leaders declared war on Spain, Britain, and the Netherlands. Fearing military defeat and counterrevolution, revo-

lutionary leaders created the Convention, a new legislative body elected by universal manhood suffrage, which abolished the monarchy and proclaimed France a republic. The Convention rallied the French

The guillotine was an efficient killing machine. In this contemporary print the executioner displays the just-severed head of King Louis XVI to the crowd assembled to witness his execution.

population by instituting the *levée en masse,* a "mass levy" that drafted people and resources for use in the war against invading forces. The Convention also rooted out enemies at home by making frequent use of the guillotine. In 1793 King Louis XVI and his wife, Queen Marie Antoinette, themselves went to the guillotine when the Convention found them guilty of treason to the principles of the revolution.

Revolutionary chaos reached its peak in 1793 and 1794 when Maximilien Robespierre (1758–1794) and the radical Jacobin party dominated the Convention. A lawyer by training, Robespierre had emerged during the revolution as a ruthless but popular radical known as "the Incorruptible," and he dominated the

Committee of Public Safety, the executive authority of the Republic. The Jacobins believed passionately that France needed complete restructuring, and they unleashed a campaign of terror to promote their revolutionary agenda. They sought to eliminate the influence of Christianity in French society by closing churches, forcing priests to take wives, and promoting a new, secular "cult of reason." They reorganized the calendar, replacing seven-day weeks with ten-day units that recognized no day of religious observance. The Jacobins also encouraged citizens to display their revolutionary zeal by wearing working-class clothes and granted increased rights to women by permitting them to inherit property and divorce their husbands.

The Jacobins made especially frequent use of the guillotine: in a yearlong "reign of terror" between the summer of 1793 and the summer of 1794, they executed about forty thousand people and imprisoned three hundred thousand others as suspected enemies of the revolution.

Eventually, such political purges undermined confidence in the regime itself. In July 1794 the Convention *The Directory* arrested Robespierre and his allies, convicted them of tyranny, and sent them to the guillotine. A group of conservative men of property then seized power and ruled France under a new institution known as the Directory (1795–1799). However, the Directory was unable to resolve the economic and military problems that plagued revolutionary France. In seeking a middle way between the ancien régime and radical revolution, they lurched from one policy to another, and the Directory faced constant challenges to its authority. It came to an end in November 1799 when a young general named Napoleon Bonaparte staged a coup d'état and seized power.

The Reign of Napoleon

Born to a minor noble family on the Mediterranean island of Corsica, Napoleon Bonaparte (1769–1821) studied at French military schools and became an officer in the army of King Louis XVI. A brilliant military leader, he became a general at age twenty-four. He was a fervent supporter of the revolution and defended the Directory against a popular uprising in 1795. In a campaign of 1796–1797, he drove the Austrian army from northern Italy and established French rule there. In

Interactive Map
Napoleon's empire

1798 he mounted an invasion of Egypt, but the campaign ended in a French defeat. Politically ambitious, Napoleon returned to France in 1799 and joined the Directory. When Austria, Russia, and Britain formed a coalition to attack France and end the revolution, he overthrew the Directory, imposed a new constitution, and named himself first consul. In 1802 he became consul for life, and two years later he crowned himself emperor.

Napoleon brought political stability to a land torn by revolution and war. He made peace with the Roman *Napoleonic* Catholic church and reversed the most radical religious policies of the Convention. In 1804 Napoleon promulgated the Civil Code, a revised body of civil law, which also helped stabilize French society. The Civil Code affirmed the political and legal equality of all adult men and established

a merit-based society in which individuals advanced in education and employment because of talent rather than birth or social standing. The Civil Code confirmed many of the moderate revolutionary policies of the National Assembly but retracted measures passed by

Image
Napoleon on his imperial throne

the more radical Convention. The code restored patriarchal authority in the family, for example, by making women and children subservient to male heads of households.

Although he approved of the Enlightenment ideal of equality, Napoleon was no champion of intellectual freedom or representative government. He limited free speech and routinely censored newspapers and other publications. He established a secret police force that relied heavily on spies and detained suspected political opponents by the thousands. He made systematic use of propaganda to manipulate public opinion. He ignored elective bodies and founded a dynasty that set his family above the people in whose name they ruled.

While working to stabilize France, Napoleon also sought to extend his authority throughout Europe. Napoleon's armies conquered the Iberian *Napoleon's* and Italian peninsulas, occupied the Neth- *Empire* erlands, and inflicted humiliating defeats on Austrian and Prussian forces. Napoleon sent his brothers and other relatives to rule the conquered and occupied lands, and he forced Austria, Prussia, and Russia to ally with him and respect French hegemony in Europe.

Napoleon's empire began to unravel in 1812, when he decided to invade Russia. Convinced that the tsar was conspiring with his British enemies, Napoleon led an army of six hundred thousand soldiers to Moscow. He captured the city, but the tsar withdrew and set Moscow ablaze, leaving Napoleon's vast army without adequate shelter or supplies. Napoleon ordered a retreat, but the bitter Russian winter destroyed his army, and only a battered remnant of thirty thousand soldiers managed to limp back to France.

Napoleon's disastrous Russian campaign emboldened his enemies. A coalition of British, Austrian, Prussian, and Russian armies converged on France and forced Napoleon to abdi- *The Fall* cate his throne in April 1814. The victors *of Napoleon* restored the French monarchy and exiled Napoleon to the tiny Mediterranean island of Elba. But in March 1815 Napoleon escaped from Elba, returned to France, and ruled France for a hundred days before a British army defeated him at Waterloo in Belgium. This time,

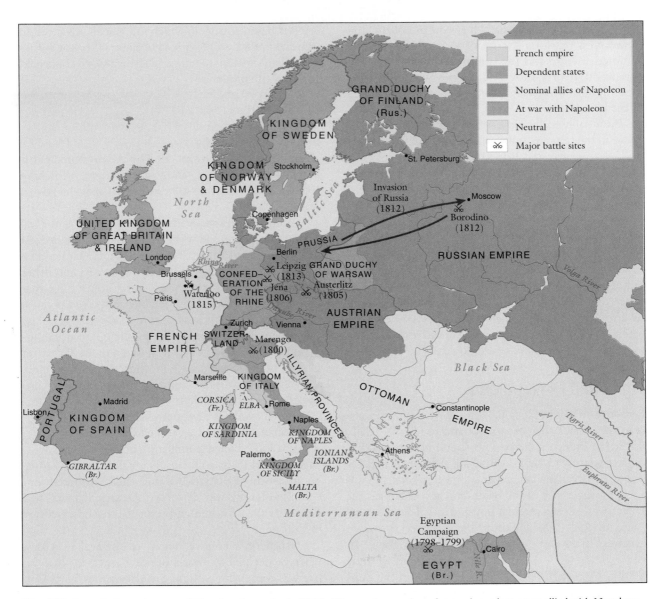

Map 26.2 Boundaries and states of Napoleon's empire in 1812. Observe the number of states dependent on or allied with Napoleon as opposed to those who were at war with him. Were there geographic conditions that allowed some states to resist Napoleon's efforts at conquest better than others?

European powers banished Napoleon to the remote and isolated island of St. Helena in the South Atlantic Ocean, where he died of natural causes in 1821.

THE INFLUENCE OF REVOLUTION

The Enlightenment ideals promoted by the American and French revolutions appealed to peoples throughout Europe and the Americas. In the Caribbean and Latin America, they inspired revolutionary movements: slaves in the French colony of Saint-Domingue rose against their overlords and established the independent republic of Haiti, and Euro-American leaders mounted independence movements in Mexico, Central America, and South America. The ideals of the American and French revolutions also encouraged social reformers to organize broader programs of liberation for women and slaves of African ancestry.

The Haitian Revolution

The only successful slave revolt in history took place on the Caribbean island of Hispaniola. The Spanish colony of Santo Domingo occupied the eastern part of the island (modern Dominican Republic), and the French colony of Saint-Domingue occupied the western part (modern Haiti). Saint-Domingue was one of the richest of all European colonies in the Caribbean: sugar, coffee, and cotton produced there accounted for almost one-third of France's foreign trade.

In 1790 the population of Saint-Domingue included about forty thousand white French settlers, *Saint-Domingue Society* thirty thousand *gens de couleur* (free people of color), and some five hundred thousand black slaves, most of whom were born in Africa. Led by wealthy planters, white residents stood at the top of society. *Gens de couleur* farmed small plots of land, sometimes with the aid of a few slaves, or worked as artisans in the island's towns. Most of the colony's slaves toiled in the fields under brutal conditions. Many slaves ran away into the mountains to escape such treatment. By the late eighteenth century, Saint-Domingue had many large communities of maroons (escaped slaves).

The American and French revolutions prepared the way for a violent political and social revolution in Saint-Domingue. Because French policy supported North American colonists against British rule, colonial governors in Saint-Domingue sent about five hundred *gens de couleur* to fight in the American war of independence. They returned to Saint-Domingue

The slave rebellion in Saint-Domingue struck fear in the hearts of European and Euro-American peoples. This French print depicts outnumbered white settlers under attack on a plantation.

with the intention of reforming society. When the French revolution broke out in 1789, white settlers in Saint-Domingue sought the right to govern themselves, but they opposed proposals to grant political and legal equality to the *gens de couleur.* By May 1791 civil war had broken out between white settlers and *gens de couleur.*

The conflict expanded dramatically when a charismatic Vodou priest named Boukman organized a slave

Slave Revolt

revolt. In August 1791 some twelve thousand slaves began killing white settlers, burning their homes, and destroying their plantations. Within a few weeks the numbers of slaves in revolt grew to almost one hundred thousand. Saint-Domingue quickly descended into chaos as white, *gens de couleur,* and slave factions battled one another. Foreign armies soon complicated the situation: French troops arrived in 1792 to restore order, and British and Spanish forces intervened in 1793 in hopes of benefiting from France's difficulties.

Eventually, slave forces overcame white settlers, *gens de couleur,* and foreign armies. Their successes were due

Toussaint L'Ouverture

largely to the leadership of François-Dominique Toussaint (1744–1803), who after 1791 called himself Louverture— from the French *l'ouverture,* meaning "the opening." The son of slaves, he himself had been a free man since 1776. Toussaint was a skilled organizer, and by 1793 he had built a strong, disciplined army. He shrewdly played French, British, and Spanish forces against one another while also jockeying for power with other black and mulatto generals. By 1797 he led an army of twenty thousand that controlled most of Saint-Domingue. In 1801 he issued a constitution that granted equality and citizenship to all residents of Saint-Domingue. He stopped short of declaring independence from France, however, because he did not want to provoke Napoleon into attacking the island.

Nevertheless, in 1802 Napoleon dispatched forty thousand troops to restore French authority in Saint-

The Republic of Haiti

Domingue. Toussaint attempted to negotiate a peaceful settlement, but the French commander arrested him and sent him to France, where he died in jail of maltreatment in 1803. By the time he died, however, the black generals who succeeded Toussaint had defeated the remaining French troops and driven them out of the colony. Late in 1803 they declared independence, and on 1 January 1804 they proclaimed the establishment of Haiti, meaning "land of mountains," which became the second independent republic in the western hemisphere.

Wars of Independence in Latin America

Revolutionary ideals traveled beyond Saint-Domingue to the Spanish and Portuguese colonies in the Americas. Though governed by *peninsulares* (colonial officials from Spain or Portugal), the Iberian colonies all had a large, wealthy, and powerful class of Euro-American *criollos,* or creoles, individuals born in the Americas of Spanish or Portuguese ancestry. In 1800 the *peninsulares* numbered about 30,000, and the creole population was 3.5 million. The Iberian colonies also had a large population—about 10 million in all— of less privileged classes such as black slaves, indigenous peoples, mestizos, and mulattoes.

Latin American Society

Creoles prospered during the eighteenth century as they established plantations in the colonies and participated in trade with Spain and Portugal. Yet the creoles also had grievances. Like British colonists in North America, the creoles resented administrative control and economic regulations imposed by the Iberian powers. Although they drew inspiration from Enlightenment political thought, the creoles desired neither radical social reform nor the establishment of an egalitarian society. Instead, they sought to displace the *peninsulares* but retain their privileged position in society. Between 1810 and 1825, creoles led movements that brought independence to all Spanish colonies in the Americas—except Cuba and Puerto Rico—and established creole-dominated republics.

The struggle for independence began in the wake of Napoleon's invasion of Spain and Portugal (1807), which weakened royal authority in the Iberian colonies. By 1810 revolts against Spanish rule had broken out in Argentina, Venezuela, and Mexico. The most serious was a peasant rebellion in Mexico led by a parish priest, Miguel de Hidalgo (1753–1811), who rallied indigenous peoples and mestizos against colonial rule. Conservative creoles who feared revolution by the masses soon captured Hidalgo and executed him, but his rebellion continued to flare for three years after his death. Hidalgo became the symbol of Mexican independence, and the day on which he proclaimed his revolt—16 September 1810—is Mexico's principal national holiday.

Mexican Independence

Colonial rule came to an end in 1821, when the creole general Augustín de Iturbide (1783–1824) de-

peninsulares (peh-neen-soo-LAH-rehs)

clared independence from Spain. In the following year, he declared himself emperor of Mexico. Iturbide was an incompetent administrator, however, and in 1823 creole elites deposed him and established a republic. Two years later the southern regions of the Mexican empire declared their own independence. They formed a Central American Federation until 1838, then split into the independent states of Guatemala, El Salvador, Honduras, Nicaragua, and Costa Rica.

In South America, creole elites such as Simón Bolívar (1783–1830) led the movement for independence. *Simón Bolívar* Born in Caracas (in modern Venezuela), Bolívar was a fervent republican steeped in Enlightenment ideas about popular sovereignty. Inspired by the example of George Washington, he took up arms against Spanish rule in 1811. In 1819, after many reversals, he assembled an army that surprised and crushed the Spanish army in Colombia. Later he campaigned in Venezuela, Ecuador, and Peru, coordinating his efforts with other creole leaders such as José de San Martín (1778–1850) in Argentina and Bernardo O'Higgins (1778–1842) in Chile. By 1825 creole forces had overcome Spanish armies and deposed Spanish rulers throughout South America.

Bolívar's goal was to weld the former Spanish colonies of South America into a confederation like the United States. During the 1820s independent Venezuela, Colombia, and Ecuador formed a repub-

lic called Gran Colombia, and Bolívar attempted to bring Peru and Bolivia into the confederation. By 1830, however, strong political and regional differences led to the breakup of Gran Colombia. As the confederation disintegrated, a bitterly disappointed Bolívar—who died shortly afterward—pronounced South America "ungovernable."

Independence came to Portuguese Brazil at the same time as to Spanish colonies, but by a different process. When Napoleon invaded Portugal in 1807, the royal court fled Lisbon *Brazilian* and established a government-in-exile in *Independence* Rio de Janeiro. In 1821 the king returned to Portugal, leaving his son Pedro in Brazil as regent. The next year Brazilian creoles called for independence from Portugal, and Pedro agreed to their demands. In 1822 Pedro declared Brazil's independence and accepted appointment as Emperor Pedro I (reigned 1822–1834).

In Brazil as in the former Spanish colonies, creole elites dominated both politics and society. Indeed, independence brought little social change in Latin America: although the *peninsulares* *Creole* returned to Europe, Latin American soci- *Dominance* ety remained stratified and unequal. The newly independent states granted military authority to local strongmen, known as caudillos, allied with creole elites. The new states also allowed the continuation of slavery, confirmed the wealth and authority of the Roman Catholic church, and repressed the lower orders. The principal beneficiaries of independence in Latin America were the creole elites.

The Emergence of Ideologies: Conservatism and Liberalism

While inspiring revolutions and independence movements in other lands, the American and French revolutions also prompted political and social theorists to crystallize the modern ideologies of conservatism and liberalism. An *ideology* is a coherent vision of human nature, human society, and the larger world that proposes some particular form of political and social organization as ideal. People who promote a given ideology seek to design a political and social order for their communities.

The modern ideology of conservatism arose as political and social theorists responded to the challenges of the American and especially *Conservatism* the French revolution. Conservatives believed that social change, if necessary at all, must be undertaken gradually and with respect for tradi-

Simón Bolívar, creole leader of the independence movement in Latin America, was a favorite subject of painters in the nineteenth century. This portrait depicts him as a determined and farsighted leader.

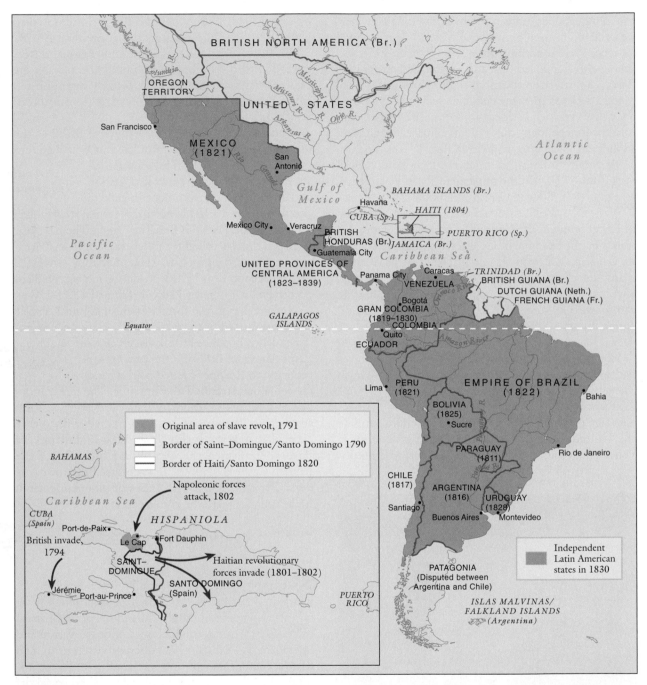

Map 26.3 States of Latin America in 1830. Note the dates each state won its independence. Since most states became independent in very close succession, what conditions prevented Latin American states from joining together in a federation like that in the United States?

tion. The English political philosopher Edmund Burke (1729–1797), for example, condemned radical or revolutionary change, which in his view could only lead to anarchy. Thus Burke approved of the American revolution, which he viewed as a natural and logical change, but he denounced the French revolution as a chaotic and irresponsible assault on society.

In contrast to conservatives, liberals viewed change as the agent of progress. Conservatism, they argued, was just a means to justify the status quo and maintain the privileges enjoyed by favored classes. For liberals

Liberalism   the trick was not to stifle change but, rather, to manage it in the best interests of society. Liberals such as the English political philosopher John Stuart Mill (1806–1873) championed the Enlightenment values of freedom and equality, which they believed would lead to higher standards of morality and increased prosperity for the whole society. They usually favored republican forms of government in which citizens elected representatives to legislative bodies, and they called for written constitutions that guaranteed freedom and equality for all citizens. Although some liberals, such as Mill, advocated universal suffrage (and in Mill's case even women's suffrage), many liberals during the nineteenth century did not go so far: for most, universal suffrage still seemed dangerous because it allowed the uneducated masses to participate in politics.

Testing the Limits of Revolutionary Ideals: Slavery and Women's Rights

The Enlightenment ideals of freedom and equality were watchwords of revolution in the Atlantic Ocean basin. Yet different revolutionaries understood the implications of freedom and equality in very different ways, and the Atlantic revolutions had produced widely varying results. Nevertheless, in the wake of the revolutions, social activists in Europe and the Americas considered the possibility that the ideals of freedom and equality would have further implications as yet unexplored. They turned their attention especially to the issues of slavery and women's rights.

Movements to End the Slave Trade   The campaign to end the slave trade and abolish slavery began in the eighteenth century. Only after the American, French, and Haitian revolutions, however, did the antislavery movement gain momentum. The leading spokesman of the movement was William Wilberforce (1759–1833), a prominent English philanthropist elected in 1780 to a seat in Parliament. There he tirelessly attacked slavery on moral and religious grounds. After the Haitian revolution he attracted supporters who feared that continued reliance on slave labor would result in more and larger slave revolts, and in 1807 Parliament passed Wilberforce's bill to end the slave trade. Under British pressure, other states also banned international commerce in slaves: the United States in 1808, France in 1814, the Netherlands in 1817, and Spain in 1845. The slave trade died slowly, but the British navy, which dominated the North Atlantic Ocean, patrolled the west coast of Africa to ensure compliance with the law.

Movements to Abolish Slavery   The abolition of slavery itself was a much bigger challenge than ending the slave trade because owners had property rights in their slaves and strongly resisted efforts to alter the system. In some places, revolution hastened slavery's end: Haiti abolished the institution in 1801 and Mexico in 1829, and in South America Simón Bolívar freed slaves who joined his forces and provided constitutional guarantees of free status for all residents of Gran Colombia. In other areas slavery was abolished as a result of extensive campaigns by antislavery activists such as Wilberforce. In 1833, one month after Wilberforce's death, Parliament provided twenty million pounds sterling as compensation to slave owners and abolished slavery throughout the British empire. Other states followed the British example: France abolished slavery in 1848, the United States in 1865, Cuba in 1886, and Brazil in 1888.

Freedom without Equality   Abolition brought legal freedom for African and African-American slaves, but it did not bring political equality. In most places, African-American peoples were prevented from voting through property requirements, literacy tests, and campaigns of intimidation. Nor did emancipation bring social and economic improvements for former slaves and their descendants. White creole elites owned most of the property in the Americas, and they kept blacks in subordination by forcing them to accept low-paying work.

Enlightenment Ideals and Women   Meanwhile, women who participated alongside men in the movement to abolish slavery came to believe that women suffered many of the same legal disabilities as slaves: they had little access to education, they could not enter professional occupations that required advanced education, and they were legally deprived of the right to vote. In making the case for their own rights, women drew on Enlightenment ideas about liberty and equality. For example, the English writer Mary Astell (1666–1731) used the political thought of John Locke to suggest that absolute sovereignty was no more appropriate in a family than in a state. Astell also reflected Enlightenment influence in asking why, if all men were born free, all women were born slaves? Mary Wollstonecraft (1759–1797), another British writer, similarly drew on Locke's ideas, especially in her 1792 essay titled *A Vindication of the Rights of Woman*. Like Astell, Wollstonecraft argued that women possessed all the rights that Locke had granted to men. She especially insisted on the right of women to education: it would make them better mothers and wives, she said, and would enable them to contribute to society by preparing them for professional occupations and participation in political life.

Women played crucial roles in the revolutions of the late eighteenth and early nineteenth centuries,

Women and Revolution from making bandages to managing farms to actively taking up arms. Yet even so, they did not win political or social rights. In France, where women did gain rights to property, education, and divorce in the early years of the revolution, they were consistently denied the right to vote or to hold public office. In the later years of the revolution, under the Directory and Napoleon's rule, women lost even the limited rights they had won earlier. In other lands, women never gained as much as they did in revolutionary France. In the United States and the independent states of Latin America, revolution brought legal equality and political rights only for adult white men, who retained patriarchal authority over their wives and families.

Nevertheless, throughout the nineteenth century social reformers pressed for women's rights as well as

Women's Rights Movements the abolition of slavery. The American feminist Elizabeth Cady Stanton (1815–1902) was an especially prominent figure in this movement. In 1840 Stanton went to London to attend an antislavery conference but found that the organizers barred women from participation. Infuriated, Stanton returned to the United States and organized a conference of feminists who met at Seneca Falls, New York, in 1848. The conference passed twelve resolutions demanding that lawmakers grant women the right to vote, to attend public schools, to enter professional occupations, and to participate in public affairs. The women's rights movement experienced only limited success in the nineteenth century: some women gained access to education, but nowhere did they win the right to vote. Yet, by seeking to extend the promises of Enlightenment political thought to blacks and women as well as white men, social reformers of the nineteenth century laid a foundation that would lead to large-scale social change in the twentieth century.

THE CONSOLIDATION OF NATIONAL STATES IN EUROPE

The Enlightenment ideals of freedom, equality, and popular sovereignty inspired political revolutions in much of the Atlantic Ocean basin, and the revolutions in turn helped spread Enlightenment values. The wars of the French revolution and the Napoleonic era also inspired the development of a particular type of community identity that had little to do with Enlightenment values—nationalism. Revolutionary wars involved millions of French citizens in the defense of their country against foreign armies and the extension of French influence to neighboring states. Wartime experiences encouraged peoples throughout Europe to think of themselves as members of distinctive national communities. Throughout the nineteenth century, European nationalist leaders worked to fashion states based on national identities and mobilized citizens to work in the interests of their own national communities, sometimes by fostering jealousy and suspicion of other national groups. By the late nineteenth century, national identities were so strong that peoples throughout Europe responded enthusiastically to ideologies of nationalism, which promised glory and prosperity to those who worked in the interests of their national communities.

Nations and Nationalism

One of the most influential concepts of modern political thought is the idea of the nation. At various times and places in history, individuals have associated themselves primarily with families, clans, cities, regions, and religious faiths. Yet, during the nineteenth century, European peoples came to identify strongly with communities they called nations. Members of a nation considered themselves a distinctive people that spoke a common language, observed common customs, inherited common cultural traditions, held common values, and shared common historical experiences.

Intense feelings of national identity fueled ideologies of nationalism. Advocates of nationalism insisted that the nation must be the focus of political loyalty. Zealous nationalist leaders maintained that members of their national communities had a common destiny that they could best advance by organizing independent national states. Ideally, in their view, the boundaries of the national state embraced the territory occupied by the national community, and its government promoted the interests of the national group, sometimes through conflict with other peoples.

Early nationalist thought often sought to deepen appreciation for the historical experiences of the national community and foster pride in its cultural accomplishments. During the late eighteenth century, for example, Johann Gottfried von Herder (1744–1803)

sang the praises of the German *Volk* ("people") and their powerful and expressive language. In reaction to

Cultural Nationalism Enlightenment thinkers and their quest for a scientific, universally valid understanding of the world, early cultural nationalists such as Herder emphasized the uniqueness of their societies through the study of history, literature, and song.

During the nineteenth century, nationalist thought became much more strident. In lands where they were

Political Nationalism minorities or where they lived under foreign rule, nationalists demanded loyalty and solidarity from the national group and sought to establish independent states. In Italy, for example, the nationalist activist Giuseppe Mazzini (1805–1872) formed a group called Young Italy that promoted independence from Austrian and Spanish rule and the establishment of an Italian national state. Austrian and Spanish authorities forced Mazzini to lead much of his life in exile, but he used the opportunity to encourage the organization of nationalist movements in new lands. By the mid–nineteenth century, Young Italy had inspired the development of nationalist movements in Ireland, Switzerland, and Hungary.

While it encouraged political leaders to work toward the establishment of national states for their

Nationalism and Anti-Semitism communities, nationalism also had strong potential to stir up conflict between different groups of people. The more nationalists identified with their own national communities, the more they distinguished themselves both from peoples in other lands and from minority groups within their own societies. This divisive potential of nationalism helps to explain the emergence of Zionism, a political movement that holds that the Jewish people constitute a nation and have the right to their own national homeland. Unlike Mazzini's Italian compatriots, Jews did not inhabit a well-defined territory but, rather, lived in states throughout Europe. As national communities tightened their bonds, nationalist leaders often became distrustful of minority populations. Suspicion of Jews fueled violent anti-Semitism in many parts of Europe. In Russia and in the Russian-controlled areas of Poland, the persecution of Jews climaxed in a series of anti-Jewish riots called pogroms, which claimed the lives and property of thousands of Jews.

During the late nineteenth and twentieth centuries, millions of Jews migrated to other European lands or to North America to escape persecution and violence. Anti-Semitism was not as severe in France as

in central and eastern Europe, but it reached a fever pitch there after a military court convicted Alfred Dreyfus, a Jewish army officer, of spying for Germany in 1894. Although he was innocent of the charges and eventually had the verdict reversed on appeal, Dreyfus was the focus of bitter debates about the trustworthiness of Jews in French society. The trial also became a key event in the evolution of Zionism.

Among the reporters at the Dreyfus trial was a Jewish journalist from Vienna, Theodor Herzl (1860–

1904). As Herzl witnessed mobs shouting "Death to the Jews" in the land of enlightenment and liberty, he concluded that anti-Semitism

Zionism

was a persistent feature of human society that assimilation could not solve. In 1896 Herzl published the pamphlet *Judenstaat,* which argued that the only defense against anti-Semitism lay in the mass migration of Jews from all over the world to a land that they could call their own. In the following year, Herzl organized the first Zionist Congress in Basel, Switzerland, which founded the World Zionist Organization. The delegates at Basel formulated the basic platform of the Zionist movement, declaring that "Zionism seeks to establish a home for the Jewish people in Palestine," the location of the ancient kingdom of Israel. During the next half century, Jewish migrants trickled into Palestine, and in 1948 they won recognition for the Jewish state of Israel. Although it arose in response to exclusive nationalism in Europe, Zionism in turn provoked a resentful nationalism among Palestinians displaced by Jewish settlers. Conflicts between Jews and Palestinians continue to the present day.

Theodor Herzl

The Emergence of National Communities

The French revolution and the wars that followed it heightened feelings of national identity throughout Europe. In France the establishment of a republic based on liberty, equality, and fraternity inspired patriotism and encouraged citizens to rally to its defense when foreign armies threatened it. Revolutionary leaders took the tricolored flag as a symbol of the French nation, and they adopted a rousing marching tune, the "Marseillaise," as an anthem that inspired pride and identity with the national community. In Spain, the Netherlands, Austria, Prussia, and Russia, national consciousness surged in reaction to the arrival of revolutionary and

Napoleonic armies. Opposition to Napoleon and his imperial designs also inspired national feeling in Britain.

The Congress of Vienna

After the fall of Napoleon, conservative political leaders feared that heightened national consciousness and ideas of popular sovereignty would undermine European stability. Meeting as the Congress of Vienna (1814–1815), representatives of Britain, Austria, Prussia, and Russia attempted to restore the prerevolutionary order. Under the guidance of the influential foreign minister of Austria, Prince Klemens von Metternich (1773–1859), the Congress dismantled Napoleon's empire, returned sovereignty to Europe's royal families, restored them to the thrones they had lost during the Napoleonic era, and created a diplomatic order based on a balance of power that prevented any one state from dominating the others. A central goal of Metternich himself was to suppress national consciousness, which he viewed as a serious threat to the multicultural Austrian empire. Yet the efforts of the Congress of Vienna to restore the ancien régime had limited success. Although the European balance of power established at Vienna survived for almost a century, it had become impossible to suppress national consciousness and ideas of popular sovereignty.

Nationalist Rebellions

From the 1820s through the 1840s, a wave of rebellions inspired by nationalist sentiments swept through Europe. The first uprising occurred in 1821 in the Balkan Peninsula, where the Greek people sought independence from the Ottoman Turks. With the aid of Britain, France, and Russia, the rebels won formal recognition of Greek independence in 1830. In the same year, liberal revolutionaries in France, Spain, Portugal, and some of the German principalities called for constitutional government based on popular sovereignty. In Belgium, Italy, and Poland, they demanded independence and the formation of national states as well as popular sovereignty. Revolution in Paris drove Charles X from the throne, and uprisings in Belgium resulted in independence from the Netherlands. In 1848 a new round of rebellions shook European states, where they brought down the French monarchy and seriously threatened the Austrian empire. Uprisings also rocked cities in Italy, Prussia, and German states in the Rhineland.

Wearing a white jacket, Otto von Bismarck (center) witnesses the crowning of King Wilhelm I of Prussia as German emperor. The coronation followed the victory of Prussia over France in 1871, and it took place in the royal palace at Versailles.

By the summer of 1849, the veteran armies of conservative rulers had put down the last of the rebellions. However, advocates of national independence and popular sovereignty remained active, and the potential of their ideals to mobilize popular support were crucial in the unification of two new European states: Italy by 1870 and Germany by 1871.

The Unification of Italy and Germany

The most striking demonstration of the power that national sentiments could unleash involved the unification of Italy and Germany. Since the fall of the Roman empire, Italy and Germany had been disunited lands. A variety of regional kingdoms, city-states, and ecclesiastical states ruled the Italian peninsula for more than a thousand years, and princes divided Germany into more than three hundred semi-autonomous jurisdictions.

The unification of Italy came about when practical political leaders such as Count Camillo di Cavour (1810–1861), prime minister to King Vittore Emmanuele II of Piedmont and Sardinia, combined forces with nationalist advocates of independence. Cavour was

a cunning diplomat, and the kingdom of Piedmont and Sardinia was the most powerful of the Italian states. In alliance with France, Cavour expelled Austrian authorities—who had gained control of the region through the Congress of Vienna—from most of northern Italy in 1859. Then he turned his attention to southern Italy, where Giuseppe Garibaldi (1807–1882), a dashing soldier of fortune and a passionate nationalist, led the unification movement. With an army of about one thousand men outfitted in distinctive red shirts, Garibaldi swept through Sicily and southern Italy, outmaneuvering government forces and attracting enthusiastic recruits. In 1860 Garibaldi met King Vittore Emmanuele near Naples. Not ambitious to rule, Garibaldi delivered southern Italy into Vittore Emmanuele's hands, and the kingdom of Piedmont and Sardinia became the kingdom of Italy. During the next decade the new monarchy absorbed several additional territories, including Venice, Rome, and their surrounding regions.

Cavour and Garibaldi

In Germany as in Italy, unification came about when political leaders harnessed nationalist aspirations. The Congress of Vienna created a German Confederation composed of thirty-nine states dominated by Austria. In 1862 King Wilhelm I of Prussia—one of the

Map 26.4 The unification of Germany. Locate the boundaries of Prussia between 1815 and 1816. Why was Prussia able to dominate the German Confederation in the period between 1866 and 1871?

Prussia, 1815–1816

Annexed by Prussia, 1866

North German Confederation, 1867

German empire, 1871

German Confederation, 1815–1866

thirty-nine states—appointed a wealthy landowner, Otto von Bismarck (1815–1898), as his prime minis-

Otto von Bismarck

ter. Bismarck was a master of Realpolitik ("the politics of reality") who argued that "the great questions of the day will not be settled by speeches or majority votes . . . but by blood and iron." It was indeed blood and iron that brought about the unification of Germany. As prime minister, Bismarck reformed and expanded the Prussian army. Between 1864 and 1870 he intentionally provoked three wars— with Denmark, Austria, and France—and whipped up German sentiment against the enemies. In all three conflicts Prussian forces quickly shattered their opponents, swelling German pride. In 1871 the Prussian king proclaimed himself emperor of the Second Reich—meaning the Second German Empire, following the Holy Roman Empire—which embraced almost all German-speaking peoples outside Austria and Switzerland in a powerful and dynamic national state.

The unification of Italy and Germany made it clear that when coupled with strong political, diplomatic, and military leadership, nationalism had enormous potential to mobilize people who felt a sense of national kinship. Italy, Germany, and other national states went to great lengths to foster a sense of national community. They adopted national flags to serve as symbols of unity, national anthems to inspire patriotism, and national holidays to focus public attention on individuals and events of special importance for the national community. They established bureaucracies that took censuses of national populations and tracked vital national statistics involving birth, marriage, and death. They built schools that instilled patriotic values in students, and they recruited young men into armies that defended national interests and sometimes went on the offensive to enhance national prestige. By the end of the nineteenth century, the national state had proven to be a powerful model of political organization in Europe.

SUMMARY

The Enlightenment ideals of freedom, equality, and popular sovereignty inspired revolutionary movements throughout much of the Atlantic Ocean basin in the late eighteenth and early nineteenth centuries. In North America colonists threw off British rule and founded an independent federal republic. In France revolutionaries abolished the monarchy, established a republic, and refashioned the social order. In Saint-Domingue rebellious slaves threw off French rule, established an independent Haitian republic, and granted freedom and equality to all citizens. In Latin America creole elites led movements to expel Spanish and Portuguese colonial authorities and found independent republics. During the nineteenth century, adult white men were the main beneficiaries of movements based on Enlightenment ideals, but social reformers launched campaigns to extend freedom and equality to African-Americans and women.

Meanwhile, as they fought one another in wars sparked by the French revolution, European peoples developed strong feelings of national identity and worked to establish states that advanced the interests of national communities. Nationalist thought was often divisive: it pitted national groups against one another and fueled tensions especially in large multicultural states. But nationalism also contributed to state-building movements that had the potential to unite. During the nineteenth and twentieth centuries, peoples throughout the world drew inspiration from Enlightenment ideals and national identities when seeking to build or restructure their societies.

CHRONOLOGY

1632–1704	Life of John Locke
1694–1778	Life of Voltaire
1712–1778	Life of Jean-Jacques Rousseau
1744–1803	Life of Toussaint Louverture
1748–1793	Life of Olympe de Gouges
1769–1821	Life of Napoleon Bonaparte
1774–1793	Reign of King Louis XVI
1775–1781	American Revolution
1783–1830	Life of Simón Bolívar
1789–1799	French Revolution
1791–1803	Haitian revolution
1799–1814	Reign of Napoleon
1810–1825	Wars of independence in Latin America
1814–1815	Congress of Vienna

FOR FURTHER READING

Benedict Anderson. *Imagined Communities: Reflections on the Origin and Spread of Nationalism*. Rev. ed. London, 1991. A pioneering work that analyzes the means and the processes by which peoples came to view themselves as members of national communities.

Bernard Bailyn. *The Ideological Origins of the American Revolution*. 2nd ed. Cambridge, Mass., 1992. A fundamental study of pamphlets and other publications that criticized British colonial policy in North America.

Aviva Chomsky and Aldo Lauria-Santiago, eds. *Identity and Struggle at the Margins of the Nation-State: The Laboring Peoples of Central America and the Hispanic Caribbean*. Durham, 1998. Discusses the impact that peasant action had on political and cultural development in different societies.

Linda Colley. *Britons: Forging the Nation, 1707–1837*. New Haven, 1992. A detailed analysis of the emergence of British national identity.

Susan Dunn. *Sister Revolutions: French Lightning, American Light*. New York, 1999. An accessible and stimulating work that traces the different legacies of the American and French revolutions of the eighteenth century.

Carolyn Fick. *The Making of Haiti: The Saint Domingue Revolution from Below*. Knoxville, 1990. A valuable study focusing on the role of slaves in the Haitian revolution.

François Furet. *Revolutionary France, 1770–1880*. Trans. by A. Nevill. Oxford, 1992. An influential interpretation emphasizing the ideological dimension of the French revolution.

Eric Hobsbawm. *Nations and Nationalism since 1780: Programme, Myth, and Reality*. 2nd ed. Cambridge, 1992. A brief interpretation of nationalism in Europe and the larger world.

Lester D. Langley. *The Americas in the Age of Revolution, 1750–1850*. New Haven, 1997. A comparative study of revolutions and wars of independence in the western hemisphere.

David Parker, ed. *Revolutions and the Revolutionary Tradition in the West, 1560–1991*. London and New York, 2000. In this comparative survey of revolutions—from the English revolution of 1649 to the revolutions within eastern Europe and the Soviet Union (1989–1991)—leading historians examine how a wider revolutionary tradition has shaped modern European history.

CHAPTER 27

The Making of Industrial Society

In 1827, shortly after marrying at the age of twenty-three, Betty Harris took a job as a drawer in a coal pit near Manchester, England. A drawer's job involved crawling down narrow mine shafts and hauling loads of coal from the bottom of the pit to the surface. Drawers performed unskilled labor for low wages, but their work was essential for obtaining the coal that fueled the factories and mills of early industrial society.

While working, Harris wore a heavy belt around her waist. Hitched to the belt was a chain that passed between her legs and attached to the coal cart that she pulled through the steep and slippery mine shafts, often on hands and knees. Every workday, even when she was pregnant, Harris strapped on her belt and chain at 6:00 A.M., removing her bindings only at the end of the shift twelve hours later.

Harris reported that drawing coal was "very hard work for a woman," and she did not exaggerate. The belts and chains worn by drawers often chafed their skin raw, and miners contributed to their physical discomfort by beating them for slow or clumsy work. The miners, many of whom worked naked in the hot, oppressive coal pits, also took sexual liberties with the women and girl drawers: Harris personally knew several illegitimate children conceived during forced sexual encounters in the mines.

Betty Harris faced her own sexual problems once she arrived home. Exhausted from twelve hours of work, with only a one-hour break for a lunch consisting of bread and butter, she often tried to discourage her husband's advances. Her husband had little patience, however, and Harris remarked that "my feller has beaten

OPPOSITE PAGE: *Young woman at work in a mechanized mill in the 1830s.*

me many a time for not being ready." Harris's work schedule made comfortable family life impossible. A cousin had to care for her two children during the day, and Harris tended to them and her husband at night. At age thirty-seven, after fourteen years in the mines, Harris admitted that "I am not so strong as I was."

Not all industrial workers worked in such difficult conditions, but Betty Harris's experience nonetheless illustrates some of the deep changes that industrialization wrought in patterns of work and family life. First in Britain, then in western Europe, North America, Russia, and Japan, machines and factories transformed agricultural societies into industrial societies. At the heart of this transformation were technological changes that led to the extensive use of machinery in manufacturing. Industrial machinery transformed economic production by turning out high-quality products quickly, cheaply, and efficiently. The process of industrialization encouraged rapid technological innovation and over the long term raised material standards of living in much of the world.

But the impact of industrialization went beyond economics, generating widespread and often unsettling social change as well. Early industrialists created a new work environment, the factory, which concentrated large numbers of workers under one roof to operate complicated machinery. By moving work outside the home, however, factories drew fathers, mothers, and children in different directions, altered traditional patterns of domestic life, and strained family relations in the industrial era.

Industrialization encouraged rapid urbanization and migration. New cities mushroomed to house workers who left the countryside for jobs in factories. Millions of migrants even crossed the seas in search of opportunities in new lands. Often, however, early industrial workers found themselves living in squalor and laboring under dangerous conditions.

Social critics and reformers worked to alleviate the problems of early industrial society. Despite their appeals, however, capitalism and industrialization flourished and spread rapidly from Britain to continental Europe, North America, and Asia. In some areas, notably western Europe and North America, industrialization was encouraged so that states could gain the economic advantages of industrialization. In other places, including Russia and Japan, industrialization was undertaken as part of a larger program of social, political, and economic reform to avoid domination by western European and American powers. Elsewhere, industrialization created a new international division of labor that made most of Africa, Asia, and Latin America economically dependent on the export of raw materials that supplied the factories and cities of the industrialized world. Thus, although industrialization and its effects spread unevenly and for different reasons, they profoundly influenced social and economic conditions all over the globe.

PATTERNS OF INDUSTRIALIZATION

Industrialization refers to a process that transformed agrarian and handicraft-centered economies into economies distinguished by industry and machine manufacture. The principal features of that process were technological and organizational changes that transformed manufacturing and led to increased productivity. Critical to industrialization were technological developments that made it possible to produce goods by machines rather than by hand and that harnessed inanimate sources of energy such as coal and petroleum. Also critical was the development of factory production, wherein workers assembled under one roof to produce goods in mass quantities. The need to invest in expensive factory equipment in turn encouraged the formation of large businesses: by the mid–nineteenth century many giant corporations had joined together to control trade through trusts and cartels.

Foundations of Industrialization

By the mid–eighteenth century, several areas of the world—Great Britain in western Europe, the Yangzi Delta in China, Japan—exhibited dynamic economies that shared many common features. High agricultural productivity resulted in significant population growth, and high population densities encouraged occupational specialization outside of agriculture. Navigable rivers and networks of canals facilitated trade and transport, and cities and towns supported sophisticated banking and financial institutions. At the same time, these sophisticated economies ran up against difficult ecological obstacles—especially soil depletion and deforestation—that threatened continued population growth and consumption levels. Despite their common features, Great Britain was the first to transcend these ecological constraints by exploiting coal deposits fortuitously found at home and natural resources found abroad.

Until the eighteenth century, wood had served as Great Britain's primary source of fuel for iron production, home heating, and cooking. Such extensive use of wood had resulted in serious wood shortages.

Coal and Colonies   However, geographic luck had placed some of western Europe's largest coal deposits in Great Britain, within easy reach of water transport, centers of commerce, and pools of skilled labor. That fortunate conjunction encouraged the substitution of coal for wood, thus creating a promising framework for industrialization. Indeed, without easily accessible coal deposits, it was unlikely that the economy could have supported an expanding iron production and the application of steam engines to mining and industry—both crucial to the industrial process in Great Britain. In that respect Britain's experience differed from that of China, because the main coal-producing regions of northwest China were quite distant from the Yangzi Delta, China's most economically promising region for the development of industrialization. Thus, geography conspired against an important early shift from wood to coal in China.

The unique economic relationship between Europe and the Americas gave Great Britain additional ecological relief. The colonized lands of the Americas lifted European land constraints by supplying European societies with a growing volume of primary products. During the eighteenth century slave-based plantations supplied Europe with huge amounts of sugar and cotton; the former increased available food calories, and the latter kept emerging textile industries going. Neither of those products could have been grown in Europe. The significance of valuable American resources grew after 1830, when large amounts of grain, timber, and beef grown on colonial acreage traveled across the Atlantic to European destinations. In addition, American lands served as outlets for European manufactured goods as well as Europe's surplus population. Access to such overseas resources, in addition to coal deposits at home, provided a context—one not available to societies such as China—that increased the odds for an industrial breakthrough.

Industrial expansion in Britain began in the mid–eighteenth century with the textile industry, when consumer demand spurred a transformation of the British cotton industry. During the seventeenth century, English consumers had became fond of calicoes—inexpensive, brightly printed cotton textiles from India. Cotton cloth came into demand because it was lighter and easier to wash than wool, which was the principal fabric of European clothes before the nineteenth century. Although British wool producers tried to protect their industry through a series of laws designed to pro-

hibit imports of cotton cloth in 1720 and 1721, they could not stifle public demand.

In fact, demand for cotton was so strong that producers had to speed up spinning and weaving to supply growing markets. To increase production they turned to inventions that rapidly mechanized the cotton textile industry. The first important *Mechanization of the Cotton Industry* technological breakthrough came in 1733 when Manchester mechanic John Kay invented the flying shuttle, which sped up the weaving process. Within a few years, inventors created several mechanical spinning devices, the most important of which was Samuel Crompton's "mule," built in 1779. In 1790 the mule was adapted for steam power, and it became the device of choice for spinning cotton. A worker using a steam-driven mule could produce a hundred times more thread than a worker using a manual spinning wheel.

The new spinning machines necessitated new weaving machines so that weavers could keep up with the production of thread. In 1785 Edmund Cartwright, a clergyman without experience in either mechanics or textiles, patented a water-driven power loom. Within two decades steam moved the power loom, and by the 1820s hand weavers were nearly obsolete. A young boy working on two power looms could produce fifteen times more cloth than the fastest hand weaver. Collectively, these technological developments permitted the mass production of inexpensive textile goods. By 1830 half a million people worked in the cotton business, Britain's leading industry, which accounted for 40 percent of exports.

The most crucial technological breakthrough of the early industrial era was the development of a general-purpose steam engine in 1765 by James *Steam Power* Watt, an instrument maker at the University of Glasgow in Scotland. Even before Watt's time, primitive steam engines had powered pumps that drew water out of coal mines, but those devices consumed too much fuel to be useful for other purposes. Watt's version relied on steam to force a piston to turn a wheel, whose rotary motion converted a simple pump into an engine. By 1800 more than a thousand of Watt's steam engines were in use in the British Isles. They were especially prominent in the textile industry, where they allowed greater productivity for manufacturers and cheaper prices for consumers.

The iron and steel industries also benefited from technological refinement, and the availability of inexpensive, high-quality iron and steel reinforced the move toward mechanization. After 1709 British

Iron and Steel

smelters began to use coke (a purified form of coal) rather than more expensive charcoal as a fuel to produce iron. As a result, British iron production skyrocketed during the eighteenth century, and prices to consumers fell.

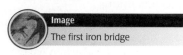
The first iron bridge

Inexpensive iron fittings and parts made industrial machinery stronger, and iron soon became common in bridges, buildings, and ships.

Steel is much harder, stronger, and more resilient than iron, but until the nineteenth century it was very expensive to produce. In 1856, however, Henry Bessemer built a refined blast furnace known as the Bessemer converter that made it possible to produce large quantities of steel cheaply. Steel production rose sharply, and steel quickly began to replace iron in tools, machines, and structures that required high strength.

Transportation

Steam engineering and metallurgical innovations both contributed to improvements in transportation technology. In 1815 George Stephenson, a self-educated Englishman, built the first steam-powered locomotive. In 1829 his *Rocket* won a contest by reaching a speed of 45 kilometers (28 miles) per hour. By the middle of the nineteenth century, refined steam engines of high efficiency also began to drive steamships.

Because they had the capacity to carry huge cargoes, railroads and steamships dramatically lowered transportation costs. They also contributed to the creation of transportation networks that linked remote interior regions and distant shores more closely than ever before in history. Between 1830 and 1870, British entrepreneurs laid about 20,000 kilometers (13,000 miles) of railroads, which carried some 322 million passengers as well as cargoes of raw materials and manufactured goods. Meanwhile, steamships proved their versatility by advancing up rivers to points that sailboats could not reach because of inconvenient twists or turns.

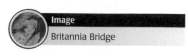
Britannia Bridge

The Factory System

The Factory

The factory system became the characteristic method of production in industrial economies. It began to emerge in the late eighteenth century, when technological advances transformed the British textile industry, and by the mid–nineteenth century most cotton production took place in factories. Many of the newly developed machines were too large and expensive for home use, so it became necessary to move work to centralized locations. That centralization of production brought together more workers doing specialized tasks than ever before.

Working Conditions

The factory system with its new machines demanded a rational organization of job functions. Thus, the factory became associated with a new division of labor that called for a production process in which each worker performed a single task, rather than one in which a single worker completed the entire job, as was typical of handicraft traditions. This new division of labor allowed managers to improve worker productivity and realize spectacular increases in the output of manufactured goods. But the new environment also had unsettling effects on the nature of work. For instance,

A woman working as a drawer in a British coal mine drags her coal cart with the aid of a belt and chain. Manually produced coal fueled the machines of early industrial society.

George Stephenson's North Star engine of 1837.

the factory system led to the emergence of an owner class whose capital financed equipment and machinery that were too expensive for workers to acquire. As a result, industrial workers became mere wage earners who depended on their employers for their livelihood. The repetitious and boring nature of many industrial jobs, moreover, left many workers alienated from their work and the products of their labor. In addition, any broad-range skills that workers may have previously acquired as artisans often became obsolete in the factory work environment. Between 1811 and 1816, that situation prompted organized bands of English handicraft workers known as Luddites to destroy textile machines that they blamed for their low wages and unemployment. Nevertheless, by hanging fourteen Luddites in 1813, the government served notice that it was unwilling to tolerate violence even against machines, and the movement gradually died out.

Equally disturbing was the new work discipline and the pace of work. Those accustomed to rural labor found that the seasons and fluctuations in the weather no longer dictated work routines. Instead, clocks, machines, and shop rules established new rhythms of work. Industrial workers commonly labored six days a week, twelve to fourteen hours a day. The factory whistle sounded the beginning and the end of each working day, and throughout the day workers had to keep pace with the movements of machines. At the same time, they faced strict and immediate supervision. Floor managers pressured men, women, and children to speed up production and punished them when they did not meet expectations.

In addition, dangerous work conditions often meant that early industrial workers faced the possibility of maiming or fatal accidents.

The Early Spread of Industrialization

For fifty years industrialization occurred only in Britain. Aware of their head start, British entrepreneurs and government officials forbade the export of machinery, manufacturing techniques, and skilled workers to other lands. Yet Britain's monopoly on industrialization did not last, because enterprising entrepreneurs ignored government regulations and sold machinery and technical know-how abroad. Moreover, European and North American businesspeople did not hesitate to bribe or even kidnap British engineers to learn the secrets of industrialization, and they also smuggled advanced machinery out of the British Isles.

As a result, by the mid–nineteenth century industrialization had spread to France, Germany, Belgium, and the United States. The earliest Continental center of industrial production was Belgium, where coal, iron, textile, glass, and armaments production flourished in the early nineteenth century. About the same time, France also moved toward industrialization. By the mid–nineteenth century, French engineers and inventors were devising refinements and innovations that led to greater efficiencies, especially in metallurgical industries. Although German industrialization started off more slowly

Industrialization in Western Europe

than in France or Belgium, German coal and iron production soared after the 1840s, and by the 1850s an extensive railroad network was under construction. After unification in 1871, Bismarck's government sponsored rapid industrialization in Germany, especially of heavy industry.

Industrialization transformed North America as well as western Europe in the nineteenth century. American industrialization began in the 1820s when entrepreneurs lured British crafts workers to New England and built a cotton textile industry. By midcentury well over a thousand mills were producing fabrics from raw cotton grown in the southern states, and New England had emerged as a site for the industrial production also of shoes, tools, and handguns. In the

Industrialization in North America

Map 27.1 Industrial Europe about 1850. Locate the places marked as emerging industrial areas. Are there any features those areas have in common? If so, what are they?

1870s heavy iron and steel industries emerged in areas such as western Pennsylvania and central Alabama where there were abundant supplies of iron ore and coal. By 1900 the United States had become an economic powerhouse, and industrialization had begun to spill over into southern Canada.

Industrial Capitalism

Cotton textiles were the major factory-made products during the early phase of industrialization, but the factory system soon spread to other industries. An important contribution to the evolving *Mass Production* factory system came from the American inventor Eli Whitney (1765–1825). Though best remembered as the inventor of the cotton gin (1793), Whitney also developed the technique of using machine tools to produce interchangeable parts in the making of firearms. This method meant that unskilled workers made only a particular part that fit every musket of the same model. Before long, entrepreneurs applied Whitney's method to the manufacture of everything from clocks and sewing machines to uniforms and shoes. By the middle of the nineteenth century, mass production of standardized articles was becoming the hallmark of industrial societies.

In 1913 Henry Ford improved manufacturing techniques further when he introduced the assembly line to automobile production. Instead of organizing production around a series of stations where workers assembled whole cars using standardized parts, Ford designed a conveyor system that allowed each worker to perform a specialized task at a fixed point on the assembly line. With the assembly line, workers churned out a complete chassis every 93 minutes instead of every 728 minutes under the old system. Such huge gains in productivity meant that car prices plummeted, allowing millions of ordinary people to purchase automobiles. The age of the motor car had arrived.

As the factory evolved, so too did the organization of business. Industrial machinery and factories were *The Corporation* expensive investments, and they encouraged businesses to organize on a large scale. During the 1850s and 1860s, government authorities in Britain and France laid the legal foundations for the modern corporation, which quickly became the most common form of business organization in industrial societies. A corporation was a private business owned by many investors who financed the business through the purchase of stocks representing shares in the company. When a corporation flourished, investors received dividends in proportion to their stake in the company. But if a corporation went bankrupt, laws protected shareholders from liability or financial loss beyond the extent of their investments—which made them extremely attractive to investors. By the late nineteenth century, corporations controlled most businesses requiring large investments in land, labor, or machinery.

To protect their investments, some big businesses of the late nineteenth century sought not only to outperform their competitors in the capitalist *Monopolies, Trusts, and Cartels* marketplace but also to eliminate competition. Business firms formed associations to restrict markets or establish monopolies in their industries. Large-scale business organizations formed trusts and cartels, both of which aimed to control the supply of a product and hence its price in the marketplace. Trusts commonly sought control of industries through vertical organization, by which they would dominate all facets of a single industry. John D. Rockefeller's Standard Oil Company and Trust, for example, controlled almost all oil drilling, processing, refining, marketing, and distribution in the United States.

Cartels, in contrast, tried to eliminate competition by means of horizontal organization, which involved the consolidation or cooperation of independent companies in the same business. Thus cartels sought to ensure the prosperity of their members by absorbing competitors, fixing prices, regulating production, or dividing up markets. By the end of the nineteenth century, some governments outlawed trusts and cartels. However, monopolistic practices continued well into the twentieth century.

Industrial Society

Industrialization brought material benefits in its train: inexpensive manufactured products, rising standards of living, and population growth. Yet industrialization also unleashed dramatic social change. Immense internal and external migrations took place as people moved from the countryside to work in new industrial cities, and as Europeans crossed the Atlantic to seek opportunities in the western hemisphere. Industrialization also encouraged the emergence of new social classes and forced men, women, and children to adjust to distinctly new patterns of family and work life. Reformers sought to alleviate the social and economic problems that accompanied industrialization and worked toward the building of a more equitable and just society.

The Fruits of Industry

Industrialization brought efficiencies in production that flooded markets with affordable manufactured goods. Indeed, industrialization raised material standards of living in many ways. Industrial production led to dramatic reductions in the cost of clothing, for example, so by the early nineteenth century all but the desperately poor could afford several changes of clothes. Industrial factories turned out tools that facilitated agricultural work, and steam-powered locomotives delivered produce quickly and cheaply to distant markets. Consumers in early industrial Europe also filled their homes with more furniture, porcelain, and decorative objects than any but the most wealthy of their ancestors.

The populations of European and Euro-American peoples rose sharply during the eighteenth and nineteenth centuries, reflecting the rising prosperity and standards of living that came *Population Growth* with industrialization. Between 1700 and 1900 the population of Europe increased from 105 to 390 million. Demographic growth in the western hemisphere—fueled by migration from Europe—was even more remarkable. Between 1700 and 1900 the

Exhibitors from around the world displayed fine handicrafts and manufactured goods at the Crystal Palace exhibition of 1851 in London. Industrial products from Britain and the United States particularly attracted the attention of visitors to the enchanting and futuristic exhibition hall.

population of North America and South America rose from 13 million to 145 million.

The rapid population growth in Europe and the Americas reflected changing patterns of fertility and mortality. In most preindustrial societies fertility was high, but so was child mortality, which held population growth in check. High birthrates were common also in early industrializing societies, but death rates fell markedly because better diets and improved disease control reduced child mortality. By the late nineteenth century, better diets and improved sanitation led to declining levels of adult as well as child mortality. In combination, these two factors allowed populations to expand rapidly.

Beginning in the nineteenth century, however, industrializing lands experienced a social change known

The Demographic Transition

as the *demographic transition*. As industrialization transformed societies, fertility began a marked decline. In the short run, mortality fell even faster than fertility, so the populations of industrial societies continued to increase. Over time, however, declining birthrates led to lower population growth and relative demographic stability. The principal reason for declining fertility in industrial lands was voluntary birth control through contraception, perhaps because raising children cost

more in industrial societies or because more children were likely to survive to adulthood than in the past.

Urbanization and Migration

Industrialization and population growth strongly encouraged migration and urbanization. Within industrial societies, migrants flocked from the countryside to urban centers in search of work. For example, in 1800 about one-fifth of the British population lived in towns and cities of 10,000 or more inhabitants. By 1900 three-quarters of the population worked and lived in cities. That pattern repeated itself elsewhere: by 1900 at least 50 percent of the population in industrialized lands lived in towns with populations of 2,000 or more. The increasing size of cities reflected this internal migration. In 1800 there were barely twenty cities in Europe with populations as high as 100,000, and there were none in the western hemisphere. By 1900 there were more than 150 large cities in Europe and North America combined.

With urbanization came intensified environmental pollution. Although cities have always been unsanitary places, the rapid increase in urban populations during the industrial age dramatically increased the magnitude and severity of water and air pollution. The widespread burning of fossil fuels fouled the air with vast quantities of chemicals and particulate matter. This pollution led to occupational diseases in some trades. Chimney sweeps, for instance, contracted cancer of the scrotum from hydrocarbon deposits found in soot. Effluents from factories and mills as well as untreated sewage dirtied virtually every major river. No part of a city was immune to the constant stench coming from air and water pollution. Worse, tainted water supplies and unsanitary living conditions led to periodic epidemics of cholera and typhus. Until the latter part of the nineteenth century, urban environments remained dangerous places in which death rates commonly exceeded birthrates, and only the constant stream of new arrivals from the country kept cities growing.

The Urban Environment

Income determined the degree of comfort and security offered by city life. The wealthy typically tried to insulate themselves from urban discomforts by retreating to their elegant homes in newly growing suburbs. The working poor, in contrast, occupied overcrowded tenements lacking in comfort and amenities. The cramped spaces in apartments obliged many to share the same bed, increasing the ease of disease transmission. The few open spaces outside the buildings were usually home to herds of pigs living in their own dung or were depositories for pools of stagnant water and human waste.

By the later nineteenth century, though, government authorities were tending to the problems of the early industrial cities. They improved municipal water supplies, expanded sewage systems, and introduced building codes that outlawed the construction of rickety tenements to accommodate poorly paid workers. Those measures made city life safer and brought improved sanitation. City authorities also built parks and recreational facilities to make cities more livable.

Rapid population growth in Europe also encouraged massive migration to the Americas, especially to the United States. During the nineteenth and early twentieth centuries, about fifty million Europeans migrated to the western hemisphere, which accounts for much of the stunning demographic growth of the Americas. Many of the migrants intended to stay for only a few years and fully expected

Transcontinental Migration

Image
Immigration map, 1853

Squalid living conditions, ca. 1885. A group of people live in crowded conditions in one room, New York, USA.

to return to their homelands with a modest fortune made in the Americas. The vast majority, however, remained in the western hemisphere. They and their descendants transformed the Americas into Euro-American lands.

Industry and Society

Industrialization radically altered traditional social structures and helped bring new social classes into being. Enterprising businesspeople became fabulously *New Social* wealthy and powerful enough to over-*Classes* shadow the traditionally privileged classes. Less powerful than this new elite was the middle class, consisting of small business owners, factory managers, engineers, and professionals such as teachers, physicians, and attorneys. A large portion of industrial wealth flowed to the middle class, which benefited greatly from industrialization. Meanwhile, laborers who toiled in factories and mines constituted a new working class. Less skilled than the artisans and crafts workers of earlier times, the new workers tended to machines or provided heavy labor for low wages.

The most basic unit of social organization—the family—also underwent fundamental change during *Industrial* the industrial age. In preindustrial societies *Families* the family was the basic productive unit. Whether engaged in agriculture, domestic manufacturing, or commerce, family members worked together and contributed to the welfare of the larger group. Industrialization challenged the family economy and reshaped family life by moving economic production outside the home and introducing a sharp distinction between work and family life. Workers left their homes each day to labor an average of fourteen hours in factories, and family members led increasingly separate lives.

Men gained increased stature and responsibility in the industrial age as work dominated public life. *Men and the* Upper-class and middle-class men enjoyed *Industrial* especially increased prestige at home, since *Revolution* they usually were the sole providers who made their families' comfortable existence possible. Working-class men also enjoyed increased prestige because they tended to make wages far in excess of those of working-class women. As a result, their earnings usually constituted the bulk of their families' income.

Industrialization dramatically changed the terms of work for women. When industry moved produc-tion from the home to the factory, married women were unable to work unless they left their homes and children in someone else's care. Millions of working-class women had no choice *Women and* but to work under such terms, but by *the Industrial* the late nineteenth century middle-class *Revolution* society promoted the idea that respectable women should devote themselves to raising children, managing the home, and preserving family values rather than to paid labor.

For middle-class women, then, industrialization brought stringent confinement to the domestic sphere and pressure to conform to new models of behavior revolving around their roles as mothers and wives. Popular books such as *Woman in Her Social and Domestic Character* (1833) insisted that the ideal woman "knows that she is the weaker vessel" and takes pride in her ability to make the home a happy place. Meanwhile, in addition to working in factories, millions of working-class women worked as domestic servants for the growing middle class. In fact, one of every three European women became a domestic servant at some point in her life.

Industrialization profoundly influenced the childhood experience. Children in preindustrial societies had always worked in and around the *Child Labor* family home. However, industrial work, which took children away from home and parents for long hours with few breaks, made child labor seem especially pitiable and exploitative. Early reports from British textile mills described sensational abuses by overseers who forced children to work from dawn until dark and beat them to keep them awake. In the 1840s the British parliament began to pass laws regulating child labor and ultimately restricted or removed children from the industrial workforce. In the long term, urban industrial societies redefined the role of children. Motivated in part by the recognition that modern society demanded a skilled and educated labor force, governments established the legal requirement that education, and not work for monetary gain, was the principal task of childhood. In England, for instance, education for children aged five to ten became mandatory by 1881.

The Socialist Challenge

Among the most vocal and influential critics of early industrial society were the socialists, who worked to alleviate the social and economic problems generated by capitalism and industrialization. Socialists deplored economic inequalities, as represented by the vast difference in wealth between a captain of industry and a factory laborer, and they condemned the system that permitted the exploitation of laborers, especially women and children. Early socialists sought to expand the Enlightenment understanding of equality: they understood equality to have an economic as well as a political, legal, and social dimension, and they looked to the future establishment of a just and equitable society.

Most prominent of the nineteenth-century socialists were the German theorists Karl Marx (1818–1883)

Marx and Engels

and Friedrich Engels (1820–1895). Marx and Engels believed that social problems of the nineteenth century were inevitable results of a capitalist economy. They held that capitalism divided people into two main classes, each with its own economic interests and social status: the capitalists, who owned industrial machinery and factories (which Marx and Engels called the means of production), and the proletariat, consisting of wageworkers who had only their labor to sell. Intense competition between capitalists trying to realize a profit resulted in ruthless exploitation of the working class. Moreover, according to Marx and Engels, the state and its coercive institutions, such as police forces and courts of law, functioned to enable capitalists to continue their exploitation of the proletariat. Even music, art, literature, and religion served the purposes of capitalists, according to Marx and Engels, since they amused the working classes and diverted attention from their misery.

Marx developed those views fully in a long, theoretical work called *Capital*. Together with Engels,

The Communist Manifesto

Marx also wrote a short, spirited tract entitled *Manifesto of the Communist Party* (1848). In the *Manifesto* Marx and Engels aligned themselves with the communists, who worked toward the abolition of private property and the institution of a radically egalitarian society. The *Manifesto* asserted that all human history has been the history of struggle between social classes. It also argued that the future lay with the working class. Crises of overproduction, underconsumption, and diminishing profits would shake the foundations of the capitalist order. Meanwhile, members of the proletariat would come to view the forcible overthrow of the existing system as the only alternative available to them. Marx and Engels believed that a socialist revolution would result in a "dictatorship of the proletariat," which would abolish private property and destroy the capitalist

order. After the revolution was secure, the state would wither away. Coercive institutions would also disappear, since there would no longer be an exploiting class. Thus socialism would lead to a fair, just, and egalitarian society infinitely more humane than the capitalist order.

The doctrines of Marx and Engels came to dominate European and international socialism, and socialist parties grew rapidly throughout the nineteenth century. Political parties, trade unions, newspapers, and educational associations all worked to advance the socialist cause. Yet socialists disagreed strongly on the best means to reform society. Revolutionary socialists such as Marx and Engels urged workers to forcibly seize control of the state. In contrast, evolutionary socialists placed their hopes in representative governments and called for the election of legislators who supported socialist reforms.

Although socialists did not win control of any government until the Russian revolution of 1917, their critiques helped persuade government authorities to attack the abuses of early

Social Reform

industrialization and provide more security for the working classes. In Britain, for example, Parliament prohibited underground employment for women and stipulated that children under the age of nine years not work more than nine hours a day. Beginning in 1832, a series of parliamentary acts also expanded the franchise for men by reducing property qualifications, preparing the way for universal male suffrage. In Germany in the 1880s, Otto von Bismarck introduced medical insurance, unemployment compensation, and retirement pensions to provide social security for working people in industrial society.

Trade unions also sought to advance the quest for a just and equitable society. As governments regulated businesses and enhanced social security,

Trade Unions

trade unions struggled to improve workers' lives by seeking higher wages and better working conditions for their members. Through most of the nineteenth century,

IWW demonstration

both employers and governments considered trade unions illegal associations whose purpose was to restrain trade. Yet trade unions persisted, and over the long run they improved the lives of working people and reduced the likelihood that a disgruntled proletariat would mount a revolution to overthrow industrial capitalist society.

SOURCES FROM THE PAST

Marx and Engels on Bourgeoisie and Proletarians

Karl Marx and Friedrich Engels were the most scathing critics of early industrial society. Indeed, their critique extended to industrial capitalism in general. In their view, contemporary society pitted capitalists (whom they called the bourgeoisie in their Manifesto of the Communist Party) *against proletarians. Marx and Engels argued that in the short term capitalists would exploit the proletarians, but that over the longer run proletarians would become aware of their misery, rise up, and destroy capitalist society.*

■ ■ ■

The history of all hitherto existing society is the history of class struggles.

Freeman and slave, patrician and plebeian, lord and serf, guild-master and journeyman, in a word, oppressor and oppressed, stood in constant opposition to one another, carried on an uninterrupted, now hidden, now open fight, a fight that each time ended, either in a revolutionary reconstitution of society at large, or in the common ruin of the contending classes. . . .

The modern bourgeois society that has sprouted from the ruins of feudal society has not done away with class antagonisms. It has but established new classes, new conditions of oppression, new forms of struggle in place of the old ones.

Our epoch, the epoch of the bourgeoisie, possesses, however, this distinctive feature: it has simplified the class antagonisms. Society as a whole is more and more splitting up into two great hostile camps, into two great classes directly facing each other: Bourgeoisie and Proletariat. . . .

The bourgeoisie has stripped of its halo every occupation hitherto honoured and looked up to with reverent awe. It has converted the physician, the lawyer, the priest, the poet, the man of science, into its paid wage-labourers. . . .

The need for a constantly expanding market for its products chases the bourgeoisie over the whole surface of the globe. It must nestle everywhere, settle everywhere, establish connexions everywhere. . . .

The weapons with which the bourgeoisie felled feudalism to the ground are now turned against the bourgeoisie itself.

But not only has the bourgeoisie forged the weapons that bring death to itself; it has also called into existence the men who are to wield those weapons—the modern working class—the proletarians.

In proportion as the bourgeoisie, i.e., capital, is developed, in the same proportion is the proletariat, the modern working class, developed—a class of labourers, who live only so long as they find work, and who find work only so long as their labour increases capital. These labourers, who must sell themselves piecemeal, are a commodity, like every other article of commerce, and are consequently exposed to all the vicissitudes of competition, to all the fluctuations of the market. . . .

The advance of industry, whose involuntary promoter is the bourgeoisie, replaces the isolation of the labourers, due to competition, by their revolutionary combination, due to association. The development of Modern Industry, therefore, cuts from under its feet the very foundation on which the bourgeoisie produces and appropriates products. What the bourgeoisie, therefore, produces, above all, is its own grave-diggers. Its fall and the victory of the proletariat are equally inevitable.

• *How did Marx and Engels's historical embrace of the concept of class struggle shape their understanding of the great forces clashing during this industrial age?*

SOURCE: Karl Marx and Friedrich Engels. *Manifesto of the Communist Party.* Trans. by Samuel Moore. London: W. Reeves, 1888.

Robert Koehler's painting *The Strike* depicts a situation verging on violence as workers mill about in a confrontation with factory owners and one angry laborer crouches to pick up a stone.

GLOBAL EFFECTS OF INDUSTRIALIZATION

Although early industrialization was a British, western European, and North American affair, it had deep global implications. In part this was because industrial powers used their tools, technologies, business organization, financial influence, and transportation networks to obtain raw materials from preindustrial societies around the world. Many lands that possessed natural resources were unable to maintain control over them because representatives of industrial countries dominated the commercial and financial institutions associated with their trade. Other societies, in particular Russia and Japan, saw the writing on the wall and embarked on huge industrialization programs of their own to stave off Euro-American domination.

The International Division of Labor

Industrialization influenced the economic and social development of many societies because it promoted a new international division of labor. Industrial societies needed minerals, agricultural products, and other raw materials to supply their factories, and they frequently obtained them from distant regions of the world.

Although large-scale global trade in agricultural products such as sugar, tea, and cotton was nothing new, industrial society fueled the demand for additional products as industrialists sought the natural resources and agricultural products of Africa, the Americas, Asia, Australia, and eastern Europe. The mechanization of the textile industry, for example, produced a demand for large quantities of raw cotton, which came mostly from India, Egypt, and the southern rim of the United States. Similarly, new industrial technologies increased demand for products such as rubber, the principal ingredient of the belts and tires that were essential to industrial machinery, which came from Brazil, Malaya, and the Congo River basin.

In some lands specialization in the production and export of primary goods paved the way for economic *Economic Development* development and eventual industrialization. That pattern was especially noticeable in lands settled by European colonists, including Canada, Argentina, Uruguay, South Africa, Australia, and New Zealand, each of which experienced economic growth through the export of primary products and the infusion of foreign capital and labor. The same societies had an additional advantage in that they were high-wage economies. High incomes fostered economic development in two ways: they created flourishing markets, and they encouraged entrepreneurs to counteract high wages and labor security by inventing new labor-saving technologies.

In most of Latin America, sub-Saharan Africa, south Asia, and southeast Asia, however, dependence *Economic Dependence* on exporting primary products such as sugar, cotton, and rubber resulted in little or no industrialization. Foreign investors owned and controlled the plantations that produced those crops, and most of the profits generated went abroad, depriving domestic economies of funds that might have contributed to the building of markets and industries. The low wages of plantation workers made the situation worse by dampening demand for manufactured goods. The result was the concentration of wealth in the hands of a small group of people, whether local or foreign, who contributed little to the creation of a domestic market. To compound the problem, both native and foreign financial interests adopted a free-trade policy that permitted unrestricted entry of foreign manufactures, further limiting opportunities for indigenous industrialization. Thus, although industrialization increasingly linked all the world's peoples in increasingly complex ways, its benefits and rewards went primarily to those who controlled the tools, capital, and trade rather than to those who provided the raw materials that made production possible.

The Continuing Spread of Industrialization: Russia and Japan

Industrialization brought great economic and military strength to societies that reconfigured themselves and relied on mechanized production. Their power encouraged other societies to seek their own paths to industrialization. Indeed, by the late nineteenth cen-

tury it had become clear to leaders in many preindustrial lands that unless they undertook programs of social, political, and economic reform, they would grow progressively weaker in relation to industrial powers. Faced with such a reality, after 1870 both Russia and Japan embarked on campaigns of rapid industrialization to strengthen their societies and enable them to resist military and economic pressures from western Europe and the United States.

Russia in 1870 was a multiethnic, multilingual, multicultural empire that stretched from Poland to the Pacific Ocean. The Romanov tsars ruled their diverse and sprawling realm through an autocratic regime in which all initiative came from the central administration. The tsars enjoyed the support of a powerful class of nobles who owned most of the land and were exempt from taxes and military duty. Peasants made up the vast majority of the population, and most of them were serfs bound to the lands that they cultivated.

Although the Russian army in the nineteenth century was huge, conflict with France and Britain in the Crimean War (1853–1856) clearly revealed the inability of Russian forces—based as they were on an agrarian economy—to compete with the industrial powers of western Europe. Military defeat compelled the tsarist autocracy to reevaluate the Russian social order and undertake an extensive program of reform along western European lines.

The key to social reform in Russia was emancipation of the serfs (1861), an institution many believed had become an obstacle to economic development. Indeed, Tsar Alexander II (reigned 1855–1881) emancipated the *Emancipation of the Serfs* serfs partly with the intention of creating a mobile labor force for emerging industries, and the tsarist government encouraged industrialization as a way of strengthening the Russian empire. Thus, although Russian industrialization took place within a framework of capitalism, it differed from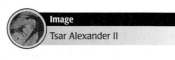

Image
Tsar Alexander II

western European industrialization in that the motivation for development was political and military and the driving force was government policy rather than entrepreneurial initiative. Industrialization proceeded slowly at first, but it surged during the last two decades of the nineteenth century.

In Russia the tsarist government promoted industrialization by encouraging the construction of rail-

tsar (ZAHR)

Map 27.2 **The Russian empire between 1801 and 1914.** Note the sheer size of Russian territory in this period, and the fact that the state included parts of Europe, central Asia, and east Asia. How would straddling so much space and so many cultures have affected the processes of industrialization and nationalism in Russia?

roads to link the distant regions of the far-flung empire. In 1860 Russia had fewer than 1,100 kilometers (700 miles) of railroads, but by 1900 there were more than 58,000 kilometers (36,000 miles). Most impressive of the Russian railroads was the trans-Siberian line, constructed between 1891 and 1904, which stretched more than 9,000 kilometers (5,600 miles) and linked Moscow with the port of Vladivostok on the Pacific Ocean. Apart from drawing the regions of the Russian empire together, railroads stimulated the development of coal, iron, and steel industries and enabled Russia to serve as a commercial link between western Europe and east Asia.

Railroads

Russian industry experienced explosive growth when Count Sergei Witte served as finance minister (1892–1903). Witte oversaw construction of the trans-Siberian railroad, and he worked to push Russian industrialization by reforming commercial law, protecting infant industries, supporting steamship companies, and promoting nautical and engineering schools. He invited foreign investors to bring their capital and expertise to Russia, and he encouraged the establishment of savings banks to raise additional investment funds at home. By 1900 Russia produced half the world's oil, and Russian steel production ranked fourth in the world, behind that of the United States, Germany, and Britain. As a result of Witte's efforts, Russia also had enormous coal and iron industries, and government demand for weapons also supported a huge armaments industry.

The Witte System

Sergei Witte (SAYR-gay VIHT-tee)

Tsar Alexander II of Russia. After signing the Treaty of Paris in 1856, ending the Crimean War, Alexander abolished serfdom in the Russian empire.

Although Russia successfully began a program of industrialization, such efforts came at a high cost. As in other lands, industrial growth generated an urban working class, which endured miserable working and living conditions. Employers kept wages of overworked and poorly housed workers at the barest minimum. Moreover, economic exploitation and the lack of political freedom made workers increasingly receptive to socialist and revolutionary propaganda, which—when combined with further military defeat and political oppression—eventually undermined the Russian state itself in the early twentieth century.

Industrial Discontent

In Japan, too, imperial authorities pushed industrialization, although under very different circumstances from those in Russia. Until 1853 Japan had largely closed itself off from interaction with European and American traders. The situation changed abruptly in that year, however, with the arrival of a U.S. naval squadron in Tokyo Bay. The American commander, Commodore Matthew C. Perry, trained his guns on the bakufu capital of Edo (modern Tokyo) and demanded that the shogun open Japan to diplomatic and commercial relations and sign a treaty of friendship. The shogun had no good alternative and so acquiesced to Perry's demands. Representatives of Britain, the Netherlands, and Russia soon won similar

Foreign Pressure

rights, all of which opened Japanese ports to foreign commerce, deprived the government of control over tariffs, and granted foreigners extraterritorial rights.

The sudden intrusion of foreign powers precipitated a domestic crisis in Japan that eventually resulted in the collapse of the Tokugawa bakufu and the restoration of imperial rule. After years of conflict and a brief civil war, the boy emperor Mutsuhito—known by his regnal name, Meiji ("Enlightened Rule")—took the reins of power on 3 January 1868.

The Meiji restoration returned authority to the Japanese emperor and marked the birth of a new Japan. Determined to gain parity with foreign powers, a conservative coalition of daimyo, imperial princes, court nobles, and samurai formed a new government dedicated to the twin goals of prosperity and strength: "rich country, strong army." The Meiji government looked to the industrial lands of Europe and the United States to obtain the knowledge and expertise to strengthen Japan. The Meiji government sent many students and officials abroad to study everything from technology to constitutions, and it also hired foreign experts to facilitate economic development and the creation of indigenous expertise.

The Meiji Restoration

Economic initiatives were critical to the process of Meiji reconstruction. Convinced that a powerful economy was the foundation of national strength, the Meiji government created a modern transportation, communications, and educational infrastructure. The establishment of telegraph, railroad, and steamship lines tied local and regional markets into a national economic network. Aiming to improve literacy rates, the government introduced a system of universal primary and secondary education. Universities provided advanced instruction for the best students, especially in scientific and technical fields. This infrastructure supported rapid industrialization and economic growth. Although most economic enterprises were privately owned, the government controlled military industries and established pilot programs to stimulate industrial development. During the 1880s the government sold most of its enterprises to private investors who had close ties to government officials. The result was a concentration of

Economic Development

Tokugawa (TOH-koo-GAH-wah)
Meiji (MAY-jee)
daimyo (DEYEM-yoh)

The Tomioka silk factory, established in the 1870s, was one of the earliest mechanized textile factories in Japan. In this factory, as in many textile mills in Europe and North America, male managers oversaw female factory workers.

enormous economic power in the hands of a small group of people, collectively known as *zaibatsu,* or financial cliques. By the early twentieth century, Japan had joined the ranks of the major industrial powers.

As in Russia, economic development came at a price, as the Japanese people bore the social and political costs of rapid industrialization. During this period, hundreds of thousands of rural families lived in destitution, haunted by malnutrition, starvation, and infanticide. In addition, those who took up work in the burgeoning industries learned that working

Costs of Economic Development

conditions were difficult and that the state did not tolerate labor organizations that promoted the welfare of workers.

Nevertheless, the desire to achieve political and economic equality with Euro-American industrial powers—and to avoid the domination and dependence experienced by preindustrial societies elsewhere—transformed Japan into a powerful industrial society in a single generation. Serving as symbols of Japan's remarkable development were the conclusion of an alliance with Britain as an equal power in 1902 and convincing displays of military prowess in victories over the Chinese empire (1894–1895) and the Russian empire (1904–1905).

zaibatsu (zeye-BAHT-soo)

SUMMARY

The process of industrialization involved the harnessing of inanimate sources of energy, the replacement of handicraft production with machine-based manufacturing, and the generation of new forms of business and labor organization. Along with industrialization came demographic growth, large-scale migration, and rapid urbanization, which increased the demand for manufactured goods by the masses of working people. Societies that underwent industrialization enjoyed sharp increases in economic productivity: they produced large quantities of high-quality goods at low prices, and their increased productivity translated into higher material standards of living. Yet industrialization brought costs as well as benefits. Family life changed dramatically in the industrial age as men, women, and children increasingly left their homes to work in factories and mines, often under appalling conditions. Socialist critics sought to bring about a more just and equitable society, and government authorities curtailed the worst abuses of the early industrial era. Meanwhile, industrialization increasingly touched the lives of peoples around the world. To avoid being dominated, Russia and Japan followed the lead of Britain, western Europe, and North America into industrialization, whereas many African, Asian, and Latin American lands became dependent on the export of raw materials to industrial societies.

CHRONOLOGY

1733	John Kay develops the flying shuttle
1765	James Watt patents an improved steam engine
1779	Samuel Crompton develops the spinning mule
1785	Edmund Cartwright develops the power loom
1797	Eli Whitney introduces interchangeable parts to the manufacturing process
1829	George Stephenson's locomotive, the Rocket, attains a speed of 45 kilometers (28 miles) per hour
1848	Karl Marx and Friedrich Engels publish *Manifesto of the Communist Party*
1849–1915	Life of Sergei Witte
1851	Crystal Palace exhibition in London
1853	Arrival of Commodore Perry in Japan
1853–1856	Crimean War
1855–1881	Reign of Tsar Alexander II
1856	Bessemer converter developed
1861	Emancipation of the Russian serfs
1868	Meiji restoration
1913	Henry Ford introduces the assembly line to the manufacture of automobiles

FOR FURTHER READING

William L. Blackwell. *The Industrialization of Russia: An Historical Perspective.* New York, 1982. A useful overview.

Daniel R. Headrick. *The Tentacles of Progress: Technology Transfer in the Age of Imperialism, 1850–1940.* New York, 1988. Concentrates on the political and cultural obstacles that hindered transfer of European technologies to colonial lands.

Marius B. Jansen and Gilbert Rozman, eds. *Japan in Transition: From Tokugawa to Meiji.* Princeton, 1986. Important collection of essays exploring economic and social change during the era of the Meiji restoration.

David S. Landes. *The Wealth and Poverty of Nations: Why Some Are So Rich and Some So Poor.* New York, 1998. A wide-ranging analysis arguing that social and cultural attitudes serve as the foundation of economic development.

Karl Marx and Friedrich Engels. *The Communist Manifesto.* Trans. by Samuel Moore. Harmondsworth, 1967. English translation of the most important tract of nineteenth-century socialism, with an excellent introduction by historian A. J. P. Taylor.

Kenneth Pomeranz. *The Great Divergence: China, Europe, and the Making of the Modern World Economy.* Princeton, 2000. Argues that the fortuitous location of coal deposits and access to the resources of the Americas created a uniquely advantageous framework for English industrialization.

Hans Rogger. *Russia in the Age of Modernisation and Revolution, 1881–1917.* New York, 1983. An important study of Russian social and economic development.

Peter N. Stearns. *The Industrial Revolution in World History.* Boulder, 1993. An excellent overview of industrialization, its European origins, its spread, and its effects in the larger world.

E. P. Thompson. *The Making of the English Working Class.* New York, 1966. A classic work that analyzes the formation of working-class consciousness in England from the 1790s to the 1830s.

Louise A. Tilly. *Industrialization and Gender Inequality.* Washington, D.C., 1993. A brief historiographical survey of debates on gender and industrialization in England, France, Germany, the United States, Japan, and China.

CHAPTER 28

The Americas in the Age of Independence

A village fish peddler, Fatt Hing Chin often roamed the coast of southern China in search of fish to sell at market. One day at the wharves, he heard a tale of mysterious but enticing mountains of gold beckoning young Chinese to cross the ocean. At nineteen years of age, Chin longed for the glittering mountains. He learned that he could purchase passage on a foreign ship, and in 1849 he boarded a Spanish ship to sail to California and join the gold rush.

Once at sea, Chin was surprised at the large number of young Chinese men crammed in with him in the ship's vomit-laden hold. Ninety-five difficult days and nights passed before the hills of San Francisco came into view. Upon arrival the travelers met Chinese veterans of life in the United States who explained the need to stick together if they were to survive and prosper.

Chin hired out as a gold miner, and after two years he accumulated his own little pile of gold. He wrote to his brothers and cousins, urging them to join him, and thus helped fuel the large-scale overseas migration of workers. Having made his fortune, though, Chin decided to return to China. Indeed, California gold provided him with the means to take a wife, build a house, and buy some land in his home country.

Although settled and prosperous, Chin longed for the excitement of California. Leaving his pregnant wife, he sailed for California again after only a year in China. He returned to mining with his brother, but the gold was more difficult to find. Inspired by the luck of another migrant, Tong Ling, who managed to get one

OPPOSITE PAGE: *Chinese immigrants employed to build the California railroads in the 1890s.*

517

dollar for each meal he sold, Chin's cousins in San Francisco decided to open a restaurant. Chin found the city much more comfortable than the mountains. "Let the others go after the gold in the hills," he said. "I'll wait for the gold to come to the city."

Fatt Hing Chin was one of the earliest Chinese migrants to settle in the Americas. His career path—from a miner in search of quick riches to an urban resident committed to a new homeland—was quite typical of Chinese migrants to the United States. Along with millions of others from Europe and Asia, Chinese migrants increased the ethnic diversity of American populations and stimulated political, social, and economic development in the western hemisphere.

During the late eighteenth and early nineteenth centuries, almost all the lands of the western hemisphere won their independence from European colonial powers. American peoples then struggled throughout the nineteenth century to build their own states and societies. The United States built the most powerful state in the western hemisphere and embarked on a westward push that brought most of the temperate regions of North America under U.S. control. Canada built a federal state under British Canadian leadership. The varied lands of Latin America built smaller states that often fell under the sway of local military leaders. One issue that most American peoples wrestled with, regardless of their region, was the legacy of the Enlightenment. The effort to build societies based on freedom, equality, and constitutional government was a monumental challenge that remained only partially realized. Indeed, Asian and European migrants joined freed slaves and native-born workers in labor systems—from plantations and factories to debt peonage—that often betrayed American promises of welcome and freedom.

The age of independence for the United States, Canada, and Latin America was a contentious era characterized by continuous mass migration and explosive economic growth, occasionally followed by deep economic stagnation, and punctuated with civil war, ethnic violence, class conflict, and battles for racial and sexual equality. Goals to build effective states, enjoy economic prosperity, and attain cultural cohesion were elusive throughout the nineteenth century and in many ways remain so even in the present day. Nevertheless, the histories of these first lands to win independence from colonial powers inspired other peoples who later sought freedom from imperial rule.

THE BUILDING OF AMERICAN STATES

After winning independence from Britain, the United States fashioned a government and began to expand rapidly to the west. Yet the United States was an unstable society composed of varied regions with diverse economic and social structures. Differences over slavery and the rights of individual states as opposed to the federal government sparked a bloody civil war in the 1860s. That conflict resulted in the abolition of slavery and the strengthening of the federal state. The experience of Canada was very different from that of the United States. Canada gained independence from Britain without fighting a war, and even though Canada also was a land of great diversity, it avoided falling into a civil war. Canada established a relatively weak federal government, which presided over provinces that had considerable power over local affairs. Latin American lands were even more diverse than their counterparts to the north, and there was never any real possibility that they could join together in a confederation. Throughout the nineteenth century Latin America was a politically fragmented region, and many individual states faced serious problems and divisions within their own societies.

The United States: Westward Expansion and Civil War

After gaining independence the United States faced the need to construct a government. During the 1780s leaders from the rebellious colonies drafted a constitution that entrusted responsibility for general issues to a federal government, reserved authority for local issues for individual states, and provided for the admission of new states and territories to the confederation. Originally, most states limited the vote to men of property, but the Enlightenment ideal of equality encouraged political leaders to extend the franchise: by the mid–nineteenth century almost all adult white men were eligible to vote.

While working to settle constitutional issues, Americans also began to expand to the west. After the American Revolution, Britain ceded to the new republic all lands between the Appalachian Mountains and the Mississippi River, and the United States doubled in size. In 1803 Napoleon Bonaparte allowed the United States to purchase France's Louisiana Ter-

Westward Expansion and Manifest Destiny

ritory, which extended from the Mississippi River to the Rocky Mountains. Overnight the United States doubled in size again. Between 1804 and 1806 a geographic expedition led by Meriwether Lewis and William Clark mapped the territory and surveyed its resources. Settlers soon began to flock west in search of cheap land to cultivate. By the 1840s many Americans spoke of a "manifest destiny" to occupy all of North America from the Atlantic to the Pacific Ocean.

Conflict with Indigenous Peoples

Westward expansion brought settlers and government forces into conflict with the indigenous peoples of North America, who resisted efforts to push them from their ancestral lands and hunting grounds. However, U.S. officials and military forces supported Euro-American settlers and gradually forced the continent open to white expansion. With the Indian Removal Act of 1830, the United States government determined to move all Native Americans west of the Mississippi River into "Indian Territory" (Oklahoma). Among the tribes affected by this forced removal from the east were the

Cherokees, who suffered a harrowing 800-mile migration from the eastern woodlands to Oklahoma on the Trail of Tears (1838–1839), so known because thousands died from disease, starvation, and the difficulties of relocation.

Interactive Map
Indian expulsion

After 1840 the site of conflict between Euro-American and indigenous peoples shifted to the plains region west of the Mississippi River. Settlers and ranchers in the trans-Mississippi west encountered peoples such as the Sioux, the Comanche, the Pawnee, and the Apache, who possessed firearms and outstanding equestrian skills. The native peoples of the plains offered effective resistance to encroachment by white settlers and at times won powerful victories over U.S. forces. In 1876, for example, thousands of Lakota Sioux and their allies annihilated an army under the command of Colonel George Armstrong Custer in the battle of Little Big Horn (in southern Montana). Ultimately, however, Native Americans on the plains lost

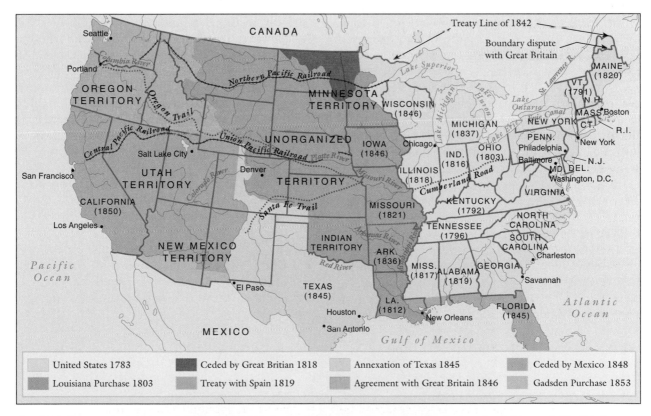

Map 28.1 Westward expansion of the United States during the nineteenth century. Note the large land claims ceded by Britain, France, and Mexico. Why were there no portions of North America purchased from or ceded by North American Indians?

the war against the forces of U.S. expansionism. U.S. forces employed cannons and deadly, rapid-fire Gatling guns against native peoples, which helped break native resistance and opened the western plains to U.S. conquest.

One last symbolic conflict took place in 1890 at Wounded Knee Creek in South Dakota. U.S. cavalry forces, hoping to suppress Sioux religious ceremonies that envisioned the disappearance of white people, chased the Sioux who were fleeing to safety in the South Dakota Badlands. At Wounded Knee Creek, a Sioux man accidentally shot off a gun, and the cavalry overreacted badly, slaughtering more than two hundred men, women, and children with machine guns. Emblematic of harsh U.S. treatment of native peoples, Wounded Knee represented the place where "a people's dream died," as a later native leader put it.

Westward expansion also generated tension between the United States and Mexico, whose territories *The Mexican-* included most of what is now the *American War* American southwest. Texas declared independence from Mexico in 1836, largely because the many American migrants who had settled there wanted to run their own affairs. In 1845 the United States accepted Texas as a new state—against vigorous Mexican protest— and moved to consolidate its hold on the territory. Those moves led to conflicts that rapidly escalated into the Mexican-American War (1845–1848). U.S. forces instigated the war and then inflicted a punishing defeat

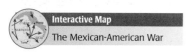

Interactive Map
The Mexican-American War

on the Mexican army. By the Treaty of Guadalupe Hidalgo (1848), the United States took possession of approximately one-half of Mexico's territory, paying a mere fifteen million dollars in exchange for Texas north of the Rio Grande, California, and New Mexico.

Westward expansion also created problems within the republic by aggravating tensions between regions. The most divisive issue had to do with slavery, which had vexed American politics since independence. The Enlightenment ideal of equality clearly suggested that the appropriate policy was to abolish slavery, but the framers of the Constitution recognized the sanctity of private property, including slaves. American independence initially promoted a surge of antislavery sentiment, and states from Delaware north abolished slavery within their jurisdictions. That move hardened divisions between slave and free states. Westward expansion aggravated tensions further by raising the question of whether settlers could extend slavery to newly acquired territories.

The election of Abraham Lincoln to the presidency in 1860 was the spark that ignited war between the states (1861–1865). Lincoln was an explicitly sectional candidate who *Sectional Conflict* was convinced that slavery was immoral and who was committed to free soil—territories without slavery. Although slavery stood at the center of the conflict, the Civil War also revolved around other important issues: the nature of the Union, states' rights as opposed to the federal government's authority, and the needs of a budding industrial-capitalist system against those of an export-oriented plantation economy.

This photograph of an 1890s Plains Indian camp in South Dakota offers an idealized, pastoral, and peaceful image of the disappearing indigenous societies in the United States.

Eleven southern states withdrew from the Union in 1860 and 1861, affirming their right to dissolve the Union and their support for states' rights.

The U.S. Civil War

Northerners saw the situation differently. They viewed secession as illegal insurrection and an act of betrayal. They fought not only against slavery but also against the concept of a state subject to blackmail by its constituent parts. They also fought for a way of life—their emerging industrial society—and an expansive western agricultural system based on free labor.

Ultimately, the northern states prevailed. They brought considerable resources to the war effort—some 90 percent of the country's industrial capacity and approximately two-thirds of its railroad lines—but still they fought four bitter years against a formidable enemy. The consequences of that victory were enormous, for it ended slavery in the United States. Indeed, once Abraham Lincoln signed the Emancipation Proclamation on 1 January 1863, which made the abolition of slavery an explicit goal of the war, it was clear that a northern victory would entail radical changes in southern life. Moreover, the victory of the northern states ensured that the United States would remain politically united, and it enhanced the authority of the federal government in the American republic. Thus, as European lands were building powerful states on the foundations of revolutionary ideals, liberalism, and nationalism, the United States also forged a strong central government to supervise westward expansion and deal with the political and social issues that divided the American republic.

The Canadian Dominion: Independence without War

Canada did not fight a war for independence, and in spite of deep regional divisions, it did not experience bloody internal conflict. Instead, Canadian independence came gradually as Canadians and the British government agreed on general principles of autonomy. The distinc-

Autonomy and Division

tiveness of the two dominant ethnic groups, the British Canadians and the French Canadians, ensured that the process of building an independent society would not be smooth, but intermittent fears about the possibility of a U.S. invasion from the south helped submerge ethnic differences. By the late nineteenth century, Canada was a land in control of its own destiny.

Originally colonized by trappers and settlers from both Britain and France, the colony of New France passed into the British empire after the British victory in the Seven Years' War (1756–1763). Until the late eighteenth century, however, French Canadians outnumbered British Canadians, so imperial officials made large concessions to their subjects of French descent to forestall unnecessary strife. After 1781, however, large numbers of British loyalists fled the newly formed United States and sought refuge in Canada, thus greatly enlarging the size of the English-speaking community there.

Ethnic divisions and political differences could easily have splintered Canada, but the War of 1812 stimulated a sense of unity against an external threat. The United States declared war on Britain in retaliation for

The grotesquely twisted bodies of dead northern soldiers lay near a fence outside Antietam, Maryland, in 1862. The Civil War was the most costly in U.S. history in number of lives lost.

encroachments on U.S. rights during the Napoleonic wars, and the British colony of Canada formed one of

The War of 1812   the front lines of the conflict. U.S. military leaders assumed that they could easily invade and conquer Canada to pressure Britain. Despite the greater resources of the United States, however, Canadian forces repelled U.S. incursions. Their victories promoted a sense of Canadian pride, and anti-U.S. sentiments became a means for covering over differences among French and British Canadians.

After the War of 1812, Canada experienced an era of rapid growth. Expanded business opportunities drew English-speaking migrants, who swelled the population. This influx threatened the identity of Quebec, and discontent in Canada reached a critical point in the 1830s. The British imperial governors of Canada did not want a repeat of the American Revolution, so between 1840 and 1867 they defused tensions by expanding home rule in Canada and permitting the provinces to govern their own internal affairs.

Fear of U.S. expansion helped stifle internal conflicts among Canadians and prompted Britain to grant independence to Canada. The British North America Act of 1867 joined Quebec, On-   *Dominion* tario, Nova Scotia, and New Brunswick and recognized them as the Dominion of Canada. Other provinces joined the Dominion later. Each province had its own seat of government, provincial legislature, and lieutenant governor representing the British crown. The act created a federal government headed by a governor-general, who acted as the British representative. An elected House of Commons and an appointed Senate rounded out the framework of governance. Without waging war, the Dominion of Canada had won control over all Canadian internal affairs, and Britain retained jurisdiction over foreign affairs until 1931.

John A. Macdonald (1815–1891) became the first prime minister of Canada, and he moved to incorpo-

Map 28.2 The Dominion of Canada in the nineteenth century. Note the provinces that make up the modern state of Canada, and the dates in which they were incorporated into the Dominion. At what date were eastern and western Canada geographically united?

rate all of British North America into the Dominion. He negotiated the purchase of the huge Northwest Territories from the Hudson Bay Company in 1869, and he persuaded Manitoba, British Columbia, and Prince Edward Island to join the Dominion. Then, to strengthen the union, he oversaw construction of a transcontinental railroad, completed in 1885. The railroad facilitated transportation and communications throughout Canada and eventually helped bring new provinces into the Dominion: Alberta and Saskatchewan in 1905 and Newfoundland in 1949. Although maintaining ties to Britain and struggling to forge an identity distinct from its powerful neighbor to the south, Canada developed as a culturally diverse yet politically unified society.

Latin America: Fragmentation and Political Experimentation

Political unity was short-lived in Latin America. Simón Bolívar (1783–1830), hailed as the region's liberator, worked for the establishment of a large confederation that would provide Latin America with the political, military, and economic strength to resist encroachment by foreign powers. The wars of independence that he led encouraged a sense of solidarity in Latin America. But Bolívar once admitted, "I fear peace more than war," and after the defeat of the common colonial enemy, Latin America fragmented into numerous independent states.

Creole Elites and Political Instability
Following the example of the United States, creole elites usually established republics with written constitutions for the newly independent states of Latin America. Yet Latin American leaders had less experience with self-government because Spanish and Portuguese colonial regimes were far more autocratic than was the British imperial government in North America. As a result, several Latin American lands lurched from one constitution to another as leaders struggled to create a machinery of government that would lead to political and social stability.

Creole elites also dominated the newly independent states and effectively prevented mass participation in public affairs. Less than 5 percent of the male population was active in Latin American politics in the nineteenth century, and millions of indigenous peoples lived entirely outside the political system. Those disillusioned with the system, then, had little choice beyond rebellion. To make matters worse, elites were divided by vocation—urban merchants versus rural landowners—as well as by ideology, whether liberalism, conservatism, secularism, or Roman Catholicism.

One thing elites agreed on was the policy of claiming land for agriculture and ranching by pushing aside indigenous peoples. Conflict was most intense on the plains of Argentina and Chile. During the mid–nineteenth century, as the United States was crushing native resistance to western expansion in North America, Argentine and Chilean forces brought modern weapons to bear in their campaign to conquer the indigenous peoples of the South American plains. By the 1870s colonists had pacified the most productive lands and forced indigenous peoples either to assimilate to Euro-American society or to retreat to marginal lands that were unattractive to cultivators and ranchers.

Conflicts with Indigenous Peoples

Image
A Chilean hacienda

Although creole elites agreed on the policy of conquering native peoples, division in the newly independent states helped *caudillos*, or regional military leaders, come to power in much of Latin America. The wars of independence had lasted well over a decade, and they provided Latin America with military rather than civilian heroes. After independence, military leaders took to the political stage by exploiting the discontent of the masses. One of the most notable caudillos was Juan Manuel de Rosas, who from 1835 to 1852 ruled an Argentina badly divided between the cattle-herding society of the pampas (the interior grasslands) and the urban elite of Buenos Aires. Rosas called for regional autonomy in an attempt to reconcile competing interests, but he worked to centralize the government he usurped. He quelled rebellions, but he did so in bloody fashion: one writer counted 22,404 victims murdered under Rosas's rule.

Caudillos

Rosas did what caudillos did best: he restored order. In doing so, however, he made terror a tool of the government, and he ruled as a despot through his own personal army. Yet although caudillo rule limited freedom and undermined republican ideals, it sometimes gave rise also to liberal opposition movements in favor of democratic forms of government.

Independent Mexico was a case in point. The Mexican-American War caused political turmoil in Mexico and helped the caudillo General Antonio López Santa Anna (1797–1876) come to power.

---

caudillos (KAHW-dee-yohs)

After the defeat and disillusion of the war, however, a liberal reform movement attempted to reshape Mexican society. Led by President Benito Juárez (1806–1872), a Mexican of indigenous ancestry, *La Reforma* of the 1850s aimed to limit the power of the military and the Roman Catholic church in Mexican society. The Constitution of 1857 set forth the ideals of *La Reforma*. It curtailed the prerogatives of priests and military elites, and it guaranteed universal male suffrage and other civil liberties, such as freedom of speech.

Mexico: War and Reform

La Reforma challenged the conservatism of Mexican elites, who led spirited opposition against it. In fact, divisions were so deep that conservatives forced the Juárez government out of Mexico City until 1861. During those difficult times, Juárez chose to suspend loan payments to foreign powers to lessen Mexico's financial woes, and that led to French, British, and Spanish intervention as Europeans sought to protect their investments in Mexico. France's Napoleon III even sent tens of thousands of troops to Mexico and proclaimed a Mexican empire.

Mexico: Revolution

Map 28.3 **The states of Latin America in the nineteenth century.** Note the many independent states that emerged from the independence movements early in the century. Why was it difficult for large, federated republics, such as the Republic of Colombia, founded by Simón Bolívar, to survive?

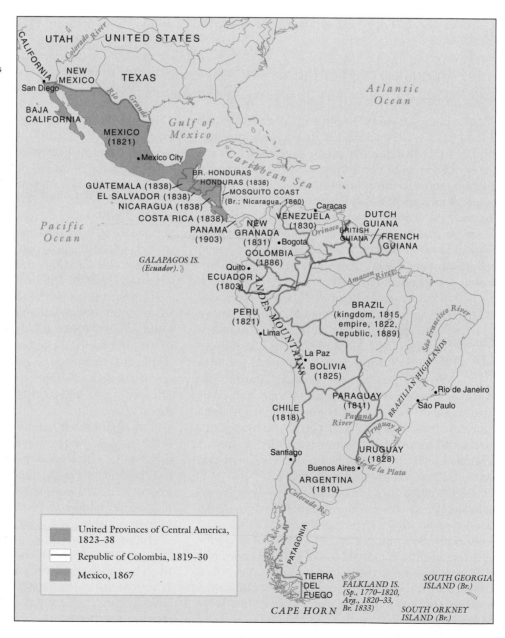

However, he was forced to withdraw French forces in 1867, and in the same year a Mexican firing squad killed the man he had appointed emperor, the Austrian archduke Maximilian (1832–1867). Juárez managed to restore a semblance of liberal government, but Mexico remained beset by political divisions.

By the early twentieth century, Mexico was a divided land moving toward civil war. The Mexican revolution (1911–1920), a bitter and bloody conflict, broke out when middle-class Mexicans joined with peasants and workers to overthrow the powerful dictator Porfirio Díaz (1830–1915). The revolt, which attempted to topple the grossly unequal system of landed estates—whereby fully 95 percent of all peasants remained landless—turned increasingly radical as rebels engaged in guerrilla warfare against government forces. The lower classes took up weapons and followed the revolutionary leaders Emiliano Zapata (1879–1919) and Francisco (Pancho) Villa (1878–1923), charismatic agrarian rebels who organized huge armies fighting for *tierra y libertad* (land and liberty). Zapata, the son of a mestizo peasant, and Villa, the son of a field worker, embodied the ideals and aspirations of the indigenous Mexican masses and enjoyed tremendous popular support. They discredited timid governmental efforts at reform and challenged governmental political control; Zapata himself confiscated hacienda lands and began distributing the lands to the peasants, while Villa attacked and killed U.S. citizens in retaliation for U.S. support of Mexican government officials.

Despite the power and popularity enjoyed by Zapata and Villa, they were unable to capture Mexico's major cities, and they did not command the resources and wealth of the government. The Mexican revolution came to an end soon after government forces ambushed and killed Zapata in 1919. Villa likewise was assassinated, on his ranch in 1923. Government forces regained control over a battered and devastated Mexico: as many as two million Mexicans may have died in the revolution. Although radicals such as Zapata and Villa were ultimately defeated, the Mexican Constitution of 1917 had already addressed some of the concerns of the revolutionaries by providing for land redistribution, universal suffrage, state-supported education, minimum wages and maximum hours for workers, and restrictions on foreign ownership of Mexican land and resources.

In the form of division, rebellion, caudillo rule, and civil war, instability and conflict plagued Latin America throughout the nineteenth century. Many

Zapata, hailing from the southern state of Morelos, was the very picture of a revolutionary leader, heavily armed and sporting his dashing, trademark moustache.

Latin American peoples lacked education, profitable employment, and political representation. Simón Bolívar himself once said that "independence is the only blessing we have gained at the expense of all the rest."

AMERICAN ECONOMIC DEVELOPMENT

During the nineteenth and early twentieth centuries, two principal influences—mass migration and British investment—shaped economic development throughout the Americas. But American states reacted in different ways to migration and foreign investment. The United States and Canada absorbed waves of migrants, exploited British capital, built industrial societies, and established economic independence. The fragmented states of Latin America were unable to follow suit, as they struggled with the legacies of colonialism, slavery, and economic dependence on single export crops. Throughout the Americas, however, life and labor for freed slaves, migrants, or industrial workers often proved arduous and at times heartbreaking, even as these American workers contributed to the economic development of the region.

Migration to the Americas

Underpinning the economic development of the Americas was the mass migration of European and Asian peoples to the United States, Canada, and Latin America. Gold discoveries in California and Canada drew prospectors hoping to make a quick fortune, but outnumbering gold prospectors were millions of European and Asian migrants who made their way to the factories, railroad construction sites, and plantations of the Americas. Following them were others who offered the support services that made life for migrant workers more comfortable and at the same time transformed the ethnic and cultural landscape of the Americas.

After the mid–nineteenth century, European migrants flocked to North America, where they filled the factories of the growing industrial economy of the United States. Their lack of skills made them attractive to industrialists seeking workers to operate machinery or perform heavy labor at low wages. By keeping labor costs down, migrants helped increase the profitability and fuel the expansion of U.S. industry. In the 1850s alone European migrants to the United States numbered 2.3 million—almost as many as had crossed the Atlantic during the half century from 1800 to 1850—and the volume of migration surged until the early twentieth century. In the first half of the century, migrants came mostly from Ireland, Scotland, Germany, and Scandinavia to escape high rents and indebtedness. By the late nineteenth century, most European migrants came from southern and eastern Europe and included Poles, Russian Jews, Slavs, Italians, Greeks, and Portuguese. Without their labor, the remarkable industrial expansion that the United States experienced in the late nineteenth century would have been inconceivable.

Industrial Migrants

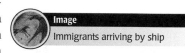
Immigrants arriving by ship

Chinese migration grew rapidly after the 1840s, when British gunboats opened China to foreign influences. Between 1852 and 1875 some two hundred

Italian migrants construct a railway in New York. Italians were just one of many European groups coming to the Americas in the nineteenth century.

thousand Chinese migrated to California. Some, like Fatt Hing Chin, negotiated their own passage, but most traveled on indentured labor contracts that required them to cultivate crops or work on the Central Pacific Railroad. An additional five thousand Chinese entered Canada to search for gold in British Columbia or work on the Canadian Pacific Railroad.

Plantation Migrants
Whereas migrants to the United States contributed to the development of an industrial society, those who went to Latin American lands mostly worked on agricultural plantations. Some Europeans figured among these migrants. About four million Italians sought opportunities in Argentina in the 1880s and 1890s, for example, and the Brazilian government paid Italian migrants to cross the Atlantic and work for coffee growers after the abolition of slavery there (1888).

Other migrants who worked on plantations in the western hemisphere came from Asia. More than fifteen thousand indentured laborers from China worked in the sugarcane fields of Cuba during the nineteenth century, and Indian migrants traveled to Jamaica, Trinidad, Tobago, and Guyana. Laborers from both China and Japan migrated to Peru, where they worked on cotton plantations, mined guano deposits, and helped build railroad lines. After the middle of the nineteenth century, expanding U.S. influence in the Pacific islands also led to Chinese, Japanese, Filipino, and Korean migrations to Hawai`i, where planters sought indentured laborers to tend sugarcane. About twenty-five thousand Chinese went to Hawai`i during the 1850s and 1860s, and later 180,000 Japanese also made their way to island plantations.

Economic Expansion in the United States

British Capital
British investment capital in the United States proved crucial to the early stages of industrial development by helping businesspeople establish a textile industry. In the late nineteenth century, it also helped spur a vast expansion of U.S. industry by funding entrepreneurs who opened coal and iron ore mines, built iron and steel factories, and constructed railroad lines. The flow of investment monies was a consequence of Britain's own industrialization, which generated enormous wealth and created a need for investors to find profitable outlets for their funds.

Perhaps the most important economic development of the later nineteenth century was the con-struction of railroad lines that linked all U.S. regions and helped create an integrated national economy.

Railroads
Because of its enormous size and environmental diversity, the United States offered an abundance of natural resources for industrial exploitation. But vast distances made it difficult to maintain close economic ties between regions until a boom in railroad construction created a dense transportation, communication, and distribution network. Before the Civil War the United States had about 50,000 kilometers (31,000 miles) of railroad lines, most of them short routes east of the Mississippi River. By 1900 there were more than 320,000 kilometers (200,000 miles) of track, and the American rail network stretched from coast to coast.

Railroads decisively influenced American economic development. They provided cheap transportation for agricultural commodities, manufactured goods, and individual travelers. Railroads hauled grain, beef, and hogs from the plains states, cotton and tobacco from the south, lumber from the northwest, iron and steel from Pittsburgh, and finished products from the eastern industrial cities. Quite apart from the transportation services they provided, railroads spurred the development of other industries: they required huge amounts of coal, wood, glass, and rubber, and by the 1880s some 75 percent of U.S. steel went to the railroad industry. Railroads also required the development of new managerial skills to operate large, complicated businesses with multiple employees.

Space and Time
Railroads led to drastic changes in the landscape. Indeed, the westward expansion driven by the railroad led to large-scale land clearing and the extension of farming and mining lands and brought about both human suffering for indigenous peoples and environmental damage through soil erosion and pollution. Railroads even shaped the American sense of time. Until rapid and regular rail transportation became available, communities set their clocks by the sun. As a result, New York time was eleven minutes and forty-five seconds behind Boston time. Those differences in local sun times created scheduling nightmares as well as the potential for train accidents. To simplify matters, in 1883 railroad companies divided the North American continent into four zones in which all railroad clocks read precisely the same time. The general public quickly adopted "railroad time," and in 1918 the U.S. government legally established the four time zones as the national standard.

In this lithograph of Frances F. Palmer's well-known painting *American Express Train* (ca. 1864), the railroad demonstrates its domination of the natural landscape and its role as the harbinger of change and industry.

AMERICAN EXPRESS TRAIN.

Economic Growth

Led by railroads, the U.S. economy expanded at a blistering pace between 1870 and 1900. Inventors designed new products and brought them to market: electric lights, telephones, typewriters, phonographs, film photography, motion picture cameras, and electric motors all made their appearance during this era. Indeed, by the early twentieth century the United States had emerged as one of the world's major industrial powers.

Canadian Prosperity

British investment deeply influenced the development of the Canadian as well as the U.S. economy in the nineteenth and early twentieth centuries. Canadian leaders, like U.S. leaders, took advantage of British capital to industrialize without allowing their economy to fall under British control.

The National Policy

After the establishment of the Dominion, politicians started a program of economic development known as the National Policy. The idea was to attract migrants, protect nascent industries through tariffs, and build national transportation systems. The centerpiece of the transportation network was the transcontinental Canadian Pacific Railroad, built largely with British investment capital and completed in 1885. The Canadian Pacific Railroad opened the western prairie lands to commerce, stimulated the development of other industries, and promoted the emergence of a Canadian national economy. The National Policy created some violent altercations with indigenous peoples who resisted encroachment on their lands and with trappers who resented disruption of their way of life, but it also promoted economic growth and independence.

As a result of the National Policy, Canada experienced booming agricultural, mineral, and industrial production in the late nineteenth and early twentieth centuries. Canadian population surged as a result of both migration and natural increase. Migrants flocked to Canada's shores from Asia and especially from Europe: between 1903 and 1914 some 2.7 million eastern European migrants settled in Canada. Fueled in part by this population growth, Canadian economic expansion took place on the foundation of rapidly increasing wheat production and the extraction of rich mineral resources, including gold, silver, copper, nickel, and asbestos. Industrialists also tapped Canadian rivers to produce the hydroelectric power necessary for manufacturing.

U.S. Investment

Canada remained wary of its powerful neighbor to the south but did not keep U.S. economic influence entirely at bay. By 1918, Americans owned 30 percent of all Canadian industry, and thereafter the U.S. and Canadian economies became increasingly interdependent. Canada began to undergo rapid industrialization after the early twentieth century, as the province of Ontario benefited from the spillover of U.S. industry in the northeast.

Latin American Dependence

Latin American states did not undergo industrialization or enjoy economic development as did the United States and Canada. Colonial legacies are part of the explanation. Even when Spain and Portugal controlled the trade and investment policies of their American colonies, their home economies were unable to supply sufficient quantities of the manufactured goods that colonial markets demanded. As a result, they opened the colonies to British, French, and German trade, which in turn snuffed out local industries that could not compete with British, French, and German producers of inexpensive manufactured goods. Moreover, both in colonial times and after independence, Latin American elites retained control over local economies. Elites profited handsomely from European trade and investment and thus had little incentive to work toward economic diversification.

Foreign influence in Latin America generally took the form of investment, which brought handsome profits and considerable control over Latin American economic affairs. In Argentina, for example, British investors encouraged the development of cattle and sheep ranching. After the 1860s and the invention of refrigerated cargo ships, meat became Argentina's largest export. British investors controlled the industry and reaped the profits, however, as Argentina became Britain's principal supplier of meat.

British Investment

In a few lands, ruling elites made attempts to encourage industrialization, but with only limited success. The most notable of those efforts came when the dictatorial general Porfirio Díaz ruled Mexico (1876–1911). Díaz represented the interests of large landowners, wealthy merchants, and foreign investors. Under his rule, railroad tracks and telegraph lines connected all parts of Mexico and the production of mineral resources surged. A small steel industry produced railroad track and construction materials, and entrepreneurs also established glass, chemical, and textile industries. The capital, Mexico City, underwent a transformation during the Díaz years: it acquired paved streets, streetcar lines, and electric street lights. But the profits from Mexican enterprises did not support continuing industrial development. Instead, they went into

Attempted Industrialization

the pockets of the Mexican oligarchy and foreign investors who supported Díaz while a growing and discontented urban working class seethed with resentment at low wages, long hours, and foreign managers. Even as agriculture, railroad construction, and mining were booming, the standard of living for average Mexicans was declining in the late nineteenth century. Frustration with that state of affairs helps explain the sudden outbreak of violent revolution in 1911.

Despite a large proportion of foreign and especially British control, Latin American economies expanded rapidly in the late nineteenth century. Exports drove this growth: copper and silver from Mexico, bananas from Central America, rubber and coffee from Brazil, beef and wheat from Argentina, copper from Chile, and tobacco and sugar from Cuba. Other areas in the world also developed many of these same products for export, however, and competition for markets tended to drive prices down. As in the United States and Canada, foreign investment in Latin America provided capital for development, but unlike the situation in the northern lands, control over industries and exports remained in foreign hands. Latin American economies were thus subject to decisions made in the interests of foreign investors, and unstable governments could do little in the face of strong foreign intervention. Controlled by the very elites who profited from foreign intervention at the expense of their citizens, Latin American governments helped promote the region's economic dependence, despite growth in industrial and export economies.

A coffee hacienda

AMERICAN CULTURAL AND SOCIAL DIVERSITY

Much of the allure of the Americas derived from their vast spaces and diverse populations. While diversity distinguished the Americas, it also provided abundant fuel for conflicts between ethnic groups, social classes, and those segregated by race or gender. The social and cultural diversity of American societies challenged their ability to achieve cultural cohesion as well as democratically inclusive states. The lingering legacies of European conquest, slavery, migration, and patriarchy highlighted contradictions between the Enlightenment ideals of freedom and equality and the realities of life for native and African-American peoples as well as recent migrants and women. In efforts to maintain their own position and preserve social stability, the dominant political forces in the Americas often repressed demands for recognition by dispossessed groups.

Multicultural Society in the United States

By the late nineteenth century, the United States had become a boisterous multicultural society whose population included indigenous peoples, Euro-American settlers, African-American laborers, and growing numbers of migrants from Europe and Asia. The poet Walt Whitman described the United States as "not merely a nation but a teeming nation of nations." Yet political and economic power rested almost exclusively with white male elites of European ancestry. The United States experienced tension and occasional conflict as members of various constituencies worked for dignity, prosperity, and a voice in society.

As they expanded to the west, Euro-American settlers and ranchers pushed indigenous peoples onto reservations. Begrudging Native Americans even those meager lands, the United States embarked in the latter half of the nineteenth century on a policy designed to reduce native

Native Peoples

autonomy even further through laws and reforms aimed at assimilating tribes to the white way of life. The U.S. government and private citizens acted to undermine or destroy outright the bases of native cultural traditions. For example, government officials removed native children from their families and tribes and enrolled them in white-controlled boarding schools. These schools, such as the Carlisle Indian School and the Toledo Indian School, illustrated the extent to which white society sought to eliminate tribal influences and inculcate Christian, U.S. values. Tribal languages as well as native dress and hair fashions were banned, further distancing the children from their cultures. Native Americans, however, resisted those forms of assimilation, and over the following decades tribes rebuilt and reaffirmed native identities.

The Civil War ended slavery, but it did not bring about equality for freed slaves and their African-American descendants. In an effort to establish a place for freed slaves in American society, northern forces sent armies of occupation to the southern states and forced them to undergo a program of social and political reconstruction (1867–1877). They extended civil rights to freed slaves and provided black men with voting rights. People in

Freed Slaves

The Apache youths at the Carlisle Indian School offer stark faces to the camera, suggesting their discontent with reform efforts directed at assimilation through education.

A lithograph from *Harper's Weekly* after the Civil War. An artisan, a middle-class African-American, and a black Union soldier are in the process of voting, perhaps for the first time in their lives.

southern states elected biracial governments for the first time in U.S. history, and freed slaves participated actively in the political affairs of the republic.

After Reconstruction, however, the armies of occupation went home, and a violent backlash soon dismantled the reforms of Reconstruction. By the turn of the century, U.S. blacks faced violence and intimidation when they tried to vote. Southern states fashioned a rigidly segregated society that deprived the African-American population of educational, economic, and political opportunities. Although freedom was better than slavery, it was far different from the hopeful visions of the slaves who had won their emancipation.

Even before the Civil War, a small but growing women's movement had emerged in the United States. At the Seneca Falls Convention in *Women* 1848, feminists issued a declaration arguing "that all men and women are created equal" and demanding equal political and economic rights. Women fought for equal rights throughout the nineteenth century, and new opportunities for education and employment offered alternatives to marriage and domesticity. Women's colleges, reform activism, and professional industrial jobs allowed some women to

pursue careers over marriage. Yet meaningful economic and political opportunities for women awaited the twentieth century.

Between 1840 and 1914 some twenty-five million European migrants landed on American shores, and in the late nineteenth century most of them *Migrants* hailed from southern and eastern European countries. Migrants introduced new foods, music, dances, holidays, sports, and languages to U.S. society and contributed to the cultural diversity of the western hemisphere. Yet white, native-born citizens of the United States began to feel swamped by the arrival of so many migrants. Indeed, concerns about growing numbers of migrants with different cultural and social traditions eventually led to the exclusion of new arrivals from Asian lands: the U.S. government ordered a complete halt to migration from China in 1882 and Japan in 1908.

Canadian Cultural Contrasts

British and French settlers each viewed themselves as Canada's founding people. That cleavage, which profoundly influenced Canadian political development, masked much greater cultural and *Ethnic Diversity* ethnic diversity in Canada. French and British settlers displaced the indigenous peoples, who remain a significant minority of Canada's population today. Slavery likewise left a mark on Canada. Slavery was legal in the British empire until 1833, and many early settlers brought their slaves with them to Canada. After emancipation, blacks in Canada were free but not equal, segregated and isolated from the political and cultural mainstream. Chinese migrants also came to Canada: lured by gold rushes such as the Fraser River rush of 1858 and by opportunities to work on the Canadian Pacific Railway in the 1880s, Chinese migrants lived mostly in segregated Chinatowns in the cities of British Columbia, and like blacks they had little voice in public affairs. Between 1896 and 1914 three million migrants from Britain, the United States, and eastern Europe arrived in Canada, bringing even greater ethnic diversity with them.

Despite the heterogeneity of Canada's population, communities descended from British and French settlers dominated Canadian society, and conflict between the two communities was the most prominent source of ethnic tension throughout the nineteenth and twentieth centuries. After 1867, as British Canadians led the effort to settle the Northwest Territories

SOURCES FROM THE PAST

The Meaning of Freedom for an Ex-Slave

Even before the conclusion of the Civil War brought slavery to an end in the United States, Jourdan Anderson had taken the opportunity to run away and claim his freedom. After the war his former master, Colonel P. H. Anderson, wrote a letter asking him to return to work on his Tennessee plantation. In responding from his new home in Dayton, Ohio, Anderson respectfully referred to the colonel as "my old master" and addressed him as "sir." Yet Anderson's letter makes it clear that his family's freedom and welfare were his principal concerns.

■   ■   ■

I want to know particularly what the good chance is you propose to give me. I am doing tolerably well here; I get $25 a month, with victuals and clothing; have a comfortable home for Mandy (the folks here call her Mrs. Anderson), and the children, Milly, Jane and Grundy, go to school and are learning well; the teacher says Grundy has a head for a preacher. They go to Sunday-School, and Mandy and me attend church regularly. We are kindly treated; sometimes we overhear others saying, "Them colored people were slaves" down in Tennessee. The children feel hurt when they hear such remarks, but I tell them it was no disgrace in Tennessee to belong to Col. Anderson. Many darkies would have been proud, as I used to was, to call you master. Now, if you will write and say what wages you will give me, I will be better able to decide whether it would be to my advantage to move back again.

As to my freedom, which you say I can have, there is nothing to be gained on that score, as I got my freepapers in 1864 from the Provost-Marshal-General of the Department at Nashville. Mandy says she would be afraid to go back without some proof that you are sincerely disposed to treat us justly and kindly—and we have concluded to test your sincerity by asking you to send us our wages for the time we served you. This will make us forget and forgive old scores, and rely on your justice and friendship in the future. I served you faithfully for thirty-two years and Mandy twenty years. At $25 a month for me, and $2 a week for Mandy, our earnings would amount to $11,680. Add to this the interest for the time our wages has been kept back and deduct what you paid for our clothing and three doctor's visits to me, and pulling a tooth for Mandy, and the balance will show what we are in justice entitled to. Please send the money by Adams Express, in care of V. Winters, esq, Dayton, Ohio. If you fail to pay us for faithful labors in the past we can have little faith in your promises in the future. We trust the good Maker has opened your eyes to the wrongs which you and your fathers have done to me and my fathers, in making us toil for you for generations without recompense. Here I draw my wages every Saturday night, but in Tennessee there was never any pay day for the negroes any more than for the horses and cows. Surely there will be a day of reckoning for those who defraud the laborer of his hire.

In answering this letter please state if there would be any safety for my Milly and Jane, who are now grown up and both good-looking girls. You know how it was with poor Matilda and Catherine. I would rather stay here and starve and die if it comes to that than have my girls brought to shame by the violence and wickedness of their young masters. You will also please state if there has been any schools opened for the colored children in your neighborhood, the great desire of my life now is to give my children an education, and have them form virtuous habits.

• *In what clever ways does Jourdan Anderson test the seriousness of his former owner's offer of employment, and what does his approach say about the meaning of black freedom?*

SOURCE: Leon F. Litwack. *Been in the Storm So Long: The Aftermath of Slavery.* New York: Knopf, 1979, pp. 334–35.

and incorporate them into the Dominion, frictions between the two groups intensified. Westward expansion brought British Canadian settlers and cultivators into conflict with French Canadian fur traders, lumberjacks, and métis of mixed French and Indian ancestry.

Indeed, a major outbreak of civil strife took place in the 1870s and 1880s. Native peoples and métis had moved west throughout the nineteenth century to preserve their land and trading rights, but the drive of British Canadians to the west threatened them. Louis Riel (1844–1885), who was himself a métis, emerged as the leader of the métis and indigenous peoples of western Canada. Of particular importance was his leadership in the resistance to the Canadian Pacific Railroad—and the white settlement it promised to bring—during the 1880s. In 1885 he organized a military force of métis and native peoples in the Saskatchewan river country and led an insurrection known as the Northwest Rebellion. Canadian forces quickly subdued the makeshift army, and government authorities executed Riel for treason. Although the Northwest Rebellion never had a chance of success, the execution of Riel nonetheless threatened to undermine the beginnings of Canadian national unity and foreshadowed a long term of cultural conflict between Canadians of British, French, and indigenous ancestry.

The Métis and Louis Riel

Ethnicity, Identity, and Gender in Latin America

The heritage of Spanish and Portuguese colonialism and the legacy of slavery inclined Latin American societies toward the establishment of hierarchical distinctions based on ethnicity and color. At the top of society stood the creoles, individuals of European ancestry born in the Americas; indigenous peoples, freed slaves, and their black descendants occupied the lowest rungs of the social ladder. In between were various groups of mixed ancestry, such as mestizos, mulattoes, zambos, and castizos. Although most Latin American states ended the legal recognition of these groups, the distinctions themselves persisted and limited their opportunities.

Large-scale migration brought cultural diversity to Latin America in the nineteenth century. Indentured laborers who went from Asian lands to Peru, Brazil, Cuba, and other Caribbean destinations carried with them many of their native cultural practices. When their numbers were relatively large, as in the case of Indian migrants to Trinidad and Tobago, they formed distinctive communities in which they observed their inherited cultural and social traditions. Migration of European workers to Argentina brought a lively diversity to the capital of Buenos Aires, which was perhaps the most cosmopolitan city of nineteenth-century Latin America. With its broad avenues, smart boutiques, and handsome buildings graced with wrought iron, Buenos Aires enjoyed a reputation as "the Paris of the Americas."

Migration and Cultural Diversity

One prominent symbol of Latin American identity was Argentina's gauchos (cowboys). Most gauchos were mestizos or castizos, but there were also white and black gauchos. In fact, anyone who adopted gaucho ways became a gaucho, and gaucho society acquired an ethnic egalitarianism rarely found elsewhere in Latin America. Gauchos were most prominent in the Argentine pampas, but their cultural practices linked them to the cowboys, or vaqueros, found throughout the Americas. As pastoralists herding cattle and horses on the pampas, gauchos stood apart from both the indigenous peoples and the growing urban and agricultural elites who gradually displaced them with large landholdings and cattle ranches that spread to the pampas.

Gauchos

Even more than in the United States and Canada, male domination was a central characteristic of Latin American society in the nineteenth century. Women could not vote or hold office, nor could they work or manage estates without permission from their male guardians. In rural areas, women were liable to rough treatment and assault by gauchos and other men steeped in the values of *machismo*—a social ethic that honored male strength, courage, aggressiveness, assertiveness, and cunning. A few women voiced their discontent with male domination and machismo. Although Latin American lands did not generate a strong women's movement, they did begin to expand educational opportunities for girls and young women after the mid–nineteenth century. In large cities most girls received some formal schooling, and women usually filled teaching positions in the public schools that proliferated throughout Latin America in the late nineteenth century.

Male Domination

---

gauchos (GAHW-chohs)
vaqueros (bah-KEH-rohs)

SUMMARY

After gaining independence from European colonial powers, the states of the western hemisphere worked to build stable and prosperous societies. The independent American states faced difficult challenges as they sought to construct viable societies on the Enlightenment principles of freedom, equality, and constitutional government. The United States and Canada built large federal societies in North America, whereas a series of smaller states governed affairs in Latin America. Throughout the hemisphere descendants of European settlers subdued indigenous American peoples and built societies dominated by Euro-American peoples. They established agricultural economies, exploited natural resources, and in some lands launched processes of industrialization. They accepted streams of European and Asian migrants, who contributed to American cultural diversity. All American lands experienced tensions arising from social, economic, cultural, and ethnic differences, which led occasionally to violent civil conflict and often to smoldering resentments and grievances. The making of independent American societies was not a smooth process, but it reflected the increasing interdependence of all the world's peoples.

CHRONOLOGY

1803	Louisiana Purchase
1804–1806	Lewis and Clark expedition
1812–1814	War of 1812
1838–1839	Trail of Tears
1845–1848	Mexican-American War
1848	Seneca Falls Convention
1849	California gold rush
1850s	*La Reforma* in Mexico
1861–1865	U.S. Civil War
1867	Establishment of the Dominion of Canada
1867	French troops withdraw from Mexico
1867–1877	Reconstruction in the United States
1869	Completion of the transcontinental railroad line in the United States
1876	Battle of Little Big Horn
1876–1911	Rule of Porfirio Díaz in Mexico
1885	Completion of the Canadian Pacific Railroad
1885	Northwest Rebellion
1890	Massacre at Wounded Knee
1911–1920	Mexican revolution

FOR FURTHER READING

Colin G. Calloway. *First Peoples: A Documentary Survey of American Indian History.* Boston, 1999. A fine text on native American history, written by a knowledgeable scholar in the field.

Fernando Henrique Cardoso and Enzo Faletto. *Dependency and Development in Latin America.* Berkeley, 1979. A sophisticated treatment of economic development in Latin America.

William Cronon. *Nature's Metropolis: Chicago and the Great West.* New York, 1991. A valuable study exploring the role of Chicago in the economic development of the American west.

Tulio Halperín Donghi. *The Contemporary History of Latin America.* Trans. by J. C. Chasteen. Durham, 1993. An influential general history of Latin America from a Latin American point of view.

Ellen C. DuBois. *Feminism and Suffrage: The Emergence of an Independent Women's Movement in America, 1848–1869.* Ithaca, 1984. Traces the rise and character of the U.S. women's movement in the nineteenth century.

Patricia Nelson Limerick. *The Legacy of Conquest: The Unbroken Past of the American West.* New York, 1987. A provocative work exploring the influences of race, class, and gender in the conquest of the American west.

Leon F. Litwack. *Been in the Storm So Long: The Aftermath of Slavery.* New York, 1979. The best study of the promises and perils of life for freed slaves after the U.S. Civil War.

J. R. Miller. *Skyscrapers Hide the Heavens: A History of Indian-White Relations in Canada.* Toronto, 1989. An important study of Canadian policies toward indigenous peoples.

Walter Nugent. *Crossings: The Great Transatlantic Migrations, 1870–1914.* Bloomington, 1992. Provides an overview and analysis of the mass migrations to North America in the nineteenth and twentieth centuries.

Ronald Takaki. *A Different Mirror: A History of Multicultural America.* Boston, 1993. A spirited account of the contributions made by peoples of European, African, Asian, and Native American ancestry to the modern American society.

CHAPTER 29

The Building of Global Empires

Few Europeans had traveled to south Africa by the mid–nineteenth century, but the discovery of diamonds and rich gold deposits brought European settlers to the region in large numbers. Among the arrivals was Cecil John Rhodes, an eighteen-year-old student at Oxford University, who in 1871 went to south Africa in search of a climate that would relieve his tuberculosis. While there, Rhodes bought claims in the diamond fields, and he bought the rights to others' claims when they looked promising. By 1889, at age thirty-five, he had almost monopolized diamond mining in south Africa, and he controlled 90 percent of the world's diamond production. With ample financial backing, Rhodes also built up a healthy stake in the gold-mining business and entered politics, serving as prime minister (1890–1896) of the British Cape Colony.

Yet Rhodes's ambitions went far beyond business and local politics. In his vision the Cape Colony would serve as a base of operations for the extension of British control to all of Africa. Under Rhodes's guidance, Cape Colony annexed Bechuanaland (modern Botswana) in 1885, and in 1895 it added Rhodesia (modern Zambia and Zimbabwe) to its holdings. But Rhodes's plan did not stop with Africa: he urged the expansion of the British empire until it embraced all the world, including the United States of America. Rhodes considered British imperial expansion as a duty to humankind: "We are the finest race in the world," he said in 1877, "and the more of the world we inhabit, the better it is for the human race." In his sense of superiority to other peoples, his compulsion to expand, and his craving to extract wealth from distant parts of the world, Rhodes

OPPOSITE PAGE: *The battle of Omdurman on the Nile River, 2 September 1898.*

represented well the views of European imperialists who carved the world into colonies during the nineteenth century.

From the days of ancient Mesopotamia and Egypt to the present, strong societies have often sought to dominate their weaker neighbors by subjecting them to imperial rule. Yet during the second half of the nineteenth century, a handful of western European states wrote a new chapter in the history of imperialism. Strong nationalist sentiments enabled them to mobilize their populations for purposes of overseas expansion. Industrialization equipped them with the most effective tools and the most lethal weapons available anywhere in the world. Three centuries of experience with maritime trade in Asia, Africa, the Americas, and Oceania provided them with unparalleled knowledge of the world and its peoples. With those advantages, western European peoples conquered foreign armies, dominated foreign economies, and imposed their hegemony throughout the world. Toward the end of the century, the United States and Japan joined European states as imperial powers.

The establishment of global empires had far-reaching effects. In many ways, imperialism tightened links between the world's societies. Imperial powers encouraged trade between dominant states and their overseas colonies, for example, and they organized mass migrations of laborers to work in agricultural and industrial ventures. Yet imperialism also fostered divisions between the world's peoples. Powerful tools, deadly weapons, and global hegemony tempted European peoples to consider themselves superior to their subjects throughout the world: modern racism is one of the legacies of imperialism. Another effect of imperialism was the development of both resistance and nationalism in subject lands. Thus, although formal empires almost entirely dissolved in the twentieth century, the influence of global imperialism continues to shape the contemporary world.

FOUNDATIONS OF EMPIRE

In nineteenth-century Europe, proponents of empire advanced a variety of political, economic, and cultural arguments to justify the conquest and control of foreign lands. The imperialist ventures that they promoted enjoyed dramatic success partly because of the increasingly sophisticated technologies developed by European industry.

Motives of Imperialism

The building of empires is an old story in world history. By the nineteenth century, however, European observers recognized that empires of their day were different from those of earlier times. Accordingly, about midcentury they began to speak of *imperialism,* and by the 1880s *Modern Imperialism* the recently coined term had made its way into popular speech and writing throughout western Europe. In contemporary usage, imperialism refers to the domination over subject lands in the larger world. Sometimes that domination came through formal imperialism, which involved military conquest and the establishment of political control. Frequently, however, it arose through what is known as informal imperialism: that is, the domination of trade, investment, and business activities that enabled imperial powers to profit from subject societies and influence their affairs without going to the trouble of exercising direct political control.

Like the building of empires, the establishment of colonies in foreign lands is a practice dating from ancient times. In modern times, however, colonialism refers not just to the settlement of colonists in new lands but also to *Modern Colonialism* the political, social, economic, and cultural structures that enabled imperial powers to dominate subject lands. In some places, such as North America, Chile, Argentina, Australia, New Zealand, and South Africa, European powers established settler colonies populated largely by migrants from the home societies. Yet contemporary scholars also speak of European colonies in India, southeast Asia, and sub-Saharan Africa, even though European migrants did not settle there in large numbers. European agents, officials, and businesspeople effectively turned such places into colonies by controlling their domestic and foreign policies, integrating local economies into the network of global capitalism, and promoting European educational and cultural preferences.

During the second half of the nineteenth century, many Europeans came to believe that imperial expansion and colonial domination were crucial for the survival of their societies. A wide range of motives encouraged European peoples to launch campaigns of domination, conquest, and control. Some advocates argued that imperialism was in the economic interests of European societies as well as individuals. They *Economic Motives of Imperialism*

Cecil Rhodes resting in the goldfields of South Africa, about 1897.

pointed out that overseas colonies could serve as reliable sources of raw materials: rubber, tin, and copper were vital industrial products, for example, and by the late nineteenth century petroleum had also become a crucial industrial resource.

Geopolitical arguments were also important for justifying imperialism. Even if colonies were not economically beneficial, imperialists held *Political Motives of Imperialism* that it was crucial for political and military reasons to maintain them. Some overseas colonies occupied strategic sites on the world's sea lanes, and others offered harbors or supply stations for commercial and naval ships. Advocates of imperialism sought to gain those advantages for their own states and to deny them to rivals.

Imperialism had its uses also for domestic politics. In an age when socialists and communists directly confronted industrialists, European politicians and national leaders sought to defuse social tension and inspire patriotism by focusing public attention on foreign imperialist ventures. Even spiritual motives fostered imperialism. Like the Jesuits in the early modern era, missionaries flocked to African and Asian lands in search of converts to Christianity, and their spiritual campaigns provided a powerful religious justification for imperialism. Furthermore, missionaries often facilitated communications between imperialists and subject peoples, and they sometimes provided European officials with information they needed to maintain control of overseas colonies.

While missionaries sought to introduce Christianity to subject peoples, their goals were compatible with those of other Europeans who sought to bring them "civilization" in the form of political order and social and cultural enlightenment. French imperialists routinely invoked the *mission civilisatrice* ("civilizing mission") as justification for their expansion into Africa and Asia, and other European powers routinely justified foreign intervention as their duty to civilize "backward" peoples.

Tools of Empire

Even the strongest motives would not have enabled imperialists to impose their rule throughout the world without the powerful technological advantages of industrialization. During the nineteenth century, industrialists devised effective technologies of transportation, communication, and war that enabled European imperialists to have their way in the larger world.

The most important innovations in transportation involved steamships and railroads. During the 1830s British naval engineers adapted steam power to military uses and built large, *Transportation Technologies* ironclad ships equipped with powerful guns. These steamships traveled much faster than any sailing vessel, and as an additional advantage they could ignore the winds and travel in any direction. Because of that, they could travel much farther upriver

SOURCES FROM THE PAST

Rudyard Kipling on the White Man's Burden

Rudyard Kipling lived in northern India for the first six years of his life. He grew up speaking Hindi, and he mixed easily with Indian subjects of the British empire. After attending a boarding school in England, he returned to India in 1882 and became a journalist and writer. Many of his works express his deep enchantment with India, but he also believed strongly in imperial rule. Indeed, he wrote his famous poem titled "The White Man's Burden" to encourage the United States to impose colonial rule in the Philippines. Although recognizing the unpopularity of foreign rule, Kipling considered it a duty to bring order to colonial lands and to serve subject peoples.

■   ■   ■

Take up the White Man's burden—
   Send forth the best ye breed—
Go bind your sons to exile
   To serve your captives' need;
To wait in heavy harness,
   On fluttered folk and wild—
Your new-caught, sullen peoples,
   Half-devil and half-child.

Take up the White Man's burden—
   In patience to abide,
To veil the threat of terror
   And check the show of pride;
By open speech and simple,
   An hundred times made plain,
To seek another's profit,
   And work for another's gain.

Take up the White Man's burden—
   The savage wars of peace—
Fill full the mouth of Famine
   And bid the sickness cease;
And when your goal is nearest
   The end for others sought,
Watch Sloth and heathen Folly
   Bring all your hope to nought.

Take up the White Man's burden—
   No tawdry rule of kings,
But toil of serf and sweeper—
   The tale of common things.

The ports ye shall not enter,
   The roads ye shall not tread,
Go make them with your living,
   And mark them with your dead.
Take up the White Man's burden—
   And reap his old reward:
The blame of those ye better,
   The hate of those ye guard—
The cry of hosts ye humor
   (Ah, slowly!) toward the light;—
"Why brought ye us from bondage,
   "Our loved Egyptian night?"

Take up the White Man's burden—
   Ye dare not stoop to less—
Nor call too loud on Freedom
   To cloak your weariness;
By all ye cry or whisper,
   By all ye leave or do,
The silent, sullen peoples
   Shall weigh your Gods and you.

Take up the White Man's burden—
   Have done with childish days—
The lightly proffered laurel,
   The easy, ungrudged praise.
Comes now, to search your manhood
   Through all the thankless years,
Cold, edged with dear-bought wisdom,
   The judgment of your peers!

• *Compare and contrast the sorts of adjectives Kipling uses to describe native peoples as opposed to Europeans; how does his very language usage convey his sense of white superiority?*

SOURCE: Rudyard Kipling. "The White Man's Burden." *McClure's Magazine* 12, no. 4 (1899): 290–91.

than sailboats, which enabled imperialists to project power deep into the interior regions of foreign lands.

The construction of new canals enhanced the effectiveness of steamships. Both the Suez Canal (constructed 1859–1869) and the Panama Canal (constructed 1904–1914) facilitated the building and main-tenance of empires by enabling naval vessels to travel rapidly be-tween the world's seas and oceans. They also lowered the costs of trade be-tween imperial powers and subject lands.

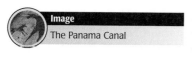

Once imperialists had gained control of overseas lands, railroads helped them to maintain their hege-mony and organize local economies to their own ad-vantage. Rail transportation enabled colonial officials and armies to travel quickly through the colonies. It also facilitated trade in raw materials and the dis-tribution of European manufactured goods in the colonies.

European industrialists also churned out enor-mous quantities of increasingly powerful weapons. By the middle of the nineteenth century, Eu-ropean armies were using breech-loading firearms with rifled bores that were far more accurate and reliable than any other firearm. By the 1870s Europeans were experimenting with rifled machine guns, and in the 1880s they adopted the Maxim gun, a light and powerful weapon that fired eleven bullets per second.

Military Technologies

These firearms provided European armies with an arsenal vastly stronger than any other in the world. Ac-curate rifles and machine guns devastated opposing overseas forces, enabling European armies to impose colonial rule against far more numerous opponents. In 1898, for example, a British army with twenty ma-chine guns and six gunboats encountered a Sudanese force at Omdurman, near Khartoum on the Nile River. During five hours of fighting, the British force lost 368 men, whereas machine guns and explosive charges fired from gunboats killed some 11,000 Su-danese. The battle of Omdurman opened the door for British colonial rule in Sudan.

Communications also benefited from industrial-ization. In the 1830s it took as long as two years for a British correspondent to receive a reply to a letter sent to India by sail-ing ship. By the 1850s, after the in-troduction of steamships, correspondence could make the round-trip between London and Bombay

Communications Technologies

in four months. With the opening of the Suez Canal in 1869,

steamships traveled from Britain to India in less than two weeks.

The invention of the telegraph made it possible to exchange messages even faster. By 1870 submarine ca-bles carried messages between Britain and India in about five hours. By 1902 cables linked all parts of the British empire throughout the world, and other Euro-pean states maintained cables to support communica-tions with their own colonies. Their monopoly on telegraphic communications allowed imperial officials to rapidly mobilize forces to deal with troubles, and the telegraph allowed merchants to respond quickly to developments of economic and commercial signifi-cance. Rapid communication was an integral structural element of empire.

EUROPEAN IMPERIALISM

Aided by powerful technologies, European states launched an unprecedented round of empire build-ing in the second half of the nineteenth century. Im-perial expansion began with the British conquest of India. Competition between imperial powers led to European intrusion into central Asia, the establish-ment of colonies in southeast Asia, and interference in the Ottoman and Qing empires in southwest and east Asia. Fearful that rivals might gain control over remaining regions, European states embarked on a campaign of frenzied expansion in the 1880s that brought almost all of Africa and Pacific Ocean terri-tories into their empires.

The British Empire in India

The British empire in south Asia and southeast Asia grew out of the mercantile activities of the English East India Company, which enjoyed a monopoly on English trade with India. The East India Company ob-tained permission from the Mughal emperors of India to build fortified posts on the coastlines. In the seven-teenth century, company merchants traded mostly for Indian pepper and cotton, Chinese silk and porcelain, and spices from southeast Asia. During the eighteenth century, tea and coffee became the most prominent trade items, and European consumers acquired a per-manent taste for both beverages.

After the death of the emperor Aurangzeb in 1707, the Mughal state entered a period of decline.

Company Rule   The East India Company took advantage of Mughal weakness to strengthen and expand its trading posts. In the 1750s company merchants began campaigns of outright conquest in India, largely to protect their commercial interests. From their forts at Calcutta, Madras, and Bombay, the merchants extended their authority inland and won official rights to rule from the Mughal emperors and local authorities. They enforced their rule with armies composed mostly of Indian troops known as sepoys.

In 1857, following widespread campaigns of conquest that left most of the subcontinent under British control, the Indian sepoys of the Bengal army revolted. The Sepoy Rebellion, as it became known, was quickly augmented by civilian peasants and disgruntled elites in north-central India who were deeply dissatisfied with recent British policies regarding taxation and law. To regain control, the British waged a bloody campaign of retribution in which many thousands of Indians—including civilians not directly involved in the rebellion—lost their lives through summary hangings and the destruction of villages. Once order was restored in 1858, the British government abolished the East India Company and assumed direct rule over the subcontinent.

Under the new administration, Queen Victoria (reigned 1837–1901) assigned responsibility for Indian policy to the newly established office of secretary of state for India. A viceroy represented British royal authority and administered the colony through an elite Indian civil service staffed almost exclusively by the English. Indians served in low-level bureaucratic positions, but *British Imperial Rule* British officials formulated all domestic and foreign policy in India.

Under both company rule and direct colonial administration, British rule transformed India. To profit from India's enormous size and wealth, British officials cleared forests and encouraged the cultivation of crops, such as tea, coffee, and opium, that were especially valuable trade items. They restructured landholdings and ensured that land taxes financed the costs of British rule. They built extensive railroad and telegraph networks that tightened links between India and the larger global economy. They also constructed new canals, harbors, and irrigation systems to support commerce and agriculture.

Especially after 1857, British colonial authorities made little effort to promote Christianity. They did, however, establish English-style schools for the children of Indian elites, and they suppressed Indian customs that conflicted with European law or values. Most prominent of those cus-

Image
Sati

toms were sati (the practice of widows burning themselves on their husbands' funeral pyres), infanticide, and slavery.

Mughal (MOO-guhl)

sati (suh-TEE)

Warships provide covering fire as British troops prepare to storm the Burmese port of Rangoon in 1824.

Imperialism in Southeast Asia

As the East India Company and British colonial agents tightened their grip on India, competition among European states kindled further empire-building efforts.

The Dutch East Indies   In southeast Asia, Dutch officials tightened their control and extended their authority throughout the Dutch East Indies, the archipelago that makes up the modern state of Indonesia. Along with cash crops of sugar, tea, coffee, and tobacco, exports of rubber and tin made the Dutch East Indies a valuable and productive colony.

In the interests of increasing trade between India, southeast Asia, and China, British imperialists moved in the nineteenth century to establish a presence in southeast Asia. By the 1880s they had established colonial authority in Burma, which became a source of teak, ivory, rubies, and jade. In 1824 Thomas Stamford Raffles founded the port of Singapore, which soon became the busiest center of trade in the Strait of Melaka. Administered by the colonial regime in India, Singapore served as the base for the British conquest of Malaya (modern Malaysia) in the 1870s and 1880s. Besides offering ports that enabled the British navy to control sea lanes linking the Indian Ocean with the South China Sea, Malaya provided abundant supplies of tin and rubber.

British Colonies in Southeast Asia

French imperialists built the large southeast Asian colony of French Indochina, consisting of the modern states of Vietnam, Cambodia, and Laos, between 1859 and 1893. Like their British counterparts in India,

Map 29.1 **Boundaries of imperial territories in Asia about 1914** (dates in parentheses indicate year of conquest). Note the claims made by various industrial powers. Which territories remained unclaimed, and why? Which power claimed the most imperial territory in Asia?

French colonial officials introduced European-style schools and sought to establish close connections with native elites. Unlike their rivals, *French Indochina* French officials also encouraged conversion to Christianity, and as a result the Roman Catholic church became prominent throughout French Indochina, especially Vietnam. By century's end, all of southeast Asia had come under European imperial rule except for the kingdom of Siam (modern Thailand), which preserved its independence largely because colonial officials regarded it as a convenient buffer state between British-dominated Burma and French Indochina.

Informal Domination in the Ottoman and Qing Empires

As in India, the Indonesian islands, and Vietnam, European powers in the nineteenth century frequently seized territories outright and ruled them as colonies. More frequently, however, European (and later U.S.) forces used their economic and military power to force concessions out of militarily weak societies. They won rights for businesses to seek opportunities on favorable terms, gained influence in political affairs, and enabled industrial capitalists to realize huge profits without going to the trouble and expense of establishing formal colonies. In the last half of the nineteenth century, two formerly powerful societies—the Ottoman and the Qing empires—increasingly came under such informal domination as each struggled with military weakness and internal problems in contrast to the industrialized and competitive nation-states of Europe. Although reform movements emerged in both lands, the results were inadequate, and by the early twentieth century both empires were still firmly in the grip of foreign domination.

By the late seventeenth century, it was already clear that Ottoman forces lagged behind European armies in strategy, tactics, weaponry, and *Military Decline* training. Loss of military power translated into declining effectiveness of the central government, which was losing power in the provinces to its own officials. In addition, although the Ottoman government managed to

Interactive Map
The Ottoman empire

maintain its authority in Anatolia as well as in Iraq, it suffered serious territorial losses in the Caucasus, central Asia, and the Balkan provinces of Greece (independent 1830) and Serbia (independent 1867).

Most significant, however, was the loss of Egypt. In 1798 the ambitious French general Napoleon invaded Egypt in hopes of using it as a springboard for an attack on the British empire in India. His campaign was a miserable failure, but the invasion sparked turmoil in Egypt, as local elites battled to seize power after Napoleon's departure. The ultimate victor was the energetic general Muhammad Ali, who built a powerful army modeled on European forces and ruled Egypt from 1805 to 1848. He also launched a program of industrialization, concentrating on cotton textiles and armaments. Although he remained nominally subordinate to the Ottoman sultan, by 1820 he had established himself as the effective ruler of Egypt, which was the most powerful land in the Muslim world. He even invaded Syria and Anatolia, threatening to capture Istanbul and topple the Ottoman state. Indeed, the Ottoman dynasty survived only because British forces intervened out of fear that Ottoman collapse would result in a sudden and dangerous expansion of Russian influence.

Meanwhile, European textiles and manufactured goods began to flow into the Ottoman empire in the eighteenth and nineteenth centuries. Because these items were inexpensive and *Economic Difficulties* high-quality products, they placed considerable pressure on Ottoman artisans and crafts workers. Gradually, the Ottoman empire moved toward financial dependency on Europe. After the middle of the nineteenth century, economic development in the Ottoman empire depended heavily on foreign loans, as European capital financed the construction of railroads, utilities, and mining enterprises. Interest payments grew to the point that they consumed more than half of the empire's revenues. In 1882 the Ottoman state was unable to pay interest on its loans and had no choice but to accept European administration of its debts.

Nothing symbolized foreign influence more than the capitulations, agreements that exempted European visitors from Ottoman law and provided European powers with extraterritorial- *The Capitulations* ity—the right to exercise jurisdiction over their own citizens according to their own laws. Capitulations also served as instruments of economic penetration by European businesspeople who established tax-exempt banks and commercial enterprises in the Ottoman empire, and they permitted foreign governments to levy duties on goods sold in Ottoman ports.

In response to recurring and deepening crises, Ottoman leaders launched a series of reforms designed to strengthen and preserve the state. In the early nineteenth century, a significant period of reform occurred under the leadership of sultan Mahmud II (reigned 1808–1839). Mahmud's program re-modeled Ottoman institutions along western European lines, especially in the creation of a more effective army. Before long, Ottoman recruits wore European-style uniforms and studied at military and engineering schools that taught European curricula. Equally important, Mahmud's government created a system of secondary education for boys to facilitate the transition from mosque schools, which provided most primary education, to newly established scientific, technical, and military academies. To make his authority more effective, the sultan established European-style ministries, constructed new roads, built telegraph lines, and inaugurated a postal service. By the time of Mahmud's death in 1839, the Ottoman empire had shrunk in size, but it was also more manageable and powerful than it had been since the early seventeenth century.

The Reforms of Mahmud II

Continuing defeats on the battlefield and the rise of separatist movements among subject peoples, however, prompted the ruling classes to undertake even more radical reforms during the Tanzimat ("reorganization") era (1839–1876). In designing their program, Tanzimat reformers drew considerable inspiration from Enlightenment thought and the constitutional foundations of western European states. One of their primary aims was to make Ottoman law more acceptable to Europeans so they could have the capitulations lifted and recover Ottoman sovereignty. Among the most important Tanzimat reforms were those that guaranteed public trials, rights of privacy, and equality before the law for all Ottoman subjects, whether Muslim or not. By 1869 educational reforms also provided free and compulsory primary education for all children. Yet even though reform and reorganization strengthened Ottoman society, the Tanzimat also provoked spirited opposition. Harsh criticism came from religious conservatives, who argued that reformers posed a threat to the empire's Islamic foundation. Perhaps most dangerously, the Ottoman bureaucracy itself criticized Tanzimat reforms because they believed that too much power was concentrated in the hands of the sultan.

The Tanzimat Era

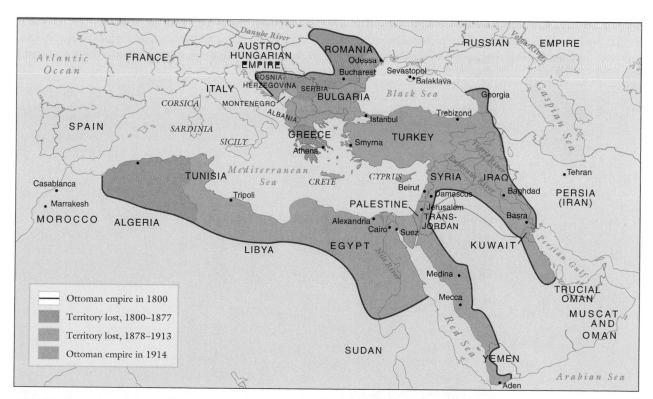

Map 29.2 Territorial losses of the Ottoman empire, 1800–1923. Compare the borders of the Ottoman empire in 1800 with what was left of the empire in 1914. What might have been the strategic value of the remaining Ottoman territories?

The despotic reign of Abdül Hamid II (reigned 1876–1909) only seemed to confirm such criticisms, *The Young Turks* and a variety of liberal opposition groups grew up to oppose his rule. Among the most articulate were those whose members were familiar with European society, and who believed above all else that Ottoman society was in dire need of a written constitution that defined and limited the sultan's power. The most active dissident organization was the Ottoman Society for Union and Progress, better known as the Young Turk Party. Founded in 1889 by exiled Ottoman subjects living in Paris, the Young Turk Party vigorously called for universal suffrage, equality before the law, freedom of religion, free public education, secularization of the state, and the emancipation of women. In 1908 the Young Turks inspired an army coup that forced Abdül Hamid to reinstate a constitution he had abandoned at the start of his reign. In 1909 they dethroned him and established Mehmed V Rashid (reigned 1909–1918) as a puppet sultan. Throughout the Young Turk era (1908–1918), Ottoman sultans reigned but no longer ruled.

Yet in spite of their efforts to shore up the ailing empire, reformers could not turn the tide of decline: Ottoman armies continued to lose wars, and subject peoples continued to seek autonomy or independence. By the early twentieth century, the Ottoman empire survived principally because European diplomats could not agree on how to dispose of the empire without upsetting the European balance of power.

The Chinese empire experienced even more difficulties than the Ottoman empire in the nineteenth century. Qing problems became serious *The Opium Trade* in the early nineteenth century when officials of the British East India Company began to trade in opium—rather than silver—in exchange for the Chinese silks, porcelains, and teas so coveted by Europeans. Trade in opium was illegal in China, but it expanded rapidly for decades because Chinese authorities made little effort to enforce the law. By the late 1830s, however, government officials had become aware that China had a trade problem and a drug problem as well. In 1839 the government took active steps to halt the trade, which included the destruction of some twenty thousand chests of opium.

Outraged, British commercial agents pressed their government into a military retaliation designed to reopen the opium trade. The ensuing *The Opium War* conflict, known as the Opium War (1839–1842), made plain the military power differential between Europe and China. The Chinese navy and infantry were no match for their British counterparts, who relied on steam power and modern firearms, and

Chinese opium smokers. Chinese efforts to stop opium imports led to a humiliating defeat in the Opium War.

in 1842 the Chinese government sued for peace. China experienced similar military setbacks throughout the second half of the nineteenth century in conflicts with Britain and France (1856–1858), France (1884–1885), and Japan (1894–1895).

In the wake of those confrontations came a series of pacts collectively known in China as unequal ***Unequal Treaties*** treaties, which curtailed China's sovereignty. The Treaty of Nanjing (1842), which ended the British war against the Chinese, ceded Hong Kong Island in perpetuity to Britain, opened five Chinese ports to commerce and residence, compelled the Qing government to extend most-favored-nation status to Britain, and granted extraterritoriality to British subjects. In later years France, Germany, Denmark, the Netherlands, Spain,

Belgium, Austria-Hungary, the United States, and Japan concluded similar unequal treaties with China. By 1900 ninety Chinese ports were under the effective control of foreign powers, foreign merchants controlled much of the Chinese economy, Christian missionaries sought converts throughout China, and foreign gunboats patrolled Chinese waters.

To make matters more difficult, China was convulsed by several large-scale rebellions in the nineteenth century, all of which reflected the increasing poverty and discontent of the Chinese peasantry. After 1850, rebellions erupted throughout China: the Nian rebellion (1851–1868) in the northeast, the Muslim rebellion (1855–1873) in the southwest, and the Tungan rebellion (1862–1878) in the northwest. Most dangerous of all was the Taiping rebellion (1850–1864), which

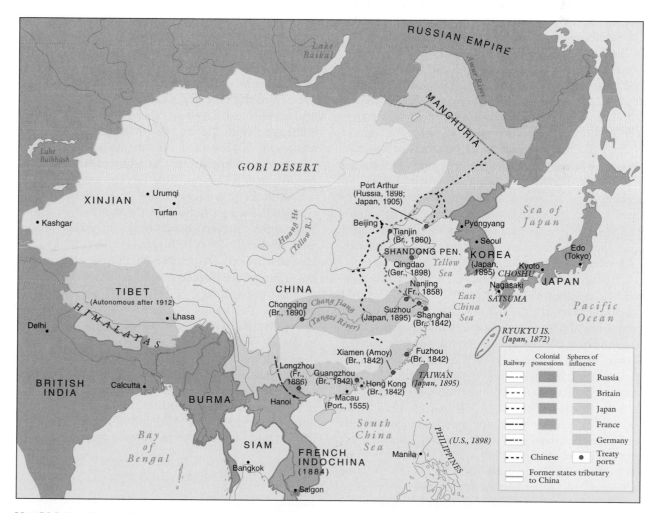

Map 29.3 East Asia in the nineteenth century. Notice the division of China, which technically remained a sovereign nation, into spheres of influence by various European nations and Japan. What impact would such spheres of influence have had on the Chinese government in Beijing?

raged throughout most of China and brought the Qing dynasty to the brink of collapse.

The village schoolteacher Hong Xiuquan provided both inspiration and leadership for the Taiping rebel-

The Taiping Rebellion

lion. He called for the destruction of the Qing dynasty and for the radical transformation of Chinese society, including the abolition of private property, the creation of communal wealth to be shared according to needs, the prohibition of foot binding and concubinage, free public education, simplification of the written language, literacy for the masses, and equality of the sexes. After sweeping through southeastern China, Hong and his followers in the Society of God Worshipers took Nanjing in 1853 and made it the capital of their Taiping ("Great Peace") kingdom. In 1855 a million Taipings were poised to attack Beijing, and in 1860 they threatened Shanghai. Although the rebellion was eventually crushed in 1864 with the aid of European advisors and weapons, in all it claimed between twenty and thirty million lives and devastated part of the Chinese countryside.

The Taiping rebellion altered the course of Chinese history. Contending with aggressive foreign pow-

The Self-Strengthening Movement

ers and lands ravaged by domestic rebellion, Qing rulers recognized that reforms were necessary for the empire to survive. Most imaginative of these programs was the Self-Strengthening Movement (1860–1895). While holding to Confucian values and seeking to reestablish a stable agrarian society, movement leaders built modern shipyards, constructed railroads, established weapons industries, opened steel foundries with blast furnaces, and founded academies to develop scientific expertise.

Yet the Self-Strengthening Movement did not introduce enough industry to bring real military and economic strength to China. It also did not prevent continuing foreign intrusion into Chinese affairs. During the latter part of the nineteenth century, foreign powers began to dismantle the Chinese system of tributary states. In 1885 France incorporated Vietnam into its colonial empire, and in 1886 Great Britain detached Burma from Chinese control. In 1895 Japan forced China to recognize the independence of Korea and cede the island of Taiwan and the Liaodong peninsula in southern Manchuria. By 1898 foreign powers had carved China itself into spheres of economic influence, and only distrust among them prevented the total dismemberment of the Middle Kingdom.

Taiping (TEYE-pihng)

These setbacks sparked the ambitious but abortive Hundred Days reforms of 1898, whose purpose was to turn China into a powerful mod-

The Hundred Days Reforms

ern industrial society. Impressed by the ideas of reform-minded scholars, the young and open-minded Emperor Guangxu launched a sweeping program to transform China into a constitutional monarchy, guarantee civil liberties, root out corruption, remodel the educational system, modernize military forces, and stimulate economic development. Yet these reform efforts produced a violent reaction from members of the imperial household, from their allies in the gentry, and especially from the young emperor's aunt, the ruthless and powerful empress dowager Cixi. After a period of 103 days, Cixi nullified the reform decrees, imprisoned the emperor in the Forbidden City, and executed six leading reformers.

Cixi then threw her support behind an antiforeign uprising known as the Boxer rebellion, a violent movement spearheaded by militia units

The Boxer Rebellion

calling themselves the Society of Righteous and Harmonious Fists. The foreign press referred to the rebels as Boxers. In 1899 the Boxers organized to rid China of "foreign devils" and their influences. With the empress dowager's encouragement, the Boxers went on a rampage in northern China, killing foreigners and Chinese who had ties to foreigners. Confident that foreign weapons could not harm them, some 140,000 Boxers besieged foreign embassies in Beijing in the summer of 1900. They were crushed, however, by a heavily armed force of British, French, Russian, U.S., German, and Japanese troops. After the rebellion, the Chinese government was forced to allow foreign powers to station troops at their embassies in Beijing and along the route to the sea. When Cixi

died in 1908, anti-Qing revolutionary movements that sought alternative methods to deal with foreign and domestic crises were rife throughout China. Indeed, revolution broke out in the autumn of 1911, and by early 1912 the child Puyi—the last emperor of the Qing dynasty—had abdicated his throne.

The Scramble for Africa

Even as European powers sponsored informal imperialism in the Ottoman and Qing empires in the last half of the nineteenth century, they also embarked on a striking outburst of formal imperialism in Africa. This was all the more remarkable, since as late as 1875 European peoples maintained a limited presence in Africa: their only sizable possessions were the Portuguese colonies of Angola and Mozambique, the French settler colony in northern Algeria, and a cluster of settler colonies populated by British and Dutch migrants in south Africa.

Between 1875 and 1900, however, the relationship between Africa and Europe dramatically changed. Within a quarter century European imperial powers partitioned and colonized almost the entire African continent. Prospects of exploiting African resources and nationalist rivalries between European powers help to explain this frenzied quest for empire, often referred to as the "scramble for Africa."

In the 1870s King Leopold II of Belgium (reigned 1865–1909) employed the American journalist Henry Morton Stanley to help develop commer-

The Belgian Congo

cial ventures and establish a colony called the Congo Free State (modern-day Democratic Republic of the Congo) in the basin of the Congo River. To forestall competition from Belgium's much larger and more powerful European neighbors, Leopold announced that the Congo region would be a free-trade zone accessible to merchants and business-people from all European lands. In fact, however, he carved out a personal colony with the sole purpose of extracting lucrative rubber using forced labor. Working conditions in the Congo Free State were so brutal, taxes so high, and abuses so many that four to eight million Africans died under Leopold's personal rule. Once those abuses became public, humanitarian pressure induced the Belgian government to take control away from Leopold in 1908 and administer the colony directly.

As Leopold colonized central Africa, Britain established an imperial presence in Egypt. In an effort to build up their army, strengthen the economy, and distance themselves from Ottoman authority, Egypt's leaders had borrowed heavily from European lenders in the mid–nineteenth century. By the 1870s crushing debt forced Egyptian officials to impose high taxes, which provoked popular unrest and a military rebellion. Concerned over the status of their financial interests and the security of the Suez Canal, British forces occupied Egypt in 1882.

The British occupation of Egypt intensified tensions between those European powers who were seeking African colonies. To avoid war, delegates from fourteen European states and the United States—not a single

This 1912 photograph shows a stark portrait of the Belgian king's inhumane treatment of Africans in the Congo.

African was present—met at the Berlin West Africa Conference (1884–1885) to devise ground rules for the colonization of Africa. According to those rules, any European state could establish African colonies after notifying the others of its intentions and occupying previously unclaimed territory.

The Berlin Conference

During the 1890s European imperialists sent armies to impose colonial rule on the African territories they claimed. Although resistance to colonial rule was often fierce, European cannons and machine guns rarely failed to defeat African forces. By the turn of the century, European colonies embraced all of Africa except for Ethiopia, where native forces fought off Italian efforts at colonization in 1896, and Liberia, a small republic in west Africa that was effectively a dependency of the United States.

In the wake of rapid conquest, Europeans struggled to identify the most cost-effective and efficient system of rule in Africa. By the early twentieth century, after some experimentation, most European governments sought to establish their own rule, which took the form of either direct rule, typical of French colonies, or indirect rule, characteristic of British colonies.

Direct and Indirect Rule

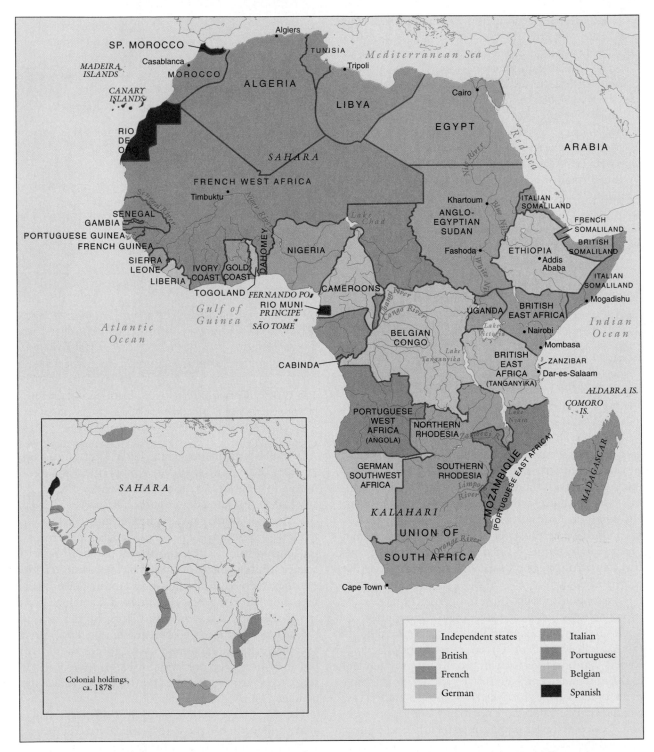

Map 29.4 Expansion of European claims to African territories from 1878 to about 1914. Note the dramatic difference between the map of 1878 and the later map. How was it possible that Europeans were able to claim so much territory in such a short span of time?

Under direct rule, colonies were headed by European personnel who assumed responsibility for tax collection, labor and military recruitment, and the maintenance of law and order. Administrative boundaries intentionally cut across existing African political and ethnic boundaries to divide and weaken potentially powerful indigenous groups. In contrast, indirect rule sought to exercise control over subject populations through indigenous institutions such as "tribal" authorities and "customary laws." Both methods of government were flawed: under direct rule, imperial powers struggled with a constant shortage of European personnel, which undermined the effectiveness of rule, and indirect rule imposed erroneous and rigid European ideas about what constituted tribal categories and boundaries onto African societies.

South Africa   Although already inhabited by Europeans long before the scramble for Africa, still the southern tip of the African continent did not escape conflict at the close of the nineteenth century. In this case, however, the main antagonists were both of European descent: one side was composed of the descendants of Dutch settlers who had founded Cape Town in 1652 (called "Boers" or "Afrikaners"), and the other of British settlers who had taken control of the Cape in 1815. Relations between the two groups had never been good. When the British established themselves at the Cape, they subjected Afrikaners to British language and law—including the abolition of slavery when it became law in 1833. The abolition of slavery was particularly contentious, as Afrikaners believed that God had given them the right to exploit both the people and the resources of the Cape—the results of which left the indigenous Khoikhoi and Xhosa peoples decimated and virtually landless. Chafing under British rule, Afrikaners left their farms in Cape Colony and gradually migrated east in what they called the Great Trek. By the mid–nineteenth century, after fierce conflict with the Ndebele and Zulu peoples indigenous to the interior of the region, the Afrikaners created several independent republics: the Republic of Natal, annexed by the British in 1843; the Orange Free State in 1854; and in 1860 the South African Republic (Transvaal territories).

Britain's lenient attitude toward Afrikaner statehood took a drastic turn with the discovery of diamonds (1867) and gold (1886) in Afrikaner territories. The influx of thousands of British miners and prospectors led to tensions between British authorities and Afrikaners, culminating in the South African War (1899–1902; sometimes called the Boer War). Al-though the brutal conflict pitted whites against whites, it also took a large toll on black Africans, who served both sides as soldiers and laborers. The internment of 100,000 black Africans in British concentration camps, for example, left more than 10,000 dead. The Afrikaners conceded defeat in 1902, and by 1910, the British government had reconstituted the four former colonies as provinces

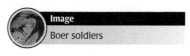

Boer soldiers

in the Union of South Africa, a largely autonomous British dominion. British attempts at improving relations between English speakers and Afrikaners centered on shoring up the privileges of white colonial society and the domination of black Africans.

European Imperialism in the Pacific

While scrambling for Africa, European imperial powers did not overlook opportunities to establish their presence in the Pacific Ocean basin. Imperialism in the Pacific took two main forms. In Australia and New Zealand, European powers established settler colonies and dominant political institutions. In most of the Pacific islands, however, they sought commercial opportunities and reliable bases for their operations but did not wish to go to the trouble or expense of outright colonization. Only in the late nineteenth century did they begin to impose direct colonial rule on the islands.

Settler Colonies in the Pacific   Settlers began to arrive in Australia in 1788, nearly two decades after Captain James Cook reported that the region would be suitable for settlement. In that year, a British fleet with about one thousand settlers, most of them convicted criminals, arrived at Sydney harbor and established the colony of New South Wales. By the 1830s voluntary migrants outnumbered convicts, and the discovery of gold in 1851 brought a surge in migration to Australia. European settlers established communities also in New Zealand, where the islands' fertile soils and abundant stands of timber drew large numbers of migrants.

European migration rocked the societies of Australia and New Zealand. Diseases such as smallpox and measles devastated indigenous peoples at the same time that European migrants flooded into their lands. The aboriginal population of Australia fell from about 650,000 in 1800 to 90,000 in 1900, whereas the European population rose from a few thousand to 3.75 million during the same period. Similarly, the population of indigenous Maori in New Zealand fell from about 200,000 in 1800 to 45,000 a century later, while European numbers climbed to 750,000.

Increasing migration also fueled conflict between European settlers and native populations. Large settler societies pushed indigenous peoples from their lands, often following violent confrontations. Because the nomadic foraging peoples of Australia did not occupy lands permanently, British settlers considered the continent *terra nullius*—"land belonging to no one"— that they could seize and put to their own uses. Despite native resistance, by 1900 the British had succeeded in brutally displacing most indigenous Australians from their traditional lands and dispersing them throughout the continent.

A similarly disruptive process transpired in New Zealand, where Maori leaders organized effective and long-lasting opposition to British attempts to usurp their land and sovereignty. Conflicts over land confiscations and disputed land sales, for example, helped to spark the New Zealand Wars, a series of confrontations between the Maori and the British that flared from the mid- to late nineteenth century. Despite that resistance, by the end of the century the British had managed to force many Maori into poor rural communities separated from European settlements.

On the smaller Pacific islands, the picture was quite different. Although indigenous peoples were ravaged by European diseases, the imperial powers had little interest in establishing direct colonial rule over the islands. Rather, they were content to use the islands as naval ports, as coaling stations, and sometimes as producers of primary products. The situation changed, however, in the late nineteenth century, as European nationalist rivalries encouraged the imperial powers to stake their claims in the Pacific as they had done in Africa. Thus, although France had established a protectorate in Tahiti, the Society Islands, and the Marquesas as early as 1841, it imposed direct colonial rule in 1880. Britain made Fiji a crown colony in 1874, and Germany annexed several of the Marshall Islands in 1876 and 1878. At the Berlin Conference, European diplomats agreed on a partition of Oceania as well as Africa, and Britain, France, Germany, and the United States proceeded to claim almost all the Pacific islands. By 1900 only the kingdom of Tonga remained independent, and even Tonga accepted British protection against the possibility of encroachments by other imperial powers.

Imperialists in Paradise

THE EMERGENCE OF NEW IMPERIAL POWERS

Nineteenth-century imperialism was mostly a European affair until the end of the century. At that point, two new imperial powers appeared on the world stage: the United States and Japan. Both lands experienced rapid

Maori (MAY-oh-ree)

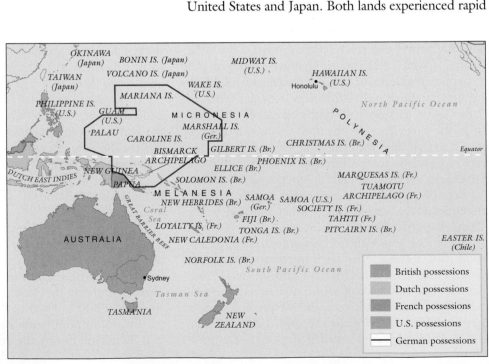

Map 29.5 Boundaries of imperial claims in Oceania about 1914. Observe the many small, distant islands of the Pacific. Why would imperial powers have thought it so important to claim these islands in the late nineteenth and early twentieth centuries?

industrialization in the late nineteenth century, and both built powerful armed forces. As European imperial powers planted their flags throughout the world, leaders of the United States and Japan decided that they too needed to establish a global imperial presence.

U.S. Imperialism in Latin America and the Pacific

The very existence of the United States was due to European imperialism. After the new republic had won its independence, U.S. leaders brought almost all the temperate regions of North America under their authority. In the process, they pushed indigenous peoples onto marginal lands and reservations. This domination of the North American continent was part of the larger story of European and Euro-American imperialism.

The fledgling United States also tried to wield power outside North America. In 1823 President James Monroe (in office 1817–1825) issued a proclamation that warned European states against imperialist designs in the western hemisphere. The Monroe Doctrine, as it came to be known, later served as a justification for U.S. intervention in hemispheric affairs.

As the United States consolidated its continental holdings, U.S. leaders became interested in acquiring territories beyond the temperate regions of North America. The United States purchased Alaska from Russia in 1867 and in 1875 claimed a protectorate over the islands of Hawai`i, where U.S. entrepreneurs had established highly productive sugarcane plantations. The Hawaiian kingdom survived until 1893, when a group of planters and businesspeople overthrew the last monarch, Queen Lili`uokalani (reigned 1891–1893), and invited the United States to annex the islands. In 1898 the pro-expansion president William McKinley (in office 1897–1901) agreed to acquire the islands.

The United States emerged as a major imperial and colonial power after the brief Spanish-Cuban-

The Spanish-Cuban-American War

American War (1898–1899). War broke out as anticolonial tensions mounted in Cuba and Puerto Rico—the last remnants of Spain's American empire—where U.S. business interests had made large investments. In 1898 the U.S. battleship *Maine* exploded and sank in Havana harbor. U.S. leaders claimed sabotage and declared war on Spain. The United States easily defeated Spain and took control and possession of Cuba and Puerto Rico. After the U.S. navy destroyed the Spanish fleet at Manila in a single day, the United States also took possession of

Queen Lili`uokalani, last monarch of Hawai`i, before her deposition in 1893. Wearing a European dress, the queen sits on a throne covered with a traditional royal cape made of bird feathers.

Guam and the Philippines to prevent them from falling under German or Japanese control.

The consolidation of U.S. authority in the Philippines was an especially difficult affair. The Spanish-Cuban-American War coincided with a Filipino revolt against Spanish rule, and U.S. forces promised to support independence of the Philippines in exchange for an alliance against Spain. After the victory over Spain, however, President McKinley decided to bring the Philippines under American control instead. In response, Filipino rebels—led by Emilio Aguinaldo—turned their arms against the new intruders. The result was a bitter insurrection that raged until 1902 and claimed the lives of 4,200 American soldiers, 15,000 rebel troops, and some 200,000 Filipino civilians.

Instability and disorder also prompted the United States to intervene in the affairs of Caribbean and Central American lands, even those that were not U.S. possessions, to prevent rebellion and protect American business interests. In the early twentieth century, U.S. military forces occupied Cuba, the Dominican Republic, Nicaragua, Honduras, and Haiti.

The Panama Canal

To facilitate communication and transportation between the Atlantic and the Pacific oceans, the United States sought to build a canal across the Isthmus of Panama in northern Colombia. However, Colombia was unwilling to cede land for the project. Under President Theodore Roosevelt (in office 1901–1909), an enthusiastic champion of imperial expansion, the United States supported a rebellion against Colombia in 1903 and helped rebels establish the breakaway state of Panama. In exchange for that support, the United States won the right to build a canal across Panama and to control the adjacent territory, known as the Panama Canal Zone. Roosevelt then added a corollary to the Monroe Doctrine in 1904, which stated that the United States has the right to intervene in the domestic affairs of nations within the hemisphere if they demonstrate an inability to maintain the security deemed necessary to protect U.S. investments. The Roosevelt Corollary, along with the Panama Canal when it opened in 1914, strengthened U.S. military and economic claims.

Imperial Japan

Strengthened by rapid industrialization during the Meiji era, Japan joined the ranks of imperial powers in the late nineteenth century. Indeed, while founding representative political institutions to demonstrate their trustworthiness to American and European diplomats, Japanese leaders also made a bid to stand alongside the world's great powers by launching a campaign of imperial expansion.

Early Japanese Expansion

The Japanese drive to empire began in the east Asian islands. During the 1870s Japanese leaders consolidated their hold on Hokkaido and the Kurile Islands to the north, and they encouraged Japanese migrants to populate the islands to forestall Russian expansion there. By 1879 they had also established their hegemony over Okinawa and the Ryukyu Islands to the south.

The Sino-Japanese War

In 1876 Japan purchased modern warships from Britain, and the newly strengthened Japanese navy immediately began to flex its muscles in Korea. In 1894 conflict erupted between Japan and China over the status of Korea. When an antiforeign rebellion broke out in Korea in 1893, Qing rulers sent an army to restore order and reassert Chinese authority in Korea. However, Japanese businesses had built substantial interests in Korea, and Meiji leaders were unwilling to recognize Chinese control over such an economically important land. Thus in August 1894 they declared war on China. The Japanese navy quickly gained control of the Yellow Sea and demolished the Chinese fleet in a battle lasting a mere five hours. Within a few months the conflict was over. When the combatants made peace in April 1895, Qing authorities recognized the independence of Korea, thus making it essentially a dependency of Japan. They also ceded Taiwan, the Pescadores Islands, and the Liaodong peninsula, which strengthened Japanese control over east Asian waters. Alongside territorial acquisitions, Japan gained unequal treaty rights in China like those enjoyed by European and American powers.

The Russo-Japanese War

The unexpected Japanese victory startled European imperial powers, especially Russia. Tensions between Japan and Russia soon mounted, because both imperial powers had territorial ambitions in the Liaodong peninsula, Korea, and Manchuria. War broke out in 1904, and Japanese forces overran Russian installations before reinforcements could arrive from Europe. The Japanese navy destroyed the Russian Baltic fleet, which had sailed halfway around the world to support the war effort. By 1905 the war was over, and Japan won international recognition of its colonial authority over Korea and the Liaodong peninsula. Furthermore, Russia ceded the southern half of Sakhalin island to Japan, along with a railroad and economic interests in southern Manchuria. Victory in the Russo-Japanese War transformed Japan into a major imperial power.

LEGACIES OF IMPERIALISM

Imperialism and colonialism profoundly influenced the development of world history. In some ways they tightened links between the world's peoples: trade and migration increased dramatically as imperial powers exploited the resources of subject lands and recruited labor forces to work in colonies throughout the world. Yet imperialism and colonialism also brought peoples into conflict and heightened senses of difference between peoples. European, Euro-American, and Japanese imperialists all came to think of themselves as superior to the peoples they overcame. Meanwhile, foreign intrusion stimulated the development of resistance in colonized lands, which over time served as a foundation for anticolonial independence movements.

Japanese infantry charging during the Russo-Japanese war.

Empire and Economy

One of the principal motives of imperialism was the desire to gain access to natural resources and agricultural products. As imperial powers consolidated their hold on foreign lands, colonial administrators reorganized subject societies so they would become efficient suppliers of timber, rubber, petroleum, gold, silver, diamonds, cotton, tea, coffee, cacao, and other products. As a result, global trade in those commodities surged during the nineteenth and early twentieth centuries. The advantages of this trade went mostly to the colonial powers, whose policies encouraged subject lands to provide raw materials for processing in the industrialized societies of Europe, North America, and Japan.

In some cases, colonial rule led to the introduction of new crops that transformed both the landscape and

Introduction of New Crops

the social order of subject lands. In the early nineteenth century, for example, British colonial officials introduced tea bushes from China to Ceylon and India. The effect on Ceylon was profound. British planters felled trees on much of the island, converted rain forests into tea plantations, and recruited Ceylonese women by the thousands to carry out the labor-intensive work of harvesting mature tea leaves.

Consumption of tea in India and Ceylon was almost negligible, but increased supplies met the growing demand for tea in Europe, where the beverage became accessible to individuals of all social classes. The value of south Asian tea exports rose from about 309,000 pounds sterling in 1866 to 6.1 million pounds sterling in 1900. Malaya and Sumatra underwent a similar social transformation after British colonial agents planted rubber trees there in the 1870s and established plantations to meet the growing global demand for rubber products.

Labor Migrations

Efforts to exploit the natural resources and agricultural products of subject lands led imperial and colonial powers to encourage mass migrations of workers during the nineteenth and early twentieth centuries. Two patterns of labor migration were especially prominent during the imperial and colonial era. European migrants went mostly to temperate lands, where they worked as free cultivators or industrial laborers. In contrast, migrants from Asia, Africa, and the Pacific islands moved largely to tropical and subtropical lands, where they worked as indentured laborers on plantations or manual laborers for mining enterprises or large-scale construction projects.

Between 1800 and 1914 some fifty million European migrants left their homes and sought opportunities overseas. Most of those migrants left the relatively poor agricultural societies of southern and eastern Europe, especially

European Migration

Italy, Russia, and Poland, although sizable numbers came also from Britain, Ireland, Germany, and Scandinavia. A majority of the migrants—about thirty-two million—went to the United States. Settler colonies in Canada, Argentina, Australia, New Zealand, and south Africa also drew large numbers of European migrants.

In contrast to their free European counterparts, migrants from Asia, Africa, and the Pacific islands generally traveled as indentured laborers.

Indentured Labor Migration

As the institution of slavery went into decline, planters sought laborers from poor and densely populated lands who could replace slaves. Between 1820 and 1914 about 2.5 million indentured laborers left their homes to work in distant parts of the world. Labor recruiters generally offered workers free passage to their destinations and provided them with food, shelter, clothing, and modest compensation for their services in exchange for a commitment to work for five to seven years.

The majority of the indentured laborers came from India, but sizable numbers also came from China, Japan, Java, Africa, and the Pacific islands. Indentured laborers went mostly to tropical and subtropical lands in the Americas, the Caribbean, Africa, and Oceania. Large numbers of Indian laborers went to work on rubber plantations in Malaya and sugar plantations in south Africa, the Pacific island of Fiji, the Guianas, and the Caribbean islands of Trinidad, Tobago, and Jamaica. After the Opium War, large numbers of Chinese laborers went to sugar plantations in Cuba and Hawai`i, guano mines in Peru, tin mines in Malaya, gold mines in south Africa and Australia, and railroad construction sites in the United States, Canada, and Peru. After the Meiji restoration in Japan, a large contingent of Japanese laborers migrated to Hawai`i to work on sugar plantations, and a smaller group went to work in guano mines in Peru. Indentured laborers from Africa went mostly to sugar plantations in Réunion, the Guianas, and Caribbean islands. Those from Pacific islands went mostly to plantations on other Pacific islands and in Australia.

All the large-scale migrations of the nineteenth century reflected the global influence of imperial powers.

Empire and Migration   European migrations were possible only because European and Euro-American peoples had established settler societies in temperate regions around the world. Movements of indentured laborers were possible because colonial officials were able to recruit workers and dispatch them to distant lands where their compatriots had already established plantations or opened mines. In combination the nineteenth-century migrations profoundly influenced societies around the world by depositing large communities of people with distinctive ethnic identities in lands far from their original homes.

Empire and Society

The policies adopted by imperial powers and colonial officials forced peoples of different societies to deal with one another on a regular and systematic basis. *Colonial Conflict* Their interactions often led to violent conflicts between colonizers and subject peoples. Indeed, the sepoy rebellion was only one among many insurrections organized by discontented Indian subjects between the mid–nineteenth and the mid–twentieth centuries. Colonized lands in southeast Asia and Africa also became hotbeds of resistance, as subject peoples revolted against foreign rule, the tyrannical behavior of colonial officials, the introduction of European schools and curricula, high

taxation, and requirements that subject peoples provide compulsory labor for colonists' enterprises.

Many rebellions drew strength from traditional religious beliefs, and priests or prophets often led resistance to colonial rule. In Tanganyika, for example, a local prophet organized the huge Maji Maji rebellion (1905–1906) to expel German colonial authorities from east Africa. Rebels sprinkled themselves with "magic water" *(maji-maji)*, which they believed would protect them from German weapons. Although the rebellion failed and resulted in the deaths of as many as seventy-five thousand insurgents, it testified to the fact that rebellion was a constant threat to colonial rule. Even when subject peoples dared not revolt, they

Scientific racists often argued that Europeans had reached a higher stage of evolution than other peoples. An illustration from a popular book by Josiah Clark Nott and G. R. Glidden, *Indigenous Races of the Earth,* deliberately distorted facial and skull features to suggest a close relationship between African peoples and chimpanzees.

resisted colonial rule by boycotting European goods, organizing political parties and pressure groups, and pursuing anticolonial policies through churches and religious groups.

Social and cultural differences were the foundation of an academic pursuit known as scientific racism, which became prominent especially after the 1840s. Theorists such as the French nobleman Count Joseph Arthur de Gobineau (1816–1882) took race as the most important index of human potential. In fact, there is no such thing as a biologically pure race, but nineteenth-century theorists assumed that the human species consisted of several distinct racial groups. In his dense, four-volume *Essay on the Inequality of the Human Races* (1853–1855), Gobineau divided humanity into four main racial groups. Gobineau characterized Africans as unintelligent and lazy; Asians as smart but docile; the native peoples of the Americas as dull and arrogant; and Europeans as intelligent, noble, and morally superior to others. Throughout the later nineteenth and early twentieth centuries, racist thinkers sought to identify racial groups on the basis of skin color, bone structure, nose shape, cranial capacity, and other physical characteristics.

Scientific Racism

After the 1860s scientific racists drew heavily from the writings of Charles Darwin (1809–1882), an English biologist whose book *On the Origin of Species* (1859) argued that all living species had evolved over thousands of years in a ferocious contest for survival. Species that adapted well to their environment survived, reproduced, and flourished, according to Darwin, whereas others declined and went into extinction. The slogan "survival of the fittest" soon became a byword for Darwin's theory of evolution. Theorists known as social Darwinists seized upon those ideas, which Darwin had applied exclusively to biological matters, and adapted them to explain the development of human societies. The English philosopher Herbert Spencer (1820–1903) relied on theories of evolution to explain differences between the strong and the weak: successful individuals and races had competed better in the natural world and consequently evolved to higher states than did other, less fit peoples. On the basis of that reasoning, Spencer and others justified the domination of European imperialists over subject peoples as the inevitable result of natural scientific principles.

Racist views were by no means a monopoly of European imperialists: U.S. and Japanese empire builders also developed a sense of superiority over the peoples they conquered and ruled. U.S. forces in the Philippines disparaged the rebels they fought there as "gooks," and they did not hesitate to torture enemies in a conflict that was supposed to "civilize and Christianize" the Filipinos. In the 1890s Japanese newspapers portrayed Chinese and Korean peoples as dirty, backward, stupid, and cowardly. After their victory in the Russo-Japanese War, political and military leaders came to believe that Japan had an obligation to oversee the affairs of their backward neighbors and help civilize their little Asian brothers.

SUMMARY

The construction of global empires in the nineteenth century noticeably increased the tempo of world integration. Armed with powerful transportation, communication, and military technologies, European peoples imposed their rule on much of Asia and almost all of Africa. They wielded enormous influence throughout the world, even where they did not establish imperial control, because of their wealth and economic power. Toward the end of the nineteenth century, the United States and Japan joined European states as global imperialists. All the imperial powers profoundly influenced the development of the societies they ruled. They shaped the economies and societies of their colonies by pushing them to supply natural resources and agricultural commodities in exchange for manufactured products. They created multicultural societies around the world by facilitating the movement of workers to lands where there was high demand for labor on plantations or in mines. They also provoked subject peoples to resist colonial expansion, which over time led them to develop a sense of national identity. From the early twentieth century forward, much of global history has revolved around issues stemming from the world order of imperialism and colonialism.

CHRONOLOGY

1805–1848	Reign of Muhammad Ali in Egypt
1808–1839	Reign of Sultan Mahmud II
1809–1882	Life of Charles Darwin
1816–1882	Life of Count Joseph Arthur de Gobineau
1824	Founding of Singapore by Thomas Stamford Raffles
1839–1842	Opium War
1839–1876	Tanzimat Era
1850–1864	Taiping rebellion
1853–1902	Life of Cecil Rhodes
1857	Sepoy rebellion
1859–1869	Construction of the Suez Canal
1860–1864	Land wars in New Zealand
1860–1895	Self-Strengthening Movement
1884–1885	Berlin West Africa Conference
1894–1895	Sino-Japanese War
1897–1901	Term of office of U.S. president William McKinley
1898–1899	Spanish-Cuban-American War
1899–1902	South African War (Boer War)
1901–1909	Term of office of U.S. president Theodore Roosevelt
1904–1905	Russo-Japanese War
1904–1914	Construction of the Panama Canal
1905–1906	Maji Maji rebellion
1908–1918	Young Turk Era

FOR FURTHER READING

Michael Adas. *Machines as the Measure of Men: Science, Technology, and Ideologies of Western Dominance*. Ithaca, 1988. Argues that European imperialists judged other peoples on the basis of their technological expertise.

W. G. Beasley. *Japanese Imperialism, 1894–1945*. Oxford, 1987. The best study of the topic, emphasizing the relationship between Japanese industrialization and imperialism.

A. Adu Boahen. *African Perspectives on Colonialism*. Baltimore, 1987. A valuable synthetic work that examines African responses to imperial intrusions and colonial regimes.

Philip D. Curtin. *The World and the West: The European Challenge and the Overseas Response in the Age of Empire*. Cambridge and New York, 2000. A work that focuses on cultural change as it examines how various peoples have responded to the establishment of European empires.

John Gallagher. *The Decline, Revival, and Fall of the British Empire*. Ed. by Anil Seal. Cambridge, 1982. A collection of essays that have deeply influenced scholarship on the British empire.

Daniel R. Headrick. *The Tentacles of Progress: Technology Transfer in the Age of Imperialism, 1850–1940*. New York, 1988. Argues that imperial powers reserved the benefits of technological innovation for themselves by limiting the expertise that they shared with subject peoples.

Adam Hochschild. *King Leopold's Ghost: A Story of Greed, Terror, and Heroism in Colonial Africa*. Boston, 1998. A ghastly story of nearly forgotten greed and crime.

Peter Hopkirk. *The Great Game: The Struggle for Empire in Central Asia*. New York, 1992. Exciting account of the contest for power known as the Great Game.

David Northrup. *Indentured Labor in the Age of Imperialism, 1834–1922*. Cambridge, 1995. Careful study of indentured labor migrations and working conditions.

Thomas Pakenham. *The Scramble for Africa, 1876–1912*. New York, 1991. Detailed popular history of empire building in sub-Saharan Africa.

At the time the Great War erupted in 1914, Europeans and their descendants in North America dominated global affairs to an unprecedented extent, exercising political and economic control over peoples and their lands in most of Asia, nearly all of Africa, the Americas, and the Pacific islands. This global dominance was the outcome of three interconnected historical developments that took place between 1750 and 1914: the formation of national states, industrialization, and imperial expansion.

Those same historical developments, which encouraged national rivalries, colonial disputes, and nationalist aspirations, plunged Europe—and then much of the world—into war in 1914. By the time the war ended in 1918, all the major European powers had exhausted much of their economic wealth and global political primacy.

Global interdependence ensured that economic instability after the Great War affected much of the world. This was especially true in the Great Depression, when political turmoil and social misery paved the way to fascist dictatorships in Italy and Germany and to nationalist movements in Asia. Meanwhile, the Soviet Union embarked on a state-sponsored program of rapid industrialization that transformed it into a major international power.

Sparked as a result of the Great War and the Great Depression, World War II began in China in 1931 when Japanese forces established a colonial empire in Manchuria. The conflict spread to Europe in the late 1930s when the Nazi regime embarked on a policy of territorial expansion. By 1941 all the world's major powers had been sucked into a maelstrom of violence and suffering that engulfed most European societies, almost all of Asia and the Pacific, and parts of Africa.

World War II completed the economic and political weakening of European societies and led to the immediate outbreak of the cold war and the dismantling of colonial empires, both of which realigned the world of the late twentieth and twenty-first centuries. The cold war conflict between the forces of capitalism and communism produced a new set of global relationships, shaping the foreign policies, economic systems, and political institutions of nations throughout the world until its abrupt end in the late 1980s.

In the three decades after World War II, an irresistible wave of independence

CONTEMPORARY GLOBAL REALIGNMENTS

movements swept away colonies and empires and led to the establishment of new nations in Africa and Asia. However, the initial euphoria that accompanied freedom from imperial control was tempered by neocolonial and postcolonial problems such as rapid population growth, lack of economic development, and regional and ethnic conflicts.

Other forces that reshaped the twentieth- and twenty-first-century world include globalization, a process that widened the extent and the forms of cross-cultural interaction among the world's peoples. Technological advances dissolved old political, social, and economic barriers. The resulting global integration encouraged similar economic and political preferences and fostered common cultural values, but forces promoting distinct cultural traditions and political identities also arose to challenge the universalizing effects of globalization.

CHAPTER 30

The Great War: The World in Upheaval

Archduke Francis Ferdinand (1863–1914) was aware that his first official visit to Sarajevo in 1914 was fraught with danger. That ancient city was the capital of Bosnia-Herzegovina, twin provinces that had been under Ottoman rule since the fifteenth century, then occupied in 1878, and finally annexed by Austria-Hungary in 1908. These provinces became the hotbed of pan-Serbian nationalism. Most Serbian nationalists hated the Austro-Hungarian dynasty and the empire represented by Ferdinand, the heir to the throne.

It was a warm and radiant Sunday morning when Ferdinand's motorcade made its way through the narrow streets of Sarajevo. Waiting for him along the designated route were seven assassins armed with bombs and revolvers, one of whom threw a bomb into the open car. Glancing off Ferdinand's arm, the bomb exploded near another vehicle and injured dozens of spectators.

Undeterred, Ferdinand went on to a reception at city hall; after the reception he instructed his driver to take him to the hospital where those wounded in the earlier attack were being treated. While Ferdinand was on his way to the hospital, a young Bosnian Serb named Gavrilo Princip (1894–1918) lunged at the archduke's car and fired a revolver. The first bullet blew a gaping hole in the side of Ferdinand's neck. A second bullet intended for the governor of Bosnia went wild and entered the stomach of the expectant Duchess Sophie, the wife of the archduke. Turning to his wife, the archduke pleaded: "Sophie, dear! Don't die! Stay alive for our children!" By the time medical

OPPOSITE PAGE: *Nurse, wounded soldier, and child.*

aid arrived, however, the archduke and the duchess were dead.

The assassination of the archduke and his wife brought to a head the tensions between the Austro-Hungarian empire and the neighboring kingdom of Serbia. As other European powers took sides, the stakes far outgrew Austro-Serbian conflicts. Nationalist aspirations, international rivalries, and an inflexible alliance system transformed that conflict into a general European war and ultimately into a global struggle involving thirty-two nations. Twenty-eight of those nations, collectively known as the Allies and the Associated Powers, fought the coalition known as the Central Powers, which consisted of Germany, Austria-Hungary, the Ottoman empire, and Bulgaria. The shell-shocked generation that survived the carnage called this clash of arms the Great War. A subsequent generation of survivors renamed the conflict World War I, because it was, sadly, only the first of two wars that engulfed the world in the first half of the twentieth century.

The Great War lasted from August 1914 to November 1918 and ushered in history's most violent century. In geographic extent the conflict surpassed all previous wars, compelling men, women, and children on five continents to participate directly or indirectly in a struggle that many did not understand. The Great War also had the distinction of being the first total war in human history, as governments mobilized every available human and material resource for the conduct of war. Moreover, the industrial nature of the conflict meant that it was the bloodiest in the annals of organized violence. The military casualties passed a threshold beyond previous experience: approximately fifteen million soldiers died, and an additional twenty million combatants suffered injuries.

The war of 1914–1918 did more than destroy individual lives. It seriously damaged national economies, it led to the redrawing of European boundaries, and it caused the demise of four dynasties and their empires—the Ottoman empire, the Russian empire, the Austro-Hungarian empire, and the German empire. The war also helped unleash the Bolshevik Revolution of 1917, which set the stage for an ideological conflict between capitalism and communism that endured to the end of the twentieth century. Finally, the Great War was responsible for an international realignment of power. It undermined the preeminence and prestige of European society, signaling an end to Europe's global primacy.

THE DRIFT TOWARD WAR

Although the catalyst for war was the assassination of Archduke Francis Ferdinand, the assassin's bullets would have had limited effect if there had not been deeper reasons for war. Indeed, the underlying causes for the war of 1914–1918 were many, including intense nationalism, abrasive colonial rivalries, and a general struggle over the balance of power in Europe and in the world at large. Between 1871 and 1914, European governments adopted foreign policies that increased steadily the danger of war. So as to not find themselves alone in a hostile world, national leaders sought alignments with other powers. The establishment and maintenance in Europe of two hostile alliances—the Allies and the Central Powers—helped spread the war from the Balkans.

Nationalist Aspirations

The nationalist fervor that spread throughout most of Europe in the nineteenth century had led many Europeans to rally behind the idea of *self-determination*, or the idea that peoples with the same ethnic origins, language, and political ideals had the right to form sovereign states. In fact, that idea helped inspire the nationalist movements that led to the creation of the new nations of Belgium (1830), Italy (1861), and Germany (1871). Yet at the end of the nineteenth century, the issue of nationalism remained unresolved in other areas of Europe, most notably in eastern Europe and the Balkans. There the nationalist aspirations of subject minorities threatened to tear apart the multinational empires of the Ottoman and Habsburg dynasties and with them the regional balance of power.

The Ottoman empire had controlled the Balkan peninsula since the fifteenth century, but after 1829 the Turkish empire shriveled, largely because of nationalist revolts. Greece was the first to gain independence (in 1830), but within a few decades Serbia, Romania, and Bulgaria followed suit. Austria-Hungary also confronted nationalism within its realms, especially the aspirations of Slavic peoples—Poles, Czechs, Slovaks, Serbs, Croats, and Slovenes. Most menacing and militant were the Serbs, who pressed for unification with the independent kingdom of Serbia. Russia and Germany added fuel to this volatile situation by supporting opposing sides. Russia supported Serbia and the notion of Slavic cultural unity, while Germany backed Austria-Hungary. Thus the stage was set for international conflict.

National Rivalries

Aggressive nationalism was also manifest in economic competition and colonial conflicts, fueling dangerous rivalries among the major European powers. All the industrialized nations of Europe competed for foreign markets and engaged in tariff wars, but the most unsettling economic rivalry involved Great Britain and Germany. By the twentieth century, Germany's rapid industrialization threatened Britain's long-standing economic predominance. Indeed, by 1914 Britain's share of global industrial output had declined to a level roughly equal to Germany's 13 percent. British reluctance to accept the relative decline of British industry vis-à-vis German industry strained relations between the two economic powers.

An expensive naval race further exacerbated tensions between the two nations. When Germany's political and military leaders announced their program to build a fleet with many large battleships, they seemed to undermine Britain's longtime mastery of the seas. The British government moved to meet the German threat through the construction of super battleships known as *dreadnoughts*. Rather than discouraging the Germans, the British determination to retain naval superiority stimulated the Germans to build their own flotilla of dreadnoughts. As the two nations raced to outdo each other, international hostilities boiled under the surface.

The Naval Race

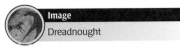

National rivalries also fomented colonial competition. During the late nineteenth and early twentieth centuries, European nations searched aggressively for new colonies or dependencies to bolster economic performance. In their haste to conquer and colonize, the imperial powers stumbled over one another, repeatedly clashing in one or the other corner of the globe: Britain and Russia faced off in Persia (modern-day Iran) and Afghanistan;

Colonial Disputes

Dissident cartoonist Walter Trier's satirical map of Europe in 1914.

Britain and France in Siam (modern-day Thailand) and the Nile valley; Britain and Germany in east and southwest Africa; Germany and France in Morocco and west Africa.

Between 1905 and 1914, a series of international crises and two local wars raised tensions and almost precipitated a general European war. The first crisis resulted from a French-German confrontation over Morocco in 1905. When the German government announced its support of Moroccan independence, which French encroachment endangered, the French responded by threatening war. An international conference in the following year prevented a clash of arms, but similar crises threatened the peace in subsequent years. Contributing to the growing tensions in European affairs were the Balkan wars. Between 1912 and 1913, the states of the Balkan peninsula—including Bulgaria, Greece, Montenegro, Serbia, and Romania—fought two wars for possession of European territories held by the Ottoman empire. The Balkan wars strained European diplomatic relations and helped shape the tense circumstances that led to the outbreak of the Great War.

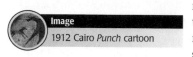

1912 Cairo *Punch* cartoon

Public pressure also contributed to national rivalries. New means of communication—especially cheap, mass-produced newspapers—nourished the public's desire to see their country "come in first," whether in the competition for colonies or in the race to the South Pole. However, public pressure calling for national greatness placed policymakers and diplomats in an awkward situation. Compelled to achieve headline-grabbing foreign policy successes, these leaders ran the risk of paying for short-lived triumphs with long-lasting hostility from other countries.

Public Opinion

Understandings and Alliances

In addition to a basic desire for security, escalating national rivalries and nationalist aspirations of subject minorities spawned a system of entangling alliances. The complexity of those obligations could not hide the common characteristic underlying all the alliances: they outlined the circumstances under which countries would go to war to support one another. Intended to preserve the peace, rival alliance systems created a framework whereby even a small international crisis could set off a chain reaction leading to global war. By 1914 Europe's major powers had transformed themselves into two hostile camps—the Triple Alliance and the Triple Entente.

The Triple Alliance, also known as the Central Powers, grew out of the close relationship that developed between the leaders of Germany and Austria-Hungary during the last three decades of the nineteenth century. In 1879 the governments of the two empires formed the Dual Alliance, a defensive pact that ensured reciprocal protection from a Russian attack and neutrality in case of an attack from any other power. Fear of a hostile France motivated Germans to enter into this pact, whereas Austrians viewed it as giving them a free hand in pursuing their Balkan politics without fear of Russian intervention. Italy, fearful of France, joined the Dual Alliance in 1882, thereby transforming it into the Triple Alliance.

The Central Powers

Meanwhile, the leaders of other nations viewed this new constellation of power with suspicion. This response was especially true of French leaders, who still remembered France's humiliating defeat during the Franco-Prussian War of 1870–1871. The tsarist regime of Russia was equally disturbed by the new alignment of powers, especially by Germany's support of Austria, and British leaders were traditionally suspicious of any arrangement that seemed to threaten the balance of power on the Continent. The result was that, in a series of agreements between 1904 and 1914, the most unlikely bedfellows formed the Triple Entente, a combination of nations commonly referred to as the Allies. The construction of such alliances made it difficult for diplomats to contain what otherwise might have been relatively small international crises.

The Allies

The preservation of peace was also difficult because the military staffs of each nation had devised inflexible military plans and timetables to be carried out in the event of war. German war plans in particular played a crucial role in the events leading to the Great War. Germany's fear of encirclement by France and Russia encouraged its military planners to devise a strategy that would avoid a war on two fronts. It was based on a strategy developed in 1905 by General Count Alfred von Schlieffen (1833–1913). The Schlieffen plan called for a swift knockout of France, followed by defensive action against Russia. German planners predicated their strategy on the knowledge that the Russians could not mobilize their soldiers and military supplies as quickly as the French, thus giving

War Plans

Triple Entente (ahn-TAHNT)

German forces a few precious weeks during which they could concentrate their full power on France. However, Germany's military strategy was a serious obstacle to those seeking to preserve the peace. In the event of Russian mobilization, Germany's leaders would feel compelled to stick to their war plans by attacking France first, thereby setting in motion a military conflict of major proportions.

GLOBAL WAR

In the capitals of Europe, people danced in the streets when their governments announced formal declarations of war. When the first contingents of soldiers left for the front, jubilant crowds threw flowers at the feet of departing men, who expected to return victorious after a short time. However, reality crushed any expectations of a short and triumphant war. On most fronts the conflict quickly bogged down and became a war of attrition in which the firepower of modern weapons slaughtered soldiers by the millions. For the first time in history, belligerent nations engaged in total war. Even in democratic societies, governments assumed dictatorial control to marshal the human and material resources required for continuous war. One result was increased participation of women in the labor force. Total war had repercussions that went beyond the borders of Europe.

Imperial ties drew millions of Asians, Africans, and residents of the British dominions into the war to serve as soldiers and laborers. Struggles over far-flung colonies further underlined the global dimension of this war. Last, the war gained a global flavor through the entry of Japan, the United States, and the Ottoman empire, nations whose leaders professed little direct interest in European affairs.

The Guns of August

The shots fired from Gavrilo Princip's revolver on that fateful day of 28 June 1914 set in motion a flurry of diplomatic activity that quickly escalated into war. Austrian leaders in Vienna were determined to teach the unruly Serbs a lesson, and on 23 July the Austrians issued an ultimatum to the government of Serbia. When the Serbian government rejected one of its terms, Austria-Hungary declared war on Serbia. The war had begun. The subsequent

Declarations of War

Image
Serbian ambulance tent

sequence of events was largely determined by two factors: complex mobilization plans and the grinding logic of the alliance system. Military planners were convinced that the timing of mobilization orders and adherence to precise timetables were crucial to the successful conduct of war.

On 29 July the Russian government mobilized its troops to defend its Serbian ally and itself from Austria. The tsar of Russia then ordered mobilization against Germany. Nicholas II (1868–1918) took that decisive step reluctantly and only after his military experts had convinced him that a partial mobilization might invite defeat should the Germans enter the war on the side of Austria. His action precipitated a German ultimatum to Russia on 31 July, demanding that the Russian army cease its mobilization immediately. Another ultimatum addressed to France demanded to know what France's intentions were in case Germany and Russia went to war. The Russians replied with a blunt "impossible," and the French never answered. Thus on 1 August the German government declared war on Russia, and France started to mobilize.

On 3 August the Germans declared war on France. On the same day, German troops invaded Belgium in accordance with the Schlieffen plan. Key to this plan was an attack on the weak left flank of the French army by an imposing German force through neutral Belgium. On 4 August the British government sent an ultimatum to Germany demanding that Belgian neutrality be respected. When Germany's wartime leaders refused, the British immediately declared war. A local conflict had become a general European war.

Mutual Butchery

Everyone expected the war to be brief. In the first weeks of August 1914, twenty million young men donned uniforms, took up rifles, and left for the front. Many of them looked forward to heroic charges, rapid promotions, and a quick homecoming. Some dreamed of glory and honor, and they believed that God was on their side. Similar attitudes prevailed among the political and military leaders of the belligerent nations, who were preoccupied by visions of sweeping assaults, envelopments, and, above all, swift triumphs. Their visions could hardly have been more wrong.

The initial German thrust toward Paris in August 1914 came to a grinding halt along the river Marne, after which each side tried to outflank the other in a race to the Atlantic coast. For the next three years, the battle lines remained virtually stationary, as both sides

The Western Front

dug in and slugged it out in a war of attrition that lasted until the late autumn of 1918. Each belligerent tried to wear down the enemy by inflicting continuous damage and casualties, only to have its own forces suffer heavy losses in return. Trenches on the western front ran from the English Channel to Switzerland. Farther south, Italy left the Triple Alliance to enter the war on the side of the Allies in 1915. Allied hopes that the Italians would pierce Austrian defenses quickly faded.

After a disastrous defeat at Caporetto in 1917, Italian forces maintained a defensive line only with the help of the French and the British.

Stalemate and New Weapons

The stalemate on the western and southern fronts reflected technological developments that favored defensive tactics. Barbed wire proved highly effective in frustrating the advance of soldiers across "no-man's-land," the deadly territory between opposing trenches. In addition, the rapid and continuous fire of machine

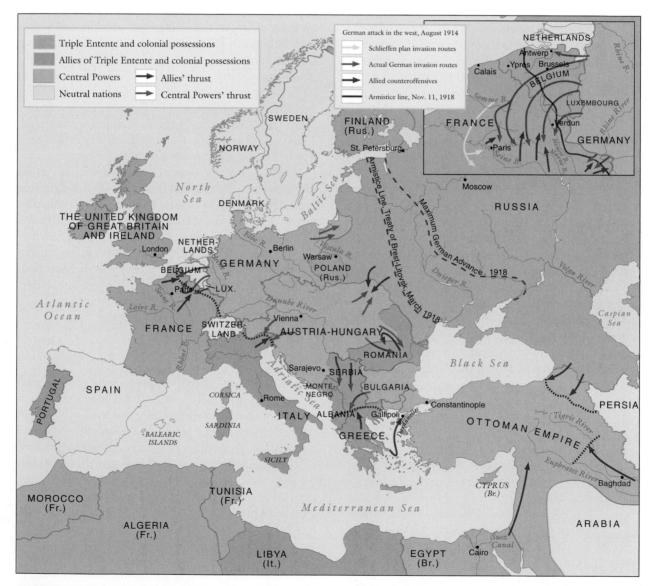

Map 30.1 The Great War in Europe and southwest Asia from 1914 to 1918. Note the locations of both the eastern and the western fronts in Europe during the war. Why didn't the same kind of trench warfare immobilize opposing armies on the eastern front the way it did on the western front?

Air raid warden in helmet and gas mask, holding a wooden gas attack rattle in his gloved hand.

guns turned infantry charges across no-man's-land into suicide missions. Both sides developed weapons to break the deadly stalemate and reintroduce movement into the war. Gas often proved lethal, and it caused its victims excruciating pain. Mustard gas, for example, rotted the body from both within and without. After blistering the skin and damaging the eyes, the gas attacked the bronchial tubes, stripping off the mucous membrane. Death could occur in four to five weeks. Yet although both sides suffered heavy casualties, totaling about 800,000 soldiers, gas attacks failed to deliver the promised strategic breakthroughs. Other novel weapons developed during the war included tanks and airplanes. Other weapons systems, such as the submarine, had made earlier appearances in warfare but were most effectively used by the German navy against Allied commercial shipping in the Great War.

The most courageous infantry charges, even when preceded by pulverizing artillery barrages and clouds of poisonous gas, were no match for *No-Man's-Land* determined defenders. Shielded by the dirt of their trenches and by barbed wire and gas masks, they unleashed a torrent of lethal metal with their machine guns and repeating rifles. In every sector of the front, those who fought rarely found the glory they sought. Instead, they encountered death. No-man's-land was strewn with shell craters, cadavers, and body parts. The grim realities of trench warfare—the wet, cold, waist-deep mud, gluttonous lice, and corpse-fed rats—contrasted sharply with the ringing phrases of politicians and generals justifying the unrelenting slaughter.

Many battles took place, but some were so horrific, so devastating, and so futile that their names are synonymous with human slaughter. The *Bloodletting* casualty figures attested to this bloodletting. In 1916 the Germans tried to break the deadlock with a huge assault on the fortress of Verdun. The French rallying cry was "They shall not pass," and they did not— but at a tremendous cost: while the victorious French counted

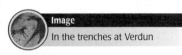
Image
In the trenches at Verdun

315,000 dead, the defeated Germans suffered a loss of 280,000. To relieve the pressure on Verdun, British forces counterattacked at the Somme, and by November they had gained a few thousand yards at the cost of 420,000 casualties. The Germans suffered similar losses, although in the end neither side gained any strategic advantage.

In eastern Europe and the Balkans, the battle lines were more fluid. After a staunch defense, a combination of Austrian and German forces over- *The Eastern* ran Serbia, Albania, and Romania. Farther *Front* north, Russia took the offensive early by invading Prussia in 1914. The Central Powers recovered quickly, however, and in the summer of 1915, combined German-Austrian forces drove the Russian armies out of East Prussia and then out of Poland and established a defensive line extending from the Baltic to the Ukraine. Russian counterattacks in 1916 and 1917 collapsed in a sea of casualties. Those Russian defeats undermined the popularity of the tsar and his government and played a significant role in fostering revolutionary ferment within Russian society.

Dying and suffering were not limited solely to combatants: the Great War established rules of engagement that made civilians targets of *New Rules of* warfare, both from air attacks and from *Engagement* naval blockades. Indeed, military leaders on both sides used blockades to deny food to whole populations, hoping that starving masses would force their governments to capitulate. The British blockade of Germany during the war contributed to the deaths of an estimated half million Germans.

Total War: The Home Front

As the Great War ground on, it became a conflict of attrition in which the organization of material and

Mutilated body on the western front.

human resources was of paramount importance. War became total, fought between entire societies, and total victory was the only acceptable outcome that might justify the terrible sacrifices made by all sides. The nature of total war created a military front and a home front. The term *home front* expressed the important reality that the outcome of the war hinged on how effectively each nation mobilized its economy and activated its noncombatant citizens to support the war effort.

As the war continued beyond Christmas 1914 and as war weariness and a decline in economic capability

The Home Front

set in, the response of all belligerents was to limit individual freedoms and give control of society increasingly to military leaders. Initially, ministers and generals shrank from compulsive measures, even conscription of recruits, but they quickly changed their minds. Each belligerent government eventually militarized civilian war production by subordinating private enterprises to governmental control and imposing severe discipline on the labor process.

Economic measures were foremost in the minds of government leaders because the war created unprecedented demands for raw materials and manufactured goods. Planning boards reorganized entire industries, set production quotas and priorities, and determined what would be produced and consumed. Government authorities also established wage and price controls, extended work hours, and in some instances restricted the movement of workers. Because bloody battlefields caused an insatiable appetite for soldiers, nations responded by extending military service. In Germany, for example, men between the ages of sixteen and sixty were eligible to serve at the front. By constantly tapping into the available male population, the war created an increasing demand for workers at home. Unemployment—a persistent feature of all prewar economies—vanished virtually overnight.

As men marched off to war, women marched off to work. Conscription took men out of the labor force, and wartime leaders exhorted women to fill the gaps in the work-

Women at War

force. A combination of patriotism and high wages drew women into many formerly "male" jobs in a wide variety of industries and public sectors. Perhaps the most crucial work performed by women during the war was the making of shells. Several million women, and sometimes children, put in long, hard hours in munitions factories. That work exposed them to severe dangers, not to mention death, from explosions and poisoning from long-term exposure to TNT.

Although some middle- and upper-class women reported that the war was a liberating experience in regard to personal and economic freedom, most working-class women found little that was liberating in war work. Most of the belligerent governments promised equal pay for equal work, but in most instances that promise remained unfulfilled. Moreover, substantial female employment was a transitory phenomenon. Once the war was over, many women workers—especially those in traditionally male occupations—found themselves forced to concede their jobs to men. Nevertheless, the extension of voting rights to women shortly after the war—in Britain (1918, for women thirty years and older), Germany (1919), and Austria (1919)—was in part due to the role women assumed during the Great War.

To maintain the spirit of the home front and to counter threats to national unity, governments resorted to the restriction of civil liberties,

Propaganda

censorship of bad news, and vilification of the enemy through propaganda campaigns. While some government officials busily censored war news, people who had the temerity to criticize their nation's war effort were prosecuted as traitors. Meanwhile, the propaganda offices of the belligerent nations tried to convince the public that military defeat would mean the destruction of everything worth living for, and to that end they did their utmost to discredit and dehumanize the enemy.

SOURCES FROM THE PAST

Dulce et Decorum Est

The Great War produced a wealth of poetry. The poetic response to war covered a range of moods from early romanticism and patriotism to cynicism, resignation, and the angry depiction of horror. Perhaps the greatest of all war poets was Wilfred Owen (1893–1918), whose poems are among the most poignant of the war. Owen, who enlisted for service on the western front in 1915, was injured in March 1917 and sent home. Declared fit for duty in August 1918, he returned to the front. German machine-gun fire killed him on 7 November, four days before the armistice, when he tried to cross the Sambre Canal.

Bent double, like old beggars under sacks,
Knock-kneed, coughing like hags, we cursed
  through sludge,
Till on the haunting flares we turned our backs
And towards our distant rest began to trudge.
Men marched asleep. Many had lost their boots
But limped on, blood-shod. All went lame; all
  blind;
Drunk with fatigue; deaf even to the hoots
Of gas-shells dropping softly behind.

Gas! GAS! Quick, boys!—An ecstasy of fumbling,
Fitting the clumsy helmets just in time;
But someone still was yelling out and stumbling
And floundering like a man in fire or lime.—
Dim, through the misty panes and thick green
  light
As under a green sea, I saw him drowning.

In all my dreams, before my helpless sight,
He plunges at me, guttering, choking, drowning.
If in some smothering dreams you too could pace
Behind the wagon that we flung him in,
And watch the white eyes writhing in his face,
His hanging face, like a devil's sick of sin;
If you could hear, at every jolt, the blood
Come gargling from the froth-corrupted lungs,
Obscene as cancer, bitter as the cud
Of vile, incurable sores on innocent tongues,—
My friend, you would not tell with such high zest
To children ardent for some desperate glory,
The old Lie: Dulce et decorum est
Pro patria mori.*

*Author's note: "Sweet and fitting is it to die for one's country" comes from a line by the Roman poet Horace (65–8 B.C.E.)

• *How does Owen poetically describe the effects of a gas attack? Is his literary depiction more or less effective than detached descriptions of war's effects?*

SOURCE: Edmund Blunden, ed. *The Poems of Wilfred Owen.* London: Chattus & Windus, 1933, p. 66.

German propaganda depicted Russians as semi-Asiatic barbarians, and French authorities chronicled the atrocities committed by the German "Hun" in Belgium. In 1917 the *Times* of London published a story claiming that Germans converted human corpses into fertilizer and food. In Germany, one widely distributed poster invoked images of bestial black Allied soldiers raping German women to suggest the horrors that would follow if the nation's war effort failed. Most atrocity stories were patently false, and they eventually engendered public skepticism and cynicism. Ironically, public disbelief of wartime propaganda led to an inability to believe in the abominations perpetrated in later wars.

Conflict in East Asia and the Pacific

The Great War quickly turned from a European war into a global conflict. There were three reasons for the war's expansion. First, European governments carried their animosities into their colonies, embroiling them—especially African societies—in their war.

"The Heroes of Belgium 1914." French propaganda poster expresses outrage at the German invasion of Belgium.

An Indian gun crew in the Somme area, 1916.

Second, because Europe's human reserves were not enough to satisfy the appetite of war, the British and the French augmented their ranks by recruiting men from their colonies. Millions of Africans and Asians were drawn into the war. Behind their trenches the French employed laborers from Algeria, China, and French Indochina, and the British did not hesitate to draft Indian and African troops for combat. The British in particular relied on troops furnished by the dominion lands, including Australia, New Zealand, Canada, Newfoundland, and South Africa. Third, the Great War assumed global significance because of the entrance into the war of Japan, the United States, and the Ottoman empire.

On 15 August 1914 the Japanese government sent an ultimatum to Germany demanding the handover of the German-leased territory of Jiaozhou (northeastern China) to Japanese authorities without compensation. The same note also demanded that the German navy unconditionally withdraw its warships from Japanese and Chinese waters. When the Germans refused to comply, the Japanese entered the war on the side of the Allies on 23 August 1914. Japanese

forces then proceeded to seize German territories in China and—aided by forces from New Zealand and Australia—in the Pacific. Next, Japan shrewdly exploited Allied support and European preoccupation to advance its own imperial interests in China. On 18 January 1915 the Japanese presented the Chinese government with twenty-one secret demands. The terms of that ultimatum, if accepted, would have reduced China to a protectorate of Japan. Chinese diplomats leaked the note to the British authorities, who spoke up for China, thus preventing total capitulation. The Twenty-One Demands reflected Japan's determination to dominate east Asia and served as the basis for future Japanese pressure on China.

Battles in Africa and Southwest Asia

The geographic extent of the conflict also broadened beyond Europe when the Allies targeted German colonies in Africa. When the war of 1914–1918 erupted in Europe, all of sub-Saharan Africa (except Ethiopia and Liberia) consisted of European colonies, with the Germans controlling four: Togoland, the Cameroons, German Southwest Africa, and German East Africa. Unlike the capture of German colonies in the Pacific, which allied forces accomplished during the first three months of the war with relative ease, the conquest of German colonies in Africa was difficult. Fighting took place on land and sea; on lakes and rivers; in deserts, jungles, and swamps; and in the air. Indeed, the German flag did not disappear from

Africa until after the armistice took effect on 11 November 1918.

The most extensive military operations outside Europe took place in the southwest Asian territories of the Ottoman empire, which was aligned with the Central Powers at the end of 1914. Seeking a way to break the stalemate on the western front, Winston Churchill (1874–1965), first lord of the Admiralty (British navy), suggested that an Allied strike against the Ottomans—a weak ally of the Central Powers—would hurt the Germans. Early in 1915 the British navy conducted an expedition to seize the approach to the Dardanelles Strait in an attempt to open a warm-water supply line to Russia through the Ottoman-controlled strait. The campaign was a disaster. Turkish defenders, ensconced in the cliffs above, quickly pinned down the Allied troops on the beaches. Trapped between the sea and the hills, Allied soldiers dug in and engaged in their own version of trench warfare. The resulting stalemate produced a total of 250,000 casualties on each side. Despite the losses, Allied leaders took nine months to admit that their campaign had failed.

THE END OF THE WAR

The war produced strains within all the belligerent nations, but most of them managed, often ruthlessly, to cope with food riots, strikes, and mutinies. In the Russian empire, the war amplified existing stresses to such an extent that the Romanov dynasty was forced to abdicate in favor of a provisional government in the spring of 1917. Eight months later, the provisional government yielded power to Bolshevik revolutionaries, who took Russia out of the war early in 1918. This blow to the Allies was more than offset by the entry of the United States into the conflict in 1917, which turned the tide of war in 1918. The resources of the United States finally compelled the exhausted Central Powers to sue for peace in November 1918.

In 1919 the victorious Allies gathered in Paris to hammer out a peace settlement that turned out to be a compromise that pleased few of the parties involved. The most significant consequence of the war was Europe's diminished role in the world. The war of 1914–1918 undermined Europe's power and simultaneously promoted nationalist aspirations among colonized peoples, who clamored for self-determination

Romanov (ROH-mah-nahv)
Bolshevik (BOHL-shih-vehk)

and national independence. For the time being, however, the major imperialist powers kept their grip on their overseas holdings.

Revolution in Russia

The Great War had undermined the Russian state. In the spring of 1917, disintegrating armies, mutinies, and food shortages provoked a series of street demonstrations and strikes in Petrograd (St. Petersburg). The inability of police forces to suppress the uprisings, and the subsequent mutiny of troops garrisoned in the capital, persuaded Tsar Nicholas II (reigned 1894–1917), to abdicate the throne.

After its success in Petrograd, this "February Revolution" spread throughout the country, and political power in Russia shifted to two new agencies: the provisional government and the Petrograd soviet of Workers' and Soldiers' Deputies. Soviets, which were revolutionary councils organized by socialists, surfaced all over Russia in 1917, wielding considerable power through their control of factories and segments of the military. The period between February and October witnessed a political struggle between the provisional government and the powerful Petrograd soviet. At first the new government enjoyed considerable public support as it eliminated the repressive institutions of the tsarist state, but it failed to satisfy popular demands for an end to war and for land reform. It claimed that, being provisional, it could not make fundamental changes such as confiscating land and distributing it among peasants. The government also promised to continue the war and to bring it to a victorious conclusion. The Petrograd soviet, in contrast, called for an immediate peace.

The Struggle for Power

Into this tense political situation stepped Vladimir Ilyich Lenin (1870–1924), a revolutionary Marxist and the leader of the small but radical Bolshevik socialist party. Although Lenin had been living in enforced exile in Switzerland, early in 1917 the German High Command helped him return to Russia in the hope that he would foment revolution and bring about Russia's withdrawal from the war. He did. Already in April 1917 Lenin began calling for the transfer of legal authority to the soviets and advocated uncompromising opposition to the war.

Lenin

Under Lenin's leadership, the Bolsheviks eventually gained control of the Petrograd soviet. Crucial to this development was the provisional government's insistence on continuing the war, its inability to feed the population, and its refusal to undertake land reform.

Vladimir Lenin makes a speech in Red Square on the first anniversary (1918) of the Bolshevik revolution.

Workers and peasants became increasingly convinced that their problems could be solved only by the soviets. In September, Lenin persuaded the Central Committee of the Bolshevik party to organize an armed insurrection and seize power in the name of the All-Russian National Congress of Soviets, which was then convening in Petrograd. During the night of 24 October and the following day, armed workers, soldiers, and sailors stormed the Winter Palace, the home of the provisional government. By the afternoon of 25 October, the virtually bloodless insurrection had run its course, and power passed from the provisional government into the hands of Lenin and the Bolshevik Party.

The Bolshevik rulers then ended Russia's involvement in the Great War by signing the Treaty of Brest-Litovsk with Germany on 3 March 1918. The treaty gave the Germans possession or control of one-third of Russia's territory (the Baltic States, the Caucasus, Finland, Poland, and the Ukraine) and one-quarter of its population. Although the terms of the treaty were harsh and humiliating, taking Russia out of the war gave the new government an opportunity to deal with internal problems. Russia's departure from the war also meant that Germany could concentrate all its resources on the western front.

Treaty of Brest-Litovsk

U.S. Intervention and Collapse of the Central Powers

The year 1917 was crucial for another reason: it marked the entry of the United States into the war on the side of the Allies. In 1914 the American public firmly opposed intervention in a European war. That sentiment soon changed. After the outbreak of the war, the United States pursued a neutrality that favored the Allies, and as the war progressed, the United States became increasingly committed economically to an Allied victory.

The official factor in the United States' decision to enter the war, however, was Germany's resumption of unrestricted submarine warfare in February 1917—a practice that had aroused American outrage in the early years of the war. Germany's leaders took this decisive step because they were desperate to break the British blockade that threatened to starve the Central powers and hoped to use their submarines to break it. German military experts calculated that submarine attacks against the ships of Great Britain and all the ships headed to Great Britain would bring about the defeat of Great Britain in six months. By that time, however, both the American public and its leadership were invested in an Allied victory, and thus Germany's decision brought the United States into the war in April 1917.

America Declares War

The corrosive effects of years of bloodletting showed. For the first two years of the conflict, most people supported their governments' war efforts, but the continuing ravages of war took their toll everywhere. The Central Powers suffered from food shortages as a result of the British blockade, and increasing numbers of people took to the streets to demonstrate against declining food rations. Food riots were complemented by strikes as prewar social conflicts reemerged. Governments reacted harshly to these challenges, pouncing on strikers, suppressing demonstrators, and jailing dissidents. Equally dangerous was the breakdown of military discipline on both sides. In France, for example, a mutiny in the spring of 1917 involved 50,000 soldiers, resulting in 23,385 courts-martial and 432 death sentences.

Collapsing Fronts

Against that grim background, Germany took the risk of throwing its remaining might at the western front in the spring of 1918. The gamble failed, and as the offensive petered out, the Allies—strengthened by fresh U.S. troops—broke through the front and started pushing the Germans back. By that time Germany had effectively exhausted its human and material means to wage war. Meanwhile, Bulgaria capitulated to the invading Allies on 30 September, the Ottomans concluded an armistice on 30 October, and Austria-Hungary surrendered on 4 November. Finally, the Germans accepted an armistice, which took effect on 11 November 1918. At last the guns went silent.

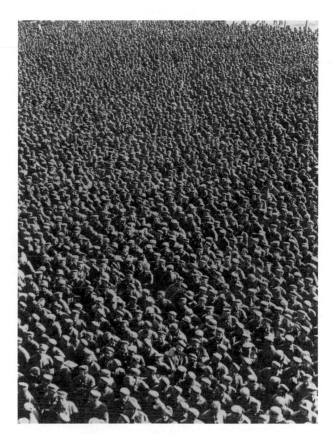

German prisoners taken in France in the fall of 1918.

The Paris Peace Conference

The immediate effects of the Great War were all too obvious. Aside from the physical destruction, which was most visible in northern France and Belgium, the war had killed, disabled, orphaned, or rendered homeless millions of people. Conservative estimates suggest that the war killed fifteen million people and wounded twenty million others. In the immediate postwar years, millions more succumbed to the effects of starvation, malnutrition, and epidemic diseases.

Before the costs of the war were assessed fully, world attention shifted to Paris. There, in 1919, the victorious powers convened to arrange a postwar settlement and set terms for the defeated nations. At the outset, people on both sides of the war had high hopes for the settlement, but in the end it left a bitter legacy. Ultimately, Georges Clemenceau (1841–1929), David Lloyd George (1863–1945), and Woodrow Wilson— the representative leaders of France, Great Britain, and the United States—dominated the deliberations. The Allies did not permit representatives of the Central Powers to participate, and the Soviet Union was not invited to the conference. Throughout this time the

British blockade of Germany remained in effect, adding a sense of urgency to the proceedings.

One year before the opening of the Paris Peace Conference, in January 1918, U.S. president Woodrow Wilson had forwarded a proposal for a just and enduring postwar peace settlement. Wilson's postwar vision subsequently prompted the defeated Central Powers to announce their acceptance of his so-called Fourteen Points as the basis for the armistice. They also expected the Allies to use them as the foundation for later peace treaties. Key among Wilson's Fourteen Points were the following recommendations: open covenants (agreements) of peace, openly arrived at; absolute freedom of navigation upon the seas in peace and war; the removal of all economic barriers and the establishment of an equality of trade conditions among all nations; adequate guarantees for a reduction in national armaments; adjustments of colonial disputes to give equal weight to the interests of the controlling government and the colonial population; and a call for "a general association of nations."

Wilson's Fourteen Points

Primary Source
Wilson's Fourteen Points

The idealism expressed in the Fourteen Points gave Wilson a position of moral leadership among the Allies. Those same allies also opposed various points of Wilson's peace formula, because those points compromised the secret wartime agreements by which they had agreed to distribute among themselves territories and possessions of the defeated nations. The defeated powers, in turn, later felt betrayed when they faced the harsh peace treaties that so clearly violated the spirit of the Fourteen Points.

The final form of the treaties represented a series of compromises among the victors. The hardest terms originated with the French, who desired the destruction or the permanent weakening of German power. Thus, in addition to requiring Germany to accept sole responsibility and guilt for causing the war, the victors demanded a reduction in the military potential of the former Central Powers. In addition, the Allies prohibited Germany and Austria from entering into any sort of political union. The French and the British agreed that the defeated Central Powers must pay for the cost of the war and required the payment of reparations either in money or in kind.

The Peace Treaties

The Paris Peace Conference resulted in additional treaties with Bulgaria, Austria, Hungary, and the Ottoman empire. Whereas Bulgaria lost only small portions of territory as a result, the Austro-Hungarian empire was destroyed: in separate treaties both Austria and Hungary suffered severe territorial losses.

Arrangements between the defeated Ottoman empire and the Allies proved to be a more complicated and protracted affair that involved two treaties. In 1920 the Treaty of Sèvres effectively dissolved the empire, calling for the surrender of Ottoman Balkan and Arab provinces and the occupation of eastern and southern Anatolia by foreign powers. However, Turkish nationalists—led by the war hero Mustafa Kemal—set out to defy those terms. Kemal organized a national army that drove out Allied occupation forces, abolished the sultanate, and replaced it with the Republic of Turkey, with Ankara as its capital. In a great diplomatic victory for Turkish nationalists, the Allied powers officially recognized the Republic of Turkey in a final peace agreement, the Treaty of Lausanne (1923).

Although the war was over, the peace settlement that resulted from it was weak. To be sure, some efforts to avoid future conflicts were made. *The League of Nations* At the urging of U.S. president Woodrow Wilson, the Covenant of the League of Na-

tions was made an integral part of the peace treaties, and every signatory to a peace treaty had to accept this new world organization. However, the league suffered from fundamental weaknesses that made it unable to enforce its decisions. Over the next two decades, it became clear that the league could not stop the aggression that would lead to World War II, and the institution closed its doors in 1940. Nevertheless, the league did establish the pattern for a permanent international organization and served as a model for its successor, the United Nations.

Another weakness of the peace was the uneven way in which key ideas of the peace-making process—especially the idea of national self-determination—were put into practice around the world. In Europe, the peacemakers in Paris did in fact try to apply the principle of self-determination and nationality to a variety of peoples, such as Slavs, Czechs, and Slovaks, although the results were far from perfect. Yet in other instances

Self-Determination

Map 30.2 Territorial changes that occurred in Europe after the Great War. Observe the territories ceded by the Central Powers and the Soviet Union. Which power lost the most territory, and why?

peacemakers pushed the principle aside for strategic and security reasons, such as in Austria and Germany, whose peoples were denied the right to form one nation.

However imperfect the results, the peacemakers at Paris tried to apply the principle of self-determination and nationality throughout Europe. Else-where, however, they did not do so. The unwillingness to apply the principle of self-determination became most obvious when the victors confronted the issue of what to do with Germany's former colonies and the Arab territories of the Ottoman empire. Because the United States rejected the establishment of old-fashioned colonies, the European powers came up with the enterprising idea of trusteeship. Article 22 of the Covenant of the League of Nations referred to the colonies and territories of the former Central Powers as areas "inhabited by peoples not yet able to stand by themselves under the strenuous conditions of the modern world." As a result, "The tutelage of such peoples should be entrusted to the advanced nations who . . . can best undertake this responsibility." The administration of the mandates fell to the victorious powers of the Great War.

The Mandate System

The Germans interpreted the mandate system as a division of colonial booty by the victors, who had conveniently forgotten to apply the tutelage provision to their own colonies. German cynicism was more than matched by Arab outrage. The establishment of mandates in the former territories of the Ottoman empire violated promises (made to Arabs) by French and British leaders during the war. They had promised Arab nationalists independence from the Ottoman empire and had promised Jewish nationalists in Europe a homeland in Palestine. Where the Arabs hoped to form independent states, the French (in Lebanon and Syria) and the British (in Iraq and Palestine) established mandates. The Allies viewed the mandate system as a reasonable compromise between the reality of imperialism and the ideal of self-determination. To the peoples who were directly affected, the mandate system smacked of continued imperial rule draped in a cloak of respectability.

Primary Source
The Balfour Declaration

Challenges to European Preeminence

When the war ended, it seemed to most Europeans that their global hegemony was more secure than ever. But the Great War did irreparable damage to European power and prestige and set the stage for a process of decolonization that gathered momentum during and after the Second World War. The decline in European power was closely related to diminished economic stature, a result of the commitment to total war. Nothing was more indicative of Europe's reduced economic might than the reversal of the economic relationship between Europe and the United States. Whereas the United States was a debtor nation before 1914, owing billions of dollars to European investors, by 1919 it was a major creditor.

The war also weakened the European hold over colonial territories. Colonial subjects in Africa, Asia, and the Pacific tended to view the Great War as a civil war among the European nations, a bloody spectacle in which the haughty bearers of an alleged superior society vilified and slaughtered one another. Because Europe seemed weak, divided, and vulnerable, the white overlords no longer appeared destined to rule over colonized subjects. The colonials who returned home from the war in Europe and southwest Asia reinforced those general impressions with their own firsthand observations. In particular, they were less inclined to be obedient imperial subjects.

The war also helped spread revolutionary ideas to the colonies. The U.S. war aims spelled out in the Fourteen Points raised the hopes of peoples under imperial rule and promoted nationalist aspirations. The peacemakers repeatedly invoked the concept of self-determination, and Wilson publicly proposed that in all colonial questions "the interests of the native populations be given equal weight with the desires of European governments." Nationalists struggling to organize anti-imperialist resistance also sought inspiration from the Soviet Union, whose leaders denounced all forms of imperialism and pledged their support to independence movements. Taken together, those messages were subversive to imperial control and had a great appeal for colonial peoples. Although nationalist movements endured many setbacks, the days of European global dominance were numbered.

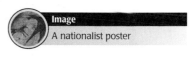

Image
A nationalist poster

SUMMARY

The assassination of the Austrian archduke Francis Ferdinand had a galvanizing effect on a Europe torn by national rivalries, colonial disputes, and demands for self-determination. In the summer of 1914, inflexible war plans and a tangled alliance system transformed a local war between Austria-Hungary and Serbia into a European-wide clash of arms. With the entry of the Ottoman empire, Japan, and the United States, the war of 1914–1918 became a global conflict. Although many belligerents organized their societies for total war and drew on the resources of their overseas empires, the war remained at a bloody stalemate until the United States entered the conflict in 1917. The tide turned, and the combatants signed an armistice in November 1918. The Great War, a brutal encounter between societies and peoples, inflicted ghastly human casualties, severely damaged national economies, and discredited established political and cultural traditions. The war also altered the political landscape of many lands as it destroyed four dynasties and their empires and fostered the creation of several new European nations. In Russia the war served as a backdrop for the world's first successful socialist revolution. In the end the Great War sapped the strength of European colonial powers while it promoted nationalist aspirations among colonized peoples.

CHRONOLOGY

1914	Assassination of Archduke Francis Ferdinand
1915	Japan makes twenty-one demands on China
1915	Gallipoli campaign
1916	Battles at Verdun and the Somme
1917	German resumption of unrestricted submarine warfare
1917	United States declaration of war on Germany
1917	Bolshevik Revolution
1918	Treaty of Brest-Litovsk
1918	Armistice suspends hostilities
1919	Paris Peace Conference
1920	First meeting of the League of Nations

FOR FURTHER READING

Joanna Bourke. *Dismembering the Male: Men's Bodies, Britain, and the Great War.* Chicago, 1996. A study that examines the most intimate site of the war—the bodies of the men who fought it.

Belinda Davis. *Home Fires Burning: Food, Politics, and Everyday Life in World War I Berlin.* Chapel Hill, 2000. Effectively covers daily life in wartime and also offers insights into how government policies during the war affected the reconstruction of society following it.

Niall Ferguson. *The Pity of War: Explaining World War I.* New York, 2000. A stimulating example of revisionist history that shifts the blame for the war away from Germany and onto England.

Paul Fussell. *Great War and Modern Memory.* Oxford, 1975. An original and deeply moving piece of cultural history.

James Joll. *The Origins of the First World War.* 2nd ed. London, 1991. The most lucid and balanced introduction to a complex and controversial subject.

John Keegan. *The First World War.* New York, 1999. A comprehensive and a stunningly vivid account of the Great War.

John Maynard Keynes. *The Economic Consequences of the Peace.* New York, 1920. A classic and devastating critique of the Versailles treaty.

John H. Morrow. *The Great War: An Imperial History.* New York, 2003. A global history of the Great War that places the conflict squarely in the context of imperialism.

Erich Remarque. *All Quiet on the Western Front.* New York, 1958. A fictional account of trench warfare.

Barbara Tuchman. *The Guns of August.* New York, 1962. Spellbinding narrative of the coming of the war.

CHAPTER 31

An Age of Anxiety

Born on a lovely spring day in 1889, in a quaint Austrian village, he was the apple of his mother's eye. He basked in Klara's warmth and indulgence as a youth, enjoying the fine life of a middle-class child. As he grew older, however, he sensed a tension between the competing expectations of his parents. Contented with the dreamy indolence allowed by Klara, he bristled at the demands of his father, Alois, who expected him to study hard and enter the Austrian civil service. He had no desire to become a bureaucrat. In fact, he envisioned a completely different life for himself. He wanted to be an artist.

Alois's unexpected death in 1903 freed him from a future as a bureaucrat. He left school in 1905, not at all dissatisfied with having achieved only a ninth-grade education, because now he could pursue an education as an artist. He followed his ambitions to Vienna, only to find bitter disappointment when the Vienna Academy of Fine Arts rejected him as an art student in 1907. His beloved Klara died the following year, and he meandered the city streets of Vienna, admiring the architecture of the city and attending the opera when his funds permitted.

Eventually, he hit bottom and began staying at a homeless shelter. It was interesting, though, to hear the different political points of view spouted by the shelter's other inhabitants. They discussed compelling issues of the day, and he listened intently to those who hailed the supremacy of the Aryan race and the inferiority of the Jews. He came to hate Jews and Marxists, who he thought had formed an evil union with the

OPPOSITE PAGE: *Edvard Munch,* Anxiety, *1896.*

goal of destroying the world. He also despised liberalism and democracy.

In 1913 he left his Austrian homeland and found refuge in Munich, Germany. In Germany he volunteered for service in the army, which had just embarked on the greatest war ever fought. He discovered in himself a real talent for military service, and he remained in the army for the duration of the war, 1914–1918. Twice wounded and decorated for bravery, he nonetheless found himself in despair at war's end. An impotent rage coursed through him when he learned of Germany's defeat. He knew with all his being that the Jews were responsible for this humiliation, and he also knew that he had to enter the political arena in his chosen fatherland and save the nation. Adolf Hitler had finally found his mission in life.

Hitler (1889–1945) stood as just one personification of Europe's age of anxiety in the early decades of the twentieth century. Embittered by a sense of dislo-

cation and fear stemming from the enormous changes engulfing the society around him, Hitler dedicated himself to discovering a way out of the anxiety for Germany. Ultimately, his solutions brought about more rather than less anxiety, but the novelty and cruelty of his political and military agendas reflected brilliantly the traumatic consequences of the Great War and the Great Depression.

Just as Adolf Hitler changed as a result of his life experiences in the early twentieth century, so too did European society as a whole. Badly shaken by the effects of war, Europeans experienced a shock to their system of values, beliefs, and traditions. Profound scientific and cultural transformations in the postwar decades also contributed to a sense of loss and anxiety. Then, as peoples in Europe and around the world struggled to come to terms with the aftermath of war, an unprecedented economic contraction gripped the international community.

Against the background of the Great Depression, dictators in Russia, Italy, and Germany tried to translate blueprints for utopias into reality. Those political innovations unsettled many Europeans and much of the world, contributing significantly to the anxiety of the age. Moreover, such innovations matched in their radicalness, however strangely, the vast alterations taking place in the intellectual and cultural realms of European society after the Great War.

PROBING CULTURAL FRONTIERS

The Great War discredited established social and political institutions and long-held beliefs about the superiority of European society. Writers, poets, theologians, and other intellectuals lamented the decline and imminent death of their society. While some wrote obituaries, however, others embarked on bold new cultural paths that established the main tendencies of contemporary thought and taste.

The discoveries of physicists undermined the Newtonian universe, in which a set of inexorable natural laws governed events, with a new and disturbing cosmos. Equally discomfiting were the insights of psychoanalysis, which suggested that human behavior was fundamentally irrational. Disquieting trends in the arts paralleled developments in science and psychology. Especially in painting, an aversion to realism and a pronounced preference for abstraction heralded the arrival of new aesthetic standards.

This is one of the few known photographic images of a young Adolf Hitler, taken in 1923.

Postwar Pessimism

"You are all a lost generation," noted Gertrude Stein (1874–1946) to her fellow American writer Ernest Hemingway (1899–1961). Stein had given a label to the group of American intellectuals and literati who congregated in Paris in the postwar years. This "lost generation" expressed in poetry and fiction the malaise and disillusion that characterized U.S. and European thought after the Great War. The brutal realities of industrialized warfare left no room for heroes or glory, and during the 1920s artists and intellectuals spat out their revulsion in a host of war novels, such as Hemingway's *A Farewell to Arms* (1929) and Erich Maria Remarque's *All Quiet on the Western Front* (1929)—works overflowing with images of meaningless death and suffering. Postwar writers lamented the decline of Western society. A retired German schoolteacher named Oswald Spengler (1880–1936) made headlines when he published *The Decline of the West* (1918–1922). In this work, which might have been seen as an obituary of civilization, Spengler proposed that all societies pass through a life cycle of growth and decay comparable to the biological cycle of living organisms. His analysis of the history of western Europe led him to conclude that European society had entered the final stage of its existence. All that remained was irreversible decline, marked by imperialism and warfare.

Theologians joined the chorus of despair. In 1919 Karl Barth (1886–1968), a notable Christian theologian, published a religious bombshell titled *Epistle to the Romans*. In his work Barth sharply attacked the liberal Christian theology that embraced the idea of progress, that is, the tendency of European thinkers to believe in limitless improvement as the realization of God's purpose. The Augustinian, Lutheran, and Calvinist message of original sin—the depravity of human nature—fell on receptive ears as many Christians refused to accept the idea that contemporary human society was in any way a realization of God's purpose. The Russian orthodox thinker Niokolai Berdiaev (1874–1948) summed up those sentiments: "Man's historical experience has been one of steady failure, and there are no grounds for supposing it will be ever anything else."

The Great War destroyed long-cherished beliefs, such as belief in the universality of human progress. Many idols of nineteenth-century progress came under attack, especially science and technology. The scientists' dream of leading humanity to a beneficial conquest of nature seemed to have gone awry, because scientists had spent the war making poisonous gas and high explosives. Democracy was another fallen idol. The idea that people should have a voice in selecting the leaders of their government enjoyed widespread support in European societies. By the early twentieth century, such sentiments had led to universal male suffrage in most societies, and after the Great War many societies also extended the franchise to women. However, many intellectuals abhorred what they viewed as weak political systems that championed the tyranny of the average person. In Germany, for example, a whole school of conservatives lamented the "rule of inferiors."

Revolutions in Physics and Psychology

The postwar decade witnessed a revolution in physics that transformed the character of science. Albert Einstein (1879–1955) struck the first blow with his theory of special relativity (1905), showing that there is no single spatial and chronological framework in the universe. According to the theory, it no longer makes

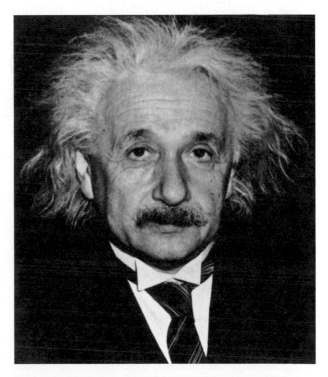

One of the best-known faces of the twentieth century, Albert Einstein was the symbol of the revolution in physics.

sense to speak of space and time as absolutes, because the measurement of those two categories always varies with the motion of the observer. That is, space and time are relative to the person measuring them. To the layperson such notions suggested that a commonsense universe had vanished, to be replaced by a radically new one in which reality or truth was merely relative.

The Uncertainty Principle More disquieting even than Einstein's discoveries was the theory formulated by Werner Heisenberg (1901–1976), who in 1927 established the "uncertainty principle." According to Heisenberg, it is impossible to specify simultaneously the position and the velocity of a subatomic particle. The more accurately one determines the position of an electron, the less precisely one can determine its velocity, and vice versa. In essence, scientists cannot observe the behavior of electrons objectively, because the act of observation interferes with them.

It quickly became evident that the uncertainty principle had important implications beyond physics. Indeed, Heisenberg's theory called into question established notions of truth. Likewise, objectivity as it was understood was no longer a valid concept, because the observer was always part of the process under observation. Accordingly, any observer—an anthropologist studying another society, for instance—had to be alert to the fact that his or her very presence became an integral part of the study.

Freud's Psychoanalytic Theory As equally unsettling as the advances in physics were developments in psychology that challenged established concepts of morality and values. Beginning in 1896, the Austrian medical doctor Sigmund Freud (1856–1939) embarked on research that focused on psychological rather than physiological explanations of mental disorders. Through his clinical observations of patients, Freud identified a conflict between conscious and unconscious mental processes that lay at the root of neurotic behavior. That conflict, moreover, suggested to him the existence of a repressive mechanism that keeps painful memories away from the conscious mind. Freud believed that dreams held the key to the deepest recesses of the human psyche. Using the free associations of patients to guide him in the interpretation of dreams, he identified sexual drives and fantasies as the most important source of repression. For example, Freud claimed to have discovered a so-called Oedipus complex, in which male children develop an erotic attachment to their mother and hostility toward their father.

A striking painted portrait of Sigmund Freud.

In the end, Freudian doctrines shaped the psychiatric profession and established a powerful presence in literature and the arts. During the 1920s, novelists, poets, and painters acknowledged Freud's influence as they focused on the inner world of their characters. The creators of imaginative literature used Freud's bold emphasis on sexuality as a tool for the interpretation and understanding of human behavior.

Experimentation in Art and Architecture

The roots of contemporary painting go back to nineteenth-century French avant-garde artists who disdained realism and instead were concerned with freedom of expression. The aversion to visual realism was heightened by the spread of photography. When everyone could create naturalistic landscapes or portraits with a camera, it made little sense for artists to do the same with paint and brush. Thus painters began to think that the purpose of a painting was not to mirror reality but to create it.

At the beginning of the twentieth century, this new aesthetic led to the emergence of a bewildering variety of pictorial schools, all of which promised an entirely new art. Regardless of whether they called themselves expressionists, cubists, abstractionists, dadaists, or surrealists, artists generally agreed on a program "to abolish the sovereignty of appearance." Paintings no longer depicted recognizable objects from the everyday world, and beauty was expressed in pure color or shape. Some painters sought to express feelings and emotions through violent distortion of forms and the use of explosive colors; others, influenced by Freudian psychology, tried to tap the subconscious mind to communicate an inner vision or a dream.

The artistic heritages of Asian, Pacific, and African societies fertilized various strains of contemporary painting. Nineteenth-century Japanese prints, for example, influenced French impressionists such as Edgar Degas (1834–1917). The deliberate violation of perspective by Japanese painters and their stress on the flat, two-dimensional surface of the picture, their habit of placing figures off center, and their use of primary colors encouraged European artists to take similar liberties with realism. In Germany a group of young artists *Artistic Influences*

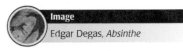
Image
Edgar Degas, *Absinthe*

known as the "Bridge" made a point of regularly visiting the local ethnographic museum to be inspired by the boldness and power of indigenous art. The early works of Pablo Picasso (1881–1973), the leading

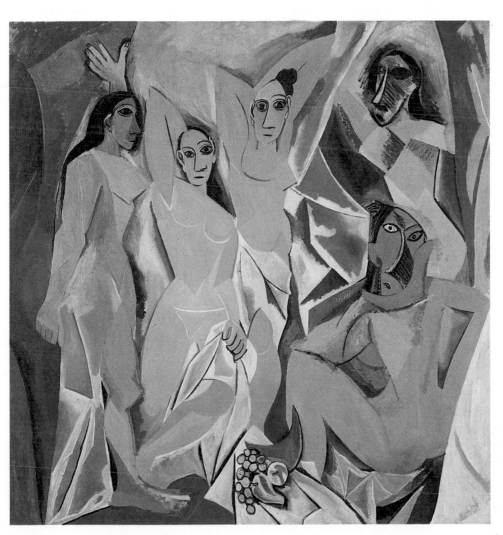

Pablo Picasso's *Les Demoiselles d'Avignon* (1907) was the first of what would be called cubist works. This image had a profound impact on subsequent art.

proponent of cubism, displayed the influence of African art forms.

By the third decade of the twentieth century, it was nearly impossible to generalize about contemporary painting. All artists were acknowledged to have a right to their own reality, and generally accepted standards that distinguished between "good" and "bad" art disappeared.

GLOBAL DEPRESSION

After the horrors and debilitating upheavals of the Great War, much of the world yearned for a return to normality and prosperity. By the early 1920s the efforts of governments and businesses to rebuild damaged economies seemed to be bearing fruit. Prosperity, however, was short-lived. In 1929 the world plunged into an economic depression that was so long-lasting, so severe, and so global that it has become known as the Great Depression. The old capitalist system of trade and finance collapsed, and until a new system took its place after 1945, a return to worldwide prosperity could not occur.

The Great Depression

By the middle of the 1920s, most countries seemed on the way to economic recovery, and industrial productivity had returned to prewar levels. But that prosperity was fragile, perhaps false, and many serious problems and dislocations remained in the international economy.

The economic recovery and well-being of Europe, for example, was tied to a tangled and interdependent financial system. In essence, the governments of Austria and Germany relied on U.S. loans and investment capital to finance reparation payments to France and England. The French and British governments, in turn, depended on those reparation payments to pay off loans taken out in the United States during the Great War. Strain on any one part of the system, then, inevitably strained them all.

Economic Problems

There were other problems as well. Improvements in industrial processes reduced worldwide demand for certain raw materials, which had devastating consequences for export-dependent areas. Technological advances in the production of automobile tires, for instance, permitted the use of reclaimed rubber. The resulting glut of natural rubber badly damaged the economies of the Dutch East Indies, Ceylon, and Malaysia, which relied on rubber exports. Similarly, the increased use of oil undermined the coal industry, and the growing adoption of artificial nitrogen virtually ruined the nitrate industry of Chile.

One of the nagging weaknesses of the global economy in the 1920s was the depressed state of agriculture. During the Great War, when Europe's agricultural output declined significantly, farmers in the United States, Canada, Argentina, and Australia expanded their own production. At the end of the war, European farmers resumed their agricultural activity, thereby contributing to worldwide surpluses. As production increased, prices collapsed throughout the world. By 1929 the price of a bushel of wheat was at its lowest level in four hundred years, and farmers everywhere became impoverished. The reduced income of farm families contributed to high inventories of manufactured goods, which in turn caused businesses to cut back production and to dismiss workers.

The United States enjoyed a boom after the Great War, which prompted many people in the United States to invest their earnings and savings in speculative and risky financial ventures, particularly in stocks. By October 1929, warnings from experts that stock prices were overvalued prompted investors to pull out of the market. On Black Thursday (24 October), a wave of panic selling on the New York Stock Exchange caused stock prices to plummet. Investors who had overextended themselves through speculative stock purchases watched in agony. Thousands of people, from poor widows to industrial tycoons, lost their life savings, and by the end of the day eleven financiers had committed suicide. The crisis deepened when lenders called in loans, thereby forcing more investors to sell their securities at any price.

The Crash of 1929

In the wake of this financial chaos came a drastic decrease in business activity, wages, and employment. When businesses realized that shrinking consumer demand meant they could not sell their inventories, they responded with layoffs. With so many people unemployed, demand plummeted further, causing more business failures and soaring unemployment. In 1930 the slump deepened, and by 1932 industrial production had fallen to half of its 1929 level. National income had dropped by approximately half, and 44 percent of U.S. banks were out of business. Because much of the world's prosperity depended on the export of U.S. capital and the strength of U.S. import markets, the con-

Economic Contraction Spreads

traction of the U.S. economy created a ripple effect that circled the globe.

Most societies experienced economic difficulties throughout the 1930s. Virtually every industrialized society saw its economy shrivel, but nations that relied on exports of manufactured goods to pay for imported fuel and food—Germany and Japan in particular—suffered the most. The depression also spread to primary producing economies in Latin America, Africa, and Asia. Hardest hit were countries that depended on the export of a few primary products such as coffee, sugar, minerals, ores, and rubber.

U.S. investors, shaken by the collapse of stock prices, tried to raise money by calling in loans and liquidating investments, and Wall Street banks refused to extend short-term loans as they became due. Banking houses in Austria and Germany became vulnerable to collapse, because they had been major recipients of U.S. loans. Devastated by the loss of U.S. capital, the German economy experienced a precipitous economic slide that by 1932 resulted in 35 percent unemployment and a 50 percent decrease in industrial production. As the German economy—which had remained a leading economic power in Europe throughout the postwar years—ground to a virtual halt, the rest of Europe sputtered and stalled with it. Likewise, because of its great dependence on the U.S. market, the Japanese economy felt the depression's effects almost immediately. Unemployment in export-oriented sectors of the economy skyrocketed as companies cut back on production.

The Great Depression destroyed the international financial and commercial network of the capitalist economies. As international cooperation *Economic Nationalism* broke down, governments turned to their own resources and practiced economic nationalism. By imposing tariff barriers, import quotas, and import prohibitions, politicians hoped to achieve self-sufficiency. Yet economic nationalism invariably backfired. Each new measure designed to restrict imports provoked retaliation by other nations whose interests were affected. After the U.S. Congress passed the Smoot-Hawley Tariff Act in 1930, which raised duties on most manufactured products to prohibitive levels, the governments of dozens of other nations retaliated by raising tariffs on imports of U.S. products. The result was a sharp drop in international trade. Between 1929 and 1932, world production declined by 38 percent and trade dropped by more than 66 percent.

Despair and Government Action

By 1933 unemployment in industrial societies had reached thirty million, more than five times higher than in 1929. Both men and women lost their jobs, and over the course of the depression most governments enacted policies restricting female employment, especially for married women. Indeed, the notion that a woman's place was in the home was widespread, and some—such as the French physician Charles Richet (1850–1935)—even insisted that removing women from the workforce would solve the problem of male unemployment.

The Great Depression caused enormous personal suffering. The stark statistics documenting the failure of economies do not convey the anguish and despair of those who lost their jobs, Image — A depression-era breadline savings, and homes. For millions of people the struggle for food, clothing, and shelter grew desperate. Shantytowns appeared overnight in urban areas, and breadlines stretched for blocks. Marriage, childbearing, and

Dorothea Lange, *Migrant Mother, Nipomo California* (1936). A famous photograph of the Great Depression.

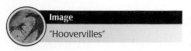
"Hoovervilles"

divorce rates declined, and suicide rates rose. Those simply trying to survive came to despise the wealthy, who, despite their own reduced incomes, remained shielded from the worst impact of the economic downturn. Adolescents completing their schooling faced an almost nonexistent job market.

Economic Experimentation

Classical economic thought held that capitalism was a self-correcting system that operated best when left to its own devices. Thus, in the initial stages of the depression most governments did nothing, hoping that the crisis would resolve itself. Faced with such human misery, however, some governments assumed more active roles, pursuing deflationary measures by balancing national budgets and curtailing public spending. Rather than lifting national economies out of the doldrums, however, those remedies only worsened the depression's impact. Far from self-correcting, capitalism seemed to be dying. Many people called for a fundamental revision of economic thought.

John Maynard Keynes (1883–1946), the most influential economist of the twentieth century, offered a novel solution. In his seminal work, *The General Theory of Employment, Interest, and Money* (1936), he argued that the fundamental cause of the depression was not excessive supply but inadequate demand. Accordingly, he urged governments to stimulate the economy by increasing the money supply, thereby lowering interest rates and encouraging investment. He also advised governments to undertake public works projects to provide jobs and redistribute incomes through tax policy. Such intervention would result in reduced unemployment and increased consumer demand, which would lead to economic revival. These measures were necessary even if they caused governments to run deficits and maintain unbalanced budgets.

Keynes

Although Keynes's theories did not become influential with policymakers until after World War II, the administration of U.S. president Franklin Delano Roosevelt (1882–1945) anticipated his ideas. Roosevelt took aggressive steps to reinflate the economy and ease the worst of the suffering caused by the depression. His program for dealing with the national calamity—called the New Deal—included legislation designed to prevent the collapse of the banking system, to provide jobs and farm subsidies, to guarantee minimum wages, and to provide social security in old age. Its fundamental premise, that the federal government was justified in protecting the social and economic welfare of the people, represented a major shift in U.S. government policy and started a trend toward social reform legislation that continued long after the depression years.

The New Deal

Primary Source
FDR on the New Deal

Human faces of the Great Depression: children bathing in the Ozark Mountains, Missouri, 1940.

CHALLENGES TO THE LIBERAL ORDER

Amid the gloom and despair of the Great Depression, some voices proclaimed the promise of a better tomorrow. Marxists believed that capitalist society was on its deathbed, and they had faith that a new and better system based on rule by the proletariat was being born out of the ashes of the Russian empire. The new rulers of Russia, Vladimir Ilyich Lenin and then Joseph Stalin, transformed the former tsarist empire into the world's first socialist society, the Union

Image
Lenin giving a speech

of Soviet Socialist Republics (1922). Other people, uncomfortable with socialism, found solace in fascist movements, which seemed to offer revolutionary answers to the economic, social, and political problems of the day. Among these fascist movements, the Italian and German ones figured most prominently.

SOURCES FROM THE PAST

Franklin Delano Roosevelt: Nothing to Fear

Franklin Delano Roosevelt (1882–1945) assumed the presidency of the United States on 4 March 1933, during the very depths of the Great Depression. In his inaugural address to the nation, he conveyed both the anxiousness of the times and the seemingly unquenchable optimism that carried him—and his nation—through hard times. A vastly wealthy man serving as president during a time of devastating penury, Roosevelt nonetheless gained the admiration and respect of the people because of his warm eloquence and compassion. Although he hid his condition quite successfully during his time in public, FDR had contracted polio in the 1920s and had lost the use of his legs. This "crippled" president became a metaphor for the United States' economic collapse but also for its ability to overcome fear itself.

■ ■ ■

I am certain that my fellow Americans expect that on my induction into the Presidency I will address them with a candor and a decision which the present situation of our Nation impels. This is preeminently the time to speak the truth, the whole truth, frankly and boldly. Nor need we shrink from honestly facing conditions in our country today. This great Nation will endure as it has endured, will revive and will prosper. So, first of all, let me assert my firm belief that the only thing we have to fear is fear itself—nameless, unreasoning, unjustified terror which paralyzes needed efforts to convert retreat into advance. In every dark hour of our national life a leadership of frankness and vigor has met with that understanding and support of the people themselves which is essential to victory. I am convinced that you will again give that support to leadership in these critical days.

In such a spirit on my part and on yours we face our common difficulties. They concern, thank God, only material things. Values have shrunken to fantastic levels; taxes have risen; our ability to pay has fallen; government of all kinds is faced by serious curtailment of income; the means of exchange are frozen in the currents of trade; the withered leaves of industrial enterprise lie on every side; farmers find no markets for their produce; the savings of many years in thousands of families are gone.

More important, a host of unemployed citizens face the grim problem of existence, and an equally great number toil with little return. Only a foolish optimist can deny the dark realities of the moment. . . .

Happiness lies not in the mere possession of money; it lies in the joy of achievement, in the thrill of creative effort. The joy and moral stimulation of work no longer must be forgotten in the mad chase of evanescent profits. These dark days will be worth all they cost us if they teach us that our true destiny is not to be ministered unto but to minister to ourselves and to our fellow men.

- *How does Roosevelt believe U.S. citizens can profit from the dark days of the Great Depression, and why is it that all they have to fear is fear itself?*

SOURCE: Franklin D. Roosevelt, First Inaugural Address, 4 March 1933, available at The Avalon Project at http://www.yale.edu/lawweb/avalon/president/inaug/froos1.htm.

Communism in Russia

In 1917 Lenin and his fellow Bolsheviks had taken power in the name of the Russian working class, but socialist victory did not bring peace and stability to the lands of the former Russian empire. After seizing power, Lenin and his supporters had to defend the world's first "dictatorship of the proletariat" against numerous internal and external enemies.

Opposition to the Bolshevik Party—by now calling itself the Russian Communist Party—erupted into a civil war that lasted from 1918 to 1920. In response, Lenin's government began a policy of terror in which 200,000 suspected

Civil War

anticommunists (known as Whites) were arrested, tried, and executed. In July 1918 the Bolsheviks executed Tsar Nicholas II, Empress Alexandra, and their five children because they feared that the Romanov family could strengthen counterrevolutionary forces. White terror was often equally as brutal as Red terror. The peasantry, although hostile to the communists, largely supported the Bolsheviks, fearing that a victory by the Whites would result in the return of the monarchy.

Meanwhile, foreign powers in Britain, France, Japan, and the United States, angry over Russia's withdrawal from the Great War and inflamed by anticommunism, supported the Whites and sent a limited number of troops and supplies to aid them. Their efforts failed, however, and in 1920 the Red Army defeated the Whites. The costs of war were devastating: estimates place the number of lives lost in the civil war at ten million, mostly from disease and starvation. Moreover, the political system that emerged from the civil war bore the imprint of political oppression, which played a significant role in the later development of the Soviet state.

Over the course of the civil war, the new rulers of Russia transformed the economy by embarking on a
War Communism
hasty and unplanned course of nationalization, known as war communism. After officially annulling private property, the Bolshevik government assumed control of banks, industry, and other privately held commercial properties. Landed estates and the holdings of monasteries and churches also became national property. Private trade was abolished, and the party seized crops from peasants to feed people in the cities. This last measure proved especially unpopular and caused peasants to drastically reduce their production. By 1920 industrial production had fallen to about one-tenth of its prewar level and agricultural output to about half its prewar level.

In 1921, as the Reds consolidated their military victories after the civil war, the Soviet economy was in
The New Economic Policy
a shambles. Workers were on strike, cities were depopulated, and factories were destroyed. Faced with economic paralysis, in the spring of 1921 Lenin decided on a radical reversal of war communism. In its place he implemented the New Economic Policy (NEP), which temporarily restored the market economy and some private enterprise in Russia. Large industries and banks remained under state control, but the government re-

turned small-scale industries to private ownership. The government also allowed peasants to sell their surpluses at free-market prices. Other features of the NEP included a vigorous program of electrification and the establishment of technical schools to train technicians and engineers. Lenin did not live to see the success of the NEP. After suffering three paralytic strokes, he died in 1924.

After a bitter political struggle for power, Joseph Stalin (1879–1953), general secretary of the Communist Party, emerged as the new leader of
Joseph Stalin
the Soviet Union in 1928. A Georgian by birth, an Orthodox seminarian by training, and a Russian nationalist by conviction, Stalin indicated his unified resolve to gain power in his surname, which meant "man of steel." His first economic program, which replaced Lenin's NEP, was both ambitious and ruthless. Indeed, Stalin's First Five-Year Plan, implemented in 1929, aimed at nothing less than transforming the Soviet Union from a predominantly agricultural country to a leading industrial power. The First Five-Year Plan set targets for increased productivity in all spheres of

Joseph Stalin at a Soviet congress in 1936.

the economy but emphasized heavy industry—especially steel and machinery—at the expense of consumer goods. As the rest of the world teetered on the edge of economic collapse, Stalin's plan offered a bold alternative to market capitalism. Stalin repeatedly stressed the urgency of this monumental endeavor, telling his people, "We are 50 to 100 years behind the advanced countries. Either we do it, or we shall go under."

Integral to the drive for industrialization was the collectivization of agriculture. The Soviet state ex-

Collectivization of Agriculture

propriated privately owned land to create collective, or cooperative, farm units whose profits were shared by all farmers. Stalin and his regime viewed collectivization as a means of increasing the efficiency of agricultural production and ensuring that industrial workers would be fed.

In some places, outraged peasants reacted to the government's program by slaughtering their livestock and burning their crops. Faced with enforced collectivization, millions of farmers left the land and migrated to cities in search of work. Those who stayed behind were often unable to meet production quotas and starved to death on the land they once owned. When Stalin called a halt to collectivization in 1931, half the farms in the Soviet Union had been collectivized. Estimates of the cost in number of peasant lives lost have fluctuated wildly, but even the most cautious place it at three million. Among them, the *kulaks*—relatively wealthy peasants who had risen to prosperity during the NEP—were nearly eliminated.

The Soviet leadership proclaimed the First Five-Year Plan a success after only four years. The Soviet Union industrialized under Stalin even though the emphasis on building heavy industry first and consumer industries later meant that citizens postponed the gratifications of industrialization. However, the scarcity or nonexistence of such consumer goods as refrigerators, radios, and automobiles was to some degree balanced by full employment, low-cost utilities, and cheap housing and food. Set against the economic collapse of the capitalist world, the ability of a centrally planned economy to create more jobs than workers could fill made it appear an attractive alternative.

Nevertheless, the disaster of collectivization and the ruthlessness with which it was carried out had raised

The Great Purge

doubts about Stalin's administration. As the Communist Party prepared for its seventeenth congress in 1934, the "Congress of

Victors," Stalin learned of a plan to bring more pluralism back into leadership. The Congress of Victors quickly became the "Congress of Victims" as Stalin purged two-thirds of the delegates from the Communist Party. Between 1935 and 1938 Stalin removed from posts of authority all persons suspected of opposition, including more than half the army's high-ranking officers. In 1939 eight million Soviet citizens faced long-term suffering in labor camps, and three million were dead as a result of the "cleansing," as Stalin's supporters termed this process.

The outside world watched the events unfolding within the Soviet Union with a mixture of contempt, fear, and admiration. The establishment of the world's first dictatorship of the proletariat challenged the values and institutions of liberal society all over the world and seemed to demonstrate the viability of communism as a social and political system.

The Fascist Alternative

While socialism was transforming the former Russian empire, another political force swept across Europe after the Great War. Fascism, a political movement and ideology that sought to create a new type of society, developed as a reaction against liberal democracy and the spread of socialism and communism. In 1919 Benito Mussolini founded the first fascist party. Movements comparable to Italian fascism subsequently developed in many European societies, most notably in Germany in the guise of National Socialism (Nazism). Although fascism enjoyed widespread popularity in many European countries, it rarely threatened the political order and overthrew parliamentary systems only in Italy and Germany. Although potential fascist movements sprang up during the 1930s in Japan, China, and South Africa; in Latin American societies such as Brazil and Argentina; and in several Arab lands, fascism nevertheless remained basically a European phenomenon in the era between the two world wars.

During the 1920s and 1930s, fascism attracted millions of followers and proved especially attractive to middle classes and rural populations. Those groups became radicalized by economic and social crises and were especially fearful of the perceived threat from the political left. Fascism also proved attractive to nationalists of all classes. Asserting that society faced a profound crisis, fascists sought to create a new national community, which they defined either as a nation-state or as a unique ethnic or racial group. Although each fascist movement had its own unique characteristics, most nevertheless shared certain common features, such as the veneration of the state, a devotion to a strong leader, and an emphasis on ultranationalism, ethnocentrism, and militarism.

Fascist ideology consistently invoked the primacy of the state, which stood at the center of the nation's life and history. Strong and charismatic leaders, such as Benito Mussolini in Italy and Adolf Hitler in Germany, embodied the state and claimed indisputable authority. Consequently, fascists were hostile to liberal democracy, which they viewed as weak and decadent. Fascism was also extremely hostile to socialism and communism. Fascist movements emphasized a belligerent form of nationalism (chauvinism) and a fear of foreign people (xenophobia), which they frequently linked to an exaggerated ethnocentrism. The typical fascist state also embraced militarism, a belief in the rigors and virtues of military life as an individual and national ideal. In practice, militarism meant that fascist regimes maintained large and expensive military establishments, tried to organize much of public life along military lines, and generally showed a fondness for uniforms, parades, and monumental architecture.

Italian Fascism

The first fascist movement grew in Italy after the Great War. Conditions conducive to the rise of fascism included a widespread disillusionment with uninspired political leadership and ineffective government, extensive economic turmoil and social discontent, and a growing fear of socialism. In addition, there was vast disappointment over Italy's skimpy territorial spoils from the peace settlement after the Great War.

Benito Mussolini The guiding force behind Italian fascism was Benito Mussolini, a former socialist who turned, after the Great War, to a political program that emphasized virulent nationalism, demanded repression of socialists, and called for a strong political leader. In 1919 he established the Fasci Italiani di Combattimento (Italian Combat Veteran League). Mussolini's movement gained widespread support after 1920, and by 1921 his league managed to have thirty-five fascists elected to the Italian parliament. Much of the newly found public support resulted from the effective use of violence against socialists by fascist armed squads known as Blackshirts. In 1922 Mussolini and his followers decided the time was ripe for a fascist seizure of power, and on 28 October they staged a march on Rome. While Mussolini

stayed safely in Milan, thousands of his black-shirted troops converged on Rome. Rather than calling on the military to oppose the fascist threat, King Victor Emmanuel III hastily asked Mussolini on 29 October to become prime minister and form a new government. Mussolini inaugurated a fascist regime in 1922.

Between 1925 and 1931, Italy's fascists consolidated their power through a series of laws that transformed the nation into a one-party dictatorship. In 1926 Mussolini seized *The Fascist State* total power as dictator and subsequently ruled Italy as Il Duce ("the leader"). The regime moved quickly to eliminate all other political parties, curb the freedom of the press, and outlaw free speech and association. A Special Tribunal for the Defense of the State, supervised by military officers, silenced political dissent. Marked as antifascist "subversives," thousands of Italians found themselves imprisoned or exiled on remote islands, and some faced capital punishment. Allying himself and his movement with business and

Italian dictator Benito Mussolini strikes a dramatic pose on horseback in 1940.

landlord interests, Il Duce also crushed labor unions and prohibited strikes. In 1932, on the tenth anniversary of the fascist seizure of power, Mussolini felt confident enough to announce that "the twentieth century will be a century of fascism, the century of Italian power."

Although racism and anti-Semitism were never prominent components of Italian fascism, in 1938 the government suddenly issued a series of anti-Semitic laws. That development may have been occasioned by Mussolini's newly found friendship with fellow dictator Adolf Hitler. In 1936 Mussolini told his followers that from now on, world history would revolve around a Rome-Berlin axis. In May 1939 the leaders of fascist Italy and Nazi Germany formalized their political, military, and ideological alliance by signing a ten-year Pact of Steel.

Axis rally

German National Socialism

After Adolf Hitler's postwar political awakening, he came into contact with an obscure political party sympathetic to his ideas. In 1921 he became chairman of the party now known as the National Socialist German Workers' Party. National Socialism (the Nazi movement) made its first major appearance in 1923 when party members and Hitler attempted to overthrow the democratic Weimar Republic, which had replaced the German empire in 1919. The revolt was a failure, however, and Hitler was jailed. When Hitler emerged from prison in 1924, he resolved to gain power legally through the ballot box and, once successful, to discard the very instrument of his success.

Hitler and the Nazi Party

National Socialism made rapid gains after 1929 because it had broad appeal. Hitler attracted disillusioned people, many of whom blamed the young German democracy for Germany's misfortunes: a humiliating peace treaty— the Treaty of Versailles—that identified Germany as responsible for the Great War and assigned reparation payments to the Allies; the hyperinflation of the early 1920s that wiped out the savings of the middle class; and the suffering brought on by the Great Depression. Adolf Hitler promised an end to all those misfortunes by creating a new order that would lead to greatness for Germany. By stressing racial doctrines, particularly anti-Semitism, the Nazis added a unique and frightening twist to their ideology. Although the Nazis

The Struggle for Power

avoided class divisions by recruiting followers from all strata of society, National Socialism in the main appealed to the members of the lower-middle classes: ruined shopkeepers, impoverished farmers, discharged white-collar workers, and disenchanted students.

As Germany slipped into the Great Depression, the government's inability to find solutions to unemployment and impoverishment radicalized the electorate and caused them to lose faith in the democratic system. Between 1930 and 1932 the Nazi Party became the largest party in parliament, and the reactionary and feeble president, Paul von Hindenburg (1847–1934), decided to offer Hitler the chancellorship. Hitler lost little time in transforming the dying republic into a single-party dictatorship. He promised a German *Reich,* or empire, that would endure for a thousand years.

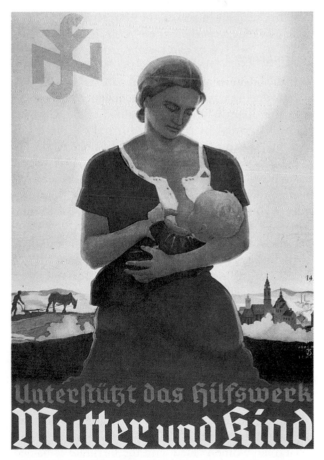

"Mother and Child" was the slogan on this poster, idealizing and encouraging motherhood. The background conveys the Nazi predilection for the wholesome country life, a dream that clashed with the urban reality of German society.

Consolidation of Power

Under the guise of a state of national emergency, the Nazis used all available means to impose their rule. They began by eliminating all working-class and liberal opposition. The Nazis suppressed the German communist and socialist parties and abrogated virtually all constitutional and civil rights. Subsequently, Hitler made the National Socialist Party the only legal party. Between 1933 and 1935 the regime replaced Germany's federal structure with a highly centralized state. The National Socialist state then guided the destruction of trade unions and the elimination of collective bargaining, subsequently prohibiting strikes and lockouts. The Nazis also purged the judiciary and the civil service, took control of all police forces, and removed enemies of the regime—both real and imagined—through incarceration or murder.

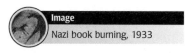

Image
Nazi book burning, 1933

Once securely in power, the Nazi regime translated racist ideology, especially the notions of racial superiority and racial purity, into practice.

The Racial State

The leaders of the Third Reich pursued the creation of a race-based national community by introducing eugenic measures designed to improve both the quantity and the "quality" of the German "race." Alarmed by declining birthrates, the Nazis launched a campaign to increase births of "racially valuable" children. Through tax credits, special child allowances, and marriage loans, the authorities tried to encourage marriage and, they hoped, procreation among young people. At the same time, the regime outlawed abortions, restricted birth control devices, and made it difficult to obtain information about family planning. The Nazis also became enamored of pronatalist (to increase births) propaganda and set in motion a veritable cult of motherhood. Annually on 12 August—the birth date of Hitler's mother—women who bore many children received the Honor Cross of the German Mother in three classes: bronze for those with more than four children, silver for those with more than six, and gold for those with more than eight. By August 1939 three million women carried this prestigious award, which many Germans cynically called the "rabbit decoration." In the long term, however, any efforts by the Nazis to increase the fecundity of German women failed, and the birthrate remained below replacement level.

The quantity of offspring was not the only concern of the new rulers, who were obsessed with "qual-

ity." Starting in 1933, the regime initiated a compulsory sterilization program for men and women whom the regime had identified as having "hereditarily determined" sicknesses, including schizophrenia, manic depression, hereditary blindness, hereditary deafness, and serious physical deformities. Between 1934 and 1939 more than thirty thousand men and women underwent compulsory sterilization. The mania for "racial health" culminated in a state-sponsored euthanasia ("mercy killing") program that was responsible for the murder of approximately two hundred thousand women, men, and children. Between 1939 and 1945 the Nazis systematically killed those people judged useless to society, especially the physically and mentally handicapped.

Anti-Semitism, or prejudice against Jews, was a key element in the designs to achieve a new racial order. Immediately after coming to power in 1933, the Nazis initiated systematic measures to suppress Germany's Jewish population. A flood of discriminatory laws and directives designed to humiliate, impoverish, and segregate Jews from the rest of society followed. In 1935 the notorious Nuremberg Laws deprived German Jews of their citizenship and prohibited marriage and sexual intercourse between Jews and other Germans. The Nazi party, in cooperation with government agencies, banks, and businesses, took steps to eliminate Jews from economic life and expropriate their wealth. Party authorities also supervised the liquidation of Jewish-owned businesses or argued for their purchase—at

A Nazi "racial expert" uses a caliper to measure the racial purity of a German.

much less than their true value—by companies owned or operated by non-Jews.

The official goal of the Nazi regime was Jewish emigration. Throughout the 1930s thousands of Jews left Germany, depriving the nation of many of its leading intellectuals, scientists, and artists. The exodus gained urgency after what came to be known as "the night of broken glass" *(Kristallnacht)*. During the night of 9–10 November 1938, the Nazis arranged for the destruction of thousands of Jewish stores, the burning of most synagogues, and the murder of more than one hundred Jews throughout Germany and Austria. This *pogrom* (a Yiddish term for devastation) was a signal that the position of Jews in Hitler's Reich was about to deteriorate dramatically. Indeed, approximately 250,000 Jews had left Germany by 1938. Those staying behind, especially the poor and the elderly, contemplated an uncertain destiny.

SUMMARY

In the decades after the Great War, European intellectuals questioned and challenged established traditions. While scientists and social thinkers conceived new theories that reshaped human knowledge and perceptions, artists forged a contemporary aesthetic. In an age of global interdependence, the U.S. stock market crash of 1929 ushered in a period of prolonged economic contraction and social misery that engulfed much of the world. As most of the industrialized world reeled under the impact of the Great Depression, the leadership of the Soviet Union embarked on a state-sponsored program of rapid industrialization that, despite causing widespread suffering, transformed the Soviet Union into a major industrial and military power.

Italians under the leadership of Mussolini rebuilt their state through fascist policies and imperial expansion. In Germany the effects of the Great Depression paved the way for the establishment of the Nazi state, which was based on the principle of racial inequality. Although many different peoples suffered under the new regime, Jews were the principal victims of the Nazi racial state. Adolf Hitler's mission in life, envisioned in the wake of the Great War, was coming to a spectacular conclusion that culminated in another world war. That war brought both the fulfillment and the destruction of the goals and dreams he had crafted in an age of anxiety.

CHRONOLOGY

1905	Einstein publishes special theory of relativity
1907	Picasso paints *Les Demoiselles d'Avignon*
1918–1920	Civil war in Russia
1919	Mussolini launches fascist movement in Italy
1921–1928	Lenin's New Economic Policy
1927	Heisenberg establishes "uncertainty principle"
1928–1932	First Soviet Five-Year Plan
1929	U.S. stock market crash
1929	Beginning of Great Depression
1929	Hemingway and Remarque publish antiwar novels
1933–1945	Hitler is ruler in Germany
1935–1938	Stalin's "Great Purge" in the Soviet Union

FOR FURTHER READING

Martin Broszat. *The Hitler State: The Foundation and Development of the Internal Structure of the Third Reich*. New York, 1981. An account that does justice to the complexity of the Nazi movement and its rule.

Robert Conquest. *Stalin: Breaker of Nations*. New York, 1991. A compelling and absorbing biography.

Sheila Fitzpatrick. *The Russian Revolution, 1917–1932*. 2nd ed. New York, 1984. This work stands out for the author's ability to make complex processes accessible to the general reader and still instruct the specialist.

George Gamow. *Thirty Years That Shook Physics*. Garden City, N.Y., 1966. A leading physicist engagingly tells the story of modern physics.

Peter Gay. *Freud: A Life for Our Time*. New York, 1988. A balanced biography of one of the most influential social thinkers of the twentieth century.

George Heard Hamilton. *Painting and Sculpture in Europe, 1880–1940*. 6th ed. New Haven, 1993. A classic that presents a discerning overview of the subject.

Ian Kershaw. *The Nazi Dictatorship: Problems and Perspectives of Interpretation*. 2nd ed. London, 1989. A superb assessment that also provides the best introduction to the enormous literature on the Third Reich.

A. J. H. Latham. *The Depression and the Developing World, 1914–1939*. London, 1981. One of the few works that look beyond the industrialized world to give a global perspective on the subject.

Robert Paxton. *The Anatomy of Fascism*. New York, 2004. A groundbreaking and fascinating history of fascism.

Richard Pipes. *The Russian Revolution*. New York, 1990. When the Communist Party collapsed in 1991, this sweeping study was quickly translated into Russian and became a national best seller.

CHAPTER 32

Nationalism and Political Identities in Asia, Africa, and Latin America

Shanfei lived in politically exciting times. The daughter of a wealthy Chinese landowner, she grew up amid luxury and opportunity. Shanfei, however, matured into a woman who rejected the rich trappings of her youth. Her formative years were marked by the unsettling political and cultural changes that engulfed the globe in the wake of the Great War. The rise of nationalism and communism in China after the revolution of 1911 and the Russian revolution in 1917 guided the transformation of Shanfei—from a girl ruled by tradition and privilege, she became an active revolutionary.

With the exception of Shanfei's father, the members of her family in Hunan province took in the new spirit of the first decades of the twentieth century. Her brothers returned from school with compelling ideas, including some that challenged the subordinate position of women in China. Shanfei's mother, to all appearances a woman who accepted her subservience to her husband, listened quietly to her sons as they discussed new views and then applied them to her daughter. She used every means at her disposal to persuade her husband to educate their daughter. He relented but still insisted that Shanfei receive an old-fashioned education and submit to foot binding and childhood betrothal.

When Shanfei was eleven years old, her father suddenly died. Shanfei's mother took the opportunity to rip the bandages off Shanfei's feet and send her to a modern school. In the lively atmosphere of her school, Shanfei bloomed into an activist. At sixteen she incited a student strike against the administration of her

OPPOSITE PAGE: *In this cigarette advertisement from 1935, Chinese women are shown challenging traditions. They are "new women," affected by the radical changes in identity and behavior taking place after the Great War and during the Great Depression.*

school, transferred to a more modern school, and became famous as a leader in the student movement. She broke tradition in both her personal and her political life. In 1926 Shanfei abandoned her studies to join the Communist Youth, and she gave up her fiancé for a free marriage to the man she loved: a peasant leader in the communist movement.

The twists of fate that altered the destiny of Shanfei had parallels throughout the colonial world after 1914. Two major events, the Great War and the Great Depression, defined much of the turmoil of those years. Disillusion and radical upheaval marked areas in Asia, Africa, and Latin America. In Japan the ravages of the Great Depression prompted militarist leaders to build national strength through imperial expansion. Latin American states worked to alter the economic domination of their "good neighbor" to the north, and African peoples suffered a contraction in living standards along with their imperial overlords.

European empires still appeared to dominate global relations, but the Great War opened fissures within the European and American spheres of influence. Beneath colonial surfaces, resistance to foreign rule and a desire for national unity were stronger than ever. This situation was especially true in India and China, but it also pertained to those in Africa and Latin America who struggled against the domination of imperial powers.

ASIAN PATHS TO AUTONOMY

The Paris peace settlement barely altered the prewar colonial holdings of Europeans, yet indirectly the Great War affected relations between Asian peoples and the imperial powers. In the decades following the Great War, nationalism developed into a powerful political force in Asia, especially in India and China. Achieving the twin ideals of independence from foreign powers and national unity became a dream of intellectuals and a goal of new political leaders. In their search for new identities untainted by the dependent past, Asians transformed and adapted European ideologies such as nationalism and socialism to fit indigenous traditions. In that sense, peoples in India and China followed in the footsteps of Japan, which had already adapted European and American economic strategies to its own advantage. Still dissatisfied with its status, Japan used militarism and imperial expansion in the interwar years to enhance its national identity.

Indian, Chinese, and Japanese societies underwent a prolonged period of disorder and struggle until a new order emerged. In India the quest for national identity focused on gaining independence from British rule but was complicated by sectarian differences between Hindus and Muslims. The Chinese path to national identity was fraught with foreign and civil war as two principal groups—the Nationalist and Communist parties—contended for power. Japanese militarists made China's quest for national unity more difficult, because Japan struggled to overcome its domestic problems through conquests that focused on China.

India's Quest for Home Rule

By the beginning of the twentieth century, Indian nationalism threatened the British empire's hold on India. The construction of a vast railway network across India to facilitate the export of raw materials contributed to national unity by bringing the people of the subcontinent within easy reach of one another. Moreover, the British had created an elite of educated Indian administrators to control and administer the vast subcontinent. A European system of education familiarized this elite with the political and social values of European society. Those values, however—democracy, individual freedom, and equality—were the antithesis of empire, and they promoted nationalist movements.

Of all the associations dedicated to the struggle against British rule, the most influential was the Indian National Congress, founded in 1885. This organization, which enlisted the support of many prominent Hindus *Indian National Congress* and Muslims, at first stressed collaboration with the British to bring self-rule to India, but after the Great War the congress pursued that goal in opposition to the British.

During the Great War, large numbers of Indians rallied to the British cause, and nationalist movements remained inactive. But as the war led to scarcities of goods and food, social discontent with British rule led to an upsurge in nationalist activity. Indian nationalists also drew encouragement from ideas emanating from Washington, D.C., and St. Petersburg. They read Woodrow Wilson's Fourteen Points, which called for national self-determination, and Lenin's appeal for a united struggle by proletarians and colonized peoples. The British government responded to increased nationalism in this period with a series of repressive measures that precipitated a wave of violence and disorder throughout the Indian subcontinent.

Into this turmoil stepped Mohandas Karamchand Gandhi (1869–1948), one of the most remarkable and charismatic leaders of the twentieth century. Gandhi grew up in a prosperous and pious Hindu household, married at thirteen, and left his hometown in 1888 to study law in London. In 1893 he went to South Africa to accept a position with an Indian firm, and there he quickly became involved in organizing the local Indian community against a system of racial segregation that made Indians second-class citizens. During the twenty-five years he spent in South Africa, Gandhi embraced a moral philosophy of tolerance and nonviolence *(ahimsa)* and developed the technique of passive resistance that he called *satyagraha* ("truth and firmness"). His belief in the virtue of simple living led him to renounce material possessions, dress in the garb of a simple Indian peasant, and become a vegetarian.

Mohandas K. Gandhi

Returning to India in 1915, Gandhi became active in Indian politics and succeeded in transforming the Indian National Congress from an elitist institution into a mass organization. Gandhi's unique mixture of spiritual intensity and political activism appealed to a broad section of the Indian population, and in the eyes of many he quickly achieved the stature of a political and spiritual leader, their Mahatma, or "great soul." Although he was himself a member of the merchant caste, Gandhi was determined to eradicate the injustices of the caste system. He fought especially hard to improve the status of the lowest classes of society, the casteless Untouchables, whom he called *harijans* ("children of God").

Under Gandhi's leadership the congress launched two mass movements: the Non-Cooperation Movement of 1920–1922 and the Civil Disobedience Movement of 1930. Convinced that economic self-sufficiency was a prerequisite for self-government, Gandhi called on the Indian people to boycott British goods and return to wearing homespun cotton clothing. Gandhi furthermore admonished his people to boycott institutions operated by the British in India, such as schools, offices, and courts. Despite Gandhi's cautions against the use of force, violence often accompanied the protest movement. The British retaliated with arrests. That the British authorities could react brutally was shown in 1919 in the city of Amritsar, where colonial troops fired on an unarmed crowd, killing 379 demonstrators.

Gandhi marches to the sea to make salt

In the face of sustained nationalist opposition and after years of hesitation, the British parliament enacted the Government of India Act, which gave India the institutions of a self-governing state. The legislation allowed for the establishment of autonomous legislative bodies in the provinces of British India, the creation of a bicameral (two-chambered) national legislature, and the formation of an executive arm under the control of the British government. Upon the urging of Gandhi, the majority of Indians approved the measure, which went into effect in 1937.

The India Act

The India Act proved unworkable, however, because India's six hundred nominally sovereign princes refused to cooperate and because Muslims feared that Hindus would dominate the national legislature. Muslims had reason for concern because they already faced economic control by Hindus, a fact underlined during the Great Depression, which had a severe impact on India. Indeed, since Muslims constituted the majority of indebted tenant farmers, during the Great Depression they found themselves increasingly unable to pay rents and debts to their Hindu landlords. As a result, many Muslims felt that they had been economically exploited by Hindus, which exacerbated tensions between the two groups. Muhammad Ali Jinnah (1876–1948), an eloquent and brilliant lawyer who headed the Muslim League—a separate nationalist organization founded in 1906 that focused on the needs of Indian Muslims—warned that a unified India represented nothing less than a threat to the Muslim faith and its Indian community. In place of one India, he proposed two states, one of which would be the "land of the pure," or Pakistan. Jinnah's proposal reflected an uncomfortable reality that society in India was split by hostility between Hindus and Muslims.

China's Search for Order

As Shanfei's life story suggested, during the first half of the twentieth century China was in a state of almost continual revolutionary upheaval. The conflict's origins dated from the nineteenth century, when the Chinese empire came under relentless pressure from imperialist powers (see chapter 29). As revolutionary

---

Satyagraha (suh-TYA-gruh-hah)

and nationalist uprisings gained widespread support, a revolution in 1911 forced the Xuantong emperor, still a child (also known as Puyi), to abdicate. The Qing empire fell with relative ease. Dr. Sun Yatsen (1866–1925), a leading opponent of the old regime, proclaimed a Chinese republic in 1912 and assumed the office of president.

Yet the revolution of 1911 did not establish a stable government. Indeed, the republic soon plunged *The Republic* into a state of political anarchy and economic disintegration marked by the rule of warlords, who were disaffected generals from the old imperial Chinese army. Although the central government in Beijing ran the post office and a few other services, the warlords established themselves as provincial rulers. Because the warlords were responsible for the neglect of irrigation projects, for the revival of the opium trade, and for the decline of economic investments, they contributed to the deterioration and instability of Chinese society. Yet warlords were just one symbol of the disintegration of the political order. The relationship between native authority and foreign powers was another. Since the nineteenth century, a collection of treaties, known in China as the unequal treaties, had established a network of foreign control over the Chinese economy that permitted foreigners to intervene in Chinese society. Foreigners did not control the state, but through their privileges they impaired its sovereignty.

After the Great War, nationalist sentiment developed rapidly in China. Youths and intellectuals, who *Chinese Nationalism* had looked to Europe and the United States for models and ideals on Chinese reform, eagerly anticipated the results of the 1919 peace conference in Paris. They expected the U.S. government to support the termination of the treaty system and the restoration of full Chinese sovereignty. Instead, the peacemakers approved increasing Japanese interference in China. That decision gave rise to the May Fourth Movement. Spearheaded by students and intellectuals in China's urban areas, all classes of Chinese protested against foreign, especially Japanese, interference. In speeches, newspapers, and novels, the movement's leaders—including student leaders such as Shanfei—pledged themselves to rid China of imperialism and reestablish national unity.

Disillusioned by the cynical self-interest of the United States and the European powers, some Chinese became interested in Marxist thought and the social and economic experiments under way in the Soviet Union. The anti-imperialist rhetoric of the Soviet lead-

ership prompted the founding of the Chinese Communist Party (CCP) in Shanghai in 1921. Among its early members was Mao Zedong (1893–1976), a former teacher and librarian who viewed a Marxist-inspired social revolution as the cure for China's problems.

The most prominent nationalist leader at the time, Sun Yatsen, did not share the communists' enthusiasm for a dictatorship of the proletariat. *Sun Yatsen* Rather, Sun's basic ideology called for elimination of special privileges for foreigners, national reunification, economic development, and a democratic republican government based on universal suffrage. To realize those goals, he was determined to bring the entire country under the control of his Nationalist People's Party, or *Guomindang*. In 1923 members of the small CCP began to augment the ranks of the Guomindang and by 1926 made up one-third of the Guomindang's membership. Both organizations availed themselves of the assistance offered by the Soviet Union, whose advisors helped reorganize the Guomindang and the CCP into effective political organizations. In the process, the Soviets bestowed upon China the basis of a new political system.

After the death of Sun Yatsen in 1925, the leadership of the Guomindang fell to Jiang Jieshi (Chiang Kai-shek, 1887–1975), a young general *Civil War* who had been trained in Japan and the Soviet Union. Before long, Jiang Jieshi launched a political and military offensive, known as the Northern Expedition, that aimed to unify the nation and bring China under Guomindang rule. Toward the end of his successful campaign, in 1927, Jiang Jieshi brutally and unexpectedly turned against his former communist allies, bringing the alliance between the Guomindang and the CCP to a bloody end. In the following year, nationalist forces occupied Beijing, set up a central government in Nanjing, and declared the Guomindang the official government of a unified and sovereign Chinese state. Meanwhile, the badly mauled communists retreated to a remote area of southeastern China to reconstitute and reorganize their forces.

The nationalist government had to deal with many concerns, but Chinese leaders evaded one major global crisis—the Great Depression. Foreign trade in such items as tea and silk, which did decline, made up only a small part of China's economy, which was otherwise dominated by its large domestic markets. Although the new government in China gener-

---

Guomindang (GWOH-mihn-dahng)

Map 32.1 **Struggle for control in China between 1927 and 1936.** Compare the continental territories controlled by Japan and the Guomindang in 1934. How would the size of Japan's territories in Manchuria and Korea influence Chinese abilities to challenge Japanese expansion?

ally avoided having to contend with global economic devastation, it did have to confront three major problems during the 1930s. First, the nationalists actually controlled only part of China, leaving the remainder of the country in the hands of warlords. Second, in the early 1930s communist revolution was still a major threat. Third, the Guomindang faced increasing Japanese aggression.

In dealing with those problems, Jiang Jieshi gave priority to eliminating the CCP. No longer able to ward off the relentless attacks of nationalist forces, the communists took flight in October 1934 to avoid annihilation, and some eighty-five thousand troops and auxiliary personnel of the Red Army began the

legendary Long March, an epic journey of 10,000 kilometers (6,215 miles). After traveling across difficult terrain and fighting for survival against hunger, disease, and Guomindang forces, those marchers who had not perished arrived in a remote area of Shaanxi province in northwestern China in October 1935 and established headquarters at Yan'an. During the Long March, Mao Zedong emerged as the leader and the principal theoretician of the Chinese communist movement. He came up with a Chinese form of Marxist-Leninism, or Maoism, an ideology grounded in the conviction that peasants rather than urban proletarians were the foundation for a successful revolution in China.

Adversaries in the struggle for power in China: at left, Jiang Jieshi (Chiang Kai-shek); at right, Mao Zedong.

Imperial and Imperialist Japan

After the Great War, Japan achieved great-power status and appeared to accept the international status quo that the major powers fashioned in the aftermath of war. After joining the League of Nations as one of the "big five" powers, in 1922 the Japanese government entered into a series of international agreements whereby Japan agreed to limit naval development, pledged to evacuate Shandong province of China, and guaranteed China's territorial integrity. In 1928 the Japanese government signed the Kellogg-Briand Pact, which renounced war as an instrument of national policy. Concerns about earlier Japanese territorial ambitions in China receded from the minds of the international community.

Japan's limited involvement in the Great War gave a dual boost to its economy. Japanese businesses profited from selling munitions and other goods to the Allies throughout the war, and they gained a bigger foothold in Asia as the war led Europe's trading nations to neglect Asian markets. Economic prosperity was short-lived, however, as the postwar economy of Japan faced a series of recessions that culminated in a giant economic slump caused by the Great Depression.

Economic contraction set the stage for social unrest and radical politics. Public demands for sweeping political and social reforms figured prominently in Japanese domestic politics throughout the 1920s. Yet conservatives blocked any major advances beyond the suffrage law of 1925, which established universal male suffrage. By the early 1930s an increasingly frustrated and disenchanted public blamed its government for the nation's continuing economic problems. Right-wing political groups called for an end to party rule, while xenophobic nationalists argued for the preservation of a unique Japanese culture and the eradication of "Western" influences. A campaign of assassinations, targeting political and business leaders, culminated in the murder of Prime Minister Inukai Tsuyoshi (1855–1932).

Politicians who supported Japan's role in the international industrial-capitalist system faced increasing opposition from those who were inclined toward a militarist vision of a self-sufficient Japan that would dominate east Asia. Indeed, the hardships of the depression only seemed to discredit the internationalist position and make the militarist vision of self-sufficiency more attractive.

Meanwhile, militarists were setting their sights on expansion in China, where political instability made it an inviting target. In 1931 Japan's military forces began their campaign of expansion in Manchuria, which had historically been Chinese territory. The choice of Manchuria was no accident: the Japanese had significant economic interests there by the twentieth century, not least of which was the Manchurian Railroad, which they had built in 1906 and continued to maintain.

On the night of 18 September 1931, Japanese troops used explosives to blow up a few feet of rail on the Japanese-built South Manchuria Railway north of Mukden, then accused the Chinese of attacking their railroad. This "Mukden incident" became the pretext for war between Japanese and Chinese troops. Although the civilian government in Japan tried to halt this military incursion, by 1932 Japanese troops controlled all of Manchuria. The Japanese established a puppet state called Manchukuo, but in reality Japan had absorbed Manchuria into its empire, challenged the international peace system, and begun a war. In response to the Manchurian invasion, the Guomindang (Nationalist Party) leader Jiang Jieshi appealed to the League of Nations to halt Japanese aggression. The league eventually called for the withdrawal of Japanese forces and for the restoration of Chinese sovereignty. The Japanese responded by leaving the league, and nothing was done to stop the aggression. That reaction set the pattern for future responses to the actions of expansionist nations like Japan. Embarking on conquests in east Asia, Japanese militarists found a sure means of promoting a new militant Japanese national identity. They also helped provoke a new global conflagration.

The Mukden Incident

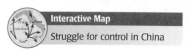

AFRICA UNDER COLONIAL DOMINATION

The Great War and the Great Depression similarly complicated quests for national independence and unity in Africa. The colonial ties that bound African colonies to European powers ensured that Africans became participants in the Great War, willing or not. European states transmitted their respective animosities and their military conflicts to African soil and drew on their colonies for soldiers and carriers. The forced recruitment of military personnel led some Africans to raise arms against their colonial overlords, but Europeans generally prevailed in putting down those uprisings. African contributions to the Great War and the wartime rhetoric of self-determination espoused by U.S. president Woodrow Wilson led some Africans to anticipate a different postwar world. The peacemakers in Paris, however, ignored African pleas for social and political reform.

In the decades following the peace settlement of 1919, colonialism grew stronger on the African continent as European powers focused on the economic exploitation of their colonies. The imposition of a rapacious form of capitalism destroyed the self-sufficiency of many African economies, and African economic life became more thoroughly enmeshed in the global economy. During the decades following the Great War, African intellectuals searched for new national identities and looked forward to the construction of nations devoid of European domination and exploitation.

Africa and the Great War

The Great War had a profound impact on Africa. The conflict of 1914–1918 affected Africans because many belligerents were colonial powers with colonies in Africa. Except for Spanish-controlled territories, which remained neutral, every African colony as well as the two independent states of Ethiopia and Liberia took sides in the war.

Although Germany had been a latecomer in the race for overseas colonies, German imperialists had managed to carve out an African empire in Togo, Cameroon, German Southwest Africa, and German East Africa. Thus, one immediate consequence of war for Africans in 1914 was that the Allies invaded those German colonies. Badly outnumbered by French and British-led troops, the Germans could not hope to win the war in Africa. Yet, by resorting to guerrilla tactics, some fifteen thousand German troops tied up sixty thousand Allied forces and postponed defeat until the last days of the war.

War in Africa

More than one million African soldiers participated directly in military campaigns, in which they witnessed firsthand the spectacle of white people fighting one another. The colonial powers also encouraged their African subjects in uniforms to kill the enemy "white man," whose life until now had been sacrosanct because of his skin color. Even more men, as well as women and children, served as carriers to support European armies, many of them serving involuntarily. In French colonies, military service became compulsory for all males between the ages of twenty and twenty-eight, and by the end of the war over 480,000 colonial troops had served in the French army. In British colonies, a compulsory service order in 1915 made all men aged eighteen to twenty-five liable for military service. In the Congo, the Belgians impressed more than half a million porters. Ultimately, more than 150,000 African soldiers and carriers lost their lives, and many suffered injury or became disabled.

While the world's attention was focused on the slaughter taking place in Europe between 1914 and 1918, Africans mounted bold challenges to European

A Senegalese regiment of the French Colonial Infantry on parade in Africa during the Great War.

colonial authority. Indeed, opportunities for rebellion and protest increased when the already thin European presence in Africa grew even thinner as commercial and administrative personnel left the colonies in large numbers to serve the war effort. The causes of those revolts varied. In some cases, as in Libya, revolts simply represented continued resistance to European rule. In other instances, religious opposition manifested itself in uprisings. The Mumbo cult in Kenya, for example, targeted Europeans and their Christian religion, declaring that "all Europeans are our enemies, but the time is shortly coming when they will disappear from our country." The major inspiration for most revolts, however, stemmed from the resentment and hatred engendered by the compulsory conscription of soldiers and carriers. No matter the cause, colonial authorities responded ruthlessly to put down the revolts.

Challenges to European Authority

The Colonial Economy

The decades following the Great War witnessed a thorough transformation of African economic life. Colonial powers pursued two key economic objectives in Africa: they wanted to make sure that the colonized paid for the institutions—bureaucracies, judiciary, police, and military forces—that kept them in subjugation; and they developed export-oriented economies characterized by the exchange of raw materials or cash crops for manufactured goods from abroad. In pursuit of those goals, colonial authorities imposed economic structures that altered, subordinated, or destroyed African economies by making them increasingly dependent on a European-dominated global economy. One result of this integration was that global economic downturns could spell disaster for African economies. During the Great Depression, for example, as international markets for primary products shrank, prices for African raw materials and cash crops dropped sharply and trade volume often fell by half. This, in turn, wreaked havoc on economies that had been geared almost completely toward the production of a single resource or crop.

Part of the process of global economic integration involved investment in infrastructures such as port facilities, roads, railways, and telegraph wires. Efficient transportation and communication networks not only facilitated conquest and rule but also linked the agricultural or mineral wealth of a colony to the outside world. Although Europeans later claimed that they had given Africa its first modern infrastructure, Europeans and their businesses were usually its main beneficiaries. Even though Africans paid for the infrastructure with their labor and taxes, Europeans designed such systems with their own needs, rather than the needs of Africans, in mind.

Infrastructure

Colonial taxation was used as an important tool to drive Africans into the labor market. To earn the money to pay colonial taxes, African farmers had to become cash-crop farmers or seek wage labor on plantations and in mines. In most colonies, farmers specialized in one or two crops destined for export to the country governing them, among them peanuts from Senegal and northern Nigeria, cotton from Uganda, cocoa from the Gold Coast, rubber from the Congo, and palm oil from the Ivory Coast and the Niger delta. In areas with extensive white settlement, such as in Kenya, Rhodesia, and South Africa, settlers expropriated African lands and grew cash crops—using African labor—themselves. In British-controlled Kenya, for example, four thousand white farmers seized seven million acres in the Kikuyu highlands, the colony's richest land.

Farming and Mining

In South Africa, the government reserved 88 percent of all land for whites, who made up just 20 percent of the total population. Colonial mining enterprises geared toward the extraction of copper, gold, and diamonds loomed large in parts of central and southern Africa. These enterprises depended on the labor of African men who were recruited from rural areas and were paid minimal wages. Such recruitment practices set in motion a vast pattern of labor migration that persisted throughout the twentieth century. In many cases, the absence of male labor and the payment of minimal wages had the effect of impoverishing rural areas, where the women left behind could not grow enough food to feed their children and elderly relatives.

Where taxation failed to create a malleable native labor force, colonial officials resorted to outright forced labor and barely disguised variants of slavery. Indeed, the construction of railways and roads often depended on forced-labor regimes. When the French undertook the construction of the Congo-Ocean railway from Brazzaville to the port at Point-Noir, for example, they rounded up some ten thousand workers annually. Within a few years, between fifteen and twenty thousand African laborers had perished from starvation, disease, and maltreatment. A white settler in Kenya candidly expressed the view held by many colonial administrators: "We have stolen his land. Now we must steal his limbs. Compulsory labor is the corollary to our occupation of the country."

Labor Practices

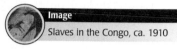
Slaves in the Congo, ca. 1910

African Nationalism

In the decades following the Great War, many Africans were disappointed that their contributions to that conflict went unrewarded. In place of anticipated social reforms or some degree of greater political participation came an extension and a consolidation of

A European colonialist takes advantage of African labor and is "Traveling in Hammock," as this 1912 photograph's title suggests.

the colonial system. Nevertheless, ideas concerning self-determination, articulated by U.S. president Woodrow Wilson during the war, gained adherents among a group of African nationalists. Those ideas influenced the growth of African nationalism and the development of incipient nationalist movements. An emerging class of native urban intellectuals, frequently educated in Europe, became especially involved in the formation of ideologies that promised freedom from colonialism and promoted new national identities.

Colonialism prompted the emergence of a new African social class, sometimes called the "new elite." *Africa's New Elite* This elite derived its status from European-style education and employment in the colonial state, in foreign companies, or in Christian missions. The upper echelons of this elite were high-ranking civil servants, physicians, lawyers, and writers who had studied abroad in western Europe or the United States. A case in point was Jomo Kenyatta (1895–1978), who spent almost fifteen years in Europe, during which time he attended various schools, including the London School of Economics. An immensely articulate nationalist, Kenyatta later led Kenya to independence from the British. Below men such as Kenyatta in status stood teachers, clerks, and interpreters who had obtained a European-derived primary or secondary education. All members of the elite, however, spoke and understood the language of the colonizer and outwardly adopted the cultural norms of the colonizer, such as wearing European-style clothes or adopting European names. It was within the ranks of this new elite that ideas concerning African identity and nationhood germinated.

Because colonialism had introduced Africans to European ideas and ideologies, African nationalists frequently embraced the European concept *Forms of Nationalism* of the nation as a means of forging unity—as well as colonial resistance— among disparate African groups. Some nationalists looked to the precolonial past for inspiration. There they found identities based on ethnicity, religion, and languages, and they believed that any future nation must reconstitute distinctively African spiritual and political institutions. Race had provided colonial powers with one rationale for conquest and exploitation; hence it was not surprising that some nationalists used the concept of an African race as a foundation for identity, solidarity, and nation building. Indeed, race figured prominently in a strain of African nationalism known as pan-Africanism, which originated in the western hemisphere among the descendants of slaves. Representative of this pan-Africanism was the Jamaican na-

tionalist leader Marcus Garvey (1887–1940), who thought of all Africans as members of a single race and who promoted the unification of all people of African descent into a single African state. Still other nationalists looked for an African identity rooted in geography rather than in race. That approach commonly translated into a desire to build the 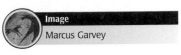 nation on the basis of borders that defined existing colonial states. Collectively those ideas influenced the development of nationalist movements during the 1930s and 1940s, which, after World War II, translated into demands for independence from colonialism.

LATIN AMERICAN STRUGGLES WITH NEOCOLONIALISM

The postcolonial history of Latin American states in the early twentieth century offered clues about what the future might hold for those areas in Asia and Africa still seeking independence from colonial rule. Having gained their independence in the nineteenth century, most sovereign nations in Latin America thereafter struggled to achieve political and economic stability in the midst of interference from foreign powers. The era of the Great War and the Great Depression proved crucial to solidifying and exposing to view the neocolonial structures that guided affairs in Latin America. Generally seen as a more subtle form of imperial control, neocolonialism refers to foreign economic domination, as well as military and political intervention, in states that have already achieved independence from colonial rule. In Central and South America, as well as in the Caribbean, this new imperial influence came not from former colonial rulers in Spain and Portugal but, rather, from wealthy, industrial-capitalist powerhouses such as Great Britain and the United States. Neocolonialism impinged on the political and economic development of Latin American states, but it did not fully prevent nationalist leaders from devising strategies to combat the newfound imperialism.

The Impact of the Great War and the Great Depression

The Great War, the Russian revolution, and the Mexican revolution spread radical ideas and the promise of new political possibilities throughout Latin America. The disparate ideals emerging from this time of politi-

SOURCES FROM THE PAST

Africa for Africans

Marcus Garvey (1887–1940) is best remembered as a pivotal figure in black nationalism, one who inspired nationalist movements as well as many African leaders. A powerful orator, Garvey preached the greatness of the African heritage and called on European colonial powers to leave Africa. Convinced that blacks in the diaspora could never secure their rights as minorities, this "Black Moses" rejected the idea of integration and instead championed a "Back to Africa" movement. According to Garvey, a Jamaican who garnered notoriety during his time in the United States, only in ancestral Africa would it be possible to establish an autonomous black state that featured its own unique culture.

■ ■ ■

George Washington was not God Almighty. He was a man like any Negro in this building, and if he and his associates were able to make a free America, we too can make a free Africa. Hampden, Gladstone, Pitt and Disraeli were not the representatives of God in the person of Jesus Christ. They were but men, but in their time they worked for the expansion of the British Empire, and today they boast of a British Empire upon which "the sun never sets." As Pitt and Gladstone were able to work for the expansion of the British Empire, so you and I can work for the expansion of a great African Empire. Voltaire and Mirabeau were not Jesus Christs, they were but men like ourselves. They worked and overturned the French Monarchy. They worked for the Democracy which France now enjoys, and if they were able to do that, we are able to work for a democracy in Africa. Lenin and Trotsky were not Jesus Christs, but they were able to overthrow the despotism of Russia, and today they have given to the world a Social Republic, the first of its kind. If Lenin and Trotsky were able to do that for Russia, you and I can do that for Africa. Therefore, let no man, let no power on earth, turn you from this sacred cause of liberty. I prefer to die at this moment rather than not to work for the freedom of Africa. If liberty is good for certain sets of humanity it is good for all. Black men, Colored men, Negroes have as much right to be free as any other race that God Almighty ever created, and we desire freedom that is unfettered, freedom that is unlimited, freedom that will give us a chance and opportunity to rise to the fullest of our ambition and that we cannot get in countries where other men rule and dominate.

We have reached the time when every minute, every second must count for something done, something achieved in the cause of Africa. . . . It falls to our lot to tear off the shackles that bind Mother Africa. Can you do it? You did it in the Revolutionary War. You did it in the Civil War; You did it at the Battles of the Marne and Verdun; You did it in Mesopotamia. You can do it marching up the battle heights of Africa. Let the world know that 400,000,000 Negroes are prepared to die or live as free men. Despise us as much as you care. Ignore us as much as you care. We are coming 400,000,000 strong. We are coming with our woes behind us, with the memory of suffering behind us—woes and suffering of three hundred years—they shall be our inspiration. My bulwark of strength in the conflict of freedom in Africa, will be the three hundred years of persecution and hardship left behind in this Western Hemisphere.

• *In his speech, how does Marcus Garvey convey the significance of Africa for both Africans and those involved in the black diaspora?*

SOURCE: Amy Jacques Garvey, compiler. *Philosophy and Opinions of Marcus Garvey or Africa for Africans.* London: Frank Cass and Co., 1967, pp. 73–74.

cal ferment found receptive audiences in Latin America, especially during the global economic crisis of the Great Depression. Marxism, Vladimir Lenin's theories on capitalism and imperialism, and a growing concern for the impoverished Indian masses as well as exploited peasants and workers in Latin American societies informed the outlooks of many disgruntled intellectuals and artists. The Enlightenment-derived liberalism that had shaped independence movements and the political systems of many post-independence nations no longer served as the only form of political legitimacy.

Some of the most radical responses to U.S. economic domination came from Latin American universities, whose students became increasingly politicized in this period. Many took their inspiration from the Mexican and Russian revolutions—both of which were inimical to the ideas of the United States. Indeed, universities became training grounds for future political leaders, including Cuba's Fidel Castro (1926–). In many Latin American countries, radicalism also expressed itself in the formation of political parties that either openly espoused communism or otherwise adopted rebellious agendas for change.

The ideological transformations apparent in Latin America became stunningly and publicly visible in the murals painted by famed Mexican artist Diego Rivera (1886–1957). Artistically trained in Mexico in his youth, Rivera went to study in Europe in 1907 and did not return to Mexico until 1921. Influenced by indigenous art forms as well as the European Renaissance artists and Cubists, Rivera's paintings reflected the turmoil and shifting political sensibilities taking place during the Great War and its aftermath. He blended his artistic and political visions in vast public murals in Mexico's cities, because he believed that art should be on display for working people.

Diego Rivera and Radical Artistic Visions

As a political activist, Rivera also used his art to level a pointed critique of the economic dependency and political repressiveness engendered by U.S. neocolonialism in Latin America. In the painting *Imperialism,* for example, Rivera depicted massive guns and tanks extending over the New York Stock Exchange. In the foreground and at the edges of the stock exchange are a variety of Latin American victims of this monied-military oppression. Indeed, Rivera made visible the

Diego Rivera's *Imperialism* was one in a series of paintings on the United States and offered a visual critique of U.S. neocolonialism in Latin America.

impact of U.S. imperialism on Latin American societies, and by doing so he helped spread political activism in the Americas.

The Evolution of Economic Imperialism

Latin American states were no strangers to foreign economic domination in the nineteenth and early twentieth centuries. Their export-oriented economies had long been tied to global finances and had been subject to controls imposed by foreign investors, largely those from Great Britain and the United States. The major evolution in economic neocolonialism during this period concerned the growing predominance of the United States in the economic affairs of Latin American nations, which was sealed by the Great War. Between 1924 and 1929, U.S. banks and businesses more than doubled their financial interests in Latin America as investments grew from $1.5 billion to $3.5 billion.

That U.S. neocolonialism was meant to be largely economic became evident in the policies of President William Howard Taft (1857–1931). In his final address to Congress in 1912, Taft argued that the United States should substitute "dollars for bullets" in its foreign policy. He wanted businesses to develop foreign markets through peaceful commerce and believed that expensive military intervention should be avoided as much as possible. This new vision of U.S. expansion abroad, dubbed "dollar diplomacy" by critics, encapsulated the gist of what those in Latin America perceived as "Yankee imperialism."

The economic crisis of the Great Depression demonstrated the extent to which Latin America had become integrated in the world economy. Indeed, the Great Depression halted fifty years of economic growth in Latin America and illustrated the region's susceptibility to global economic crises. For one thing, U.S. capital investments for nascent industries and other financial concerns during the 1920s could not be

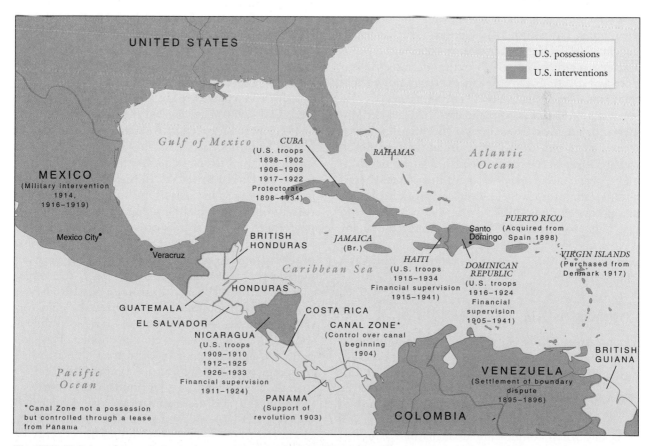

Map 32.2 U.S. interference in Latin America between 1895 and 1941. Note the number of states where U.S. troops intervened in local politics. On what basis did U.S. policymakers justify those interventions?

maintained during this disastrous economic downturn. Moreover, most Latin American states, because they exported agricultural products or raw materials, suffered from plummeting prices. Indeed, the prices of sugar from the Caribbean, coffee from Brazil and Colombia, wheat and beef from Argentina, tin from Bolivia, nitrates from Chile, and many other products fell sharply after 1929. Throughout Latin America unemployment rates increased rapidly. The drastic decline in the price of the region's exports and the drying-up of foreign capital prompted Latin American governments to raise tariffs on foreign products and impose various other restrictions on foreign trade.

Although the weaknesses of export-oriented economies and industrial development financed by foreigners became evident during the Great Depression, the international crisis also allowed Latin American nations to take alternative paths to economic development. Economic policy stressing internal economic development was most visible in Brazil, where dictator-president (1930–1945, 1950–1954) Getúlio Dornelles Vargas (1883–1954) turned his nation into an *estado novo* (new state). Ruling with the backing of the military but without the support of the landowning elite, Vargas and his government during the 1930s and 1940s embarked on a program of industrialization that created new enterprises. Key among them was the iron and steel industry. The Vargas regime also implemented protectionist policies that shielded domestic production from foreign competition, which pleased both industrialists and urban workers. Social welfare initiatives accompanied industrial development, protecting workers with health and safety regulations, minimum wages, limits on working hours, unemployment compensation, and retirement benefits. Thus the Great Depression contributed in many ways to the evolution of both economic neocolonialism and economic experimentation within Latin American states.

Conflicts with a "Good Neighbor"

The pressures of the Great Depression and the instability of global politics led to a reassessment of U.S. foreign policy in Latin America during the late 1920s and 1930s. U.S. leaders realized the costliness and the ineffectiveness of direct interventions in Latin America, especially when committing U.S. marines as peacekeeping forces. To extricate U.S. military forces and

The "Good Neighbor Policy"

rely more fully on "dollar diplomacy," policymakers instituted certain innovations that nonetheless called into question any true change of heart among U.S. neocolonialists. They approved "sweetheart treaties" that guaranteed U.S. financial control in the Caribbean economies of Haiti and the Dominican Republic, for example, and the U.S. Marines provided training for indigenous police forces to keep the peace and maintain law and order. This revamped U.S. approach to relations with Latin America became known as the "Good Neighbor Policy," and it was most closely associated with the administration of Franklin D. Roosevelt (1882–1945).

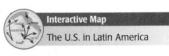

Interactive Map
The U.S. in Latin America

Under Roosevelt, the Good Neighbor Policy evolved into a more conciliatory U.S. approach to Latin American relations. The interventionist corollary to the Monroe Doctrine enunciated previously by President Theodore Roosevelt (1859–1919) was formally renounced in December 1933, when Secretary of State Cordell Hull attended the Seventh International Conference of American States in Montevideo, Uruguay. Hull signed the Convention on the Rights and Duties of States, which held that "no state has the right to intervene in the internal or external affairs of another." That proposition faced a severe challenge in March 1938 when Mexican president Lázaro Cárdenas (1895–1970) nationalized the oil industry, much of which was controlled by foreign investors from the United States and Great Britain.

Given the history of tempestuous relations between the United States and Mexico, including multiple U.S. military incursions into Mexico during the revolution, it seemed there was little chance for a peaceful resolution to this provocative move on the part of Cárdenas. The reluctance of U.S. and British oil companies to grant concessions to Mexican oil workers prompted him to this drastic act. Yet despite calls for a strong U.S. and British response, Roosevelt and his administration officials resisted the demands of big businesses and instead called for a cool, calm response and negotiations to end the conflict. This plan prevailed, and the foreign oil companies ultimately had to accept only $24 million in compensation rather than the $260 million that they initially demanded.

Although the nationalization crisis in Mexico ended in a fashion that suggested the strength of the Good Neighbor Policy, a good deal of the impetus for this policy came from economic and political concerns

This Hollywood publicity photo of Carmen Miranda features the type of lively costuming that made her a colorful favorite in both the United States and Latin America.

associated with the Great Depression and the deterioration of international relations in the 1930s. The United States wanted to cultivate Latin American markets for its exports, and it wanted to distance itself from the militarist behavior of Asian and European imperial powers. The U.S. government knew it needed to improve relations with Latin America, if only to secure those nations' support in the increasingly likely event of another global war. Widespread Mexican migration to the United States during and after the Great

War suggested the attractiveness of the United States for at least some Latin Americans.

Filling the migration void left by Europeans prevented from coming to the United States by the war and by the U.S. immigration restriction laws of the 1920s, Mexican men, women, and children entered the United States in the hundreds of thousands to engage in agricultural and industrial work. The migrants suffered the animosity of some U.S. citizens, who considered them "cheap Mexican labor," but the political power of agribusinesses prevented the government from instituting legal restrictions on Mexican migration. Federal and local officials managed, however, to deport thousands of Mexicans during the Great Depression.

Trying to contribute to the repairing of relations and the promoting of more positive images of Latin American and U.S. relations, Hollywood adopted a Latin American singing and dancing sensation, Carmen Miranda (1909–1955). Born in Portugal but raised from childhood in Brazil, Miranda found fame on a Rio de Janeiro radio station and recorded hundreds of hit songs. In the United States, she gained her greatest visibility in films produced during World War II, such as *Down Argentine Way* (1940). Carmen Miranda appeared as an exotic Latin American woman, usually clothed in sexy, colorful costumes that featured headdresses adorned with the fruits grown in Latin America—such as bananas. She softened representations of Latin Americans for audiences in the United States, providing a less threatening counterpoint to laboring migrants or women guerrilla fighters in Mexico's revolution. She also became a source of pride for Brazilians, who reveled in her Hollywood success. Hollywood's espousal of Roosevelt's Good Neighbor Policy proved a success.

SUMMARY

In the decades after the Great War, and in the midst of the Great Depression, intellectuals and political activists in Asia, Africa, and Latin America challenged the ideological and economic underpinnings of empire and neocolonialism. Often embracing the ideas and theories that disseminated around the globe as a result of the war, including self-determination, socialism, communism, and anti-imperialism, radicals and nationalists revised understandings of political identity in the colonial and neocolonial worlds.

Japanese and U.S. imperial practices incited military and civil discord within their respective spheres, while European colonial rulers continued to limit, often brutally, the freedom of peoples in India and Africa. Like Shanfei, young intellectuals and older political leaders alike emerged transformed in these years. Their efforts to inspire nationalism and to achieve economic and political autonomy came to fruition later—after another world war had come and gone.

CHRONOLOGY

1912	Taft establishes "dollar diplomacy" as U.S. foreign policy
1914–1918	2.5 million African troops and carriers serve in the Great War
1919	May Fourth Movement in China
1920	Non-Cooperation Movement in India
1921	Rivera returns to Mexico to paint
1928	Socialist Party of Peru is founded
1929	Beginning of Great Depression
1930	Civil Disobedience Movement in India
1931	Japanese invasion of Manchuria
1933	Roosevelt begins practice of the Good Neighbor Policy
1934	Long March by Chinese communists
1935	Government of India Act is passed
1938	Cárdenas nationalizes oil industry in Mexico

FOR FURTHER READING

A. Adu Boahen, ed. *Africa under Colonial Domination, 1880–1935.* Berkeley, 1985. Part of the ambitious UNESCO General History of Africa (vol. 7), this work reflects how different Africans view their own history.

Tulio Halperin Donghi. *The Contemporary History of Latin America.* Translated and edited by John Charles Chasteen. Durham, 1993. An exhaustive historical survey of Latin American social and political change.

Cynthia Enloe. *Bananas, Beaches & Bases: Making Feminist Sense of International Politics.* Berkeley, 1989. A gendered analysis of U.S. and other foreign policies through such categories as tourism and diplomats' spouses.

Robert E. Hannigan. *The New World Power: American Foreign Policy, 1898–1917.* Philadelphia, 2002. A detailed account of U.S. foreign relations that links class, race, and gender influences to policymakers.

John Iliffe. *Africans: The History of a Continent.* New York, 1995. A well-written introductory text that is organized thematically rather than chronologically.

Jim Masselos. *Indian Nationalism: A History.* 3rd ed. Columbia, 1998. A keen work that remains the standard, most readable introduction to Indian leaders and movements.

Michael E. Parish. *Anxious Decades: America in Prosperity and Depression, 1920–1941.* New York, 1992. A detailed portrait of the United States between the world wars, featuring treatments of foreign relations with Latin America.

Jonathan D. Spence. *Mao Zedong.* New York, 1999. Blending history with cultural analysis, this intimate portrait of Mao is informative despite its brevity.

Odd Arne Westad. *Decisive Encounters: The Chinese Civil War, 1946–1950.* Stanford, 2003. An engagingly written work that introduces the reader to the salient political and military events that led to the eventual defeat of the Guomindang.

Louise Young. *Japan's Total Empire: Manchuria and the Culture of Wartime Imperialism.* Berkeley, 1999. An important and penetrating work on the nature of Japanese imperialism.

CHAPTER 33

New Conflagrations: World War II

O n 6 August 1945, as he listened to the armed services radio on Saipan (a U.S.-controlled island in the North Pacific), U.S. marine Victor Tolley heard the president of the United States announce that a "terrible new weapon" had been deployed against the city of Hiroshima, Japan. Tolley and the other marines rejoiced, realizing that the terrible new weapon—the atomic bomb—might end the war. A few days later Tolley heard that the city of Nagasaki had also been hit with an atomic bomb and that radio announcers suggested it might be decades before either city would be inhabitable.

Imagine Tolley's astonishment when he was assigned to the U.S. occupation forces in Nagasaki just a few weeks after the Japanese surrender. Assured that Nagasaki was "very safe," Tolley lived there for

three months, during which he became very familiar with the devastation wrought by the bomb. Tolley also became acquainted with some of the Japanese survivors in Nagasaki, which proved to be an eye-opening experience. After seeing "young children with sores and burns all over," Tolley, having become separated from his unit, befriended a young boy who took Tolley home to meet his surviving family. Tolley recalled that while speaking to the boy's father about his missing son-in-law, "it dawned on me that they suffered the same as we did. They lost sons and daughters and relatives, and they hurt too."

Before his chance meeting with this Japanese family, Tolley had felt nothing except contempt for the Japanese. He pointed out, "We were trained to kill them. They asked for it and now we're

OPPOSITE PAGE: *A Japanese child crouches and cries in the rubble of Hiroshima in the aftermath of the atomic bombing, expressing the profound sadness of war and its devastating weapons.*

gonna give it to 'em. That's how I felt until I met this young boy and his family." But after coming face-to-face with his enemies, Tolley saw only their common humanity, their suffering, and their hurt.

The civility that reemerged at the end of the war was little evident during the war years. The war began and ended with Japan. In 1931 Japan invaded Manchuria, and the United States concluded hostilities by dropping atomic bombs on Hiroshima and Nagasaki. By 1941 World War II was a truly global war. Hostilities spread from east Asia and the Pacific to Europe, north Africa, and the Atlantic. Beyond its immense geographic scope, World War II exceeded even the Great War (1914–1918) in demonstrating the willingness of societies to make enormous sacrifices in lives and other resources to achieve complete victory. Moreover, World War II redefined gender roles and relations between colonial peoples and their colonizers. The cold war and the atomic age that began almost as soon as World War II ended also inaugurated a new global order. In particular, the United States and the Soviet Union gained geopolitical strength during the early years of the cold war as they competed for global influence.

ORIGINS OF WORLD WAR II

In 1941 two major alliances squared off against each other. Japan, Germany, and Italy, along with their conquered territories, formed the Axis powers. The Allied powers included France and its empire; Great Britain, its empire, and its Commonwealth allies (such as Canada, Australia, and New Zealand); the Soviet Union; China; and the United States and its allies in Latin America. Driven in part by a desire to revise the peace settlements that followed the Great War and compelled by the economic distress of the worldwide depression, Japan, Italy, and Germany engaged in a campaign of territorial expansion that ultimately broke apart the structure of international cooperation that had kept the world from violence in the 1920s. These revisionist powers, so called because they revised or overthrew the terms of the post–Great War peace, confronted nations that were committed to the avoidance of another world war. To expand their global influence, the revisionist nations remilitarized and conquered territories they deemed central to their needs. The Allies acquiesced to the revisionist powers' early aggressive actions, but in the late 1930s and early 1940s they decided to engage the Axis powers in a total war.

Japan's War in China

The global conflict opened with Japan's attacks on China in the 1930s: the conquest of Manchuria between 1931 and 1932 was the first step in the revisionist process of expansionism and aggression. In 1933, after the League of Nations condemned its actions in Manchuria, Japan withdrew from the league and followed an ultranationalist and promilitary policy. Four years later, Japan launched a full-scale invasion of China. Japanese troops first took Beijing and then moved south toward Shanghai and Nanjing, the capital of China. Japanese naval and air forces bombed Shanghai, killing thousands of civilians, and secured it as a landing area for armies bound for Nanjing. By December 1937 Shanghai and Nanjing had fallen, and during the following six months Japanese forces won repeated victories.

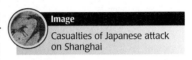
Image
Casualties of Japanese attack on Shanghai

China became the first nation to experience the horrors of World War II: brutal warfare against civilians and repressive occupation. Chinese civilians were among the first to feel the effects of aerial bombing of urban centers; the people of Shanghai died by the tens of thousands when Japanese bombers attacked the city. What became known as the Rape of Nanjing demonstrated the brutality of the war as the residents of Nanjing became victims of Japanese troops inflamed by war passion and a sense of racial superiority. Over the course of two months, Japanese soldiers raped seven thousand women, murdered hundreds of thousands of unarmed soldiers and civilians, and burned one-third of the homes in Nanjing. Four hundred thousand Chinese lost their lives as Japanese soldiers used them for bayonet practice and machine-gunned them into open pits.

The Rape of Nanjing

Despite Japanese military successes, Chinese resistance persisted throughout the war. Japanese aggression aroused feelings of nationalism among the Chinese that continued to grow as the war wore on. By September 1937 nationalists and communists had agreed on a "united front" policy against the Japanese, uniting themselves into standing armies of some 1.7 million soldiers. Although Chinese forces failed to defeat the Japanese, who retained naval and air superiority, they tied up half the Japanese army, 750,000 soldiers, by 1941.

Chinese Resistance

Throughout the war, the coalition of nationalists and communists threatened to fall apart as the two groups competed for control of enemy territory and

Japanese soldiers execute Chinese prisoners.

for political control within China. Those clashes rendered Chinese resistance less effective. While the nationalists shied away from direct military confrontation with Japanese forces and kept the Guomindang government alive by moving inland to Chongqing, the Chinese communists carried on guerrilla operations against the Japanese invaders. The guerrillas did not defeat the Japanese, but they captured the loyalty of many Chinese peasants through their resistance to the Japanese and their moderate policies of land reform. At the end of the war, the communists were poised to lead China.

The Japanese invasion of China met with intense international opposition, yet other world powers, distracted by depression and military aggression in Europe, could offer little in the way of an effective response to Japanese actions. The government of Japan aligned itself with the other revisionist nations, Germany and Italy, by signing a ten-year military and economic pact, the Tripartite Pact, in September 1940. Japan also cleared the way for further empire building in Asia and the Pacific basin by concluding a neutrality

pact with the Soviet Union in April 1941, thereby precluding hostilities in Manchuria. Japan did not face determined opposition to its expansion until it ran into conflict with the United States in December 1941.

Italian and German Aggression

Italy's expansionism helped destabilize the post–Great War peace. Italians suffered tremendously in World War I. Six hundred thousand Italian soldiers died, and the national economy was badly damaged. Many Italians expected far greater recompense and respect than they received at the conclusion of the Great War.

Benito Mussolini promised to bring glory to Italy through the acquisition of territories that it had been denied after the Great War. Italy's conquest of *Italy* Ethiopia in 1935 and 1936, when added to the previously annexed Libya, created an overseas empire. Italy also intervened in the Spanish Civil War (1936–1939) on the side of General Francisco Franco (1892–1975), and it annexed Albania in 1939. The invasion and conquest of Ethiopia in particular infuriated other

Ethiopian soldiers train with outmoded equipment that proves no match for Italian forces.

nations, but as with Japan's invasion of Manchuria, the League of Nations offered little effective opposition.

What angered nonrevisionists about Italy's conquest of Ethiopia was not just the broken peace but also the excessive use of force. Mussolini sent an army of 250,000 soldiers armed with tanks, poison gas, artillery, and aircraft to conquer the Ethiopians, who were entirely unprepared for the assault. The mechanized Italian troops mowed them down. Italy lost 2,000 soldiers, whereas 275,000 Ethiopians lost their lives.

Japan and Italy were the first nations to challenge the post–World War I settlements through territorial **Germany** conquest, but it was Germany that systematically undid the Treaty of Versailles and the fragile peace of the interwar years. Most Germans deeply resented the harsh terms imposed on their nation in 1919. Adolf Hitler (1889–1945) came to power in 1933, riding a wave of public discontent with Germany's postwar powerlessness and the suffering caused by the Great Depression. Hitler referred to the signing of the 1918 armistice as the "November crime" and blamed it on those he viewed as Germany's internal enemies: Jews, communists, and liberals of all sorts. Hitler's scheme for ridding Germany of its enemies and reasserting its power was remilitarization—which was legally denied to Germany under the Versailles Treaty. Hitler's aggressive foreign policy helped relieve the German public's feeling of war shame and depression trauma. After withdrawing Germany from the League of Nations in 1933, his government carried out a large-scale plan to strengthen the German armed forces. Hitler reinstated universal

military service in 1935, and in the following year his troops entered the previously demilitarized Rhineland, which bordered France. In 1938 Hitler began the campaign of expansion that ultimately led to the outbreak of World War II in Europe.

Germany's forced *Anschluss* ("union") with Austria took place in March 1938. Hitler justified this annexation as an attempt to reintegrate all Germans into a single homeland. Europe's major powers, France and Britain, did nothing in response, thereby enhancing Hitler's reputation in the German military and deepening his contempt for the democracies. Soon thereafter, using the same rationale, the Nazis attempted to gain control of the Sudetenland, the western portion of Czechoslovakia, which was inhabited largely by ethnic Germans. In September 1938 Hitler demanded the immediate cession of the Sudetenland to the German Reich. Against the desires of the Czechoslovak government, the leaders of France and Britain accommodated Hitler and allowed Germany to annex the Sudetenland. Neither the French nor the British were willing to risk a military confrontation with Germany to defend Czechoslovakian territory.

At the Munich Conference, held in September 1938, European politicians formulated the policy that came to be known as appeasement. In conceding demands to Hitler, or "appeasing" him, the British and French governments extracted a promise that Hitler would cease further efforts to expand German territorial claims. Their goal was to keep peace in Europe, even if it meant making major concessions. Britain's prime minister, Neville Chamberlain (1869–1940), arrived home from Munich to announce that the meeting had achieved "peace for our time." Unprepared for war and distressed by the depression, nations sympathetic to Britain and France also embraced peace as an admirable goal in the face of aggression by the revisionist nations.

Hitler, however, refused to be bound by the Munich agreement, and in the next year German troops occupied most of Czechoslovakia. As Hitler next threatened Poland, it became clear that the policy of appeasement was a failure, which caused Britain and France to abandon it by guaranteeing the security of Poland. By that time Joseph Stalin (1879–1953) was convinced that British and French leaders were conspiring to deflect German aggression toward the Soviet Union, which made him seek an accommodation with the Nazi regime. In August 1939 the foreign ministers of the Soviet Union and Germany signed the Russian-German Treaty of Nonaggression, an agreement that promised neutrality in the event of war with a third party and prevented the possibility of a war on two fronts. Additionally, a secret protocol divided eastern Europe into German and Soviet spheres of influence. Hitler was ready to conquer Europe.

TOTAL WAR: THE WORLD UNDER FIRE

Two months after the United States became embroiled in World War II, President Franklin Roosevelt (1882–1945) delivered one of his famous radio broadcasts, known as fireside chats. In it he explained: "This war is a new kind of war. It is warfare in terms of every continent, every island, every sea, every air lane." There was little exaggeration in FDR's analysis. Before World War II was over, almost every nation had participated in it, and virtually every weapon known to humanity had been used. More so than the Great War, this was a conflict in which entire societies engaged in warfare and mobilized every available material and human resource.

The war between Japan and China had been in progress for eight years when European nations stormed into battle in 1939. By 1941 nations outside Europe were also drawn into the conflict, including the French and British colonies in Africa and India, as well as Canada, Australia, and New Zealand. As the war dragged on, only eleven countries avoided direct involvement: Afghanistan, Greenland, Iceland, Ireland, Mongolia, Portugal, Spain, Sweden, Switzerland, Tibet, and Yemen.

Blitzkrieg: Germany Conquers Europe

During World War II it became common for aggressor nations to avoid overt declarations of war. Instead, the new armed forces relied on surprise and swiftness for their conquests. Germany demonstrated the advantages of that strategy in Poland, when their air force and *Panzer* ("armored") columns moved into Poland unannounced on 1 September 1939. Within a month they had subdued its western expanses while the Soviets took the eastern sections in accordance with the Nazi-Soviet pact. The Germans stunned the world with their *Blitzkrieg* ("lightning war") and sudden victory.

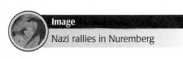
Nazi rallies in Nuremberg

With Poland subdued, Germany prepared to break through European defenses. In April 1940 the Germans occupied Denmark and Norway, then launched a full-scale attack on western Europe. Their offensive against Belgium, France, and the Netherlands began in May, and again the Allies were jolted by Blitzkrieg tactics. Belgium and the Netherlands fell first, and the French signed an armistice in June. After the fall of France, Italy's Benito Mussolini entered the conflict in the hopes of reaping any potential benefits his partnership with the Germans might offer. *The Fall of France*

Before the battle for France, Hitler had boasted to his staff, "Gentlemen, you are about to witness the most famous victory in history!" Given France's rapid fall, Hitler was not far wrong. In a moment of exquisite triumph, Hitler had the French sign their armistice in the very railroad car in which the Germans had signed the armistice in 1918. Meanwhile, the British, in an attempt to rescue the remaining Allied troops in France, engineered a stunning retreat from Dunkirk across the English Channel, but it could not hide the bleak failure of the Allied troops. Britain now stood alone against the German forces.

Germany therefore launched the Battle of Britain, led by its air force, the Luftwaffe. "The Blitz," as the British called this air war, rained bombs on heavily populated metropolitan areas, especially London, and killed more than forty thousand British civilians. The Royal Air Force staved off defeat, however, forcing Hitler to abandon plans to *The Battle of Britain*

Adolf Hitler proudly walks through conquered Paris in 1940, with the Eiffel Tower as a backdrop.

invade Britain. Yet despite the setback in Britain, Hitler had plenty of reasons to be happy by the summer of 1941, for the swastika-bedecked Nazi flag waved from the streets of Paris to the Acropolis in Athens, and he had succeeded beyond his dreams in his quest to reverse the outcome of World War I.

The German Invasion of the Soviet Union

Flush with victory in the spring of 1941, Hitler turned his sights on the Soviet Union. This land was the ultimate German target, from which Jews, Slavs, and Bolsheviks could be expelled or exterminated to create more Lebensraum ("living space") for resettled Germans. Believing firmly in the bankruptcy of the Soviet system, Hitler was confident that in the Soviet Union

---

Lebensraum (LAY-behnz-rahwm)

"you only have to kick in the door, and the whole rotten structure will come crashing down."

On 22 June 1941, Adolf Hitler ordered the initiation of Operation Barbarossa, the invasion of the Soviet Union. For that, the German military assembled the largest and most powerful invasion force in history, attacking with 3.6 million soldiers, thirty-seven hundred tanks, twenty-five hundred planes, and thirty divisions from the governments of Hungary, Finland, and Romania. The invasion along a front of 3,000 kilometers (1,900 miles) took Stalin by surprise and caught the Red Army off guard. By December 1941 German troops had reached the gates of Moscow. Germany seemed assured of victory.

Operation Barbarossa

However, German Blitzkrieg tactics that had earlier proved so effective in Poland and western Europe failed the Germans in the vast expanses of Russia. Hitler and his military leaders underestimated Soviet personnel reserves and industrial capacity. Within a matter of weeks, for example, the 150 German divisions faced 360 divisions of the Red Army. By the time the German forces reached the outskirts of Moscow, fierce Soviet resistance had produced eight hundred thousand German casualties.

The arrival of winter—the most severe in decades— also helped Soviet military efforts. So sure of an early victory were the Germans that they did not bother to supply their troops with winter clothing and boots. One hundred thousand soldiers suffered frostbite, and two thousand of them underwent amputation. The Red Army, in contrast, prepared for winter and found further comfort in the thirteen million pairs of felt-lined winter boots sent by their allies in the United States. By early December, Soviet counterattacks along the entire front had stopped German advances.

In the spring of 1942 the Germans briefly regained the military initiative, and by June they were approaching the city of Stalingrad. As the Germans came upon Stalingrad in September, the Russians dug in. "Not a step back," Stalin ordered. The Russians did indeed hold Stalingrad, but only at the price of waging a bloody street-by-street defense of the city until the Red Army could regroup for a counterattack.

Battles in Asia and the Pacific

Before 1941 the United States was inching toward greater involvement in the war. In 1939 it instituted a cash-and-carry policy of supplying the British, in which the British paid cash and carried the materials on their own ships. More significant was the lend-lease program initiated in 1941, in which the United States "lent" destroyers and other war goods to the British in return for the lease of naval bases. The program later extended such aid to the Soviets, the Chinese, and many others.

German victories in 1940 and Great Britain's precarious military position in Europe encouraged the Japanese to project their influence into southeast Asia in their quest for raw materials such as tin, rubber, and petroleum. Between September 1940 and July 1941, and with the blessings of the German-backed Vichy government of France, Japanese forces occupied French Indochina (now Vietnam, Laos, and Cambodia). The government of the United States—supported by Great Britain, the Commonwealth of Nations, and the Dutch East Indies—responded to this situation by freezing Japanese assets in the United States and by imposing a complete embargo on oil. To Japanese militarists faced with the alternative either of succumbing to U.S. demands—which included the withdrawal of Japanese forces from China and southeast Asia—or of engaging the United States in war, war seemed the lesser of two evils.

The Japanese hoped to destroy American naval capacity in the Pacific with an attack at Pearl Harbor. On 7 December 1941, "a date which will live in infamy," as Franklin Roosevelt concluded, more than 350 Japanese bombers, fighters, and torpedo planes struck in two waves, sinking or disabling eighteen ships and destroying more than two hundred. Except for the U.S. aircraft carriers, which were out of the harbor at the time, American naval power in the Pacific was devastated.

Pearl Harbor

Primary Source
FDR's declaration of war

On 11 December 1941, though not compelled to do so by treaty, Hitler and Mussolini declared war on the United States. That move provided the United States with the only reason it needed to declare war on Germany and Italy. The United States, Great Britain, and the Soviet Union came together in a coalition that linked two vast and interconnected theaters of war, the European and Asian-Pacific theaters, and ensured the defeat of Germany and Japan. Winston Churchill (1874–1965), prime minister of Britain, expressed a vast sense of relief when he said: "So we had won after all!"

Flames consumed U.S. battleships in Pearl Harbor after the Japanese attack on 7 December 1941.

Yet after Pearl Harbor the Japanese swept on to one victory after another. The Japanese coordinated their strike against Pearl Harbor with simultaneous attacks against the Philippines, Guam, Wake Island, Midway Island, Hong Kong, Thailand, and British Malaya. For the next year the Japanese military maintained the initiative in southeast Asia and the Pacific, capturing Borneo, Burma, the Dutch East Indies, and several Aleutian islands off Alaska. Australia and New Zealand were now within striking distance. Moreover, the humiliating surrender of British-held Singapore in February 1942 dealt a blow to British prestige and shattered any myths of European military invincibility.

Japanese Victories

The slogan under which Japan pursued expansion in Asia was "Asia for Asians," according to which the Japanese would lead Asian peoples to independence from the despised European imperialists. In this struggle for Asian independence, Japan required the region's resources, arguing that this was necessary to build a "Greater East Asia Co-Prosperity Sphere." The appeal to Asian independence at first struck a responsive chord among Asians, but conquest and brutal occupation soon made it obvious to most Asians that the real agenda was "Asia for the Japanese." Proponents of the Greater East Asia Co-Prosperity Sphere advocated Japan's expansion in Asia and the Pacific while cloaking their territorial and economic designs with the idealism of Asian nationalism.

Map 33.1 The high tide of Axis expansion in Europe and north Africa between 1942 and 1943. Observe the number of nations occupied by or allied with the Axis powers. Given Axis dominance in Europe, what factors finally allowed the Allies to turn the tide of war in their favor?

Defeat of the Axis Powers

The entry of the Soviet Union and the United States into the war in 1941 was decisive, because personnel reserves and industrial capacity were the keys to the Allied victories in the European and Asian-Pacific theaters. The U.S. automotive industry alone, for instance, produced more than four million armored, combat, and supply vehicles of all kinds during the war. Not until the United States joined the struggle in 1942 did the tide in the battle for the Atlantic turn in favor of the Allies.

By 1943 German forces in Russia faced bleak prospects. Moscow never fell, and the battle for Stalingrad, which ended in February 1943, *Allied Victory* resulted in the first large-scale victory *in Europe* for Soviet forces. The Red Army, drawing on enormous personnel and material reserves, then pushed the German invaders out of Russian territory. By April 1945 the Soviets had reached the suburbs of Berlin. At that point, the Soviets had inflicted more than six million casualties on the German enemy—twice the number of the original German invasion force. The Red Army had broken the back of the German war machine.

With the eastern front disintegrating under the Soviet onslaught, British and U.S. forces attacked the Germans from North Africa and then through Italy. In August 1944 the Allies forced Italy to withdraw from the Axis and to join them. In the meantime, the Germans also prepared for an Allied offensive in the west, where the British and U.S. forces opened a front in France. On D-Day, 6 June 1944, British and U.S. troops landed on the French coast of Normandy and overwhelmed the Germans. With the two fronts collapsing around them and round-the-clock strategic bombing by the United States and Britain leveling German cities, German resistance faded. Indeed, the British firebombing raid on Dresden alone killed 135,000 people in February

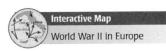

Interactive Map
World War II in Europe

1945. As Germans and Russians engaged in a brutal street-by-street battle in Berlin and U.S. and British forces advanced through western Germany, the Germans surrendered unconditionally on 8 May 1945. A week earlier, on 30 April, as fighting flared right outside his Berlin bunker, Hitler committed suicide. He therefore did not live to see the Soviet red flag flying over the Berlin Reichstag, Germany's parliament building.

The turning point in the Pacific war came at Midway (4 June 1942), the last U.S.-controlled island in the Pacific. The victory was accomplished by a code-breaking operation known as *Magic,* which enabled *Turning the Tide in the Pacific* a cryptographer to discover the plan to attack Midway. On the morning of 4 June, thirty-six carrier-launched dive-bombers attacked the Japanese fleet, sinking three Japanese carriers in one five-minute strike and a fourth one later in the day. After Midway, the Allies took the offensive in the Pacific. They adopted an island-hopping strategy, capturing islands from which they could make direct air assaults on Japan. Deadly, tenacious fighting characterized these battles in which the United States and its allies gradually retook islands in the Marianas and the Philippines and then, early in 1945, moved toward areas more threatening to Japan: Iwo Jima and Okinawa.

The fighting on Iwo Jima and Okinawa was savage. On Okinawa the Japanese introduced the kamikaze—pilots who volunteered to fly planes with just enough fuel to reach an Allied ship and dive-bomb into it. In the two-month battle for Okinawa, the Japanese flew nineteen hundred kamikaze missions, sinking dozens of ships and killing more than five thousand U.S. soldiers. The kamikaze, and the defense mounted by Japanese forces and the 110,000 Okinawan civilians who died refusing to surrender, convinced many people in the United States that the Japanese would never capitulate.

The fall of Saipan in July 1944 and the subsequent conquest of Iwo Jima and Okinawa brought the Japanese homeland within easy reach of U.S. strategic bombers. The release of napalm *Japanese Surrender* firebombs during low-altitude sorties at night met with devastating success. The firebombing of Tokyo in March 1945 destroyed 25 percent of the city's buildings and annihilated approximately one hundred thousand people. The final blows came on 6 and 9 August 1945, when the United States used its revolutionary new weapon, the atomic bomb, against the cities of Hiroshima and Nagasaki. The atomic bombs either instantaneously vaporized or slowly killed by radiation poisoning upward of two hundred

Image
Mushroom cloud over Nagasaki

thousand people. The Soviet Union declared war on Japan on 8 August 1945, and that new threat, combined with the devastation caused by the bombs,

---

kamikaze (kah-mih-KAH-zee)

Map 33.2 Progress of World War II in Asia and the Pacific. Compare the geographical conditions of the Asian-Pacific theater with those of the European theater. What kinds of resources were necessary to win in the Asian-Pacific theater as opposed to the European theater?

persuaded Emperor Hirohito (1901–1989) to surrender unconditionally on 15 August. On 2 September 1945, the war officially ended.

LIFE DURING WARTIME

The widespread bombing of civilian populations during World War II, from its beginning in China to its end in Hiroshima and Nagasaki, meant that there was no safe home front during the war. So too did the arrival of often brutal occupation forces in the wake of Japanese and German conquests in Asia and Europe. In this total war, civilian death tolls far exceeded military casualties. In spite of the war's brutality, however, the human spirit endured, personified in the contributions of resistance groups and mobilized women, and in the survivors of bombings or concentration camps.

A Hiroshima Maiden's Tale

Yamaoka Michiko, at fifteen years of age, worked as an operator at a telephone exchange in Hiroshima and attended girls' high school. Many young women had been mobilized for work during World War II, and they viewed even civilian work on telephone exchanges as a means of helping to protect Japan during wartime. On the morning of 6 August 1945, when the first U.S. atomic bomb used in battle devastated Hiroshima, Yamaoka Michiko had just started off for work.

That morning I left the house at about seven forty-five. I heard that the B-29s [U.S. bomber planes] had already gone home. Mom told me, "Watch out, the B-29s might come again." My house was one point three kilometers from the hypocenter [the exact point of the atomic bomb's impact]. My place of work was five hundred meters from the hypocenter. I walked toward the hypocenter. . . . I heard the faint sound of planes. . . . The planes were tricky. Sometimes they only pretended to leave. I could still hear the very faint sound of planes. . . . I thought, how strange, so I put my right hand above my eyes and looked up to see if I could spot them. The sun was dazzling.

That was the moment. There was no sound. I felt something strong. It was terribly intense. I felt colors. It wasn't heat. You can't really say it was yellow, and it wasn't blue. At that moment I thought I would be the only one who would die. I said to myself, "Goodbye, Mom."

They say temperatures of seven thousand degrees centigrade hit me. You can't really say it washed over me. It's hard to describe. I simply fainted. I remember my body floating in the air. That was probably the blast, but I don't know how far I was blown. When I came to my senses, my surroundings were silent. There was no wind. I saw a threadlike light, so I felt I must be alive. I was under stones. I couldn't move my body. I heard voices crying, "Help! Water!" It was then I realized I wasn't the only one. . . .

"Fire! Run away! Help! Hurry up!" They weren't voices but moans of agony and despair. "I have to get help and shout," I thought. The person who rescued me was Mom, although she herself had been buried under our collapsed house. Mom knew the route I'd been taking. She came, calling out to me. I heard her voice and cried for help. Our surroundings were already starting to burn. Fires burst out from just the light itself. It didn't really drop. It just flashed. . . .

My clothes were burnt and so was my skin. I was in rags. I had braided my hair, but now it was like a lion's mane. There were people, barely breathing, trying to push their intestines back in. People with their legs wrenched off. Without heads. Or with faces burned and swollen out of shape. The scene I saw was a living hell.

Mom didn't say anything when she saw my face and I didn't feel any pain. She just squeezed my hand and told me to run. She was going to rescue my aunt. Large numbers of people were moving away from the flames. My eyes were still able to see, so I made my way toward the mountain, where there was no fire, toward Hijiyama. . . .

I spent the next year bedridden. All my hair fell out. When we went to relatives' houses later they wouldn't even let me in because they feared they'd catch the disease. There was neither treatment nor assistance for me. . . . It was just my Mom and me. Keloids [thick scar tissue] covered my face, my neck. I couldn't even move my neck. One eye was hanging down. I was unable to control my drooling because my lip had been burned off. . . .

The Japanese government just told us we weren't the only victims of the war. There was no support or treatment. It was probably harder for my Mom. Once she told me she tried to choke me to death. If a girl had terrible scars, a face you couldn't be born with, I understand that even a mother could want to kill her child. People threw stones at me and called me Monster. That was before I had my many operations.

- *What did Yamaoka Michiko's psychological and physical reactions to the atomic bombing of Hiroshima suggest about the nature of these new weapons? Why did friends and relatives treat her as if she were a "monster"?*

SOURCE: Yamaoka Michiko. "Eight Hundred Meters from the Hypocenter." In Haruko Taya Cook and Theodore F. Cook, *Japan at War: An Oral History.* New York: The New Press, 1992, pp. 384–87.

Occupation, Collaboration, and Resistance

The administration imposed on conquered territories by Japanese and German forces varied in character. In territories such as Manchukuo, Japanese-controlled China, Burma, and the Philippines, Japanese authorities installed puppet governments. Other conquered territories either were considered too unreliable for "self-rule" or were deemed strategically too important to be left alone. Thus territories such as Indochina, Malaya, the Dutch East Indies, Hong Kong, Singapore, Borneo, and New Guinea came under direct military control.

In Europe, Hitler's racist ideology played a large role in determining how occupied territories were administered. Hitler intended that most areas of western and northern Europe—populated by racially valuable people, according to him—would become part of a Greater Germanic Empire. Accordingly, Denmark retained its elected government and monarchy under German supervision. In Norway and Holland, the Germans left the civilian administration intact. Though northern France and the Atlantic coast came under military rule, the so-called Vichy government remained the civilian authority in the unoccupied southeastern part of the country. In contrast, most conquered territories in eastern Europe and the Balkans came under direct military rule as a prelude for harsh occupation, economic exploitation, and German settlement.

Japanese and German authorities administered their respective empires for economic gain and pro-
Exploitation   ceeded to ruthlessly exploit the resources of the lands under their control for their own benefit. The most notorious form of economic exploitation involved the use of slave labor. In Poland, the Soviet Union, France, Italy, and the Balkan nations, German occupiers forced millions of people to labor in work camps and war industries, and the Japanese did likewise in China and Korea. These slave laborers worked under horrific conditions and received little in the way of sustenance.

Reaction to Japanese and German occupation varied from willing collaboration and acquiescence to
Collaboration and Resistance   open resistance. In both Asia and Europe, local notables often joined the governments sponsored by the conquerors because collaboration offered them the means to gain power or because they thought native rule was better than foreign rule. Businesspeople and companies often collaborated because they prospered financially from foreign rule. Still other people assisted occupation forces to get revenge for past grievances.

Nevertheless, occupation and exploitation created an environment for resistance that took various forms. The most dramatic forms of resistance were campaigns of sabotage, armed assaults on occupation forces, and assassinations. Resistance fighters as diverse as Filipino guerrillas and Soviet partisans blew up ammunition dumps and destroyed communication and transportation facilities. More quietly, other resisters gathered intelligence or hid and protected refugees.

Resistance also comprised simple acts of defiance such as scribbling anti-German graffiti or walking out of bars and restaurants when Japanese soldiers entered. German and Japanese citizens faced different decisions about resistance than conquered peoples did, since they had no antiforeign axe to grind. Moreover, many institutions that might have formed the core of resistance in Japan and Germany, such as political parties, labor unions, and churches, were weak or had been destroyed. As a result, there was little or no opposition to the state and its policies in Japan, while in Germany resistance remained generally sparse and ineffective.

Occupation forces reacted swiftly and brutally to resistance. When in May 1942 members of the Czech resistance assassinated the Nazi official Rein-
hard Heydrich, the Nazis eliminated the en-   *Atrocities*
tire village of Lidice as punishment. Likewise, when a group of officers and civilians tried to kill Adolf Hitler in July 1944, many of the conspirators were hanged with piano wire suspended from meat hooks, a process recorded on film for Hitler. The Japanese were equally brutal. After eight hundred Chinese slave laborers were captured after escaping from their camp in the small Japanese town of Hanaoka, at least fifty were beaten and tortured to death as they hung by their thumbs from the ceiling of the town hall. Yet despite such deadly retaliation meted out to people who resisted occupation, widespread resistance movements grew throughout the war.

The Holocaust

By the end of World War II, the Nazi regime and its accomplices had physically annihilated millions of Jews, Slavs, Gypsies, homosexuals, Jehovah's Witnesses, communists, and others targeted as undesirables. Jews were the primary target of Hitler's racially motivated genocidal policies, and the resulting Holocaust nearly wiped out the Jewish population of Europe.

Titled "Abyss of Human Horror," this photograph shows a survivor of the concentration camp at Nordhausen, Germany, upon its liberation by Allies in 1945.

The murder of European Jews was preceded by centuries of anti-Semitism in Europe, where Jews were routinely marked as outsiders. Thus Europeans' passive acceptance of anti-Semitism, combined with Nazi determination to destroy the Jewish population, laid the groundwork for genocide. Initially, the Nazi regime encouraged Jewish emigration. Although tens of thousands of Jews availed themselves of the opportunity to escape from Germany and Austria, many more were unable to do so because most European nations limited the migration of Jewish refugees and because German victories in Europe brought an ever-larger number of Jews under Nazi control. Early in the war, Nazi "racial experts" toyed with the idea of mass deportation of Jews, but that idea proved to be impractical as well as threatening, since the concentration of Jews in one area led to the dangerous possibility of the creation of a separate Jewish state, hardly a solution to the so-called Jewish problem in the Nazi view.

The Final Solution   The German occupation of Poland in 1939 and the invasion of the Soviet Union in the summer of 1941 gave Hitler an opportunity to solve what he considered the problem of Jews throughout Europe. When German armies invaded the Soviet Union in June 1941, the Nazis dispatched three thousand troops in mobile detachments known as SS *Einsatzgruppen* ("action squads") to kill entire populations of Jews and Roma (Gypsies), and many non-Jewish Slavs in the newly occu-

pied territories. By the end of 1941, the special units had killed 1.4 million Jews.

Sometime during 1941 the Nazi leadership committed to the "final solution" of the Jewish question, which entailed the attempted murder of every Jew living in Europe. At the Wannsee Conference, on 20 January 1942, fifteen leading Nazi

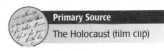

Primary Source

The Holocaust (film clip)

bureaucrats agreed to evacuate all Jews from Europe to camps in eastern Poland, where they would be worked to death or exterminated. Soon German forces—aided by collaborating authorities in foreign countries—rounded up Jews and deported them by rail to specially constructed concentration camps in occupied Poland. The Jewish victims packed into those suffocating railway cars never knew their destinations, but rumors of mass deportations and mass deaths spread among Jews remaining at large and among the Allied government leaders, who were apparently apathetic to the fate of Jews.

In camps such as Belzec, Treblinka, and Auschwitz, the final solution took on an organized and technologically sophisticated character. Nazi camp personnel subjected victims from all corners of Europe to industrial work, starvation, medical experiments, and outright extermination. The German commandant of Auschwitz—the largest camp, where at least one million Jews perished—explained proudly how his camp became the most efficient at killing Jews: by using the fast-acting

Map 33.3 **The major concentration, extermination, and euthanasia sites of the Holocaust in Europe.** Observe the geographical locations of the concentration and extermination camps. Why were there more concentration camps in Germany and more extermination camps in Poland?

crystallized prussic acid Zyklon B as the gassing agent, by enlarging the size of the gas chambers, and by lulling victims into thinking they were going through a delousing process. At Auschwitz and elsewhere, the Germans also constructed large crematories to incinerate the bodies of gassed Jews and hide the evidence of their crimes. Even though Jews put up fierce resistance throughout the war, by 1945 approximately 5.7 million Jews had perished in the Holocaust.

Women and the War

Observing the extent to which British women mobilized for war, the U.S. ambassador to London noted, "This war, more than any other war in history, is a woman's war." While hundreds of thousands of women in Great Britain and the United States joined the armed forces or entered war industries, women around the world were affected by the war in a variety of ways. In some nations, such as the Soviet Union

and China, women took up arms. So, too, did female members of resistance groups, who often excelled at resistance work because they were less suspect in the eyes of occupying security forces and less subject to searches. Nazi forces did not discriminate, though, when rounding up Jews for transport and extermination: Jewish women and girls died alongside Jewish men and boys.

Although women's roles changed during the war, often in dramatic ways, those new roles were temporary. After the war, women warriors and workers were expected to return home and assume their traditional roles as wives and mothers. In the meantime, though, women made the most of their opportunities. In Britain, more than half a million women joined British military services, and approximately 350,000 women did the same in the United States.

Women's experiences in war were not always ennobling or empowering. The Japanese army forcibly conscripted as many as three hundred thousand

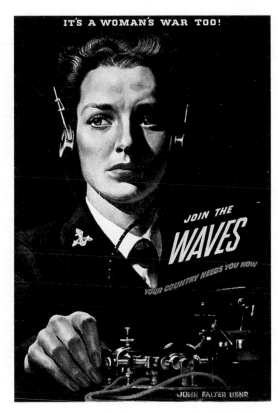

A WAVE recruitment poster proclaims "It's A Woman's War Too!"

women aged fourteen to twenty to serve in military brothels, called "comfort houses" or "consolation centers." Most of the women came from Japanese colonies such as Korea, Taiwan, and Manchuria and from occupied territories in the Philippines and elsewhere in southeast Asia. Eighty percent of the women came from Korea.

Once forced into this imperial prostitution service, "comfort women" catered to between twenty and thirty men each day. Some were killed by Japanese soldiers, especially if they tried to escape or contracted venereal diseases. At the end of the war, soldiers massacred large numbers of comfort women to cover up the operation. The impetus behind the establishment of comfort houses came from the horrors of Nanjing, where Japanese soldiers had engaged in the mass rape of Chinese women. In trying to avoid such atrocities, however, the Japanese army created another. Comfort women who survived the war experienced deep shame and hid their past or faced shunning by their families. They found little comfort or peace after the war.

NEITHER PEACE NOR WAR

The end of World War II produced moving images of peace, including those of Soviet and U.S. soldiers clasping hands in camaraderie at the Elbe River, celebrating their victory over the Germans. Indeed, the Soviet Union and the United States emerged as the two strongest powers after the war, and each played a central role in shaping, influencing, and rebuilding the postwar world. It quickly became clear that both powers sought to create a world in their own image. Initially, the struggle to align postwar nations on one side or the other centered on areas liberated at the end of the war. Ultimately, however, it spread to the whole world.

Postwar Settlements and Cold War

Although the peoples of victorious nations danced in the streets on Victory in Europe (V-E) Day and Victory in Japan (V-J) Day, they also gazed at a world transformed by war. At least sixty million people perished in World War II. The Soviets lost more than twenty million, one-third of whom were soldiers; fifteen million Chinese, mostly civilians, died; Germany and Japan suffered the deaths of four million and two million people, respectively; six million Poles were also dead; in Great Britain four hundred thousand people died; and the United States lost three hundred thousand. The Holocaust claimed the lives of almost six million European Jews. In Europe and Asia tens of millions of displaced persons further contributed to the difficulty of rebuilding areas destroyed by war.

At the same time, the cold war between the Soviet Union and the United States began. That long-drawn-out conflict (1947–1991) divided humans and nations as sympathetic either to the Soviet Union or to the United States. The cold war came to define the postwar era as one of political, ideological, and economic hostility between the two superpowers and affected nations around the globe.

Throughout most of World War II, Hitler had believed that the alliance of the communist Soviet Union, the imperialist Great Britain, and the unwarlike U.S. democracy would break up over ideological differences. Yet Hitler underestimated the extent to which opposition to his regime could unite such unusual allies. Winston Churchill had put it like this: "If Hitler invaded Hell, I would at least make favorable reference to the Devil in the House of Commons."

The Origins of the Cold War

Comfort women playing mah-jongg.

The necessity of defeating the Axis nations glued the Allies together, although there were tensions among them. Some of those tensions began to surface at the second wartime conference between the Allied leaders, at Yalta (4–11 February 1945), but they became obvious at the third and final wartime conference, at Potsdam (16 July–2 August 1945). By the time of the Yalta Conference, the Soviets were 64 kilometers (40 miles) from Berlin, and they controlled so much territory that Churchill and Roosevelt could do little to alter Stalin's plans for eastern Europe. They attempted to persuade Stalin to allow democracy in Poland, but Stalin's plans for Soviet-occupied nations prevailed. The Soviets suppressed noncommunist political parties and prevented free elections in Poland, Czechoslovakia, Hungary, Romania, and Bulgaria. They also installed a communist government in Poland and took similar steps elsewhere in eastern Europe.

At Yalta Stalin ensured that the Red Army's presence would dictate the future of states liberated by the Soviets, and at Potsdam Truman initiated the pro-capitalist, pro-democracy stance of the United States. The successful test of the atomic bomb while Truman was at Potsdam stiffened the president's re-

solve, and tensions over postwar settlements intensified. Having just fought a brutal war to guarantee the survival of their ways of life, neither the United States nor the Soviet Union would easily forgo the chance to remake occupied territories as either capitalist or communist allies.

In the end, all the Allies agreed on was the dismemberment of the Axis states and their possessions. The Soviets took over the eastern sections of Germany, and the United States, Britain, and France occupied the western portions. The capital city of Berlin, deep within the Soviet area, remained under the control of all four powers. In 1946, Churchill proclaimed that an "iron curtain" had come down on Europe, separating the Soviet-controlled nations of eastern Europe from the capitalist nations of western Europe. A somewhat similar division occurred in Asia. Whereas the United States alone occupied Japan, Korea remained occupied half by the Soviets and half by the Americans.

The enunciation of the Truman Doctrine on 12 March 1947 crystallized the new U.S. perception of a world divided between free and enslaved peoples. Articulated partly in response to crises in Greece and Turkey, where communist movements seemed to threaten democracy and U.S. strategic interests, the Truman Doctrine starkly drew the battle lines of the cold war. As Truman explained to the U.S. Congress: "I believe that it must be the policy of the United States to support free peoples who are resisting attempted subjugation by armed minorities or by outside pressures."

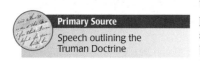

Primary Source

Speech outlining the Truman Doctrine

Thus the United States committed itself to an interventionist foreign policy, dedicated to the "containment" of communism, which meant preventing any further expansion of Soviet influence. As a result, the world was polarized into two armed camps, each led by a superpower that provided economic and military aid to nations within its sphere of influence.

Global Reconstruction and the United Nations

As an economic adjunct to the Truman Doctrine, the U.S. government developed a plan to help shore up the destroyed infrastructures of western Europe. The European Recovery Program, commonly called the Marshall Plan after U.S. secretary of state George C. Marshall (1880–1959), proposed to rebuild European economies to forestall Soviet influence in the devastated nations of Europe. Beginning in 1948, the Marshall Plan provided more than $13 billion to reconstruct western Europe.

The Marshall Plan

In response, the Soviet Union countered with a plan for its own satellite nations. The Soviet Union established the Council for Mutual Economic Assistance (COMECON) in 1949, offering increased trade within the Soviet Union and eastern Europe as an alternative to the Marshall Plan.

The creation of the U.S.-sponsored North Atlantic Treaty Organization (NATO) and the Soviet-controlled Warsaw Pact signaled the militarization of the cold war.

In 1949 the United States established NATO as a regional military alliance against Soviet aggression. The original members included Belgium, Canada, Denmark, France, Great Britain, Iceland, Italy, Luxembourg, the Netherlands, Norway, Portugal, and the United States. The intent of the alliance was to maintain peace in postwar Europe through collective defense. When NATO admitted West Germany and allowed it to rearm in 1955, the Soviets formed the Warsaw Pact as a countermeasure. A military alliance of seven communist European nations, the Warsaw Pact matched the collective defense policies of NATO.

NATO and the Warsaw Pact

Despite their many differences, the superpowers were among the nations that agreed to the creation of the United Nations (UN), a supranational organization dedicated to keeping world peace. The commitment to establish a new international organization derived from Allied cooperation during the war, and in 1945 the final version of the United Nations charter was hammered out by delegates from fifty nations at the United Nations Conference in San Francisco. The United Nations was dedicated to maintaining international peace and security and promoting friendly relations among the world's nations. It offered an alternative for global reconstruction that was independent of the cold war.

The United Nations

It rapidly became clear, however, that international peace and security eluded both the United Nations and the superpowers. The cold war dominated postwar reconstruction efforts. It remained cold for the most part, characterized by ideological and propaganda campaigns, but it became "hot" in places, such as Korea between 1950 and 1953, and it had the potential to escalate into a war more destructive than World War II. The Soviet Union broke the U.S. monopoly on the atomic bomb in September 1949, and from that point on the world held its collective breath at the possibility of a nuclear war.

SUMMARY

At the end of World War II, it was possible for a U.S. marine to enjoy the hospitality of a Japanese family in Nagasaki, but not for Soviet and U.S. troops to continue embracing in camaraderie. World War II was a total global war that forced violent encounters between peoples and radically altered the political shape of the world. Beginning with Japan and China in 1931, this global conflagration spread to Europe and its empires and to the Pacific Ocean and the rest of Asia. Men, women, and children throughout the world became intimate with war as victims of civilian bombing campaigns, as soldiers and war workers, and as slave laborers and comfort women. When the Allies defeated the Axis powers in 1945, destroying the German and Japanese empires, the world had to rebuild as the cold war began. The cold war helped determine the new shape of the world as nations reconstructed under the auspices of either the United States or the Soviet Union, the two superpowers of the postwar era.

CHRONOLOGY

1937	Invasion of China by Japan
1937	The rape of Nanjing
1938	German *Anschluss* with Austria
1939	Nazi-Soviet pact
1939	Invasion of Poland by Germany
1940	Fall of France, Battle of Britain
1941	German invasion of the Soviet Union
1941	Attack on Pearl Harbor by Japan
1942	U.S. victory at Midway
1943	Soviet victory at Stalingrad
1944	D-Day, Allied invasion at Normandy
1945	Capture of Berlin by Soviet forces
1945	Atomic bombing of Hiroshima and Nagasaki
1945	Establishment of United Nations
1947	Truman Doctrine
1948	Marshall Plan
1949	Establishment of NATO
1955	Establishment of Warsaw Pact

FOR FURTHER READING

Ian Buruma. *The Wages of Guilt: Memories of War in Germany and Japan*. New York, 1995. A moving account of how societies deal with the war crimes of World War II.

Haruko Taya Cook and Theodore F. Cook. *Japan at War: An Oral History*. New York, 1992. Views of World War II in the words of the Japanese who witnessed it.

John Dower. *War without Mercy: Race and Power in the Pacific War*. New York, 1986. An insightful and important work on how race influenced the Japanese and U.S. war in the Pacific.

Paul Fussell. *Understanding and Behavior in the Second World War*. Oxford, 1989. A dissection of the culture of war; see the author's similar treatment of World War I.

Margaret Higgonet, Jane Jenson, Sonya Michel, and Margaret Weitz, eds. *Behind the Lines: Gender and the Two World Wars*. New Haven, 1987. A penetrating series of articles on women in both world wars, focusing generally on U.S. and European experiences.

Raul Hilberg. *The Destruction of the European Jews*. New York, 1967. One of the most important works on the Holocaust.

Akira Iriye. *The Origins of the Second World War in Asia and the Pacific*. New York, 1987. An examination of the Asian and Pacific origins of the war by one of the field's leading scholars.

Studs Terkel. *"The Good War": An Oral History of World War II*. New York, 1984. A valuable collection of oral histories on the war from a U.S. perspective.

Sun, You-Li. *China and the Origins of the Pacific War, 1931–1941*. New York, 1993. An account of the origins of the war in which China takes center stage.

Gerhard Weinberg. *A World at Arms: A Global History of World War II*. Cambridge, 1994. An exhaustive look at the war from a global perspective.

CHAPTER 34

The Bipolar World

In the summer of 1959, the world was treated to a verbal slugfest—subsequently known as the kitchen debate—between United States vice president Richard M. Nixon (1913–1994) and Soviet premier Nikita S. Khrushchev (1894–1971). In July of that year, Nixon arrived in Moscow to open the American National Exhibition, a rare display of U.S. goods on Russian soil. Khrushchev, however, was not in a welcoming mood: the U.S. Congress had just passed the "captive nations" resolution, which openly criticized the Soviet Union for mistreating its satellite nations, and Khrushchev was convinced that Nixon's visit to Moscow was timed to humiliate the Soviet leader. Before visiting the exhibit, Khrushchev and Nixon met privately and exchanged heated words about captive nations. Ac-

cording to Nixon's memoirs, the colorful and candid Soviet premier initiated the conversation by remarking: "It stinks like fresh horse shit, and nothing smells worse than that." The equally frank Nixon—aware that Khrushchev had tended pigs in his youth—quickly replied: "There is something that smells worse than horse shit and that is pig shit." Having thus set the mood, Nixon and Khrushchev descended on the exhibit, where they continued their barbed exchange.

The high point of their vocal showdown took place in the kitchen of a U.S. model house built expressly for the exhibit. Without hesitation, Khrushchev mocked the many modern appliances in the kitchen. In his opinion they epitomized "the capitalist attitude toward women." Besides, he argued, the working class could

OPPOSITE PAGE: *The visceral beauty of nuclear explosions, such as this one in the Marshall Islands in 1954, masked the terror and tensions that beset the Soviet Union, the United States, and the rest of the world during the cold war.*

never afford such useless gadgets. In response, Nixon poked a finger at the chest of the Soviet premier and declared that any U.S. steelworker could purchase this $14,000 home. What followed was an unrehearsed polemical discourse on communism and capitalism that climaxed with a debate on the relative merits of everything from dishwashers to missiles.

The kitchen debate between Nixon and Khrushchev took place at the height of the cold war and illustrated how deep the rift between the United States of America and the Union of Soviet Socialist Republics (USSR) had grown since 1945. The cold war was a strategic struggle that developed after World War II between the United States and its allies on the one hand and the USSR and its allies on the other. Yet the confrontation was more than great-power rivalry; it was also an encounter between rival social and economic systems and competing political ideologies. This clash in turn gave rise to a new set of global relationships, shaping the foreign policies, economic systems, and political institutions of nations throughout the world.

The geopolitical and ideological rivalry between the Soviet Union and the United States lasted almost five decades and affected every corner of the world. The cold war was responsible for the formation of military and political alliances, the creation of client states, and an arms race of unprecedented scope. In the end, however, the United States and the Soviet Union always avoided a direct clash of arms, hence the term *cold war.* Nevertheless, the ideological exchanges of the cold war inspired significant changes in social and economic practices in both the Soviet Union and the United States.

THE FORMATION OF A BIPOLAR WORLD

By the time Germany surrendered in the spring of 1945, the wartime alliance between the Soviet Union and the United States was disintegrating. With the advent of peace, the one-time partners increasingly sacrificed cooperation for their own national interests. The competing ideologies of capitalism and communism shaped the postwar aims of the two superpowers, and their mutual hostility resulted in a divided world.

The Cold War in Europe

Among the first manifestations of the cold war was the division of the European continent into competing political, military, and economic blocs—one dependent on the United States and the other subservient to the USSR—separated by what Winston Churchill called an "iron curtain." In essence, both blocs adopted the political institutions, economic systems, and foreign policies of the two superpowers. Thus western European nations that were tied to the United States embraced parliamentary political systems and capitalist economic structures and

Interactive Map
The cold war

Soviet premier Nikita Khrushchev and U.S. vice president Richard Nixon sharing a rare "lighter" moment during the kitchen debate.

adjusted their foreign policies to the U.S. vision of the postwar world. On the other hand, the governments of eastern European states adopted Soviet political and economic institutions and supported Moscow's foreign policy goals.

The fault lines of cold war Europe were most visible in Germany. After the collapse of Hitler's Third *A Divided Germany* Reich, the forces of the United States, the Soviet Union, Britain, and France occupied Germany and its capital, Berlin, both of which they divided into four administrative zones. Specific travel corridors running through the Soviet occupation zone of Germany gave the French, British, and Americans access from their zones of occupation in western Germany to their sectors in Berlin, which lay deep within Soviet territory. Tensions mounted between Soviet authorities and their Western counterparts in 1947–1948 after the Western powers decided to merge their occupation zones in Germany into a single economic unit and to introduce a new currency, the German mark, throughout their occupation zones and in their sectors of Berlin.

The Soviets retaliated by blockading all road, rail, and water links between Berlin and western Germany. The Soviet Union maintained that Western economic measures violated wartime agreements and, on 24 June 1948, announced that the four-power administration of Berlin was no longer in effect *Blockade and* and that the Allies no longer had any ju- *Airlift* risdiction there. Two days later, in the first serious test of the cold war, the Americans and British responded with an airlift designed to keep the city's inhabitants fed and warm. For eleven months, American and British aircrews flew around-the-clock missions to supply West Berlin with the necessities of life. Finally, the Soviet leadership called off the blockade in May 1949, though the airlift continued until September. The blockade failed to force the British, French, and Americans to vacate Berlin. In May 1949 the U.S., British, and French zone of occupation coalesced to form the Federal Republic of Germany (West Germany). In October the German Democratic Republic (East Germany) emerged out of the Soviet zone of occupation. A similar process repeated itself in Berlin: the Soviet sector formed East Berlin and became the capital of the new East Germany, and the remaining three sectors united to form West Berlin.

By 1961 the communist East German state was hemorrhaging from a steady drain of refugees who preferred life in capitalist West Germany. Much to the

Map 34.1 Boundaries of occupied Germany between 1945 and 1949. Locate the city of Berlin in Soviet-controlled territory. How was it possible for the British, American, and French to maintain their zones of control in Berlin, given such geographical distance from western Germany?

Barbed wire and a concrete wall in front of the Brandenburg Gate in Berlin symbolized the cold war division of Europe.

embarrassment of East Germany's communist leaders, between 1949 and 1961 nearly 3.5 million East Germans—many of them young and highly skilled—left their homeland. To remedy the problem, in August 1961 the communists built a fortified wall—replete with watchtowers, searchlights, antipersonnel mines, and border guards ordered to shoot to kill—dividing the city of Berlin. In subsequent years several thousand East Germans escaped to West Germany, but several hundred others paid with their lives for attempting to do so.

Berlin Wall

A central feature of the cold war world was a costly arms race and the terrifying proliferation of nuclear weapons. The struggle between the United States and the Soviet Union led to the creation of two military blocs: the North Atlantic Treaty Organization, or NATO (1949), and the Warsaw Treaty Organization, or Warsaw Pact (1955). Because the United States was determined to retain military superiority and because the Soviet Union was equally determined to reach parity with the United States, both sides amassed enormous arsenals of thermonuclear weapons and developed a multitude of systems for deploying those weapons. By 1970 both superpowers had ac-

The Nuclear Arms Race

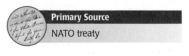
Primary Source
NATO treaty

quired the capacity for mutually assured destruction, or MAD. Yet the balance of terror restrained the contestants and stabilized their relationship, with two important exceptions.

Confrontations in Korea and Cuba

With the unforeseen outbreak of hostilities on the Korean peninsula in the summer of 1950, the focus of the cold war shifted from Europe to east Asia. At the end of World War II, the leaders of the Soviet Union and the United States had partitioned Korea along the thirty-eighth parallel of latitude into a northern Soviet zone and a southern U.S. zone. Because the superpowers were unable to agree on a framework for the reunification of the country, in 1948 they consented to the establishment of two separate Korean states: in the south, the Republic of Korea, with Seoul as its capital and the conservative anticommunist Syngman Rhee (1875–1965) as its president; in the north, the People's Democratic Republic of Korea, with Pyongyang as its capital and the revolutionary communist Kim Il Sung (1912–1995) as its leader. After arming their respective clients, each of which claimed sovereignty over the entire country, U.S. and Soviet troops withdrew.

Early on the morning of 25 June 1950, the unstable political situation in Korea came to a head. Determined to unify Korea by force, the Pyongyang regime ordered more than one hundred thousand troops across the thirty-eighth parallel in a surprise attack, capturing Seoul on 27 June. Convinced that the USSR had sanctioned the invasion, and armed with UN support, the U.S. military went into action. Within two weeks U.S. forces had pushed North Koreans back to the thirty-eighth parallel. However, sensing an opportunity to unify Korea under a pro-U.S. government, they pushed on into North Korea, occupied Pyongyang, and made advances toward the Chinese border. Those advances caused the government of the People's Republic of China to issue a warning: the U.S. incursion across the thirty-eighth parallel threatened Chinese national interests and could result in Chinese intervention in the Korean conflict.

The Korean War

When U.S. leaders gave no indication of heeding China's warning, some three hundred thousand Chinese soldiers surged into North Korea. A combined force of Chinese and North Koreans pushed U.S. forces and their

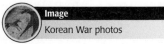
Image
Korean War photos

allies back into the south, and the war settled into a protracted stalemate near the original border at the thirty-eighth parallel. After two more years of fighting that resulted in three million deaths—mostly Korean civilians—both sides finally agreed to a cease-fire in July 1953.

Beyond the human casualties and physical damage it wrought, the Korean conflict also encouraged the globalization of containment. *The Globalization of Containment* After Korea, the U.S. government extended military protection and economic aid to the noncommunist governments of Asia to bolster them against communism. It also entered into security agreements that culminated in the creation of the Southeast Asian Treaty Organization (SEATO), an Asian counterpart of NATO. In 1954 U.S. president Dwight D. Eisenhower (1890–1969) accepted the famous "domino theory," which rationalized worldwide U.S. intervention on the assumption that if one country became communist, neighboring ones would collapse as well. Subsequent U.S. administrations extended the policy of containment to real or imagined communist threats in Central and South America, Africa, and Asia.

Ironically, the cold war confrontation that came closest to unleashing nuclear war took place not at the expected flashpoints in Europe or Asia but on the island of Cuba. In 1959 a revolutionary movement headed by *Cuba: Nuclear Flashpoint* Fidel Castro Ruz (1926–) overthrew the autocratic Fulgencio Batista y Zaldivar (1901–1973), whose regime had gone to great lengths to maintain the country's traditionally subservient relationship with the United States. Denouncing Yankee imperialism, Castro seized foreign properties and businesses, most of which were U.S. owned. He also accepted assistance from the Soviet Union. The U.S. government promptly retaliated by cutting off Cuban sugar imports to the U.S. market and imposing a severe export embargo of U.S. goods on Cuba. U.S. officials also cut diplomatic relations with Cuba and secretly began planning an invasion of the island.

The severing of ties between Cuba and the United States gave the Soviet Union an unprecedented opportunity to contest the dominant position of the United States in its own hemisphere. Castro's regime accepted a Soviet offer of extensive military and economic aid, including an agreement to purchase half of Cuba's sugar production. In return for the Soviet largesse, Castro loudly declared his support for the USSR's foreign policy at the UN General Assembly on 26 September 1960.

Cuba's alignment with the Soviet Union spurred newly elected president John F. Kennedy (1917–1963) to approve a plan to invade Cuba and overthrow Castro. In April 1961 a force *The Bay of Pigs* of 1,500 anti-Castro Cubans trained, armed, and transported by the Central Intelligence Agency (CIA) landed on Cuba at a place called the Bay of Pigs. The invasion, however, was a complete failure and actually strengthened Castro's position in Cuba as well as his commitment to communism. It also likely encouraged Castro to accept and the Soviets to deploy nuclear missiles in Cuba as a deterrent to any future invasion.

On 22 October 1962 President Kennedy went on national television to inform the public about the U.S. discovery of offensive nuclear missiles and launch sites in Cuba. The Soviet *The Cuban Missile Crisis* government apparently took that bold step to protect the Castro government, give the USSR greater diplomatic leverage vis-à-vis the United States,

In August 1950, U.S. troops marched toward North Korea while South Koreans moved in the opposite direction to escape the fighting.

undermine U.S. credibility in the region, and gain more influence in Latin America. Whatever the precise motives, the deployment of nuclear missiles in Cuba represented an unacceptable threat to U.S. national security. In response, President Kennedy delivered a public ultimatum calling on the Soviets to

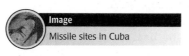

withdraw all missiles from Cuba and stop the arrival of additional nuclear armaments. To back up his demand, Kennedy imposed an air and naval quarantine on the island, which went into effect two days later. The superpowers seemed poised for nuclear confrontation, and for a week the world's peoples held their collective breath.

Understanding the seriousness of a nuclear showdown over Cuba, Nikita Khrushchev agreed to Kennedy's demand that he withdraw the missiles on the condition that the United States pledge not to invade Cuba. He also received a private promise from Kennedy

that U.S. missiles in Turkey would be removed. Khrushchev informed the public of the end of the crisis in a worldwide radio broadcast on 28 October, and global tension finally began to ebb.

Cold War Societies

The global political arena after World War II resounded with clashes stemming from the cold war and decolonization. The conflicts emanating from those dual forces naturally had repercussions in societies around the world. Postwar social transformations demonstrated how domestic policies and international affairs often become linked, particularly as peoples living in disparate parts of the world discover commonalities and differences, mutual sympathies and antipathies.

When Nikita Khrushchev and Richard Nixon squared off in the kitchen debate in Moscow, their argument highlighted the different ways that capitalist

Map 34.2 Allies of the United States and the Soviet Union between 1949 and 1962. Note the size of the territories and the number of states allied to both sides. Were these alliances a source of global stability or global instability?

and communist societies understood the importance of women and domesticity. Citizens of the United States, like Nixon, celebrated the home appliances that made the lives of housewives so comfortable and that distinguished them from their toiling Soviet counterparts. Women did not need to work, as they did in the Soviet Union, because their husbands earned enough to support the family in suburban splendor and because a mother's most important job was keeping the family happy and loyal.

Domestic Containment and Female Liberation

Indeed, in the United States cold war concerns about the spread of communism reached into the domestic sphere. Politicians, FBI agents, educators, and social commentators warned of communist spies trying to undermine the institutions of U.S. life. Thus, many believed that U.S. women best served their families and their nation by staying home and rearing patriotic, anticommunist children. The idea of families providing the best defense against communist infiltration has been dubbed by scholars as "domestic containment," indicating its similarity to the U.S. foreign policy of containment.

Women were deeply affected by the restraints imposed by domestic containment. Not all women aspired to the domestic ideals being showcased on new television shows such as *Leave It to Beaver* (1957–1963), and female discontent with postwar domesticity in the United States helped to fuel the modern feminist movement. In 1963 U.S. author Betty Friedan (1921–2006) published *The Feminine Mystique*, laying bare the severe unhappiness of women who presumably enjoyed the best life the United States could offer. Aligning themselves to some extent with women in societies such as the Soviet Union and taking inspiration from women in Asia and Africa who fought for their independence from the colonial powers, women activists adopted the language and terms of Marxism and anticolonialism in their own quest for equality and independence. They referred to women as an "oppressed class" and argued for "women's liberation." Support for domestic containment, and containment itself, wavered.

As the ideals of domestic containment clearly indicate, cross-fertilization between domestic and foreign policies took place throughout the early cold war years. Another arena in which those links could be seen was the coinciding of the cold war with the modern civil rights movement in the United States. The Soviet Union could and did use the appalling conditions of African-Americans to expose the weaknesses of the capitalist

Black Nationalism

system in the United States. In virtually every sphere of life, southern U.S. states institutionalized segregation, a system of laws and customs designed to separate blacks and whites. African-Americans contended with segregation and the loss of voting rights, widespread discrimination, and extralegal violence. Discrimination was less pronounced in northern states, but informal segregation practices also influenced northern society. U.S. politicians and lawmakers recognized the adverse propaganda value of this institutionalized racism during the cold war, and in 1954 the U.S. Supreme Court ruled segregation in the schools illegal in *Brown v. the Board of Education*. However, it was direct action on the part of African-Americans—through the civil rights movement—that brought segregation down.

Indeed, the civil rights movement was first and foremost a challenge to segregation. In 1955, when Rosa Parks, an African-American woman living in Montgomery, Alabama, refused to give up her seat on a bus to a white man—as required by law—she accelerated a civil rights revolution that resulted in major advances for blacks in the United States. African-Americans in Montgomery refused to ride city buses until they were desegregated, and the Montgomery bus boycott—led by Dr. Martin Luther King Jr. (1929–1968)—proved the effectiveness of Mohandas Gandhi's methods of nonviolence in a new social context. King went on to lead numerous marches and demonstrations and, despite the violence visited on him and his followers, to win major civil rights battles. Until his assassination in 1968, King clung to his dream of black equality in the United States, a nation pressured by the cold war and African liberation movements to accede rights to its black population.

The Civil Rights Movement

The United States fell short in cold war ideological battles in its treatment of African-Americans, but the Soviet Union had difficulty matching the United States and its allies in the provision of material wealth, leisure, and consumer goods. Like women and domesticity, consumerism became a means of distinguishing communist and capitalist societies.

Cold War Consumerism

The contrasting economic and social conditions of western and eastern Europe after World War II demonstrated the different lifestyles that emerged in Europe during the cold war. Western European nations experienced what many people termed an economic miracle, recovering swiftly from the war's devastation. Starting with an infusion of $13 billion from the U.S. Marshall Plan between 1948 and 1952, west European government leaders rebuilt their nations by

Nikita Khrushchev on the Capitalist Iron Curtain

In early 1946 Winston Churchill (1874–1965) delivered his "Iron Curtain" speech, stirring audiences with its image of a Europe firmly and frighteningly divided between communist nations and marking, for some, the beginning of the cold war. Fifteen years after Churchill delivered his speech, Nikita Khrushchev (1894–1971) acknowledged the power of Churchill's imagery by using it in his own speech to the Communist Party Congress. In his 1961 "Report to the Communist Party Congress," Soviet premier Khrushchev blasted capitalism with the same force Churchill had employed in his earlier condemnation of communism.

■ ■ ■

Comrades! The competition of the two world social systems, the socialist and the capitalist, has been the chief content of the period since the 20th Party Congress [February 1956]. It has become the pivot, the foundation of world development at the present historical stage. Two lines, two historical trends, have manifested themselves more and more clearly in social development. One is the line of social progress, peace and constructive activity. The other is the line of reaction, oppression and war.

In the course of the peaceful competition of the two systems, capitalism has suffered a profound moral defeat in the eyes of all peoples. The common people are daily convinced that capitalism is incapable of solving a single one of the urgent problems confronting mankind. It becomes more and more obvious that only on the paths to socialism can a solution to these problems be found. Faith in the capitalist system and the capitalist path of development is dwindling. Monopoly capital, losing its influence, resorts more and more to intimidating and suppressing the masses of the people, to methods of open dictatorship in carrying out its domestic policy and to aggressive acts against other countries. But the masses of the people offer increasing resistance to reaction's acts.

The ruling circles of some imperialist powers have elevated subversive activities against the socialist countries to the level of state policy. With cynical frankness, the United States of America is spending hundreds of millions of dollars on espionage and subversion against socialist countries and organizing so-called "guerrilla units," assembling in them criminal elements and cut-throats prepared to undertake the vilest crimes for money. For several successive years the United States has been holding provocational "captive nations weeks." The hired agents of the monopolies call "captive" all those peoples who have liberated themselves from imperialist bondage and taken the path of free development. Truly, imperialist demagogy and hypocrisy know no bounds!

Our society is open to those people who come to us from abroad with open hearts. It is open to honest trade, to scientific, technical and cultural exchanges, to the exchange of truthful information. If it's an iron curtain we're talking about, where it really exists is in the world of capitalism, which, though dubbing itself the "free world," every now and then fearfully slams its gates shut to Soviet people, one moment to our cooks, the next to our chess players. There was a case where one state, which calls itself the "most open," was afraid to let in Soviet dancers. Can they really have feared that Russian folk dancing might shake the foundations of the capitalist world?!

We have long proposed to the capitalist world that we compete not in an arms race but in improving the working people's lives. We are confident that capitalism cannot stand up under that kind of competition! We are confident that in the end all peoples will make the correct choice, will give their preference to the truly free world of communism and turn their backs on the so-called "free world" of capitalism.

- *Why did Khrushchev contend that faith in capitalism had dwindled and that the true "iron curtain" closed capitalist nations to outside contacts?*

SOURCE: Nikita Khrushchev. "Report to the Communist Party." In *Current Soviet Policies IV,* ed. Charlotte Saikowski and Leo Gruliow, from the translations of *The Current Digest of the Soviet Press.* 1962.

encouraging economic growth and by providing social services that outpaced those in the United States—including, over time, the guarantee of a thirty-day paid vacation. Western Europeans also enjoyed increased access to consumer goods such as automobiles, supermarkets, and record albums.

In contrast, the peoples of the Soviet Union and eastern European nations experienced less economic *The Space Race* growth and enjoyed far fewer consumer items and far less leisure than did their counterparts in western Europe and North America. They could, however, take pride and some comfort from the technological triumphs enjoyed by the Soviet Union in the late 1950s and early 1960s. Soviet experts demonstrated to the world their apparent superiority in science and technology when they tested a workable intercontinental ballistic missile (ICBM) in

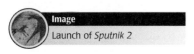

the late 1950s. That success was overshadowed on 4 October 1957 by the more spectacular Soviet launching into space of the first satellite, *Sputnik*. Between the ICBM and *Sputnik*, the Soviets grabbed the initiative in the newly dubbed space race, an extraterrestrial form of the cold war. The Soviet head start in that race provoked panic among U.S. citizens and politicians, which intensified in April 1961 when the Soviets rocketed cosmonaut Yuri Gagarin (1934–1968) into space, where he became the first man to orbit the earth.

The United States soon copied those Soviet successes in space with its own—launching the satellite *Explorer I* in 1958 and sending astronaut John Glenn (1921–) into orbit in 1962. When John F. Kennedy became president, he dedicated himself and the National Aeronautics and Space Administration (NASA) to the task of landing a man on the moon. That came to fruition on 20 July 1969 when *Apollo XI* gently set down on the moon's Sea of Tranquility. The moon landing reassured U.S. citizens of their world status, but the earlier years of the cold war had left them insecure about missile gaps and diminished scientific ingenuity in a society relentlessly devoted to consumerism.

Societies in the Soviet Union and the United States may have resembled each other in their space racing, in *Peaceful Coexistence* their pursuit of nuclear superiority, and in their quest for cold war supremacy, but they also resembled each other in their basic humanity: a fact that may have prevented the ultimate tipping of the balance of terror. A few weeks after the famous kitchen debate, Khrushchev became the first

Soviet leader to visit the United States. Despite some tense moments, Khrushchev's tour of the United States contributed to a thaw in the cold war, however brief. In his September 1959 travels, which included stops in New York, California, and Iowa, he showed himself to be a warm and witty man. Television coverage of his trip allowed millions in the United States to see the previously demonized Soviet premier as a human being as he talked with U.S. farmers and thanked his U.S. hosts for their hospitality. That encounter between a Soviet leader and a U.S. audience suggested the ever-shifting possibilities for peace in the perilous cold war world.

CHALLENGES TO SUPERPOWER HEGEMONY

The global preeminence of the two new superpowers evoked challenges from several quarters. In western Europe, French politicians sought to free their nation from superpower dominance by transforming Europe into an independent strategic bloc. Eastern European states also tried to become their own masters, or at least to gain a measure of autonomy from the Soviet Union. The leadership of the People's Republic of China mounted the most serious challenge to Soviet hegemony within the communist world when a quarrel over national interests and disagreements concerning ideology grew into a schism. Finally, in Vietnam and Afghanistan, respectively, the United States and the Soviet Union suffered serious political and military setbacks that signaled the decline of superpower hegemony.

Defiance, Dissent, and Intervention in Europe

The first direct assault on the bipolar world emanated from France under the leadership of President Charles de Gaulle (1890–1970), who dreamed of a Europe that could act as a third force in *France under* world affairs. In particular, de Gaulle *de Gaulle* regarded subservience to U.S. authority and unqualified support for U.S. global objectives intolerable, because he believed that France could never regain great-power status if it depended for security on U.S. military protection. Moreover, military dependence carried with it the risk that a nuclear confrontation between the superpowers over issues unrelated to European interests could engulf Europe by virtue of its alliance with the United States.

The focus of French policy under de Gaulle was disengagement from the U.S.-dominated NATO and the development of an independent nuclear strike force, which became a realistic proposition in 1964 when the French detonated their first atomic bomb in the Sahara desert. Four years later the French military put together a nuclear delivery system consisting of long-range bombers and land- and submarine-based missiles. French military doctrine and capability failed to persuade Europeans to leave the protective fold of the United States, however, and by the time de Gaulle left office in 1969 his vision for France and Europe had nearly disappeared.

There were many challenges to the hegemonic position of the Soviet Union during the cold war decades.

Tito's Yugoslavia   The first opposition from within the communist world emanated from Yugoslavia, where a postwar communist regime under Josip Broz, known as Marshal Tito (1892–1980), came to power without the assistance of the Soviet Union. Tito's resistance to Soviet control led to a major split with Stalin, and in 1948 Stalin expelled Yugoslavia from the Soviet bloc.

Developments within the Soviet Union caused more serious changes in eastern Europe. Three years after Stalin's death in 1953, Nikita

De-Stalinization   Khrushchev attacked Stalin and questioned his methods of rule during a secret speech at the Twentieth Party Congress. Khrushchev subse-

quently embarked on a policy of de-Stalinization, that is, the end of the rule of terror and the partial liberalization of Soviet society. Government officials removed portraits of Stalin from public places, renamed localities bearing his name, and commissioned historians to rewrite textbooks to deflate Stalin's reputation. The de-Stalinization period, which lasted from 1956 to 1964, also brought a "thaw" in government control and resulted in the release of millions of political prisoners. One of those was Alexandr Solzhenitsyn (1919–), who, thanks to Khrushchev, was able to publish his novel *One Day in the Life of Ivan Denisovich* (1962), a moving description of life in a Siberian forced-labor camp. With respect to foreign policy, Khrushchev emphasized the possibility of "peaceful coexistence" between different social systems and the recognition that a nuclear war was more likely to lead to mutual annihilation than to victory. The peaceful coexistence that Khrushchev fostered with the United States appeared to apply to domestic Soviet and eastern European societies also and tempted communist leaders in eastern Europe to experiment with domestic reforms and seek a degree of independence from Soviet domination.

The most serious challenge to Soviet control in eastern Europe came in 1956 from nationalist-minded communists in Hungary. When the communist regime in Hungary embraced the process of de-Stalinization,   *The Hungarian Challenge*
large numbers of Hungarian citizens demanded democracy and the breaking of ties to Moscow and

Czech citizens confront Warsaw Pact troops in Prague during the Soviet invasion in the spring of 1968.

the Warsaw Pact. In the wake of huge street demonstrations joined by the Hungarian armed forces, communist Imre Nagy (1896–1958) gained power and visibility as a nationalist leader who announced Hungary's withdrawal from the Warsaw Pact. Yet there were limits to Soviet tolerance for reform: viewing Hungary's demands as a threat to national security, Soviet officials sent tanks into Budapest and crushed the uprising in the late autumn of 1956.

Twelve years after the Hungarian uprising, Soviets again intervened in eastern Europe, this time in Czechoslovakia. In 1968 the Communist Party leader, Alexander Dubček (1921–1992), launched a liberal movement known as the "Prague Spring" and promised his fellow citizens "socialism with a human face." But Khrushchev's successor, Leonid Ilyich Brezhnev (1906–1982), fearful that such reforms might undermine Soviet control in eastern Europe, sanctioned military intervention by the Soviet army and brought an end to the Prague Spring. Brezhnev justified the invasion of Czechoslovakia by the Doctrine of Limited Sovereignty, better known as the "Brezhnev doctrine," which reserved the right to invade any socialist country that was deemed to be threatened by internal or external elements "hostile to socialism." The destruction of the Prague Spring served to reassert Soviet control over its satellite nations in eastern Europe and led to tightened controls within the Soviet Union.

The Prague Spring

The People's Republic of China

The birth of a communist China further transformed the cold war. With the defeat of Japan in 1945, the civil war in China resumed. By mid-1948 the strategic balance favored the communists, who inflicted heavy military defeats on the nationalists throughout 1948 and 1949. Faced with communist control, the national government under Jiang Jieshi (Chiang Kaishek) fled to the island of Taiwan, all the while continuing to claim its legitimacy as the government of all China. Nevertheless, Mao Zedong, the chairman of the Chinese Communist Party, proclaimed the establishment of the People's Republic of China on 1 October 1949. That declaration brought to an end the long period of imperialist intrusion in China and spawned a close relationship between the world's largest and most powerful socialist states.

Although the new Chinese constitution that took effect in 1954 created a national assembly chosen by popular election, it was the Communist Party that monopolized political power through a central committee and a politburo, chaired by Mao. To protect its authority, the government orchestrated campaigns to remove from power—by execution as well as through forced-labor camps—all of those likely to be a threat to the new leaders.

Next came the economic and social transformations of Chinese society, which centered on rapid industrialization and the collectivization of agriculture. Emulating the Soviet experiment of 1929, the Chinese introduced their first Five-Year Plan in 1955, which was designed to speed up economic development and expand heavy industry at the expense of consumer goods. A series of agrarian laws confiscated the landholdings of rich peasants and landlords and redistributed the land so that virtually every peasant had at least a small plot of land. After the government took over the grain market and prohibited farmers from marketing their crops, however, collective farms replaced private farming. Health care and primary education anchored to collectives permitted the extension of social services to a larger part of the population. Social reforms challenged and often eliminated Chinese family traditions, including child and forced marriages. Women also gained equal access to divorce as well as legal abortions. Foot binding, a symbol of women's subjugation, became a practice of the past.

Social and Economic Transformations

Moscow and Beijing drew closer during the early years of the cold war. That relationship was hardly astonishing because the leaders of both communist states felt threatened by a common enemy, the United States, which sought to establish anticommunist bastions throughout Asia, especially in Japan, South Korea, and Taiwan. In the early 1950s the Chinese-Soviet partnership took on a distinct form when Beijing recognized Moscow's authority in world communism in exchange for Russian military equipment and economic aid. In return, Soviet diplomats instigated a campaign in the United Nations to transfer the Chinese seat in the Security Council from Taiwan to the communist government on the mainland.

Fraternal Cooperation

As the Chinese embarked on a crash program of industrialization, the Soviet Union rendered valuable assistance in the form of economic aid and technical advisors. Before long, however, cracks appeared in the Soviet-Chinese alliance. From the Chinese perspective, Soviet aid programs were far too modest and had too many strings attached. For example, Soviet military aid to China

Cracks in the Alliance

during the Korean War had to be repaid in full at a time when China was in desperate need of capital. Another source of friction was the conflict between China and India over Tibet. After forcibly restoring Chinese sovereignty over Tibet in 1950, the Chinese ruthlessly quelled an armed insurrection in favor of Tibetan independence eleven years later. Beijing accused the government of India of fomenting the revolt, and the two sides subsequently became involved in border clashes in the Himalayas. Most infuriating to the Chinese, however, was Moscow's announcement of neutrality in the conflict, which the Soviets belied by giving a loan to India that exceeded any similar loan ever granted to China.

By the end of 1964, the rift between the Soviet Union and the People's Republic of China had become embarrassingly public, with both sides engaging in name-calling and in open competition for influence among the newly independent nations of Africa and Asia.

Détente and the Decline of Superpower Influence

In the late 1960s the leaders of the Soviet Union and the United States agreed on a policy of *détente,* or a reduction in hostility, trying to cool the costly arms race and slow their competition in developing countries. Although détente did not resolve the deep-seated antagonism between the superpowers, it did signal the relaxation of cold war tensions and prompted a new spirit of cooperation.

Between 1972 and 1974, U.S. and Soviet leaders exchanged visits and signed agreements calling for cooperation in areas such as health research, environmental protection, space ventures, and cultural exchange programs. However, the spirit of détente was most visible in negotiations designed to reduce the threat posed by strategic nuclear weapons. In 1972 U.S. and Soviet negotiators concluded their Strategic Arms Limitations Talks (SALT) with two agreements and reached another accord in 1979. The two cold war antagonists cooperated despite the tensions caused by the U.S. incursion into Vietnam, Soviet involvement in Angola and other African states, and continued Soviet repression of dissidents in eastern Europe.

An Era of Cooperation

Ironically, the era of détente coincided with a marked decline in superpower influence and prestige. This became clearly evident in the military and political setbacks experienced by the United States in Vietnam. After the Vietnamese defeated their French colonizers

in 1954, the United States extended aid to noncommunist Vietnamese in the south as a way of countering the influence of communists who had installed themselves in the north. Thereafter, U.S. involvement in South Vietnam steadily escalated and militarized under Presidents Eisenhower, Kennedy, and Lyndon B. Johnson (1908–1973), until by 1968 more than half a million U.S. troops served in-country in defense of South Vietnam. Heavy bombing campaigns were also unleashed on North Vietnam. Yet even with such a major U.S. presence, U.S. and South Vietnamese military leaders and troops could only achieve a stalemate in their struggles against communists in both North and South Vietnam. In the face of such a stalemate as well as mounting U.S. casualties, militant protests against the U.S. role in Vietnam spread in the United States, signaling a public distancing from U.S. cold war policy.

The U.S. Defeat in Vietnam

Primary Source
Gulf of Tonkin Resolution

Recognizing his country's distaste for the U.S. role in the Vietnam War, presidential candidate Richard Nixon pledged in 1968 to end the war. After escalation of the conflict in 1969 and 1970, U.S. troops began to withdraw, leaving the war in the hands of the South Vietnamese. In January 1973 the U.S. phase of the Vietnam War ended with the Paris Peace Accords. Within two years, however, the North Vietnamese, with help from the communist National Liberation Front in the south, had torn up the peace accords and defeated South Vietnam. In 1976 they unified the nation. In addition to being a bloody and expensive conflict, the Vietnam War severely damaged U.S. prestige at home and abroad.

Although the Vietnam War caused tension between the United States and the Soviet Union, it did not destroy the détente. By the early 1980s, however, relations between the superpowers had deteriorated notably, in large part due to another conflict—this time between the Soviet Union and Afghanistan. Until 1978 Muslim Afghanistan had quietly remained aloof from the cold war as a nonaligned nation. In that year, however, a pro-Soviet coup drew the republic into the cold war, precipitated foreign intervention, and fomented civil war. Once in power, the leftist People's Democratic Party of Afghanistan (PDPA) wasted little time in introducing radical social and legal reforms, which quickly caused a backlash. Especially in rural areas, Islamic religious and ethnic leaders objected to rapid

Soviet Setbacks in Afghanistan

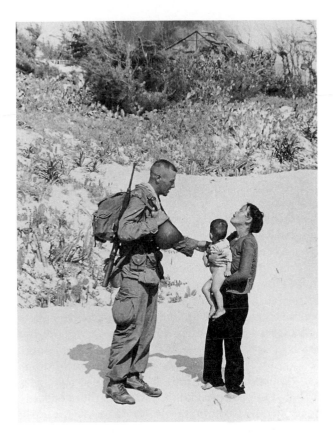

The Vietnam War: with her home going up in flames behind her, a Vietnamese woman pleads with a U.S. soldier.

social change and to the PDPA's brutal methods and called for armed resistance. By the summer of 1979, antigovernment rebels controlled much of the Afghan countryside. At that point the Soviet Union intervened, installing the Marxist Babrak Karmal as president. This Soviet-backed government was highly unpopular, and a national resistance movement spread throughout the country.

For nine years, well-equipped Soviet forces fought a brutal, unsuccessful campaign against Afghan mujahideen, or Islamic warriors, who gradually gained control of most of the countryside. Weapons and money from the United States, Saudi Arabia, Iran, Pakistan, and China sustained the mujahideen in their struggle. In 1986 the Kremlin decided to pull its troops out of the costly, unpopular, and unwinnable war. A cease-fire negotiated by the United Nations in 1988 led to a full Soviet withdrawal in 1989. However, the shared Islamic identity that mobilized and unified the mujahideen in their struggle against Soviet forces gave way to tribal, ethnic, and religious rival-

ries. In 1994 the Taliban, an organization claiming to be an army of religious students, began a campaign to unify the Afghan lands. In 1996 they captured the capital of Kabul after an eleven-month siege and proclaimed the Islamic State of Afghanistan.

Like the U.S. involvement in Vietnam, the Soviet experience in Afghanistan taxed the nation financially and also caused internal dissatisfaction with cold war politics. And as the Vietnam conflict had done to the United States, the war in Afghanistan undermined Soviet prestige and exposed the hollowness of its claims to military superiority.

Indeed, anxiety about nuclear weapons and doubts about cold war policies flourished in the 1960s and 1970s, and the world's youth formed the vanguard in a countercultural revolution that challenged the basic *Countercultural Protests* political and cultural precepts of post–World War II societies. Disturbed by their nations' apparent commitment to war and social conformity, European and American students in particular took to the streets in massive demonstrations designed to promote peace, end the nuclear arms race and the war in Vietnam, and abolish unfair university rules and restrictions. In the United States, students at the University of California at Berkeley formed the Free Speech Movement in 1964 to encourage free political expression on campus; four years later, students in France erected barricades in Paris reminiscent of nineteenth century French revolts.

THE END OF THE COLD WAR

Between 1989 and 1991 the Soviet system in Europe collapsed with stunning speed. During most of the 1980s, U.S. president Ronald Reagan (in office 1981–1989) reinvigorated cold war animosities, zeroing in on communism and the

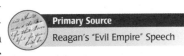

Primary Source
Reagan's "Evil Empire" Speech

USSR, which he called "the evil empire." In addition, Reagan called for enormous military spending to stay ahead of the Soviets.

Yet although Reagan's cold war rhetoric and budgets challenged détente and the Soviet ability to match U.S. spending, internal changes in the Soviet Union and eastern Europe worked most effectively to end communism and the cold war. Between 1989 and 1990, through a series of mostly nonviolent revolutions, the peoples of eastern and central Europe

At a U.S./USSR summit in 1985, a Soviet flag served as a dramatic backdrop and counterpoint to U.S. president Ronald Reagan's speech.

tegration by restructuring the economy and liberalizing society. Caught between the rising tide of radical reforms and the opposition of entrenched interests, however, he could do little except watch as events unfolded beyond his control. By the time the Soviet Union collapsed in 1991, the cold war system of states and alliances had become irrelevant to international relations.

Revolutions in Eastern and Central Europe

The inability to connect communism with nationalism left communist regimes vulnerable throughout eastern and central Europe. Those regimes were born in Moscow, transplanted by the Soviet army, and shored up by tanks and bayonets. To most eastern and central Europeans, the Soviet-imposed governments lacked legitimacy from the beginning, and despite the efforts of local communist leaders, the regimes never became firmly established. Moreover, the brutal Soviet interventions in 1956 (Hungary) and 1968 (Czechoslovakia) dashed the aspirations and dreams of reformers who had hoped to establish less harsh, more enlightened forms of communist rule. Thus, by the early 1970s, intellectuals and dissidents had abandoned all hope for a humane socialism. The Polish intellectual Leszek Kolakowski echoed the sentiments of many reformers when he complained in 1971 that "the dead and by now also grotesque creature called Marxist-Leninism still hangs at the necks of the rulers like a hopeless tumor."

Despite economic stagnation, an accelerated arms race with the Reagan administration that further strained the Soviet economy, and obvious signs of discontent, the rulers of eastern and central Europe were reluctant to restructure their ailing systems. It remained for a new Soviet leader, Mikhail S. Gorbachev, to unleash the forces that resulted in the disappearance of the Soviet empire in Europe. By the time Gorbachev visited East Berlin in 1989 on the fortieth anniversary of the German Democratic Republic, he had committed himself to a restructuring of the Soviet Union and to unilateral withdrawal from the cold war. In public interviews he surprised his grim-faced hosts with the announcement that the Brezhnev doctrine was no longer in force and that from then on each country would be responsible for its own destiny. The new Soviet orientation led in rapid succession to the collapse or overthrow of regimes in Poland, Bulgaria, Hungary, Czechoslovakia, Romania, and East Germany.

regained their independence, instituted democratic forms of government, and adopted market-based economies.

The downfall of communist regimes in Europe was the direct consequence of interrelated economic and political developments. The economic weakness of the communist regimes in eastern and central Europe and the Soviet Union became so apparent as to require reforms. The policies espoused by Soviet leader Mikhail Gorbachev (1931–), who came to power in 1985, represented an effort to address this economic deterioration, but they also unleashed a tidal wave of revolution that brought down governments from Czechoslovakia to the Soviet Union. As communism unraveled throughout eastern and central Europe, Gorbachev desperately tried to save the Soviet Union from disin-

The end of communism came first in Poland, where Solidarity—a combined trade union and nationalist movement—put pressure on the crumbling rule of the Communist Party. The Polish government legalized the previously banned Solidarity movement and agreed to multiparty elections in 1989 and 1990. The voters favored Solidarity candidates, and Lech Walesa (1943–), the movement's leader, became president of Poland. In Bulgaria popular unrest forced Todor Zhivkov (1911–1998), eastern Europe's longest-surviving communist dictator, to resign in November 1989. Two months later a national assembly began dismantling the communist state. In 1990 Hungarians also held free elections and launched their nation on the rocky path toward democracy and a market economy.

The disintegration of communism continued elsewhere in eastern Europe. In Czechoslovakia a "velvet revolution"—so called because it entailed little violence—swept communists out of office and restored

---

Lech Walesa (LEHK wah-LEHN-sah)

Berliners climb the wall after it fell on 9 November 1989.

democracy by 1990. In 1993 disagreements over the time frame for shifting to a market economy led to a "velvet divorce," breaking Czechoslovakia into two new nations, the Czech Republic and Slovakia. In Romania, in contrast, the regime of dictator Nicolae Ceaușescu (1918–1989) savagely repressed demonstrations, setting off a national uprising that ended within four days and left Ceaușescu and his wife dead.

East Germany had long been a staunchly communist Soviet satellite. Its aging leader, Erich Honecker (1912–1994), openly clung to Stalinist policies. It was too late for anything other than radical changes, however. Honecker's own party removed him from power and decided to open the Berlin Wall to intra-German traffic on 9 November 1989. The end to a divided Berlin was in sight, literally, as thousands of East and West Berliners tore down the Berlin wall in the last weeks of 1989. In 1990 the two Germanies, originally divided by the cold war, formed a united nation.

The Collapse of the Soviet Union

The desire to concentrate attention and resources on urgent matters at home motivated Gorbachev's decision to disengage his nation from the cold war and its military and diplomatic extensions. Although he never intended to abolish the existing political and economic system, it proved impossible to fix parts of the system without undermining the whole. The desire of the Communist Party to control every aspect of the system precluded partial reforms.

Gorbachev's reform efforts focused on the ailing economy. Antiquated industrial plants and obsolete technologies resulted in shoddy and out-moded products, and in any case the diversion of crucial resources to the military *Gorbachev's Reforms* made it impossible to produce enough consumer goods. The failure of state and collective farms to feed the population compelled the Soviet government to import grains from the United States, Canada, and elsewhere. By 1990 the government had imposed rationing to cope with the scarcity of essential consumer goods and food. Economic stagnation in turn contributed to the decline of the Soviet standard of living and the disintegration of the state-sponsored health care system. Funding of the educational system dropped precipitously, and pollution threatened to engulf the entire country. Demoralization affected ever-larger numbers of Soviet citizens as divorce rates climbed, corruption intensified, and alcoholism became more widespread.

When it was clear that the old methods of boosting productivity through bureaucratic exhortation and harassment would not work, Gorbachev contemplated different kinds of reform, using the term *perestroika,* or "restructuring," to describe his efforts to decentralize the economy. To make perestroika work, the Soviet leader linked it to *glasnost,* the opening of Soviet society to public criticism and admission of past mistakes.

Perestroika and Glasnost

Perestroika proved more difficult to implement than Gorbachev had imagined, and glasnost unleashed a torrent of criticism that shook the Soviet state to its foundations. When Gorbachev pushed economic decentralization, the profit motive and the cost-accounting methods he instituted engendered the hostility of those whose privileged positions depended on the old system. Many of Gorbachev's comrades and certain factions of the mili-

perestroika (payr-eh-STROY-kuh)
glasnost (GLAHS-nohst)

tary objected to perestroika and worked to undermine or destroy it. Moreover, as glasnost allowed discontent with Soviet life to burst into the open, long-repressed ethnic and nationalist sentiments bubbled to the surface, posing a threat to the multiethnic Soviet state.

By the summer of 1990, it was clear that Gorbachev's reforms could not halt the downward slide of industrial and agricultural production or control skyrocketing inflation. As the Soviet economy disintegrated, many minorities contemplated secession from the Soviet Union. The Baltic peoples—Estonians, Latvians, and Lithuanians—were first into the fray, declaring their independence in August 1991. In the following months the remaining twelve republics of the Soviet Union followed suit. The largest and most prominent of the Soviet republics, the Russian Soviet Federated Socialist Republic, and its recently elected president, Boris N. Yeltsin (1931–), led the drive for independence. Soviet leaders vacillated between threats of repression and promises of better treatment, but neither option could stop the movement for independence.

Map 34.3   Collapse of the Soviet Union and the European communist regimes. Note the number of states suddenly created by the breakup of the Soviet Union. How would this affect the ability of each to survive, both economically and politically?

Some did try. While Gorbachev was vacationing in the Crimea in August 1991, a group of conspirators—including discontented party functionaries, disillusioned KGB (secret police) officials, and dissatisfied military officers—decided to seize power. Gorbachev's former friend and ally, the flamboyant Boris Yeltsin, crushed the coup with the help of loyal Red Army units. Gorbachev emerged unscathed from house arrest, but his political career had ended. He watched from the sidelines as Yeltsin dismantled the Communist Party and pushed the country toward market-oriented economic reforms. On 25 December 1991 the Soviet flag fluttered for the last time atop the Kremlin, and by the last day of that year the Union of Soviet Socialist Republics had ceased to exist.

Toward an Uncertain Future

In many ways the cold war provided comfort to the world—however cold that comfort seemed at the time. World War II left most of the major imperialist, fascist, and militarist nations in shambles, and the United States and the Soviet Union stepped into what could have been an uncomfortable vacuum in global leadership. Perilous and controlling it may have been, but the cold war that resulted from the ideological contest between the superpowers ordered and defined the world for almost fifty years. The cold war also shaped how the nations and peoples of the world perceived themselves—as good capitalists fighting evil communists, as progressive socialists bat-

tling regressive capitalists, or as nonaligned peoples striving to follow their own paths. Although those perceptions placed constraints on the choices open to them, particularly given the control exerted by the United States and the USSR at the peak of their power, the choices nonetheless were familiar. At the end of the cold war, those easy choices disappeared.

The most immediate and obvious loss that accompanied the end of the cold war involved the alliance systems built by the two former superpowers. Indeed, many observers praised the cold war system for providing peace and security around the world despite the nuclear balance of terror. The loss of deterrence against global disorder and violence was matched by a corresponding lack of certainty regarding the future and by a declining sense of purpose in an era no longer characterized by ideological struggle.

The disappearance of communist regimes in eastern Europe, the dissolution of the Soviet Union, and the increasing market orientation of the People's Republic of China virtually guaranteed the diminishing popularity of the communist model. To be sure, a few states, such as Cuba and North Korea, clung to communism, but without the support once furnished by the Soviet Union their long-term viability as communist regimes was doubtful. The end of the cold war suggested the possibility of a radical shift in power relations, a global realignment that marked a new era of world history devoid of the categories embraced during the cold war.

SUMMARY

The cold war defined much of the global political landscape after World War II. The United States and the Soviet Union stepped into the void created by the disappearance of European empires after 1945, and global encounters between these proponents of democracy and communism stretched from a divided Europe to Korea, Cuba, Vietnam, and Afghanistan. Adding elements of tension to these conflicts were the increasingly sophisticated nuclear weapons and delivery systems that threatened human annihilation. The cold war evolved from mutual hostility to peaceful coexistence and détente, finally reaching extinction at the close of the twentieth century. Facing opposition at home and military humiliation abroad, the superpowers relinquished their hegemonic dreams of world control. From its beginning to its end, the cold war suggested powerful new global forces at work in the wake of World War II. The process of decolonization—itself complicated by the cold war—also symbolized that same phenomenon of radical postwar alterations in the global balance of power.

CHRONOLOGY

1948–1949	Berlin blockade and airlift
1949	Division of Berlin and Germany
1949	Establishment of People's Republic of China
1950–1953	Korean War
1956	Uprising in Hungary
1959	Castro comes to power in Cuba
1961	Bay of Pigs invasion
1961	Construction of Berlin Wall
1962	Cuban missile crisis
1964	Sino-Soviet rift
1965–1973	U.S. troops to Vietnam
1968	Prague Spring
1973	U.S. defeat in Vietnam
1989	Soviet withdrawal from Afghanistan
1989	Fall of Berlin Wall
1990	Reunification of Germany
1991	Collapse of the Soviet Union
1991	End of the cold war

FOR FURTHER READING

David Calleo. *Beyond American Hegemony: The Future of the Western Alliance*. New York, 1987. A broad treatment of Europe during and after the cold war.

John Lewis Gaddis. *Strategies of Containment: A Critical Appraisal of Postwar American National Security Policy*. New York, 1982. Insightful work that traces the U.S. policy of containment from its inception to the late 1970s.

Margot A. Henriksen. *Dr. Strangelove's America: Society and Culture in the Atomic Age*. Berkeley, 1997. Analyzes the crucial role the bomb played in shaping postwar U.S. society.

Akira Iriye. *The Cold War in Asia: A Historical Introduction*. Englewood Cliffs, N.J., 1974. A leading diplomatic historian provides an excellent introduction to the subject.

Madeline Kalb. *The Congo Cables: The Cold War in Africa—from Eisenhower to Kennedy*. New York, 1982. Proper attention for an often neglected aspect of the cold war.

Bruce Kuniholm. *The Origins of the Cold War in the Near East*. Princeton, 1980. A dissection of great power diplomacy and conflicts that focuses on Greece, Turkey, and Iran.

Walter Lafeber. *America, Russia, and the Cold War, 1945–1992*. 7th ed. New York, 1993. A standard work that emphasizes the corrosive effects the cold war had on democratic values in the United States.

Elaine Tyler May. *Homeward Bound: American Families in the Cold War Era*. New York, 1988. An insightful analysis of how the cold war and the atomic age affected family and gender roles in U.S. society.

William Taubman. *Stalin's American Policy: From Entente to Détente to Cold War*. New York, 1982. An important work that focuses on the Soviet perspective of the cold war.

Stephen Whitfield. *The Culture of the Cold War*. Baltimore, 1991. An in-depth analysis of how the cold war and domestic anti-communism shaped U.S. culture from the 1940s to the early 1960s.

CHAPTER 35

The End of Empire and the Emergence of a World without Borders

"Hé Ram" were the last words that escaped his lips after three bullets savagely ripped through his frail body. Roughly translated, he uttered "O! God" and then died. It had begun as a day much like any other in the life of Mohandas K. Gandhi (1869–1948), or "Bapuji" as he was fondly called—a dear father of the country of India. On 30 January 1948, a few months after India gained its independence from Great Britain, he awakened at 3:00 A.M. to work on a draft of a new constitution for the Indian National Congress. The draft emphasized his major concerns for the newly independent India: that villages be empowered, that discrimination based on the caste system be abolished, and that religious intolerance and violence between Hindus and Muslims cease. Still distraught over the partitioning of his land into a Hindu India and a Muslim Pakistan, he had weakened himself after independence through fasts and hunger strikes to protest the killings of Hindus and Muslims that had ensued. He weighed a mere 107 pounds that day.

Alternating between working, talking with visitors, and napping, Gandhi finally took a meal at 4:30 P.M. A little over half an hour later, he made his way to the evening prayer meeting he was to lead. As he approached the dais, he stopped to press his palms together, offering the traditional Hindu greeting to the waiting crowd. At that moment, out of the crowd stepped the Hindu extremist Nathuram Godse, who suddenly pulled a Beretta pistol from his pants pocket and fired the three shots that ended the life of the man many credited with

OPPOSITE PAGE: *This saintly image of Mohandas K. Gandhi captures his spiritual significance to the independence movement in India both before and after his death.*

Indian independence, the man seen as the very soul and conscience of India.

Gandhi's murder suggested the troubles and traumas faced by nations and peoples adjusting to independence from colonial rule. Yet despite the hazards of life in a world without empires, peoples in the colonial world fought tenaciously for independence and then for national unity after World War II. In conjunction with the cold war, decolonization reshaped the world in the latter half of the twentieth century. Indeed, the end of empire was one of the most important outcomes of World War II, as dozens of new, independent nations emerged from the British, French, Dutch, Spanish, and Portuguese empires established in previous centuries. With the emergence of two superpowers dedicated to the overthrow of empire, the stage was set for a wholesale overturning of colonial rule. As cold war animosities deepened, however, emerging nations were often confronted by the demand that they take sides and choose between capitalism and communism. At times that demand compromised their newly won independence, particularly in nations deemed strategically important by the superpowers.

In the years between the end of World War II and 1980, more than ninety nations gained independence. Nations achieved independence at different times: whereas India and Pakistan became independent in 1947, for example, Zimbabwe (Southern Rhodesia) became independent only in 1980. Algerians in North Africa fought a long, hard war against the French for freedom, whereas others followed less torturous routes to independence. Vietnam became deeply embroiled in the cold war even as it successfully fought French imperial domination; other countries managed to avoid such entanglement. Regardless of freedom's timetable, new and developing nations around the world discovered, as Gandhi had, that independence was just the first step on a much longer, and often much more difficult, road to national unity and social and economic stability.

With the end of empires and also of the cold war, a new world order emerged: one without borders. One pronounced feature of that world was an increased level of economic interaction and integration between countries. The forces driving the world economy in that direction, often referred to as *globalization,* included advances in communications technology, an enormous expansion of international trade, and the emergence of new international organizations that favored market-oriented economics. Many of these same forces have also driven global cultural integration through consumer goods, television, computers, and popular culture. Although global economic and cultural integration are not new, the more recent phenomenon of globalization has been different and unprecedented both in scope and in speed, and it has transformed the social and political as well as the economic contours of the world. Some of those transformations have taken the form of global problems—such as poverty, terrorism, and environmental degradation—that now face all of humanity. Whatever the transformations, one thing is increasingly clear: the national borders so long fought for, and fought over, are no longer as significant as they once were.

INDEPENDENCE IN ASIA

In the wake of World War II, the power of Asian nationalism was irrepressible. New nations emerged throughout Asia, from India and Pakistan in south Asia to diverse Arab nations in southwest Asia and to Vietnam, Cambodia, and Laos in southeast Asia. These lands encountered different conditions in their quests for independence and freedom from imperial control, but everywhere Asian nationalists rallied their people against colonialism and imperialism.

India's Partitioned Independence

After World War II, it became painfully obvious to the British government that it could not continue to bear the financial burden of governing India, particularly since nationalists made it clear that they would accept nothing less than complete independence. As the probability of Indian *The Coming of Self-Rule* independence became more pronounced, the issue of Muslim separatism grew in importance, and Muslims increasingly feared their minority status in a free India dominated by Hindus. Muhammad Ali Jinnah (1876–1948), leader of the Muslim League, felt no qualms about frankly expressing Muslim concerns and desires for a separate Muslim state, even as Congress Party leaders such as Jawaharlal Nehru (1889–1964) and Gandhi urged all Indians to act and feel as one nation, undivided by what came to be known as communalism—emphasizing religious over national identity.

Jinnah had his way, however, and when the British withdrew from India in 1947 two new flags were raised in place of the British Union Jack. Gandhi condemned

Zimbabwe (zihm-BAHB-way)

the division as a "vivisection" of his homeland and prophesied that "rivers of blood" would flow in its wake. His vision came true as the terms of partition were announced and hundreds of thousands of Muslim and Hindu refugees migrated to either Muslim Pakistan (divided between parts of Bengal in the east and Punjab in the west) or Hindu India to escape religious per-

Partition and Violence

secution. By mid-1948 an estimated ten million refugees had made the tortuous journey to one or the other state, and between half a million and one million people had died in the violence that accompanied those mass migrations. Through it all, Gandhi continually urged all Indians

Image
Partition of India

Map 35.1 Decolonization in Asia. (Date is year of independence.) Note the dates of independence for the colonies of Great Britain, the Netherlands, the United States, and France. Why did independence occur in such a short span of time for most of these colonies?

and Pakistanis to adhere to the practice of nonviolence. When Gandhi was shot he became a martyr to his own cause, killed by the violence he so abhorred.

Though mired in violence, Indian independence became a reality, with momentous consequences for the process of decolonization. Just as Gandhi's nonviolent resistance to British rule inspired nationalists around the globe before and after World War II, independence in India and Pakistan further encouraged anti-imperial movements throughout Asia and Africa. Moreover, once India left the British empire, there could be little doubt about the fate of Britain's remaining imperial possessions.

Unlike the Dutch and the French, who at times tenaciously battled to maintain imperial control in Asia, the British recognized that Europeans could not rule in Asia without the cooperation of colonial peoples. Also unlike the Dutch and the French, the British could rely on their own models of decolonization, previously tested in Canada. Like Canada, India and Pakistan gained independence yet retained ties to Britain, becoming Dominion members in the British Commonwealth and adopting English as their official language.

Another way in which Indian independence inspired other nations and set a pattern for grappling

Nonalignment   with decolonization in the midst of a cold war was through Nehru's promotion of a nonalignment strategy. Nehru proved instrumental in fashioning a compelling position for newly independent nations caught in the cold war and in the superpower tug-of-war contests for the loyalties of new nations. He became one of the impassioned defenders of nonalignment, arguing that "each country has not only the right to freedom but also to decide its own policy and way of life."

Nehru made that assertion at the Bandung Conference, where in April 1955 leaders from twenty-three Asian and six African nations met in Bandung, Indonesia, to discuss alternatives to choosing between the United States and the Soviet Union. Besides neutrality in the cold war, the Bandung Conference stressed the struggle against colonialism and racism. Bandung was the precursor of the broader Nonaligned Movement, which held occasional meetings so that its members could discuss their relations with the United States and the Soviet Union. The movement's primary goal was to maintain formal neutrality. However, although theoretically nonaligned with either cold war superpower, many member states had close ties to one or the other, and that situation caused dissension within the movement. For example, the Philippines and Cuba clearly

supported the U.S. and Soviet camps, respectively. Nevertheless, other individual states avoided becoming pawns in the cold war by announcing the policy of nonalignment advocated by Nehru.

Since winning its independence, India has stood out among decolonized nations not just for its advocacy of nonalignment but also for its ability to maintain its political stability and its democratic system. Indeed, even though India has faced many of the same crises that have shaken other developing nations—ethnic and religious conflict, wars, poverty, political assassinations, and overpopulation—Nehru's heirs have remained committed to free elections and a critical press.

Nationalist Struggles in Vietnam

In contrast to India, Vietnam could not keep its nationalist struggle for independence separate from the complications of the cold war. Rather, Vietnam became deeply enmeshed in the contest between capitalism and communism, which meant that decolonization there was a long and bloody process.

Vietnam's nationalist communist leader, Ho Chi Minh (1890–1969), had been struggling for autonomy from French imperialism for two decades when World War II broke out in Europe. Thus the Japanese invasion of his homeland after the fall of France in 1940 seemed to Ho like the replacement of 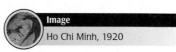 one imperialist power with another. During the war, Ho fought against the Japanese and in the waning days of the war helped oust them from Vietnam altogether. With both the French and the Japanese gone, Ho took the opportunity to establish himself as leader of an independent Vietnam, complete with a Declaration of Independence modeled on the U.S. declaration.

However, the French, humiliated by their country's easy defeat and occupation by the Germans, sought to reclaim their imperial possessions as a way of regaining their world-power status. In 1945 they invaded Vietnam, and by 1947 they seemed to have secured their power. However, that security proved to be temporary. Much like the Chinese communists in their battles against the Japanese and then against the nationalists in the postwar years, the Vietnamese resistance forces, led by Ho Chi Minh and General Vo Nguyen Giap (1911–), mounted a campaign of guerrilla warfare. The Vietnamese communists increasingly regained control of their country, especially after 1949, when communist China sent aid and arms to the Viet Minh. Thus strengthened, they defeated the French at

Image

Ho Chi Minh, 1920

their fortress in Dienbienphu in 1954. The French had to sue for peace at the conference table.

The peace conference, held in Geneva in 1954, determined that Vietnam should be temporarily divided at the seventeenth parallel; North Vietnam would be controlled by Ho Chi Minh and the communist forces, whereas South Vietnam remained in the hands of non-communists. Leaving all of Vietnam in the hands of Ho's communists was unthinkable for the United States, especially after the globalization of the cold war that had accompanied the Korean War. The United States had already aided the French in their struggle against Ho—now they did the same for the government of South Vietnam. Violating the terms of the Geneva Agreements, which required elections that would likely have brought Ho to power, South Vietnam's leaders, with U.S. support, avoided elections and sought to build a government that would prevent the spread of communism in South Vietnam and elsewhere in Asia. However, the leaders of South Vietnam did not have the support of the people, who quickly grew discontented enough to resort to arms.

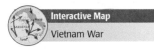
Interactive Map
Vietnam War

In 1960 South Vietnamese nationalists—with the aid of weapons and troops from the north—formed the National Liberation Front to fight for freedom from South Vietnamese rule. In turn, the government in the north received economic and military assistance from the Soviet Union and China. This ensured that the war would be a long, bloody, and expensive stalemate. Ultimately, United States forces withdrew from this unwinnable war in 1975, and in 1976 North Vietnam conquered the south, united the country, and at long last declared independence.

Although the Vietnamese ultimately did achieve their long-awaited independence, their experience demonstrated what could occur when independence movements became entangled with the politics and logic of the cold war.

Arab National States and the Problem of Palestine

With one exception, the Arab states of southwest Asia—including Syria, Iraq, Lebanon, and Jordan—had little difficulty freeing themselves from the colonial powers of France and Britain by the end of World War II. The issue of Palestinian independence, however, highlighted the difficulties of decolonization in an area where more than one group claimed the right to establish a nation.

Great Britain served as the mandate power in Palestine after the Great War, and before and during its mandate made conflicting promises both to Palestinian Arabs and to Jews who hoped to establish a secure homeland in Palestine. With the Balfour Declaration of 1917, the British government committed itself to the support of a Jewish homeland. The declaration was due in part to pressure by Zionists, who were dedicated to combating the violent anti-Semitism prevailing in central and eastern Europe by establishing a national Jewish state. Zionists received an additional boost when their aims were supported by the Allies at the Paris Peace Conference in 1919. Thus the British were compelled to allow Jewish migration to Palestine under their mandate, but they also had to allay the fears of those in possession of the land—the Palestinian Arabs.

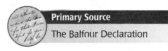
Primary Source
The Balfour Declaration

This British attempt to balance the causes of two conflicting groups was unsuccessful, and large-scale violence was prevented only through the use of imperial military forces. The Palestinian Muslims perceived the Jews as alien interlopers in their own land. At the same time, European Jews were dangerously under attack by the Nazis, and Zionists in Palestine armed themselves to protect Jewish settlers against Arab reprisals. At the end of World War II, a battle brewed. As Arab states around Palestine gained their freedom from imperial rule, they developed a pan-Arab nationalism

Ho Chi Minh, leader of North Vietnam from 1945 to 1969 and one of southeast Asia's most influential communist leaders.

sparked by support for their fellow Arabs in Palestine and opposition to the possibility of a Jewish state there. The Holocaust, however, intensified the Jewish commitment to build a state capable of defending the world's remaining Jews.

While the Arabs in Palestine insisted on complete independence under Arab rule, in 1945 the Jews embarked on a course of violent resistance to the British to compel recognition of Jewish demands for self-rule. The British could not resolve the dispute and instead gave up. In 1947 they turned the region over to the newly created United Nations, which came up with a plan, in November 1947, to divide Palestine into two distinct states. Both Arabs and Jews found the terms unacceptable and began to battle each other. In May 1948 the Jews in Palestine further provoked Arab outrage when they announced the creation of the independent state of Israel. In response, the Arab states of Egypt, Jordan, Syria, Lebanon, and Iraq joined Palestinians in a war to destroy the new state.

However, Arab attacks and campaigns, although boldly fought, were uncoordinated, and the Israelis managed to achieve a stunning victory, gaining territories far larger than those that would have been granted to the Jewish state under the United Nations partition plan. A truce went into effect in early 1949 under UN auspices, and the partition of Palestine resulted. Jerusalem and the Jordan River valley were divided between the new Israeli state and the Kingdom of Jordan, and Israel controlled the coastal areas of Palestine and the Negev Desert to the Red Sea.

The problem of Palestine, then, demonstrated the difficulties and dangers of decolonization in contested areas. In the case of Palestine, it seems safe to say that the transfer of power from the British mandate system resulted in an outcome that has created long-term instability and mutual hatreds.

Map 35.2 Arab-Israeli conflict between 1949 and 1982. Compare the boundaries proposed by the UN partition of Palestine with those claimed by Israel after 1948–49. What were the strategic advantages of the extra territories claimed by Israel in 1948–49?

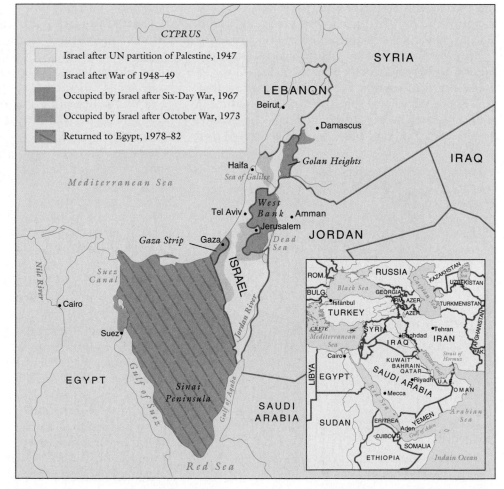

DECOLONIZATION IN AFRICA

In the 1950s the superpowers' influence intensified. For African lands, that situation often meant delays in decolonization. Also complicating the decolonization process were internal divisions in African societies, which undermined attempts to forge national or pan-African identities. Tribal, ethnic, religious, and linguistic divides within and between state boundaries, all of which colonial rulers had exploited, posed a challenge to African leaders, particularly once independence came and the imperial enemy departed. Given the variety of barriers to African independence, then, it is not astonishing that independence came more slowly in Africa than in other regions of the world.

Forcing the French out of North Africa

In Africa as in southeast Asia, the French resisted decolonization. In Algeria the French fought a bloody war that began in 1954, the year France suffered its defeat at Dienbienphu. Somewhat ironically, while it focused its efforts on Algeria in the 1950s and 1960s, France allowed all its other territories in Africa to gain independence. In

France in Africa

1956 France granted independence to its colonies in Morocco and Tunisia, and thirteen French colonies in west and equatorial Africa won

Interactive Map
Imperialism in Africa

their independence in 1960, a year that came to be known as "the year of Africa."

In Algeria, however, France was determined to remain in control. The two million French settlers who lived there by the mid-1940s demanded that the government in Paris defend their cause in north Africa. Yet after World War II, Algerians embarked on a revitalized campaign for independence from France and for freedom from domination by white settlers. The event that touched off the Algerian revolt came in May 1945. French colonial police in the town of Sétif fired shots into an otherwise peaceful demonstration in support of Algerian and Arab nationalism. The resulting melee killed more than eight thousand Algerian Muslims and approximately one hundred French.

In 1954 the Algerian war of liberation began in earnest under the command of the Front de Libération Nationale (National Liberation Front, *War in Algeria* or FLN). France sent thousands of troops to Algeria to put down the revolution, and by 1958 it had committed half a million soldiers to the war. The war became ugly and brutal: Algerians serving with the French had to kill fellow Algerians or be killed by them; Algerian civilians became trapped in the crossfire of war, often accused of and killed for aiding FLN guerrillas; thousands of French soldiers died. By the time Algerians finally gained independence from France in 1962, hundreds of thousands of Algerians had lost their lives. Thereafter, thanks in large part to the writings of the West Indian Frantz Fanon (1925–1961), who became an Algerian revolutionary, the Algerian war of liberation became synonymous

French paratroopers search for terrorists near Algiers, January 1957.

with the utility of using whatever violent means necessary to achieve independence from colonial oppressors.

Black African Nationalism and Independence

Before and during World War II, nationalism flourished in sub-Saharan Africa. African nationalists celebrated their blackness and Africanness in contrast to their European colonial rulers. Drawing from the pan-African movements that emerged in the United States and the Caribbean, African intellectuals, especially in French-controlled west Africa, established a movement to promote *Négritude* ("Blackness"). Reviving Africa's great traditions and cultures, poets and writers expressed a widely shared pride in Africa.

This celebration of African culture was accompanied by grassroots protests against European imperialism. However, although most Europeans came to believe in the inevitability of decolonization in the decades after World War II, their beliefs about the incapacities of Africans for self-government convinced them that the transition to independence would be very slow indeed. Also complicating the process of decolonization in sub-Saharan Africa were the presence of white settlers in certain African colonies as well as cold war politics, which allowed imperial powers to justify oppressive actions in the name of rooting out a subversive communist presence. Despite the delays, however, sub-Saharan states slowly but surely won their independence.

Growth of African Nationalism

Agitation for independence in sub-Saharan Africa took on many forms, peaceful and violent, and decolonization occurred at a different pace in different nations. Ghana became independent in 1957, but independence came much later to Angola (1975) and Zimbabwe, formerly Southern Rhodesia (1980). In many instances, African nations sealed their severance from imperial control by adopting new names that shunned the memory of European rule and drew from the glory of Africa's past empires. Ghana set the pattern, and the map of Africa soon featured similar references to precolonial African places: Zambia, Malawi, Zimbabwe.

African Independence

Freedom and Conflict in Sub-Saharan Africa

Ghana's success in achieving its freedom from British rule in 1957 served as a hallmark in Africa's end of empire. Under the leadership of Kwame Nkrumah (1909–1972), political parties and strategies for mass action took shape. Although the British initially subjected Nkrumah and other nationalists to jail terms and repressive control, gradually they allowed reforms and negotiated the peaceful transfer of power in their Gold Coast colony. After it became independent in 1957, Ghana emboldened and inspired other African nationalist movements. Nkrumah, as a leader of the first sub-Saharan African nation to gain independence from colonial rule, became a persuasive spokesperson for pan-African unity.

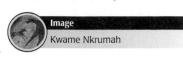
Image
Kwame Nkrumah

The process of attaining independence did not always prove as nonviolent as in Ghana. The battle that took place in the British colony of Kenya in east Africa demonstrated the complexity and difficulty of African decolonization. The situation in Kenya turned tense and violent in a clash between powerful white settlers and nationalists, especially the Kikuyu, one of Kenya's largest ethnic groups. Beginning in 1947, Kikuyu rebels embarked on a violent campaign against Europeans and African collaborators. The settlers who controlled the colonial government in Nairobi refused to see the uprisings as a legitimate expression of discontent with colonial rule. Rather, they branded the Kikuyu tribes as radicals—calling them Mau Mau subversives or communists—bent on a racial struggle for primacy. As one settler put it, "Why the hell can't we fight these apes and worry about the survivors later?"

Anticolonial Rebellion in Kenya

In reality, Kikuyu radicalism and violence had much more to do with nationalist opposition to British colonial rule, especially land policies in Kenya. In the 1930s and 1940s, white settlers had pushed many Kikuyu off the most fertile highland farm areas and reduced them to the status of wage slaves or relegated them to overcrowded "tribal reserves." Resistance began in the early 1940s with labor strikes and violent direct-action campaigns, but attacks on white settlers and black collaborators escalated in the 1950s. In 1952 the British established a state of emergency to crush the anticolonial guerrilla movement. Unable or unwilling to distinguish violent activism from nonviolent agitation, the British moved to suppress all nationalist groups and jailed Kenya's nationalist leaders, including Jomo Kenyatta (1895–1978), in 1953. Amid growing resistance to colonial rule, the British mounted major military offenses against rebel forces, supporting their army troops with artillery, bombers, and jet fighters. By 1956 the British had effectively

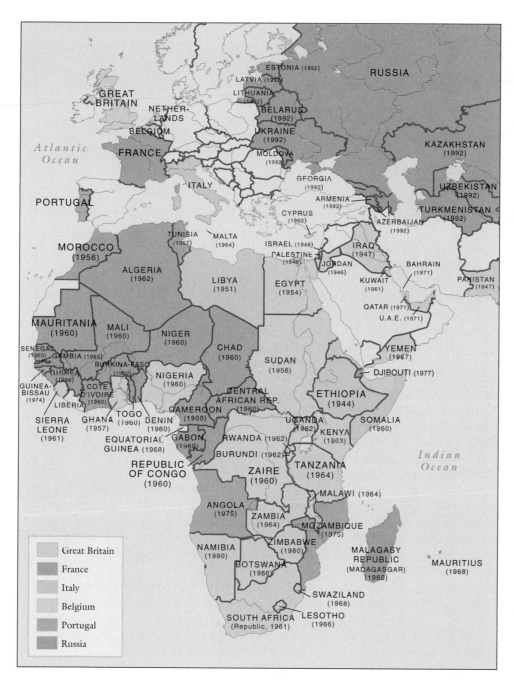

Map 35.3 Decolonization in Africa. (Date is year of independence.) Compare this map with Map 29.4. How do the borders of the newly independent African states compare with those drawn by European powers in the late nineteenth century?

crushed all military resistance in a conflict that claimed the lives of twelve thousand Africans and one hundred Europeans.

Despite military defeat, Kikuyu fighters broke British resolve in Kenya and gained increasing international recognition of African grievances. The British resisted the radical white supremacism and political domineering of the settlers in Kenya and instead responded to calls for Kenya's independence. In 1959 the British lifted the state of emergency, and as political parties formed, nationalist leaders such as Kenyatta reemerged to lead those parties. By December 1963 Kenya had negotiated its independence.

The experience of some African countries also demonstrated the dangers of becoming entangled in cold war politics. That was the case in the land once known as the Belgian Congo, which was reconfigured as Zaire in 1971 and renamed the Democratic Republic of the

Kwame Nkrumah on African Unity

As the leader of the first African nation to gain independence, Kwame Nkrumah (1909–1972) became a respected spokesperson for African unity as a strategy for dealing with decolonization during the cold war. In his book I Speak of Freedom: A Statement of African Ideology *(1961), Nkrumah made an eloquent case for an African solution for the problems of African independence during a global cold war.*

■ ■ ■

It is clear that we must find an African solution to our problems, and that this can only be found in African unity. Divided we are weak; united, Africa could become one of the greatest forces for good in the world.

Never before have a people had within their grasp so great an opportunity for developing a continent endowed with so much wealth. Individually, the independent states of Africa, some of them potentially rich, others poor, can do little for their people. Together, by mutual help, they can achieve much. But the economic development of the continent must be planned and pursued as a whole. A loose confederation designed only for economic cooperation would not provide the necessary unity of purpose. Only a strong political union can bring about full and effective development of our natural resources for the benefit of our people.

The political situation in Africa today is heartening and at the same time disturbing. It is heartening to see so many new flags hoisted in place of the old; it is disturbing to see so many countries of varying sizes and at different levels of development, weak and, in some cases, almost helpless. If this terrible state of fragmentation is allowed to continue it may well be disastrous for us all.

Critics of African unity often refer to the wide differences in culture, language and ideas in various parts of Africa. This is true, but the essential fact remains that we are all Africans, and have a common interest in the independence of Africa. The difficulties presented by questions of language, culture and different political systems are not insuperable. If the need for political union is agreed by us all, then the will to create it is born; and where there's a will there's a way.

The greatest contribution that Africa can make to the peace of the world is to avoid all the dangers inherent in disunity, by creating a political union which will also by its success, stand as an example to a divided world. A union of African states will project more effectively the African personality. It will command respect from a world that has regard only for size and influence.

We have to prove that greatness is not to be measured in stock piles of atom bombs. I believe strongly and sincerely that with the deep-rooted wisdom and dignity, the innate respect for human lives, the intense humanity that is our heritage, the African race, united under one federal government, will emerge not as just another world bloc to flaunt its wealth and strength, but as a Great Power whose greatness is indestructible because it is not built on fear, envy and suspicion, nor won at the expense of others, but founded on hope, trust, friendship and directed to the good of all mankind.

• *How does Nkrumah's call for African unity rather than fragmentation reflect the tensions between decolonization and the ongoing cold war?*

SOURCE: Kwame Nkrumah. *I Speak of Freedom: A Statement of African Ideology.* New York: Frederick A. Praeger, 1961, x–xii.

Congo in 1997. The region won independence from Belgium in 1960 under the popular leadership of Patrice Lumumba (1925–1961), who was also a Maoist Marxist. The general Mobutu Sese Seko (1930–1997), a contender for power, killed Lumumba the very next year in a military coup supported by the United States. Although Mobutu ruled Zaire as a dictator and devastated the economy in the process of enriching himself, his government continued to receive support from the United States and other European

Rebel suspects in a British internment camp, Nairobi, Kenya.

of them followed a communist or socialist path of political development. Under Mao Zedong (1893–1976), China served as a guide and inspiration *Mao's China* for those countries seeking a means of political development distinct from the ways of their previous colonial masters. Mao reunified China for the first time since the collapse of the Qing dynasty, transforming European communist ideology into a distinctly Chinese form. After 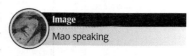 1949 he embarked on programs designed to accelerate development in China and to distinguish Chinese communism from Soviet communism. Unfortunately, the Great Leap Forward (1958–1961) and the Great Proletarian Cultural Revolution (1966–1976) hampered the political and economic development that Mao so urgently sought.

Mao envisioned his Great Leap Forward as a way to overtake the industrial production of more developed nations, and to that end he worked to collectivize all land, business, and industrial enterprises. Private ownership was abolished, and farming and industry became largely rural and communal. The Great Leap Forward—or "Giant Step Backward" as some have dubbed it—failed. Most disastrous was its impact on agricultural production in China: peasants could not meet quotas, and a series of bad harvests contributed to one of the deadliest famines in history, resulting in the deaths of as many as twenty million people between 1959 and 1962.

In 1966 Mao tried to reignite the revolutionary spirit with the inauguration of the Great Proletarian Cultural Revolution. Designed to root out the revisionism Mao perceived in Chinese life, the Cultural Revolution subjected millions of people to humiliation, persecution, and death. The elite—intellectuals, teachers, professionals, and managers—constituted the major targets of the Red Guards, youthful zealots empowered to cleanse Chinese society of opponents to Mao's rule. Victims were beaten and killed, jailed, or sent to corrective labor camps or to toil in the countryside. The Cultural Revolution, which cost China years of stable development and gutted its educational system, did not end until after Mao's death in 1976. It fell to one of Mao's heirs, Deng Xiaoping—himself a one-time victim of the Cultural Revolution—to heal the nation.

Deng came to power in 1981, and the 1980s are often referred to as the years of "Deng's Revolution." Deng moderated Mao's commitment to Chinese self-sufficiency and isolation and engineered China's entry into the international financial and trading system. In

democracies hoping to quell the growth of communism in Africa. Thus the convergence of decolonization with the politics of the cold war helped to undermine the possibilities for lasting stability in an independent Zaire.

The Democratic Republic of the Congo

AFTER INDEPENDENCE: LONG-TERM STRUGGLES IN THE POSTCOLONIAL ERA

Political and economic stability often proved elusive after independence, particularly in those developing nations struggling to build political and economic systems free from the domination of more powerful nations. The legacies of imperialism, either direct or indirect, hindered the creation of democratic institutions in many parts of the world. In Asia and the Islamic world, some governments staved off interference by relying on tightly centralized rule, as in China, or on religion, as in Iran after the 1979 revolution. Few developing or newly industrialized countries, however, escaped the disruption of war or revolution that also characterized the postcolonial era.

Communism and Democracy in Asia

Except for Japan and India, the developing nations in south, southeast, and east Asia adopted some form of authoritarian or militarist political system, and many

A 1966 poster shows Mao Zedong inspiring the people to launch the Great Proletarian Cultural Revolution.

addition, Deng sent tens of thousands of Chinese students to foreign universities to rebuild the profes-

Deng's Revolution

sional, intellectual, and managerial elite needed for modern development. These students were exposed to the democratic societies of western Europe and the United States. However, when they staged pro-democracy demonstrations in Beijing's Tiananmen Square in 1989, Deng approved a bloody crackdown. Indeed, having successfully negotiated a path that halted imperial interference, China entered the global economy facing the issue of how (or whether) to reap economic benefits without compromising its identity and its authoritarian political system.

Islamic Resurgence in Southwest Asia and North Africa

The geographic convergence of the Arab and Muslim worlds in southwest Asia and north Africa encouraged the development of Arab nationalism in states of those regions that gained independence after World War II.

Whether in Libya, Algeria, or Egypt in north Africa or in Syria, Saudi Arabia, or Iraq in southwest Asia, visions of Arab nationalism, linked to the religious force of Islam, dazzled nations that wished to fend off European and U.S. influence. In north Africa, Egypt's Gamal Abdel Nasser provided the leadership for this Arab nationalism, and Arab-Muslim opposition to the state of Israel held the dream together.

The hopes attached to pan-Arab unity did not materialize. Although Arab lands shared a common language and religion, divisions were frequent and alliances shifted over time. The cold war split the Arab-Muslim world as some states allied themselves

Muslim Revival and Arab Disunity

with the United States and others associated with the Soviet Union. Religious divisions also complicated the attainment of Arab unity, because Sunni and Shia Muslims followed divergent theologies and foreign policies.

In southwest Asia, peace seemed a distant prospect, given the political turmoil caused by the presence of Israel in the midst of Arab-Islamic states, many of which allied themselves with the Soviet Union as Israel became a staunch ally of the United States. Intermittent Arab-Israeli wars also greatly intensified the tensions in the region. Although Egyptian president Anwar Sadat (1918–1981) did in fact make significant progress in improving relations between Egypt and Israel, those efforts also raised the ire of the other Arab states and ultimately resulted in Sadat's assassination in 1981 by anti-Israeli opponents.

In Palestine, violence between Israelis and Palestinians—under the leadership of Yasser Arafat's (1929–2004) Palestinian Liberation Organization (PLO)—continued into the 1990s. However, in 1993 and 1995 Arafat and Israeli prime minister Yitzhak Rabin (1922–1995) signed peace treaties that advanced the notion of limited Palestinian self-rule in Israeli-occupied territories. Yet the assassination of Rabin in 1995 by a Jewish extremist who opposed the peace agreements, as well as other hurdles, blocked the peace process.

Elsewhere in southwest Asia and north Africa, a revival of Muslim traditions found expression in Islamism. At the heart of Islamism was the desire for the reassertion of Islamic values

Islamism

in Muslim politics. Many Muslims had become skeptical about European and American models of economic development and political and cultural norms, which they blamed for economic and political failure as well as the breakdown of traditional social and religious values. The solution to the problems faced by Muslim societies lay, according to Islamists, in the revival of Islamic identity, values, and power. Although the vast majority of Islamic activists have sought to bring about change through peaceful means, an extremist minority has called for violent transformations. Convinced that the Muslim world is under siege, extremists use the concept of *jihad*—the right and duty to defend Islam and the Islamic community from unjust attack—to rationalize and legitimize violence and revolution.

The Iranian revolution of 1979 demonstrated the power of Islam as a means of staving off secular foreign influences. Islamist influences grew in *The Iranian Revolution* Iran during the lengthy regime of Shah Mohammed Reza Pahlavi (1919–1980), whom the CIA helped bring to power in 1953. Money from Iran's lucrative oil industry helped finance industrialization under the shah, and the United States provided Iran with the necessary military equipment to fight communism in the region. By the late 1970s, however, opposition to the shah's government came from many quarters. Shia Muslims despised the shah's secular regime, Iranian small businesses detested the influence of U.S. corporations on the economy, and leftist politicians rejected the shah's repressive policies. The shah fled the country in early 1979, and power was captured by the Islamist movement under the direction of Ayatollah Ruhollah Khomeini (1900–1989).

The revolution took on a strongly anti-U.S. cast, partly because the shah was allowed to travel to the United States for medical treatment. In retaliation, Shia militants captured sixty-nine hostages at the U.S. embassy in Tehran, fifty-five of whom remained captives until 1981. In the meantime, Iranian leaders shut U.S. military bases and confiscated U.S.-owned economic ventures. This Islamic power play against a developed nation such as the United States inspired other Muslims to undertake terrorist actions.

The resurgent Islam of Iran did not lead to a new era of Islamic solidarity, however. Instead, Iran's neighbor Iraq—led by President Saddam Hussein (in office 1979–2003)—attempted *The Iran-Iraq War* to take advantage of the revolution to invade Iran. Although Iraqi troops were initially successful, they faced a determined counterattack by Iranian forces, and the conflict became a war of attrition—as many as one million soldiers were killed—that did not end until 1988.

Although Hussein's bid to conquer Iran was unsuccessful, Iraq continued on a militant course. Two years after the end of the Iran-Iraq War, Hussein's troops invaded Kuwait (1990) and incited the Gulf War (1991). Hussein suffered another defeat, creating further hardship for Iraqis and much of southwest Asia. His troubles deepened in the wake of the 11 September 2001 terrorist attacks against the United States as President George W. Bush (1946–) vastly expanded his nation's war on terror. A coalition of forces aligned with the United States launched a preemptive invasion of Iraq in 2003 to destroy Hussein's "weapons of mass destruction" and Iraq's capacity to harbor global terrorists. Iraqi military units suffered defeat and coalition forces captured Saddam Hussein in December 2003.

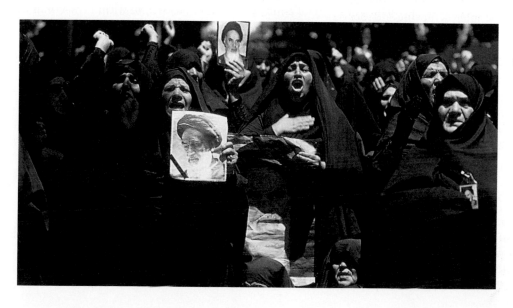

Iranians show their devotion to the Ayatollah Khomeini at his funeral in 1989.

A WORLD WITHOUT BORDERS

The United States' war on terror, which legitimized the invasion of Iraq in 2003, offered a telling testament to the emergence of a new world order. By the turn of the twenty-first century, empires had given way to a multiplicity of national states, and the collapse of the Soviet system had destroyed the bipolar world. Even the name of the conflict—the war on terror—does not feature nation-states or locations: rather, it denotes a more far-reaching, extensive conflict that could be anywhere, at any time. It implies connections between civilians all over the world who could be victims of terrorism in their home countries, while moving from place to place, or even on their computers. It is a global conflict in an increasingly globalized world.

Indeed, the problem of terrorism highlights one of the darker sides of the new international order, in which small groups, connected across borders by financial flows and communications technology, can utilize resources to control or combat the actions of even the most powerful nations. Yet there is far more to this new, globalized world than terrorism. The world's peoples have become connected in many other ways—economically through global trade networks, and culturally through mass media and consumerism. The world's peoples are also connected through the global problems that now face all of humanity, including overpopulation, environmental degradation, and poverty. Opinions differ as to the costs and benefits of this new globalized world, but few can deny its realities. It is somewhat ironic, however, that within a few decades of nearly all the world's peoples achieving independence from colonial rule and creating long-wished-for nation-states, national borders have become increasingly vulnerable to supranational influences such as global financial networks, corporations, and media. And although the joys of independence and decolonization were surely real, it is nevertheless the case that many of the world's newest nations have found that they receive few dividends in this new world order.

Economic Globalization

The early origins of economic globalization derived from the establishment of international organizations such as the International Monetary Fund (IMF). Founded in 1944, the IMF began the promotion of market economies, free trade, and high growth rates.

In addition to the IMF, U.S. politicians and business leaders wanted to establish an international trading system that suited their interests, and they pushed for the elimination of restrictive trading practices that stood in the way of free trade across national borders. The main vehicle for the promotion of unrestricted global trade was the General Agreement on Tariffs and Trade (GATT), which was signed by the representatives of twenty-three noncommunist nations in 1947. After the round of negotiations that ended in 1994, the member nations of GATT (now totaling 123) signed an agreement to establish the World Trade Organization (WTO), which took over the activities of GATT in 1995. The WTO has developed into a forum for settling international trade disputes, with the power to enforce its decisions. Numbers tell the story of the fortunes of free trade. World trade (exports and imports) grew by 6.6 percent annually between 1948 and 1966 and by 9.2 percent annually between 1966 and 1977. Although trade slowed in the 1980s, by 1990 world trade exceeded six trillion U.S. dollars, roughly double the figure for 1980.

GATT and WTO

The emergence of a new breed of corporation played another key role in the development of the new economic order. Global corporations have increasingly replaced the more traditional international or multinational forms of corporate enterprises. International companies were born out of the desire to extend business activities across borders in pursuit of specific activities such as importation, exportation, and the extraction of raw materials. International companies evolved into multinationals, which conducted their business in several countries but had to operate within the confines of specific laws and customs of a given society. During the last twenty-five years, the transformation of the corporate landscape has resulted in the birth of some fifty thousand global corporations. In contrast to the multinational, the typical global corporation relies on a small headquarters staff while dispersing all other corporate functions across the globe in search of the lowest possible operating costs. For example, global corporations move jobs from high-wage facilities to foreign locations where wages are low and environmental laws are weak or nonexistent. Global corporations treat the world as a single market and act as if the nation-state no longer exists. Many multinational corporations, such as General Motors, Siemens AG, and Nestlé, have transformed themselves into global enterprises, both benefiting from and contributing to the ongoing process of globalization.

Global Corporations

One response to the increasingly competitive global economy has been the creation of national economic alliances designed to achieve advantages and greater strength for their partners. One of the earliest and most successful of these alliances was the Organization of Petroleum Exporting Countries (OPEC), a producer cartel established in 1960 by the oil-producing states of Iran, Iraq, Kuwait, Saudi Arabia, and Venezuela and later joined by Qatar, Libya, Indonesia, Abu Dhabi, Algeria, Nigeria, Ecuador, and Gabon. The mostly Arab and Muslim member states of OPEC sought to raise the price of oil through cooperation, but OPEC demonstrated during the Arab-Israeli War of 1973 that cooperation had political as well as economic potential. The cartel ordered an embargo on oil shipments to the United States, Israel's ally, and quadrupled the price of oil between 1973 and 1975. The huge increase in the cost of petroleum triggered a global economic downturn.

Trading Blocs

OPEC's policies therefore demonstrated that the alliance could exert control over the developed world and its financial system. The most famous and most strongly integrated regional bloc is the European Union, which is characterized by a common market and free trade. In March 1957 representatives of six nations—France, West Germany, Italy, the Netherlands, Belgium, and Luxembourg—took a significant step in this direction by establishing the European Economic Community (renamed the European Community in 1967). At the heart of this new community of nations lay the dismantling of tariffs and other barriers to free trade among member nations. Subsequent treaties creating political institutions such as the Council of Ministers and the European Parliament facilitated the long-range goal of European political integration. The development of a supranational organization dedicated to increasing European economic and political integration culminated in the Maestricht Treaty of 1993, which established the European Union. Fifteen European nations have submerged much of their national sovereignty in the European Union, and since 1999 eleven members have adopted a common currency. In the future, this tight economic integration is expected to lead to a European Political Union.

Cross-Cultural Exchanges and Global Communications

Like trade and business organizations, cultural practices have become increasingly globalized, thriving on a continuous flow of information, ideas, tastes, and values. At the turn of the twentieth century, local traditions—commonly derived from gender, social class, or religious affiliation—still determined the cultural identity of the vast majority of people. At the end of the twentieth century, thanks in part to advances in technology and communications, information and cultural practices were becoming truly global.

One of the hallmarks of this new global cultural integration is consumption. Although the desire to consume is hardly novel, one of the tendencies of the modern consumer culture is toward the homogenization of cultural products. Critics sometimes refer to the homogenizing aspect of global culture as the "Americanization" or "McDonaldization" of the world. Those terms suggest that the consumer culture that developed in the United States during the mid–twentieth century has been exported throughout the world, principally through advertising. Thus it is no accident that young people clad in blue jeans and T-shirts sing the same Usher or Eminem lyrics in San Francisco, Sarajevo, and Beijing. Still, nothing symbolizes the global marketing of U.S. mass culture more than the spread of its food and beverage products. While Pepsi and Coca-Cola fight battles over the few places on earth that their beverages have not yet dominated, fast-food restaurants such as Burger King, McDonalds, and Pizza Hut sell their standardized foods throughout the world. The closing of many bistros and cafés in France, for instance, is the result of more French people opting for fashionable fast food instead of taking the time for more traditional and lengthy lunches. So successful has the global spread of U.S. mass culture been that it seems to threaten local or indigenous cultures everywhere.

Consumption and Cultural Interaction

The export of U.S. products and services is not the sole determinant of global cultural practices, however. Indeed, the experiences in the Americas demonstrate that U.S. patterns of cultural consumption have not simply dominated the globe without competition or critical evaluation. One example in Latin America is Music Television (MTV) Latino, perceived by many critics as another case of foreign cultural intrusion, where Latin video deejays speak "Spanglish" or "Chequenos" ("check us out"), mixing Spanish and English. Yet, whereas Latin Americans once had called for protection against such alien influence, by the 1990s many had relaxed their guard. They see evidence of increased cultural sharing among Latin societies, noting that MTV and cable television have come to serve as a means of communication and unity by making the

A citizen of Kuwait lugs a television through streets filled with European and U.S. consumer products. From tennis shoes to automobiles to English-language signs, cultural interpenetration is occurring around the globe.

nations of Latin America more aware of one another. Although the sheer dominance and size of the U.S. entertainment-technology industry keeps cultural sharing lopsided, cultural dominance is also limited by those societies' ability to blend and absorb a variety of foreign and indigenous practices.

Global Problems in a Borderless World

One of the consequences of a globalized world is the rapid development of global problems, which in turn demand global solutions. One of the most important of those problems is the rapid growth of the human population and attendant questions about human poverty and the environmental capacity of the earth. Indeed, in the past three hundred years the world has experienced a fivefold population increase: from 500 million people in 1650 to 2.5 billion in 1950. After World War II the widespread and successful use of vaccines, antibiotics, and insecticides, along with improvements in water supplies and increased agricultural yields, caused a dramatic decline in worldwide death rates. By 1994 roughly 5.5 billion people shared the planet, and the population division of the United Nations has estimated that the earth's population will stabilize around 11.6 billion in 2200.

A large population changes the earth and its environment, raising an important question: How many people can the earth support? The exact carrying capacity of the planet is, of course, a matter of debate, but by many measures the earth seems to strain already to support the current population. Scientists and concerned citizens have become increasingly convinced that human society cannot infinitely expand beyond the physical limits of the earth and its resources.

The prodigious growth of the human population is also at the root of many environmental problems. As people are born, pollution levels increase, more habitats and animal and plant species disappear, and more natural resources are consumed. This process, in turn, contributes to the atmospheric pollution that causes global warming. Indeed, if global warming caused even a modest rise of one to three degrees Celsius in the temperature of the atmosphere, that could allow sea levels to rise to levels that would inundate low-lying islands and coastal areas on all continents.

Global poverty—caused by a combination of overpopulation and an unequal distribution of global wealth—is another serious problem of the contemporary world. Several hundred million people, especially in the developing areas of eastern Europe, Africa, Latin America, and Asia, struggle daily for sufficient food, clean water, adequate shelter, and other basic necessities. Poverty has correlated strongly with higher-than-average infant mortality rates and lower-than-average life expectancies.

It is no accident that many of the poorest areas in the world share a legacy of colonialism, defined by the appropriation of labor and natural resources. Indeed, pervasive poverty characterizes many former colonies and dependencies. All of these developing societies have tried to raise income levels and eliminate poverty through diversified economic development, but only a few, such as South Korea, Singapore, Malaysia, and Indonesia, have accomplished their aims. In the meantime, economic globalization has generated unprecedented wealth for developed nations, creating an even deeper divide between rich and poor countries.

The global economy—and the globalized world more generally—is still very much a work in progress, and it not clear what the long-term effects will be on the societies it touches. To its supporters, the global economy delivers markets that operate with maximum efficiency. Proponents of globalization also argue that the new economy is the only way to bring prosperity to the developing world. To its critics, the global economy is a force that rewards the few and impoverishes the many. Specifically, antiglobalization groups assert that globalization diminishes the sovereignty of local and national governments and transfers the power to shape economic and political destinies to transnational corporations and global institutions such as the IMF and the WTO. Detractors of globalization also claim that the hallmark of globalization—rapid economic development—is responsible for the destruction of the environment, the widening gap between rich and poor societies, and the worldwide homogenization of local, diverse, and indigenous cultures.

SUMMARY

In the years immediately before and after World War II, a few nations controlled the political and economic destiny of much of the world. The decades following 1945 witnessed the stunning reversal of that state of affairs, as European empires fell and dozens of newly independent nations emerged. Decolonization changed the world's political, economic, and social landscape in often radical ways, and the peoples of these newly free countries thereafter labored to reshape their own national identities and to build workable political and economic systems. The effervescence of liberty and independence at times gave way to a more sober reality in the days, years, and decades after liberation. Religious and ethnic conflict, political instability, economic dependency, and foreign interference dampened spirits and interfered with the ability of nations to achieve peace and stability. Yet the global balance of power had been irrevocably altered by this attainment of worldwide independence. The fall of those age-old empires, along with the disappearance of the superpowers' bipolar cold war world, reshaped the world's landscape once again and intensified the globalization of economies and cultures around the world. National boundaries became increasingly irrelevant and ushered in a world order based more than ever on connections and encounters. This new world order is replete with problems, and in contemporary times those problems are shared by all humanity.

CHRONOLOGY

1947	Partition of India
1947	Establishment of GATT
1948	Creation of Israel
1954	French defeat at Dienbienphu
1954–1962	Algerian war of liberation
1955	Bandung Conference
1957	Ghana gains independence
1958–1961	Great Leap Forward in China
1960	Creation of OPEC
1967	Birth of European Community
1973	Arab-Israeli War
1979	Revolution in Iran
1980–1988	Iran-Iraq war
1990–1991	Gulf War
1995	WTO supersedes GATT
2000	World population at 6 billion
2001	Terrorist attacks against the United States

FOR FURTHER READING

Franz Ansprenger. *The Dissolution of the Colonial Empires*. New York, 1989. A discerning and thorough treatment of the dismantling of European empires and colonies.

Mark Borthwick, ed. *Pacific Century: The Emergence of Modern Pacific Asia*. Boulder, 1992. An excellent source for an overview of southeast and east Asia.

Michael J. Cohen. *Palestine and the Great Powers 1945–48*. 2nd ed. Princeton, 1992. An evenhanded assessment of the role played by the great powers in the partition of Palestine and the creation of Israel.

Basil Davidson. *The Black Man's Burden: Africa and the Curse of the Nation State*. New York, 1992. A critical postindependence account that emphasizes the shortcomings of nationalism and the national state.

Thomas L. Friedman. *The Lexus and Olive Tree*. New York, 1999. A readable overview that docs justice to the complexities of globalization.

Sunil Khilani. *The Idea of India*. New York, 1988. A lively and incisive analysis of the contracts between India and Pakistan.

Naomi Klein. *No Space, No Choice, No Jobs, No Logo: Taking Aim at the Brand Bullies*. New York, 2000. Part cultural analysis and part political manifesto, this work makes an angry case against multinational corporations.

J. R. McNeill. *Something New under the Sun: An Environmental History of the Twentieth-Century World*. New York, 2000. A brilliant but dark tale of the past century's interaction between humans and the environment.

Robert A. Mortimer. *The Third World Coalition in International Politics*. New York, 1980. Surveys the political evolution of the nonaligned world.

Jeffrey N. Wasserstrom and Elizabeth J. Perry, eds. *Popular Protest and Political Culture in Modern China*. 2nd ed. Boulder, 1994. A collection of essays in which scholars from various disciplines take a critical look at contemporary China.

Glossary and Pronunciation Guide

A	short *a* sound, as in *asp, fat, parrot*
AH	*a* sound, as in *car, father*
AHW	diphthong *au* in Romance languages, similar to vowel sound in *ouch*
AHY	diphthong *ai* in Romance languages, similar to vowel sound in *die*
AW	diphthong *a* sound, as in *awful, paw, law*
AY	long *a* sound, as in *ape, date, play*
EE	long *e* sound, as in *even, meet, money*
EH	short *e* sound, as in *ten, elf, berry, how, haw*
EHY	diphthong *ei* in Romance languages, similar to "ay" in *day*
EW	diphthong *iu* in Romance languages, similar (but shorter than) *you*
EYE	long *i* sound, as in *ice, high, bite*
IH	short *i* sound, as in *fit, his, mirror*
KH	hard *h* sound
OH	long *o* sound, as in *open, go, tone*
OHI	diphthong *oi* in Romance languages, similar to "oy" in *toy*
OO	long *o* sound, as in *ooze, tool, crew*
'R	tapped *r* like *dd* or *tt* in *latter* and *butter*
RR	trilled *r* (repeated taps)
UH	short *u* sound, as in *up, cut, color*
WA	diphthong *ua* in Romance languages, similar to the "wa" in *want* and *waffle*
WE	diphthong *ui* in Romance languages, similar to the word *we*
Y	like *ll* in *million* or *ny* in *canyon*
YA	diphthong *ia* in Romance languages, similar to "ya" in *yacht*
YE	diphthong *ie* in Romance languages, similar to "ye" in *yet*
YO	diphthong *io* in Romance languages, similar to "yo" in the suffix *yoke*

Note on emphasis: Syllables in capital letters receive the stress. If there is no syllable in capitals, then all syllables get equal stress.

Abbasid (ah-BAH-sihd) Cosmopolitan Arabic dynasty (750–1258) that replaced the Umayyads; founded by Abu al-Abbas and reaching its peak under Harun al-Rashid.

Abolitionism Antislavery movement.

Absolutism Political philosophy that stressed the divine right theory of kingship: the French king Louis XIV was the classic example.

Abu Bakr (ah-BOO BAHK-uhr) First caliph after the death of Muhammad.

Achaemenid empire (ah-KEE-muh-nid) First great Persian empire (558–330 B.C.E.), which began under Cyrus and reached its peak under Darius.

Aeschylus (ES-kuh-luhs) Greek tragedian, author of the *Oresteia*.

Age grades Bantu concept in which individuals of roughly the same age carried out communal tasks appropriate for that age.

Agricultural transition The gradual transition from a dependence on hunting and gathering for subsistence to a dependence on cultivation and animal husbandry. First evidence of transition is from around 12,000 B.C.E.

Ahimsa (uh-HIM-suh) Jain term for the principle of nonviolence to other living things or their souls.

Ahmosis (AH-moh-sis) Egyptian pharaoh (c. 1500 B.C.E.), founder of the New Kingdom.

Ahura Mazda (uh-HOORE-uh MAHZ-duh) Main god of Zoroastrianism who represented truth and goodness and was perceived to be in an eternal struggle with the malign spirit Angra Mainyu.

Al-Andalus (al-ahn-dah-LOOS) Islamic Spain.

Allah (AH-lah) God of the monotheistic religion of Islam.

Aliæi nui Hawaiian class of high chiefs.

Amon-Re (AH-mohn RRAY) Egyptian god, combination of the sun god Re and the air god Amon.

Ancestor worship Belief that dead ancestors can influence one's fortunes in this life. People who practice ancestor worship characteristically practice rituals and ceremonies to the memory or remains of their ancestors.

Ancien régime The political structure of prerevolutionary France, characterized by an absolute monarchy, a feudal aristocracy, and a vast class of powerless peasants.

Angkor (AHN-kohr) Southeast Asian Khmer kingdom (889–1432) that was centered around the temple cities of Angkor Thom and Angkor Wat.

Anti-Semitism Term coined in late nineteenth century that was associated with a prejudice against Jews and the political, social, and economic actions taken against them.

Antonianism African syncretic religion, founded by Doña Beatriz, that taught that Jesus Christ was a black African man and that heaven was for Africans.

Apartheid (ah-PAHR-teyed) South African system of "separateness" that was implemented in 1948 and that maintained the black majority in a position of political, social, and economic subordination.

Appeasement British and French policy in the 1930s that tried to maintain peace in Europe in the face of German aggression by making concessions.

Arianism Early Christian heresy that centered around teaching of Arius (250–336 C.E.) and contained the belief that Jesus was a mortal human being and not coeternal with God; Arianism was the focus of Council of Nicaea.

Artha Hindu concept for the pursuit of economic well-being and honest prosperity.

Arthashastra (UHRR-th-sha-strrah) Ancient Indian political treatise from the time of Chandragupta Maurya; its authorship was traditionally ascribed to Kautalya, and it stressed that war was inevitable.

Aryans (AYR-ee-uhns) Indo-European tribes who settled in India after 1500 B.C.E.; their union with indigenous Dravidians formed the basis of Hinduism.

Association of Southeast Asian Nations (ASEAN.) Regional alliance established in 1967 by Thailand, Malaysia, Singapore, Indonesia, and the Philippines; the alliance was designed to promote economic progress and political stability; it later became a free-trade zone.

Assyrians (uh-SEER-ee-uhns) Southwest Asian people who built an empire that reached its height during the eighth and seventh centuries B.C.E.; it was known for a powerful army and a well-structured state.

Astrolabe Navigational instrument for determining latitude.

Aten Monotheistic god of Egyptian pharaoh Akhenaten (r. 1353–1335 B.C.E.) and arguably the world's first example of monotheism.

Audiencias Spanish courts in Latin America.

Australopithecus (ah-strah-loh-PIHTH-uh-kuhs) "Southern ape," oldest known ancestor of humans; it lived from around four million down to around one million years ago, and it could walk on hind legs, freeing up hands for use of simple tools.

Austronesians People who, by as early as 2000 B.C.E., began to explore and settle islands of the Pacific Ocean basin.

Avesta Book that contains the holy writings of Zoroastrianism.

Aztec empire Central American empire constructed by the Mexica and expanded greatly during the fifteenth century during the reigns of Itzcoatl and Motecuzoma I.

Axum African kingdom centered in Ethiopia that became an early and lasting center of Coptic Christianity.

Balfour Declaration British declaration from 1917 that supported the creation of a Jewish homeland in Palestine.

Bantu (BAHN-too) African peoples who originally lived in the area of present-day Nigeria; around 2000 B.C.E. they began a centuries-long migration that took them to most of sub-Saharan Africa; the Bantu were very influential, especially linguistically.

Bedouins (BEHD-oh-ihnz) Nomadic Arabic tribespeople.

Benefice Grant from a lord to a vassal, usually consisting of land, which supported the vassal and signified the relationship between the two.

Berlin Conference Meeting organized by German chancellor Otto von Bismarck in 1884–1885 that provided the justification for European colonization of Africa.

Bhagavad Gita (BHUHG-vuhd GEE-tuh) "Song of the Lord," an Indian short poetic work drawn from the lengthy *Mahabharata* that was finished around 400 C.E. and that expressed basic Hindu concepts such as karma and dharma.

Bhakti (BHUK-tee) Indian movement that attempted to transcend the differences between Hinduism and Islam.

Black Hand Pre–World War I secret Serbian society; one of its members, Gavrilo Princip, assassinated Austrian archduke Francis Ferdinand and provided the spark for the outbreak of the Great War.

Blitzkrieg German style of rapid attack through the use of armor and air power that was used in Poland, Norway, Denmark, Belgium, the Netherlands, and France in 1939–1940.

Boddhisatvas (BOH-dih-SAT-vuhs) Buddhist concept regarding individuals who had reached enlightenment but who stayed in this world to help people.

Bolshevik (BOHL-shih-vehk) Russian communist party headed by Lenin.

Bourgeoisie Middle class in modern industrial society.

Boyars (BOY-ahrs) Russian nobles.

Brahmins (BRAH-minz) Hindu caste of priests.

Brezhnev Doctrine Policy developed by Leonid Brezhnev (1906–1982) that claimed for the Soviet Union the right to invade any socialist country faced with internal or external enemies; the doctrine was best expressed in Soviet invasion of Czechoslovakia.

Bubonic plague Epidemic that swept Eurasia, causing devastating population loss and economic disruption. It was known as the Black Death in Europe after around 1350 C.E.

Buddha (BOO-duh) The "enlightened one," the term applied to Siddhartha Gautama after his discoveries that would form the foundation of Buddhism.

Buddhism (BOO-diz'm) Religion, based on Four Noble Truths, associated with Siddhartha Gautama (563–483 B.C.E.), or the Buddha; its adherents desired to eliminate all distracting passion and reach nirvana.

Bunraku (boon-RAH-koo) Japanese puppet theater.

Bushido (BOH-shee-DOH) The "way of the warrior," the code of conduct of the Japanese samurai that was based on loyalty and honor.

Byzantine (BIHZ-uhn-teen) Long-lasting empire centered at Constantinople; it grew out of the end of the Roman empire and carried legacy of Roman greatness and was the only classical society to survive into the early modern age; it reached its early peak during the reign of Justinian (483–565).

Caesaropapism Concept relating to the mixing of political and religious authority, as with the Roman emperors, that was central to the church versus state controversy in medieval Europe.

Cahokia (kuh-HOH-kee-uh) Large structure in modern Illinois that was constructed by the mound-building peoples; it was the third largest structure in the Americas before the arrival of the Europeans.

Caliph (KAH-leef) "deputy," Islamic leader after the death of Muhammad.

Capetian (cah-PEE-shuhn) Early French dynasty that started with Hugh Capet.

Capitalism An economic system with origins in early modern Europe in which private parties make their goods and services available on a free market.

Capitulation Highly unfavorable trading agreements that the Ottoman Turks signed with the Europeans in the nineteenth century that symbolized the decline of the Ottomans.

Carolingians Germanic dynasty that was named after its most famous member, Charlemagne.

Carthage Northern African kingdom, main rival to early Roman expansion, that was defeated by Rome in the Punic Wars.

Caste A social class system with distinctions that are transferred through generations or through occupation. Restrictions are placed on marriage, occupation, handling of food, and other matters, according to caste. Caste usually refers to the social system of India.

Çatal Hüyük Important Neolithic settlement in Anatolia (7250–6150 B.C.E.).

Cathars Medieval heretics, also known as the Albigensians, who considered the material world evil; their followers renounced wealth and marriage and promoted an ascetic existence.

Catholic Reformation Sixteenth-century Catholic attempt to cure internal ills and confront Protestantism; it was inspired by the reforms of the Council of Trent and the actions of the Jesuits.

Caudillos (kahw-DEE-yohs) Latin American term for nineteenth-century local military leaders.

Central Powers World War I term for the alliance of Germany, Austria-Hungary, and the Ottoman empire.

Chaghatai One of Chinggis Khan's sons, whose descendants ruled central Asia through the Chaghatai khanate.

Chan Buddhism (CHAHN BOO-diz'm) Most popular branch of Buddhism in China, with an emphasis on intuition and sudden flashes of insight instead of textual study.

Chan Chan (chahn chahn) Capital of the pre-Incan, South American Chimu society that supported a large population of fifty thousand.

Chavín cult Mysterious but very popular South American religion (1000–300 B.C.E.).

Chimu Pre-Incan South American society that fell to Incas in the fifteenth century.

Chinampas Style of agriculture used by Mexica (Aztecs) in which fertile muck from lake bottoms was dredged and built up into small plots.

Chivalry European medieval concept, a code of conduct for the knights based on loyalty and honor.

Chola Southern Indian Hindu kingdom (850–1267), a tightly centralized state that dominated sea trade.

Christianity Religious doctrine that emerged in southeast Asia in the first century C.E. and then spread through Europe, north Africa, parts of Asia, and eventually to the Americas. Central to the religion is the belief that Jesus was the son of God and sacrificed himself on behalf of humankind.

Chucuito (choo-CWE-toh) Pre-Incan South American society that rose in the twelfth century and fell to the Incas in the fifteenth century.

City-state Urban areas that controlled surrounding agricultural regions and that were often loosely connected in a broader political structure with other city-states.

Cohong Specially licensed Chinese firms that were under strict government regulation.

Collectivization Process beginning in the late 1920s by which Stalin forced the Russian peasants off their own land and onto huge collective farms run by the state; millions died in the process.

Columbian Exchange The trans-Atlantic exchange of plants, animals, and diseases that followed European contact with the Americas at the end of the fifteenth century.

COMECON The Council for Mutual Economic Assistance, which offered increased trade within the Soviet Union and eastern Europe; it was the Soviet alternative to the United States's Marshall Plan.

Communalism A term, usually associated with India, that placed an emphasis on religious rather than national identity.

Communism Philosophy and movement that began in middle of the nineteenth century with the work of Karl Marx; it has the same general goals as socialism, but it includes the belief that violent revolution is necessary to destroy the bourgeois world and institute a new world run by and for the proletariat.

Confucianism (kuhn-FEW-shuhn-iz'm) Philosophy, based on the teachings of the Chinese philosopher Kong Fuzi (551–479 B.C.E.), or Confucius, that emphasizes order, the role of the gentleman, obligation to society, and reciprocity.

Congress of Vienna Gathering of European diplomats in Vienna, Austria, from October 1814 to June 1815. The representatives of the "great powers" that defeated Napoleon—Britain, Austria, Prussia, and Russia—dominated the proceedings, which aimed to restore the prerevolutionary political and social order.

Conquistadores (kohn-kees-tah-DOH-rays) Spanish adventurers like Cortes and Pizarro who conquered Central and South America in the sixteenth century.

Conservatism A political philosophy that emphasizes gradual change, continuity of traditions and established authority. Although the word has taken on many shades of meaning, nineteenth-century conservatives generally opposed democracy and supported traditional institutions such as church, monarchy, and nobility.

Constitutionalism Movement in England in the seventeenth century that placed power in Parliament's hands as part of a constitutional monarchy and that increasingly limited the power of the monarch; the movement was highlighted by the English Civil War and the Glorious Revolution.

Containment Concept associated with the United States and specifically with the Truman Doctrine during the cold war that revolved around the notion that the United States would contain the spread of communism.

Corporation A concept that reached mature form in 1860s in England and France; it entailed private business owned by thousands of individual and institutional investors who financed the business through the purchase of stocks.

Corpus iuris civilis (KOR-poos EW-rees sih-BEE-lees) *Body of the Civil Law,* the Byzantine emperor Justinian's attempt to codify all Roman law.

Cossacks (KAW-sacks) Russian "free men" recruited by Ivan III to settle conquered land in return for their freedom; the strategy eventually played a key role in Russian expansion eastward.

Criollos (KRYO-yohs) Creoles, people born in the Americas of Spanish or Portuguese ancestry.

Cro-Magnon (CROH MAHG-nohn) *Homo sapiens sapiens,* who appeared forty thousand years ago during the Paleolithic age and were the first human beings of the modern type.

Cross staff Device that sailors used to determine latitude by measuring the angle of the sun or pole star above the horizon.

Cuneiform Written language of the Sumerians, probably the first written script in the world.

Daimyo (DEYEM-yoh) Powerful territorial lords in early modern Japan.

Dao Key element in Chinese philosophy that means the "way of nature" or the "way of the cosmos."

Daodejing (DOW-DAY-JIHNG) Book that is the fundamental work of Daoism.

Daoism (DOW-i'zm) Chinese philosophy with origins in the Zhou dynasty; it is associated with legendary philosopher Laozi, and it called for a policy of inaction.

Dar al-Islam The "house of Islam," a term for the Islamic world.

Declaration of Independence Drafted by Thomas Jefferson in 1776; the document expressed the ideas of John Locke and the Enlightenment, represented the idealism of the American rebels, and influenced other revolutions.

Declaration of the Rights of Man and Citizen Document from the French Revolution (1789) that was influenced by the American Declaration of Independence and in turn influenced other revolutionary movements.

Decolonization Process by which former colonies achieved their independence, as with the newly emerging African nations in the 1950s and 1960s.

Deism (DEE-iz'm) An Enlightenment view that accepted the existence of a god but denied the supernatural aspects of Christianity; in deism, the universe was an orderly realm maintained by rational and natural laws.

Demographic transition Adjustments in the rate of births and deaths that usually accompany industrialization. The demographic transition is often triggered by improvements in health and nutrition, which result in lower death rates. Birthrates remain high initially, but after a period of rapid population growth, birthrates fall in response to the lower death rates. Eventually, in highly industrialized societies, birthrates and death rates stabilize at low levels.

Descamisados "Shirtless ones," Argentine poor who supported Juan and Eva Perón.

Détente A reduction in cold war tension between the United States and the Soviet Union from 1969 to 1973.

Devshirme Ottoman requirement that the Christians in the Balkans provide young boys to be slaves of the sultan.

Dharma (DHUHR-muh) Hindu concept of obedience to religious and moral laws and order.

Dhimmi (DIHM-mee) Islamic concept of a protected people that was symbolic of Islamic toleration during the Mughal and Ottoman empires.

Dhow Indian, Persian, and Arab ships, one hundred to four hundred tons, that sailed and traded throughout the Indian Ocean basin.

Diaspora People who have settled far from their original homeland but who still share some measure of ethnic identity.

Dionysus Greek god of wine, also known as Bacchus; Greek plays were performed in his honor.

Dravidians Peoples who produced the brilliant Harappan society in India, 3000–1500 B.C.E.

Dreadnoughts A class of British battleships whose heavy armaments made all other battleships obsolete overnight.

Duma Russian parliament, established after the Revolution of 1905.

Dutch learning European knowledge that reached Tokugawa Japan.

East India Company British joint-stock company that grew to be a state within a state in India; it possessed its own armed forces.

Eastern Orthodox Christianity An eastern branch of Christianity that evolved after the division of the Roman Empire and the subsequent development of the Byzantine Empire in the east and the medieval European society in the west. The Eastern Orthodox Church acknowledged what became known as the Byzantine rite and recognized the primacy of the patriarch of Constantinople.

Eight-legged essay Eight-part essays that an aspiring Chinese civil servant had to compose, mainly based on a knowledge of Confucius and the Zhou classics.

Encomienda (ehn-koh-MYEN-dah) System that gave the Spanish settlers (*encomenderos*) the right to compel the indigenous peoples of the Americas to work in the mines or fields.

Engenho (ehn-GEN-yo) Brazilian sugar mill; the term also came to symbolize the entire complex world relating to the production of sugar.

Enlightenment Eighteenth-century philosophical movement that began in France; its emphasis was on the preeminence of reason rather than faith or tradition; it spread concepts from the Scientific Revolution.

Epicureans (ehp-ih-KYOOR-eeuhns) Hellenistic philosophers who taught that pleasure—as in quiet satisfaction—was the greatest good.

Equal-field system Chinese system during the Han dynasty in which the goal was to ensure an equitable distribution of land.

Essenes Jewish sect that looked for the arrival of a savior; they were similar in some of their core beliefs to the early Christians.

Etruscans (ih-TRUHS-kuhns) Northern Italian society that initially dominated the Romans; the Etruscans helped convey Greek concepts to the expanding Romans.

Eunuchs (YOO-nihks) Castrated males, originally in charge of the harem, who grew to play major roles in government; eunuchs were common in China and other societies.

European Community (EC) Organization of European states established in 1957; it was originally called the European Economic Community and was renamed the EC

in 1967; it promoted economic growth and integration as the basis for a politically united Europe.

European Union Established by the Maastricht Treaty in 1993, a supranational organization for even greater European economic and political integration.

Fascism Political ideology and mass movement that was prominent in many parts of Europe between 1919 and 1945; it sought to regenerate the social, political, and cultural life of societies, especially in contrast to liberal democracy and socialism; fascism began with Mussolini in Italy, and it reached its peak with Hitler in Germany.

Fief (FEEF) A grant of land from a lord to a vassal.

Five Pillars The foundation of Islam; (1) profession of faith, (2) prayer, (3) fasting during Ramadan, (4) alms, and (5) pilgrimage, or hajj.

Five-year plans First implemented by Stalin in the Soviet Union in 1928; five-year plans were a staple of communist regimes in which every aspect of production was determined in advance for a five-year period; five-year plans were opposite of the free market concept.

Four Noble Truths The foundation of Buddhist thought: (1) life is pain, (2) pain is caused by desire, (3) elimination of desire will bring an end to pain, (4) living a life based on the Noble Eightfold Path will eliminate desire.

Free trade Economic doctrine, first argued by Adam Smith in the late eighteenth century, of unrestricted trade between nations without protective tariffs or duties. Smith and his followers argue that, through free trade and competition, the forces of supply and demand will ensure that the best product is available at the best price. Free trade has gained wide acceptance since World War II.

Front de Libération Nationale (FLN) The Algerian organization that fought a bloody guerilla war for freedom against France.

Fulani (foo-LAH-nee) Sub-Saharan African people who, beginning in the seventeenth century, began a series of wars designed to impose their own strict interpretation of Islam.

Gathas (GATH-uhs) Zoroastrian works believed to be compositions by Zarathustra.

Gauchos (GAHW-chohs) Argentine cowboys, highly romantic figures.

General Agreement on Tariffs and Trade (GATT) Free trade agreement first signed in 1947; by 1994 it had grown to 123 members and formed the World Trade Organization (WTO).

Ghana (GAH-nuh) Kingdom in west Africa during the fifth through the thirteenth centuries whose rulers eventually converted to Islam; its power and wealth was based on dominating trans-Saharan trade.

Ghaznavids Turkish tribe under Mahmud of Ghazni who moved into northern India in the eleventh century and began a period of greater Islamic influence in India.

Ghazi (GAH-zee) Islamic religious warrior.

Gilgamesh Legendary king of the Mesopotamian city-state of Uruk (ca. 3000 B.C.E.), subject of the *Epic of Gilgamesh,* world's oldest complete epic literary masterpiece.

Glasnost (GLAHS-nohst) Russian term meaning "openness" introduced by Mikhail Gorbachev in 1985 to describe the process of opening Soviet society to dissidents and public criticism.

Globalization The breaking down of traditional boundaries in the face of increasingly global financial and cultural trends.

Global warming The emission of greenhouse gases, which prevents solar heat from escaping the earth's atmosphere and leads to the gradual heating of the earth's environment.

Golden Horde Mongol tribe that controlled Russia from the thirteenth to the fifteenth centuries.

Greater East Asia Co-Prosperity Sphere Japanese plan for consolidating Asia under their control during World War II.

Great Game Nineteenth-century competition between Great Britain and Russia for the control of central Asia.

Great Zimbabwe Large sub-Saharan African kingdom in the fifteenth century.

Greenpeace An environmental organization founded in 1970 and dedicated to the preservation of earth's natural resources.

Guild Organizations whose membership is based on occupation. They often regulate the production and sale of goods and serve as mutual aid societies for their members. They were particularly powerful in medieval European cities.

Guomindang (GWOH-mihn-dahng) Chinese nationalist party founded by Sun Yat-sen (1866–1925) and later led by Jiang Jieshi; it has been centered in Taiwan since the end of the Chinese civil war.

Gupta (GOOP-tah) Indian dynasty (320–550 C.E.) that briefly reunited India after the collapse of the earlier Mauryan dynasty.

Hacienda (ah-SYEN-dah) Large Latin American estates.

Hagia Sophia (HAH-yah soh-FEE-uh) Greek orthodox temple constructed by the Byzantine emperor Justinian and later converted into a mosque.

Hajj (HAHJ) Pilgrimage to Mecca.

Hammurabi's Code (hahm-uh-RAH-beez cohd) Sophisticated law code associated with the Babylonian king Hammurabi (r. 1792–1750 B.C.E.).

Harappan (huh-RUHP-puhn) Early brilliant Indian society centered around Harappa and Mohenjo-Daro.

Harijans "Children of God," Gandhi's term for the Untouchables.

Hebrews Semitic-speaking nomadic tribe influential for monotheistic belief in Yahweh.

Heian (HAY-ahn) Japanese period (794–1185), a brilliant cultural era notable for the world's first novel, Murasaki Shikibu's *The Tale of Genji.*

Hellenic Era First phase in Greek history (ca. 2000–328 B.C.E.), which was highlighted by the Golden Age of Athens in the fifth century B.C.E.

Hellenistic Era Second phase in Greek history (328–146 B.C.E.), from the conquest of Greece by Philip of Macedon until Greece's fall to the Romans; this era was a more cosmopolitan age facilitated by the conquests of Alexander the Great.

Hieroglyphics (heye-ruh-GLIPH-iks) Ancient Egyptian written language.

Hijra Muhammad's migration from Mecca to Medina in 622, which is the beginning point of the Islamic calendar and is considered to mark the beginning of the Islamic faith.

Hinayana (HEE-nah-yah-nuh) Branch of Buddhism known as the "lesser vehicle," also known as Theravada Buddhism; its beliefs include a strict, individual path to enlightenment, and it is popular in south and southeast Asia.

Hinduism Main religion of India, a combination of Dravidian and Aryan concepts; Hinduism's goal is to reach spiritual purity and union with the great world spirit; its important concepts include dharma, karma, and samsara.

Holocaust German attempt in World War II to exterminate the Jews of Europe.

Holy Roman Empire A confederation of states mostly in central and western Europe. It began in 962 C.E. with the crowning of Otto I by the pope.

Humanism Cultural movement during the Renaissance that drew inspiration from the humanities, that is, literature, history, philosophy, and the arts. In contrast to medieval theologians, humanists argued that one could live a moral life and still be actively engaged in the affairs of the world.

Home front Term made popular in World War I and World War II for the civilian "front" that was symbolic of the greater demands of total war.

Hominid (HAW—mih-nihds) A creature belonging to the family Hominidae, which includes human and humanlike species.

Homo erectus (HOH-moh ee-REHK-tuhs) "Upright-walking human," which existed from 1.5 million to two hundred thousand years ago; *Homo erectus* used cleavers and hand axes and learned how to control fire.

Homo sapiens (HOH-moh SAY-pyans) "Consciously thinking human," which first appeared around two hundred fifty thousand years ago and used sophisticated tools.

Homo sapiens sapiens (HOH-moh SAY-pyans SAY-pyans) First human being of the modern type, which appeared roughly one hundred thousand years ago; Cro-Magnon falls into this category.

Huitzilopochtli (we-tsee-loh-POCK-tlee) Sun god and patron deity of the Aztecs.

Hundred Days of Reform Chinese reforms of 1898 led by Kang Youwei and Liang Qichao in their desire to turn China into a modern industrial power.

Hunting/gathering culture Any culture whose primary means of subsistence is through hunting and gathering from the environment. Humans survived this way for millions of years before the agricultural transition, and some hunting/gathering cultures persisted into the twenty-first century C.E.

Hyksos (HICK-sohs) Invaders who seized the Nile delta and helped bring an end to the Egyptian Middle Kingdom.

Iconoclasts (eye-KAHN-oh-klasts) Supporters of the movement, begun by the Byzantine Emperor Leo III (r. 717–741), to destroy religious icons because their veneration was considered sinful.

Ilkhanate (EEL-kahn-ate) Mongol state that ruled Persia after abolition of the Abbasid empire in the thirteenth century.

Imperialism Term associated with the expansion of European powers and their conquest and colonization of African and Asian societies, mainly from the sixteenth through the nineteenth centuries.

Inca empire Powerful South American empire that would reach its peak in the fifteenth century during the reigns of Pachacuti Inca and Topa Inca.

Indentured labor Labor source in the Americas; wealthy planters would pay the European poor to sell a portion of their working lives, usually seven years, in exchange for passage.

Indo-Europeans Series of tribes from southern Russia who, over a period of millennia, embarked on a series of migrations from India through western Europe; their greatest legacy was the broad distribution of Indo-European languages throughout Eurasia.

Indra Early Indian god associated with the Aryans; Indra was the king of the gods and was associated with warfare and thunderbolts.

Intelligentsia Refers to an educated and literate class in Russia that often advocated social and political reform. In the late nineteenth century the Russian intelligentsia became frustrated when reform efforts failed, and many turned to anarchism and violence. Some members of the intelligentsia supported the Bolshevik rise to power in the revolution of 1917.

Investiture (ihn-VEHST-tih-tyoor) The granting of church offices by a lay leader; one aspect of the medieval European church versus state controversy.

Iroquois (EER-uh-kwah) Eastern American Indian confederation made up of the Mohawk, Oneida, Onondaga, Cayuga, and Seneca tribes.

Islam Monotheistic religion of the prophet Muhammad (570–632); influenced by Judaism and Christianity, Muhammad was considered the final prophet because the earlier religions had not seen the entire picture; the Quran is the holy book of Islam.

Jainism (JEYEN-iz'm) Indian religion associated with the teacher Vardhamana Mahavira (ca. 540–468 B.C.E.) in which

every physical object possessed a soul; Jains believe in complete nonviolence to all living beings.

Jati Indian word for a Hindu subcaste.

Jihad Arabic word meaning "struggle." In Islam this word is understood to be one's duty to struggle on behalf of the faith. Although this struggle might be a personal and spiritual effort, it has frequently been a call for holy war against perceived enemies. In recent years, radical Islamists such as al-Qaeda have called for a *jihad* against the United States and other "nonbelievers."

Jizya (JIHZ-yuh) Tax in Islamic empires that was imposed on non-Muslims.

Joint-stock companies Early forerunner of the modern corporation; individuals who invested in a trading or exploring venture could make huge profits while limiting their risk.

Judaism The monotheistic religion of the Jewish people that traces its origins to Abraham (ca. 2000 B.C.E.). It emerged in the Middle East, and constitute a majority, believers were widespread in Europe, north Africa, and southeast Asia.

Ka'ba (KAH-bah) Main shrine in Mecca, goal of Muslims embarking on the hajj.

Kabuki (kah-BOO-kee) Japanese theater in which actors were free to improvise and embellish the words.

Kama Hindu concept of the enjoyment of physical and sexual pleasure.

Kamikaze (KAH-mih-kah-zee) A Japanese term meaning "divine wind" that is related to the storms that destroyed Mongol invasion fleets; the term is symbolic of Japanese isolation and was later taken by suicide pilots in World War II.

Kanun (KUH-noon) Laws issued by the Ottoman Süleyman the Magnificent, also known as Süleyman Kanuni, "the Lawgiver."

Kapu Hawaiian concept of something being taboo.

Karma (KAHR-mah) Hindu concept that the sum of good and bad in a person's life will determine his or her status in the next life.

Khoikhoi Sub-Saharan African society referred to pejoratively as the Hottentots by Europeans.

Kin-based society A society that governs itself primarily through family and clan relationships; many existed in sub-Saharan Africa throughout history.

Kongo Central African state that began trading with the Portuguese around 1500; although their kings, such as King Affonso I (r. 1506–1543), converted to

Christianity, they nevertheless suffered from the slave trade.

Koumbi-Saleh Important trading city along the trans-Saharan trade route from the eleventh to the thirteenth centuries.

Kshatriayas (SHUHT-ree-uhs) Hindu caste of warriors and aristocrats.

Kulaks Land-owning Russian peasants who benefited under Lenin's New Economic Policy and suffered under Stalin's forced collectivization.

Kush Nubian African kingdom that conquered and controlled Egypt from 750 to 664 B.C.E.

Lamaist Buddhism (LAH-muh-ihst BOO-diz'm) Branch of Buddhism that was similar to shamanism in its acceptance of magic and supernatural powers.

La Reforma Political reform movement of Mexican president Benito Juárez (1806–1872) that called for limiting the power of the military and the Catholic church in Mexican society.

Latifundia (lah-tee-FOON-dya) Huge state-run and slave-worked farms in ancient Rome.

League of Nations Forerunner of the United Nations, the dream of American president Woodrow Wilson, although its potential was severely limited by the refusal of the United States to join.

Lebensraum (LAY-behnz-rahwm) German term meaning "living space"; the term is associated with Hitler and his goal of carving out territory in the east for an expanding Germany.

Legalism Chinese philosophy from the Zhou dynasty that called for harsh suppression of the common people.

Levée en Masse (leh-VAY ahn MAS) A term signifying universal conscription during the radical phase of the French revolution.

Lex talionis (lehks tah-LYO-nihs) "Law of retaliation," laws in which offenders suffered punishments similar to their crimes; the most famous example is Hammurabi's Laws.

Li (LEE) Confucian concept, a sense of propriety.

Liberalism A political philosophy inspired by John Locke and the ideals of the Enlightenment that advocated individual liberty, constitutional government, and free trade. Nineteenth-century liberals favored representative government but not necessarily democracy.

Liberation theology The beliefs of Christian thinkers and social activists who emphasize Jesus' role in helping those who were oppressed, a view that gained wide support in Latin America in the late twentieth century. Liberation theologians question the historic role of the church in supporting traditional regimes.

Linear A Minoan written script.

Linear B Early Mycenaean written script, adapted from the Minoan Linear A.

Luddites Early-nineteenth-century artisans who were opposed to new machinery and industrialization.

Machismo (mah-CHEEZ-moh) Latin American social ethic that honored male strength, courage, aggressiveness, assertiveness, and cunning.

Madrasas (MAH-drahs-ahs) Islamic institutions of higher education that originated in the tenth century.

Magyars (MAH-jahrs) Hungarian invaders who raided towns in Germany, Italy, and France in the ninth and tenth centuries.

Mahabharata (mah-hah-BAH-rah-tah) Massive ancient Indian epic that was developed orally for centuries; it tells of an epic civil war between two family branches.

Mahayana (mah-huh-YAH-nah) The "greater vehicle," a more metaphysical and more popular northern branch of Buddhism.

Majapahit Southeast Asian kingdom (1293–1520) centered on the island of Java.

Mali (MAH-lee) West African kingdom founded in the thirteenth century by Sundiata; it reached its peak during the reign of Mansa Musa.

Manchus Manchurians who conquered China, putting an end to the Ming dynasty and founding the Qing dynasty (1644–1911).

Mandate of Heaven Chinese belief that the emperors ruled through the mandate, or approval, of heaven contingent on their ability to look after the welfare of the population.

Mandate system System that developed in the wake of World War I when the former colonies ended up mandates under European control, a thinly veiled attempt at continuing imperialism.

Manichaeism (man-ih-KEE-iz'm) Religion founded by the prophet Mani in the third century C.E., a syncretic version of Zoroastrian, Christian, and Buddhist elements.

Manifest destiny The idea, popular in the United States in the mid-nineteenth century, that the North American continent was intended by God to be settled by white Americans. This notion helped justify the Mexican war of 1846–1848 and the Indian wars of the 1870s and 1880s.

Manor Large estates of the nobles during the European middle ages, home for the majority of the peasants.

Maori (MAY-oh-ree) Indigenous peoples of New Zealand.

Marathon Battlefield scene of the Athenian victory over the Persians in 490 B.C.E.

Marae Polynesian temple structure.

Maroons Runaway African slaves.

Marshall Plan U.S. plan, officially called the European Recovery Program, that offered financial and other economic aid to all European states that had suffered from World War II, including Soviet bloc states.

Mauryan empire Indian dynasty (321–185 B.C.E.) founded by Chandragupta Maurya and reaching its peak under Ashoka.

Maya (MAH-uh) Brilliant Central American society (300–1100) known for math, astronomy, and a sophisticated written language.

May Fourth Movement Chinese movement that began 4 May 1919 with a desire to eliminate imperialist influences and promote national unity.

Medes (meeds) Indo-European branch that settled in northern Persia and eventually fell to another branch, the Persians, in the sixth century.

Meiji Restoration (MAY-jee) Restoration of imperial rule under Emperor Meiji in 1868 by a coalition led by Fukuzawa Yukichi and Ito Hirobumi; the restoration enacted western reforms to strengthen Japan.

Melaka (may-LAHK-ah) Southeast Asian kingdom that was predominantly Islamic.

Mesopotamia Term meaning "between the rivers," in this case the Tigris and Euphrates; Sumer and Akkad are two of the earliest societies.

Mestizo (mehs-TEE-soh) Latin American term for children of Spanish and native parentage.

Metallurgy The process of extracting metal from ores, or purifying metals, and of creating objects from metals.

Métis (may-TEE) Canadian term for individuals of mixed European and indigenous ancestry.

Millet An autonomous, self-governing community in the Ottoman empire.

Ming Chinese dynasty (1368–1644) founded by Hongwu and known for its cultural brilliance.

Minoan (mih-NOH-uhn) Society located on the island of Crete (ca. 2000–1100 B.C.E.) that influenced the early Mycenaeans.

Missi dominici (MEE-see doh-mee-NEE-chee) "Envoys of the lord ruler," the noble and church emissaries sent out by Charlemagne.

Mithraism (MIHTH-rah-iz'm) Mystery religion based on worship of the sun god Mithras; it became popular among the Romans because of its promise of salvation.

Mochica (moh-CHEE-kah) Pre-Incan South American society (300–700) known for their brilliant ceramics.

Moksha Hindu concept of the salvation of the soul.

Monotheism (mah-noh-THEE-iz'm) Belief in only one god, a rare concept in the ancient world.

Monroe Doctrine American doctrine issued in 1823 during the presidency of James Monroe that warned Europeans to keep their hands off Latin America and that expressed growing American strength and also growing American imperialistic views regarding Latin America.

Mughals (MOO-guhls) Islamic dynasty that ruled India from the sixteenth through the eighteenth centuries; the construction of the Taj Mahal is representative of their splendor; with the exception of the enlightened reign of Akbar, the increasing conflict between Hindus and Muslims was another of their legacies.

Muhammad (muh-HAHM-mahd) Prophet of Islam (570–632).

Muslim A follower of Islam.

Mycenaean (meye-suh-NEE-uhn) Early Greek society on the Peloponese (1600–1100 B.C.E.) that was influenced by the Minoans; the Mycenaeans' conflict with Troy is immortalized in Homer's *Odyssey*.

Nara era Japanese period (710–794), centered around city of Nara, that was the highest point of Chinese influence.

National Policy Nineteenth-century Canadian policy designed to attract migrants, protect industries through tariffs, and build national transportation systems.

NATO The North Atlantic Treaty Organization, which was established by the United States in 1949 as a regional military alliance against Soviet expansionism.

Ndongo (n'DAWN-goh) Angolan kingdom that reached its peak during the reign of Queen Nzinga (r. 1623–1663).

Neandertal (nee-ANN-duhr-tawl) Early humans (100,000 to 35,000 years ago) who were prevalent during the Paleolithic period.

Negritude (NEH-grih-tood) "Blackness," a term coined by early African nationalists as a means of celebrating the heritage of black peoples around the world.

Neo-Confucianism (nee-oh-kuhn-FYEW-shuhn-iz'm) Philosophy that attempted to merge certain basic elements of Confucian and Buddhist thought; most important of the early Neo-Confucianists was the Chinese thinker Zhu Xi (1130–1200).

Neolithic New Stone Age (10,000–4000 B.C.E.), which was marked by the discovery and mastery of agriculture.

Nestorian (neh-STOHR-eeuhn) Early branch of Christianity, named after the fifth-century Greek theologian Nestorius, that emphasized the human nature of Jesus Christ.

New Economic Policy (NEP) Plan implemented by Lenin that called for minor free market reforms.

Nirvana (nihr-VAH-nuh) Buddhist concept of a state of spiritual perfection and enlightenment in which distracting passions are eliminated.

Noble Eightfold Path Final truth of the Buddhist Four Noble Truths that called for leading a life of balance and constant contemplation.

North American Free Trade Agreement (NAFTA) Regional alliance established in 1993 between the United States, Canada, and Mexico; it formed world's second largest free-trade zone.

Nubia (NOO-bee-uh) Area south of Egypt; the kingdom of Kush in Nubia invaded and dominated Egypt from 750 to 664 B.C.E.

Oceania Term referring to the Pacific Ocean basin and its lands.

Olmecs Early Central American society (1200–100 B.C.E.) that centered around sites at San Lorenzo, La Venta, and Tres Zapotes and that influenced later Maya.

Oprichnina (oh-PREEK-nee-nah) A Russian term meaning the "land apart," Muscovite territory that the Russian Tsar Ivan IV (r. 1533–1584) demanded to control; the tsar created a new class of nobles called the *oprichniki* for this territory.

Oracle bones Chinese Shang dynasty (1766–1122 B.C.E.) means of foretelling the future.

Organization of African Unity (OAU) An organization started in 1963 by thirty-two newly independent African states and designed to prevent conflict that would lead to intervention by former colonial powers.

Organization of Petroleum Exporting Countries (OPEC) An organization begun in 1960 by oil-producing states originally for purely economic reasons but that later had more political influence.

Osiris Ancient Egyptian god that represented the forces of nature.

Ottoman empire Powerful Turkish empire that lasted from the conquest of Constantinople (Istanbul) in 1453 until 1918 and reached its peak during the reign of Süleyman the Magnificent (r. 1520–1566).

Paleolithic Old Stone Age, a long period of human development before the development of agriculture.

Palestinian Liberation Organization (PLO) Organization created in 1964 under the leadership of Yasser Arafat to champion Palestinian rights.

Paris Peace Accords Agreement reached in 1973 that marked the end of the United States's role in the Vietnam War.

Parsis (pahr-SEES) Indian Zoroastrians.

Parthians Persian dynasty (247 B.C.E.–224 C.E.) that reached its peak under Mithradates I.

Pater familias (PAH-tehrr fah-MEE-lyas) Roman term for the "father of the family," a theoretical implication that gave the male head of the family almost unlimited authority.

Patriarch (PAY-tree-ahrk) Leader of the Greek Orthodox church, which in 1054 officially split with the Pope and the Roman Catholic church.

Patriarchy A system of social organization in which males dominate the family and in which the public institutions and descent and succession are traced through the male line.

Patricians Roman aristocrats and wealthy classes.

Pax Americana "American Peace," a term that compares American domination in the years after World War II with the power of Rome at its peak.

Pax Romana (Pahks roh-MAH-nah) "Roman Peace," a term that relates to the period of political stability, cultural brilliance, and economic prosperity beginning with unification under Augustus and lasting through the first two centuries C.E.

Peninsulares (peh-neen-soo-LAH-rehs) Latin American officials from Spain or Portugal.

Perestroika (PAYR-eh-stroy-kuh) "Restructuring," a Russian term associated with Gorbachev's effort to reorganize the Soviet state.

Pharaohs (FARE-ohs) Egyptian kings considered to be gods on earth.

Plebeians (plih-BEE-uhns) Roman common people.

Polis (POH-lihs) Greek term for the city-state.

Popol Vuh (poh-pohl VOO) Mayan creation epic.

Prehistory The period before the invention of writing.

Proletariat Urban working class in a modern industrial society.

Protestant Reformation Sixteenth-century European movement during which Luther, Calvin, Zwingli, and others broke away from the Catholic church.

Putting-out system Method of getting around guild control by delivering unfinished materials to rural households for completion.

Ptolemaic (tawl-oh-MAY-ihk) Term used to signify both the Egyptian kingdom founded by Alexander the Great's general Ptolemy and the thought of the philosopher Ptolemy of Alexandria (second century C.E.), who used mathematical formulas in an attempt to prove Aristotle's geocentric theory of the universe.

Qadis Islamic judges.

Qanat (kah-NAHT) Persian underground canal.

Qi (chee) Chinese concept of the basic material that makes up the body and the universe.

Qin (chihn) Chinese dynasty (221–207 B.C.E.) that was founded by Qin Shihuangdi and was marked by the first unification of China and the early construction of defensive walls.

Qing (chihng) Chinese dynasty (1644–1911) that reached its peak during the reigns of Kangxi and Qianlong.

Qizilbash (gih-ZIHL-bahsh) Term meaning "red heads," Turkish tribes that were important allies of Shah Ismail in the formation of the Safavid empire.

Quetzalcoatl (keh-tzahl-koh-AHT'l) Aztec god, the "feathered serpent," who was borrowed originally from the Toltecs; Quetzalcoatl was believed to have been defeated by another god and exiled, and he promised to return.

Quinto (KEEN-toh) The one-fifth of Mexican and Peruvian silver production that was reserved for the Spanish monarchy.

Quipu (KEE-poo) Incan mnemonic aid comprised of different colored strings and knots that served to record events in the absence of a written text.

Quran (koorr-AHN) Islamic holy book that is believed to contain the divine revelations of Allah as presented to Muhammad.

Ramayana (rah-MAHY-yuh-nah) Ancient Indian masterpiece about the hero Rama that symbolized the victory of *dharma* (order) over *adharma* (chaos).

Rape of Nanjing Japanese conquest and destruction of the Chinese city of Nanjing in the 1930s.

Realpolitik (ray-AHL-poh-lih-teek) The Prussian Otto von Bismarck's "politics of reality," the belief that only the willingness to use force would actually bring about change.

Reconquista (ray-kohn-KEES-tah) Crusade, ending in 1492, to drive the Islamic forces out of Spain.

Reconstruction System implemented in the American South (1867–1877) that was designed to bring the Confederate states back into the union and also extend civil rights to freed slaves.

Renaissance The cultural flowering of western Europe in the fourteenth and fifteenth centuries. Arts and literature of this period reflected greater individualism and secularism than in the medieval period and often drew inspiration from classical models.

Repartimiento (ray-pahrr-tee-MYEN-toh) Spanish labor system in Latin America, supposed to replace the *encomienda* system, in which native communities were compelled to provide laborers for the farms or mines and the Spanish employers were expected to pay fair wages.

Romanov (ROH-mah-nahv) Russian dynasty (1610–1917) founded by Mikhail Romanov and ending with Nicholas II.

Rubaiyat (ROO-beye-aht) "Quatrains," famous poetry of Omar Khayyam that

was later translated and transformed by Edward Fitzgerald.

Safavid (SAH-fah-vihd) Later Persian empire (1501–1722) that was founded by Shah Ismail and that became a center for Shiism; the empire reached its peak under Shah Abbas the Great and was centered around the capital of Isfahan.

Sakk Letters of credit that were common in the medieval Islamic banking world.

Saljuqs (sahl-JYOOKS) Turkish tribe that gained control over the Abbasid empire and fought with the Byzantine empire.

Samsara (suhm-SAH-ruh) Hindu term for the concept of transmigration, that is, the soul passing into a new incarnation.

Samurai (SAM-uhr-eye) A Japanese warrior who lived by the code of *bushido*.

Sasanids (suh-SAH-nids) Later powerful Persian dynasty (224–651) that would reach its peak under Shapur I and later fall to Arabic expansion.

Sati (suh-TEE) Also known as *suttee*, Indian practice of a widow throwing herself on the funeral pyre of her husband.

Satraps (SAY-traps) Persian administrators, usually members of the royal family, who governed a satrapy.

Satyagraha (suh-TYA-gruh-hah) "Truth and firmness," a term associated with Gandhi's policy of passive resistance.

Scholar-bureaucrats Describes the administrative apparatus of China created by the Ming dynasty (1368–1644) and continued by the Qing dynasty (1644–1911). Under this system, Confucian scholars, chosen through a highly competitive series of examinations, ran the country. This system meant that China was a meritocracy, but a very conservative one.

Scholasticism Medieval attempt of thinkers like St. Thomas Aquinas to merge the beliefs of Christianity with the logical rigor of Greek philosophy.

Scientific racism Nineteenth-century attempt to justify racism by scientific means; an example would be Gobineau's *Essay on the Inequality of the Human Races.*

Self-determinism Belief popular in World War I and after that every people should have the right to determine their own political destiny; the belief was often cited but ignored by the Great Powers.

Self-strengthening movement Chinese attempt (1860–1895) to blend Chinese cultural traditions with European industrial technology.

Seleucids (sih-LOO-sihds) Persian empire (323–83 B.C.E.) founded by Seleucus after the death of Alexander the Great.

Semitic (suh-MIHT-ihk) A term that relates to the Semites, ancient nomadic herders who spoke Semitic languages; examples of Semites were the Akkadians, Hebrews, Aramaics, and Phoenicians, who often interacted with the more settled societies of Mesopotamia and Egypt.

Sepoys Indian troops who served the British.

Seppuku A Japanese term for ritual suicide committed by the samurai when he had been dishonored.

Serfs Peasants who, while not chattel slaves, were tied to the land and who owed obligation to the lords on whose land they worked.

Shamanism (SHAH-mah-niz'm) Belief in shamans or religious specialists who possessed supernatural powers and who communicated with the gods and the spirits of nature.

Sharia (shah-RREE-ah) The Islamic holy law, drawn up by theologians from the Quran, and accounts of Muhammad's life.

Shia (SHEE-ah) Islamic minority in opposition to the Sunni majority; their belief is that leadership should reside in the line descended from Ali.

Shintoism (SHIHN-toh-iz'm) Indigenous Japanese religion that emphasizes purity, clan loyalty, and the divinity of the emperor.

Shiva (SHIH-vuh) Hindu god associated with both fertility and destruction.

Shogun (SHOH-gun) Japanese military leader who ruled in place of the emperor.

Shudras (SHOO-druhs) Hindu caste of landless peasants and serfs.

Siddhartha Gautama (sih-DHAR-thuh GAHW-tah-mah) Indian *kshatriya* who achieved enlightenment and became known as the Buddha, the founder of Buddhism.

Sikhs (SIHKS) Indian syncretic faith that contains elements of Hinduism and Islam.

Silk roads Ancient trade routes that extended from the Roman empire in the west to China in the east.

Social Darwinism Nineteenth-century philosophy, championed by thinkers such as Herbert Spencer, that attempted to apply Darwinian "survival of the fittest" to the social and political realm; adherents saw the the elimination of weaker nations as part of a natural process and used the philosophy to justify war.

Socialism Political and economic theory of social organization based on the collective ownership of the means of production; its origins were in the early nineteenth century, and it differs from communism by a desire for slow or moderate change compared to the communist call for revolution.

Solidarity Polish trade union and nationalist movement in the 1980s that was headed by Lech Walesa.

Song (SOHNG) Chinese dynasty (960–1279) that was marked by an increasingly urbanized and cosmopolitan society.

Soviets Russian elected councils that originated as strike committees during the 1905 St. Petersburg disorders; they represented a form of local self-government that went on to become the primary unit of government in the Union of Soviet Socialist Republics. The term was also used during the cold war to designate the Soviet Union.

Spanish Inquisition Institution organized in 1478 by Fernando and Isabel of Spain to detect Protestant heresy and the secret practice of Judaism or Islam.

Spheres of influence A region dominated by an outside power. Generally refers to the intrusion of western imperial powers into China in the late nineteenth century. China, although technically a sovereign state, was divided into "spheres," each one occupied by a European state that had license to conduct business without any interference.

Srivijaya (sree-vih-JUH-yuh) Southeast Asian kingdom (670–1025), based on the island of Sumatra, that used a powerful navy to dominate trade.

Stateless societies Term relating to societies such as those of sub-Saharan Africa after the Bantu migrations that featured decentralized rule through family and kinship groups instead of strongly centralized hierarchies.

Stoics (STOH-ihks) Hellenistic philosophers who encouraged their followers to lead active, virtuous lives and to aid others.

Stoicism A Hellenistic philosophy that emphasized strict adherence to duty and

personal self-discipline. It became very popular among the Roman upper classes.

Strabo (STRAH-boh) Greek geographer (first century C.E.).

Strategic Arms Limitations Talk (SALT) Agreement in 1972 between the United States and the Soviet Union.

Stupas (STOO-pahs) Buddhist shrines.

Sufis (SOO-fees) Islamic mystics who placed more emphasis on emotion and devotion than on strict adherence to rules.

Sui (SWAY) Chinese dynasty (589–618) that constructed Grand Canal, reunified China, and allowed for the splendor of the Tang dynasty that followed.

Süleyman (SOO-lehy-mahn) Ottoman Turkish ruler Süleyman the Magnificent (r. 1520–1566), who was the most powerful and wealthy ruler of the sixteenth century.

Sumerians (soo-MEHR-ee-uhns) Earliest Mesopotamian society.

Sundiata (soon-JAH-tuh) Founder of the Mali empire (r. 1230–1255), also the inspiration for the *Sundiata,* an African literary and mythological work.

Sunni (SOON-nee) "Traditionalists," the most popular branch of Islam; Sunnis believe in the legitimacy of the early caliphs, compared to the Shiite belief that only a descendent of Ali can lead.

Suu Kyi, Aung San (SOO KEE, AWNG SAHN) Opposition leader (1945–) in Myanmar; she was elected leader in 1990 but she was not allowed to come to power; she was a Nobel Peace Prize recipient in 1991.

Swahili (swah-HEE-lee) East African city-state society that dominated the coast from Mogadishu to Kilwa and was active in trade.

Taino (tah-EE-noh) A Caribbean tribe who were the first indigenous peoples from the Americas to come into contact with Christopher Columbus.

Taiping rebellion (TEYE-pihng) Rebellion (1850–1864) in Qing China led by Hong Xiuquan, during which twenty to thirty million were killed; the rebellion was symbolic of the decline of China during the nineteenth century.

Taliban Strict Islamic organization that ruled Afghanistan from 1996 to 2002.

Tang Taizong (TAHNG TEYE-zohng) Chinese emperor (r. 627–649) who founded the Tang dynasty (618–907).

Tanzimat "Reorganization" era (1839–1876), an attempt to reorganize

the Ottoman empire on Enlightenment and constitutional forms.

Temnjin (TEM-oo-chin) Mongol conqueror (ca. 1167–1227) who later took the name Chinggis Khan, "universal ruler."

Tenochtitlan (teh-noch-tee-TLAHN) Capital of the Aztec empire, later Mexico City.

Teotihuacan (tay-oh-tee-wa-KAHN) Central American society (200 B.C.E.–750 C.E.); its Pyramid of the Sun was the largest structure in Mesoamerica.

Teutonic Knights Crusading European order that was active in the Baltic region.

Third Rome Concept that a new power would rise up to carry the legacy of Roman greatness after the decline of the Second Rome, Constantinople; Moscow was referred to as the Third Rome during the fifteenth century.

Three Principles of the People Philosophy of Chinese Guomindang leader Sun Yat-sen (1866–1925) that emphasized nationalism, democracy, and people's livelihood.

Tian (TEE-ehn) Chinese term for heaven.

Tikal (tee-KAHL) Maya political center from the fourth through the ninth centuries.

Timur-i lang (tee-MOOR-yee LAHNG) "Timur the Lame," known in English as Tamerlane (ca. 1336–1405), who conquered an empire ranging from the Black Sea to Samarkand.

Tokugawa (TOH-koo-GAH-wah) Last shogunate in Japanese history (1600–1867); it was founded by Tokugawa Ieyasu who was notable for unifying Japan.

Toltecs Central American society (950–1150) that was centered around the city of Tula.

Trail of Tears Forced relocation of the Cherokee from the eastern woodlands to Oklahoma (1837–1838); it was symbolic of U.S. expansion and destruction of indigenous Indian societies.

Triangular trade Trade between Europe, Africa, and the Americas that featured finished products from Europe, slaves from Africa, and American products bound for Europe.

Triple Alliance Pre–World War I alliance of Germany, Austria-Hungary, and Italy.

Triple Entente (ahn-TAHNT) Pre–World War I alliance of England, France, and Russia.

Truman Doctrine U.S. policy instituted in 1947 by President Harry Truman in which the United States would follow an interventionist foreign policy to contain communism.

Tsar (ZAHR) Old Russian term for king that is derived from the term *caesar*.

Twelver Shiism (SHEE'i'zm) Branch of Islam that stressed that there were twelve perfect religious leaders after Muhammad and that the twelfth went into hiding and would return someday; Shah Ismail spread this variety through the Safavid empire.

Uighurs (WEE-goors) Turkish tribe.

Ukiyo Japanese word for the "floating worlds," a Buddhist term for the insignificance of the world that came to represent the urban centers in Tokugawa Japan.

Ulama (oo-lah-MAH) Islamic officials, scholars who shaped public policy in accordance with the Quran and the *sharia*.

Ulaanbaatar (OO-lahn-bah-tahr) Mongolian city.

Umayyad (oo-MEYE-ahd) Arabic dynasty (661–750), with its capital at Damascus, that was marked by a tremendous period of expansion to Spain in the west and India in the east.

Umma (UM-mah) Islamic term for the "community of the faithful."

United Nations (UN) Successor to the League of Nations, an association of sovereign nations that attempts to find solutions to global problems.

Upanishads (oo-pan-NIH-shuhds) Indian reflections and dialogues (800–400 B.C.E.) that reflected basic Hindu concepts.

Urdu (OOR-doo) A language that is predominant in Pakistan.

Uruk (OO-rook) Ancient Mesopotamian city from the fourth millennium B.C.E. that was allegedly the home of the fabled Gilgamesh.

Vaishyas (VEYESH-yuhs) Hindu caste of cultivators, artisans, and merchants.

Vaqueros (bah-KEH-rohs) Latin American cowboys, similar to the Argentine gaucho.

Varna (VUHR-nuh) Hindu word for caste.

Varuna (vuh-ROO-nuh) Early Aryan god who watched over the behavior of mortals and preserved the cosmic order.

Vedas (VAY-duhs) "Wisdom," early collections of prayers and hymns that provide information about the Indo-European Aryans who migrated into India around 1500 B.C.E.; *Rig Veda* is most important collection.

Velvet revolution A term that describes the nonviolent transfer of power in Czechoslovakia during the collapse of Soviet rule.

Venta, La (BEHN-tah, lah) Early Olmec center (800–400 B.C.E.).

Venus figurines Small Paleolithic statues of women with exaggerated sexual features.

Vernacular (ver-NA-kyoo-lar) The language of the people; Martin Luther translated the Bible from the Latin of the Catholic church into the vernacular German.

Versailles (vehr-SEYE) Palace of French King Louis XIV.

Viet Minh North Vietnamese nationalist communists under Ho Chi Minh.

Vijayanagar (vih-juh-yuh-NUH-guhr) Southern Indian kingdom (1336–1565) that later fell to the Mughals.

Vishnu (VIHSH-noo) Hindu god, preserver of the world, who was often incarnated as Krishna.

Vodou (VOO-doo) Syncretic religion practiced by African slaves in Haiti.

Volksgeist (FOHLKS-geyest) "People's spirit," a term that was coined by the German philosopher Herder; a nation's volksgeist would not come to maturity unless people studied their own unique culture and traditions.

Volta do mar (VOHL-tah doh MAHR) "Return through the sea," a fifteenth-century Portuguese sea route that took advantage of the prevailing winds and currents.

Voltaire (vohl-TAIR) Pen name of French philosophe Francois-Marie Arouet (1694–1778), author of *Candide*.

Walesa, Lech (WAH-lehn-sah, LEHK) Leader of the Polish Solidarity movement.

Waldensians Twelfth-century religious reformers who criticized the Roman Catholic church and who proposed that the laity had the right to preach and administer sacraments; they were declared heretics.

Wanli (wahn-LEE) Chinese Ming emperor (r. 1572–1620) whose refusal to meet with officials hurried the decline of Ming dynasty.

War Communism The Russian policy of nationalizing industry and seizing private land during the civil war.

Warsaw Pact Warsaw Treaty Organization, a military alliance formed by Soviet bloc nations in 1955 in response to rearmament of West Germany and its inclusion in NATO.

Wind wheels Prevailing wind patterns in the Atlantic and Pacific Oceans north and south of the equator; their discovery made sailing much safer and quicker.

Witte, Sergei (VIHT-tee, SAYR-gay) Late-nineteenth-century Russian minister of finance who pushed for industrialization.

World Health Organization (WHO) United Nation organization designed to deal with global health issues.

World Trade Organization (WTO) An organization that was established in 1995 with more than 120 nations and whose goal is to loosen barriers to free trade.

Wuwei (woo-WAY) Daoist concept of a disengagement from the affairs of the world.

Xia (shyah) Early Chinese dynasty (2200–1766 B.C.E.) that is known mainly from legend.

Xianyang (SHYAHN-YAHNG) Capital city of Qin empire.

Xiao (SHAYOH) Confucian concept of respect for one's parents and ancestors.

Xinjiang (shin-jyahng) Western Chinese province.

Xuanzang (SHWEN-ZAHNG) Seventh-century Chinese monk who made a famous trip to India to collect Buddhist texts.

Yahweh (YAH-way) God of the monotheistic religion of Judaism that influenced later Christianity and Islam.

Yangshao (YAHNG-shahw) Early Chinese society (2500–2200 B.C.E.).

Yangzi (YAHNG-zuh) River in central China.

Yongle (YAWNG-leh) Chinese Ming emperor (r. 1403–1424) who pushed for foreign exploration and promoted cultural achievements such as the *Yongle Encyclopedia*.

Young Turks Nineteenth-century Turkish reformers who pushed for changes within the Ottoman empire, such as universal suffrage and freedom of religion.

Yu (yoo) Legendary founder of the Xia dynasty (ca. 2200 B.C.E.).

Yuan (yoo-AHN) Chinese dynasty (1279–1368) that was founded by the Mongol ruler Khubilai Khan.

Yucatan (yoo-kah-TAN) Peninsula in Central America, home of the Maya.

Yurts (yuhrts) Tents used by nomadic Turkish and Mongol tribes.

Zaibatsu (zeye-BAHT-soo) Japanese term for "wealthy cliques," which are similar to American trusts and cartels but usually organized around one family.

Zambos (SAHM-bohs) Latin American term for individuals born of indigenous and African parents.

Zamudio, Adela (sah-MOO-dyo, ah-DEH-lah) Nineteenth-century Bolivian poet, author of "To Be Born a Man."

Zarathustra (zar-uh-THOO-struh) Persian prophet (ca. 628–551 B.C.E.) who founded Zoroastrianism.

Zen Buddhism Japanese version of Chinese Chan Buddhism, with an emphasis on intuition and sudden flashes of insight instead of textual study.

Zhou (JOH) Chinese dynasty (1122–256 B.C.E.) that was the foundation of Chinese thought formed during this period: Confucianism, Daoism, Zhou Classics.

Zhu Xi (ZHOO-SHEE) Neo-Confucian Chinese philosopher (1130–1200).

Ziggurats (ZIG-uh-rahts) Mesopotamian temples.

Zimbabwe (zihm-BAHB-way) Former colony of Southern Rhodesia that gained independence in 1980.

Zemstvos (ZEHMST-voh) District assemblies elected by Russians in the nineteenth century.

Zoroastrianism (zohr-oh-ASS-tree-ahn-iz'm) Persian religion based on the teaching of the sixth-century B.C.E. prophet Zarathustra; its emphasis on the duality of good and evil and on the role of individuals in determining their own fate would influence later religions.

Credits

p. 613, Courtesy Everett Collection
Chapter 33 p. 616, © Bettmann/Corbis;
p. 619, © Hulton-Deutsch Collection/
Corbis; p. 620, © Popperfoto; p. 622,
© Harwood/Getty Images; p. 623, 629,
© Bettmann/Corbis; p. 631, Library of
Congress; p. 632, © Bettmann/Corbis
Chapter 34 p. 636, © Corbis; p. 638,
© Authenticated News/Getty Images;
p. 640, © Fritz Henle/Photo Researchers,
Inc.; p. 641, © UPI/Corbis; p. 646,
© Josef Koudelka/Magnum Photos;
p. 649, © James Pickerell/Camera Press,
London/Retna, Ltd.; p. 650, © Peter
Turnley/Corbis; p. 651, © Tom Stoddart/
Katz Pictures/Woodfin Camp and Asso-
ciates **Chapter 35** p. 656, © Bettmann/
Corbis; p. 661, © Baldwin H. Ward/
Corbis; p. 663, © UPI/Corbis; p. 667,
© Bert Hardy/Getty Images; p. 668,
© Sovfoto; p. 669, © Alexandra Avakian/
Woodfin Camp and Associates; p. 672,
© Bruno Barbey/Magnum Photos

TEXT CREDITS

Chapter 1 Pritchard, James, *Ancient Near Eastern Texts Relating to the Old Testa-ment.* Third Edition with Supplement. © 1950, 1955, 1969, renewed 1978 by Princeton University Press. Reprinted by permission of Princeton University Press. **Chapter 2** Miriam Lichtheim, ed., *Ancient Egyptian Literature.* Three volumes. Berkeley: University of California Press,

1973. Vol. 1, pp. 25–27. Reprinted by permission of the University of California Press. **Chapter 4** Reprinted with permis-sion of Simon & Schuster Adult Publishing Group, from *Popul Vuh: The Definitive Edition of the Mayan Book of the Dawn of Life.* Translated by Dennis Tedlock. Copy-right © 1985, 1996 by Dennis Tedlock. All rights reserved. **Chapter 10** From *The Alexiad of Anna Comnena.* Translated by E. R. A. Sewter (Penguin Classics, 1969) copyright © E. R. A. Sewter, 1969. Pp. 496–505. Reproduced by permission of Penguin Books Ltd. **Chapter 13** From *Sources of Indian Tradition.* Volume 1, pp. 325–26, 328 edited by Ainslie T. Embree and Stephen Hay. © 1988 Colum-bia University Press. **Chapter 16** From D. T. Niane, *Sundiata: An Epic of Old Mali,* pp. 80–82. © Pearson Education Limited, 1965. Used by permission of Pearson Education Limited. **Chapter 18** Teuira Henry and others, Dennis Kawaharada, ed., *Voyaging Chiefs of Havai'i.* Copyright 1995. pp. 138–39, 144–46. Kalamaku Press. Reprinted by permission of Kalamaku Press. **Chapter 19** From Said Hamdun and Noel King, *Ibn Battuta in Black Africa.* Princeton: Markus Wiener Publishers, 1994, pp. 49–50, 58–59. Reprinted by permission. **Chapter 20** Christopher Columbus, *The Diario of Christopher Columbus's First Voyage to America.* Trans. By Oliver Dunn and

James E. Kelley, Jr. Norman: University of Oklahoma Press, 1989, pp. 65–69, 143–45. Reprinted by permission of the University of Oklahoma Press. **Chapter 22** Bernardino de Sahagun, *Florentine Codex: General History of the Things of New Spain.* 13 vols. Trans. By Arthur J. O. Anderson and Charles E. Dibble. Salt Lake City: University of Utah Press, 1950–82, 13:19–20. Used by permission of the University of Utah Press. **Chapter 23** Copyright © 1964 by Basil Davidson. Reprinted by permission of Curtis Brown, Ltd. **Chapter 28** From *Been in the Storm So Long* by Leon F. Litwack, copyright © 1979 by Leon F. Litwack. Used by permission of Alfred A. Knopf, a division of Random House, Inc. **Chapter 32** Amy Jacques Garvey, compiler, *Philosophy and Opinions of Marcus Garvey or Africa for Africans.* Reprinted courtesy of The Majority Press Inc. PO Box 538, Dover, MA 02030. **Chapter 33** Haruko Taya Cook and Theodore F. Cook, *Japan at War.* Copyright © 1993. Reprinted by permission of The New Press. www.thenewpress.com. **Chapter 34** Nikita Khrushchev, "Report to the Communist Party," in *Current Soviet Policies IV,* ed. Charlotte Saikowski and Leo Gruliow, from the translations of *The Current Digest of the Soviet Press,* 1962. Used by permis-sion of the Current Digest of the Post-Soviet Press.

Index

communication *(continued)*
telegraphs, 541; in African colonies, 606; globalization of, 658, 671–72. *See also* railroads; roads; silk roads

communism: Marx and Engels on, 507, 508 *(source document)*; in Russia, 589–91; war communism, 590; in China, 602–3, 603 *(map)*, 647–48, 667–68, 668 *(illus.)*; Holocaust and, 628; in Poland, 632; in North Korea, 640–41; globalization of containment of, 641; in Vietnam, 648, 661; after the collapse of the Soviet Union, 653

compasses, 219, 339, 360

complex society: defined, 2; characteristics of, 2–3; in Mesopotamia, 6, 13–22; in the Nile River Valley, 32–37, 33 *(illus.)*

concentration camps, Nazi, 629–30, 630 *(illus.)*

concrete construction, Roman, 149

Confucianism: origin of, 100–103; educational system in, 108; Han dynasty collapse and, 168; Neo-Confucianism, 223–24, 448, 451; under Mongol rule, 276–77; in Ming dynasty China, 439, 447–48; in Qing dynasty China, 440, 442, 447–48

Confucius (551–479 B.C.E.), 100–103, 101 *(illus.)*, 102 *(source document)*

Congo, Belgian, 549, 549 *(illus.)*, 550 *(map)*, 605, 665–67

Congo, Democratic Republic of the, 665–67

Congo Free State, 549, 549 *(illus.)*

Congo-Ocean railway, 607

Congress of Vienna (1814–1815), 492

conquistadores, 402

conscription: in French revolution, 482; during World War I, 570, 571–72, 605; in African colonies, 605–6, 606 *(illus.)*; in World War II, 620, 630–31

conservatism, 487–88

Constantine, Roman Emperor (c. 275–337), 169, 169 *(illus.)*, 171, 179–80

Constantinople (Istanbul): founding of, 169, 178; seige from Islamic forces, 182, 182 *(illus.)*; importance in trade, 184–85; urban life in, 185; tensions with Rome, 187; Norman invasion of, 190; Ottoman Turks in, 190, 281, 458–59; Viking raids on, 255

constitutional states: Dutch Republic, 384–85; England, 385; United States, 479, 518; France, 480; Haiti, 486; Portugal, 492; Spain, 492; in Latin America, 523; Mexico, 524, 525; Ottoman empire, 546

Constitution of the United States (1787), 479

consumerism, 643–45, 671–73, 672 *(illus.)*

containment, globalization of, 641

Continental Congress (1774), 477

Convention (French), 481–82

"Convention on the Rights and Duties of States," 612

Cook, Capt. James (1728–1779), 364–65, 366 *(map)*, 413–14, 551

Copernicus, Nicolaus (1473–1543), 394

copper metallurgy, 13

Coptic scripts, 36

Córdoba, 312, 313 *(map)*

corporations, 503, 670

Corpus iuris civilis (Justinian), 181

Cortés, Hernán (1485–1547), 399–400, 402, 403 *(source document)*

Costa Rica, 487

cotton, 67, 429, 499, 601. *See also* textiles

Council for Mutual Economic Assistance (COMECON), 633

Council of Chalcedon (451), 172

Council of Nicaea (325), 172, 186

Council of Trent (1545–1563), 380

Cranach, Lucas (sixteenth century), 376 *(illus.)*

creation stories, Maya, 69, 71

creoles, 407, 486, 487, 523, 533

Crete, Minoan society on, 133

Crimean peninsula, Mongols in, 278

Crimean War (1853–1856), 510

criollos, 407, 486, 487, 523, 533

Croesus, King of Lydia (c. 560–546 B.C.E.), 83

Crompton, Samuel (1753–1827), 499

crop rotation, 305

cross staffs, 360, 360 *(illus.)*

Crusades, 189, 313–14, 313 *(map)*, 314 *(illus.)*, 359

Crystal Palace exhibition (1851), 504 *(illus.)*

Ctesiphon (Parthian empire), 89, 90 *(map)*

Cuba: emancipation of slaves in, 432, 489; Spanish-Cuban-American War, 553; U.S. military forces in, 553–54, 611 *(map)*; Cuban missile crisis, 641–42

cubism, 585 *(illus.)*, 586, 610 *(illus.)*

cult of motherhood, 594

"cult of reason," 482

Cultural Revolution (China, 1966–1976), 667, 668 *(illus.)*

culture: Harappan, 45–46; Spartan, 133–34; classical Greek, 140–44, 141 *(illus.)*; in post-Han dynasty China, 167–68; Islamic, 206–7, 207 *(illus.)*; in post-classical China, 220–22, 220 *(illus.)*; in southern India, 239 *(illus.)*; in Ming and Qing dynasties, 344, 448; African-American, 430–31; in Tokugawa shogunate Japan, 451–52; in Islamic empires, 456 *(illus.)*, 467–68, 467 *(illus.)*, 468 *(illus.)*, 470–71; cultural nationalism, 491; motives for imperialism, 539; after World War I, 582–83; homogenizing of, 671. *See also* architecture; art

cuneiform writing, 15, 21

currency. *See* money and coinage

Custer, George Armstrong (1839–1876), 519

Cuzco (Peru), 325–26, 402

Cybele (goddess), 151

Cyprian, Saint, bishop of Carthage (third century), 166 *(source document)*

Cyril, Saint, 190

Cyrillic alphabet, 190–91

Cyrus, King of Persia (585–530 B.C.E.), 83, 84–85, 136

Czechoslovakia: in World War II, 620, 628, 632; Soviet invasion of, 646 *(illus.)*, 647; separation of, 651; "velvet revolution" in, 651

Czech Republic, 651

da Gama, Vasco (c. 1460–1524), 348, 349–350 *(map)*, 357–62, 366

Dahomey, slave trade in, 428

daimyo (great names), 450

Damascus (Syria), 201

dao, 103, 222

Daodejing (Laozi), 103–4

Daoism, 103–4, 104 *(illus.)*, 168, 222–23

dar al-Islam (house of Islam), 196, 201, 202, 206–7

Darius, King of Persia (reigned 521–486 B.C.E.), 85–86, 87 *(illus.)*, 94, 118, 136–37

Darwin, Charles (1809–1882), 557

David, Hebrew king (reigned 1000–970 B.C.E.), 17

D-Day (6 June 1944), 625

Declaration of Independence (United States), 477–78

Declaration of Independence (Vietnam), 660

Declaration of the Rights of Man and the Citizen, 475, 480, 481 *(source document)*

Declaration of the Rights of Woman and the Female Citizen, 475

The Decline of the West (Spengler), 583

deforestation, of Harappan lands, 45

Degas, Edgar (1834–1917), 585

de Gaulle, Charles (1890–1970), 645–46

deism, 395–96

Delacroix, Eugène, 474 *(illus.)*

Delhi, India, in Mughal empire, 461

Delian League, 136–37

roads *(continued)*
Roman empire, 148–49, 148 *(map);* in Islamic realm, 204; in Inca empire, 326
Robespierre, Maximilien (1758–1794), 482–83
Roman Catholic Church: papacy, 172, 260–61; schism with Eastern Orthodox Church, 183, 185, 187; medieval Italian city-states and, 187, 303 *(map),* 304; in early medieval Europe, 260–62, 261 *(illus.);* Holy Roman Empire and, 302–3; as the First Estate, 306; on code of chivalry, 307; works of Aristotle and, 309; Dominicans, 311; Franciscans, 311; Waldensians and, 311; Crusades, 313–14, 313 *(map),* 314 *(illus.);* missionaries, 338–39, 347, 359–60, 368–69, 380; indulgences in, 377; Protestant Reformation and, 377–79; Catholic Reformation, 379–80, 380 *(illus.);* Council of Trent (1545–1563), 380; Jesuits (Society of Jesus), 380, 411–12, 448–49, 452–53; Spanish Inquisition, 383 *(illus.),* 384; Enlightenment and, 395–96; in the Americas, 411–12; in China, 448; in Japan, 452. *See also* Christianity
The Romance of the Three Kingdoms, 448
Roman Colosseum, 149
Roman forum, 144, 145 *(illus.)*
Romania, 632, 651
Romanov tsars, 386–87, 391, 510, 573, 590
Roman Republic, 144–46, 146 *(map)*
Rome and Roman empire: invasion of Persian empire, 89–90; Etruscans and, 144; founding of Rome, 144; kingdom of Rome, 144; Roman Republic, 144–46, 146 *(map);* Punic Wars (264–146 B.C.E.), 146; civil wars (second and first centuries B.C.E.), 147; Julius Caesar, 147–48, 147 *(illus.);* Augustus Caesar, 147–48; in *pax romana,* 148–49, 148 *(map);* Ju-

daism and early Christianity and, 132,151–52, 171–72; epidemic diseases in, 165–66; internal decay in, 168–69, 169 *(illus.);* fall of western Roman Empire, 169–71, 170 *(map);* formation of Byzantium from, 178–80, 179 *(map)*
Romulus and Remus, 144
Romulus Augustulus, Roman Emperor (c. 476), 170
Roosevelt, Franklin Delano (1882–1945): New Deal policies of, 588; inaugural speech of, 589 *(source document);* "Good Neighbor Policy," 612; in World War II, 621, 623, 632
Roosevelt, Theodore (1859–1919), 554, 612
Roosevelt Corollary, 554
Rosas, Juan Manuel de (ruled 1835–1852), 523
Rousseau, Jean-Jacques (1712–1778), 477
Royal Mosque of Isfahan, 467, 468 *(illus.)*
Royal Road (Persia), 85 *(map),* 87, 92
rubber, 510, 549, 586
rudders, 360
Rule (St. Benedict), 261
Russia: Byzantine empire and, 191; serfs in, 257, 262, 391, 510; Mongol conquests in, 273, 275, 275 *(map);* exploration of the Pacific by, 364; expansion into central Asia and Siberia, 369–70, 370 *(map);* under Peter I, 386–87; Romanov tsars, 386–87, 391, 510, 573, 590; under Catherine II, 387; early capitalism and, 391–92; during French revolution, 483; invasion by Napoleon, 483; anti-Semitism in, 491; nationalism in, 491–92; Crimean War (1853–1856), 510; industrialization of, 510–12, 511 *(map);* Russo-Japanese War (1904–1905), 513, 554, 555 *(illus.);* in World War I, 564–67, 568 *(map),* 569, 573–74; revolution in, 573–74, 574 *(illus.);* civil war in, 589–90; formation of the Soviet Union, 588. *See also* Soviet Union

Russian-German Treaty of Nonaggression (1939), 621
Russian Orthodox Church, 191
Russian Soviet Federated Socialist Republic, 652, 652 *(map)*
Russo-Japanese War (1904–1905), 554, 555 *(illus.)*
Ryukyu Islands, 554

sacrifices: Maya, 64, 69, 69 *(illus.);* Persian, 93; Aztec, 318, 322, 322 *(illus.)*
Sadat, Anwar (1918–1981), 668
Safavid empire: boundaries of, 459 *(map);* formation of, 460–61, 461 *(illus.);* political organization of, 463–64; women in, 464; agriculture in, 464–65; population growth in, 465; trade in, 465–66; religion in, 466, 469; culture in, 467, 468 *(illus.),* 470–71; decline of, 468–70
Safi al-Din (1252–1334), 460
Sahara desert, 27, 288–92, 289 *(map)*
sail shapes, 204, 360
Saint-Domingue, 429, 484–86, 485 *(illus.)*
saints, Roman Catholic, 310
Sakhalin Island, 554
sakk (letter of credit), 205
Salah al-Din (Saladin, c. 1137–1193), 314
Saljuq Turks, 190, 270, 271 *(map)*
salons, 395 *(illus.)*
Samoa, 75, 75 *(map),* 328, 330
samsara, doctrine of, 51
Samudra Gupta (335–375), 119
samurai, 226, 450
Sandeleur dynasty (Caroline Islands), 330
San Lorenzo site (Mexico), 65, 66
San Martín, José de (1778–1850), 487
Santa Anna, Gen. Antonio López (1797–1876), 523
Santeria religion, 430
Santo Domingo. *See* Saint-Domingue
Sanxingdui (China), 53
São Jorge da Mina (Ghana), 360, 361 *(map)*
São Tomé, 425
Sappho (c. 600 B.C.E.), 140

Saramaka people, 429
Sargon of Akkad (2370–2315 B.C.E.), 10–11
Sasanid empire, 89–90, 90 *(map),* 94, 165, 179 *(map),* 201. *See also* Persia
sati, 542
satrapies, 86, 89
satyagraha (technique of passive resistance), 601
Saudi Arabia. *See* Arab lands
Sauma, Rabban (thirteenth century), 277
Saxons, 171, 260
Scandinavia, Christianity in. *See also names of specific countries*
Schlieffen, Count Alfred von (1833–1913), 566
Schlieffen plan, 566–67, 568 *(map)*
scholar-bureaucrats, 442, 445
Scholastica, Saint (482–543), 261
scholasticism, 208, 310
science: Mesopotamian, 17; Mesoamerican, 68; Islamic, 208; Crusades and, 314; Egyptian, second-century, 393, 394 *(illus.);* Copernicus and, 394; in the Enlightenment, 394–96, 395 *(illus.);* theory of evolution, 557; physics revolution, 583–84; psychology, 584; space race, 645. *See also* astronomy
scientific racism, 556 *(illus.),* 557, 594 *(illus.)*
scroll paintings, 223 *(illus.)*
sculpture: Sumerian, 11 *(illus.),* 14 *(illus.);* Mesopotamian, 14 *(illus.);* Aryan, 50 *(illus.);* Olmec, 66, 66 *(illus.);* Maya, 69 *(illus.);* Mochican, 74 *(illus.);* Persian, 87 *(illus.),* 89 *(illus.),* 92 *(illus.),* 93 *(illus.);* Chinese, 104 *(illus.),* 107 *(illus.),* 220 *(illus.);* Mauryan, 114 *(illus.),* 118 *(illus.);* in classical India, 121–22, 121 *(illus.),* 123 *(illus.),* 124 *(illus.),* 126 *(illus.);* Greek, 141 *(illus.);* Roman, 147 *(illus.),* 169 *(illus.);* Bactrian, 162 *(illus.);* in Tang dynasty China, 225 *(illus.);* southeast Asian, 244 *(illus.);* tenth-century European, 249 *(illus.);* Frank-